Social Research Methods

A reader

Social Research Methods: A Reader brings together many of the core classic and contemporary works in social and cultural research methods, giving students direct access to methodological debates and examples of practical research across the qualitative/quantitative divide. The book is designed to be used both as a collection of readings and as an introductory research methods book in its own right. Topics covered include:

- Research methodology
- Research design, data collection and preparation
- Analysing data
- Mixing qualitative and quantitative methods
- Validity and reliability
- Methodological critique: postmodernism, post-structuralism and critical ethnography
- Political and ethical aspects of research
- Philosophy of social science
- Reporting research.

In addition to containing an extensive introduction, each Part is preceded by a short introduction placing the readings in context. This reader-text also includes features such as discussion questions and practical exercises.

Social Research Methods: A Reader will be essential reading for students taking social and cultural research methods courses.

Clive Seale is Professor of Sociology in the Department of Human Sciences, Brunel University.

Routledge Student Readers

Series Editor: Chris Jenks, Professor of Sociology, Goldsmiths College, University of London

| MarketPlace : AUS | Order Number : 114-0015016-6807400 |
| Order Date : 2017-04-17 | Email : vc35p3dj3h6b2kc@marketplace.amazon.com |

Items : 1

Item		**Locator**
Social Research Methods: A Reader (Routledge Stude	RY	MUL-2-BE-03-005-5
ISBN : 0415300843		

PrintID: 100009498176

Please note:

Items are dispatched individually. If you have ordered multiple books they will

arrive in separate packages

We hope that you are completely satisfied with your purchase and ask you to leave positive feedback accordingly.

However, if you are unsatisfied with your order, please contact us by telephone or email. We will do whatever it takes to resolve the issue.

Mulberry House, Woods Way, Goring By Sea, West Sussex, BN12 4QY. Tel:+44(0)1903 507544
Email: international@worldofbooks.com | Twitter: @WorldofBooksltd | Web: www.worldofbooks.com

Social Research Methods

A reader

Edited by

Clive Seale

Routledge
Taylor & Francis Group

LONDON AND NEW YORK

First published 2004
by Routledge
11 New Fetter Lane, London EC4P 4EE

Simultaneously published in the USA and Canada
by Routledge
29 West 35th Street, New York, NY 10001

Routledge is an imprint of the Taylor & Francis Group

Typeset in Perpetua and Bell Gothic by RefineCatch Limited, Bungay Suffolk

British Library Cataloguing in Publication Data
A catalogue record for this book is available from the British Library

Library of Congress Cataloging in Publication Data
Social research methods: a reader / Edited by Clive Seale.
    —p. cm. – (Routledge student readers)
Includes bibliographical references and index.
1.   Sociology – Research – Methodology. 2. Social sciences – Research – Methodology. I. Seale, Clive.
II. Series.

HM511.S65 2004
301'.01–dc21   2003010537

ISBN 0-415-30083-5 (hbk)
ISBN 0-415-30084-3 (pbk)

Contents

Illustrations

Figures

Tables

Acknowledgements

Editor's acknowledgements

I would like to thank Routledge editors Mari Shullaw and James McNally for their help in preparing this book.

Publisher's acknowledgements

The publishers would like to thank the following for permission to reprint their material:

American Educational Research Association for permission to reprint from John K. Smith and Lous Heshusius, 'Closing down the conversation: the end of the quantitative–qualitative debate among educational inquirers,' *Educational Researcher* 15: 4–12, 1986. Copyright © American Educational Research Association.

Ashgate Publishing Ltd for permission to reprint from Alan Bryman, 'Quantitative and qualitative research: further reflection, on their integration', in Brannen, J. (ed.) *Mixing Methods: Qualitative and Quantitative Research*, Avebury, 1992.

Basic Books, a member of Perseus Books LLC for permission to reprint from Claude Lévi-Strauss *Structural Anthropology: Volume 1*, Penguin Books, 1968. Copyright © 1963 Basic Books, Inc

Blackwell Publishing Ltd for permission to reprint from Jenny Kitzinger, 'The methodology of focus groups: the importance of interaction between research participants', *Sociology of Health and Illness* 16 (1): 104–121, 1994; David Silverman, *Harvey Sacks: Social Science and Conversation Analysis*, Polity Press,

1998; Zygmunt Bauman, *Legislators and Interpreters: On Modernity, Post-modernity and Intellectuals*, Polity Press, 1987; Carol H. Weiss, 'The many meanings of research utilization', from Bulmer, M. (ed.) *Social Science and Social Policy*, Allen and Unwin, 1986.

British Medical Journal for permission to reprint from Julienne Meyer, 'Using qualitative methods in health related action research', *British Medical Journal* 320: 178–181, 2000.

British Sociological Association for permission to reprint from British Sociological Association, 'Statement of ethical practice', http://www.britsoc.org.uk/about/ethic.htm, 2002; Maureen Cain and Janet Finch, 'Towards a rehabilitation of data' in Abrams, P., Deem. R., Finch J., Rock, P. (eds), *Practice and Progress: British Sociology 1950–1980*, George Allen and Unwin, 1981.

Cambridge University Press for permission to reprint from Ian Hacking, *The Taming of Chance*, Cambridge University Press, 1990; Hanneke Houtkoop-Steenstra, 'Quality of life assessment interviews,' from *Interaction and the Standardised Survey Interview*, Cambridge University Press, 2000; John M. Swales, 'Episodes in the history of the research article', from *Genre Analysis: English in Academic and Research Settings*, Cambridge University Press, 1990.

Council of American Survey Research Organizations for permission to reprint from Council of American Survey Research Organizations (CASRO), 'Code of standards and ethics for survey research', http://www.casro.org/codeofstandards.cfm, 2002.

Elsevier Science for permission to reprint from Catherine Kohler Riessman, 'Strategic uses of narrative in the presentation of self and illness: a research note', *Social Science and Medicine* 30 (11): 1195–1200, 1990, copyright © 1990.

The Free Press, an imprint of Simon and Schuster Adult Publishing Group, for permission to reprint from Paul F. Lazarsfeld, 'Interpretation of statistical relations as a research operation', from Lazarsfeld, P.F. and Rosenberg, M., *The Language of Social Research: A Reader in the Methodology of Social Research*, Free Press and Collier-MacMillan, 1955, copyright © by The Free Press; copyright renewed 1983 by Patricia Kendall Lazarsfeld; Aaaron V. Cicourel, 'Fixed-choice questionnaires', from Cicourel, A.V., *Method and Measurement in Sociology*, Free Press and Collier-MacMillan, copyright © 1964 by The Free Press; copyright renewed 1992.

Barney G. Glaser and Anselm L. Strauss for permission to reprint from *The Discovery of Grounded Theory: Strategies for Qualitative Research*, Aldine and London: Weidenfeld and Nicolson, 1967. Copyright © 1967 by Barney G. Glaser and Anselm L. Strauss.

Robin Hamman for permission to reprint from his 'The application of ethnographic methodology in the study of cybersex', *Cybersociology Magazine* 18/06/02; www.socio.demon.co.uk/magazine

Sandra Harding for permission to reprint from Harding S. (ed.) *Feminism and Methodology* (1987), Indiana University Press and Open University Press.

The Haworth Press for permission to reprint from Ann Oakley, 'Who's afraid of the randomised controlled trial? Some dilemmas of the scientific method and "good" research practice', *Women and Health* 15 (4): 25–59, 1989.

Journal of Computer Mediated Communications for permission to reprint from Kim Sheehan and Mariea Hoy, 'On-line surveys', from 'Using e-mail to survey internet users in the United States: methodology and assessment', *Journal of Computer Mediated Communications* 4 (3) March 1999.

The New York Review of Books and Professor R.C. Lewontin for permission to reprint from 'Sex, lies, and social science', *New York Review of Books 20*: April 24–29, 1995 and associated subsequent correspondence.

Open University Press for permission to reprint from Graham Gibbs, *Qualitative Data Analysis: Explorations with NVIVO*, Open University Press, 2002.

Oxford University Press Inc. for permission to reprint from C. Wright Mills, 'On intellectual craftsmanship', from his *The Sociological Imagination*, Oxford University Press, 2000; H.G. Widdowson, 'The theory and practice of critical discourse analysis', *Applied Linguistics* 19 (1): 136–151, 1998.

Pearson Education Ltd for permission to reprint from Madan Sarup, *An Introductory Guide to Post-structuralism and Postmodernism*, Harvester Wheatsheaf, 1993.

Sage Publications Inc. for permission to reprint from K. Jill Kiecolt and Laura E. Nathan, *Secondary Analysis of Survey Data*, Sage, 1985; Anselm L. Strauss and Juliet Corbin, 'Open coding', in *Basics of Qualitative Research: Grounded Theory Procedures and Techniques*, Sage, 1998; Laurel Richardson, 'The consequences of poetic representation', from Ellis C. and Flaherty M. (eds), *Investigating Subjectivity*, Sage, 1992; Arthur W. Frank, 'Can we research suffering?' *Qualitative Health Research* 11 (3): 353–362, 2001; Thomas A. Schwandt, 'Farewell to criteriology', *Qualitative Inquiry* 2 (1): 58–72, 1996; William Foote Whyte, 'Qualitative sociology and deconstructionism', *Qualitative Inquiry* 2 (2): 220–226, 1996. Norman K. Denzin, 'The facts and fictions of qualitative inquiry', *Qualitative Inquiry* 2 (2): 230–241, 1996.

Sage Publications Ltd for permission to reprint from Michael Billig, 'Methodology and scholarship in understanding ideological explanation', in *Analysing Everyday Explanation: A Case Book of Methods*, edited by Charles Antaki, Sage, 1988; Ray Pawson and Nick Tilley, 'Go forth and experiment', from *Realistic Evaluation*, Sage, 1997; Martyn Hammersley, 'Qualitative data archiving: some reflections on its prospects and problems', *Sociology* 31 (1): 131–142, 1997; John D. Brewer, 'The ethnographic critique of ethnography: sectarianism in the RUC', *Sociology* 28 (1): 231–244, 1994; Anssi Peräkylä, 'Reliability and validity in research based on tapes and transcripts', in Silverman, D. (ed.) *Qualitative Research: Theory, Method and Practice*, Sage, 1997; Stuart Hall, 'Foucault and discourse', from his *Representation: Cultural Representation and Signifying Practices*, Sage, 1997; Jonathan Potter and Margaret Wetherell, 'Unfolding discourse analysis', from *Discourse and Social Psychology: Beyond Attitudes and Behaviour*, Sage, 1987; Norman Fairclough and Ruth Wodak, 'Critical discourse analysis', in van Dijk, T. (ed) *Discourse Studies: A Multidisciplinary Introduction, Volume 2*, Sage, 1997; Paul Atkinson, *Understanding Ethnographic Texts*, Sage, 1992; Martyn Hammersley, 'On feminist methodology', from his *The Politics of Social Research*, Sage, 1995.

Sociological Research Online for permission to reprint from Udo Kelle, 'Theory building in qualitative research and computer programs for the management of textual data', *Sociological Research Online* 2, 2. *http://www.socresonline.org.uk/socresonline/2/2/1.html*, 1997.

Stanford University Press for permission to reprint from Clifford Geertz, *Works and Lives: The Anthropologist as Author*, Stanford University Press, 1988.

Taylor and Francis for permission to reprint from Angela Dale, Sara Arber and Michael Procter, 'A sociological perspective on secondary analysis', from their *Doing Secondary Analysis*, Unwin Hyman, 1988; Cathie Marsh, 'The critics of surveys', from *The Survey Method: The Contribution of Surveys to Sociological Explanation*, Allen and Unwin, 1982; Ann Oakley 'Interviewing women: a contradiction in terms?' in H. Roberts (ed.) *Doing Feminist Research*, Routledge, 1981; Ken Plummer, 'On the diversity of life documents', from *Documents of Life: An Introduction to the Problems and Literature of a Humanistic Method*, George Allen and Unwin, 1983; Mary Maynard 'Methods, practice and epistemology: the debate about feminism and research' in Maynard, M. and Purvis, J. (eds) *Researching Women's Lives from a Feminist Perspective*, Taylor and Francis, 1994; Les Back and John Solomos, 'Doing research, writing politics: the dilemmas of political intervention in research on racism', *Economy and Society* 22 (2): 178–199, 1993. www.tandf.co.uk

Transaction Publishers for permission to reprint from Julius A. Roth, 'Hired hand research', *The American Sociologist* 1 (4): 190–196: 1966. Copyright © 1996 by Transaction Publishers.

University of California Press for permission to reprint from James Clifford, 'Partial truths', from Clifford, J. and Marcus, G.E. (eds) (1986) *Writing Culture: The Poetics and Politics of Ethnography*, University of California Press; Patti Lather 'Fertile obsession: validity after poststructuralism', *Sociological Quarterly* 34 (4): 673–693, 1993 (JAI Press).

University of Chicago Press for permission to reprint from Herbert Hyman with Cobb W. J., Feldman J. J., Hart C. W., Stember C. H., *Interviewing in Social Research*, University of Chicago Press, 1954; Thomas S. Kuhn, from *The Structure of Scientific Revolutions*, University of Chicago Press, 1970; William Foote Whyte from 'Methodological appendix' in *Street Corner Society: The Social Structure of an Italian Slum* University of Chicago Press, 1981, (third edition); Buford H. Junker 'The field work situation: social roles for observation' from *Field Work: An Introduction to the Social Sciences*. University of Chicago Press, 1960.

Verso for permission to reprint from Paul Feyerabend, *Against Method: Outline of an Anarchistic Theory of Knowledge*, Verso, 1975.

Walter L. Wallace for permission to reprint from *The Logic of Science in Sociology*, (Aldine-Atherton) Copyright © 1971 by Walter L. Wallace.

Introduction to the reader

THIS BOOK CONTAINS CAREFULLY edited extracts from writings on methods and methodology, relevant to a wide variety of students and practitioners in the social science and cultural studies disciplines. The collection contains theoretically driven discussions of methodological principles and debates, and accounts of practical techniques in use by social and cultural researchers, including both qualitative and quantitative approaches. A combination of foundational classics and pieces by contemporary writers who are leading research practice in new directions is included. The book, therefore, is suitable for use as a general methods textbook on courses in research methods, as well as being a 'reader' in the more traditional sense of a collection of interesting readings.

It is this double nature of the book that has made it so exciting for me to produce, and I hope for you to use. In preparing this book I have drawn on experience in writing and editing books about research methods. Some of this experience has been at introductory textbook level where the primary concern is to outline various areas of research practice for an undergraduate audience learning about these things for the first time (Seale 1998), other work has been at a more advanced level, being my own reflections on the state of the field (Seale 1999), hopefully to be read by practising researchers and postgraduate students. This experience, combined with some perceptions about the nature of existing methods texts, has helped me edit and write the present text. Let me list some dissatisfactions that I have, as a practising researcher as well as a teacher, with existing books on method so that you can see what I think this book has to offer.

Books on research methods

First, there are many introductory texts around, whose authors attempt to survey some area of social research practice, or even all research practice, so as to help readers do their own research. A selection of these is at the end of this introduction. One of the best of these books is by Alan Bryman (who has written one of the pieces in this volume) called *Social Research Methods* published by Oxford University Press (2002). Now this, as I say, is a really good book, one which will definitely help you do thoughtful research, and in a variety of styles. Bryman is a very clear writer, and the text is organized in an exemplary manner, with teaching aids, a dedicated website, and all the other helpful paraphernalia that accompany a great new teaching book.

Yet the book – as any introductory textbook must be – is fundamentally a summary of the ideas of other people. Just about all of the methods described were originally invented or developed by other people, and these authors put things in their own way, not in Bryman's way. The resonance of the words they used to describe their ideas was different for them, and for their original readers, than the resonance for Bryman. Often, the original research workers who developed the techniques of 'discourse analysis', 'attitude measurement' or whatever, or who were in at the early stages of such methodological developments, were really excited by these ideas. The excitement may have died down a bit now, and by the time even a talented textbook writer like Bryman is dealing with them, they have lost quite a bit of their original fizz.

That's why textbooks are often so boring, and that is why editors produce 'readers' in which classic writings in an area are reprinted – so that readers can see under one convenient cover a collection of the originals which formed the field. But there are some problems with these too.

First, a lot of these readers – at least in the methods sphere – do not reproduce very many articles and this means they tend to focus on specialist topics rather than the full range of methods and methodological debate. Below are details of twelve readers on methods (ancient and modern), demonstrating this.

Abbott, P. and Sapsford R. (1992) *Research into Practice: A Reader for Nurses and the Caring Professions,* Buckingham: Open University Press. (10 readings)

Bulmer M. (1984) *Sociological Research Methods,* London: MacMillan. (18 readings)

Burgess, R. (1982) *Field Research: A Sourcebook and Field Manual,* London: Unwin Hyman. (34 readings)

Bynner J. and Stribley K.M. (1979) *Social Research: Principles and Procedures,* London: Longman. (24 readings)

Denzin, N. (1970) *Sociological Methods: A Sourcebook,* London: Butterworth. (36 readings)

Hammersley, M. (1986) *Controversies in Classroom Research: A Reader,* Buckingham: Open University Press. (18 readings)

Hammersley, M. (1993) *Social Research: Philosophy, Politics and Practice,* London: Sage. (17 readings)

Lazarsfeld, P.F. and Rosenberg, M. (1955) *The Language of Social Research: A Reader in the Methodology of Social Research,* Glencoe, Ill.: Free Press. (64 readings)

McCall, G.J. and Simmons, J.L. (1969) *Issues in Participant Observation: A Text and Reader*, Reading, Mass. and London: Addison-Wesley. (30 readings)

Murphy, R. and Torrance, H. (1987) *Evaluating Education: Issues and Methods*, London: Paul Chapman. (25 readings)

Taylor S. (2002) *Ethnographic Research: A Reader*, London: Sage. (10 readings)

Weinberg, D. (2002) *Qualitative Research Methods*, Oxford: Blackwell. (17 readings)

The one with the most readings is Lazarsfeld and Rosenberg, followed by the Denzin, Burgess and McCall and Simmons readers. The first of these is almost entirely devoted to quantitative techniques; the Burgess and McCall and Simmons readers are concerned with qualitative methods, and the Denzin reader is largely oriented towards this too. Some of the smaller readers also focus on a particular set of approaches: the Bynner and Stribley volume is largely quantitative; the Taylor and the Weinberg books are wholly about qualitative work. Others (for example, the volumes by Murphy and Torrance, Hammersley (1986), Abbott and Sapsford) are aimed at a particular field of activity, either teaching or nursing.

Clearly the mere quantity of readings isn't necessarily an indicator of the quality or usefulness of a book, otherwise it would be too easy to put together an edited collection! But when an editor wants to reprint original pieces in full – or almost full – it is inevitable that this will constrain coverage. The strategy of limiting the scope of the book to just one aspect of research practice means that the book cannot be used to introduce a reader to the full scope of contemporary practice in social research. Focusing on issues that concern a particular profession is also limiting. Such books are used as supplementary texts on courses, are bought by libraries, read largely by more adventurous or hard-working undergraduate students, or by postgraduates and practising researchers. They do not become key introductory texts in their own right.

This book tries to solve this tension, so that the apparently dull subject of research methods is presented to a student audience as far as possible using the texts, and generating the excitement that methodological developments had when they were first invented and developed. Of course, there is an argument against this: sometimes the 'original authors' expressed themselves in impossibly dense ways, or did not themselves have a sufficiently clear vision to see the wood from the trees – to distinguish the essential points, the highlights, the main contributions of the methods they were developing.

This, dear reader, is where I come in. First, I have not *always* gone for the original author. The writings of Foucault are a good example of why. I looked hard for something written by him that would capture the essence of his views, asking a couple of Foucauldian 'experts' that I know for guidance, as well as rereading likely parts of his intricately expressed *œuvre* myself. I was defeated in my search for something that a beginner might be able to understand, so I turned to someone else's (textbook) summary of his ideas. That is why you will find in this book a reading by Stuart Hall (who of course is himself quite a thinker) called 'Foucault and discourse'. Additionally, I am a great admirer of some textbook writings: the art of explaining complicated things clearly and simply is undervalued in an academic environment that often seems to revere complexity for the sake of it. That is why you will find readings such as

'Searching for text' by Graham Gibbs, or 'Attitude scaling methods' by A.N. Oppenheim. This latter is from an early textbook that has become a classic, and the Gibbs textbook deserves to be a future classic. These are authors describing other people's ideas, but they put things in a lovely way.

And then you must know that I have edited the original texts quite radically in order to extract the essential ideas, also eliminating repetition and unnecessary complexity where I can see it. I got a lot of practice in doing this when I took part in editing successive editions of a student reader on *Health and Disease* (Davey *et al.*, 1995, 2001). There, we were trying to achieve some similar things to the present volume. But above all, I think, I have tried in this book to apply a lifelong habit that I have developed as a practising researcher and academic, and I think maybe you should know a bit about this habit because it could be helpful to you. I call it 'getting the essentials'. Like the craft skills described by Michael Billig and C. Wright Mills in the first two readings in this book, this is a habit that could assist you across a range of academic activities.

Getting the essentials

Something I have noticed in students, and I saw evidence of this practice as I trawled the library shelves for extracts to place in the present book, is that there is a very prevalent habit nowadays, when reading a book, to place marks on it. These may be done with highlighter pens, or by underlining passages in ink or pencil. I see this more and more in library books and, since some of the books I needed to consult for the present reader were quite popular ones, particularly in those books. This upsets me a lot, because when I then try to read texts that have these marks on them it is hard to have my own fresh encounter with the author's ideas: I am always looking at the text through the lens of one (or more) of these other readers.

So don't do that to this text please, unless you own it. Even if you do own it, there may be a better way of getting what you want, and also learning a really useful skill, which I describe below.

My education, I suppose, was 'traditional', in the sense that we learned things in a way that maybe people do not believe in quite so strongly any more. One of the things we had to do a lot was to write summaries, or *précis*, of other writers. These are a bit like the 'abstracts' that you find at the start of academic journal articles, in which the writer summarizes the findings, or the argument. As children, we didn't like doing this very much, but we were made to do it anyway. It pains me to say this, because I feel somehow that I am betraying that little person I once was, who felt all of this was a silly exercise imposed by thoughtlessly authoritarian adults, but I confess now that the ability to write short summaries of other people's ideas has proved really useful. Because I was also brought up to believe books were precious things, I never wrote in them either. Photocopying wasn't an option, because there weren't any copiers. My memory was, and still is, terrible. If I wanted to remember what I had read, therefore, I had to write down a summary of it.

I have now got six filing cabinet drawers in my office, containing my notes and summaries of other writers. This is an amazingly helpful resource. I don't have to rely on memory, nor do I have to get hold of the books again and leaf through to find highlighted passages. If I need to recall what someone said about something, it doesn't take long to do this, as there are only 4 or 5 pages to read instead of a whole book. Sometimes I used to copy out good quotations that I could use in essays or other writing. Nowadays I tend to just note that a good quote exists on page 453 or whatever, and then I photocopy just that page before I give the book back to the library, and add it to my notes. It's a great method for doing academic work, because out of these notes I can stitch together my own arguments and I can show my readers that I have done justice to existing people in the field.

But more importantly, I have found that it helps me 'cut through the crap' in understanding someone else's ideas. I get tired, writing notes. I don't want to copy out the whole text, or summarize every little aside that the author makes. So I have learned to look at the text and extract the main points. I have done this for hundreds and hundreds of articles and books over a period of twenty or more years, so I would claim I am pretty good at it now. I find it influences my writing too. If you can deconstruct someone else's text in this way, it influences how you put together your own arguments. Hopefully, it means there's less diversionary material (the 'crap') and you focus on the important things.

That is a lot of claims to make, and you may be feeling that they are a bit self-serving by now, as they seem to consist of me complimenting myself on being such a clever fellow. But I hope you'll see, too, that this is something that informs how this book has been put together. I have used this trained capacity to get to the essentials of someone's ideas to generate quite brief extracts from a large variety of writers. I have surprised myself in having been able to fit into a single volume the essentials of a wide survey of writings on social research methods, including a variety of qualitative and quantitative techniques, as well as more abstract philosophical and theoretical considerations. I think the text that is presented is fairly straightforward to understand, and I have done my best to preserve some of the excitement conveyed in the original words of these great writers. This returns me to why I am so excited about this book, and why I hope you will be too.

One objection that can be made to this approach is that my reading of what is essential may not be the same as another reader's. This actually touches on some pretty deep philosophical and political issues about how knowledge is constructed, as you will discover when you read some of the extracts in Part Twelve – particularly 'Partial truths' by James Clifford. Of course, any book presents one version out of many that are possible. There is no doubt that I have blind spots, I have interests that others do not share, I bring my biography as a researcher with particular preferences to this text, to the selection of extracts, to the editing out of some 'crap' and the editing in of 'the essentials'. Who is to say I am right in what I have done, that my reading of the field should prevail?

In one sense, I can't escape from this problem on my own. Editing something heavily has the advantages I have outlined, but may increase the 'danger' of promoting a particular reading. I am not going to make a special plea that I am a particularly liberal, experienced or enlightened person, interested in a wide variety of research practices rather than narrowly committed to a single form, such that I am less likely to impose 'my own views' on the extracts than many others (though, as you can see, I am pretty tempted to go down this route). Instead, I can only point you in the direction of further work that you can do, so that you can form your own opinion about how selective I have been. First, you can read the originals themselves and check out the material I have chosen to ignore. The references are all listed under the chapter headings and it is likely that most can be found in your local university library. Second, you can start to read some authors that I have not read, so that you can make your own personal selection of what you consider to be great methodological writing. Again the 'Further reading' at the end of the introduction to each part contains suggestions for this. These are all things you could do, and in fact you should do if you are to emerge from the sheltering canopy of your teachers and exercise some independence of thought. But you have got to start somewhere, and I offer you this book as a good place to begin.

Organization of the book

The book, as you will have seen from the Contents page, is organised into fifteen parts of varying lengths. The shortest is the first part, containing just two readings. These, by Michael Billig and C. Wright Mills, contain general reflections and tips that are likely to be helpful in orienting you to research practice, and to the business of doing academic work in general. These kinds of preliminary considerations can be useful to start with, and helpful to return to from time to time. In a sense, they continue the discussion I am constructing in parts of this introduction, about what it is to be an independent thinker, about the role that methodological procedures may, or may not play, in doing good work, about some tips or tricks that can sometimes help.

Thereafter, the book proceeds in a quasi-chronological fashion, starting with sections on scientific conceptions of social research, and quantitative method, continuing with attempts to criticize or 'overthrow' this paradigm that emerged particularly powerfully in the 1960s and 1970s, accompanied by a large variety of qualitative or interpretive alternatives, in which philosophical and political considerations loom increasingly large. Although this is a convenient way of organizing things, I would urge you not too read too much of a story into this organization. Quantitative and scientific conceptions of research have not been overthrown or superseded by other methods in contemporary research practice; interpretive and qualitative methods were around in various guises long before the 1960s. Many practising researchers share the view, nowadays, that a variety of approaches to social research have emerged at various times, and that it is best to learn skills in all of them if possible, since different approaches are suited to different kinds of research problem.

Be that as it may, the book continues with sections outlining classic readings on social research as science, followed by sections on the techniques involved in collecting quantitative data through surveys and other methods such as observation or content analysis, as well as methods for using numbers for reasoning about the social world. Following this, in Part Five of the book a variety of quite practical critiques of quantification are shown, before a section in which philosophers of science weigh in with more fundamental issues. These concern the limitations of a simple progress narrative of social science (which some people like to call a 'positivist' approach) in which its methods are seen as equivalent to those of the natural sciences.

This then opens the way for an extended exploration of a variety of qualitative or interpretive methods. First, in Part Seven, there are a variety of conceptions of ethnography – that umbrella term for the application of a variety of techniques of data gathering and thinking about cultures. Then, perhaps the most common form of qualitative research, the interview (either individual or group), is considered. Other sources of qualitative data – pictures, documents, archives, the internet, are then considered before moving on to Part Ten, in which practical techniques for analysing qualitative material are outlined.

Conversation analysis, in Part Ten, is chosen for particularly detailed treatment in order to demonstrate the technical proficiency and rigour that some researchers bring to qualitative analysis, in contrast to its reputation with some uninformed critics as a research style that is impressionistic, subjective or non-rigorous. In the part that follows, a similarly rigorous approach to qualitative analysis, discourse analysis (and its varieties) is described, and it becomes clear that this method, like many that have emerged in recent years, can be explicitly related to some profound shifts of thinking at the philosophical level in the human sciences.

There is then a part entitled 'Reflexivity and representation'. Here, it becomes clear that what has been called the 'crisis of legitimation and representation' (Denzin and Lincoln, 2000: 17) that is seen by some to characterize contemporary academic practice in the various arenas of social research has its roots in earlier moves by sociologists such as Alvin Gouldner (reading 56) to question the politics of knowledge produced in Western sociology. The consequences of this crisis, its relevance for research practice, and the implications of postmodernist ideas are all explored in both this part and the one on 'Postmodernism' that follows.

This is a suitable point at which to consider the political and ethical aspects of social research in the context of more general debates about the relationship that is appropriate between universities and the state in Western countries. These rather grand considerations impinge on researchers in a variety of ways, and awareness of gendered, racialized and other divisions are the hallmark of intelligent research practice in contemporary times. As you will see, though, there is no easy consensus to be had on these matters.

The final part (fifteen) of the book considers the phenomenon of paradigm disputes, a term made possible by the work of Thomas Kuhn, himself represented in an earlier reading (number 27). Like the natural scientists described by Kuhn, social researchers like to form tribes, or bands, or networks that share similar assumptions and preferences. Unlike natural science, though, where there is often a dominant paradigm, social researchers seem to lack consensus around a single set of issues, and 'paradigm wars' (Hammersley, 1992) often break out, with rather dispiriting consequences for people who want to learn a broad variety of research skills. In particular, in British sociology, this has led to a damaging neglect of the quantitative tradition in sociology (though not in other disciplines involved in social research). Fortunately, there exist researchers who have seen fit to build bridges, and others who have changed earlier more trenchant views: the writings of some of these individuals are in this section.

How to use this book

There remains the question of how someone planning to do research ought to use a book on methods. Obviously, a textbook can be used to write essays on method and to pass exams that show you know the content of some methodological debate, can explain some procedure, or construct an argument about methodology for yourself. But that begs the question of why we need to learn about method at all. My reason for teaching people research methods is that they can thereby learn how to do research, or do better research. The purpose of this subject is to help people generate knowledge out of research practice – it is not an end in itself; it is a means to an end. (A secondary aim is to help people evaluate the results of research.)

How, then, can a person use a methodology text to learn or to improve research practice? I said a lot about this in another book I wrote, so I'll quote this here:

> methodological writing is of limited use to practising social researchers, who are pursuing a craft occupation, in large part learned 'on the job', through apprenticeship, experience, trial and error, rather than by studying general accounts of method. The general thrust of the argument is that methodology, if it has any use at all, benefits the quality of research by encouraging a degree of awareness about the methodological implications of particular decisions made during the course of a project. Intense methodological awareness, if engaged in too seriously, can create anxieties that hinder practice, but if taken in small doses can help to guard against more obvious errors. It may also give ideas for those running short on these during the course of a project. Reading methodology, then, is a sort of intellectual muscle building exercise, time out in the brain gymnasium, before returning to the task at hand, hopefully a little stronger and more alert.
>
> (Seale, 1999: ix)

That, though, was from a book (on qualitative research) written largely for people who were already doing research projects, or at least knew quite a lot about research already. Of course, I hope that the present book will attract such readers too, but there is the additional audience now of people who want to learn about research from scratch. I have ensured, therefore, that many of the readings contain quite detailed, concretely described examples of elements of research practice (for example, coding (reading 44), question design (reading 9), writing field notes (reading 33)) as well as more abstract, philosophical or political considerations. This will, I hope, assist in making clear the nature of research practices, both so that you can learn to do these yourself, and so that the abstract considerations (which are otherwise somewhat free floating discussions) are more easily related to what researchers actually do on the ground. Additionally, you will find that there are, at the end of each part introduction, some teaching and learning exercises (Discussion points) that are likely to be of assistance in translating what you have read into better research practice.

Essentially, though, I would stick to the points made in the quote above. Learning to do research is best done through having a go. You can't learn how to swim, or play a piano, from a book. Eventually you have to get into the water and try to float, or open the lid and press the keys. If you do it enough times, and think hard about what you are doing, you should get better fast. Doing research is pretty similar to this. Try gathering materials ('data') in one of the ways described; try analysing some such materials using the analytic techniques covered; think about the philosophical, political and theoretical implications of what you have done, using the readings contained here. This book should help get you started and, for those already skilled in one area of research, will assist you in learning some new approaches.

References

Bryman, A. (2002) *Social Research Methods*, Oxford: Oxford University Press.

Davey, B., Gray, A. and Seale, C.F. (eds) (1995) *Health and Disease: a Reader*, Buckingham: Open University Press. (second edition)

Davey, B., Gray, A. and Seale, C.F. (eds) (1995) *Health and Disease: a Reader*, Buckingham: Open University Press. (third edition)

Denzin, N.K. and Lincoln, Y.S. (2000) 'Introduction: the discipline and practice of qualitative research', in Denzin, N.K. and Lincoln, Y.S. (eds) *Handbook of Qualitative Research*, Thousand Oaks, Cal.: Sage.

Hammersley, M. (1992) 'The paradigm wars: reports from the front', *British Journal of Sociology of Education*, 13 (1): 131–143.

Seale, C.F. (ed.) (1998) *Researching Society and Culture*. London: Sage.

—— (1999) *The Quality of Qualitative Research*. London: Sage.

Further reading
General methods texts

Bernard, H.R. (2000) *Social Research Methods: Qualitative and Quantitative Approaches*, Newbury Park, Cal.: Sage.

—— (2001) *Research Methods in Anthropology: Qualitative and Quantitative Approaches*, 3rd edition, Walnut Creek, Cal.: Altamira Press.

Bryman, A. (2001) *Social Research Methods*, Oxford: Oxford University Press.

Crotty, M. (1998) *The Foundations of Social Research: Meaning and Perspective in the Research Process*, London: Sage.

Denzin, N.K. (1989) *The Research Act: A Theoretical Introduction to Sociological Methods*, 3rd edition, Englewood Cliffs, N.J.: Prentice Hall.

Gilbert, N. (ed.) (2001) *Researching Social Life*, London: Sage.

May, T. (1997) *Social Research: Issues, Methods and Process*, Buckingham: Open University Press.
Pelto, P.J. and Pelto, G.H. (1978) *Anthropological Research: The Structure of Inquiry*, Cambridge: Cambridge University Press.
Rose, G. (1982) *Deciphering Social Research*, London: Macmillan.
Seale, C.F. (1998) (ed.) *Researching Society and Culture*, London: Sage.

Philosophy of science

Fay, B. (1996) *Contemporary Philosophy of Social Science*, Oxford: Blackwell.
Hollis, M. (1994) *The Philosophy of Social Science: An Introduction*, Cambridge: Cambridge University Press.
Smith, M.J. (1998) *Social Science in Question*, London: Sage.
Williams, M. and May, T. (1996) *Introduction to the Philosophy of Social Research*, London: University College London Press.

Quantitative method

Cozby, P.C. (2003) *Methods in Behavioral Research*, New York: McGraw-Hill.
de Vaus, D.A. (2002) *Surveys in Social Research*, 5th edition, London: Routledge.
Sapsford, R. (1999) *Survey Research*, London: Sage.

Qualitative method

Alasuutari, P. (1995) *Researching Culture: Qualitative Method and Cultural Studies*, London: Sage.
Denzin, N.K. and Lincoln, Y.S. (1994) *Handbook of Qualitative Research*, Thousand Oaks, Cal.: Sage.
—— (2000) *Handbook of Qualitative Research, 2nd edition*, Thousand Oaks, Cal.: Sage.
Gubrium, J.F. and Holstein, J.A. (1997) *The New Language of Qualitative Method*, Oxford: Oxford University Press.
Seale, C.F. (1999) *The Quality of Qualitative Research*, London: Sage
Seale, C.F., Gobo, G., Gubrium, J. and Silverman D. (eds) (2004) *Qualitative Research Practice*, London: Sage.

PART ONE

Methodological awareness

INTRODUCTION

THERE ARE JUST TWO readings in this opening section. The first, by Michael Billig, outlines an opposition between the methodologist and the scholar. On the one hand, the methodologist is characterized as a rule follower, devoted to the application of an impersonal and objective system. The scholar, on the other hand, is an independent thinker or intellectual – individually quirky, seeing links between texts that are particular to his or her own network of ideas and experience, breaking methodological rules if they are not appropriate to the task at hand. Billig illustrates these approaches by describing how each type of person might approach the analysis of a political speech.

Mills gives a detailed account of his own working practice as an 'intellectual craftsman', describing his note-taking and filing practices, how his work and his life are intermingled, and how he 'plays' with and explores his filed materials in a variety of ways to generate ideas for research projects and writing.

I have included these extracts because I think it is potentially very helpful for researchers and academics to share knowledge about these less formal processes of doing academic work. Both writers strike me as particularly thoughtful about their working practices and mental processes. They are discussing topics that are hardly ever covered in conventional methods texts, but which are quite central to many aspects of research practice.

DISCUSSION POINTS

- To what extent does Billig's depiction of research practice promote stereotypes and feed 'paradigm warfare'? For example, does his depiction of content analysis tally with that described by Weber in reading 14? What aspects of his account give useful hints on how to proceed with your own work?

- Is Mills a methodologist or a scholar (in Billig's terms)? What aspects of his account give useful hints on how to proceed with your own work? How does his use of notes and files compare with the outline given of Clive Seale's practices in the general introduction to this book?
- Mills writes about 'men' and uses 'he' and 'his' to refer to people in general. This is something shared by other writers in this book (e.g. Lazarsfeld in reading 19, Lofland in reading 33). How does this affect you? Find out how someone else felt about this when they read the piece. Did they have the same reaction as you?

FURTHER READING

Back, L. (2002) 'Dancing and wrestling with scholarship: things to do and things to avoid in a PhD career', *Sociological Research Online* 7 (4). www.socresonline.org.uk/7/4/back.html

Becker, H.S. (1998) *Tricks of the Trade: How To Think About Your Research While You're Doing It,* Chicago: University of Chicago Press.

Chapter 1

Michael Billig

METHODOLOGY AND SCHOLARSHIP IN UNDERSTANDING IDEOLOGICAL EXPLANATION

From Antaki, C. (ed.) *Analysing Everyday Explanation: A Case Book of Methods,* London: Sage (1988).

THIS CHAPTER WILL NOT outline the whys and wherefores of a particular methodology as such. In fact, it will challenge the use of methodology, and the importance which social scientists give to methodological matters. When social scientists advocate the use of a methodology, whether for understanding explanations or for anything else, they are prescribing a set of procedures which the analyst is to follow. Social scientific investigation is frequently presented as being based upon the following of methodological rules. However, this chapter will recommend an alternative approach: that of traditional scholarship. The approach of the traditional scholar can be considered anti-methodological, in that hunches and specialist knowledge are more important than formally defined procedures. This anti-methodological stance will be illustrated by considering the issue of ideology and, in particular, the conspiracy theory of politics. . . . It will be suggested that more understanding is to be gained by using the traditional, ill-defined skills of scholarship than by following a rigorous, up-to-date methodology.

Theoretical background

There are a number of ways in which traditional scholarship can be distinguished from what modern investigators mean by methodology. A *methodology* involves presenting rules of procedure about matters such as the collection of data and their analysis. The rules are impersonal, in that they are meant to apply equally to all researchers. It is assumed that any two researchers who approach the same problem should arrive at identical results, as long as neither infringes the methodological rules. Thereby, it is hoped that individual bias is excluded from the research process. In this way, methodology attempts to standardize the practice of the social sciences and to eliminate quirkiness. To the modern methodologist, traditional scholarship seems a haphazard and biased affair. The traditional scholar does not seem obsessed with laying bare the methodological procedures, which can be followed by anyone with sufficient training.

Individual quirkiness is very much part of traditional *scholarship*. It was taken for granted by the traditional scholar that one should read as widely as possible, and in as many languages as possible. Through wide reading, breadth and depth of knowledge would be gained, as well as the ability to make connections between seemingly disparate phenomena. The learned scholar would be able to interpret individual texts with an acuity not available to those of restricted reading. Traditional scholars are not particularly bothered with the origins of their insights, in the sense that they do not attempt the impossible task of laying bare all the intellectual experiences which lead up to the ability to make a scholarly judgement. Nor do they presume that other scholars will read the same texts in just the same way as they have. In fact, scholars spend a great deal of energy in criticizing the readings of their fellow scholars.

[The] traditional skills of scholarship have much to offer the study of ideology. . . . [For example] the ideology of conspiracy seeks to explain all major political events in the world in terms of an evil conspiracy, or series of conspiracies. The conspiracy theorist tells a story of hidden machinations by small groups who are plotting to subvert the natural order of the world. According to Lipset and Raab (1970), the conspiracy theorist offers a monomanic explanation for social events, in that all major happenings are explained in precisely the same way: no matter what happens, the conspiracy theorist sees the malign hand of hidden conspirators. In this sense conspiracy theory represents an extreme form of personal explanation, in that nothing happens by chance, since all is to be explained in terms of deliberate plotting . . . Over and above the conspiracy theorist's use of a particular type of explanation, there is the matter of explanatory style. The conspiracy theorist employs apocalyptic terms, asserting that the masses have been duped: unless people awake soon to the conspiratorial reality, all will be lost. The conspiracy theorist is like a prophet, who has glimpsed a higher reality and is berating the masses for their unseeing complacency in the face of imminent danger. . . .

In his study of British contemporary fascism, Billig (1978) showed that quantitative methodologies are insufficient for investigating the ideological heritage of conspiracy theory. He showed that a content analysis of UK National Front propaganda only revealed the surface characteristics of that group's ideology. To probe further the deeper meanings and traditions of the ideology it was necessary to explore the wider traditions of conspiracy theory. It was necessary to show how National Front ideologists had absorbed notions from an unbroken ideological tradition, which includes overtly Nazi theorists, non-Nazi groups such as the John Birch Society and eighteenth-century writers such as Auguste de Barruel and John Robison. The identification of this common political culture was not achieved by methodological means as much as by the practices of traditional scholarship. Texts had to be sought out and read and half-hinted allusions had to be noticed and then interpreted. The ideologies of different extremist groups had to be compared, to see whether they were drawing upon common ideological heritages. Only by so doing is it possible to discover when an ideologist is alluding to a writer or a set of ideas firmly situated within the conspiracy tradition. . . .

If such an investigation is to be undertaken, it is not enough merely to see if one or other conservative politician uses conspiracy as a political explanation for a particular event. More is required if an individual conservative is to be located within the ideological traditions of conspiracy theory. The individual must show evidence of possessing an ideological structure which ties together the untidiness of the social world into a tale of deception and conspiracy. In addition there should be evidence of a linkage with the ideological tradition itself. We can consider these problems in relation to the beliefs of a particular UK Conservative Party politician, Enoch Powell, posing the question of whether Powell's beliefs should be located within the ideological traditions of the conspiracy theory. . . .

A sound methodological procedure for attempting to produce an answer would be to opt for a quantitative 'content analysis' . . . The speeches of Enoch Powell could be systematically sampled – perhaps every fifth or tenth of his published orations could be selected. Word counts could be made, with or without computer assistance. Perhaps the word 'conspiracy' could be chosen for special attention. The analysis might then show how many times, per 10 000 other words, Enoch Powell uses the key term 'conspiracy'. Powell's ratio could then be compared statistically to the ratios of other speakers, whose texts had been chosen with as much methodological care.

All this might be quite interesting, but, as Beardsworth (1980) has shown in an important critique, the techniques of such content analysis are essentially limited. This sort of methodology can count words, but it cannot interpret them. Under some circumstances mere counting can lead to misleading conclusions. For example, someone who is continually scoffing at the ideas of conspiracy theories might have just as high a usage of the word 'conspiracy' as the most obsessed believer. Furthermore, the question about Powell is not whether he talks about conspiracies, but whether any such talk should be located within the conspiracy ideological tradition. As will be shown, mere talk about conspiracy, even belief in a conspiracy, is not of itself sufficient evidence for such a location. Over and above statistical identification, such beliefs need to be interpreted by the ideological analyst. Interpretation cannot be achieved by handing over the whole business of scholarship to a programme of computation.

It is one feature of traditional scholarship that attention is not confined exclusively to a single text. Perhaps the scholar might be perplexed by the meaning of a particular text, but that will often signal the start of a search which will embrace other texts and wider reading. Part of the scholar's skill is not to follow a preset programme, laid down in advance by a methodologist, but to gather up clues which can nudge the search one way or another. Scholars have to feel their way around their library and archival sources, backing hunches as they proceed. . . .

[An] extraordinary speech [was] delivered [by Powell] in Bridgnorth on 28 August 1969 and reported in *The Times*. It is a significant speech because it is his first upon Northern Irish matters. Ostensibly, the speech comments upon the report that a French and a German student had been gaoled at Londonderry for throwing petrol bombs. Yet Powell reads wider designs into the report of the single incident. The event was part of a pattern which is subverting nationality and which 'has all but destroyed governments and states in Asia, in Europe and in America'. This wider pattern could explain all manner of phenomena in contemporary life, including racial tensions in Britain and the payment of local property taxes or rates: 'The pattern is recognizable enough and it belongs in an international, a worldwide context.' The moral of all this was that 'We must simply have more control over the admission, the movement and the activities of aliens in this country.'

These themes of national destruction and international plotting seem familiar enough, but what marked this speech out was a remark at the beginning. Having mentioned the newspaper report of the two gaoled students, Powell declared that 'We shall do well to ponder the news item deeply: for, as Douglas Reed used to say in the 1930s; "This means you."' No individual is cited in the speech other than Douglas Reed. Nor is any information given about Reed. To most of the audience and to most of the readers of the written text the name of Douglas Reed would be unfamiliar. But it would be recognizable to those with a knowledge of the traditions of British anti-semitism and the conspiracy ideology. In this way, knowledge of the subject area can lead to insights which fall outside the range of methodological expertise.

Douglas Reed had been a prewar correspondent of *The Times* in Germany. He left Germany in 1935, an opponent of Hitler but not of National Socialism. He was a strong advocate of the Strasser brothers' form of National Socialism. When he died in 1976, *The Times* obituary declared that 'Reed had his own hobby-horses, some of which were indeed not so very unlike Nazi hobby horses.' The writer specified the allusion by mentioning Reed's 'virulent anti-semitism'. It was not merely that Reed was an anti-semite, but that he allied his anti-semitism to conspiratorial fantasies. Reed, in books such as *Far and Wide* and *The Controversy of Zion*, outlined his notions about Jewish plans to take power of the world by subverting independent nations. As Thurlow (1984) points out in his study of British fascism, Reed was one of the first anti-semitic writers to deny the reality of Hitler's persecution of the Jews.

Today Reed's work is unread by mainstream political thinkers, but continues to be much venerated by anti-semitic and fascist groups on the extreme right. Reed is an especial favourite of the UK National Front, which is currently following a Strasserite line. His books, alleging Jewish conspiracies for world domination, are distributed in fascist circles and frequently quoted in anti-semitic publications. For example, *Candour* (July/August 1986) quoted conspiratorial notions from Reed's *Far and Wide* in 'an effort to persuade readers that there is a very cogent argument in support of the Conspiracy Theory' (p. 62). The National Front's magazine, *Nationalism Today*, recently ran a series featuring quotations from writers who 'laid the foundations' of its ideology: issue 19 featured Reed and his ideas about Jews, conspiracies and Jewish conspiracies. It is unsurprising that the sayings of Douglas Reed should appear in National Front publications. It is more noteworthy, to say the least, when they are quoted by Enoch Powell.

Advantages and disadvantages

The procedures followed in this brief examination of Powell have scarcely been methodological in the accepted sense. The starting point was a single text, which needed to be interpreted in terms of other texts before the ideological patterns could emerge. A methodologist might prescribe a system of sampling other texts, but the scholar knows that as much as possible should be read, lest something important be missed. Nor can the results of reading be reduced to a quantitative matrix. A single quotation might have more ideological significance than an oft-repeated one. George (1959), describing the analysis of Nazi propaganda during the war, stressed the importance of uniquely occurring messages. Similarly, in the analysis of Powell, the ideological significance of the quotation from Reed is not diminished by its unusualness; if anything, it is increased by it.

Moreover, the scholar knows that the task of scholarship cannot be reduced to getting through a list of set reading. It is not, for example, merely a matter of ploughing through the collected works of Enoch Powell, in the belief that all necessary reading then will have been completed. Wider reading is also required. . . . Of course the preceding analysis is a very limited sketch. A fuller analysis would have required more details, and scholars must hope to deepen their expertise, not merely as a result of having engaged in study, but as part of the process of studying.

The main drawback of such traditional scholarship is that it places a burden of responsibility upon the scholar. The procedures of methodology make the individual expert anonymous, in the hope of reducing the vagaries of individual bias. Yet this abolition of bias also involves abolishing judgement. The traditional scholar cannot avoid the task of judging whether a piece of evidence is important or not. Moreover, the scholar cannot avoid responsibility for making judgements which can be criticized by other scholars with different views about the essential features of the issue in question. Thus, judgements about the patternings of ideology are potentially controversial. Scholars, with different complexions to their expertise, will argue matters, putting different interpretations on each others' evidence. This is particularly true when one is asserting what are the essential features of an ideological patterning. It cannot be expected that the foregoing analysis is the last word on the subject of Enoch Powell and the shape of his ideology. At best it raises further questions, even as it suggests possibilities for answers.

Moreover, it must be recognized that the analyses of traditional scholarship, or the judgements of traditional scholars, are potentially controversial. In this sense, scholarship is located firmly within the domain of argumentative rhetoric (Billig, 1987 [. . .]). The traditional scholar, amongst many other responsibilities, also has the responsibility not to shirk the possibility of receiving and administering criticism. There are no neutral methodological procedures to hide behind. The analyses of others, even of colleagues, must be criticized if the scholar finds their judgement to be lacking. Moreover, each scholar exposes himself or herself to the danger of criticism, especially to that most damaging accusation of being unscholarly. In consequence, the so-called cosy world of scholarship is, or should be, a controversial place of criticism.

References

Beardsworth, A. (1980) 'Analyzing Press Content: some Technical and Methodological Issues', *Sociological Review Monograph*, 29: 371–95.

Billig, M. (1978) *Fascists: a Social Psychological View of the National Front*. London: Academic Press.

—— (1987) *Arguing and Thinking: A Rhetorical Approach to Social Psychology*. Cambridge: Cambridge University Press.

George, A.L. (1959) *Propaganda Analysis*. Evanston, Ill.: Row, Peterson.

Lipset, S.M. and E. Raab (1970) *The Politics of Unreason*. London: Heinemann.

Thurlow, R. (1984) 'Anti-Nazi. Anti-semite', *Patterns of Prejudice*, 18: 23–34.

Chapter 2

C. Wright Mills

ON INTELLECTUAL CRAFTSMANSHIP

From *The Sociological Imagination,* Oxford: Oxford University Press (1959).

EVERYONE SERIOUSLY CONCERNED WITH teaching complains that most students do not know how to do independent work. They do not know how to read, they do not know how to take notes, they do not know how to set up a problem nor how to research it. In short, they do not know how to work intellectually. Everyone says this, and in the same breath asserts: 'But then, you just can't teach people how to think,' which they someties qualify by: 'At least not apart from some specific subject matter,' or 'At least not without tutorial instruction.'

There is the complaint and there are the dogmatic answers to the complaint all of which amount to saying: 'But we cannot help them much.' This essay is an attempt to help them. It is neither a statement of formal method nor an attempt to inspire. Perhaps there are already too many formal discourses on method, and certainly there are too many inspirational pieces on how to think. Neither seem to be of much use to those for whom they are apparently intended. The first does not usually touch the realities of the problem as the beginning student encounters them: the second is usually vulgar and often nonsense. . . .

Only by conversations in which experienced thinkers exchange information about their actual, informal ways of working can 'method' ever really be imparted to the beginning student. I know of no other way in which to begin such conversations, and thus to begin what I think needs to be done, than to set forth a brief but explicit statement of one man's working habits.

I must repeat that I do not intend to write about method in any formal sense, nor, under the guise of methodology, to take up a statesman-like pose concerning the proper course for social science. So many social scientists nowadays, it seems to me, seem always to be writing about something: and, in the end to be thinking only about their own possible thinking. This may indeed be useful to them and to their future work. But it seems to me rather less than useful to the rest of those at work in the social studies, to those who are just beginning their studies, or to those who have lived with them for quite a while.

Useful discussions of method and theory usually arise as marginal notes on work in progress or work about to get under way. In brief, 'methods' are simply ways of asking and answering questions, with some assurance that the answers are more or less durable. 'Theory' is simply paying close attention to the words one uses, especially their degree of generality and their interrelations. What method and theory properly amount to is clarity of conception and ingenuity of procedure, and most important, in sociology just now, the release rather than the restriction of the sociological imagination.

To have mastered 'theory' and 'method' in short, means to have become a self-conscious thinker, a man ready for work and aware of the assumptions and implications of every step he will take as he tries to find out the character and the meaning of the reality he is working on. On the contrary, to be mastered by 'method' and 'theory' means simply to be kept from working: from trying, that is, to find out about some area of reality. Just as the result of work is infirm without insight into the way it was achieved, so is the way meaningless without a determination that the study shall come to an end and some result be achieved. Method and theory are like the language of the country you live in: it is nothing to brag about that you can speak it, but it is a disgrace, as well as an inconvenience, if you cannot. . . .

Life and work

In joining the scholarly community, one of the first things I realized was that most of the thinkers and writers whom I admired never split their work from their lives. They seemed to take both too seriously to allow such dissociation, and they wanted to use each for the enrichment of the other. Yet such a split is the prevailing convention among men in general, deriving. I supposed, from the hollowness of the work which men in general now do.

I recognized that insofar as I might become a scholar, I would have the exceptional opportunity of designing a way of living which would encourage the habits of good workmanship. It was a choice of how to live as well as a choice of career: whether he knows it or not, the intellectual workman forms his own self as he works towards the perfection of his craft. And so, I came early to the conviction that to realize my own potentialities and opportunities I had to try to construct a character which had as its core the qualities of the good workman. Somehow I realized that I must learn to use my life experience in my intellectual work: continually to interpret it and to use it. It is in this sense that craftsmanship is the center of oneself and that one is personally involved in every intellectual product upon which one may work.

To say that one can 'have experience', means, in part, that past experience plays into and affects present experience, and that it limits the capacity for future experience. But I have to control this rather elaborate interplay, to capture experience and sort it out: only thus can I use it to guide and test my reflection and in the process shape myself as an intellectual craftsman. A personal file is the social organization of the individual's memory: it increases the continuity between life and work, and it permits a continuity in the work itself, and the planning of the work: it is a crossroads of life experience, professional activities, and way of work. In this file the intellectual craftsman tries to integrate what he is doing intellectually and what he is experiencing as a person. Here he is not afraid to use his experience and, as it were, to cross-classify them with various projects which he has under way. It is the link between life and work: in it the two become one.

By serving as a check on repetitious work, my file enables me to conserve what little energy I have. It also encourages me to capture 'fringe-thoughts': various ideas occur, which may be byproducts of everyday experience, snatches of conversation overheard on the street, or for that matter, dreams. Once noted these may lead to more systematic thinking, as well as lend intellectual relevance to more directed experience.

I have often noticed how carefully accomplished thinkers treat their own minds, how closely they observe their development and codify their experience. The reason they treasure their smallest experiences is because, in the course of a lifetime, a modern man has so very little personal experience, and yet experience is so important as a source of good intellectual work. To be able to trust one's own experience, even if it often turns out to be inadequate, is one mark of the mature workman. Such confidence in one's own experience is indispensable to originality in any intellectual pursuit, and the file is one tool by which I have tried to develop and justify such confidence.

If the intellectual workman is a man who has become self-confidently aware of himself as a center of experience and reflection, the keeping of a file is one way of stabilizing, even institutionalizing, this state of being. By the keeping of an adequate file and the self-reflective habits this fosters, one learns how to keep awake one's inner world. Whenever I feel strongly about events or ideas I try not to let them pass from my mind but instead to formulate them for my files and in so doing draw out their implications, show myself either how foolish these feelings or ideas are, or how [they] might be developed into articulate and productive shape. The file also maintains the habit of writing. I cannot 'keep my hand in' if I do not write something at least every week. In the file, one can experiment as a writer and thus develop one's own powers of expression.

Arrangement of file

Under various topics in this file there are ideas, personal notes, and excerpts from books; there are bibliographic items and outlines of projects – it is, I suppose, a matter of arbitrary habit, but I have found it best to blend all these items into a master file of topical projects, with many subdivisions. The topics, of course, are frequently changed. For instance, when as a student I was working toward the preliminary oral examination, the writing of a thesis, and at the same time, doing term papers, files were arranged in these three focal areas of endeavor. But after a year or so of graduate work I began to reorganize the whole file in relation to the main project of the thesis. Then as I pursued my work I noticed that no one project ever dominated my work, nor set the master categories in which the file was arranged. In fact, the use of this file encouraged an expansion of the categories with which I was actively thinking. And the way in which these categories changed, some being dropped out and others being added, was an index of my own intellectual progress and breadth. Eventually, the file came to be arranged according to several larger projects, having many subprojects, which changed from year to year.

All this involves the taking of notes. It is my habit to take a very large volume of notes from any book I read which I feel worth remembering. For the first step in translating experience, either of other men's symbols or of one's own life, into the intellectual sphere is to give it form. Merely to name an item of experience often invites us to explain it: the mere taking of a note from a book is often a prod to reflection. At the same time, the taking of a note is an additional mechanism for comprehension of what one is reading.

My notes seem to be of two sorts. In reading certain very important books I try to grasp the structure of the writer's thoughts, and take notes accordingly. But more frequently, in the last ten years, I do not read whole books, but rather parts of many books, from the point of view of some particular theme in which I am interested, and concerning which I usually have plans in my file. Therefore, I take notes which do not fairly represent the books I read. I am using this particular passage, this particular experience, for the realization of my own projects. Notes taken in this way form the contents of memory upon which I may have to call. . . .

The sociological imagination

But, the reader may ask, how do ideas come? How is the imagination spurred to put all the images and facts together and lend meaning to them? I do not think I can really answer that; all I can do is talk about the general conditions and a few simple techniques which have seemed to increase my chances to come out with something.

I do not believe that workmanlike imagination is an absolute gift. I, at least, have got to work in order to call it forth, and when I am really in the middle of some set of problems, I am working for it all the time, even when I do not know it. I have to develop and nurse it, and I must live as well as work in such a way as to allow it to occur. I believe that there are techniques of imagination and definite ways of stimulating it, although I do not want to acquire any technique of work that would limit the play of fancy. Naturally, I hope that beginning students might gather a few hints for their own ways of work, and some encouragement to pursue them, but I am not suggesting any rigid technique. Yet, there are several ways I have found useful to invite the sociological imagination:

1   The rearranging of the file . . . is one way. One simply dumps out heretofore disconnected folders, mixing up their contents, and then re-sorts them many times. How often and how extensively one does this will of course vary with different problems and the development of their solutions. But in general the mechanics of it are as simple as that.

2   A second technique which should be part of the intellectual workman's way of life consists of a kind of relaxed browsing in libraries, letting the mind play

over books and new periodicals and encyclopedias. Of course, I have in mind the several problems on which I am actively working, and try to be passively receptive to unforeseen and unplanned linkages.

3   Closely related to playing with the file and relaxing in the library is the idea of actively using a variety of perspectives. I will, for instance, ask myself how would a political scientist whom I recently read approach this, or that experimental psychologist, or this historian. One thinks in multiple perspectives which are here represented by men of different specialties. I try in this way to let my mind become a moving prism that catches light from as many angles as possible. In this connection, the writing of dialogues is often very useful.

4   One of the things meant by 'being soaked in the literature' is being able to locate the opponents and the friends of every available viewpoint. I very often try to think against something, and in trying to understand and advance an intellectual field, one of the first things I do is lay out the arguments. . . .

5   An attitude of playfulness toward the phrases and words with which various issues are defined often loosens the imagination. I look up synonyms for each of my key terms in dictionaries as well as in various scholarly books, in order to know the full range of their connotations. This simple procedure seems to prod me to a conceptual elaboration of the problem and hence to a more precise definition of terms. Only if I know the several meanings which might be given to terms or phrases can I select the precise ones with which I want to work. As a student, I kept a notebook containing the vocabularies for handling given problem areas.

6   On all work, but especially on existing theory, I try to keep close watch on the level of generality of every key term, and I often find it useful to take a high-level statement and break it down to more concrete levels. When that is done, the statement often falls into two or three components, each lying along different dimensions. I also try to move up the level of generality: remove the specific qualifiers and examine the re-formed statement more abstractly, to see if I can stretch it or elaborate it. From above and from below, I try to probe.

7   Almost any general idea I come upon will, as I think about it, be cast into some sort of types. A new classification is often the beginning of fruitful developments. The skill required to make up types and then to search for the conditions and consequences of each type has become an automatic procedure with me. Rather than resting content with Democratic vs. Republican voters, I have to make up a classification of voters along the motivational line, and another along the intensity line, and so forth. I am searching for common denominators within Democratic types and Republican types and for differentiating factors within and between all of the types built.

8   The technique of cross-tabulating is not limited to quantitative materials, but as a matter of fact, is a good way to get hold of new types. Charts, tables and diagrams of a qualitative sort not only display models for work already done: they are often genuinely productive in their effects.

9   On almost any problem with which I am concerned, I try to get a comparative grip on the materials. The search for comparative cases in one civilization or historical period or several, or in two samples, gives me leads. I would never

think of describing an institution in twentieth-century America without trying to bear in mind similar institutions in other types of milieu and structure.

10   In the search for comparative cases, I seem to get the best insights from extreme types – from thinking of the opposite of that with which I am directly concerned. If I think about despair, then I also think about elation: if I study the miser, then also the spendthrift. That is also a general characteristic of anchor projects, which, if it is possible, I design in terms of 'polar types'. The hardest thing in the world for me is to study one object: but when I try to contrast objects, I get a sort of grip on the materials and I can then sort out the dimensions in terms of which the comparisons are made. I find the shuttling between these dimensions and the concrete types very illuminating. This technique is also logically sound, for without a sample, you can only guess about statistical frequencies: what you can do is give the range and major types of some phenomenon, and for that it is more economical to begin by constructing 'polar types', opposites along various dimensions. This does not mean that I do not strive to gain and to maintain a sense of proportion, some lead in the frequencies of given types. One continually tries, in fact, to combine this quest with the search for indices for which one might find statistics.

11   I seem automatically to try to put historical depth into my reflection, and I think this is the reason for it: often what you are examining is limited in number, so to get a comparative grip on it, you have got to place it inside a frame with historical depth. To put it another way, the contrasting-type approach often requires the examination of historical cases. This sometimes results in points useful for a trend analysis, or it leads to a typology of stages. I use historical materials, then, because of the desire for a fuller range, or for a more convenient range of some phenomena – by which I mean one that includes the variations along some known set of dimensions. Some knowledge of world history is indispensable to the sociologist: without such knowledge, he is simply a provincial, no matter what else he knows.

From these considerations, I hope the reader will understand that in a way I never 'start' writing on a project: I am writing continuously, either in a more personal vein, in the files, in taking notes after browsing, or in more guided endeavors. I always have, in following this way of living and working, many topics which I want to work out further. After I decide on some 'release' out of this work, I try to use the entire file, the browsing in libraries and periodicals, my conversations and my selection of people – all on this topic. I am trying, you see, to build a framework containing all the key elements which enter into the work: then to put each section in separate folders and continually readjust the whole framework around changes in them. Merely to lay out such a skeleton is to suggest what flesh is needed: facts, tables, more ideas.

So one discovers and describes, constructing typologies for the ordering of what one has found out, focusing and organizing experience by distinguishing items by name. This search for order pushes one to seek out underlying patterns and trends, to find relations that may be typical and causal. One searches, in short, for the meanings of what one has come upon, for what seems capable of being interpreted as a visible token of something else that is invisible. One makes an inventory of everything that seems involved in some phenomena, pares it down to essentials, then carefully and systematically relates these items to one another, thus forming a sort of working model. And then one relates this model to the systematically-defined phe-nomenon one wants to explain. Sometimes it is that easy: sometimes it just will not come.

But always, among all these details, one searches for indicators that might point to the main drift, to the underlying forms and tendencies of society . . . in the middle of the twentieth century. For that is what, in the end, one is always writing about.

Thinking is a simultaneous struggle for conceptual order and empirical com-prehensiveness. You must not close it up too soon – or you will fail to see all that you should: you cannot leave it open forever – or you yourself will burst. It is this dilemma that makes reflection, on those rare occasions when it is more or less successful, the most passionate endeavor of which a man is capable.

PART TWO

Social research as science

INTRODUCTION

THIS SECTION CONTAINS READINGS on the application of scientific method in social research from both a broad philosophical point of view, and from the point of view of researchers designing particular studies. Durkheim (reading 3), writing in 1897 in the preface to his great study of suicide, presents a classic statement of sociological research as science, devoted to the objective discovery of the laws governing society. In it, he reveals his commitment to the building of theories and explanations on a bedrock of facts, which facts stand separately from interpretations. Social facts, such as marriage, the family or religion, are 'things', exercising an external, determining influence over individuals. The discovery of regular causal patterns in which, for example, different kinds of religion influence different rates of suicide, becomes the task of the researcher. Findings like this acquire an independent life of their own, being different in this respect from personally biased social commentary, and can be built upon by other researchers in the future.

The contribution from Walter Wallace (reading 4) continues the distinction between scientific and non-scientific ways of knowing. Conveniently, for our purposes, Wallace uses Durkheim's study of suicide to illustrate the scientific approach he is describing, in which theories arise to explain facts, and propositions, or hypotheses, are tested by reference to new facts that either support or refute theories. This is followed by reading 5 in which Cook and Campbell explain and explore a core idea of the philosopher Karl Popper (falsificationism). In this conception of the research process, theories survive because they explain facts, but a good theory is always potentially falsifiable, not just by contradictory facts, but by a combination of such contradictory observations with plausible rival theories that explain them. Theorizing is thus an inevitable part of the research process; gathering facts alone is never enough. At the same time, there are those ('post positivists' such as Kuhn (reading 27) or Feyerabend (reading 26)) who question the distinction between facts and theories, arguing that all 'facts' are the product not only of observation, but of prior theorizing (whether recognized or not by the researcher). In the view of Cook and Campbell, though, this point can be given an exaggerated importance, and they maintain a belief in the value of falsificationism as a framework for research practice devoted to establishing causal relations.

Reading 6, by Cook and Campbell again, focuses on the topic of the 'internal validity' of quasi-experimental research studies using quantitative data. This refers to the adequacy with which different research designs provide evidence of causal effects. It is not enough to know that two variables (for example, religious belief and suicide attempts) vary together if a causal relationship is to be claimed. Cook and Campbell list a variety of 'threats' to such a claim, which need to be ruled out by a careful research design. This provides a general framework for statistical analysis of the sort described in the readings by Lazarsfeld and Rosenberg (readings 19 and 20) in Part Four. Experimental design is outlined in reading 7 from Pawson and Tilley, who also point out that reviews of large numbers of such experimental research studies in certain areas (crime control, for example) have shown contradictory or inconclusive results. They advocate looking inside the 'black box' of the experimental intervention itself, in order to understand how the intervention is working.

DISCUSSION POINTS

- Summarize Durkheim and Wallace's depiction of scientific and non-scientific ways of knowing, the role of observation in science, and their discussion of objectivity and bias.
- Think of a published research project that you have read. Can you identify theories, hypotheses, observations and empirical generalisations? Do these relate to each other in the way in which Wallace's Figure 4.1 suggests?
- Choose an area of social theory, or a social issue (eg: globalization, deviance, inequalities, racism). What causal propositions might be relevant to this area? In the case of a theory, try to find a proposition that would have to be true for the theory to be supported. What facts would assist in testing or falsifying these propositions? To what extent are such facts pre-constituted by existing theories and assumptions? Are there some facts that are not like this?
- Design an experimental study to discover whether prison is effective in reducing the likelihood of people offending again. Draw on the first part of the Pawson and Tilley reading here. Then assess which of the 'threats' listed by Cook and Campbell apply. How would you design a study that overcomes these threats? (Alternatively, do this for a study of whether an educational programme has helped pupils learn a subject.)
- How could social researchers evaluate the effectiveness of an intervention programme (such as a school, or a 'treatment' programme for offenders) without

using an experimental design, using qualitative rather than quantitative methods?

FURTHER READING

American Psychological Association (1954) 'Validity: technical recommendations for psychological tests and diagnostic techniques', *Psychological Bulletin* (*supplement*): 13–28.

Campbell, D.T. (1969) 'Reforms as experiments', *American Psychologist* 24: 409–429.

Campbell, D.T. and Stanley, J.C. (1966) *Experimental and Quasi-Experimental Design for Research*, Chicago, Ill.: Rand McNally.

Durkheim, E. (1982) *The Rules of Sociological Method*, London: Macmillan.

Popper, K.R. (1963) *Conjectures and Refutations*, London: Routledge and Kegan Paul.

——(1972) *Objective Knowledge*, Oxford: Clarendon Press.

Weber, M. (1949) *The Methodology of the Social Sciences*, New York: Free Press.

Chapter 3

Emile Durkheim

LAWS AND SOCIAL FACTS

From 'Preface' to *Suicide: A Study in Sociology,* translated by Spaulding, J.A. and
Simpson, G., London: Routledge and Kegan Paul (1952).

SOCIOLOGY HAS BEEN IN vogue for some time. Today this word, little
known and almost discredited a decade ago, is in common use. Representatives
of the new science are increasing in number and there is something like a public
feeling favorable to it. Much is expected of it. It must be confessed, however, that
results up to the present time are not really proportionate to the number of publications nor the interest which they arouse. The progress of a science is proven by the
progress toward solution of the problems it treats. It is said to be advancing when
laws hitherto unknown are discovered, or when at least new facts are acquired
modifying the formulation of these problems even though not furnishing a final
solution. Unfortunately, there is good reason why sociology does not appear in this
light, and this is because the problems it proposes are not usually clear-cut. It is still
in the stage of system-building and philosophical syntheses. Instead of attempting to
cast light on a limited portion of the social field, it prefers brilliant generalities
reflecting all sorts of questions to definite treatment of any one. Such a method may
indeed momentarily satisfy public curiosity by offering it so-called illumination on
all sorts of subjects, but it can achieve nothing objective. Brief studies and hasty
intuitions are not enough for the discovery of the laws of so complex a reality. And,
above all, such large and abrupt generalizations are not capable of any sort of proof.
All that is accomplished is the occasional citation of some favorable examples
illustrative of the hypothesis considered, but an illustration is not a proof. Besides,
when so many various matters are dealt with, none is competently treated and only
casual sources can be employed, with no means to make a critical estimate of them.
Works of pure sociology are accordingly of little use to whoever insists on treating

only definite questions, for most of them belong to no particular branch of research and in addition lack really authoritative documentation.

Believers in the future of the science must, of course, be anxious to put an end to this state of affairs. If it should continue, sociology would soon relapse into its old discredit and only the enemies of reason could rejoice at this. The human mind would suffer a grievous setback if this segment of reality which alone has so far denied or defied it should escape it even temporarily. There is nothing necessarily discouraging in the incompleteness of the results thus far obtained. They should arouse new efforts, not surrender. A science so recent cannot be criticized for errors and probings if it sees to it that their recurrence is avoided. Sociology should, then, renounce none of its aims; but, on the other hand, if it is to satisfy the hopes placed in it, it must try to become more than a new sort of philosophical literature. Instead of contenting himself with metaphysical reflection on social themes, the sociologist must take as the object of his research groups of facts clearly circumscribed, capable of ready definition, with definite limits, and adhere strictly to them. Such auxiliary subjects as history, ethnography and statistics are indispensable. The only danger is that their findings may never really be related to the subject he seeks to embrace; for, carefully as he may delimit this subject, it is so rich and varied that it contains inexhaustible and unsuspected tributary fields. But this is not conclusive. If he proceeds accordingly, even though his factual resources are incomplete and his formulae too narrow, he will have nevertheless performed a useful task for future continuation. Conceptions with some objective foundation are not restricted to the personality of their author. They have an impersonal quality which others may take up and pursue; they are transmissible. This makes possible some continuity in scientific labor, – continuity upon which progress depends.

It is in this spirit that the work here presented has been conceived. Suicide has been chosen as its subject, among the various subjects that we have had occasion to study in our teaching career, because few are more accurately to be defined and because it seemed to us particularly timely; its limits have even required study in a preliminary work. On the other hand, by such concentration, real laws are discoverable which demonstrate the possibility of sociology better than any dialectical argument. The ones we hope to have demonstrated will appear. Of course we must have made more than one error, must have overextended the facts observed in our inductions. But at least each proposition carries its proofs with it and we have tried to make them as numerous as possible. Most of all, we have striven in each case to separate the argument and interpretation from the facts interpreted. Thus the reader can judge what is relevant in our explanations without being confused.

Moreover, by thus restricting the research, one is by no means deprived of broad views and general insights. On the contrary, we think we have established a certain number of propositions concerning marriage, widowhood, family life, religious society, etc., which, if we are not mistaken, are more instructive than the common theories of moralists as to the nature of these conditions or institutions. There will even emerge from our study some suggestions concerning the causes of the general contemporary maladjustment being undergone by European societies and concerning remedies which may relieve it. One must not believe that a general condition can only be explained with the aid of generalities. It may appertain to specific causes which can only be determined if carefully studied through no less definite manifestations expressive of them. Suicide as it exists today is precisely one of the forms through which the collective affection from which we suffer is transmitted; thus it will aid us to understand this.

Finally, in the course of this work, but in a concrete and specific form, will appear the chief methodological problems elsewhere stated and examined by us in greater detail.[1] Indeed, among these questions there is one to which the following work makes a contribution too important for us to fail to call it immediately to the attention of the reader.

Sociological method as we practice it rests wholly on the basic principle that social facts must be studied as things, that is, as realities external to the individual. There is no principle for which we have received more criticism; but none is more fundamental. Indubitably for sociology to be possible, it must above all have an object all its own. It must take cognizance of a reality which is not in the domain of other sciences. But if no reality exists outside of individual consciousness, it wholly lacks any material of its own. In that case, the only possible subject of observation is the mental states of the individual, since nothing else exists. That, however, is the field of psychology. From this point of view the essence of marriage, for example, or the family, or religion, consists of individual needs to which these institutions supposedly correspond: paternal affection, filial love, sexual desire, the so-called religious instinct, etc. These institutions themselves, with their varied and complex historical forms, become negligible and of little significance. Being superficial, contingent expressions of the general characteristics of the nature of the individual, they are but one of its aspects and call for no special investigation. Of course, it may occasionally be interesting to see how these eternal sentiments of humanity have been outwardly manifested at different times in history; but as all such manifestations are imperfect, not much importance may be attached to them. Indeed, in certain respects, they are better disregarded to permit more attention to the original source whence flows all their meaning and which they imperfectly reflect. On the pretext of giving the science a more solid foundation by establishing it upon the psychological constitution of the individual, it is thus robbed of the only object proper to it. *It is not realized that there can be no sociology unless societies exist, and that societies cannot exist if there are only individuals.* Moreover, this view is not the least of the causes which maintain the taste for vague generalities in sociology. How can it be important to define the concrete forms of social life, if they are thought to have only a borrowed existence?

But it seems hardly possible to us that there will not emerge, on the contrary, from every page of this book, so to speak, the impression that the individual is dominated by a moral reality greater than himself: namely, collective reality. When each people is seen to have its own suicide-rate, more constant than that of general mortality, that its growth is in accordance with a coefficient of acceleration characteristic of each society; when it appears that the variations through which it passes at different times of the day, month, year, merely reflect the rhythm of social life; and that marriage, divorce, the family, religious society, the army, etc., affect it in accordance with definite laws, some of which may even be numerically expressed –

---

1 *Les Règles de la méthode sociologique*, Paris, F. Alcan, 1895. (Translated into English as *The Rules of Sociological Method*, and published by the Free Press, Glencoe, Illinois, 1950.)

these states and institutions will no longer be regarded simply as characterless, ineffective ideological arrangements. Rather they will be felt to be real, living, active forces which, because of the way they determine the individual, prove their independence of him; which, if the individual enters as an element in the combination whence these forces ensue, at least control him once they are formed. Thus it will appear more clearly why sociology can and must be objective, since it deals with realities as definite and substantial as those of the psychologist or the biologist. . . .

Chapter 4

Walter L. Wallace

THE LOGIC OF SCIENCE IN SOCIOLOGY

From *The Logic of Science in Sociology,* Chicago: Aldine-Atherton (1971).

WHATEVER ELSE IT MAY be, science is a way of generating and testing the truth of statements about events in the world of human experience. But since science is only one of several ways of doing this, it seems appropriate to begin by identifying them all, specifying some of the most general differences among them, and thus locating science within the context they provide.

There are at least four ways of generating, and testing the truth of, empirical statements: 'authoritarian,' 'mystical,' 'logico-rational' and 'scientific.' A principal distinction among these is the manner in which each vests confidence in the *producer* of the statement that is alleged to be true (that is, one asks, *Who* says so?); in the *procedure* by which the statement was produced (that is, one asks, *How* do you know?): and in the *effect* of the statement (that is, one asks, What *difference* does it make?).

In the authoritarian mode, knowledge is sought and tested by referring to those who are socially defined as qualified producers of knowledge (for example, oracles, elders, archbishops, kings, presidents, professors). Here the knowledge-seeker attributes the ability to produce true statements to the natural or supernatural occupant of a particular social position. The procedure whereby the seeker solicits this authority (prayer, petition, etiquette, ceremony) is likely to be important to the nature of the authority's response, but not to the seeker's confidence in that response. Moreover, although the practical effects of the knowledge thus obtained can contribute to the eventual overthrow of authority, a very large number of effective disconfirmations may be required before this happens.

The mystical mode (including its drug- or stress-induced hallucinatory variety) is partly related to the authoritarian, insofar as both may solicit knowledge from

prophets, mediums, divines, gods, and other supernaturally knowledgeable authorities. But the authoritarian mode depends essentially on the social position of the
knowledge-producer, while the mystical mode depends more essentially on manifestations of the knowledge-consumer's personal 'state of grace,' and on his personal psychophysical state. For this reason, in the mystical mode far more may
depend on applying ritualistic purification and sensitizing procedures to the consumer. This mode also extends its solicitations for knowledge beyond animistic gods,
to more impersonal, abstract, unpredictably inspirational, and magical sources, such
as manifest themselves in readings of the tarot, entrails, hexagrams, and horoscopes.
Again, as in the case of the authoritarian mode, a very large number of effective
disconfirmations may be needed before confidence in the mystical grounds for
knowledge can be shaken.

In the logico-rational mode, judgment of statements purporting to be true rests
chiefly on the procedure whereby these statements have been produced; and the
procedure centers on the rules of formal logic. This mode is related to the authoritarian and mystical ones, insofar as the latter two can provide grounds for accepting
both the rules of procedure and the axioms or 'first principles' of the former. But
once these grounds are accepted, for whatever reasons, strict adherence to correct
procedure is held infallibly to produce valid knowledge. As in the two preceding
modes, disconfirmation by effect may have little impact on the acceptability of the
logico-rational mode of acquiring knowledge.

Finally, among these four modes of generating and testing empirical statements,
the scientific mode combines a primary reliance on the observational effects of the
statements in question, with a secondary reliance on the procedures (methods) used
to generate them. Relatively little weight is placed on characteristics of the producer
per se; but when they are involved, achieved rather than ascribed characteristics are
stressed – not for their own sakes, but as *prima facie* certifications of effect and
procedure claims.

In emphasizing the role of methods in the scientific mode, I mean to suggest that
whenever two or more items of information (for example, observations, empirical
generalizations, theories) are believed to be rivals for truth-value, the choice
depends heavily on a collective assessment and replication of the procedures that
yielded the items. In fact, all of the methods of science may be thought of as
relatively strict cultural conventions whereby the production, transformation, and
therefore the criticism, of proposed items of knowledge may be carried out collect-
ively and with relatively unequivocal results. This centrality of highly conventionalized criticism seems to be what is meant when *method* is sometimes said to be the
essential quality of science; and it is the relative clarity and universality of this
method and its several parts that make it possible for scientists to communicate
across, as well as within, disciplinary lines.

Scientific methods deliberately and systematically seek to annihilate the individual scientist's standpoint. We would like to be able to say of every statement of
scientific information (whether observation, empirical generalization, theory,
hypothesis, or decision to accept or reject an hypothesis) that it represents an
unbiased image of the world – not a given scientist's *personal* image of the world, and
ultimately not even a *human* image of the world, but a *universal* image representing
the way the world 'really' is, without regard to time or place of the observed events

and without regard to any distinguishing characteristics of the observer. Obviously, such disembodied 'objectivity' is impossible to finite beings, and our nearest approximation to it can only be *agreement* among individual scientists. Scientific methods constitute the rules whereby agreement about specific images of the world is reached. The methodological controls of the scientific process thus annihilate the individual's standpoint, not by an impossible effort to substitute objectivity in its literal sense, but by substituting rules for intersubjective criticism, debate, and, ultimately, agreement. The rules for constructing scales, drawing samples, taking measurements, estimating parameters, logically inducing and deducing, etc., become the primary bases for criticizing, rejecting, and accepting items of scientific information. Thus, ideally, criticism is not directed first to what an item of information says about the world, but to the method by which the item was produced.

But I have stressed that reliance on the *observational effects* of statements purporting to be true is even more crucial to science than is its reliance on methodological conventions. By this I mean that if, after the methodological criticism mentioned above, two information components are still believed to be rivals, the extent to which each is accepted by the scientific community tends to depend heavily on its resistance to repeated attempts to refute it by observations. Similarly, when two methodological procedures are believed to be rivals, the choice between them tends to rest on their relative abilities to generate, systematize, and predict new observations. Thus, Popper says: 'I shall certainly admit a system as empirical or scientific only if it is capable of being tested by experience. . . . It must be possible for an empirical scientific system to be refuted by experience' (1961: 40–41).

Assuming that observation is partly independent of the observer (that is, assuming that he can observe something other than himself, even though the observation is shaped to greater or lesser degree by that self – assuming, in short, that observations refer, partly, to something 'out there,' external to any observer), it becomes apparent that reliance on observation seeks the same goal as reliance on method: the annihilation of individual bias and the achievement of a 'universal' image of the way the world 'really' is. But there is an important difference in the manner in which the two seek this goal. Reliance on method attacks individual bias by subjecting it to highly conventionalized criticism and subordinating it to collective agreement. It thus seeks to overpower personal bias with shared bias. Reliance on observation (given the 'independence' assumption mentioned above), however, introduces into both biases an element whose ultimate source is independent of all human biases, whether individual and unique or collective and shared. In a word, it seeks to temper shared bias, as well as individual bias, with *un-bias*.

Therefore, the scientific mode of generating and testing statements about the world of human experience seems to rest on dual appeals to rules (methods) whose origin is human convention, and to events (observables) whose origin is partly nonhuman and nonconventional. From these two bases, science strikes forcibly at the individual biases of its own practitioners that they may jointly pursue, with whatever falter and doom, a literally superhuman view of the world of human experience.

Finally, in this brief comparison of modes of generating and testing knowledge, one should remember that neither the scientific, nor the authoritarian, nor the mystical, nor the logico-rational mode excludes any of the others. Indeed, a typical effort will involve some scientific observation and method, some authoritarian foot-noting and documentation, some invocations of ritually purified (that is, trained) imagination and insight, and some logico-rational induction and deduction; only relative emphasis or predominance among these modes permits classifying actual cases. It is perhaps just as well so, since none of the modes can be guaranteed, in the long run, to produce any more, or any more accurate, or any more important, knowledge than another. And even in the short run, a particular objective truth discovered by mystical, authoritarian, or logico-rational (or, indeed, random) means is no less true than the same truth discovered by scientific means. Only our con-fidence in its truth will vary, depending on which means we have been socialized to accept with least question.

Given this initial perspective on science as compared to other ways of testing the truth of statements about the world of human experience, a more focused approach to it can be made.

Overview of elements in the scientific process

The scientific process may be described as involving five principal information components whose transformations into one another are controlled by six principal sets of methods, in the general manner shown in Figure 4.1. . . . In brief translation, Figure 4.1 indicates the following ideas:

Individual observations are highly specific and essentially unique items of information whose synthesis into the more general form denoted by empirical generalizations is accomplished by measurement, sample summarization, and par-ameter estimation. Empirical generalizations, in turn, are items of information that can be synthesized into a theory via concept formation, proposition for-mation, and proposition arrangement. A theory, the most general type of information, is transformable into new hypotheses through the method of logical deduction. An empirical hypothesis is an information item that becomes trans-formed into new observations via interpretation of the hypothesis into observables, instrumentation, scaling, and sampling. These new observations are transformable into new empirical generalizations (again, via measurement, sample summariza-tion, and parameter estimation), and the hypothesis that occasioned their con-struction may then be tested for conformity to them. Such tests may result in a new informational outcome: namely, a decision to accept or reject the truth of the tested hypothesis. Finally, it is inferred that the latter gives confirmation, modifica-tion, or rejection of the theory. . . . Although Figure 4.1 and the discussion in this book are intended to be *systematic* renderings of science as a field of socially organized human endeavor, they are not intended to be inflexible. The task I have chosen is to set forth the principal common elements – the themes – on which a very large number of variations can be, and are, developed by different scientists. . . .

But as C. Wright Mills implied, . . . in practice any element in the scientific process may vary widely in the degree of its formalization and integration with other elements. Mills argued specifically that the relationship of theorizing to other phases in the scientific process can be so tenuous that theory becomes distorted and

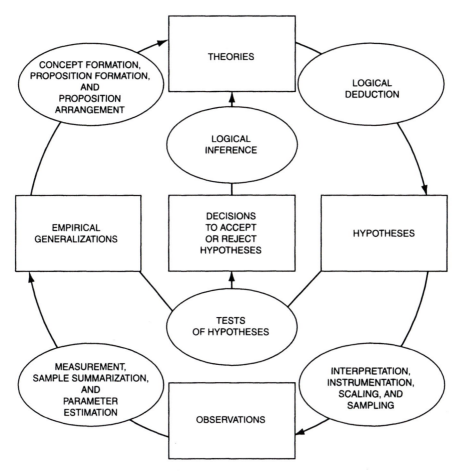

Figure 4.1 The principal informational components, methodological controls and information transformations of the scientific process.

Note: Informational components are shown in rectangles; methodological controls are shown in ovals; information transformations are shown by arrows.

enslaved by 'the fetishism of the Concept.' Similarly, he claimed, the relationship of research methods to hypotheses, observations, and empirical generalizations can be so rigid that empirical research becomes distorted by 'the methodological inhibition.' . . . Mills dubbed these two distortions 'grand theory' and 'abstracted empiricism' (1959: 25–75). Glaser and Strauss also derisively contrast 'logico-deductive theory, which . . . was merely thought up on the basis of *a priori* assumption and a touch of common sense, peppered with a few old theoretical speculations made by the erudite,' with 'grounded' theory – theory generated 'from data systematically obtained from social research' (1967: 29, 2).

[. . .]

An illustration based on Durkheim's *Suicide*

The formulations presented so far are relatively abstract. An illustration based on Durkheim's famous study (first released in 1897) may convey the overall sense of the process . . . (It must be emphasized that in this illustration I am not concerned with how empirically true my statements about suicide are, nor am I much concerned with how accurately they reproduce Durkheim's statements; instead, I am concerned chiefly that the form of my statements illustrates Figure 4.1, and thus illustrates how scientific statements about suicide *would* be generated and their truth tested.)

Suppose a scientist became interested in explaining why suicide rates are higher among some people than others. Such an interest is almost certain to be generated by prior theory and hypotheses (Durkheim indicated in the Preface to *Suicide*, pages 35–39, that his own interest was so generated), even though they may be vague, implicit, and unconsciously held. But the first explicit step in satisfying one's research interest would be to interpret the concept 'suicide' in terms of phenomena on which observations can actually be made.

Following that, one might choose or construct the scales that are to be applied to these observations. Durkheim used the ratio scale of counting; the nominal scales of religious affiliation, sex, nationality, etc.; the interval scale of calendar year; and the (obviously) ordinal scale of marital status.

Next, the instruments whereby observations will be made are determined. Durkheim relied on official documents (which he accepted as accurately recording observations on suicide as he interpreted the term) and the published works of others.

Then, decisions regarding sampling procedures are made. Durkheim sampled suicides presumably committed during given years of the nineteenth century, in various geopolitical units of Europe, by persons in given age categories, by persons of given sex, etc.

Finally, by acting in accord with the above methodological decisions, a large number of individual observations would be collected. These observations would be measured by the appropriate scales and the measures would then be summarized in the form of rates, averages, totals, maps, tables, graphs, and the like. Since these summaries would refer only to the observations that were actually in the samples, some estimate would be made of the corresponding true (that is, error-free) values of these measures in the populations from which the samples were drawn. Durkheim does not seem to have considered this question explicitly, and simply treated his sample statistics as if they were population parameters.

At this point, the large number of observations so laboriously collected might be reduced to a brief but informationally heavy-laden empirical generalization: 'suicide varies with Catholic and Protestant religious affiliation.'

The next information transformation (of empirical generalization into theory) involves four entirely mental steps: (1) forming a concept (explanans) that identifies some characteristic that the examined religious affiliation populations, together with other populations still unexamined, may have in different degree, and that may logically or causally account for their having different suicide rates; (2) forming a concept (explanandum) that identifies some characteristic that suicide rates have in common with other conceivable rates, by virtue of which they might all be logical or causal consequences of the explanans; (3) forming a proposition in which the explanans and explanandum are related in a way consistent with the relationship stated in the originating empirical generalization; and (4) forming several such propositions, all sharing a common explanandum or a common explanans, and arranging them in such a way that further hypotheses can be deduced and tested.

To continue the Durkheim-based example, the first step (forming the explanans) means that one might arrive at a statement such as, 'Suicide rates vary inversely with the *social integration of individuals* in its very-low-to-moderate range.' Here only religious affiliation – the independent variable of the originating empirical generalization – has been theoretically conceptualized. After the second step, one might say, 'The *incidence of deviant behavior* varies inversely with the social integration of individuals in its very-low-to-moderate range,' thus adding a more abstract conceptualization of suicide rate – the original dependent variable. The third step might yield a theoretic proposition of the following kind: 'The social integration of individuals, in its very-low-to-moderate range, causes, in inverse ratio, the incidence of deviant behavior.' Here the explanans and explanandum are related as cause and effect – a relationship consistent with that in the original empirical generalization, but going beyond observable 'covariation' to the more abstract 'causation.'

Finally, in the fourth step, through reiterations of the above process (beginning with the transformation of observations into empirical generalizations) one might develop three other Durkheim-like propositions. Then, all four propositions (together with necessary definitions) might be arranged into the following concatenated theory:

Definitions:

1   'Deviant behavior' refers to individuals' violations of particular behavioral prescriptions or proscriptions promulgated by others.
2   'Social integration' refers to the degree to which individuals objectively receive benefits and injuries provided by others, and so are integrated into the latter's social system.
3   'Normative integration' refers to the degree to which individuals subjectively accept behavioral prescriptions and proscriptions promulgated by others, and so are integrated into the latter's normative system.

Propositions:
The incidence of deviant behavior is caused:

1   In inverse ratio by social integration in its very-low-to-moderate (egoism) range;
2   In direct ratio by social integration in its moderate-to-very-high (altruism) range;
3   In inverse ratio by normative integration in its very-low-to-moderate (anomie) range; and
4   In direct ratio by normative integration in its moderate-to-very-high (fatalism) range.

From such a theory, one could deduce, interpret, and finally test new hypotheses purporting to explain the incidence of kinds of deviant behavior other than suicide by referring to manifestations of social and normative integration other than those actually examined in the process of generating the theory. For example (again drawn from Durkheim), if it could be shown that unmarried persons experience less social integration than married persons, and that both are in the very-low-to-moderate range of social integration, then the theory predicts that the unmarried will have a higher suicide rate, and a higher incidence of other deviant behavior, than the married. New observations and new empirical generalizations to test the truth of this new hypothesis could be generated as before, by interpreting the hypothesis into directly observable terms, scaling, instrumentation, and sampling; and by measurement, summarization, and parameter estimation. Then the new empirical generalizations could be compared with the hypothesis; and if the comparison were judged favorable, a decision to accept the hypothesis would be made and confirmation for the theory would be inferred (or, more precisely, no disconfirmation would be inferred). If the theory were to remain unchanged, results of tests of many such hypotheses would describe the limits of the theory. That is, such results would indicate which varieties of 'deviant behavior,' 'social integration,' and 'normative integration' fall within its explanatory scope, and which varieties do not. But since scientists are usually more interested in expanding than in describing the limits of a theory, it would almost certainly be modified under the impact of each test that did not give positive results. . . .

References

Durkheim, Emile. *Suicide*. New York: Free Press, 1951.

Glaser, Barney G. and Anselm L. Strauss. *The Discovery of Grounded Theory*. Chicago: Aldine Publishing, 1997.

Mills, C. Wright. *The Sociological Imagination*. New York: Oxford University Press, 1959.

Popper, Karl R. *The Logic of Scientific Discovery*. New York: Science Editions, 1961.

Chapter 5

Thomas D. Cook and Donald T. Campbell

POPPER AND FALSIFICATIONISM

From *Quasi-experimentation: Design and Analysis Issues for Field Settings,* Chicago: Rand McNally (1979).

A MONG MORE CONTEMPORARY PHILOSOPHERS of science, Popper (1959) has been the most explicit and systematic in recognizing the necessity of basing knowledge on ruling out alternative explanations of phenomena so as to remain, the researcher hopes, with only a single conceivable explanation. Such a theory has general implications for all knowledge processes, and our discussion will reflect this. However, we urge the reader to interpret the following discussion particularly in terms of ruling out alternative interpretations of *causal hypotheses*.

Popper's thinking is based on an acceptance of Hume's critique of induction (e.g., to say that night has always followed day does not logically justify the inductive conclusion that night will always follow day). Accepting this critique entails denying the possibility of confirmatory knowledge based on generalizing from particular observations to general scientific propositions. However, Popper claims that deductive knowledge is logically possible and that deductions from a general scientific proposition can be tested by comparing obtained data with a deduced pattern. If the data fit the pattern, this supports the theory to the provisional extent that no other known theory can account for the pattern. But such corroboration can never prove the theory to be true, although failures to confirm the prediction can falsify the theory under test.

The debate between the 'confirmationist' position of the logical positivists and Popper's 'falsificationist' alternative needs discussion even in a brief review such as this, particularly since both points of view have been rejected by recent post-positivists. Both points of view assume that experimental and observational 'facts' can often be generated that are relevant to the validity of a theory and yet independent enough of the theory to be used in evaluating its validity. This shared assumption has come under vigorous attack, as we will discuss below.

Both the confirmationist and falsificationist assume that scientific theories can be used to generate quantitative predictions as to the outcome of scientific experiments and that these predictions, many of which are about causal relations, can be compared with the data. Let us grant this assumption while noting that such predictions also require many background assumptions. . . . However, let us tentatively agree that on important issues the relevant scientific community can divide outcomes into three categories that are clear in the extremes even if blurred at the borders: (1) confirmed (or corroborated) predictions, (2) ambiguous outcomes, and (3) disconfirmed or falsified predictions. (The degree of precision required for a confirmation varies widely at various stages of a science and even within the same stage for various data types.) . . .

It is in relating these outcomes to the choice among theories that a central distinction between the confirmationist and falsificationist positions emerges. Let us first consider confirmations. The empiricist monism of the positivist leads to the interpretation that the theory which produced the prediction remains a useful, economical summary and predictor of experience. The ambiguity that comes from recognizing that this theory is only one of many different theories that might do equally well with present and past data is not regarded as relevant, for theory is not regarded as a description of real unobserved underlying processes, but rather as but a convenient summarizer and predictor. The 'confirmation' achieved is confirmation of usefulness, rather than of the truth of the theory in any realist sense.

Popper's falsificationism, on the other hand, stresses the ambiguity of confirmation. For him, corroboration gives only the comfort that the theory has been tested and has survived the test that, even after the most impressive corroborations of predictions, it has only achieved the status of 'not yet disconfirmed.' This status of 'not yet disconfirmed' is of course a rare and precious status in any advanced science where rigorous experimentation is possible. . . .

It is our inescapable predicament that we cannot prove a theory or other causal proposition. We must [. . .] try in some practical way to expand as much as we can the number, range, and precision of confirmed predictions. The larger and more precise the set, the fewer will be the alternative explanations, even though this number still remains in some sense infinite. But as practicing scientists, we in fact pay little or no attention to the mere logical possibility of alternative theories. . . . Toulmin (1961, pp. 113–15) has stated the point well:

> Again, philosophers sometimes assert that a finite set of empirical observations can always be explained in terms of an infinite number of hypotheses. The basis for this remark is the simple observation that through any finite set of points an infinite number of mathematical curves can be constructed. If there were no more to 'explanation' than curve-fitting, this doctrine would have some bearing on scientific practice. In fact, the scientist's problem is very different: In an intellectual situation which presents a variety of demands, his or her task is — typically — to accommodate some new discovery to the scientist's own

inherited ideas, without needlessly jeopardizing predecessors' intellectual gains. This kind of problem has an order of complexity quite different from that of simple curve-fitting: Far from a scientist having an infinite number of possibilities to choose between, it may be a stroke of genius to imagine even a single one.

It is only when there exist actually developed alternative explanations that validity questions arise for theories and other causal hypotheses whose predictions have been confirmed. It was because there were no actually developed rivals that Newton's theory was regarded as certainly true for 200 years, even by such critical epistemologists as Kant. . . . But the logical correctness of Hume's analysis of scientific truth is brought home as a relevant problem for scientific induction by the subsequent overthrow of Newton's theory for that of Einstein.

The situation is in fact even sloppier than this. When a theory such as Newton's has no near rivals and predicts exquisitely well an enormous range of phenomena, we tend to forgive it a few wrong predictions. Thus, as Kuhn (1962) emphasizes, there were known in Newton's day systematic errors of prediction, as of the precession of the perihelion of Mercury, which would have invalidated the theory at that time had Einstein's theory been available. The truer picture is one of a competition between developed and preponderantly corroborated theories for an overall superiority in pattern matching (Campbell 1966), that is, in matching a pattern of predictions to a pattern of data.

Thus the only process available for establishing a scientific theory is one of eliminating plausible rival hypotheses. Since these are never enumerable in advance, or at all, and since these are usually quite particular and require quite unique modes of elimination, this is inevitably a rather unsatisfactory and inconclusive procedure. But the logical analysis of our predicament as scientific knowers, from Hume to Popper, convinces us that this is the best we can do.

Let us grant that . . . singular discordant facts, or discordant facts alone, rarely falsify theories unless they are accompanied by alternative theories that are more in accord with the facts. While it would be wrong to state simply that theories are falsified by alternative theories alone, the usual essential is a combination of alternative theory *and* discordant facts. This leads to an emphasis upon a rivalry of theories in an environment of experimental and observational facts. For this rivalry, Popper has used a natural selection analogy in his 1935 presentation (1959), . . . and he stresses the use of critical evidence of all kinds. The rigid thesis that *any* discordant observation falsifies a theory is an oversimplified stereotype of Popper's views created almost entirely by his critics. Popper himself emphasizes tests with multiple validation criteria that permit one theory to be preferred over another. He does not stress a single test being used to reject the theory in the absence of a competitor.

Popper's perspective on falsification depends on the assumption that theories can be compared with each other. This assumption is currently under attack by postpositivists (Hanson 1958; Kuhn 1962; Feyerabend 1975). In challenging positivist beliefs in the possibility of uninterpreted observation statements which provide a theoretically neutral basis for testing theories, the postpositivists have claimed that all observations ('facts') are presumptive and are impregnated with the theory or paradigm under which they were collected. The relevant slogan is one of the 'theory-ladenness of facts.' Our concern is with the corollary that, because facts are laden with a particular theory, the relative merits of theories cannot be estimated by comparing each theory's predictions with 'objective (i.e., theory-free) facts.'

We share the postpositivists' belief that observations are theory-laden and that the construction of sophisticated scientific apparatus and procedures for data presentation usually involve the explicit or implicit acceptance of well-developed scientific theories, over and above the theory being tested. However, we reject the position that observations are laden with only a single theory or paradigm. . . . In the great scientific revolutions, most of the facts and apparatus, as theory laden as they are, still remain available for comparative tests which help assess the relative merits of extant and new rival theories. . . .

Our objection to current connotations of the postpositivist critique goes further. We find much to value in the laboratory scientist's belief in 'stubborn facts' that 'speak for themselves' and which have a firm dependability greater than the fluctuating theories with which one tries to explain them. Modern theorists of science – Popper, Hanson, Polanyi, Kuhn, and Feyerabend included – have exaggerated the role of comprehensive theory in scientific advance and have made experimental evidence seem almost irrelevant. Instead, exploratory experimentation unguided by formal theory, and unexpected experimental discoveries tangential to whatever theory motivated the research, have repeatedly been the source of great scientific advances, providing the stubborn, dependable, replicable puzzles that have justified theoretical efforts at solution. The experimental physicists feel that their incontrovertible laboratory data serve to keep the speculative theorists honest – an indispensable role in the process of science. Of course, when analytically examined, these stubborn, incontrovertible facts turn out to involve both commonsense presumptions and trust in the truth of many well-established theories that are no longer challenged and that make up the shared core of belief of the science in question. In addition, some of these stubborn facts prove to be undependable, become reinterpreted as experimental artifacts, or prove to be laden with the dominant focal theory under attack and disappear once it has been replaced. But the great bulk of factual base is not so, and remains dependable. In some areas of psychology, the difficulties of replicating experimental results are so great that this emphasis will seem inappropriate. Perhaps such areas should put more emphasis on achieving such stubborn facts and less emphasis on elaborate theorization until there are indeed dependable factual puzzles worthy of the theoretical effort.

Popper's work relates to epistemology in general rather than the epistemology of causal inferences in particular. However, his work is totally germane to the logic of drawing causal inferences. Indeed, it implies (1) a logical stress on falsifying causal propositions and on giving the status of 'not yet disproven' to data patterns that corroborate a particular causal hypothesis but do not rule out all plausible alternative causal hypotheses; (2) a need to collect data which will confront the causal propositions under test, recognizing that convincing data-based refutations require multiple disconfirmations from a variety of strong tests and that the data from any one refutation test are not 'objective' in the sense of being free of all theoretical assumptions; and (3) a need to collect data which confronts causal propositions by putting them in competition with other plausible causal propositions, so that a winnowing of the weaker causal hypotheses can take place and a smaller number of hypotheses remains. But whereas Popper is concerned with differentiating between alternative grand theories, the perspective we shall adopt in differentiating among causal hypotheses is less grandiose in implication. Most of the alternatives to the proposition that, say, school desegregation causes an increase in white flight to the suburbs revolve around the possibility that an observed increase in white flight would have occurred without school desegregation, or is an artifact of how white flight is measured, and so on. Such alternatives are threats to the validity of causal inferences but are hardly alternative theories as that term is generally used. Rather, they are more in the nature of theoretical 'nuisance factors.' Yet these are the alternatives most often confronting practicing researchers who attempt to probe causal relationships by trying to rule out alternative explanations for an observed change, particularly when this change conforms to an expected data pattern suggesting that it could be due to the presumed causal aspect whose influence is being tested. . . .

References

Campbell, D.T. 'Pattern matching as an essential in distal knowing.' In K.R. Hammond (ed.), *The Psychology of Egon Brunswik*. New York: Holt, Rinehart, 1966.

Feyerabend, P. *Against Method: Outline of an Anarchist Theory of Knowledge*. London, England: New Left Books, 1975.

Hanson, N.R. *Patterns of Discovery: An Inquiry into the Conceptual Foundations of Science*. Cambridge, England: Cambridge University Press, 1958.

Kuhn, T.S. *The Structure of Scientific Revolutions*. Chicago: University of Chicago Press, 1962.

Popper, K.R. *The Logic of Scientific Discovery*. New York: Basic Books, 1959. (Originally *Die Logik der Forschung*, 1935.)

Toulmin, S.E. *Foresight and Understanding: An Inquiry into the Aims of Science*. Bloomington: Indiana University Press, 1961.

Chapter 6

Thomas D. Cook and Donald T. Campbell

VALIDITY

From *Quasi-experimentation: Design and Analysis Issues for Field Settings,* Chicago: Rand McNally (1979).

W E SHALL USE THE concepts *validity* and *invalidity* to refer to the best available approximation to the truth or falsity of propositions, including propositions about cause. . . . We should always use the modifier 'approximately' when referring to validity, since one can never know what is true. At best, one can know what has not yet been ruled out as false. Hence, when we use the terms valid and invalid in the rest of this book, they should always be understood to be prefaced by the modifiers 'approximately' or 'tentatively.'

One could invoke many types of validity when trying to develop a framework in which to understand experiments in complex field settings. Campbell and Stanley (1963) invoked two, which they called 'internal' and 'external' validity. Internal validity refers to the approximate validity with which we infer that a relationship between two variables is causal or that the absence of a relationship implies the absence of cause. External validity refers to the approximate validity with which we can infer that the presumed causal relationship can be generalized to and across alternate measures of the cause and effect and across different types of persons, settings, and times. . . .

Internal validity

Once it has been established that two variables covary, the problem is to decide whether there is any causal relationship between the two and, if there is, to decide whether the direction of causality is from the measured or manipulated *A* to the measured *B*, or vice versa.

The task of ascertaining the direction of causality usually depends on knowledge of a time sequence. Such knowledge is usually available for experiments, as opposed to most passive correlational studies. In a randomized experiment, the researcher knows that the measurement of possible outcomes takes place after the treatment has been manipulated. In quasi-experiments, most of which require both pretest and posttest measurement, the researcher can relate some measure of pretest-posttest change to differences in treatments.

It is more difficult to assess the possibility that A and B may be related only through some third variable (C). If they were, the causal relationship would have to be described as: $A \rightarrow C \rightarrow B$. This is quite different from the model $A \rightarrow B$ which most clearly implies that A causes B. To conclude that A causes B when in fact the model $A \rightarrow C \rightarrow B$ is true would be to draw a false positive conclusion about cause. Accounting for third-variable alternative interpretations of presumed A-B relationships is the essence of internal validity and is the major focus of this book. . . .

It is possible for more than one internal validity threat to operate in a given situation. The net bias that the threats cause depends on whether they are similar or different in the direction of bias and on the magnitude of any bias they cause independently. Clearly, false causal inferences are more likely the more numerous and powerful the validity threats and the more homogeneous the direction of their effects. Though our discussion will be largely in terms of threats *taken singly*, this should not blind readers to the possibility that multiple internal validity threats can operate in cumulative or countervailing fashion in a single study.

Threats to internal validity

Bearing this brief introduction in mind, we want to define some specific threats to internal validity.

History

'History' is a threat when an observed effect might be due to an event which takes place between the pretest and the posttest, when this event is not the treatment of research interest. In much laboratory research the threat is controlled by *insulating* respondents from outside influences (e.g., in a quiet laboratory) or by *choosing dependent variables* that could not plausibly have been affected by outside forces (e.g., the learning of nonsense syllables). Unfortunately, these techniques are rarely available to the field researcher.

Maturation

This is a threat when an observed effect might be due to the respondent's growing older, wiser, stronger, more experienced, and the like between pretest and posttest and when this maturation is not the treatment of research interest.

Testing

This is a threat when an effect might be due to the number of times particular responses are measured. In particular, familiarity with a test can sometimes enhance performance because items and error responses are more likely to be remembered at later testing sessions.

Instrumentation

This is a threat when an effect might be due to a change in the measuring instrument between pretest and posttest and not to the treatment's differential impact at each time interval. Thus, instrumentation is involved when human observers become more experienced between a pretest and posttest. . . .

Statistical regression

This is a threat when an effect might be due to respondents' being classified into experimental groups at, say, the pretest on the basis of pretest scores or correlates of pretest scores. When this happens and measures are unreliable, high pretest scorers will score relatively lower at the posttest and low pretest scorers will score higher. It would be wrong to attribute such differential 'change' to a treatment because it might be due to statistical regression.

Statistical regression is not an easy concept to grasp intuitively. It might help you understand it if you think of your own academic test taking. You may sometimes have surprised yourself by doing worse than you expected, perhaps because you didn't sleep well the night before, you read the questions too quickly and misunderstood them, there may have been someone with an infuriating cough in front of you, or because the test just happened to have had a disproportionately high number of items from a part of the curriculum that you had not studied in detail. Any or all of these factors could have depressed your scores, and they can be conceptualized as error factors that do not reflect true ability. Consequently, the next time you took a test on the same or similar subject matter your scores would probably be higher and would more accurately reflect your ability. This is because, all things being equal, you will be less likely to have been deprived of sleep, less likely to have read the questions too quickly, less likely to have had someone with a cough sit in front of you, and less likely to have received questions from parts of the curriculum that you had studied the least. . . .

Selection

This is a threat when an effect may be due to the difference between the kinds of people in one experimental group as opposed to another. Selection is therefore pervasive in quasi-experimental research, which is defined in terms of different groups receiving different treatments as opposed to probabilitistically equivalent groups receiving treatments as in the randomized experiment.

Mortality

This is a threat when an effect may be due to the different kinds of persons who dropped out of a particular treatment group during the course of an experiment. This results in a selection artifact, since the experimental groups are then composed of different kinds of persons at the posttest.

Interactions with selection

Many of the foregoing threats to internal validity can interact with selection to produce forces that might spuriously appear as treatment effects. Among these are selection-maturation, selection-history, and selection-instrumentation. . . .

Ambiguity about the direction of causal influence

It is possible to imagine a situation in which all plausible third-variable explanations of an *A-B* relationship have been ruled out and where it is not clear whether *A* causes *B* or *B* causes *A*. This is an especially salient threat to internal validity in simple correlational studies where it will often not be clear whether, for example, less foreman supervision causes higher productivity or whether higher productivity causes less supervision. This particular threat is not salient in most experiments since the order of the temporal precedence is clear. Nor is it a problem in those correlational studies where one direction of causal influence is relatively implausible (e.g., it is more plausible to infer that a decrease in the environmental temperature causes an increase in fuel consumption than it is to infer that an increase in fuel consumption causes a decrease in outside temperature). Nor is it necessarily a problem in correlational studies when the data are collected at more than one time interval, for then one knows something about temporal antecedence. However, ambiguity about the direction of causal influence is a problem in many correlational studies that are cross-sectional.

Diffusion or imitation of treatments

When treatments involve informational programs and when the various experimental (and control) groups can communicate with each other, respondents in one treatment group may learn the information intended for others. The experiment may, therefore, become invalid because there are no planned differences between experimental and control groups. This problem may be particularly acute in quasi-experiments where the desired similarity of experimental units may be accompanied by a physical closeness that permits the groups to communicate. For example, if one of the New England states were used as a control group to study the effects of changes in the New York abortion law, any true effects of the law would be obscured if New Englanders went freely to New York for abortions.

Compensatory equalization of treatments

When the experimental treatment provides goods or services generally believed to be desirable, there may emerge administrative and constituency reluctance to tolerate the focused inequality that results. Thus, in nationwide educational experiments such as Follow Through, the control schools, particularly if equally needy, tended to be given Title I funds earmarked for disadvantaged children. Since these funds were given to the supposed 'no-treatment controls' in amounts approximately equivalent to those coming to the experimental schools, the planned contrast obviously broke down. Several other experimental evaluations of compensatory education have encountered the same problem. It exemplifies a problem of administrative equity that must certainly occur elsewhere, including among units of industrial organizations. Such focused inequities may explain some administrators' reluctance to employ random assignment to treatments which their constituencies consider valuable.

Compensatory rivalry by respondents receiving less desirable treatments

Where the assignment of persons or organizational units to experimental and control conditions is made public (as it frequently must be), conditions of social competition may be generated. The control group, as the natural underdog, may be motivated to reduce or reverse the expected difference. . . . Saretsky (1972) . . . calls this a 'John Henry effect' in honor of the steel driver who, when he knew his output was to be compared to that of a steam drill, worked so hard that he outperformed the drill and died of overexertion. . . .

Resentful demoralization of respondents receiving less desirable treatments

When an experiment is obtrusive, the reaction of a no-treatment control group or groups receiving less desirable treatments can be associated with resentment and demoralization, as well as with compensatory rivalry. This is because persons in the less desirable treatment groups are often relatively deprived when compared to others. In an industrial setting the persons experiencing the less desirable treatments might retaliate by lowering productivity and company profits, while in an educational setting, teachers or students could 'lose heart' or become angry and 'act up.' Any of these forces could lead to a posttest difference between treatment and no-treatment groups, and it would be quite wrong to attribute the difference to the planned treatment. . . .

Estimating internal validity in randomized experiments and quasi-experiments

Estimating the internal validity of a relationship is a deductive process in which the investigator has to systematically think through how each of the internal validity threats may have influenced the data. Then, the investigator has to examine the data to test which relevant threats can be ruled out. In all of this process, the researcher has to be his or her own best critic, trenchantly examining all of the threats he or she can imagine. When all of the threats can plausibly be eliminated, it is possible to make confident conclusions about whether a relationship is probably causal. When all of them cannot, perhaps because the appropriate data are not available or because the data indicate that a particular threat may indeed have operated, then the investigator has to conclude that a demonstrated relationship between two variables may or may not be causal. Sometimes the alternative interpretations may seem implausible enough to be ignored and the investigator will be inclined to dismiss them. They can be dismissed with a special degree of confidence when the alternative interpretations seem unlikely on the basis of findings from a research tradition with a large number of relevant and replicated findings.

Invoking plausibility has its pitfalls, since it may often be difficult to obtain high inter-judge agreement about the plausibility of a particular alternative interpretation. Moreover, theory testers place great emphasis on testing theoretical predictions that seem so implausible that neither common sense nor other theories would make the same prediction. There is in this an implied confession that the 'implausible' is sometimes true. Thus, 'implausible' alternative interpretations should reduce, but not eliminate, our doubt about whether relationships are causal.

When respondents are randomly assigned to treatment groups, each group is similarly constituted on the average (no selection, maturation, or selection-maturation problems). Each experiences the same testing conditions and research instruments (no testing or instrumentation problems). No deliberate selection is made of high and low scorers on any tests except under conditions where respondents are first matched according to, say, pretest scores and are then randomly assigned to treatment conditions (no statistical regression problem). Each group experiences the same global pattern of history (no history problem). And if there are treatment-related differences in who drops out of the experiment, this is interpretable as a consequence of the treatment. Thus, randomization takes care of many threats to internal validity.

With quasi-experimental groups, the situation is quite different. Instead of relying on randomization to rule out most internal validity threats, the investigator has to make all the threats explicit and then rule them out one by one. His task is, therefore, more laborious. It is also less enviable since his final causal inference will not be as strong as if he had conducted a randomized experiment. The principal reason for choosing to conduct randomized experiments over other types of research design is that they make causal inference easier. . . .

References

Campbell, D.T., and Stanley, J.C. 'Experimental and quasi-experimental designs for research on teaching.' In N. L. Gage (ed.), *Handbook of Research on Teaching*. Chicago: Rand McNally, 1963. (Also published as *Experimental and Quasi-experimental Designs for Research*. Chicago: Rand McNally, 1966.)

Saretsky, G. 'The OEO P.C. experiment and the John Henry effect'. *Phi Delta Kappan*, 1972, 53, 579–581.

Chapter 7

Ray Pawson and Nick Tilley

GO FORTH AND EXPERIMENT

From *Realistic Evaluation,* London: Sage (1997).

. . . **UNDERLYING EVERYTHING IN THE** early days of evaluation research was the *logic of experimentation.* Its basic framework is desperately simple and disarmingly familiar to us all. Take two more or less matched groups (if they are really matched through random allocation, you call it real experimentation; quasi-experimentation follows from the impracticality of this in many cases). Treat one group and not the other. Measure both groups before and after the treatment of the one. Compare the changes in the treated and untreated groups, and lo and behold, you have a clear measure of the impact of the program. The practitioner, policy adviser, and social scientist are at one in appreciating the beauty of the design. At one level it has the deepest roots in philosophical discourse on the nature of explanation, as in John Stuart Mill's *A System of Logic* (1961); at another it is the hallmark of common sense, ingrained into advertising campaigns telling us that Washo is superior to Sudz. The basic design . . . is set down as Figure 7.1 using Campbell's classic *OXO* notation (Campbell and Stanley, 1963).

	Pre-test	Treatment	Post-test
Experimental group	O_1	X	O_2
Control group	O_1		O_2

Figure 7.1 The classic experimental design.

The sheet anchor of the method is thus a *theory of causation*. Since the experimental and control groups are identical to begin with, the only difference between them is the application of the program and it is, therefore, only the program which can be responsible for the outcomes. On this simple and elegant basis was constructed the whole edifice of experimental and quasi-experimental evaluation. This way of thinking about causality is known in the epistemological literature as a 'successionist' or 'molar' understanding of causality. The basic idea is that one cannot observe 'causation' in the way one observes teaching schemes and changes in reading standards, or burglar alarms and changes in crime rates. Causation between treatment and outcome has to be *inferred* from the repeated succession of one such event by another. The point of the method, therefore, is to attempt to exclude every conceivable rival causal agent from the experiment so that we are left with one, secure causal link.

At this juncture experimentalists acknowledge a fundamental distinction between their work in the laboratory and in the field. A simple ontological distinction is drawn which regards the social world as inherently 'complex', 'open', 'dynamic' and so forth. This renders the clear-cut 'program causes outcome' conclusion much more problematic in the messy world of field experiments. Additional safeguards thus have to be called up to protect the 'internal validity' of causal inferences in such situations. For instance, there is the problem of 'history', where during the application of the program an unexpected event happens which is not part of the intended treatment but which could be responsible for the outcome. An example might be the comparisons of localities with and without neighbourhood watch schemes, during which police activity suddenly increases in one in response to some local policy directive. The neat experimental comparison is thus broken and needs to be supplemented with additional monitoring and statistical controls in order that we can be sure the scheme rather than the increased patrols is the vital causal agent. Such an example can be thought of as a shorthand for the development of the entire quasi-experimental method. The whole point is to wrestle with the design and analysis of field experimentation to achieve sufficient *control* to make the basic causal inference secure.

Following these principles of method comes a theory of *policy implementation*. In Campbell's case we can properly call this a 'vision' of the *experimenting society* – a standpoint which is best summed up in the famous opening passage from his 'Reforms as experiments' (1969):

> The United States and other modern nations should be ready for an experimental approach to social reform, an approach in which we try out new programs designed to cure specific social problems, in which we learn whether or not these programs are effective, and in which we retain, imitate, modify or discard them on the basis of their apparent effectiveness on the multiple imperfect criteria available.

What we have here, then, is a clear-cut Popperian (1945) view of the open society, always at the ready to engage in piecemeal social engineering, and to do so on the basis of cold, rational calculations which evaluate bold initiatives. . . .

For us, the experimental paradigm constitutes a heroic failure, promising so much and yet ending up in ironic anticlimax. The underlying logic (as above) seems meticulous, clear-headed and militarily precise, and yet findings seem to emerge in a typically non-cumulative, low-impact, prone-to-equivocation sort of way. . . . The experimental approach has always been gripped by anxiety about its own track record. . . . The real 'quake occurred with the publication of Martinson's 'What works? Questions and answers about prison reform' (1974). . . . Martinson's (1974) paper is a summary of a 1,400 page manuscript which itself was a summary of *all* published reports in English on attempts at the rehabilitation of offenders from 1945 to 1967. These programs are sorted into a series of broad 'treatments', so that Martinson reviews, in turn, educational and vocational training, individual counselling, milieu therapy, drug and surgical treatment, sentence variation, decarceration, community psychotherapy, probation and parole, and intensive supervision. Curiously, he never uttered the verdict 'nothing works' directly in the whole paper, yet he managed to flatten the aspirations of reformers in fields way beyond his own with these words:

> I am bound to say that these data, involving over two hundred studies and hundreds of thousands of individuals as they do, are the best available and give us very little reason to hope that we have in fact found a sure way of reducing recidivism through rehabilitation. This is not to say that we have found no instances of success or partial success; it is only to say that these instances have been isolated, producing no clear pattern to indicate the efficacy of any particular method of treatment.
>
> (1974, p. 49)

Reading Martinson's paper (or indeed this very passage) from the point of view of the rhetorical practices involved, we can say that *it works* through the construction of an impossibly stringent criterion for 'success'. To count as a body of treatment that 'works', such programs have to provide positive changes in favour of the experimental group in all trials in all contexts. He is thus able to discount successful experiments by dint of them being 'isolated' and thus producing an 'inconsistent' pattern of outcomes.

Thanks to this loaded logic Martinson managed to throw a spanner in the works of evaluation which has rattled around ever since. He certainly hit the spot in terms of political reaction, for indeed, in the 1970s, 'reaction' was growing. The merest possibility that 'nothing works' was just the spur needed for a backlash demanding 'retribution' and 'just deserts' as the proper engines of criminal justice, a clamour which students of the political ebb and flow report as lasting comfortably into the 1980s (Nuttall, 1992).

Although overshadowed politically, the 'mainstream' evaluation community never took Martinson's pessimism seriously. Palmer (1975) 'revisited' Martinson's study in the year following its publication and pointed to the skulduggery involved in bundling programs into broad treatment groups which would inevitably show mixed results. Palmer observes that, if programs are taken on an individual basis, Martinson details and actually uses the term 'success' to describe dozens of conditional positive achievements in which certain portions of programs had worked for a portion of their clientele. Following the same example through, we note that 'revivification' of faith in rehabilitation was symbolized with the publication of two massive, Martinson-like overviews of corrections programs (Ross and Gendreau, 1980; Gendreau and Ross, 1987). On the basis of fresher but much the same types of evidence as that surveyed by their gloomy predecessor, they opined (hopefully) to the effect that *most things have been found sometimes to work. . . .*

Palmer cocks the gun for our second blast at the experimental approach, in his recommendation, following his review of Martinson, that:

> Rather than ask 'What works for offenders as a whole?' we must increas-ingly ask, 'Which methods work best for which types of offenders and under what conditions or in what types of settings?
>
> (1975, p. 150)

Reviewing a rather different literature, Rosenbaum makes a remarkably similar point when he says in relation to crime prevention:

> [There is] a compelling need to open up the black box . . . and test the many presumed causal links in our theoretical models. We are past the point of wanting to report that crime prevention does or does not work, and now are interested in specifying the conditions under which particu-lar outcomes are observed.
>
> (1988, p. 382)

These are indeed words of wisdom for evaluators. . . . Festering away in both these challenges is the dilemma that experimental evaluation might be incapable of asking the right question. The aim of *OXO* outcome investigation is to achieve sufficient control to tell us in any particular trial whether an initiative has 'worked' or not. To understand why there is inconsistency of outcomes we need to ask the rather different question of 'why' or 'how' the measure has its effect. We need a method which seeks to understand what the program actually does to change behaviours and why not every situation is conducive to that particular process. . . .

References

Campbell, D. (1969) 'Reforms as experiments,' *American Psychologist*, 24: 409–429.

Campbell, D. and Stanley, J. (1963) *Experimental and Quasi-Experimental Evaluations in Social Research*, Chicago: Rand McNally.

Gendreau, P. and Ross, R. (1987) 'The revivification of rehabilitation,' *Justice Quarterly*, 4: 349–408.

Martinson, R. (1974) 'What works? Questions and answers about prison reform,' *Public Interest*, 35: 22–45.

Mill, J.S. (1961) *A System of Logic*. London: Longman.

Nuttall, C. (1992) 'What works?' in *Proceedings of the Annual Conference of the Association of Chief Officers of Probation*. Wakefield: Association of Chief Officers of Probation.

Palmer, T. (1975) 'Martinson revisited,' *Journal of Research in Crime and Delinquency*, July: 133–152.

Popper, K. (1945) *The Open Society and its Enemies*. London: Routledge.

Rosenbaum, D. (1988) 'Community crime prevention: a review and synthesis of the literature,' *Justice Quarterly*, 5: 325–395.

Ross, R. and Gendreau, P. (1980) *Effective Correctional Treatment*. Toronto: Butterworths.

PART THREE

Collecting quantitative data

INTRODUCTION

A VARIETY OF METHODS for producing quantitative data are available to social and cultural researchers. In the modern world we live, as Ian Hacking (reading 15) suggests, in the midst of an 'avalanche of printed numbers', and social researchers play a key part in this quantification of life, often through the application of survey methods. The readings in this section are designed to provide practical guidance on the conduct of social surveys and other methods for the production of statistical information about social processes.

The first reading, by Hedges (reading 8), concerns the selection of samples for social surveys. A sample is a selection from a wider population to whom it is hoped the results found in the sample can be generalized. Random sampling can be done in various ways, and it is important to distinguish these from non-random methods whose representativeness of relevant populations cannot be estimated. Ways of dealing with the problems of non-response and inadequate listings ('sampling frames') of populations are also addressed.

The next three readings consider questionnaires and interviewing, the methods most commonly used for collecting data in social surveys. Moser and Kalton (reading 9) distinguish first between questions asking for facts and questions asking for opinions, noting that the latter are hardest to ask about. They then present a list, with examples, of some common problems with question wording before considering the relative merits of pre-coded (often called 'fixed choice') questions and open questions and discussing considerations that may influence the order in which questions are put. Trying out drafts of questionnaires and interview schedules before using them in the study proper is recommended. The reading by Hyman et al. (reading 10) discusses the substantial body of methodological work that has addressed the phenomenon of error in interviewing, including a research project done by the authors into the conduct of interviews. This piece was written in the context of large-scale social survey work, in which teams of interviewers are generally hired to gather data for projects designed by researchers. A major concern of these authors is to discover ways of eliminating various forms of interviewer bias, including attention to the motivation and working conditions of interviewers, an issue close to the heart of a later contributor to this book (Roth, reading 21).

Oppenheim (reading 11) tackles techniques for measuring attitudes, identified as a difficult area in the earlier reading by Moser and Kalton. To do this, he takes us back to the first principles of measurement, identifying the criteria a good measure should meet, before considering the degree to which different approaches to attitude meas-urement fulfil these criteria. In this extract, only his account of the Likert method is reproduced for reasons of space. Importantly, Oppenheim then discusses methods for ensuring the validity of such scales, for ensuring in other words that they measure the underlying dimensions that their makers intend. It becomes clear that while methods for improving validity exist, the relation of measurable 'attitudes' to actual behaviour is a somewhat open question.

The next three readings demonstrate the potential of less conventional sources of quantitative (and some qualitative) data. It is clear that the internet and email (read-ing 12) offer many advantages in gathering information from members of certain kinds of population. Sheehan and Hoy demonstrate the advantages and disadvantages of different forms of on-line surveys, as well as comparing these with conventional survey methods. Flanders (reading 13) describes a schedule for 'interaction analysis' that, with practice, can be used by a classroom observer to generate quantitative data about significant patterns of interaction as they occur. This schedule and others like it have been widely used in educational research. Weber (reading 14) outlines the method of quantitative content analysis, usually applied to texts, whether these be documents or transcripts of speeches. His comments on reliability and validity demon-strate similar concerns to those of Oppenheim in relation to attitude measurement (reading 11).

The section ends with a reflective piece from Hacking (reading 15), who relates the popularity of quantification and statistics to historical changes in society, and a growth in interest in explaining human behaviour as the outcome of laws of chance. Accompanying this arose a vision of what it is to be normal, such 'normalcy' being defined by statistical distributions and in some cases policed by state regulations. Quantification, Hacking argues, affects the way we think of ourselves. Clearly social researchers who participate in quantification are not just discovering facts; they are constructing a particular version of human affairs.

DISCUSSION POINTS

- You are planning a study of the mass media portrayal of gender stereotypes, using content analysis. Using the information in reading 8, outline the steps you would take in designing a representative, randomly selected sample.

- Design a structured interview schedule on any topic using a combination of fixed choice and open questions. Try it out on potential respondents. Use this experience and the accounts provided in readings 9 and 10 to assess what problems of interviewer bias and/or question wording arise.
- How would you assess the validity of a scale measuring parental acceptance of children made up of the items listed in Oppenheim's Figure 11.1 (reading 11)?
- Outline the advantages and disadvantages of on-line surveys compared with (a) interview surveys and (b) postal surveys.
- Design a category system for analysing significant aspects of interaction in a discussion or seminar group in a university. What differences does it have in comparison with that of Flanders (designed for use in schools)? How would a schedule for analysing doctor–patient interaction compare with these?
- Re-examine the criticisms made by Billig of content analysis and 'methodology' in reading 1. Are these applicable to the approach described by Weber?
- One view of quantitative social research is that it is a process of data collection, done for the purposes of discovering facts about human social and cultural life. Another view (see Hacking in reading 15) is that quantification involves the construction of a particular version of what it is to be a person. Where do you stand on this issue? How might such considerations affect the conduct of a social research project?

FURTHER READING

Best, J. (2001) *Damned Lies and Statistics: Untangling Numbers from the Media, Politicians and Activists*, Berkeley, Cal.: University of California Press.

Cannell, C.F. and Kahn, R.O. (1954) 'Interviewing', in Lindzey, G. and Arondson, E. (eds) *The Handbook of Social Psychology*, New York: Addison-Wesley.

Cronbach, L.J. and Meehl, P.E. (1955) 'Construct validity in psychological tests', *Psychological Bulletin* 52:281–302.

de Vaus, D.A. (2002) *Surveys in Social Research*, 5th edition, London: Routledge.

Dillman, D. (2000) *Mail and Internet Surveys: The Tailored Design Method*, New York: Wiley.

Foddy, W. (1993). *Constructing Questions for Interviews and Questionnaires: Theory and Practice in Social Research*, Cambridge: Cambridge University Press.

Gubrium, J.F. and Holstein, J.A. (2002) *Handbook of Interview Research*, Thousand Oaks, Cal.: Sage.

Henry, G.T. (1990) *Practical Sampling*, Thousand Oaks, Cal.: Sage.

Kahn, R.L. and Cannell, C.F. (1957). *The Dynamics of Interviewing: Theory, Techniques, and Cases*, Malabar, Fl.: Krieger.

Neuendorf, K.A. (2001b). *The Content Analysis Guidebook*, Thousand Oaks, Cal.: Sage.

Salant, P. and Dillman, D.A. (eds) (1994). *How to Conduct Your Own Survey*, John Wiley.

Sapsford, R. (1999) *Survey Research*, London: Sage.

Schuman, H. and Presser, S. (1996) *Questions and Answers in Attitude Surveys Experiments on Question Form, Wording, and Context*, Thousand Oaks, Cal.: Sage.

Chapter 8

Barry Hedges

SAMPLING

From Hoinville, G., Jowell R. *et al.* (1978) *Survey Research Practice*. London: Heinemann Educational Books (1978)

. . .

T HE FIRST STEP IN the sampling process is to define the survey population, which might be the entire population of the United Kingdom, but it is more likely to be a sub-set of that population: a large sub-set, such as all adults, or a small sub-set, such as university students, or something in between.

At an early stage of planning the survey, only an approximate definition of the survey population is needed. Even this may not be easy to achieve, because the purpose of the survey may not make it immediately obvious what part of the population should be studied. . . . In studying, for example, people likely to be affected by a new road development – as residents, motorists or pedestrians – there is probably no entirely satisfactory way of defining a suitable population, although workable solutions can be found. As so often happens, the difficulty is the conceptual one of deciding to whom a new road is or is not relevant rather than the technical one of finding a suitable sampling method.

[. . .]

The principles of sampling

Thus far, . . . little or no statistical or specialized sampling skill is required. . . . But now, as we move from defining the survey population to sampling it, we will need to draw upon a variety of theoretical concepts. Sample design requires both a knowledge of sampling theory and a practical knowledge of what is possible and economic. . . . In condensing so broad a subject, we have decided to concentrate on probability sampling methods. Other less rigorous sampling methods such as quota sampling are only briefly touched on in the final section.

A sample is a small-scale representation – a kind of miniature model – of the population from which it was selected. Because it includes merely a part, not all, of the parent population, it can never be an exact replica of that population. But in many respects it will resemble it closely, and it is this resemblance that makes sampling so useful in the study of populations too large to survey in their entirety: the proportions, ratios, averages and other similar measures computed from the sample are likely to correspond to those of the parent population.

How close the resemblance is depends on several factors, in particular the size of the sample and the way in which it was selected. The securest basis for sample selection is chance, although in most practical sample designs certain constraints must be placed on its operation. There is plenty of empirical evidence to show that when selections are made by non-probability methods results are liable to distortions that may be serious. That is why in this chapter we deal mainly with probability methods.

Estimating population values

In probability sampling the differences between sample estimates and population values constitute *sampling error*, of which the central ideas are explained in the following paragraphs.

Suppose a sample survey estimates the mean height of adult men as 68.2″. Would another sample survey give an identical result? Probably not; it might, let us say, provide an estimate of 67.9″. If we continued selecting fresh samples and obtaining fresh estimates of the population mean, after a time we would observe a definite pattern emerging.

This can be illustrated by imagining that we plot the mean height from each fresh survey as a square on graph paper (Figure 8.1). As more results come to hand their frequency distribution (or sampling distribution) begins to take on a definite pattern (2, 3), which is seen to approximate to a bell-shaped curve – the *normal distribution*. The mean of that normal distribution will correspond to the population mean.

The normal distribution has certain fixed properties that are very useful to us. There is a widely used statistical measure of dispersion, known as the *standard deviation*, and in a normal distribution about 95 per cent of the observations lie within two standard deviations of its mean. It follows that there are 95 chances out of 100 that the mean of any particular sample, chosen at random, will be within two 'standard deviations' of the true population mean. It also follows that if we have selected only one sample, the population value is likely to lie within two standard deviations of our sample estimate. If we knew the standard deviation of the sampling distribution (a quantity usually referred to as the 'standard error'), we could tell how near our single sample's result was likely to be to the population mean. In practice we do not know this, but we can estimate it from our single sample. We do not need to repeat our survey time after time to build up the pattern shown in the

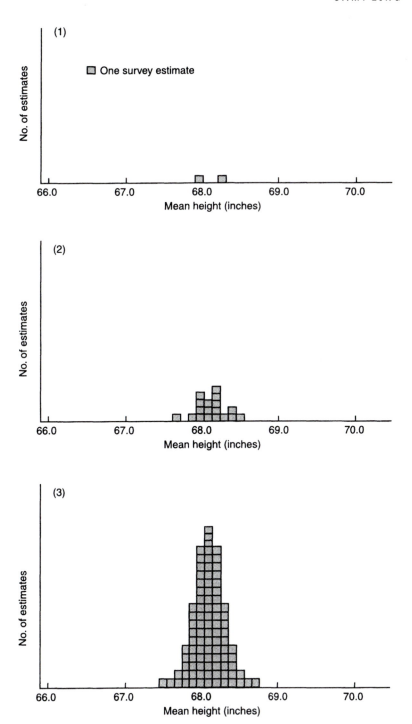

Figure 8.1 Plotting sample survey estimates of the mean height of adult men: frequency distribution taking on the bell-shaped curve of a normal distribution.

figure; by carrying out our survey only once – which is of course the real situation – we have the basic elements we need: an estimate from our sample of the population mean, and a statement of how likely it is that this sample estimate will be within any distance we choose to nominate of the population mean. We do not know exactly where our particular sample lies in relation to the population mean but we know how close it is likely to be.

For example, if our sample estimates the average height of men at 68.2″, and the standard deviation of the sampling distribution at 1.0″, we can say that we are 95 per cent confident that the true average height of men is between 66.2″ and 70.2″ (the observed value plus or minus twice the standard deviation). But we could equally well say that we are 90 per cent confident that the true average height is between 66.5″ and 69.9″ (1⅔ times the standard deviation). Or that we are roughly 99 per cent confident that it is between 65.6″ and 70.8″ (2½ times the standard deviation).

The intervals in these statements are known as *confidence intervals* and the different probabilities – 95 per cent, 90 per cent, 99 per cent – as *confidence levels*. The researcher can choose to run very little risk that the interval will fail to cover the population value by opting for, say, a 99 per cent confidence level (which gives him a wide interval), or he can choose a lower confidence level in order to narrow the confidence interval. The 95 per cent confidence level is the most commonly used.

Bias and precision

The foregoing discussion can now be used to explain two basic ideas. We have said that if we carry out repeated sampling to produce a sampling distribution, then the mean of that distribution will coincide with the true population mean. But if there is *selection bias* in drawing members of the sample, repeated sampling will produce results that would centre on some value other than the true mean. If, for example, some feature of the sampling method means that tall men have a greater chance of being sampled than short men, the average of the means produced by repeated sampling would be higher than the population mean. Estimates from samples with this biased selection procedure will thus generally tend to be too high (although it is still possible that some of these samples may produce estimates exactly corresponding to the population mean).

The other essential idea is that of *precision*. The narrower the sampling distribution (the more tightly the estimates are bunched together), the narrower the confidence intervals, the greater the precision of the estimate, and the smaller the sampling error.

Sampling error and bias are not connected. A sampling method which involves a selection bias may nevertheless yield results of high precision. Another sampling method may be unbiased but yield results of such low precision that sampling error is too large for the results to have any practical value.

Sampling error depends on three factors. First, the variability of the characteristic under study in the population in question: the more varied the population is with respect to that characteristic, the larger the potential sampling error will be. Second, the size of the sample selected: the larger the sample the smaller the sampling error. People sometimes think that the proportion of the population sampled (*the sampling fraction*) determines the amount of sampling error, but unless this fraction is fairly large – more than 1 in 10 – its effect on sampling error is negligible. Where large populations are being sampled, it is rare to reach a 1 in 10 fraction, and even with smaller populations such a fraction seldom occurs. The important factor is thus the sample size rather than the sampling fraction. The third factor influencing the amount of the sampling error is the sample design. The aim of the sampler is to construct a sample design that minimizes sampling error and bias within the available resources.

Sample size

For a given sample design and survey population, the likely amount of sampling error, and hence the width of the confidence interval for a specified confidence level, depends on the sample size: the larger the sample, the smaller the amount of sampling error to be expected, and the narrower the confidence interval.

Deciding what sample size to use is almost always a matter more of judgement than of calculation. Textbook methods demand that the survey designer should start from information about the distribution of the variable to be measured and about the precision (width of confidence interval) required by those who are to use the results. In most surveys, the first condition is difficult to apply because surveys have more than one purpose, with many variables to be studied, each of them having a different distribution. The second usually cannot be applied, because research users are rarely able to specify the degree of precision they require.

In practice, the main determinant of sample size is almost always the need to look separately at the results of different subgroups of the total sample (separate age groups, socio-economic groups, and so on). The total sample size is usually governed by the sample size required for the smallest subgroup: as a rough guide, the smallest subgroup will need to have between fifty and a hundred members.

In most surveys, therefore, samples of fewer than 1,000 people are of limited use for exploring variations within the total population. But samples do not often need to comprise more than 5,000 people; among the exceptions are transportation studies, where analyses of a great many geographical subdivisions are usually required, and general purpose population descriptions such as the General Household Survey conducted by the Office of Population Censuses and Surveys.

Sampling error decreases as sample size increases, but not in direct proportion. The decrease is proportionate to the square root of the relative increase in sample size. The additional cost that an increase in sample size entails is more nearly proportionate, although the increase usually brings some economies of scale.

Systematic sampling

The method of sampling in which selections are made by chance alone is called *simple random sampling*. To draw a simple random sample of, say, 100 people from a list of 2,500, every person in the list would be numbered and then 100 numbers would be chosen at random; in this way every member of the population would have an equal chance of being selected into the sample. It is a laborious procedure, little used in practice. The alternative method of *systematic sampling* is more commonly used. With this method the first sample member is selected from the list by a random number and subsequent members are selected according to a fixed *sampling interval*. This interval is calculated by dividing the total number of names on the list by the required sample size. The random starting number must lie within the sampling interval. To select 100 people from 2,500 the sampling interval would be 25, and a random starting number would be chosen between 1 and 25. If this were 14 then the people selected would be those numbered 14, 39, 64 . . . and so on. Like simple random sampling, systematic sampling gives every member of the population the same chance of being selected.

Care needs to be taken in the application of systematic sampling. If, for example, on a list of married couples the husband's name always precedes the wife's, and the interval is an even number, the sample will be all men or all women, depending on the random starting number. But lists are usually arranged in alphabetical or other orders in which this type of regular pattern rarely occurs: systematic sampling is then satisfactory. Sometimes the order of a list can help rather than hinder the survey designer. For instance, if all the men are listed in the first half of the list and all the women in the second half, systematic sampling ensures that the sexes are represented in their correct proportions. This is an example of *stratification*.

Proportionate stratification

Stratification is the process of dividing the population to be sampled into distinct groups or strata and selecting a separate sample from each stratum. If we choose the separate sample sizes so that they are proportionate to the population of each stratum, the procedure is known as *proportionate stratification*. . . .

Several stratification factors can be employed simultaneously. If our list of individuals included their income and age, we could stratify by both. . . .

Disproportionate stratification

. . . If the sample designer wants to study a small stratum on its own he may need to depart from a proportionate allocation of the sample, because such an allocation would yield too small a sample in that stratum of separate analysis. He may therefore decide to over-represent it by employing a larger sampling fraction than in the other strata. *Variable sampling fractions* are used so that more selections are made in that stratum than would be the case with proportionate stratification; and a large enough sample for separate analysis is thus obtained from it. . . .

Clustering

In a national interview survey it would be highly uneconomic for the sample to be scattered over the country at random. A way of *clustering* it usually has to be found so that each interviewer has a substantial batch of interviews in a single area. Working there for, say, between two and three weeks will give the interviewer time to call back in a systematic way on people out at the first or second visit. . . .

The disadvantage of clustering is that it reduces the precision of the sample. The sampling error for a given sample size will usually be larger when clustering is used, because people in the same area will tend to be similar in respect of the survey variables. If the area is small they may all live in the same type of housing, or be mostly in the same socio-economic group. The greater the similarity of people within the clusters, the more a clustering scheme will increase the sampling error relative to that of a simple random sample of the same size.

But clustering has the advantage of allowing a larger sample to be interviewed for a given cost which in turn reduces the sampling error. . . .

Achieving population coverage

At the beginning of the chapter we stressed that before the sample could be designed it was necessary to have a definition of the survey population. This definition could in the early stages be broad, but subsequently needed to be given precision as a first step towards evolving a satisfactory sample design. We pick up the thread again here, beginning at the point where a precise definition of the survey population has been agreed. Our first requirement is a suitable sampling frame.

Sampling frames

A sampling frame is (usually) a list of population elements from which a sample can be drawn, and if it is to fulfil its purpose satisfactorily it must meet a number of criteria. Few frames do in fact meet all of them; sometimes the deficiency can be remedied, sometimes not. A number of primary considerations must be taken into account.

First, is the frame composed of the same kind of population elements as the survey population? Or if it is not, are its elements capable of being translated into those of the survey population? As an example of the latter, consider the use of the electoral register as a frame for sampling households: it does not list households, but it does list addresses, which can be translated to households during fieldwork.

Second, is it complete? Are any members of the target population likely to be missing? If so, why, and how many? Are there any means of bringing the missing elements into the sampling process?

Third, are any elements listed more than once? If they are, their probabilities of inclusion in the sample will be correspondingly greater, introducing a bias. It is not sufficient to look for duplicates among those actually selected for the sample; the problem must be dealt with either at the outset by eliminating duplicate entries, or by re-weighting in the analysis.

Fourth, are there elements in the frame that do not belong, or no longer belong, to the survey population? Interviewers will make wasted calls on these: they are out-of-scope, or 'deadwood'. Provided they are not numerous, the wastage will not involve heavy costs, but if they comprise the majority of elements of the frame a major 'screening' exercise will be involved in eliminating them in the field – or, better, at the sample selection stage if this is possible.

Fifth, does the information given provide an adequate means of finding the sampled units, and is it up-to-date? If addresses are no longer current, for example, it may not be possible to trace people at all – or, if it is, it may be very expensive.

Sixth, is there information on the frame that could be used for stratification? And if there is, can it be effectively used? . . . If it is in the form of, say, an index of cards to which access for re-sorting is limited, stratification may be, if not impossible, at any rate too expensive to be worthwhile. The physical form of the frame can exercise an important influence on the sampling procedure.

Seventh, if the survey is to be conducted by personal interview rather than by post, is there any means of selecting a clustered sample that will lend itself to an efficient allocation of interviewers? Like stratification, this depends a good deal on the physical form of the list, but it is a rather more important issue since the costs of unclustered interviews can be very high indeed and the design consequently inefficient when both precision and cost are considered together. One solution, if the frame is very large, is to select an unclustered sample much smaller than the frame but considerably larger than the eventual sample. This 'subframe' may be small enough to make a clustering operation manageable, though of course the resulting clusters will be much looser than would have resulted from clustering the entire frame.

If there is no extant frame, it is sometimes a practical proposition to construct one. For example, if no complete list of hospital nurses exists, a list of hospital management committees may be found (or compiled) which permits a sample of hospitals to be selected, contacted and asked to provide lists of nurses from their records. Or school leavers may be sampled by first sampling schools and utilizing their records. . . .

Non-response

It is rarely possible to obtain a response from all those selected for the sample. In a typical national household interview survey, the level of response is likely to be around 80 per cent, and non-response therefore around 20 per cent. Non-response can be a source of bias, since non-respondents may well differ in their characteristics from respondents, and it is essential to reduce it to a minimum. Increasing the sample size will compensate for the numerical loss, but will do nothing to remove any bias. Achieving high response levels is largely a matter of field training and procedures, though other factors, such as questionnaire design, play their part.

Non-response must be carefully distinguished from elements being out-of-scope (deadwood). Selected sample elements that turn out not to be, or no longer to be, members of the survey population are out-of-scope: they should not have been included in the sampling frame and, when found, can simply be deleted. Selected sample elements that prove to be in the survey population but do not yield any data are non-respondents; they should have yielded data and the fact that they have not done so opens the door to bias. Every survey report should contain a clear statement of the number selected, the number that proved to be out-of-scope and the number that responded. The base for calculating the response rate is the number of in-scope elements selected (not the total number initially selected), The analysis of response should also break down non-response into its various categories – refusals and failure to make contact usually being the most prominent. . . .

But perhaps the most common method of assessing non-respondent characteristics is to compare known population characteristics with those of the achieved sample. If this, or any of the methods mentioned above, tells the researcher that non-respondents have different characteristics from respondents, what should he do? In general, it is desirable to *re-weight* the sample to bring it into line with the known population distribution. This will usually improve the survey estimates. . . .

Samples of minority populations

A great many surveys are concerned not with the population as a whole, but with small groups within it. In principle, a sample of any small group can be achieved by sampling the general population and discarding those people who do not qualify for inclusion, but this can be a wasteful procedure. . . . Some very small groups, notably immigrant groups, tend to be concentrated in particular areas of the country and in particular districts. This fact has been utilized in designing samples of such groups. . . .

The basis of the method is that if a sufficiently large proportion of the survey population is concentrated in sufficiently few districts, it may be justifiable to confine the survey to such districts, accepting the consequent bias that arises from giving members of the survey population resident elsewhere a zero probability of inclusion. Such a bias is clearly not desirable in itself, but it may be an acceptable price to pay for converting what might otherwise be an unviable survey into a manageable one. . . .

Non-probability sampling methods

In the methods of selecting respondents described so far the assumption has been made that the research designer will employ a probability sample as the basis for the sample design. Even though interviewers may be required to carry out the final stages of sample selection, neither they nor the respondent should exercise any choice concerning the person to be interviewed.

Many market research surveys, however, use a non-probability method of sampling households or individuals at the final selection stage within the sampling areas, though the areas themselves are normally selected by probability methods.

The most commonly used non-probability method is quota sampling. Interviewers are supplied with 'quotas' or set specifications regarding the number of people of various kinds that they must interview. Provided that the specification is fulfilled, they are free to interview whom they wish within the designated area.

The idea behind quota sampling is that much of the variability in human behaviour is accounted for if the sample is made properly representative in respect of the 'quota' variables – usually sex, age and social class. It is argued that the quota controls, which are in effect a stratifying procedure, reduce variability and that any bias that may arise in the selection of individuals within the quota groups is unlikely to be serious, provided that the interviewer operates intelligently and with an understanding of what is required. But while quota sampling has undoubtedly often produced results that are satisfactory for particular purposes, and although it offers advantages of being cheaper in the field and easier to organize, the risk of bias of perhaps a major kind must make the user of quota sampling uneasy. For this reason, probability sampling is generally to be preferred. . . .

Other variants of quota sampling methods exist but none can guarantee that every member of the population has an equal (or at least calculable) chance of being selected. None of these methods can therefore provide the security of a properly conducted probability sample.

Chapter 9

Sir Claus Moser and Graham Kalton

QUESTIONNAIRES

From *Survey Methods in Social Investigation* (2nd edition), Aldershot: Gower (1971).

. . .

THE FIRST STEP IN designing a questionnaire is to define the problem to be tackled by the survey and hence to decide on what questions to ask. The temptation is always to cover too much, to ask everything that might turn out to be interesting. This must be resisted. Lengthy, rambling questionnaires are as demoralizing for the interviewer as for the respondent, and the questionnaire should be no longer than is absolutely necessary for the purpose. Certain questions will, so to speak, include themselves, but a problem of choice inevitably arises with marginal ones. Let us consider a hypothetical survey to ascertain what daily newspapers different kinds of people read. A number of newspaper questions, together with those asking for necessary personal data, automatically suggest themselves. Then, as the discussion of the planning of the survey warms up, many extensions of interest occur to those taking part. Would it be useful to include reading of periodicals and books? Would the main results be more meaningful if they could be viewed against the background of the respondents' leisure habits as a whole? Would it be wise to find out something about how much money and time different people have available for newspaper buying and reading? Should one ask a question or two about the use of libraries? Should one go beyond the facts of reading and ask people's opinions on individual newspapers?

And so it goes on, with the questionnaire growing from a short list of questions to a document many pages long. . . . It is obvious that the survey planner must rigorously examine every question, and exclude any that are not strictly relevant to the survey's objectives. In this, the pilot survey is his most helpful tool. Here all the marginal questions can be tested out and dummy tabulations made from the results. Questions likely to prove of small importance in the final analysis can be spotted, as can those which turn out to be not worth asking unless a host of others is also included.

In settling the scope of a questionnaire, one other criterion should be applied, namely that the questions should be practicable. This merits emphasis, even though no amount of textbook admonition can take the place of common sense. It is no good asking a person's opinion about something he does not understand; about events too long ago for him to remember accurately; about matters which, although they concern him, he is unlikely to have accurate information on or that are so personal or emotional that valid answers cannot be expected by formal direct questioning.

Question content

In considering any question, then, it is wise to ask oneself whether respondents are likely to possess the knowledge, or have access to the information, necessary for giving a correct answer. It is unsafe to *assume* that respondents will voluntarily admit ignorance. On the contrary it has often been shown that they will give some kind of answer to most questions, even if they are ill-informed and know it. Similarly, they will express opinions on matters they have given little thought to or which they barely understand. . . .

The surveyor should aim to ask questions only from those likely to be able to answer them accurately; to ask about past events only if he can reasonably expect people to remember them accurately (perhaps with the help of recall methods); and to ask their opinions only if he can be reasonably sure that they understand what is involved and are able to give meaningful answers. It is always well to remember that most survey questions are addressed to a variety of people very differently qualified to answer them. . . .

Most survey questions are concerned with either facts or opinions. There are also questions dealing with motivation ('Why did you go to the cinema last night?'), and knowledge questions ('What do the initials NATO stand for?'), but the main points of methodology will emerge if we consider factual and opinion questions. . . .

The chief difficulties with factual questions are to ensure that interviewers understand, and manage to convey to the respondents, precisely what facts are wanted. Some of the definitions may be tricky but, in most cases, the chances of either interviewer or respondent misunderstanding the question, not understanding it at all, or the latter being influenced in his answer by the words chosen are much slighter than with opinion questions.

With opinion questions the problems are much more fundamental. Though we would not venture into the psychologist's territory and discuss concepts of opinion and attitude in any detail, some attempt must be made to analyse why the study of opinions is basically so much more troublesome than that of facts. Why would one be more confident with a question asking a respondent whether he owns a wrist-watch than with one asking whether he is in favour of capital punishment? There are several related reasons:

(a) A respondent either does or does not possess a watch, and one may reasonably assume that he knows whether he does or not. All the surveyor has to do is to make clear to the respondent what he wants to know, and to be sure he understands the respondent's answer. It may be that the respondent wishes not to give the correct answer, but at least he knows what it is. With the opinion question it is not so simple. The respondent's attitude to capital punishment may be largely latent, and he may never have given the matter any conscious thought until he was confronted by the question. The first problem with opinion questions thus arises from the uncertainty whether the respondent, in any meaningful sense, 'knows' the correct answers. To say whether he possesses a watch or not needs no 'thinking' on the respondent's part; to give a genuine opinion on capital punishment may require thought and 'self-analysis'.

(b) A person's opinion on virtually any issue is many-sided. On capital punishment there are moral, medical, legal and other aspects: it is possible to be against it on moral grounds, in favour on legal ones. A person may be against it in all but certain circumstances, or against it whatever the situation. He may be in favour of abolishing it experimentally, or as an irrevocable step whatever the consequences. In short, there probably is *no one correct answer* to the survey question as there is to that on watch ownership. The answer the respondent actually gives will depend on the aspect of the issue that is uppermost in his mind – quite possibly because the wording of the question, or the context created by previous ones, has put it there.

(c) Closely related to this is the problem of intensity. On any given subject some people feel strongly, some are indifferent, some have settled and consistent views, others are highly changeable in their attitude. In any attempt to get more than snap answers, the problem of assessing the intensity of opinion and attitude must be faced.

(d) Finally, it must be repeated that answers to opinion questions are more sensitive to changes in wording, emphasis, sequence and so on than are those to factual questions. . . . This established sensitivity of opinion questions does not imply instability of opinion among respondents. Rather it is a reflection of the point made in (b) above. Opinion is many-sided, and questions asked in different ways will seem to 'get at' different aspects of the opinion: if they result in different answers, it is largely because respondents are in effect answering different questions.

There is a secondary difficulty here. With factual questions, it is often feasible to compare the merits of different forms of the same question by checking the answers against known data. With opinion questions this is impossible, although checks on validity can and should be made; where, for instance, opinions are closely related to measurable behaviour, a check on behaviour can be used to test the validity of an expressed opinion. . . .

Question wording

The literature on the wording of questions is bewildering. Numerous papers have appeared showing the relative advantages of various specific questions, the danger of using a certain word or phrase, the sensitivity of answers to changes in wording and presentation: but it is exceedingly difficult to build out of them any general principles. We shall confine ourselves to some aspects of wording which are of general importance in social research surveys.

(a) *Questions that are insufficiently specific.* A common error is to ask a general question when an answer on a specific issue is wanted. If one is interested specifically in a canteen's meal prices and the quality of its service, the question 'Are you satisfied or dissatisfied with your canteen?' is unsatisfactory, since it fails to provide the respondent with the necessary frames of reference. As there are two distinct frames of reference of interest here, two questions are needed, perhaps 'Are you satisfied or dissatisfied with the prices of meals in your canteen?' and 'Are you satisfied or dissatisfied with the service in your canteen?' Although these two questions now cover the topics required in a seemingly straightforward way, they still need to be pre-tested to check on their suitability for the particular situation. It may, for instance, be the case that the canteen serves special meals once a week at a higher cost and that, although generally satisfied with the canteen's prices, a respondent objects to the cost of the special meals; or he may be dissatisfied only with one particular aspect of the service. In cases like these he would have difficulty answering the questions. Such problems are brought to light by pre-testing and pilot work, the importance of which for question wording cannot be overrated. . . .

(b) *Simple language.* In choosing the language for a questionnaire the population being studied should be kept in mind. The aim in question wording is to communicate with respondents as nearly as possible in their own language. A survey of the members of a particular profession, for instance, can usefully employ the profession's common technical terms; not only are such terms part of the informants' common language, but they also normally have a single precise meaning, unlike everyday terms, which particularly to professionals are often vague and ambiguous.

Technical terms and jargon are, however, obviously to be avoided in surveys of the general population. We would not ask a respondent whether his household is run on matriarchal lines, what he thinks about bilateral trading, amortization of the National Debt, and fiscal policy.

Much less easy to recognize and reject are words which, though everyday usage to the university-trained survey expert, are far from common in ordinary conversation. Words like hypothetical, irrespective, aggravate, deprecate, and hundreds more are in this category. . . .

With surveys of the general population, the first principles in wording are that questions should use the simplest words that will convey the exact meaning, and that the phrasing also should be as simple and informal as possible. It is more natural to ask: 'Do you think . . . ?' than: 'Is it your opinion . . . ?'; 'What is your attitude to . . . ?' than: 'What is your attitude with regard to . . . ?' In fact the more questions sound like ordinary conversation the smoother the interview will be. Of course, this should not be overdone. Bad grammar may be more common than good, but one would not advocate its deliberate use in survey questions. Nor are slang expressions advisable; as with technical jargon, not everyone uses the same expressions. It is not indeed enough to know that a word or phrase is commonly used; one must equally be sure that it is used in the same sense by all groups of respondents. Even words like 'dinner' and 'tea' have different meanings in different parts of the country. A simple case is the word 'book', which in some parts of the population is taken to include magazines. Hence the phrasing of the following question in a readership survey by Stuart (1952): 'During the past week roughly how many hours would you say you had spent reading *books* – I mean books not magazines or papers?' . . .

There is a temptation to ask complex questions when the subject matter is inherently complicated, involving a variety of different facets. This, for example, would be the case in a housing survey in which one wanted to discover how many households comprised three-generation families, that is grandparents, parents and children. Once the term 'three-generation family' has been precisely defined (how about widowed grandparents, unmarried mothers, divorced or separated parents?), one might with ingenuity design a single question to obtain the information, but many respondents would certainly fail to understand it. Rather than rely on a single complex question, a series of simple questions should be asked, the number of such questions depending on the degree of simplicity required. Household composition is generally a complex subject and one for which several descriptive indices are required; the information is usually best obtained by using a 'household box' on the questionnaire in which the household members are listed together with their relevant characteristics, e.g. age, sex, marital status, working status and educational level. . . . From these basic data the surveyor can determine for himself all the indices he requires for his analysis. . . .

(c) *Ambiguity*. Ambiguous questions are to be avoided at all costs. If an ambiguous word creeps in, different people will understand the question differently and will in effect be answering different questions. The following example is taken from a university research survey: 'Is your work made more difficult because you are expecting a baby?' The question was asked of all women in the survey, irrespective of whether they were expecting a baby or not. What, then, did a 'No' answer mean? Depending on the respondent, it might have meant 'No, I'm not expecting a baby' or 'No, my work is not made more difficult by the fact that I'm expecting a baby'.

Ambiguity also arises with double barrelled questions, such as the following question on public transport: 'Do you like travelling on trains and buses?' Respondents liking one and disliking the other would be in a dilemma in answering this question. Clearly it needs to be divided into two questions, each concerned with a single idea, in this case with a single mode of transport.

(d) *Vague words*. Vague questions encourage vague answers. If people are asked whether they go to the cinema regularly or occasionally, the meaning of their answers will be vague. (This common choice of alternatives is strictly illogical; the word 'occasional' refers to frequency, the word 'regular' does not. However, this may be a case where logic can give way to common usage.) The meaning can easily be made more precise, as in the following question from the 1968 National Readership Survey: 'How often these days do you go to the cinema? Would it be nearer to – twice a week or more often; once a week; once a fortnight; once a month; three or four times a year; less often; or do you never go these days?'

Vague words and phrases like 'kind of', 'fairly', 'generally', 'often', 'many', 'much the same', 'on the whole' should be avoided, unless one is only seeking vague answers. If one asks 'What kind of house do you have?' without specifying a frame of reference, some people will answer that it is semi-detached, others that it is sub-urban, others that it is very pleasant, and so on.

A similar type of vagueness occurs in 'Why' questions. In answering the question: 'Why did you go to the cinema last night?' some respondents will say that they wanted to see that particular film, some that they did not want to stay at home, others that 'the wife suggested it', or that they hadn't been since last week. The word 'Why' in this question – as the phrase 'kind of' in the previous one – can mean so many different things that its use would produce a useless mixture of answers. Lazarsfeld (1935) discusses the problems of the 'Why' question.

(e) Leading questions. A leading question is one which, by its content, structure or wording, leads the respondent in the direction of a certain answer. The question form: 'You don't think . . . do you?' as obviously leads to a negative answer as the form: 'Should not something be done about . . . ?' leads to a positive one.

Equally, a question which suggests only some of the possible answers may lead in their direction. Take the question: 'Do you read any weekly newspapers, such as the *New Statesman* or *Punch?*' Respondents, especially if they are not sure of their correct or complete reply, may seek refuge in the answers named; either all or none of the alternatives should be stated.

There are numerous words that have been shown on occasion to have a 'leading' influence in survey questions (see Payne 1951, and Cantril 1944). The word 'involved' in a question like: 'Do you think that the Government should get involved in . . . ?' may have a sufficiently sinister ring to lead people in the negative direction. Similarly, the wording: 'Do you agree that the Government is right in staying out of . . . ?' invites a 'Yes' answer. The 'leading' nature of these examples is obvious, but more subtle leads can often creep unnoticed into survey questions . . .

(f) Presuming questions. Questions should not, generally speaking, presume anything about the respondent. They should not imply that he necessarily possesses any knowledge or an opinion on the survey subject, or that he engages in the activity about which he is being asked. Questions like: 'How many cigarettes a day do you smoke?' or 'How did you vote in the last General Election?' are best asked only after a 'filter' question has revealed that the respondent does smoke cigarettes and did vote in the last election.

On occasion, however, one might deliberately depart from this procedure. Kinsey and others (1948) did not first ask respondents *whether* they had engaged in certain sexual practices, but went straight into questions about frequency and detail. Respondents were thus spared the embarrassment of admitting the experiences directly and were made to feel that these represented perfectly usual behaviour: thus they found themselves able to talk freely and give detailed answers. The case for such an approach is obvious, but one cannot ignore the possibility that it may discourage 'I never do' answers and thus cause an upward bias in the results.

(g) *Hypothetical questions.* Questions of the 'Would you like to live in a flat?' type are of very limited value. Most people would like to try anything once, and an affirmative answer would have little value as a prediction of behaviour. It is another matter if one has first made sure that the person has experience of both flat and house dwelling. Equally, answers to the 'What would you do if . . . ?' kind of question, although perhaps a good reflection of wishful thinking or of what people feel to be right and proper, are unsafe pointers to future behaviour.

Yet prediction of future behaviour on the basis of survey questions plays, and must be expected to play, a central role in survey applications. Market researchers would like – and try – to predict how people will react to a proposed change in the price of a product, to an alteration to its quality or packaging; how many people are likely to buy cars, radios or television sets in a given period, and so on. They may rely on straight questions (a Gallup Poll question in 1950 was: 'Supposing the price of (a certain newspaper) went up from 1d. to 1½d. would you change over to another paper where the price hadn't gone up?') but the answers are recognized to be imperfect guides to future behaviour. People are not good at predicting their behaviour in a hypothetical situation and the prediction has somehow to be taken out of their hands and made by the researcher himself – naturally on the basis of the information he has obtained.

Another kind of hypothetical question is 'Would you like a more frequent bus service?' or 'Would you like an increase in wages?' Such questions are unlikely to be of any value because the respondent is being asked if he would like something for nothing. It is hard to see how he could possibly say 'No'. If he did, it could only be because he has taken into account some hidden factors of his own, or because he has failed to understand the question.

(h) *Personalized questions.* It is often necessary to decide whether a question should be asked in a personalized form or not. This is well illustrated by the following questions which appeared, one after the other, in a schedule dealing with health matters (see David, 1952): 'Do you think it is a good idea to have everyone's chest regularly checked by X-ray?' and 'Have you ever had yours checked?' Some 96 per cent of the respondents answered 'Yes' to the first question, but only 54 per cent to the second. As the author suggested, the opinion given in answer to the first question 'is more a pious hope for some vague corporate decision than a considered aim involving personal action'.

(i) *Embarrassing questions.* Subjects which people do not like to discuss in public present a problem to the questionnaire designer. Respondents are often embarrassed to discuss private matters, to give low-prestige answers, and to admit to socially unacceptable behaviour and attitudes. If, for instance, questions on sexual behaviour, frequency of taking a bath, cheating in examinations or attitudes to Communism were asked in the usual way, many respondents would probably refuse to reply and others would distort their answers. There are several ways of attempting to deal with this problem.

One method of reducing the threatening nature of a question is to express it in the third person; instead of asking the respondent for his views, he is asked about the views of others. An example from market research of an indirect question of this sort is given by Smith (1954): 'Some women who use this cleanser find a lot of faults with it. I wonder if you can guess what they are objecting to'. The purpose of this wording was to make the housewives feel free to criticize the product. The aim of such questions is to obtain the respondent's own views, but he may of course answer the question asked, and give what he believes to be the views of others. For this reason it is often advisable to follow the indirect question by a direct one asking the respondent whether he holds the views he has described.

There are several other indirect methods which can be useful in dealing with embarrassing topics. The respondent can for instance be shown a drawing of two persons in a certain setting, with 'balloons' containing speech coming from their mouths, as in comic strips and cartoons. One person's balloon is left empty and the respondent is asked to put himself in the position of that person and to fill in the missing words. Another method is that of sentence completion; the respondent is given the start of a sentence and is asked to complete it, usually under time pressure to ensure spontaneity. Oppenheim (1966) describes the use of the following two examples of sentence completion in a study among psychiatric nurses in a mental hospital:

'I wish that doctors . . .'
'Patients who are incontinent . . .'

The different ways in which a group of student nurses and a group of nurses with twelve or more years of experience completed these sentences showed the difference of attitude and approach of the two groups. . . .

Belson (1968) describes a study of a randomly derived sample of London teenage boys on the sensitive subject of stealing. A variety of procedures were employed in this study to make it easier for the boys to admit that they had stolen things. On arrival at the interviewing centre a boy chose a false name and, in order to preserve his anonymity, he was introduced under his false name to the interviewer, who knew him only by that name. After an extended initial phase, the interview proceeded to the card-sorting technique by which the information on stealing was to be obtained. The interviewer and the boy sat on either side of a table, with a screen in between so that they could not see each other. Through a slot in the screen the interviewer passed to the boy a card on which one type of stealing (e.g. 'I have stolen cigarettes') was recorded. The boy was asked to put the card in a box labelled 'Yes' if he had ever done what was recorded on it, and in a box labelled 'Never' if not. This was repeated for 44 kinds of theft. At the end of this sorting stage, the interviewer went through a procedure which tried to reduce the force of a boy's resistances, and to strengthen his feeling of willingness, to admitting thefts. Then the boy was asked to re-sort all the cards he had put in the 'Never' box. Finally he was asked for further details on each type of theft he had admitted. This detailed procedure elicited reports of many types of theft from many boys with, for example, 69 per cent of boys admitting 'I have stolen something from a shop' and 58 per cent 'I have stolen money' at least once in their lives. . . .

(j) Questions on periodical behaviour. An interesting choice arises in studying the frequency of periodical behaviour. The main choice of questions can be illustrated with reference to cinema-going:

(i)   'How often have you been to the cinema during the last fortnight (or any other period chosen)?'
(ii) 'How often do you go to the cinema on the average?'
(iii) 'When did you last go to the cinema?'

The first question covers a number of different possibilities corresponding to the period chosen, and answers will depend on the type of activity and on the extent to which one is willing to rely on the respondent's memory (see (*k*) below). In any case, the three question types might produce different results, and there is little evidence on which to choose between them. At first sight, (i) seems to be most specific, but many people's answers might simply be an estimate of their average cinema-going rather than the actual figure; i.e. if they normally go twice a fortnight, they may give this as an answer, although they went only once in the last fortnight. As a case in point, Belson (1964a) reports that an intensive interview follow-up enquiry of respondents to the National Readership Survey suggested that people frequently answered in terms of what publications they *usually* looked at, rather than what they had *actually* looked at, which was what was required. Of course the two answers will often be the same, and it is only when a difference arises that an answer in the wrong terms produces error.

Many survey questions involve this type of choice, e.g. questions on newspaper reading, radio listening, television watching, and consumer purchases. It is a matter deserving further research.

(k) Questions involving memory. Most factual questions to some extent involve the respondent in recalling information. His degree of success in doing this accurately is thus a basic determinant of the quality of his response. With certain questions, such as 'Are you married, single or widowed?', there is no such problem, but with a large range of survey questions recalling information does present a problem, the severity of which depends on what is to be recalled. Two factors of primary importance in memory are the length of time since the event took place and the event's importance to the respondent; events the respondent considers insignificant are likely to be forgotten almost immediately and even the recollection of significant events decreases as time elapses. Moreover, for events not forgotten in their entirety, memory acts selectively, retaining some aspects and losing others, thus producing distorted images. For questions dealing with the past, serious attention must therefore be given to the respondents' abilities to recall the required information accurately, and to ways by which they can be helped to do so.

As an example . . . a memory problem arises with questions asking respondents to provide a list, as would be the case for instance if they were asked which television programmes they had viewed yesterday, or which newspapers they had read or looked at in the preceding seven days; without help many respondents would be unable to give a complete list. A sensible way to aid recall in this case is to provide the respondent with a list of all television programmes transmitted yesterday (or a list of all newspapers), from which he can pick out the ones he had seen (or read, or looked at). In the National Readership Surveys, for example, respondents are asked about their readership of each publication from a complete list of every publication with which the surveys are concerned. With the interviewer they go through book-lets containing the title blocks of the publications, and are asked about each one in turn. The use of the title blocks in these recall-aid booklets is an example of another useful device, visual aids, to assist recall.

With questions like the readership one, there are two types of memory error. The first is the 'recall loss', occurring when the respondent fails to report an activity in the recall period because he has forgotten about it, and this loss is likely to be more serious the longer the period. The second occurs when he reports an activity in the recall period when it actually took place outside that period: the tendency to report as occurring in the current period events which in fact occurred earlier has been termed the 'telescoping effect'. A greater telescoping effect for shorter recall periods has been suggested as part of the explanation for the commonly found effect of relatively greater reporting rates for short recall periods. . . .

With serious memory errors having been demonstrated in many studies, it is natural to look for a procedure which does not rely heavily on an informant's ability to recall information. One obvious possibility is to persuade informants to keep diaries of the events of interest, as is done in the Family Expenditure and National Food Surveys. Diaries, however, have their own limitations. First, the amount of work asked of the respondent is much greater with the diary method, and this may make it difficult to gain the co-operation of the selected sample – the refusal rate may be high. Secondly, the diary method is likely to be more expensive, for inter-viewers will probably need to contact informants at least twice. One visit is needed to gain the informant's co-operation and to explain the recording procedure, and another is needed to collect the completed diaries. During the recording period other visits may be made to ensure that the instructions have been understood, to check that the data are being correctly recorded, and to maintain morale. The last visit serves not only for the collection of the diary, but also as an opportunity for the interviewer to edit the diary with the respondent; were it not for this editing, the last visit could perhaps be dispensed with, for the diaries could be returned by post.

Even with careful editing, however, the standard of informants' recording can-not be expected to reach that achieved by well-trained interviewers. Surveys of the general population contain people from a wide range of educational levels and with varying amounts of form-completing experience; it can be anticipated that some of them will fail to understand from one interview exactly what they are to do. In addition, others may lack the motivation to complete the diaries as accurately as is required. One particular way in which informants may deviate from instructions is by failing to record the events while they are fresh in their memories; the main strength of the diary approach is the avoidance of reliance on memory, but, if the informant does not keep the diary up-to-date, at least part of that strength is lost. Another source of error is that, although instructed not to change their habits as the result of their recording, some informants will do so; in consumer expenditure surveys, for instance, housewives keeping log-books of their purchases may become more aware of their shopping habits, and this may for example persuade them of the advantages of buying larger items and of shopping in supermarkets. . . .

These limitations of the diary method must be balanced against the memory errors involved in the recall method. The choice between the methods depends on the subject matter of the survey and, in particular, on the ability of respondents to recall accurately the necessary details of the information required. In situations where, even with assistance from the interviewer, informants are unable to recollect details accurately, the recall method is inappropriate and the diary method may be the only possible approach.

Open and pre-coded questions

The relative merits of open and pre-coded questions have been the subject of a good deal of research and debate. In an open question the respondent is given freedom to decide the aspect, form, detail and length of his answer, and it is the interviewer's job to record as much of it as she can. In the case of pre-coded questions, either the respondent is given a limited number of answers from which to choose or the question is asked as an open question and the interviewer allocates the answer to the appropriate code category. . . .

The essential difference thus lies in the stage at which the information is coded, whether in the office, by the respondent or by the interviewer. If the researcher wants a very detailed answer, or wishes to find out what aspects of an issue are uppermost in the respondent's mind, [an open question] is to be preferred. Even if it has to be summarized subsequently, all the detail is there, not merely a number representing the nearest code answer. Any summarizing or coding can be carried out uniformly in the office, uninfluenced by the circumstances of the interview or the reaction of the respondent to the interviewer. But, of course, open questions have their problems. The detail obtained is partly a reflection of the respondent's loquacity, so that different amounts (as well as different items) of information will be available for different people. A second difficulty lies in the task of compressing a written, qualitative answer into code categories. Again, although the remoteness of the office from the interview situation ensures some gain in coding objectivity, it also has drawbacks. Just as questions can sound different if asked by different people, so the meaning of an answer is communicated partly by the way it is given, and this will not be reflected in the written record. Finally, there is the difficulty of getting a verbatim report of what is said. All interviewers probably exercise some selection in recording answers and, to the extent that this happens, bias may creep in.

Pre-coded questions may offer two or more alternative answers (referred to respectively as dichotomous and multiple-choice – or 'cafeteria' – questions) and their advantages are evident. To combine the recording and coding of answers in one operation simplifies the whole procedure; and, in a very real sense, the interviewer is the person best placed to arrive at an accurate coding, since she hears the answers in full and thus has more data to work on than the office coder. On the other hand, once she has ringed a code there is little hope of detecting errors of recording or judgement. Also, she is working under pressure and may be unable to give sufficient time and attention to the needs of a complex coding operation.

If the range of answers to a question is limited and well established, pre-coding is generally to be preferred. Most factual questions – with regular exceptions like questions on occupation – belong to this category. If, however, one cannot reasonably determine in advance what the main categories will be, it is best to begin with open questions, progressing to pre-coded ones as the range and distribution of answers become clear. This is why open questions play such a valuable role in pilot surveys.

The alternatives offered in pre-coded questions must above all be exhaustive and mutually exclusive. (The code 'Other, specify . . .' is usually added for rare or unthought-of answers.) In such questions all the possible answers must be given. The following question occurred in an opinion survey: 'What happens to the copy of the . . . (newspaper); for instance, does anyone take it to work?'

Stays in house	1
Regularly taken to work, left there	2
Occasionally taken to work, left there	3
Taken to work, brought home	4

It is likely that the form of the question disfavoured the first code answer. If any of the answers are to be suggested, *all* should be. A respondent who has never considered the subject of the question carefully may seize upon any lead given by the mention of a possible answer.

A risk with pre-coded questions is that answers may be forced into a category to which they do not properly belong. Take the hypothetical question: 'Do you think the present Government is doing a good or bad job?' Many people will have clear views and will unhesitatingly say 'Good' or 'Bad'. But what of those who are inclined to say 'Good, but . . .' or 'Bad, except that . . . '? The coding demands a decision one way or the other and may result in qualified responses being forced into categories to which they do not genuinely belong. To try to avoid this, survey designers leave space for qualifications or allow in the codes for finer shades of opinion. Up to a point, a greater number of codes has the added advantage that more information is collected. But there is a limit: if too many codes are used, respondents will be unable to make a rational choice between several of the alternatives and, faced with so many codes, they may have difficulty in making a choice at all.

Besides fixing the number of codes to be used, with opinion questions the survey designer has also to decide whether or not to code for a neutral position, in other words he must decide whether he wants to force respondents to come down on one side or other of the fence. If he does provide a neutral code, he may well find that many people take up that option. The following question was included in a schedule on saving habits: 'During the coming year do you think things will get much better or worse for people in your position or do you think there is not likely to be much change?' The last phrase offered a neutral escape, and 44 per cent of the respondents chose it. These answers may of course express genuine opinions, but there is clearly a risk in suggesting a non-committal answer to the respondent. . . .

Question order

In putting the individual questions together to form the questionnaire, the order of questions needs to be planned. The order may affect the refusal rate and there is plenty of evidence that it may also influence the answers obtained (e.g. Mosteller and others 1949, Cantril 1944, Whitfield 1950), especially so when one is concerned with opinions that are unstable or marginal.

At the start of the interview the respondent is unsure of himself and so the opening questions should be ones to put him at ease and build up rapport between him and the interviewer. They should be interesting questions which he will have no difficulty in answering, and they should not be on sensitive topics, for otherwise he may refuse to continue with the interview. The questions should then proceed in a logical manner, moving from topic to topic in a way that indicates to the respondent the relationship between the questions; where an obvious break in subject matter occurs it is usually advisable to give a sentence or two explaining the break and the relevance of the new set of questions. Since questions on highly sensitive topics may lead to the respondent refusing to continue with the interview, they may be best left until last; then, if a refusal is met, relatively little information is lost.

When determining the order of questions within a topic (and also, for that matter, between topics) the conditioning effect of earlier questions should be considered. It is no good asking: 'Can you name any washing powder?' if a previous question has mentioned 'Tide' or 'Dreft'; in other words knowledge questions must not be preceded by others giving relevant information. Even though interest may centre on specific issues, it can be a good idea to start with broad questions about the subject and then to narrow down to the specific issues, using what is known as a *funnel sequence* of questions (Kahn and Cannell 1957). Thus a general open question on the achievements of the present Government may be the beginning of a sequence leading to specific questions on the Government's actions in the field of labour relations; a mention of labour relations in reply to the first question suggests that the respondent attaches some importance to the subject. On the other hand, if one is interested in the broader question and one thinks the respondents do not hold considered opinions about it, an inverted funnel sequence may be useful. In this case, the early questions ask about the range of issues involved and, in answering them, the respondent is led towards forming a considered opinion on the broader question.

A fairly common situation is one in which the respondent is taken through a list of items by the interviewer, who asks the same initial question about each item in turn. If the respondent answers this question in a certain way the interviewer asks supplementary questions: otherwise she proceeds to the next item. Respondents soon learn in this situation that they can complete the interview more rapidly by avoiding the replies leading to supplementary questions, and this may tempt some to falsify their replies. This risk is easily avoided, however, by asking the supplementary questions only after answers to the initial question have been obtained for all the items on the list.

Another problem with long lists of items is that of respondent fatigue: towards the end of a list of, say, 90 items (about the number of publications in the National

Readership Surveys) the respondent can be expected to experience fatigue, which may result in him failing to recall the later items and hence answering the questions about them negatively. In the National Readership Surveys, for instance, it has been found that the readership level for the group of weeklies when they appeared last in the presentation order (after the groups of dailies, Sundays and monthlies) was only about three-quarters of that when they appeared first (Belson 1964); fatigue probably provides at least a partial explanation of this finding. In these surveys, to avoid bias arising from the order of presentation, the order of the four groups is varied by a rotation scheme throughout the sample; in addition, for one half of the sample the publications within a group are presented in one order and in the other half in the reverse order. This procedure may mean that somewhat better comparisons can be made between the readership levels of different publications, because they have on average about the same presentation position (although account must also be taken of the variation in the 'rotation effect' for the different publications), but it does not make the absolute readership levels for all publications more accurate.

Concluding remarks

We have not attempted to deal comprehensively with the subject of question wording. The points selected for discussion have been those thought to be of most interest to the student or researcher embarking on a survey. To the problem of questionnaire design in general there is no easy solution. Even if one follows all the accepted principles, there usually remains a choice of several question forms, each of which seems satisfactory. Every surveyor tries to phrase his questions in simple, everyday language, to avoid vagueness and ambiguity and to use neutral wording. His difficulty lies in judging whether, with any particular question, he has succeeded in these aims. He may appreciate perfectly that leading questions are to be avoided, but how can he know for sure which words will be 'leading' with the particular question, survey and population that confront him, perhaps for the first time?

The answer to this question lies in detailed pre-tests and pilot studies: more than anything else, they are the essence of a good questionnaire. However experienced the questionnaire designer, any attempt to shortcut these preparatory stages will seriously jeopardize the quality of the questionnaire; past experience is a considerable asset, but in a fresh survey there are always new aspects which may perhaps not be immediately recognized, but which exist and must be investigated through pre-tests and pilot studies. . . .

Question designing remains a matter of common sense and experience and of avoiding known pitfalls. It is not as yet, if indeed it ever can be, a matter of applying theoretical rules. Alternative versions of questions must be rigorously tested in pre-tests and the pilot survey, for in the absence of hard and fast rules, tests of practicability must play a crucial role in questionnaire construction.

References

Belson, W.A. (1964) 'Readership in Britain'. *Business Review* (Australia), **6**, 416–420.

—— (1968) 'The extent of stealing by London boys and some of its origins'. *Advancement of Science*, **25**, 171–184.

Cantril, H., ed. (1944) *Gauging Public Opinion*. Princeton University Press, Princeton.

David, S.T. (1952) 'Public opinion concerning tuberculosis'. *Tubercle (Journal of the British Tuberculosis Association)*. **33**, 78–90.

Kahn, R.L. and Cannell, C.F. (1957) *The Dynamics of Interviewing; Theory, Technique, and Cases*. Wiley, New York.

Kinsey, A.C., Pomeroy, W.B. and Martin, C.E. (1948) *Sexual Behavior in the Human Male*. Saunders, Philadelphia.

Lazarsfeld, P.F. (1935) 'The art of asking why'. *National Marketing Review*, **1**, 26–38.

Mosteller, F., Hyman, H., McCarthy, P.J., Marks, E.S. and Truman, D.B. (1949) *The Pre-election Polls of 1948: Report to the Committee on Analysis of Pre-election Polls and Forecasts*. US Social Science Research Council (Bulletin, no. 60), New York.

Oppenheim, A.N. (1966) *Questionnaire Design and Attitude Measurement*. Heinemann, London; Basic Books, New York.

Payne, S.L.B. (1951) *The Art of Asking Questions*. (Studies in Public Opinion, no. 3.) Princeton University Press, Princeton.

Smith, G.H. (1954) *Motivation Research in Advertising and Marketing*. McGraw-Hill, New York.

Stuart, A. (1952) 'Reading habits in three London boroughs'. *Journal of Documentation*, **8**, 33–49.

Whitfield, J.W. (1950) 'The imaginary questionnaire'. *Quarterly Journal of Experimental Psychology*, **2**, 76–87.

Chapter 10

Herbert H. Hyman with William J. Cobb, Jacob J. Feldman, Clyde W. Hart and Charles Herbert Stember

INTERVIEWING IN SOCIAL RESEARCH

From *Interviewing in Social Research,* Chicago: University of Chicago Press (1954)

. . .

IT IS NECESSARY TO learn as much as possible about how, under what conditions, and to what extent interviewer effects operate. . . .

Approaches to the problem of reducing error may be classified into three groups:

1   Empirical methods which attempt to remove or diminish the *source* of error, so that minimum error will occur in the interview.
2   Empirical methods which may allow effects to operate in the interview, but seek to bring about a cancellation of effects over all interviewers or to produce homogeneity among interviewers so as to eliminate at least the differential effects of different interviewers.
3   Formal or mathematical methods which allow effects to operate in the interview, but attempt by analysis or measurement of the magnitude of the effects to minimize or estimate their influence on final results.

The methods employed to remove the *source* of error will depend on what the source is. Methods which aim at the cancellation of effects or at minimizing or estimating them by analysis and measurement apply generally to error from all sources.

Control of error arising from factors within the interviewer

Empirical approaches to the control of interviewer effects through the manipulation of the interviewer may take the form of improvements in selection and training of interviewers or improvements in general personnel policy which will reduce turnover among the better interviewers or attract people of superior ability to interviewing work.

Improvement in the selection of interviewers requires some decision on the part of survey agencies as to what particular traits are desirable in an interviewer. If all kinds of interviewer error were positively and highly correlated, this problem would not arise, but in so far as skills are independent, some choice has to be made as to which skills are primary.

The essential phases of the interviewer's work are:

1   *Sampling.* The interviewer must be able to follow instructions for probability sampling or to use good judgment in selection under quota controls.
2   *Obtaining accurate information.* The interviewer must be able to get respondents to answer fully and truthfully, so that the opinions they express are not influenced by the interviewer. Social skills, accuracy in asking questions, and skill in probing are required in this phase of the work.
3   *Recording.* The interviewer must be thorough and accurate in recording the respondent's answers.

An interviewer may be skilful in one of these phases but not in another. The interviewer who is careless in the clerical work of recording answers may use excellent judgment in probing equivocal or vague answers in an unbiased manner. An interviewer skilful at getting the respondent to 'open up' may find it difficult to follow complicated sampling instructions or may be prone to obtain or record too many responses in accord with his own expectations or opinions.

Before improvement in selection of interviewing personnel can come, it is essential to know to what degree these skills are compatible with each other and what types of individuals are most likely to have combined skills. . . .

[Our evidences suggests] that, although social skill plays some part in the survey interviewer's work, it is not closely related to the other skills demanded by the job, and that excessive social orientation of the interviewer is not conducive to superior performance. This view is reinforced by the qualitative material we have presented. Earlier conceptions of the interview process have emphasized its social nature and in consequence have tended to enthrone good rapport as the *sine qua non* of the successful interview, and to over-evaluate the socially oriented personality as the most desirable interviewer type. Some of the current interviewer manuals sound like the pep talks of sales managers. But the phenomenological investigation of the nature of the interview situation seems to show that the analogy with 'selling' has been pressed too far. True, a moderate degree of sociableness and ability to meet people is an essential for getting respondents to consent to the interview and to answer questions willingly. Survey agencies are not likely to hire people for inter-viewing work who do not possess at least this minimum degree of 'sociality.' Beyond this point, however, there seems to be little relation between social skills and interviewing success over most of the range, and, in fact, there is reason to believe that too great rapport or too much social orientation in the interviewer may actually be detrimental. 'The Creep' and 'Tough Guy' cases cited [earlier] were instances where, from the usual point of view, rapport was poor, hostility of either interviewer or respondent was present, and yet there was no evidence that bias was introduced. In the 'Hen Party' case, on the other hand, the respondent was completely 'sold,' rapport was excellent, but there was evidence that the respondent was aware of the interviewer's opinions and may have deferred to those opinions in giving her answers. The kind of situation which the salesman attempts to produce may be precisely the one which is least suitable for the accurate measurement of opinion. And the interviewer who is most adept at producing such situations may be as unsuitable for the interviewing task as the one who encounters too many refusals.

Other evidence was presented [earlier] to show that the respondent is often much more detached from the social aspects of the interview situation and from the personality of the interviewer than he is usually considered to be; and that the interviewer himself usually has a kind of professional task orientation which enables him to preserve objectivity; that interviewers themselves regard over-involvement in the interview socially as a fault to be avoided, and that interviewers as a group show less 'sociality,' as measured by the inclination to discuss personal problems with others, than the general norm of college-educated women with whom they may be compared.

Some general conclusions of a tentative nature emerge. Over-all skill, in the various phases of the interviewing task (getting respondents to answer easily and truthfully, recording answers accurately, and sampling efficiently) show a fair degree of association. However, each element of the job requires social skills and other abilities – carefulness, judgment, intelligence, etc. – in varying proportions, and these underlying skills, particularly the social and nonsocial, do not appear to be closely related.

The implications for the survey agency are that the current practice of rejecting applicants who are *markedly* lacking in either ability to approach people or ability to understand and follow instructions, and fill out questionnaires accurately is a sound one; but also that caution should be exercised in having interviewers who are excessively socially oriented. In order to apply these findings efficiently, these skills and traits need to be measured. Hence we need to know how they are related to other more easily determined characteristics. If we can find correlations between skills and independent variables, such as test scores or interviewer characteristics, we would have some basis for the selection of good interviewers within the limitations imposed by interviewer labor market conditions. Before taking up this question, however, we need to examine the relationship of interviewer performance in the routine tasks to his biasing tendencies. . . .

. . . [The] main sources of bias are misunderstanding of instructions; mistakes in judgment of equivocal responses; idiosyncratic definition of his role by the interviewer himself, proceeding from his own beliefs as to the nature of attitudes and of respondent behavior; and nonobservance of prescribed procedures when situational pressures are strong.

Since at least a substantial part of the biased errors occurring in the interview seem to arise from the same set of causes that produce errors in general, the selection of interviewers on the basis of skill in the routine tasks of the interview should also have the effect of minimizing at least one of the determinants of interviewer bias. . . .

Minimizing bias through training procedures

Research agencies depend largely on careful instruction and training of interviewers in correct interviewing procedures for the avoidance of bias. These training procedures have been developed naturally out of experience and from the experimental studies of interviewer bias which have appeared in the literature, and the emphasis in training manuals reflects the prevalent beliefs as to the sources and locus of bias. Examination of a number of the training manuals currently in use by market and opinion survey agencies discloses that the principal source of bias is conceived to be ideological and that the locus of bias is considered to be chiefly in the process of asking questions. By contrast, biases arising in the process of recording respondents' answers have received less attention, and the operation of perceptual and cognitive factors such as expectations has been almost completely neglected. We may hope that one result of this study of interviewer effect will be to shift some of the emphasis in training to those sources and loci of error which this study has shown to be of hitherto unsuspected importance.

Every one of the interviewing manuals examined has included admonitions to the interviewer to ask questions using the exact wording of the questionnaire and in the exact sequence in which the questions appear on the questionnaire, and every one of them has cautioned the interviewer to avoid influencing the answer of the respondent either by actual suggestion of answers or by conscious or unconscious verbal emphasis or mannerisms, and to refrain from expressing his own opinions, even when asked to do so by the respondent. But with the exception of the NORC manual, most of them have scant material on the biases which may arise in the recording process. None of them that we have seen makes any mention of possible biases arising from interviewer expectations, including the NORC interview manual, which is the most voluminous and has twenty-five separate references to biasing factors, including even a warning concerning biases arising from differences in race, economic class, or sex between interviewer and respondent.

Curiously enough, one manual contains an admonition which would seem to encourage the introduction of bias through the employment of attitude-structure expectations. We quote: 'Should the respondent change his opinion during the course of an interview, you must check over the questionnaire from the beginning and make sure all answers are consistent.' And again: 'Make sure *all* answers are properly co-ordinated and provide a complete story.'

This insistence on consistency seems to require that the interviewer *reject* any answer not in accord with his expectations based on the attitudes revealed by answers to the earlier questions!

However, it should be stated that agencies have made and are making continuous efforts to eliminate or reduce bias in interviewing by intensive instruction and training, by means of manuals, specifications for particular surveys, and by continuing supervision and inspection of the interviewer's work. Every effort is made to enforce uniform practices in interviewing so that the results will at least be comparable. The degree of supervision exercised varies depending on the kind of work and the size of staff of the particular agency. Some of the larger agencies have regional supervisors who are in at least occasional contact with the interviewers. NORC training and supervision procedures are described at length in an appendix to this report. Each interviewer's work is rated regularly, and upon the completion of each assignment, the interviewer receives a personal letter from the central office in which errors of procedure, in so far as they can be detected from examination of the completed schedules, are pointed out to him. For example, marked or unusual patterns in the responses, the repetition of particular words or phrases in free-answer replies, indications that suggestive probes have been used, deviant behavior as revealed by comments on the interviewer's report form, and the like faults are noted and called to the attention of the interviewers.

Similar procedures are used by other agencies. This intensive training is designed not only to reduce error but to produce homogeneity, which is useful in itself in error control, as we shall have occasion to elaborate later on.

When the interviewer is first hired, he receives individual training in NORC techniques and procedures under the personal direction of an office or regional supervisor. This training includes study of the manual, basic instructions, and trial interviews, which are observed and criticized by the supervisor. During the course of this training, the supervisor will point out weaknesses and biasing tendencies in the interviewer's work. Applicants with obviously biasing personal characteristics are never hired, and the new interviewer is indoctrinated early in his training with such precepts as 'Never suggest an answer,' 'Ask all questions exactly as worded,' 'Never show surprise at a person's answer,' 'Never reveal your own opinions,' etc. The interviewer manual devotes particular and detailed attention to the subjects of field ratings and probing behavior – two of the areas in which studies have found greatest evidence of bias. The specifications for each survey point out the areas in which bias is most likely to occur on the survey.

Improvement in personnel policies and working conditions

To one familiar with the status of present-day interviewing and the conditions under which interviewers work, there must appear to be a certain futility in elaborate research to find methods of selecting the best interviewers, without at the same time finding ways to make interviewing work sufficiently attractive to appeal to such hypothetically superior personnel. Lists of the qualifications required for good interviewers have been made to sound like a catalog of all the virtues – a high degree of intelligence, pleasing personality, carefulness, dependability, honesty, good physical condition, good education, and many others. But what does the research agency offer for this paragon? Work which is physically and mentally demanding, low pay, sporadic assignments given with little advance notice, and no opportunity for advancement. Present average pay rates for interviewing work run as low as $1.00 per hour, compared with the average rates of 70–75 cents common ten years ago. Although we sometimes see interviewing characterized as 'professional' work, such pay rates could hardly be expected to attract persons with professional qualifications, certainly not for full-time work.

But interviewing, as market and opinion research is currently organized, is not full-time work. The frequency and size of assignments varies somewhat from one agency to another, but the range is probably from about eight to twenty assignments per year, of a few hours to four or five days in length. Hence, most of the agencies rely on housewives and others who do not have to work full-time for a living, who may be able to use a little pin-money, or who accept the work because it relieves the tedium of household duties. . . . If current limitations imposed by financial and operating conditions are accepted as fixed and unalterable, it is doubtful if any thoroughgoing improvement in interviewing standards can be achieved. . . . inter-viewer turnover would be greatly reduced if the job could be made to offer greater security, more regularity, higher pay, and higher status. On the other hand, as long as interviewing remains an occasional or part-time job at low pay, turnover in the staff will be minimized by hiring persons who are not in the full-time labor market and who will therefore not be attracted by other jobs. Under present conditions, the frequency and size of assignments and the type of work determine almost com-pletely the type of interviewer hired. The cities and counties in which the services of interviewers are required are specified by the sampling requirements, and hence the field department is restricted in its ability to act on independent applications, or to increase the frequency of assignments. If interviewing were to be made a full-time job, research agencies would probably not only have to pool their interviewing staffs (a practice already followed to some extent) but might also be forced to use the same national samples of primary areas. And higher rates of pay for interviewing would mean drastic changes in the economics of the industry. It is unlikely that such changes will come about without great pressure from outside.

Control of errors arising from respondent reactions

. . . Bias arising from the group membership disparities between interviewers and respondents has long been recognized by research agencies, which have modified certain practices to control error. As Sheatsley remarks:

> It has become more and more unlikely that any research agency today, except for experimental purposes, would use white interviewers to survey the opinions of a cross-section of Negroes, would hire 'Jewish-looking' interviewers to conduct a poll on the subject of anti-Semitism or would employ a crew of upper class clubwomen to carry out a survey on the attitudes of the slum dwellers.

But aside from such precautions in special cases where it is clear that the group membership disparity could seriously affect the results, such disparities continue to exist as a potential source of bias. In his study of the composition of existing field staffs, Sheatsley shows that interviewers are of a considerably higher education and socio-economic status than the general population. 'The "typical" interviewer, in fact, is an upper-middle class woman, about 40 years old, with at least one or two years of college.' . . .

Selection of respondents under quota sampling, as has been shown re-peatedly, tends to produce an under-representation of lower-income and lower-education groups, and such an under-representation also distorts results in the conservative direction. This compounded bias against lower-class opinion is probably the largest and most systematic of all biases operating in opinion survey work and is probably responsible for the Republican bias in the results of many of past election polls. More serious in its effects would be the continual pro-conservative bias in the studies of opinion on important public issues in the interim between elections.

What can survey agencies do to minimize such biases? An approach involving matching or dovetailing characteristics of interviewer and respondent is severely limited by labor market and administrative conditions. . . . Under existing conditions, the general composition of interviewing staffs cannot be greatly altered. . . .

However, some of the survey agencies have made some attempt to achieve a partial 'matching' by trying to make the field staff a miniature sample of the population being studied – usually a national cross section with respect to certain characteristics, e.g., by hiring approximately equal numbers of men and women or proportionate numbers of Republicans and Democrats, on the theory that biases will cancel out. . . . Such attempts have not been completely successful, and in any case, do not greatly affect potential reactional biases, since they are directed mainly toward minimizing ideological bias of the *interviewer* rather than differential *respondent* reaction to the interviewer.

Smaller agencies cannot use this approach and hence rely largely on training methods to avoid bias. It is possible for these agencies to exercise closer supervision over their smaller staffs and to train each interviewer in talking to all kinds of people. No matter how intensive the training in correct interviewing procedures may be, however, it cannot eliminate biases from respondent reactions to the *appearance* of the interviewer himself.

Control of error through modification of the situation

Perhaps the most practical approach to the reduction of interviewer effect lies in greater control over or modification of the situational factors which mediate effects. . . .

Although the mere presence of the interviewer is often sufficient to induce *some* bias, effects will increase in the degree that the personality of the interviewer enters the situation as a focus for the respondent. The available techniques for collecting information may be scaled according to the degree to which they 'socially involve' the respondent in this manner from minimum to maximum involvement.

1. Self-administered questionnaires, which may be mail questionnaires or self-enumeration schedules picked up by the interviewer.

2. Secret ballots, handed to the respondent by the interviewer, but filled out in the interviewer's presence.

3. The 'deliberative' technique, by which the interviewer leaves the questionnaire for the respondent to 'think about' and returns later to conduct the interview.

4. The personal interview of the usual type. . . .

Where the respondent's prestige is involved in the answer to the question, or where the questions are of a highly personal nature or otherwise embarrassing to either interviewer or respondent, there is some evidence that effects will tend to be greater as the technique employed increases the ratio of 'social involvement' to 'total involvement.' For questions of this type, research agencies might consider more frequent employment of the less socially involving techniques, or at least a combination of techniques, with the usual type of personal interview reserved for those questions which experience has shown are less productive of bias, unless other gains to be derived through the agency of the interviewer are paramount.

. . . Types of questions which are likely to produce psychological difficulties for the interviewer or unfavorable reactions in the respondent should be avoided as much as possible or special techniques employed to mitigate the psychological difficulties involved.

Now of course, it is evident that all such questions cannot be eliminated. Frequently they may be essential objectives of the survey or essential to the analysis of survey results. However, it may be possible to lessen their biasing possibilities in other ways: (1) By use of the less 'socially involving' data collecting technique. Income questions might, for example, be obtained via the secret ballot, even where the rest of the questions are asked personally by the interviewer. (2) By careful attention to *question sequence* on the schedule. Personal questions or other types likely to arouse resentment, embarrassment, or apathy should not be placed at the beginning of the interview, where they may destroy rapport at the outset, unless the survey purpose makes this order mandatory, as, for example, when necessary to determine whom to interview. (3) By greater attention to simplification of wording.

In some cases, attitude-structure expectation effects might be minimized by embedding the significant attitude questions in a context of questions which have no presumptive attitudinal relation to each other, or by placing related questions as far apart as possible to prevent the carry-over in the interviewer's mind.

The situational pressures which bring into play certain biasing tendencies as an aid in coping with the difficulties of the interviewing task are attenuated by experience. The experienced interviewer has had practice in learning how to overcome many of the difficulties that arise in interviewing, and hence he is less hostile to such difficulties, is able to maintain a more detached or professional attitude in cases where the inexperienced interviewer might try to find a way out of his troubles by the conscious or unconscious employment of his own preconceptions or expectations. Thus the implications [. . .] for the modification or control of the situation to minimize bias are most relevant when inexperienced interviewers have to be employed. . . .

Reference

Sheatsley, P.B. (1951) 'An analysis of interviewer characteristics and their relationship to performance – Part III', *International Journal of Opinion and Attitude Research*, V, 193–197.

Chapter 11

A. N. Oppenheim

ATTITUDE SCALING METHODS

From *Questionnaire Design and Attitude Measurement,* London: Heinemann (1966)

THE WORLD IS FULL of well-meaning people who believe that anyone who can write plain English and has a modicum of common sense can produce a good questionnaire. This book is not for them. . . .

Attitude scales consist of from half-a-dozen to two dozen or more attitude statements, with which the respondent is asked to agree or disagree. Since so much depends on the way the issue is put into words, a single item or a single question is often unreliable and, because it usually approaches an attitude from one particular direction only, may give rather one-sided results. Thus, agreement with the statement 'Divorce should be made easier' can hardly, by itself, be a reliable index of a broader attitude, such as the respondent's radicalism, since his agreement may, in any case, be due to personal circumstances; but by having many items we can reduce the effects of one-sided responses. However, more important than the number of attitude statements used is the fact that they have been scaled: they have been selected and put together from a much larger number of attitude statements according to certain statistical procedures. Because of this, we must not judge the relatively small number of attitude statements in a finished scale at their face value; they are the outcome of a process of complicated sifting. . . .

Public-opinion polls frequently use a single question to obtain a rough guide to people's attitudes. While this is commonly excused on the grounds of expediency, such questions are the outcome of much trial and error, and, since they are used repeatedly in various surveys, a good deal is known about their correlates.

Attitude scales are relatively crude measuring instruments, and we must not expect too much from them. Their chief function is to divide people roughly into a number of broad groups, with regard to a particular attitude. Such scales cannot, by themselves, be expected to provide us with subtle insights in an individual case. They are techniques for placing people on a continuum in relation to one another, in relative and not in absolute terms.

Principles of measurement

Let us examine, for a moment, what is involved in the construction and evaluation of any measurement tool. We shall take as our example an ordinary ruler.

1   Unidimensionability or homogeneity. This means that the scale should be about one thing at a time, as purely as possible. Thus, the ruler should measure length, not temperature or viscosity. In the case of attitude scales, problems arise because the manifest contents of the items may be a poor guide to what the items actually measure. We need correlation techniques to find out how the items 'hang together' and which of them are 'purest.'

2   Linearity and equal intervals or equal-appearing intervals. This means that the scale should follow the straight-line model and that some sort of scoring system should be devised, preferably one based on interchangeable units. Such units are convenient to handle statistically, though they may be psychologically dubious. With a ruler, it is relatively easy to make sure that it is straight rather than bent and that it is marked off in equal units of inches or centimeters. Attitude scales assume the straightline model (though this may not be adequate), but the creation of scoring units is difficult, and they are, at best, of doubtful interchangeability. An inch is an inch, whether it lies at one end of a ruler or at the other, but numerically similar attitude-scale differences may represent very different psychological distinctions. Also, how can we ensure comparability of units from one attitude to another? For both these reasons, ranking is often preferable when constant scale units are hard to come by.

3   Reliability. This is the indispensable attribute of consistency. If the same measure were applied to the same object today and next week, the results should be near-identical (unless a real change in the object has meanwhile taken place). A ruler can be applied, say, to the leg of a table and the results, for all practical purposes, will be quite consistent over time. The greater length and diversity of attitude scales make them more reliable than single questions, but even so, complete consistency is difficult to achieve; people are bound to react somewhat differently to a scale when they are confronted by it a second time. Nevertheless, reliability coefficients of .80 or higher are quite common. . . .

4   Validity. This tells us whether the scale measures what it is supposed to measure. We may have obtained unidimensionality by keeping only those items which intercorrelate highly, yet the scale may not measure what we want it to measure. Instead of measuring authoritarianism, for instance, it may just be a measure of acquiescence. Sometimes, it is possible to correlate the new scale with an older, well-established one. At other times, it may be possible to use criterion groups, such as membership in religious congregations or political

parties, between which the scale should be able to distinguish; but behavior is often not a simple manifestation of an underlying attitude, and so there are dangers and pitfalls in this approach. At present, there is no way of making sure that an attitude scale is valid. . . .

5   Reproducibility. When we say that a man weighs 150 pounds, we mean that the pointer on the scales will move from 0 to 150, but will cover none of the remainder; in other words, the figure of 150 refers, not to just any odd 150 pound units, but to the first 150 pounds on the scale. From the 'score' of 150, we can reproduce exactly which units on the scale were covered and which were not. This is not an essential requirement when we are dealing with constant and interchangeable units, such as pounds or inches; but if we were dealing, say, with the symptoms of the different stages of an illness, it would be helpful if they could be ordered or scaled in terms of their degree of seriousness in such a way that the presence of symptom D would mean that the patient also must have symptoms A, B, and C. Similarly, a score on an attitude scale might show us, by means of a single figure, which statements the respondent agreed with and which he disagreed with, thus telling us his place on the attitude continuum. This is a requirement that in practice is difficult to achieve, for many attitude pools are not amenable to this kind of cumulative or progressive scaling – partly because they may not be unidimensional.

Apart from these main requirements, there may be others. For instance, it is helpful to have norms or standards derived from the scores of large numbers of respondents, so that we can compare an individual's score with those of others and interpret its meaning.

In the sections that follow we will discuss the four best-known methods of attitude scaling. One might well ask why we need more than one method. This has come about because . . . different research workers have developed methods of scale-building in which they have laid particular stress on one or another of the above requirements and have paid less attention to the others. One method has concentrated on unidimensionality, another on finding equivalent scale units, a third on obtaining reproducibility, and so on. There does not seem to be a method that combines the advantages of all of them, and it is therefore very important that we understand their respective aims and the differences between them.

It follows that, for the present, it is impossible to say which method is best. Each has important desirable features, but each of them is also open to criticism. For our own inquiry, the best method is the one which is most appropriate to our particular problem. If we wish to study attitude-patterning or explore theories of attitudes, then probably the Likert procedure will be the most relevant. If we wish to study attitude change, or the hierarchical structure of an attitude, then Guttman's method might be preferable. If we are studying group differences, then we'll probably elect to use the Thurstone procedures, and so on. Each type of scale does one thing rather well, and, if this is what our research needs, then this is the type of scale we will want to use. . . .

[Editor's note: Oppenheim's account of social distance and Thurstone methods are omitted from this extract.]

Likert scales

The construction of a Thurstone scale always means a lot of work, and it is often difficult to obtain an adequate group of judges. The Likert procedure[1] may have its disadvantages, but it is certainly less laborious, and this – together with the discovery that Likert scales correlate well with Thurstone scales[2] – has helped to make it more popular.

Likert's primary concern was with unidimensionality – making sure that all the items would measure the same thing. He also wanted to eliminate the need for judges by getting subjects in a trial sample to *place themselves* on an attitude continuum for each statement – running from 'strongly agree' to 'agree,' 'uncertain,' 'disagree,' and 'strongly disagree.' These five positions were given simple weights of 5, 4, 3, 2, and 1 for scoring purposes (or sometimes 4–0), after more complex scoring methods had been shown to possess no advantage.

To produce a Likert scale we proceed as follows: First, as usual, we compose an item pool. However, for the Likert procedure it is best not to have many neutral items nor many extreme items at either end of the continuum. Next, we need a sample of respondents on whom to try the items – the entire pool of items together. Probably 100 respondents would suffice for most purposes, but numbers of the order of 250 or 300 are not unusual. Each respondent will be asked, not merely whether he agrees or disagrees with each statement, but to check one of the five positions given above. Respondents should be similar to those on whom the scale will be used.

Next, we score the record of each respondent. To do this, we must decide whether we want a high scale score to mean a favorable or an unfavorable attitude. It does not matter what we decide, but from then on we must be consistent. If we decide that a high score on the scale will mean a favorable attitude, then favorable statements must be scored 5 for 'strongly agree,' down to 1 for 'strongly disagree' – and unfavorable statements must be scored 1 for 'strongly agree,' up to 5 for 'strongly disagree.' If we decide that a high score will mean an *un*favorable attitude, then the opposite system of scoring will apply. It helps, therefore, if we have few neutral items, so that we can readily tell from the wording of the statement whether it is positive or negative. But if we feel uncertain about some statements, we can score them arbitrarily from 1–5 or from 5–1; the correlations will subsequently show us whether we are right. Research workers often get into difficulties over this problem of scoring reversals, so it is important to be meticulous about it from the start.

Having scored each item from 1–5 or from 5–1, we next add up the item scores to obtain a total score. For instance, if we have 132 items in our pool, then the possible range of total scores will be from 132 to 660 (5 × 132) for each subject. Figure 11.1 illustrates some items from a scale for mothers, dealing with acceptance or rejection of children. It becomes obvious, on reading through the items, that

---

1 Rensis Likert, 'A technique for the measurement of attitudes,' *Archives of Psychology*, no. 140 (1932). Source book for the Likert scaling method.
2 A.L. Edwards and K.C. Kenney, 'A comparison of the Thurstone and Likert techniques of attitude scale construction,' *Journal of Applied Psychology*, XXX (1946), 72–83.

	Strongly agree 5	Agree 4	Uncertain 3	Disagree 2	Strongly disagree 1
(1) Children bring a husband and wife closer to each other.			✓		
(2) It is fun showing children how to do things.		✓			
(3) Children need some of their natural meanness taken out of them.					✓
(4) A mother with young children badly misses adult company and conversation.	✓				
(5) On balance, children are more of a blessing than a burden.		✓			
(6) It is often difficult to keep one's temper with a child.				✓	
(7) Looking after children really demands too much of me.				✓	
(8) If we could afford to do so, we would prefer to send our children to a boarding school.			✓		
(9) When things are difficult, children are often a great source of courage and inspiration.				✓	
(10) If I had my life to live over again, I should again want to have children.	✓				

Figure 11.1 An attitude scale, relating to mothers' acceptance or rejection of children.

some of them express greater or lesser acceptance, others express degrees of hostility or rejection, and one or two may not fit on this particular dimension. Thus, agreement with statement (2) 'It is fun showing children how to do things' would seem to imply positive feelings for children; agreement with statement (3) 'Children need some of their natural meanness taken out of them' would seem to indicate hostility to children on the part of the respondent; while the implications of statement (8) 'If we could afford to do so, we would prefer to send our children to a boarding school' are a little unclear: agreement might signify rejection of the children, or it might mean the desire to lavish money on them in order to give them a better education (which could, however, be a form of overcompensation for unconscious feelings of rejection).

We now come to the problem of scoring. If we decide that a high scale score is going to mean a positive attitude to children, then agreement with the statements that imply love of children should be scored 4 or 5, and agreement with statements that imply rejection of children should be scored 1 or 2 – in other words, the scoring of these latter statements is reversed. If, on the other hand, we decide that a high scale score will mean a negative attitude to children, then the scoring on the items that imply positive feelings toward children (items 1, 2, 5, 9, and 10) should be reversed. The important thing is to be consistent; likewise, we must make sure that we write our scoring instructions correctly and that in the case of punch-card analysis of each statement we know whether the respondents' checks were punched as they stood or were reversed before punching, where necessary.

In our example we have given but ten items, and we have shown the responses of one particular individual. Just glancing at her responses we get the impression of a mother with a mildly positive attitude toward children (items 2, 5, 7, and 10) who is able to express some moderately negative feelings (items 4 and 9) but shies away from extreme hostility (item 3) or inspired love (item 9). She also expresses some doubts (items 1 and 8); this may be because she is uncertain of her feelings or uncertain of the implications of the items. Perhaps these items do not belong in this scale because they contain other powerful attitude components (to marriage, to social class, to private boarding schools, to separation) besides acceptance or rejection of children. Item-analysis would show us whether these items should be retained.

How should this mother's responses be scored? Let us assume that we have decided that a high scale score shall mean a positive attitude to children. In that case, all the positive items can be scored as they stand:

5 = strongly agree
4 = agree
3 = uncertain
2 = disagree
1 = strongly disagree.

The scoring for items 3, 4, 6, 7, and 8 will, however, have to be reversed, as follows:

1 = strongly agree
2 = agree

3 = uncertain
4 = disagree
5 = strongly disagree.

Note, by the way, that the scoring of 'uncertain' is the same (namely 3) in both cases. We can now give a numerical score to each check (in large-scale scoring operations it may be best to write such scores on the scale itself next to each check or in the margin) and calculate a total score, as follows:

```
      item   1 = 3
             2 = 4
             3 = 5
             4 = 1
             5 = 4
             6 = 4
             7 = 4
             8 = 3
             9 = 2
            10 = 5
total score   35
```

Since there are ten items, we have a maximum possible score of $5 \times 10 = 50$, and a necessary minimum score of $1 \times 10 = 10$. A score of 35 is thus a little above the midway point toward the positive end of the scale – which confirms our earlier impression of someone with mildly positive attitudes toward children.

Now we shall want to carry out an item-analysis to decide which are the best statements for our scale. To do this, something like an act of faith is required. Ideally, the item-analysis should take place by correlating each item with some reliable outside criterion of the attitude that it is supposed to measure and retaining only the items with the highest correlations. Such external criteria are, however, almost never available. It would not be safe to infer from the fact that a woman has children that she necessarily loves them; nor can we be sure that people who vote for a certain political party necessarily occupy a given position on a political spectrum; or that professional military men are necessarily more war-minded; in other words, it is dangerous to infer a person's attitudes from his behavior or from his group membership. We must therefore say to ourselves that, for the moment at least, the best available measure of the attitude concerned is the total item pool that we have so carefully constructed. By purifying this, the items will at least be consistent and homogeneous – they will all be measuring the same thing – and the scale may possibly also be valid. It is rather like trying to pull ourselves up by our own bootstraps!

However, this kind of procedure is not uncommon in the field of mental measurement and, if we are prepared to make this assumption, then the rest is plain sailing. We simply work out correlation coefficients for each item with the total score and retain those with the highest correlations. This is known as the internal-consistency method of item-analysis, since no external criterion is available. There is, however, one practical snag: we should really use, not the total score, but the total score minus the score for the item in question. This means that, for each item in turn, we will have a slightly different set of total scores. However, since we will probably group the total scores to work out the correlations, this subtraction procedure will not often make much difference, especially if the item pool is at all large; many research workers do not bother with it. . . .

Reliability of Likert scales tends to be good and, partly because of the greater range of answers permitted to respondents, is often higher than that of corresponding Thurstone scales; a reliability coefficient of .85 is often achieved. The scale makes no pretence at equal-appearing intervals but by using the internal-consistency method of item selection it approaches unidimensionality in many cases. The number of items in a Likert scale is arbitrary, but is sometimes very small. . . .

In practice, if we remember that equal score intervals do not permit us to make assertions about the equality of underlying attitude differences and that identical scores may have very different meanings, the Likert scales tend to perform very well when it comes to a reliable, rough ordering of people with regard to a particular attitude. Apart from their relative ease of construction, these scales have two other advantages: first, they provide more precise information about the respondent's degree of agreement or disagreement, and respondents usually prefer this to a simple agree/disagree score. Second, it becomes possible to include items whose manifest content is not obviously related to the attitude in question, so that the subtler and deeper ramifications of an attitude can be explored. These 'long shots,' such as the item about sending children to boarding schools in our earlier example . . . enable us to make use of the links that an attitude may have with neighboring areas and to uncover the strands and interconnections of its various components. . . .

The problem of validation

[In an earlier chapter] we discussed the problems of validity, and we remarked then on the difference between factual and attitudinal measures and the greater difficulty of validating the latter because of their abstract and indirect nature and because of the absence of suitable criteria. Attitude scales share this problem with other forms of mental measurement. The literature contains but a small number of attempts at direct validation against a criterion, and we may well ask whether the measures employed as criteria were themselves valid. Such attempts have included the use of essay-type questions, experts' judgments, membership in groups with known policies or interests, pictorial material, interviews and case studies, judgments by friends or co-workers, self-ratings, political votes, and such overt behavior as church attendance. New scales are often correlated with older, well-known scales which, however, may themselves be of questionable validity. Scales are often given names or labels that help to create a spuriously high impression of validity. The very fact that they look like tests and can be scored may create expectations of validity and exactitude that may not be fulfilled.

It may be helpful to remind ourselves of the different approaches to the problem of validity. We have repeatedly pointed out the weaknesses in the criterion-group approach, sometimes known as pragmatic validation. For more theoretically oriented research the concept of construct validity has been developed, which hinges on the relationship of our scale with other measures. Much depends on the quality of the attitude statements and the feelings that they arouse in the respondents; in this sense, validity depends on the respondents' candor and willingness to cooperate and the absence of stereotyped answers or 'façade' responses. Some investigators simply state that what the scale measures is indicated by the manifest content of the items; others rely on groups of judges for ascertaining what the items measure. Of particular importance is predictive validity, usually in the sense of predicting some future aspect of behavior. We can see from this that a great deal depends on our purpose in building a scale. It is one thing to require a purely descriptive device, which can roughly divide our sample into several groups with regard to a given attitude, but quite another to ask for a technique that will predict people's actions at some time in the future. Speaking very generally, many of our scales will probably do quite an adequate descriptive job, as long as not too much precision is required of them, but the problems of predictive validity are a long way from being solved.

To illustrate the lack of correspondence that is found at times between verbal attitudes and behavior (predictive validity), the classic demonstration of LaPiere[3] is often cited. In 1934, he traveled through the United States in the company of a Chinese couple. When he later questioned the managers of hotels and restaurants that had served them, over 90 per cent said that they would not accept Chinese guests! Kutner, Wilkins, and Yarrow[4] carried out a study in 1952, similarly showing that ethnic prejudice may not necessarily express itself in discriminatory behavior in a face-to-face situation. Wilkins,[5] on the other hand, found it possible to predict the demand for British campaign stars and medals after World War II with considerable accuracy from an attitude questionnaire.

Can attitude scales, then, predict behavior? As we have seen, behavior does not have a simple one-to-one relationship with one type of inner determinant such as an attitude. The relationship is complex and will involve both other attitudes and character traits and environmental determinants. . . .

An attitude scale may indicate inclinations toward cheating, but the respondent will probably act honestly if he thinks he will be found out. Behavior is a compromise, a resultant of the interaction of multiple forces. . . .

More research is needed on internal conflict between contradictory attitudes or between attitudes and other aspects of personality: we have some measures of these variables in isolation, but we do not know how conflicts between them are resolved within the individual. We also need to make a serious start with the measurement of the perceived environment, such as threats, role expectations, and conformity needs. Not until we have arrived at a fuller measurement and understanding of all the components in the behavioral equation and their interaction will we be able to make valid predictions.

3 Richard T. LaPiere, 'Attitudes versus actions,' *Social Forces*, XIV (1934), 230–237.
4 B. Kutner, Carol Wilkins, and Penny R. Yarrow, 'Verbal attitudes and overt behavior involving racial prejudice,' *Journal of Abnormal and Social Psychology*, XLVII (1952), 647–652.
5 Leslie T. Wilkins, *Prediction of the Demand for Campaign Stars and Medals* (London: Central Office of Information, 1948).

Chapter 12

Kim Sheehan and Mariea Hoy

ON-LINE SURVEYS

From 'Using e-mail to survey internet users in the United States: methodology and assessment,' *Journal of Computer Mediated Communication* 4(3) March 1999

. . .

THE INTERNET PRESENTS ENORMOUS potential for interaction between on-line users and researchers. . . . [We present] evidence based on previous research that discusses the strengths and limitations of web page-based surveys and assesses the viability of using e-mail as a survey data collection method. . . .

Web-based surveys

To date, the Internet offers both web page-based surveys and e-mail for prospective researchers to use for data collection. Web page-based surveys tend to collect broad-based data from individuals all over the world who self-select to respond to surveys that are posted on web sites. These web page-based polls can collect demographic information, as well as other types of purchase, psychographic and opinion data. Numerous benefits to web-based surveys have been noted.

A web page-based survey can take advantage of the graphic power available through programming languages such as HTML and JavaScript to create an attractive, interesting, and compelling survey that is inviting to respondents. . . . The use of CGI scripts allow adaptive questioning, which means that the questions that a respondent is asked depend on his or her answers to previous questions (Kehoe and Pitkow 1996). This allows for follow-up questions that can enrich responses as well as easier navigation for respondents.

Web page-based polls have been noted for their ability to generate a high number of responses (Kehoe and Pitkow 1995): the GVU polls at Georgia Institute of Technology generate more than 10,000 responses per poll. The sheer number of responses suggests that the results represent a diverse set of users. For example, it was estimated that one out of every 100 on-line users responded to each of the GVU polls (Kehoe and Pitkow 1996).

This high volume of responses can be collected very quickly. . . . For example, studies have shown that several hundred responses can be generated over the course of a single weekend (McCullough 1998). This time factor alone suggests huge benefits over traditional surveying techniques in terms of being able to collect and analyze data quickly, and implement decisions based on the findings.

The costs of both data collection and analysis can be minimized by the use of web-based surveys (McCullough 1998). Outside of high start-up costs for equipment and web page design, the actual implementation of a survey can be almost free, with no costs for paper or postage. Data analysis can be simplified by a direct transfer from the form to the analysis software, where limited data cleaning would be necessary (McCullough 1998).

Web page-based surveys allow for anonymity in responses, since the respondent can choose whether to provide his or her name or not. Previous research (Kiesler and Sproull 1986) has indicated that anonymity may affect response rates positively, as respondents may be more willing to respond without fear that their answers may be identifiable to them.

Since respondents type in their answers directly to a form on a web page, there is no need for an interviewer to have contact with the respondents. . . . Therefore, survey responses will be free from errors caused by interviewers, resulting in cleaner data (McCullough 1998).

Similarly, the lack of an interviewer eliminates any potential for bias that the interviewer brings to the survey. An interviewer's mood, prejudices or opinions will not be reflected in the data (McCullough 1998).

However, web-based surveys do present some limitations that researchers must recognize when they are considering this method.

Web page-based surveys must attract respondents to the web page with messages posted in news groups, links on other web pages, banner ads, and other types of methods. As a result, all segments of a Web population may not be represented in the sample (Kehoe and Pitkow 1996). All Internet users do not use the same browsers, and different browsers may not present images and text on web pages in the same manner. For example, some users (such as those subscribing to freenets) use only a text-based web browser (such as Lynx), and may not be able to respond to the survey. Some web based-polls are announced in Usenet newsgroups. Therefore, if potential respondents are not a frequent visitor to newsgroups, they may not be aware of the survey announcement posted in newsgroups, and thus may not have the opportunity to complete the survey. The self-select nature of web page-based surveys also may affect their generalizability. . . .

Web page-based polls generally allow for multiple responses from a single individual, as well as responses from individuals outside of the population of interest (e.g. persons in countries where a product or service is not available, or from persons who are younger or older than the population of interest). This could also bias the results.

One way to validate a method is to compare it to other methods that are accepted within the research community. Since it is almost impossible to develop response rates to web page-based surveys (Kehoe and Pitkow 1996), it is difficult to compare web page-based survey methods to traditional survey data collection methods such as postal mail and telephone surveys. This leads to another generalizability issue. Without an understanding of the size of the respondent pool in comparison to the size of the universe and the sampling pool, it is also difficult to generalize research findings beyond the universe of those responding to the survey.

E-mail as a data collection method

Using e-mail as a survey data collection method comparable to postal mail may ameliorate some of the issues inherent in web page-based data collection. Previous research presents several reasons to support the idea the e-mail offers much promise as a means of administering surveys as well as pitfalls to be avoided.

Today, as many as 100 million people worldwide have access to e-mail (DOC 1998). Eighty per cent of all users use the Internet daily, with many reporting that 'surfing' replaces 'TV viewing' as entertainment (Kehoe, Pitkow and Morton 1997). The sheer number of individuals using the medium coupled with the frequency and ease with which they could be contacted suggest that e-mail is a viable survey method.

A lack of a national directory of e-mail addresses could be seen as a limitation to e-mail surveys. For example, Schuldt and Totten (1994) reported a problem with obtaining names for their sample. This situation has changed in recent years. Many content providers compile their own databases and should be able to access names quickly from these sources. Some organizations (such as universities and trade associations) publish directories, both paper and on-line, with e-mail addresses. On-line search engines such as Lycos provide 'People finders' for e-mail addresses.

When respondents use the 'reply' function of their e-mail programs to return their completed surveys, their names and e-mail addresses can be automatically written on the electronic message (i.e. the survey) the researcher would receive. While previous research (Kiesler and Sproull 1986) has indicated that anonymity may have affected response rates positively, other researchers (Couper, Blair and Triplett 1997) suggest that the lack of anonymity may not have any effect on response rates. With e-mail surveys, anonymity could be guaranteed through the use of encryption technology, and confidentiality can be guaranteed through confidentiality assurances. This study chose to guarantee confidentiality. Assuring that responses will be confidential throughout the data collection process should help to build respondent trust and enhance response rates.

An additional benefit to using e-mail is that duplicate responses can be eliminated. Steel, Schwendig and Kilpatrick (1992) suggested that duplicate responses can become problematic since researchers using postal mail often send out multiple copies of questionnaires to their entire sample in order to increase response rates.

E-mail presents a benefit over postal mail, then, since e-mail responses can be tracked and previous respondents can be eliminated from follow-up e-mail.

E-mail surveys may allow the researcher to develop a profile of non-respondents. Depending on the search engine used and the respondents' server, some demographic information about persons with e-mail accounts is available on-line and some demographic information such as gender and location may be compiled. It might also be possible to attempt to contact non-respondents using an alternative method (such as postal mail or telephone) to solicit responses that could be compared to the e-mail sample for similarities. It should be noted that demographic information about persons with e-mail accounts may not be completely accurate, as individuals may have changed locations or jobs since the information was provided. However, the availability of such data allows for options that the researcher can consider when assessing non-response.

As with web page-based surveys, there appears to be some cost savings inherent in using new technology. Parker (1992) indicates that cost savings from e-mail compared to traditional mail and telephone surveys are based on low transmission costs and elimination or reduction of paper costs. E-mail may also present cost savings over web page-based surveys, as costs for page design and posting to a server would not be incurred. However, some savings may be offset by the on-line server used (costs vary by Internet service provider) and time considerations (transmission costs may increase by the minute, which may impact the length of the survey).

When respondents perceive technology as easy to use, they seem more likely to respond (Parker 1992). As more people become familiar with the Internet, these individuals should become comfortable using the technology to answer surveys. An additional advantage to e-mail is that respondents can return it in one of three ways: e-mail, fax or postal mail (Parker 1992). This flexibility may enhance the perception of ease of use. Unless the respondent purposely deletes the survey, it cannot be accidentally tossed or misplaced like a mail survey. Yet, comparable to a mail survey, the respondents still have the benefits of completing the survey at their own pace and convenience.

There is not clear evidence that new technology produces a higher response than postal mail. In a review of nine studies that have used both postal mail and e-mail four studies show postal mail achieving higher response rates than e-mail, three studies indicate that e-mail response rates are higher than postal mail, and two studies did not show significant differences in response rates. Researchers indicated that the lack of familiarity with the technology may have impacted some of the response rates. It is also important to note that many of these studies are from small, homogenous populations, and thus may not represent larger population groups' response tendencies.

Past studies found direct marketers can collect data more quickly using e-mail than with postal mail methods. In the five studies that reported response time results, e-mail responses were collected significantly faster than postal mail responses. The variety of populations used in these studies suggest that this rapid rate of response might be seen among larger Internet populations.

Current research has also identified two key limitations unique to e-mail that must be considered when planning an e-mail survey. First, researchers must recognize that unsolicited surveys may be considered aggressive by respondents, and not in keeping with Internet culture (Mehta and Sivadas 1995). Minimizing a perception of intrusiveness should help to address this problem (Schillewaert, Langerak and Duhamel 1998). Second, the changing nature of the Internet suggests that it is possible that e-mail addresses may become out-of-date fairly quickly (Smith 1997). Addressing this issue early on can prepare the researcher for dealing with delivery failures. . . .

Considerations

. . . It would not be possible to generalize results to mass markets including both Internet users and non-Internet users based on knowledge attained solely from on-line respondents. This has also been shown as a limitation to web based polls (Coomber 1997; Kehoe and Pitkow 1996). However, depending on the research question, it is possible that sample information can be used to generalize to the on-line population.

One of the most challenging limitations is the changing nature of the Internet. The composition of the Internet changes daily with new individuals logging on and others adding or switching Internet service providers. Thus, some directories may contain information that is out of date or incomplete. . . . The changing nature of the Internet is also seen in changes to how search engines operate. Any ownership changes of a search engine or other web content provider may result in unanticipated changes to this methodology. Additionally, the technology allows individuals to set up mail filters, which delete messages from those senders not on the receiver's 'approved' list. This deletion may or may not be reported to the sender. As use of mail filters grows, response rates may be affected. Researchers should anticipate these changes by testing search engines prior to address generation to make sure that the method is still appropriate and pre-testing the study with a random sample of names to determine and plan for non-deliverable mail.

While response rates now appear promising, respondent distrust of data collection may influence response rates in the future. . . . One respondent wrote, 'if you are a student then I am the Emperor of Japan'. The novelty of using e-mail to collect data may be partly to blame. Until this method becomes more ingrained with academics and popularized among on-line users, respondent concern and distrust is likely to continue.

Additionally, individual ISPs have policies and procedures that may limit the success of e-mail surveys. We encountered one ISP that monitored the number of e-mails delivered to its users that originated from a single address. If the number was very large, the ISP assumed that the sender was 'spamming', and the system operator blocked the originator from sending additional messages to the ISP's subscribers. . . .

How government regulation will affect the promise of e-mail remains to be seen. Federal courts have barred specific companies from sending unsolicited e-mail advertisements to subscribers of CompuServe (Kanaley 1997). The courts are ruling that ISPs have the right to restrict access by 'spammers', mostly for economic reasons. Users who pay hourly access rates complain about spending too much time and money reading messages they have no interest in. How this will affect mailing in the future is not yet clear. Options being discussed include charging mailers a fee for each piece of mail sent. Some believe this will cause companies to be more selective in the addresses to which they send mail. Obviously, this would increase the costs of e-mail surveying. . . .

While e-mail surveying will probably never replace the broad-based data available via postal mail surveys, it will probably provide adequate data for the study of on-line populations, and given the propensity of 'hard to reach' individuals to respond, may provide richer data about on-line behavior than postal mail surveys. As on-line usage continues to grow, and as more and more consumers have access to e-mail, it is conceivable that this method may be eventually used in place of postal mail to gather information about broad-based consumer segments.

References

Coomber, R. (1997) 'Using the Internet for survey research.' *Sociological Research Online* 2 (2) [On-line]. Available: http://www.socresonline.org.uk/2/2/2.html

Couper, M.P., Blair, J. and Triplett, T. (1997) 'A comparison of mail and e-mail for a survey of employees in federal statistical agencies.' Paper presented at the annual conference of the American Association for Public Opinion Research, Norfolk, Va.

Kanaley, R. (1997, February 5) 'Judge bars bulk mailer from online.' *Philadelphia Inquirer*, p. C1.

Kehoe, C., and Pitkow, J. (1996) 'Surveying the territory: GVU's five WWW user surveys.' *The World Wide Web Journal*, 1, (3). [Also on-line]. Available: http://www.cc.gatech.edu/gvu/user surveys/papers/w3j.html

Kehoe, C., Pitkow, J., and Morton, K. (1997) *Eighth WWW user survey* [On-line]. Available: http://www.gvu.gatech.edu/user_surveys/survey-1997–10/

Kiesler, S., and Sproull, L. S. (1986) 'Response effects in the electronic survey.' *Public Opinion Quarterly*, 50: pp. 402–413.

McCullough, D. (1998) 'Web-based market research, the dawning of a new era.' *Direct Marketing* 61 (8), pp. 36–39.

Mehta, R. and Sivada, E. (1995) 'Comparing response rates and response content in mail versus electronic mail surveys.' *Journal of the Market Research Society* 17 (4), pp. 429–440.

Parker, L. (1992) 'Collecting data the e-mail way.' *Training and Development*, July: pp. 52–54.

Schillewaert, N., Langerak, F., and Duhamel, T. (1998) 'Non probability sampling for WWW surveys: a comparison of methods.' *Journal of the Market Research Society* 4, (40), pp. 307–313.

Schuldt, B.A., and Totten J.W. (1994) 'Electronic mail vs. mail survey response rates.' *Marketing Research*, Winter: pp. 1–7.

Smith, C. (1997) 'Casting the net: Surveying an Internet population.' *Journal of Computer Mediated Communication* 3 (1). Available: http://www.ascusc.org/jcmc/vol3/issue1/smith.html.

Steele, T.J., Schwendig, L.W., and Kilpatrick, J.A. (1992) 'Duplicate responses to multiple survey mailings: A problem?' *Journal of Advertising Research* 32 (1): pp. 26–33.

Chapter 13

Ned Flanders

INTERACTION ANALYSIS

From *Analyzing Teacher Behavior,* Addison-Wesley (1970).

CLASSROOM INTERACTION ANALYSIS REFERS not to one system, but to many systems for coding spontaneous verbal communication, arranging the data into a useful display, and then analyzing the results in order to study patterns of teaching and learning. Each system is essentially a process of encoding and decoding, i.e., categories for classifying statements are established, a code symbol is assigned to each category, and a trained observer records data by jotting down code symbols. Decoding is the reverse process: a trained analyst interprets the display of coded data in order to make appropriate statements about the original events which were encoded, even though he may not have been present when the data were collected. A particular system for interaction analysis will usually include (a) a set of categories, each defined clearly, (b) a procedure for observation and a set of ground rules which governs the coding process, (c) steps for tabulating the data in order to arrange a display which aids in describing the original events, and (d) suggestions which can be followed in some of the more common applications.

Most of the category systems which have been developed thus far have been restricted to verbal communication, but any kind of spontaneous behavior could presumably be encoded, provided a practical procedure was available.

Coding systems of all sorts are used constantly in our daily affairs. We use zip codes for addressing our letters, area codes to facilitate a telephone call, and we distinguish ourselves from other animals by our use of language, which is the most elaborate and flexible encoding-decoding system used by man. Language permits man to abstract phenomena and classify them within category systems, thus providing the foundation upon which modern science has been built.

Knowing language and how it is used provides a firm basis for understanding interaction analysis systems. Speakers and writers encode. Listeners and readers decode. The words used are code symbols which stand for ideas, and the purpose of language is to communicate these ideas accurately, excluding ideas which are not relevant. So it is with interaction analysis. The code symbol stands for a category which defines a particular type of statement. All statements judged to be of this type are assigned the same code symbol, regardless of certain differences which may be obvious, but are considered to be not relevant. The tabulated code symbols represent the statements which were made, and a display of these data can be interpreted to recreate some aspects of the original flow of communication within the relatively severe limitations of the category system.

Classroom interaction analysis systems seek to abstract communication by ignoring most of its characteristics. For example, a category such as 'teacher asks a question' is used to code many different statements, provided they are all questions. Once the same code symbol is used for all of these statements, the differences among them are ignored and lost forever. Yet this loss is offset by keeping an accurate record of the number of times that a teacher attempts to solicit verbal expression from the pupils, which is the characteristic common to all statements with this code symbol. This process is sensible only when keeping an accurate record of teacher questions is crucial to some investigation. This procedure makes no sense at all when what is lost by the process is more important than what is gained. . . .

Classroom interaction analysis can be used for in service and preservice education in order to help teachers improve classroom instruction. Usually such training requires some kind of objective feedback to the person who is trying to change his behavior. . . . Interaction analysis is also used for research on the teaching-learning process. The technique provides a method of quantifying concepts which refer to spontaneous behavior and which heretofore could be measured only indirectly. When measures of teaching behavior are associated with pupil attitudes and achievement, it is possible to start building primitive theories of instruction.

A ten-category system

The system you will study in this section was developed by Flanders and others[1] at the University of Minnesota between 1955 and 1960. The category system still has many useful applications, although efforts to increase the number of categories and modify the procedures have already been successfully completed.

Figure 13.1 lists ten categories: seven are used when the teacher is talking, two are used when any pupil is talking, and the last category is used to indicate silence or confusion. So far as communication is concerned, these three conditions, (a) teacher talk, (b) pupil talk, and (c) silence or confusion, are said to exhaust all the possi-

---

1   Individuals at Minnesota who influenced the early development include: Sulo Hayumaki, Thomas Filson, Edmund Amidon, Theodore Storlie, and J. Paul Anderson. Earlier work at the University of Chicago also influenced the shape of the ten categories. These individuals include: Herbert Thelen, John Withall, and John Glidewell. In fact, the work of John Withall provided the first experiences of the author in the field of interaction analysis.

Teacher talk	Response	1. *Accepts feeling.* Accepts and clarifies an attitude or the feeling tone of a pupil in a nonthreatening manner. Feelings may be positive or negative. Predicting and recalling feelings are included. 2. *Praises or encourages.* Praises or encourages pupil action or behavior. Jokes that release tension, but not at the expense of another individual; nodding head, or saying "Um hm?" or "go on" are included. 3. *Accepts or uses ideas of pupils.* Clarifying, building, or developing ideas suggested by a pupil. Teacher extensions of pupil ideas are included but as the teacher brings more of his own ideas into play, shift to category five.
	Initiation	4. *Asks questions.* Asking a question about content or procedure, based on teacher ideas, with the intent that a pupil will answer. 5. *Lecturing.* Giving facts or opinions about content or procedures; expressing *his own* ideas, giving *his own* explanation, or citing an authority other than a pupil. 6. *Giving directions.* Directions, commands, or orders to which a pupil is expected to comply. 7. *Criticizing or justifying authority.* Statements intended to change pupil behavior from nonacceptable to acceptable pattern; bawling someone out; stating why the teacher is doing what he is doing; extreme self-reference.
Pupil talk	Response	8. *Pupil-talk—response.* Talk by pupils in response to teacher. Teacher initiates the contact or solicits pupil statement or structures the situation. Freedom to express own ideas is limited.
	Initiation	9. *Pupil-talk—initiation.* Talk by pupils which they initiate. Expressing own ideas; initiating a new topic; freedom to develop opinions and a line of thought, like asking thoughtful questions; going beyond the existing structure.
Silence		10. *Silence or confusion.* Pauses, short periods of silence and periods of confusion in which communication cannot be understood by the observer.

Figure 13.1 Flanders' Interaction Analysis Categories (FIAC).

Note: There is *no* scale implied by these numbers. Each number is classificatory; it designates a particular kind of communicative event. To write these numbers down during observation is to enumerate, not to judge a position on a scale.

bilities. Category systems which exhaust all possibilities are *totally inclusive* of all possible events, and since any event can be classified, a totally inclusive system permits coding at a constant rate throughout the observation. This is essential whenever you wish to reach conclusions about the proportion of time spent in one or more categories. . . .

The major feature of this category system lies in the analysis of *initiative* and *response* which is a characteristic of interaction between two or more individuals. To initiate, in this context, means to make the first move, to lead, to begin, to introduce an idea or concept for the first time, to express one's own will. To respond means to take action after an initiation, to counter, to amplify or react to ideas which have already been expressed, to conform or even to comply to the will expressed by others. We expect the teacher, in most situations, to show more initiative than the pupils.

With this ten-category system, an estimate of the balance between initiative and response can be inferred from the percent time of teacher talk, pupil talk, and silence or confusion. These percents alone are not very good predictors of pupil learning and attitudes because the *quality* of the statements is associated with educational outcomes just as much, if not more, than the *quantity*. Since the teacher has more authority than any pupil, it is not surprising to discover that the teacher's communication, which is a sample of his total behavior, will be the most potent single factor in establishing a balance of initiation and response. It is for this reason that seven of the ten categories are devoted to discriminations among teacher statements.

A more accurate estimate of the initiative-response balance of classroom interaction can be reached by comparing the teacher tallies in Categories 1, 2, and 3 with those in 5, 6, and 7. The teacher is responding to pupil behavior in a supportive manner when he uses ideas expressed by pupils, praises or encourages their behavior, and makes constructive reactions to their attitudes or feelings. He is initiating his own will and making use of his authority whenever he expresses his own ideas, gives directions with the expectation of compliance, or becomes critical of pupil behavior.

We usually find, but not always, a complementary and logical relationship between the initiative-response balance of teacher statements and the same balance expressed by the pupils. An above average use of Categories 5, 6, and 7 is more likely to be associated with a higher incidence of Category 8. The above average use of 1, 2, and 3 is more likely to be associated with Category 9. . . . A relatively small shift in the tallies located in 1, 2, and 3 versus 5, 6, and 7 – say 10 percent – appears to have a consistent and logical effect on the behavior and perceptions of the pupils. . . . This balance can be used to predict how much subject matter pupils learn and their general attitudes – toward the teacher and the class activities – at levels which are higher than would be expected by chance. Such evidence indicates that the teacher's verbal communication pattern is associated with pupil learning and pupil attitudes toward learning.

As you might expect, the balance of initiation and response for the teacher, as well as the pupils, will vary from one learning activity to the next, even with the same class. It will also vary according to the teacher's preferred style of instruction, the subject matter being taught, the age and maturity of the pupils, and various other characteristics of the classroom learning situation. Tracing this variation provides us with knowledge about teaching behavior and about relationships between what a teacher does and how pupils react.

By way of summary, then, every category system has a purpose, and this category system can be used to study the balance between initiation and response. With seven categories of teacher talk, and only two for pupil talk, more information is provided about the teacher, and therefore how teacher statements influence this balance can be studied with this particular set of categories. A different category system would be needed in order to investigate other problems of teaching and learning, for example, how different pupil reactions affect class learning. . . .

The procedure of observation

An observer sits in the classroom in the best position to hear and see the participants. Almost as often as possible, he decides which category best represents the
communication events just completed. He then writes down this category number
while he simultaneously assesses the continuing communication. Observation continues at a rate of 20 to 25 tallies per minute, *keeping the tempo as steady as possible.*
This usually works out to about one tally every 3 seconds. There is nothing magical
about a 3-second period. An experienced observer, after considerable practice,
tends to classify at this rate with this particular category system. A gifted observer
might settle down to a faster rate, after considerable experience, and another category system might force a slower rate, even for a gifted observer. Having a regular
tempo is much more important than achieving a particular rate because most conclusions depend on rate consistency, not on speed. For example, a comparison
between two categories in one observation or the same category in two different
observations is possible only when the tempo of coding is the same for both categories and for both observations, whether or not that tempo is one tally every 2, 2½, 3,
or 3½ seconds. There is a tendency to increase the rate of coding during rapid
interchanges, especially if rare events are occurring. Apparently, experienced observers hate to miss rare events, like Categories 1, 2, 7, and 9. On the other hand,
during a long period of lecture, the observer may relax and inadvertently slow his
tempo compared to periods of more rapid exchanges. No observer is a perfect
metronome, but with experience two observers can train themselves to code at
quite similar and regular rates. . . .

Recording procedures for live classroom observation, video or sound recordings, will require various printed forms, depending on what is to be done with the
data. During practice observations designed to check your reliability with another
observer, a histogram, on its side, such as the form shown in Figure 13.2 may be

Category number		Completed tally marks made by an observer	Total tallies	Percent
Teacher	1	॥।	3	0.8
	2	ℍℋ ।	6	2.5
	3	ℍℋ ℍℋ ॥	12	5.0
	4	ℍℋ ℍℋ ℍℋ ℍℋ ॥	22	9.2
	5	ℍℋ ℍℋ	130	54.2
	6	ℍℋ ℍℋ ℍℋ ।	16	6.7
	7	॥॥।	4	1.6
Pupils	8	ℍℋ ℍℋ ℍℋ ℍℋ ॥	22	9.2
	9	ℍℋ ℍℋ ॥	12	5.0
Silence	10	ℍℋ ℍℋ ॥॥॥	14	5.8
		Total	240	100.0

Figure 13.2 Tallying hash marks by categories.

most convenient. In other applications, an ordinary sheet of paper may be used. If you draw ½-inch columns on yellow legal pads, there is often enough room for about 400 coded symbols to be written down in their original sequence, top to bottom, left to right. A zero is used for Category 10. It is also possible to use IBM mark-sense cards in the classroom by marking with a soft pencil. These can be punched automatically in later processing. Forms which preserve the original sequence permit the tabulation of a matrix display. A form that can be used in microteaching, which usually consists of short 4- to 6-minute teaching segments, might be best recorded on a time line display. In automatic recording, which makes use of electronic equipment or the remote terminal of a shared-time computer, the observer uses a pushbutton device, similar to the base of a pushbutton telephone. This is by far the most convenient. In short, there are many different ways to record code symbols. Choose the best procedure for the task at hand. . . .

Chapter 14

Robert Philip Weber

CONTENT ANALYSIS

From *Basic Content Analysis* (2nd edition), Thousand Oaks, Cal.: Sage (1990)

CONTENT ANALYSIS IS a research method that uses a set of procedures to make valid inferences from text. . . . Compared with other data-generating and analysis techniques, content analysis has several advantages:

- Communication is a central aspect of social interaction. Content-analytic procedures operate directly on text or transcripts of human communications.
- The best content-analytic studies use both qualitative and quantitative operations on texts. Thus content analysis methods combine what are usually thought to be antithetical modes of analysis.
- Documents of various kinds exist over long periods of time. Culture indicators generated from such series of documents constitute reliable data that may span even centuries. . . .
- In more recent times, when reliable data of other kinds exist, culture indicators can be used to assess quantitatively the relationships among economic, social, political, and cultural change.
- Compared with techniques such as interviews, content analysis usually yields unobtrusive measures in which neither the sender nor the receiver of the message is aware that it is being analyzed. Hence, there is little danger that the act of measurement itself will act as a force for change that confounds the data.
  . . .

Two very different studies show some ways content analysis has been used. . . .

Walker (1975) analyzed differences and similarities in American black and white popular song lyrics, 1962–1973. Using computer-aided content analysis, Walker investigated differences in narrative form. He found that compared with popular white song lyrics, 'rhythm and blues' and 'soul' song lyrics showed greater emphasis on action in the objective world, less concern with time, and greater emphasis on what Walker calls 'toughmindedness' or 'existential concreteness.' . . .

In another study, Aries (1973) . . . studied differences in female, male, and mixed-sex small groups. She found that differential sex-role socialization and sex-role stereotyping affect thematic content and social interaction. In female groups, women show much concern with interpersonal issues. Women discuss 'themselves, their homes and families, and their relationships, defining themselves by the way they relate to the significant others who surround them' (Aries 1973: 254).

In male groups, members do not address interpersonal matters directly. Instead, men indirectly relate personal experiences and feelings through stories and metaphors. Men 'achieve a closeness through the sharing of laughter and stories of activities, rather than the sharing of the understanding of those experiences' (Aries 1973: 254). Also, all-male groups manifest more themes involving aggression than do all-female groups.

In mixed groups, Aries found that women talked less of their homes and families. Women also spoke less of achievement and institutions. In short, women in these groups 'orient themselves around being women with men by assuming the traditional female role' (Aries 1973: 256). Men in mixed groups expressed their competitiveness less through storytelling than through assuming leadership roles in the group. Moreover, in the presence of women, men shift more toward reflection of themselves and their feelings. . . .

A central idea in content analysis is that the many words of the text are classified into much fewer content categories. Each category may consist of one, several, or many words. Words, phrases, or other units of text classified in the same category are presumed to have similar meanings. Depending on the purposes of the investigator, this similarity may be based on the precise meaning of the words (such as grouping synonyms together), or may be based on words sharing similar connotations (such as grouping together several words implying a concern with a concept such as WEALTH or POWER). To make valid inferences from the text, it is important that the classification procedure be reliable in the sense of being consistent: Different people should code the same text in the same way. Also, the classification procedure must generate variables that are valid. A variable is valid to the extent that it measures or represents what the investigator intends it to measure. . . .

Content classification and interpretation

. . . In content analysis, reliability problems usually grow out of the ambiguity of word meanings, category definitions, or other coding rules. Classification by multiple human coders permits the quantitative assessment of achieved reliability. Classification by computer, however, leads to perfect coder reliability. . . . Once correctly defined for the computer, the coding rules are always applied in the same way.

A much more difficult set of problems concerns the validity of variables based on content classification. A content analysis variable is valid to the extent that it measures the construct the investigator intends it to measure. As happens with reliability, validity problems also grow out of the ambiguity of word meanings and category or variable definitions.

As an introduction to these problems, consider two sample texts and some simple coding rules. Using commonsense definitions, imagine that the coding instructions define five categories: CITIZENS' RIGHTS, ECONOMIC, GOVERNMENT, POLITICAL DOCTRINE, and WELFARE. Imagine also that coders are instructed to classify each entire paragraph in one category only. Consider first a portion of the Carter 1980 Democratic Platform:

> Our current economic situation is unique. In 1977, we inherited a severe recession from the Republicans. The Democratic Administration and the Democratic Congress acted quickly to reduce the unacceptably high levels of unemployment and to stimulate the economy. And we succeeded. We recovered from that deep recession and our economy was strengthened and revitalized. As that fight was won, the enormous increases in foreign oil prices – 120 percent last year – and declining productivity fueled an inflationary spiral that also had to be fought. The Democrats did that, and inflation has begun to recede. In working to combat these dual problems, significant economic actions have been taken.
>
> (Johnson 1982: 38)

Now consider another paragraph from the Reagan 1980 Republican platform:

> Through long association with government programs, the word 'welfare' has come to be perceived almost exclusively as tax-supported aid to the needy. But in its most inclusive sense – and as Americans understood it from the beginning of the Republic – such aid also encompasses those charitable works performed by private citizens, families, and social, ethnic, and religious organizations. Policies of the federal government leading to high taxes, rising inflation, and bureaucratic empire-building have made it difficult and often impossible for such individuals and groups to exercise their charitable instincts. We believe that government policies that fight inflation, reduce tax rates, and end bureaucratic excesses can help make private effort by the American people once again a major force in those works of charity which are the true signs of a progressive and humane society.
>
> (Johnson 1982: 179)

Most people would code the first excerpt in the *economic* category, but the proper coding of the second is less obvious. This paragraph could be taken to be mainly about the rights of citizens, the desirability of restricting the government's *role*, the welfare state, or to be the espousal of a political doctrine. In fact, it occurs at the end of a section titled *Improving the Welfare System*.

The difficulty of classifying the second excerpt is contrived partly by the present author, because it results from the lack of clear and detailed coding rules for each category and from the variety of the subject matter. Large portions of text, such as paragraphs and complete texts, usually are more difficult to code as a unit than smaller portions, such as words and phrases, because large units typically contain more information and a greater diversity of topics. Hence they are more likely to present coders with conflicting cues.

These examples show the kind of difficulties investigators face with coding text. The next two sections look more systematically at coding problems, first from the perspective of reliability assessment and then from the perspective of validity assessment.

Reliability

Three types of reliability are pertinent to content analysis: stability, reproducibility, and accuracy (Krippendorff 1980: 130–154). *Stability* refers to the extent to which the results of content classification are invariant over time. Stability can be determined when the same content is coded more than once by the *same* coder. Inconsistencies in coding constitute unreliability. These inconsistencies may stem from a variety of factors, including ambiguities in the coding rules, ambiguities in the text, cognitive changes within the coder, or simple errors, such as recording the wrong numeric code for a category. Because only one person is coding, stability is the weakest form of reliability.

Reproducibility, sometimes called *intercoder reliability*, refers to the extent to which content classification produces the same results when the same text is coded by *more than one* coder. Conflicting codings usually result from cognitive differences among the coders, ambiguous coding instructions, or from random recording errors. High reproducibility is a minimum standard for content analysis. This is because stability measures the consistency of the individual coder's private understandings, whereas reproducibility measures the consistency of shared understandings (or meaning) held by two or more coders.

Accuracy refers to the extent to which the classification of text corresponds to a standard or norm. It is the strongest form of reliability. As Krippendorff notes (1980: 131), it has sometimes been used to test the performance of human coders where a standard coding for some text has already been established. Except for training purposes, standard codings are established infrequently for texts. Consequently, researchers seldom use accuracy in reliability assessment.

Krippendorff (1980: 132) also points out that many investigators fail totally to assess the reliability of their coding. Even when reliability is assessed, some investigators engage in practices that often make data seem more reliable than they actually are. In particular, where coders have disagreed, investigators have resolved these disagreements by negotiations or by invoking the authority of the principal investigator or senior graduate assistant. Resolving these disagreements may produce judgments biased toward the opinions of the most verbal or more senior of the coders. Consequently, the reliability of the coding should be calculated *before* these disagreements are resolved. . . .

Validity

. . . Perhaps the weakest form of validity is *face* validity, which consists of the correspondence between investigators' definitions of concepts and their definitions of the categories that measured them. A category has face validity to the extent that it appears to measure the construct it is intended to measure. Even if several expert judges agree, face validity is still a weak claim because it rests on a single variable. Stronger forms of validity involve more than one variable. Unfortunately, content analysts often have relied heavily on face validity; consequently, some other social scientists have viewed their results skeptically.

Much stronger validity is obtained by comparing content-analytic data with some external criterion. Four types of external validity are pertinent. [For example,] a measure has *predictive validity* to the extent that forecasts about events or conditions external to the study are shown to correspond to actual events or conditions. These predictions may concern future, past (postdiction), or concurrent events. Predictive validity is powerful because the inferences from data are generalized successfully beyond the study to situations not under the direct control of the investigator. . . .

Semantic validity exists when persons familiar with the language and texts examine lists of words (or other units) placed in the same category and agree that these words have similar meanings or connotations. Although this seems an obvious requirement for valid content analysis, many difficulties arise because words and category definitions are sometimes ambiguous. For example, some systems for computer-aided content analysis cannot distinguish among the various senses of words with more than one meaning, such as *mine*. Does this refer to a hole in the ground, the process of extraction, or a possessive pronoun? Because of this failure, word counts including the frequency of *mine* lack semantic validity. . . .

Creating and testing a coding scheme

Many studies require investigators to design and implement coding schemes. Whether the coding is to be done by humans or by computer, the process of creating and applying a coding scheme consists of several basic steps. If investigators have identified the substantive questions to be investigated, relevant theories, previous research, and the texts to be classified, they next proceed with the following necessary steps:

1. *Define the recording units.* One of the most fundamental and important decisions concerns the definition of the basic unit of text to be classified. There are six commonly used options:

- *Word* – One choice is to code each word. As noted, some computer software for text analysis cannot distinguish among the various senses of words with more than one meaning, and hence may produce erroneous conclusions.
- *Word sense* – Other computer programs are able to code the different senses of words with multiple meanings and to code phrases that constitute a semantic unit, such as idioms (e.g., *taken for granted*) or proper nouns (e.g., *the Empire State Building*).

- *Sentence* – An entire sentence is often the recording unit when the investigator is interested in words or phrases that occur closely together. For example, coders may be instructed to count sentences in which either positive, negative, or affectively neutral references are made to the Soviet Union. A sentence with the phrase *evil empire* would be counted as NEGATIVE EVALUATION, whereas *Talks with the Soviet Union continue* would be coded NEUTRAL EVALUATION, and *The President supports recent efforts to extend economic and political rights in the Soviet Union* would be coded POSITIVE EVALUATION.
- *Theme* – Holsti (1963: 136, emphasis in the original) defines a theme as a unit of text 'having *no more than one each of the following elements:* (1) the *perceiver*, (2) the *perceived* or agent of action, (3) the *action*, (4) the *target* of the action.' For example, the sentence *The President/hates/Communists* would be divided as shown. Numeric or other codes often are inserted in the text to represent subject/verb/object. This form of coding preserves important information and provides a means of distinguishing between the sentence above and the assertion that *Communists hate the President*.

Sometimes long, complex sentences must be broken down into shorter thematic units or segments. Here, parts of speech shared between themes must be repeated. Also, ambiguous phrases and pronouns must be identified manually. These steps are taken before coding for the content. Holsti (1963: 136–137) gives the following example of editing more complex sentences before coding for themes and content.

> The sentence, 'The American imperialists have perverted the peace and are preparing to attack the Socialist Camp,' must be edited to read: The American imperialists have perverted the peace + (the Americans) are preparing to attack the Socialist Camp.'

This form of coding is labor-intensive, but leads to much more detailed and sophisticated comparisons. . . .

- *Paragraph* – When computer assistance is not feasible and when resources for human coding are limited, investigators sometimes code entire paragraphs to reduce the effort required. Evidence discussed later in this chapter shows that it is more difficult to achieve high reliability when coding large units, such as paragraphs, than when coding smaller units, such as words.
- *Whole text* – Unless the entire text is short – like newspaper headlines, editorials, or stories – it is difficult to achieve high reliability when coding complete texts.

2. *Define the categories.* In creating category definitions, investigators must make two basic decisions. The first is whether the categories are to be mutually exclusive. Most statistical procedures require variables that are not confounded. If a recording unit can be classified simultaneously in two or more categories and if both categories (variables) are included in the same statistical analysis, then it is possible that,

because the basic statistical assumptions of the analysis are violated, the results are dubious. This is likely to be the case when using common multivariate procedures such as factor analysis, analysis of variance, and multiple regression.

The second choice concerns how narrow or broad the categories are to be. Some categories are limited because of language. For example, a category indicating self-references defined as first person singular pronouns will have only a few words or entries. A category defined as concern with ECONOMIC matters may have many entries. For some purposes, however, it may make sense to use much more narrow or specific categories, such as INFLATION, TAXES, BUDGET, TRADE, AGRI-CULTURE, and so on.

3. *Test coding on sample of text.* The best test of the clarity of category definitions is to code a small sample of the text. Testing not only reveals ambiguities in the rules, but also often leads to insights suggesting revisions of the classification scheme.

4. *Assess accuracy or reliability.* Accuracy in this sense means the text is coded correctly by the computer, not in the sense of the type of reliability that was discussed earlier. If human coders are used, the reliability of the coding process should be estimated *before* resolving disputes among the coders.

5. *Revise the coding rules.* If the reliability is low, or if errors in computer procedures are discovered, the coding rules must be revised or the software corrected.

6. *Return to Step 3.* This cycle will continue until the coders achieve sufficient reliability or until the computer procedures work correctly.

7. *Code all the text.* When high coder reliability has been achieved or when the computer programs are functioning correctly, the coding rules can then be applied to all the text.

8. *Assess achieved reliability or accuracy.* The reliability of human coders should be assessed after the text is classified. Never assume that if samples of text were coded reliably then the entire corpus of text will also be coded reliably. Human coders are subject to fatigue and are likely to make more mistakes as the coding proceeds. Also, as the text is coded, their understanding of the coding rules may change in subtle ways that lead to greater unreliability.

If the coding was done by computer, the output should be checked carefully to insure that the coding rules were applied correctly. Text not in the sample(s) used for testing may present novel combinations of words that were not anticipated or encountered earlier, and these may be misclassified. . . .

References

Aries, E. (1973) 'Interaction patterns and themes of male, female, and mixed groups'. Unpublished PhD dissertation, Harvard University.

Holsti, O.R. (1963) 'Computer content analysis,' in R.C. North, O.R. Holsti, M.G. Zaninovich, and D.A. Zinnes, *Content Analysis: A Handbook with Applications for the Study of International Crises.* Evanston: Northwestern University Press.

Johnson, D.B. (1982) 'National party platforms of 1980.' Urbana: University of Illinois Press.

Krippendorff, K. (1980) 'Content analysis: an introduction to its methodology.' Beverly Hills, Cal.: Sage.

Walker, A.W. (1975) 'The empirical delineation of two musical taste cultures: a content analysis of best-selling soul and popular recordings from 1962–1973.' Unpublished PhD dissertation, New School for Social Research.

Chapter 15

Ian Hacking

THE TAMING OF CHANCE

From *The Taming of Chance*, Cambridge: Cambridge University Press (1990).

THE MOST DECISIVE CONCEPTUAL event of twentieth century physics has been the discovery that the world is not deterministic. Causality, long the bastion of metaphysics, was toppled, or at least tilted: the past does not determine exactly what happens next. This event was preceded by a more gradual transformation. During the nineteenth century it became possible to see that the world might be regular and yet not subject to universal laws of nature. A space was cleared for chance.

This erosion of determinism made little immediate difference to anyone. Few were aware of it. Something else was pervasive and everybody came to know about it: the enumeration of people and their habits. Society became statistical. A new type of law came into being, analogous to the laws of nature, but pertaining to people. These new laws were expressed in terms of probability. They carried with them the connotations of normalcy and of deviations from the norm. The cardinal concept of the psychology of the Enlightenment had been, simply, human nature. By the end of the nineteenth century, it was being replaced by something different: normal people. . . .

The transformations that I shall describe are closely connected with an event so all-embracing that we seldom pause to notice it: an avalanche of printed numbers. The nation-states classified, counted and tabulated their subjects anew. Enumerations in some form have been with us always, if only for the two chief purposes of government, namely taxation and military recruitment. Before the Napoleonic era most official counting had been kept privy to administrators. After it, a vast amount was printed and published.

The enthusiasm for numerical data is reflected by the United States census. The first American census asked four questions of each household. The tenth decennial census posed 13,010 questions on various schedules addressed to people, firms, farms, hospitals, churches and so forth. This 3,000-fold increase is striking, but vastly understates the rate of growth of printed numbers: 300,000 would be a better estimate.

The printing of numbers was a surface effect. Behind it lay new technologies for classifying and enumerating, and new bureaucracies with the authority and continuity to deploy the technology. There is a sense in which many of the facts presented by the bureaucracies did not even exist ahead of time. Categories had to be invented into which people could conveniently fall in order to be counted. The systematic collection of data about people has affected not only the ways in which we conceive of a society, but also the ways in which we describe our neighbour. It has profoundly transformed what we choose to do, who we try to be, and what we think of ourselves. Marx read the minutiae of official statistics, the reports from the factory inspectorate and the like. One can ask: who had more effect on class consciousness, Marx or the authors of the official reports which created the classifications into which people came to recognize themselves? These are examples of questions about what I call 'making up people'. . . .

What has the avalanche of printed numbers to do with my chief topic, the erosion of determinism? One answer is immediate. Determinism was subverted by laws of chance. To believe there were such laws one needed law-like statistical regularities in large populations. How else could a civilization hooked on universal causality get the idea of some alternative kind of law of nature or social behaviour? . . . Statistical laws that look like brute, irreducible facts were first found in human affairs, but they could be noticed only after social phenomena had been enumerated, tabulated and made public. That role was well served by the avalanche of printed numbers at the start of the nineteenth century.

On closer inspection we find that not any numbers served the purpose. Most of the law-like regularities were first perceived in connection with deviancy: suicide, crime, vagrancy, madness, prostitution, disease. This fact is instructive. It is not common to speak of information and control as a neutral term embracing decision theory, operations research, risk analysis and the broader but less well specified domains of statistical inference. We shall find that the roots of the idea lie in the notion that one can improve – control – a deviant subpopulation by enumeration and classification.

We also find that routinely gathering numerical data was not enough to make statistical laws rise to the surface. The laws had in the beginning to be read into the data. They were not simply read off them. Throughout this book I make a contrast of a rough and ready sort between Prussian (and other east European) attitudes to numerical data, and those that flourished in Britain, France, and other nations of western Europe. Statistical laws were found in social data in the West, where libertarian, individualistic and atomistic conceptions of the person and the state were rampant. This did not happen in the East, where collectivist and holistic attitudes were more prevalent. Thus the transformations that I describe are to be understood only within a larger context of what an individual is, and of what a society is. . . .

Probability and statistics crowd in upon us. The statistics of our pleasures and our vices are relentlessly tabulated. Sports, sex, drink, drugs, travel, sleep, friends – nothing escapes. There are more explicit statements of probabilities presented on American prime time television than explicit acts of violence (I'm counting the ads). Our public fears are endlessly debated in terms of probabilities: chances of melt-downs, cancers, muggings, earth-quakes, nuclear winters, AIDS, global green-houses, what next? There is nothing to fear (it may seem) but the probabilities themselves. This obsession with the chances of danger, and with treatments for changing the odds, descends directly from the forgotten annals of nineteenth century information and control.

This imperialism of probabilities could occur only as the world itself became numerical. We have gained a fundamentally quantitative feel for nature, how it is and how it ought to be. This has happened in part for banal reasons. We have trained people to use numerals. The ability to process even quite small numbers was, until recently, the prerogative of a few. Today we hold numeracy to be at least as import-ant as literacy. . . .

Measurement and positivism are close kin. Auguste Comte coined the word 'positivism' as the name of his philosophy, holding that in all the European languages the word 'positive' had good connotations. His own philosophy did not fare espe-cially well, but the word caught on. Positive science meant numerical science. Nothing better typified a positive science than a statistical one – an irony, for Comte himself despised merely statistical inquiries.

The avalanche of numbers, the erosion of determinism, and the invention of normalcy are embedded in the grander topics of the Industrial Revolution. The acquisition of numbers by the populace, and the professional lust for precision in measurement, were driven by familiar themes of manufacture, mining, trade, health, railways, war, empire. Similarly the idea of a norm became codified in these domains. Just as the railways demanded timekeeping and the mass-produced pocket watch, they also mandated standards, not only of obvious things such as the gauge of the lines but also of the height of the buffers of successive cars in a train. It is a mere decision, in this book, to focus on the more narrow aspects that I have mentioned, a decision that is wilful but not arbitrary. My project is philosophical: to grasp the conditions that made possible our present organization of concepts in two domains. One is that of physical indeterminism; the other is that of statistical information developed for purposes of social control.

This study can be used to illustrate a number of more general philosophical themes. I have mentioned one above: the idea of making up people. I claim that enumeration requires categorization, and that defining new classes of people for the purposes of statistics has consequences for the ways in which we conceive of others and think of our own possibilities and potentialities. . . .

PART FOUR

Analysing quantitative data

INTRODUCTION

CARRYING OUT A LARGE social survey is beyond the resources of most students, and for many researchers it may be unnecessary too. This is because data from many different social surveys on a great variety of topics are already stored in data archives, available in increasingly easy and accessible formats for 'secondary' analysis. These are frequently high-quality surveys, using careful question design and sampling, with high response rates. The first two readings in this section (Kiecolt and Nathan (reading 16) and Dale *et al.* (reading 17)) describe pertinent considerations when assessing and using such data sources, clarifying their advantages and disadvantages.

If, though, you collect information in your own survey, you will need to prepare it for analysis. The reading by Oppenheim (reading 18) explains how to code answers to both fixed-choice and open-ended questions so that these can be entered into a computer for analysis. The second half outlines a plan for the analysis of newly entered survey data, moving from frequency counts of single variables to tabulations of two or more variables.

Lazarsfeld (reading 19) and Rosenberg (reading 20) continue with this form of analysis, using tables to explore causal propositions and test out alternative explanations for associations between variables in tables. The logic of elaborating two-variable relationships by entering third variables as 'test factors' is one that is general to a number of forms of multivariate statistical analysis. In a worked example taken from media audience research, Lazarsfeld conveys the essence of this logic. Rosenberg uses several examples to illustrate the elaboration of survey data, pointing out that a *variety of outcomes can emerge* once a third variable is introduced to elaborate a bivariate relationship. The data analyst is characterized as being in 'hot pursuit of an idea', in an interplay of theory and data. This has its exploratory aspect, but is also an enactment of the Popperian falsificationist approach described by Cook and Campbell (readings 5 and 6).

DISCUSSION POINTS

- Visit a data archive on the web. For example, the UK data archive is at http://www.data-archive.ac.uk Imagine you want to find out more about the influence of social class, gender and ethnicity on health, illness and use of health care. Which data sets in the archive would you use? In the light of the issues raised in readings 16 and 17, what are the advantages and disadvantages of collecting original data yourself as opposed to using an archived data set?
- With a partner, ask the same, open-ended question of ten people and write down their answers as fully as possible (for example 'How is your health?' or 'What is your view of the current president/prime minister?'). Without consulting each other, each devise a coding scheme to quantify these answers, using the advice given in reading 18. Compare coding schemes. Construct a new coding scheme together.
- For this exercise you will need to be familiar with a statistical software programme (such as SPSS) and have access to a statistical data set such as the UK General Household Survey. You should produce frequency counts of variables that interest you and recode them by collapsing categories where appropriate. Cross-tabulate two variables where one might be considered cause and the other effect. Carry on doing this with pairs of variables until you find a tabulation that shows a strong relationship between the variables (e.g., gender and participation in paid work; age and the experience of long-standing illness). What third variable might modify this relationship (e.g. whether a couple has young children; gender)? If this variable is also contained in the data set, break the original table down by different values of this third 'test' variable. What do you conclude? What would you need to do next to test this conclusion?

FURTHER READING

Babbie, E. (1995) *Adventures in Social Research: Data Analysis Using SPSS for Windows,* Thousand Oaks, Cal.: Pine Forge Press.

Bryman, A. and Cramer, D. (2001) *Quantitative Data Analysis with SPSS Release 10 for Windows,* London: Routledge.

Campbell, D.T. and Fiske, D.W. (1959) 'Convergent and discriminant validation by the multitrait-multimethod matrix', *Psychological Bulletin* 56 (2): 81–105.

de Vaus, D.A. (2002) *Surveys in Social Research,* 5th edition, London: Routledge.

Field, A. (2000) *Discovering Statistics Using SPSS for Windows,* London: Sage.

Hellevik, O. (1989) *Introduction to Causal Analysis: Exploring Survey Data by Cross-Tabulation,* Oxford: Oxford University Press.

Hirschi, T. and Selvin, H.C. (1967) *Delinquency Research: An Appraisal of Analytic Methods*, New York: Free Press/Collier-Macmillan.

Hyman, H. (1955) *Survey Design and Analysis*, New York: Free Press.

Hyman, H.H. (1972) *Secondary Analysis of Sample Surveys: Principles, Procedures and Potentialities*, New York: John Wiley.

Levitas, R. and Guy, W. (1996) *Interpreting Official Statistics*, London: Routledge.

Sapsford, R. (1999) *Survey Research*, London: Sage.

Chapter 16

K. Jill Kiecolt and Laura E. Nathan

SECONDARY ANALYSIS OF SURVEY DATA

From *Secondary Analysis of Survey Data,* Thousand Oaks: Sage (1985).

. . .

THE PRIMARY ADVANTAGE OF secondary survey analysis is its potential for resource savings. Secondary research requires less money, less time, and fewer personnel and is therefore attractive in times of economic fluctuations, when the funds available for research are limited or uncertain. With data already collected, the costs are only those of obtaining the data, preparing them for analysis (such as ensuring that all data are computer-ready and compatible with the system), and conducting the analysis. Compared with the time normally required to collect data in social research, the time necessary for acquiring an appropriate data set is miniscule. Further, a researcher can complete a research project independently, thereby eliminating the need for ancillary research staff. Secondary analysis also obviates the need for researchers to affiliate with a large organization in order to command the backing necessary for acquiring adequate survey data.

Another advantage is that secondary analysis circumvents data collection problems. Data archives furnish a large quantity of machine-readable survey data spanning many topics, time periods, and countries. Many available data sets provide the benefits of nationally representative samples, standard items, and standard indices. Both data availability and improvements in technology facilitate research. Growing numbers of researchers have access to computer facilities and computer software packages. . . .

A variety of research projects can be accomplished with precollected data. When used in exploratory research prior to fielding a new survey, secondary analysis can uncover aspects of a research problem that require elaboration, groups that need to be oversampled, grounds for hypothesis revision, and the need to refine and improve existing measures . . . Secondary analysis may be employed for a variety of research designs, including trend, cohort, time-series, and comparative studies. Existing data can also be combined with other types of data to investigate a problem more thoroughly. For example, they can be combined with primary data to render an analysis dynamic, or they can be used to supplement in-depth interviews. Demographic and historical studies and research conducted under time constraints, such as policy-related projects, often require the use of existing data.

Our increased familiarity with and use of preexisting data encourage social scientific progress. Data sets such as the General Social Survey and the American National Election Study are widely used, and investigators who employ these data sets can turn to other researchers with questions on data handling. The widespread use of particular data sets also allows authors greater ease of reporting. On the basis of earlier articles which have used or discussed a particular data set, most readers will be familiar with relevant aspects of the survey such as the sampling procedure and question wording. . . .

The better acquainted researchers become with existing databases, the greater the potential for creative new research. Ideas for studies often emerge from interaction between a researcher's substantive interests and his or her intimate knowledge of information contained in data files.

Although the advantages of secondary analysis clearly outweigh the disadvantages, there are limitations. Many of the problems that secondary analysts encounter are intrinsic to the survey method, but some are unique to secondary analysis. A major problem is data availability. Despite the development of data archives, researchers sometimes have trouble locating what they need. Some topics lend themselves more readily to secondary analysis than others; for example, researchers interested in drug abuse, crime, and physical health are likely to have an easy time finding data. In more specialized areas, such as mental health epidemiology, however, there are relatively few publicly available databases, and investigators must depend on the generosity of individuals who own private data files. Often primary researchers are reluctant to share their data, as reputations are made by publishing work from a controlled body of data. A different sort of data availability problem stems from a major mismatch of primary and secondary research objectives. Sometimes when information on specific items or individuals is desired, data are available only in scaled or aggregated form. . . .

Errors made in original surveys often are no longer visible, and it is impossible to differentiate interviewing, coding, and keypunching errors. Moreover, the survey procedures that were followed may not have been sufficiently documented to enable secondary analysts to appraise errors in data. Trivial sources of error, such as that from sampling design, may be magnified when a survey is put to other than its original use, and such errors may be compounded by combining surveys. For example, a study using a national sample that excludes the institutionalized population could draw misleading conclusions about very young or very old adults because of the relatively high proportions of these groups who reside in various institutions. The problem would be compounded by using such samples for a trend study of old or young adults to the extent that the proportions of these groups in institutions have changed over time. . . .

Data quality is another reason that some researchers are leery of secondary research. Data files from surveys employing nationally representative samples, properly designed questionnaires, and rigorous procedures for interviewing and coding do not always exist. Even surveys of high quality may have measurement problems. Invalidity is of concern to the extent that survey items are imprecise measures of the concepts a secondary analyst has in mind, or that the variables have been poorly operationalized. Surveys rarely contain all the variables of interest to the secondary researcher, and even when they do there may be too few indicators of a concept for reliable measurement. Thus researchers sometimes need to use a number of surveys to assemble arguments that cannot be developed with the data from one survey alone. Using multiple surveys compounds potential error, however, and issues of comparability arise when measures of a concept are not strictly equivalent. In sum, secondary analysts must frequently make do with measures that are not precisely those desired. Often this results in criticism from peers for lacking hypothetically perfect indicators, or for proceeding atheoretically with research.

Another disadvantage of secondary analysis is the possible inhibition of creativity. If researchers use the same data sets repeatedly and are limited by the variables contained therein, scientific progress will be thwarted to some extent. More globally, continued use of the same indices and data sets may limit the scope of social science research. However, we believe that the inclusion of the same measures is necessary to ensure comparability. As long as new items are continually incorporated into surveys, advances will be made in the social sciences.

The increased availability of good survey data for secondary analysis is something of a mixed blessing to the degree that it has contributed to so-called 'trendy' social research. That is, some researchers obtain a data set, apply a currently popular statistical technique, and then look for a problem to investigate. Without theory, however, the utility of social research is called into question. The proliferation of survey data for secondary analysis offers tremendous opportunity, but the 'data set in search of analysis' approach yields only trivial findings.

Chapter 17

Angela Dale, Sara Arber and Michael Procter

A SOCIOLOGICAL PERSPECTIVE ON SECONDARY ANALYSIS

From *Doing Secondary Analysis,* London: Unwin Hyman (1988)

. . .

BY COMPARISON WITH THE primary analyst – the researcher who conducted the survey – the secondary analyst sidesteps all the time-consuming and difficult problems of obtaining funding for the survey, working out an interview schedule, carrying out a pilot study, briefing interviewers, sorting out coding problems, devising categories for the open-ended questions, coding the data and getting it into a form that can be read by computer. While these may be seen by some as mundane run-of-the-mill procedures to which those who carry out surveys have routinely to attend, they serve a *crucial* role in the research process. They not only form the interface between the respondent and the researcher, but also ensure that the researcher has though through the issues, clarified the concepts to be used and, through the process of the fieldwork, become familiar with the respondent's understanding of the issues and interpretation of the interview questions.

Preliminary consideration

Having neatly sidestepped all these tasks, the secondary analyst must, in order to use the available data sensitively and with validity, confront a different, but equally important set of issues. Stewart (1984) suggests six different kinds of question that those embarking upon secondary analysis should ask themselves. These questions form the basis of those listed below:

1. First, what was the purpose of the study? Was it an academic study designed

to explore background issues? Was it a very quick poll aimed at capturing attitudes at one point in time? What was the conceptual framework that informed the study? The study may have been a fact-gathering exercise that was concerned with drawing together as much information on one particular topic as possible. Alternatively, the researcher may have been trying to establish an explanatory framework and has sought information on a range of topics believed to be significant. Therefore, the purpose of the study – whether descriptive or explanatory – as well as the topic, becomes of relevance to the secondary analyst.

Where a study has used a particular theoretical perspective to explore an issue, the questions asked will relate not just to the subject of investigation, but also to other areas that may be expected to have explanatory value. For example, a study of school truancy, if it is merely a fact-gathering exercise, may collect data on who plays truant, which type of schools are most affected and the number of days off school. However, if the study is interested in explaining the reasons behind truancy, and the researcher is concerned to test the hypothesis that the reasons lie within the school – in the teacher–pupil relationship and the discipline procedures used – then these will form additional areas about which detailed information is gathered. A secondary analyst who wants to use this data to explore truancy using a model that postulates the importance of relationships between home and school and the extent of parental involvement in a child's education, is likely to find that a number of key questions have been omitted. Therefore, if the data has been collected in order to answer a specific hypothesis, it may not lend itself to re-analysis using a different explanatory model.

With either a descriptive or explanatory survey the analyst may find it necessary to derive new variables by combining information from a number of items of data. This is one of the distinctive features of secondary analysis . . . .

2. What information has been collected? Does it cover the range of issues in which the researcher is interested? What categories have been used for classifying, say, occupation or marital status? Does the data incorporate the distinctions required by the secondary analyst?

The questions asked here will, to some extent, be answered by knowing the purpose of the study and the theoretical framework employed. However, it is essential for the secondary analyst to study with care the documentation relating to the survey and to establish exactly the topics that it covers. This involves obtaining not just the interview schedule but also the instructions to interviewers, the coding frames used and, if possible, the results of the pilot study and any qualitative work that was done as a preliminary exercise. For example, if the researcher is concerned with making a detailed investigation of the occupational structure, then it is essential to find out beforehand what classification has been used and to ensure that it is adequate for the required purpose. It is similarly important to know the basis upon which categories such as 'self-employed' and 'manager' have been assigned, if distinctions of employment status are likely to be important. If the secondary analyst thinks that she may need to distinguish between people who are legally married and those who are cohabiting, then, again, it is necessary to check that the survey to be used incorporates such a distinction. This often entails thinking through, with great care, each stage of the analysis in an attempt to foresee the likely analytical requirements.

3. What sampling frame was used, and what is the sampling unit – that is, has

the survey sampled individuals, or households, or employers? What are the potential biases in the data? What is the response rate?

The sampling frame will be chosen to give, as accurately as possible, a listing of the population to be surveyed. . . . While sampling frames are generally chosen as the best available to draw a particular sample, all have their weaknesses. . . .

Knowledge of the sampling frame used can give the secondary analyst an indication of the extent to which the population sampled is likely to correspond to the 'true' population and the sampling unit used can indicate the kinds of analyses that are appropriate to that dataset. For example, a household-based survey . . . although recording details of employment, cannot adequately support an analysis of *employers' use* of fixed contract labour, although it can provide an estimate of the number of contract workers, the occupations which they fill and their personal characteristics. By contrast, an employer-based survey can focus directly on the ways in which employers use contract workers.

It is always important to know the limitations of the data that is being used. Although we may fall back on the slogan that 'any data is better than none', this is not a very adequate excuse for using poor data, and it is an even less adequate reason for failing to identify and assess the impact of the weaknesses. . . .

4. The secondary analyst needs to establish the credentials of the data which she is going to use. Who was responsible for collecting the data? What is the quality of the data?

However good the the credentials of the agency responsible for collecting the data, there must always be a degree of healthy scepticism about both the reliability and the validity of the data. In fact, the more professional the data collection, the more likely it is that the shortcomings of the data will be recognized and assessed. OPCS publish a biannual series of *Survey Methodology Bulletins* (available from OPCS for a small subscription), which report in-house research into topics that include the effects of non-response, question wording tests for the next Census, the use of particular sample designs, an assessment of interviewer variance effects, and an evaluation of the use of the Postcode Address File as an alternative sampling frame to the Electoral Register. Although the British Social Attitudes Survey, carried out by SCPR, has been the vehicle for methodological comparisons of cross-sectional versus panel data (Lievesley and Waterton 1986), this kind of methodological work is beyond the means of most of the academic researchers and social and market research organizations who make their data available for secondary analysis. . . .

5. Is the survey nationally representative? Will it support generalizations about the population sampled? Are any weighting procedures needed?

One of the main reasons for using secondary analysis is because it is the only feasible way of obtaining a nationally representative sample. It is becoming increasingly difficult for social scientists to carry out their own large-scale surveys. The cost of mounting a national sample survey, together with the reductions in funding available to the social sciences, make this a rare option for academic researchers. If it is important to the analyst that her research findings can be generalized, then the secondary analyst should check that the sampling frame and the sampling procedure used allows this . . .

6. When was the data collected? Is it still relevant, or have there been substantial changes that make the data source of little value?

For much academic research the fact that the data is five or six years old may not detract from its value. Many theoretically interesting issues concern structures of society that are not liable to short-term change and fluctuation. . . . Whatever the importance attached to the age of the data, the analyst should always take into account the political and economic circumstances that may have influenced the results of the survey. For example, a researcher concerned with divorce should be aware of the legislative framework existing at the time of the survey, as well as the prevailing social mores of the period. . . .

Preliminary questions relating to the proposed analysis

Having listed those questions which should be asked about the data to be analysed, it may also be useful to suggest another set of questions, which the secondary analyst should ask *herself* before beginning work.

1. Is secondary analysis an appropriate method for tackling the research problem?

. . . Secondary analysis is only one method among many and may not be appropriate for all kinds of research. Considerable creativity may be employed in the derivation of a new variable to produce measures which were not included in the original questionnaire but there are, none the less, limitations to this, and it may be important to recognize the possibility that secondary analysis is not going to permit you to measure adequately the concepts of importance in your research.

2. What theoretical framework will be used in analysing the data? What are the hypotheses to be tested? What are the questions to be answered?

There is little to prevent the secondary analyst approaching a dataset with a complete absence of both theoretical concepts and understanding of the issues to which the data relate. There is no *requirement* on the secondary analyst to do any of the preliminary thinking that has to be done before designing an interview schedule; nor is there any need to have first-hand experience of the issues covered by the survey.

The relationship between theory and data is one that has always troubled sociologists. C. Wright Mills (1959) adopted the term 'abstracted empiricism' to describe the trend that he saw in American sociology in the 1950s towards increasingly sophisticated quantification, which was replacing the traditional role of theory. He refers to 'the blindness of empirical data without theory and the emptiness of theory without data' (ibid., p. 77) and attacks vigorously his fellow social scientist Lazarsfeld for equating 'theory' with the 'variables useful in interpreting statistical findings' and 'empirical data' with such 'statistically determined facts and relations as are numerous, repeatable and measureable'. These sharp warnings are, perhaps, particularly relevant to the secondary analyst who may be tempted to view her readymade survey data as 'manna from heaven'.

Clearly it is important that the secondary analyst approaches the research with a carefully thought-out conceptual framework, if worthwhile results are to be achieved. It is also important, and perhaps more difficult, to ensure that there is a close relationship between theory and data: there is little value in adopting a theoretical framework that cannot be operationalized. . . .

3. Has the secondary analyst acquired a good knowledge of the substantive area under investigation?

It is to be hoped that an interest in the substantive area will be the propelling factor behind the planned research, but, if not, it is essential to acquire a good grounding in the subject material if the specification and interpretation of analyses are to be meaningful. There is no doubt that it is possible for researchers with very little substantive knowledge to engage in secondary analysis, but the results of such work are unlikely to stand up to scrutiny by those with greater experience of the area and may also fail to build upon work already done. Although a thorough review of all publications in the research area is always important, reports based upon qualitative research may have a particular role to play in giving insight and understanding of the conceptual problems involved and the issues of interpretation that may arise. Mills (1959, p.80), again writing on the topic of 'abstracted empiricism', gives a timely warning of the danger of doing a hasty review of the literature *after* data analysis and of using it to surround an empirical study with a 'cloak of theory'.

4. Does the secondary analyst understand the meaning of the categories used and the methods of coding open-ended questions?

This question leads on directly from the previous one; an understanding of the meanings behind the categories used is likely to produce much better analyses than if no effort has been made to understand the way in which responses are coded. The process of assigning responses to categories plays a crucial role in the interpretation and negotiation that, at least implicitly, goes on between the respondent, the interviewer and the coder. It is during this process that the 'reality' of the respondent is turned into a numerical category in a data file . . .

If worthwhile and meaningful results are to be produced by the secondary analyst, as much preliminary thinking, background reading and theoretical development needs to go into the study as would be required if it were a primary survey. Further, the results need to be understood in the context of other studies that approach the issues by using qualitative methods. . . .

References

Lievesley, D. and Waterton, J. (1986) 'Measuring individual attitude change', in R. Jowell and S. Witherspoon (eds) *British Social Attitudes: The 1985 Report* (Aldershot: Power).

Mills, C. W. (1959) *The Sociological Imagination* (Harmondsworth: Penguin).

Stewart, D. W. (1984) *Secondary Research: Information Sources and Methods* (Beverly Hills, Calif.: Sage).

Chapter 18

A.N. Oppenheim

THE QUANTIFICATION OF
QUESTIONNAIRE DATA

From *Questionnaire Design and Attitude Measurement,* London: Heinemann (1966).

THE PURPOSE OF THE questionnaire and of the survey as a whole is measurement. The final product is likely to consist of a series of tabulations and statistical analyses, together with a few selected quotations from the raw data, and these will be turned into a report showing in what way our findings bear on the hypotheses with which we set out. During the quantification stage of a survey the words and phrases spoken or written by the respondent will be processed, they will be turned into figures and symbols that can be counted and added up. In this way we obtain the entries for the tables that we need in order to draw conclusions.

In the case of precoded questions, attitude scales, grids, indexes, and other 'closed' techniques there is little difficulty: we assign, or have assigned beforehand, numerical symbols to the various answer categories, and as soon as the questionnaires return from the field they can be made ready for analysis or other forms of processing. In precoded questions each answer will usually carry a number, and that number can be used in the analysis. With scales and other devices, some simple scoring operations may have to be carried out, but, essentially, the nature of the techniques will determine the process of analysis in a routine fashion.

This is not so in the case of free-answer or 'open' questions, probes, and some projective techniques. Here, the data reach the office in the form of words and sentences written down either by the interviewer, or by the respondent, or perhaps in the form of tape recordings, and before we can start any kind of statistical analysis we first have to convert the data into numerical form. Usually we do this with the aid of a classification system, and the process of classifying responses in this way is known as coding. . . .

Coding frames

Each free-answer question, probe, sentence-completion item, or other 'open' technique in our questionnaire will require its own classification scheme. Only rarely can we use a scheme devised for some other inquiry. Our first task will therefore be the design of all the classification schemes, usually known as 'codes' or 'coding frames,' required for our particular study. . . .

How do we set about designing a coding frame?

Probably the first step should be the examination of a representative sample of responses. In practice, we select a convenient number of questionnaires (say, fifty or sixty cases) on a representative basis and copy all the responses to a particular question onto sheets of paper. At the top of each sheet will be the text of the question as it appeared in the questionnaire, and below that will be copied all the various answers given to that question by our subsample of fifty or sixty cases, each answer preceded by the case number. Where answers are few, for instance if the question applied to only part of the sample, more cases will be needed, until we have a sufficiently large and varied selection of answers. When we come to design the coding frame of the next free-answer question, we go through the entire batch of selected questionnaires again, copying all the responses to that particular question together, so that we can look at them.

From this point on we must bear in mind very clearly what it is that we are trying to do. By imposing a set of classificatory categories, perhaps eight or ten in number, on a very much larger and probably very varied set of responses, we are inevitably going to *lose information*. Bearing in mind the aims and hypotheses of the survey and the particular purpose of the question under consideration, we must so design the coding frame that this loss of information will occur where it matters least, enabling us to run our comparisons or test our hypotheses with the greatest accuracy. This means that our set of categories will not necessarily be designed simply 'to do justice to the responses'; other considerations may apply, and compromises often have to be made.

For a start, how many categories should we have? If there were no constraints, and we were anxious not to cause any distortion, we might like to have almost as many categories as there are responses, grouping under one heading only those responses that are identical. This is obviously not a practical proposition. Even if we could afford to follow so elaborate a coding scheme, we would probably find during the statistical analysis that each category contained only one case or a very few cases. Therefore, *the number of categories we can afford to have will in part be determined by the number of cases in the sample and the number of statistical breakdowns we shall use;* a category that will, in the final analysis and after subdivision of the sample, hold fewer than two or three dozen cases must usually be regarded as a luxury. However much it offends our semantic sensibilities or philosophical finesse, we must realize that it is pointless to retain a category that is used by too few people.

There is one exception to this argument. It sometimes happens that we have a hypothesis about a certain type of response being absent or very rare. In that case we might reserve a category for it in order to show just how rare it is. . . .

What other considerations guide us in the composition of coding frames? Let us take, for example, a question asking for the respondent's favorite film star. Let us assume that we have copied the replies of five dozen people, and that we are now faced with the problem of classifying these responses. One approach might simply be by frequency. We allot, say, seven categories to the seven names occurring most often and lump the remaining names in one or two other categories. Or perhaps we wish to expand the frame; we could have dozens of categories, each with one film star's name, if we chose. Or we might decide to group the names under different labels, such as 'romantic,' 'Western,' 'musical,' and so on, according to the type of role with which such film stars are associated. Then again, we may decide to have two coding frames, one for male and one for female film stars. Or we may wish to group together those stars who also appear on other mass media and those who do not. We may classify stars by their ages, or by their ethnic background, or by the number of divorces they have had. So we see that it is often not a simple matter to design a coding frame that will 'do justice to the data,' and that, moreover, the type of coding frame we need will depend on what we wish to find out. Suppose, for instance, that we wish to examine the hypothesis that men will most often admire female film stars, whereas women will more often mention male film stars. In that case, all we need to do, strictly speaking, is to classify the responses by sex into just two categories, male stars and female stars. This would tell us all we needed to know – though it would not enable us to go very much further. On the other hand, suppose we had the hypothesis that a lot depends on the star's age in relation to one's own age, with younger respondents admiring a somewhat older and more mature person, while middle-aged respondents prefer a younger star. In that case we would need a fairly complex coding frame giving categories of age differentials, up or down from one's own age, and to do the coding we would need to know both the respondent's age and that of his most admired film star.

When we copy out the responses, it is helpful to group the respondents in terms of one or more variables of concern, such as sex, age, social mobility, and so on. This often suggests differences in content, flavor, or expression between subgroups, and a coding frame can be designed to highlight these. For this reason, the copied responses must not merely be regarded as a try-out; they should be most carefully studied and perused.

Usually, the order of the categories is unimportant, and the categories are quite independent of one another. Sometimes, however, we may need a coding frame that is more like a rating scale. For instance, we may use some of our categories to indicate the degree of favorableness with which the respondent views a certain person or object; some responses would be classified as 'Highly favorable,' others as 'Moderately favorable' or as 'Favorable with reservations,' and so on. . . .

It should also be mentioned that for some questions, typically those used for classificatory purposes, there are probably some well-designed and elaborate coding frames available ready-made. A classification of occupational prestige might be one example. . . .

Every coding frame is likely to need two or three categories that are standard, namely 'miscellaneous,' 'don't know,' and 'no answer' or 'not ascertained.' When we are pressed for space, the latter two categories are frequently grouped together. On the other hand, sometimes it is important to know how many respondents said that they did not know the answer, or which ones refused to commit themselves, these two categories may not be just 'waste categories.' Into 'miscellaneous' go all those responses that cannot readily be fitted into one of our prepared categories. In cases of doubt, it is better practice to classify a response as 'Miscellaneous' than to force it into another category. One reason for this is that it is best not to blur the limits of the categories. Another is that if such doubtful responses occur with unexpected frequency, then at some point they can be 'rescued,' by making the decision to amend the coding frame and introducing a new category; in that case we merely have to look again at the responses coded 'Miscellaneous' with a view to reclassification, instead of having to recode every response category. Such a course of action should be seriously considered if the frequency of 'Miscellaneous' responses rises above, say, 15 per cent or so.

It should be realized that code categories can always be combined, putting together all the male film stars, or all the favorable plus moderately favorable responses, or all the respondents doing manual labor of any kind. This is sometimes necessary when we are dealing with small subanalyses, where the lack of cases is making itself felt.

Each category in a coding frame should be designated in the clearest possible way. It should be described in words, or given a label, and it is always helpful to give many illustrative examples taken from actual responses. Suppose we have asked people a question about the platform of a given political party and that we wish to classify the answers in terms of the amount of knowledge revealed by the respondents. In such a case it would not be enough, to set up a coding frame with categories such as 'very good,' 'adequate,' 'poor,' and so forth. Obviously, this would lead to inconsistencies among the coders and might not be clear to our readers. We have to set up definite criteria, such as: 'Very good: gives at least three different items of party policy correctly' together with some examples of actual responses. This is particularly important when numerous coders will be engaged on the same survey, in order to ensure consistency and reliability, but even where the investigator does all his own coding the categories should be as clear and as unambiguous as possible, for it is only too easy to change one's standards as one goes on. It is also necessary that the future reader know what is the precise meaning of each category; often verbal labels are ambiguous, but examples can make the meaning clear.

In the entire coding operation it is necessary to introduce frequent checks, both with others and with oneself, for statistics based on inconsistent coding can be very misleading. Some coding frames are relatively objective and merely require consistency and attention to detail on the part of the coder, for instance the coding of favorite school subjects. Other coding frames, however, require a certain amount of interpretation on the part of the coder, for instance coding the job dissatisfactions of teachers or the reasons people give for not saving more than they do. We then have to face the delicate problem of designing a coding frame that goes 'deep' enough, yet one that can be used consistently by the coding staff available, bearing in mind their training and experience. In some investigations it is necessary to check every coded response or to have two coders working independently on the same data and then discussing and resolving the differences between them. The primary aim must be consistency and the elimination of ambiguities; a coder who 'stretches' a category in order not to have to classify a response under 'Miscellaneous,' or one who 'improves' a category from one day to the next, or who finds that he 'knows' what the respondent 'really meant,' merely does the study a disservice. The better and clearer the coding frame, the fewer such occasions will arise. . . .

The plan of analysis

Once the data are in numerical form, we can start with the tabulations. But what tables do we need? In the smaller and simpler surveys, where we can proceed step by step, the first tabulations we want will usually be the 'straight runs,' the simple frequency distributions of the answers of the entire sample to each question in the questionnaire. If the sample is a representative one, considerable interest may attach to these over-all tabulations, while any further tables will merely be in the nature of elaborations. But if we are dealing with a more complex sampling design then the real interest of the survey analyst will lie in the interrelations between the variables, and the over-all distributions will merely enable him to plan the study of these interrelationships more carefully. At this stage, we can see for the first time how often a much-discussed code category has actually been used, or how many twins there are in the sample, or whether it contains enough users of Product X to make comparisons possible with the users of other products. . . .

We must now turn to our design, reminding ourselves which are our experimental variables, and set up some kind of grouping within the sample. We shall essentially be engaged in making comparisons between fairly stable sets of subgroups on a number of dependent variables. . . . Of course, the better and tighter our design is, the more the analysis will 'run itself'; if, for instance, we have utilized a factorial design then the main classifying variables are known from the start. If we have employed control groups, then a matching operation (which may first have to be checked by tabulation) will have preceded the analysis, and the comparisons will be between experimental and control groups. The same applies to the before-and-after type of design.

After this stage, there is usually a third one, which is much more difficult to plan. It comes after the main results of the survey have been tabulated and digested and have begun to give rise to new problems. At this point, we will very likely want to undertake a series of 'cross-breaks,' to study the relationships between certain subsidiary variables that were not part of the main analysis. Often such cross-breaks require that certain other variables be held constant, so that we either have to carry out a 'within-within' tabulation (for instance, studying the relationship between family size and maternal strictness within each social class in turn) or else engage in the compilation of matched subsamples. This part of the analysis is both interesting and time-consuming, and in a sense there is no end to it, for there always seem to be further interesting possibilities just beyond the horizon. Most surveys are never 'analyzed-out' completely; the analysis stops for lack of money or lack of time.

Unless this kind of detailed cross-analysis is planned for from the beginning and the sample collected accordingly, we tend very soon to run out of cases. Perhaps this is just as well, for there are distinct disadvantages in going on a 'fishing expedition.' The chances are that we will end up with a great many wasted tables, with a few substantial and interesting differences that we will be unable to interpret, and with a large number of small trends that may whet our curiosity; the latter are still more difficult to interpret and are not likely to emerge again in similar surveys. Quite possibly, we will obtain a finding that shows, for example, that men who marry women older than themselves also like their children to learn Latin at school, or that people with strong beliefs in the hereafter look at television less often – but unless we can say how these findings have come about and thus derive a new explanatory variable that might have wider applications, such results are of doubtful value. Up to a point, cross-breaks are useful and may yield important findings, but we must learn to curb our urge to do too many.

Sometimes there may be a fourth stage, which may be contrasted with the previous one in that it tries to 'build up' rather than 'break down' the data. Carrying out a principal-components analysis or developing a new composite index would come under this heading. Quite often such new variables will then require us to undertake new 'production runs,' to show how they are linked with our question-naire data. This stage, too, is likely to present serious problems of interpretation, but at least we can hope to replicate these new measures in subsequent studies.

It is, perhaps, worth mentioning that only a small fraction of all the tabulations are eventually published, perhaps less than 5 per cent. This kind of 'wastage' is inevitable; many results can be summed up in a few words, quoting perhaps one or two figures for illustrative purposes without publishing the entire table. This is especially true if the results are negative; if we have a questionnaire with 114 questions, and we wish to find out which of these are related to the respondent's religion, then this will require 114 tables, none of which will be published if the results are altogether negative. When writing a report it is important to ask our-selves constantly: 'Is this table really necessary?' Otherwise, the reader will not be able to see the forest for the trees. In some cases, a number of tables can be accommodated in appendixes.

Statistical comments

Competence in statistics is a necessary requirement for the research worker in any field. There is no shortage of textbooks in this field covering sampling, tests of significance, and correlational and multivariate techniques, and computer programs are available for many of these calculations.

One way of approaching this entire field is to distinguish between quantitative and qualitative data. Quantitative data have additive properties, equal intervals, and usually a zero point; in social surveys age, family size, income, savings, and number of cigarettes smoked per day are all examples of quantitative variables. The statistical techniques applicable to them are means and standard deviations, t-tests and F-tests, analysis of variance, product-moment correlation coefficients, and so on. Qualitative data are not measured along a continuum; they lack additive or even ordinal proper-ties and can best be thought of as frequencies in discrete categories. Qualitative data in social surveys might be the answers to the question 'Who is your favorite film star?' or the reasons for not liking frozen peas, or a person's religious beliefs. Applicable statistical techniques are percentages, chisquared tests and most other nonparametric devices, tetrachoric correlation coefficients (sometimes), and so on. It is very much worth bearing this fundamental distinction in mind, since the entire pattern of further analysis will be determined by it. If we are dealing with a variable which is quantitative, then we must ask the machines to produce sums, sums of squares, means, medians, standard deviations, t-tests, sums of cross-products, correlation coefficients, and perhaps analyses of variance or of principal components; if the variable is qualitative, then we must ask, first of all, for percentages and then find some way of applying nonparametric and multivariate techniques. In most surveys, the majority of the data will be of the latter kind.

It is worth pointing out that quantitative data can readily be turned into qualitative ones (albeit with some loss of information), by arranging them into frequency distributions. Thus, instead of giving the average age of a subsample, we say that 24 per cent were over 45 years old. However, qualitative data cannot be turned into quantitative data except in a very few instances and then only with the aid of certain assumptions. Social class is one such variable, which, though qualitative in the strict sense, is often used as a quantitative variable by making the necessary assumptions about equality of intervals and additive properties – a procedure that some regard as rather dubious. Measures of IQ or any other psychological test results, attitude scale scores, and index scores are all examples where such assumptions can, perhaps, be made with more justification.

In between the quantitative and the qualitative extremes lie variables that have ordinal properties, such as sociometric results, rating and ranking data, measures of relative interest, worry or liking, orderings of prestige or priority, and others. Here we can use Kendall's Tau and sometimes other rank correlation co-efficients or, with some loss of information, the usual techniques applicable to qualitative data (percentages and chi-squared tests). This latter approach is often resorted to, for the sake of uniformity and simplicity, though it takes no account of the ordering of the classes.

Many types of experimental design, including the factorial design, have been developed in relation to quantitative techniques of analysis, in particular analysis of variance, and to employ these designs in relation to the usual survey data, which tend to be qualitative, requires some ingenuity. Fortunately, a great deal can be done with the aid of simple percentages. For many surveys it is worthwhile obtaining or calculating percentage conversion tables for the subsamples that occur most frequently (for instance, for a cell and all possible combinations of cells of a factorial design) and designing special analysis sheets showing the percentages within the various subsamples – unless, of course, all this can be obtained directly in the form of a computer printout. Suppose we require breakdowns by sex, age, and social class; we might set up the following analysis shown in Figure 18.1.

We start by filling in the cells, showing the frequency with which each subsample has given response x to question q (say, voting preference for a particular party). Since we know the total number of cases for each cell, we can calculate percentages within each cell. We next proceed to compute the various marginal percentages (each time by recalculating the percentages to the new base and not by averaging them). Now we have a set of figures from which we can, by inspection, derive some tentative conclusions, for instance that voting preference for this party seems to be associated with lower social class for males, but not for females; or that younger women tend to prefer this party in every social class. Note that we have here the analysis of just one category from a coding frame; for a code with twelve categories

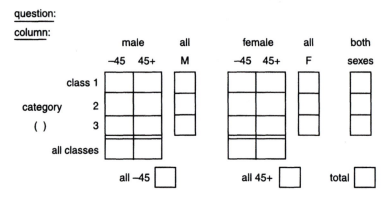

Figure 18.1 An analysis sheet for showing breakdowns by sex, age and social class.

we must do this analysis twelve times over, in order to understand the pattern of response to a single question. Obviously, such analysis will vary from survey to survey; a before-and-after design, for instance, would need quite a different pattern.

The most readily applicable test of statistical significance to data of this kind is the chi-squared test, which is usually outlined in almost any textbook of elementary statistics. This test is applicable to 2 × 2, 2 × n, or m × n tables, any of which may be used in the above example, depending on the issue to which we seek an answer. If we are interested in the over-all relationship between voting and sex, voting and age, voting and class, or voting and any combination of these three variables, then we should calculate m × n or 2 × n chi-squared tests (assuming that we are dealing with categories that are mutually exclusive and that do not contain multiple-mention responses). If the particular overall relationship that we have tested is statistically significant, then we may wish to go further and test for significance in relation to a particular category or party, for instance the relationship between age and voting for a particular party M. The reasoning here is analogous to the use of t-tests within an analysis of variance. . . .

One other general point is worth making here. Suppose that we have asked a number of questions in an effort to measure attitude to saving, and suppose further that we now find 22 per cent of middle-class respondents to be 'in favor' of saving on our first question. This figure, by itself, is very nearly meaningless. It only acquires meaning when we can compare it, say, to a response of 32 per cent 'in favor' among working-class respondents. But perhaps, if we look at a differently worded question on attitude to savings we will find a different result. Perhaps now we will find 28 per cent, or 50 per cent, of our middle-class respondents giving a favorable reply. Again, let us look at the working-class figures; quite likely we will find them running at around 40 per cent, or 60 per cent, for that question. In other words, it is often impossible to say, in absolute terms, how many respondents have a particular attitude to a given extent, because so much depends on the wording of the question; nevertheless, the *relative* differences (in terms of class, age, sex, or some other variable of concern) may well be quite stable and consistent, no matter how the question is phrased. In social research we have few absolute measures, but relative differences are well worth having if they are consistent, since they can give us an indication of relationships between variables.

Chapter 19

Paul F. Lazarsfeld

INTERPRETATION OF STATISTICAL RELATIONS AS A RESEARCH OPERATION

From Lazarsfeld, P.F. and Rosenberg, M., *The Language of Social Research: A Reader in the Methodology of Social Research*, Glencoe, Ill.: Free Press (1955).

The role of test factors

THE STARTING POINT FOR the present discussion is a research procedure which is applied almost automatically in empirical research. Whenever an investigator finds himself faced with the relationship between two variables he immediately starts to 'cross-tabulate,' i.e., to consider the role of further variables. The procedure may be demonstrated by using data that represent in somewhat stylized form the results obtained in many studies of radio listening tastes. By relating age of respondent to the program to which he usually listens, it is found that older people listen more to religious programs and political discussions on the air than do younger people, while there is practically no age difference in listening to classical music (Table 19.1).

Every research man knows that age is related to education; because of the recent extension of formal education, younger people in a community are usually better educated than the older ones. In the present sample the relation between age and education is as in Table 19.2. (The education break is between those who completed high school and those who did not; the age break is at 40.)

We thus deal with three variables: age, education, and type of listening. To simplify matters, we converted each variable into a dichotomy. Education, which is introduced here to elaborate and to clarify the original relationship, is called the *test variable* (t). Age is conventionally called the independent variable (x) and listening the dependent variable (y). Sometimes for brevity of expression we will use the symbols xyt, in the sense indicated in the previous sentence. But, otherwise, no mathematics will be used in this exposition.

Simple reflection will show that three relations can be drawn between three such variables. One relates age to listening: [xy], and the corresponding information has been given in Table 19.1, for each of the three program types. Then we have the relation between age and the test factor, education: [xt]. This is, of course, the same for all program types and the figures, rounded out but substantially correct, are reported in Table 19.2. Finally, we have [ty], the relation between education and listening. This again is different for all the programs, and the data will be given presently.

Table 19.1 Proportion of listeners in two age groups

	Young % Listen	Old % Listen
Religious programs	17	26
Discussion programs	34	45
Classical music programs	30	29
(Total cases)	(1,000)	(1,300)

For better understanding, one should take into account at this point that the entire fourfold Table 19.2, and any one line in Table 19.1, give the same type of information. The content of Table 19.2 could be summarized by stating that 60% of the young people but only 31% of the old people are in the high education group. Inversely, we could convert any line of Table 19.1 into a fourfold table, giving for the two age classes the number of people who listen or do not listen to a certain type of program. We shall use both types of presentation, according to which is convenient. . . .

Table 19.2 Relation between age and education

	Young	Old	Total
High education	600	400	1,000
Low education	400	900	1,300
Total	1,000	1,300	2,300

The research operation we are describing here thus starts out with an original relation [xy], then introduces a test variable, and thus creates two more relations [xt] and [ty]. But the most important results obtained with the help of the test variable are two *partial relations*. We can now raise the following question. If we study people in the high education and low education groups separately, what happens to the relation between age and listening? The answer is given in Table 19.3.

The figures pertain to religious programs. To make them more comparable with the first line of Table 19.1, we use the per cent presentation and then see that *within*

Table 19.3 Relation between age and listening to religious programs, by education

	High education				Low education		
	Young	Old			Young	Old	
Listen	55	45	100	Listen	115	285	400
Don't listen	545	355	900	Don't listen	285	615	900
	600	400	1,000		400	900	1,300

Table 19.4 Proportion of listeners to religious programs (%)

Young	Old
17	26

High education		Low education	
Young	Old	Young	Old
9	11	29	32

each educational group the relation between age and listening has practically disappeared. (The first line of Table 19.4 repeats information presented in Table 19.1.)

We can now perform the same analysis for the other two program types listed in Table 19.1. The results are reported without discussing all the intermediate steps. The main point to note is how different the role of the test variable is from one example to the next. We begin with listening to discussion programs on the radio.[1]

The data of Table 19.1 are repeated in the first line of Table 19.5, as they were in Table 19.4. Table 19.5 shows that, *within* educational groups, age makes an even larger difference than for the sample as a whole.

Now, how about listening to classical music? From Table 19.1 it might appear that age plays no role here. However, notice: the footnote shows that educated people listen more to this type of program, and we know that younger people are more highly educated.

---

1 To complete our information we still need to know how education is related to listening; or, in other words, we need to know [ty]. The data are as follows:

Listen to discussion programs				Listen to classical music			
	Yes	No			Yes	No	
High education	460	540	1,000	Low education	280	1,020	1,300
Low education	460	840	1,300	High education	404	596	1,000
Total	920	1,380	2,300	Total	684	1,616	2,300

Table 19.5 Proportion of listeners to discussion programs (%)

Young		Old	
34		45	

High education		Low education	
Young	Old	Young	Old
40	55	25	40

Carrying out the full tabulation scheme reveals indeed a rather complex structure, exhibited in Table 19.6.

Table 19.6 Proportion of listeners to classical music (%)

Young		Old	
30		29	

High education		Low education	
Young	Old	Young	Old
32	52	28	19

Table 19.6 shows that age plays a different role for high and low educated respondents. In a more sophisticated environment, maturation leads to more attention to such cultural matters as good music. In a 'culturally impoverished' environment, the peak of such interest seems to come near to the age when school influence still prevails; with increasing age, cultural interests decline.

It is the logic, not the substantive details, of these three examples, to which one should attend. The introduction of age had a different effect in each example cited in Table 19.1. With religious programs it decreased the original difference; with discussion programs it led to an increase; with classical music it brought to light two counter trends which were concealed in the original findings. . . .

Chapter 20

Morris Rosenberg

THE STRATEGY OF SURVEY ANALYSIS

From *The Logic of Survey Analysis,* New York: Basic Books (1968)

IT IS SOMETIMES ASSUMED, either explicitly or implicitly, that there is a single correct approach to survey analysis and that approaches which deviate from this path are in error. We would suggest, on the contrary, that several approaches are available and that the research worker should be flexible in conducting his analysis in a way which will maximize theoretical fruitfulness and will permit more confident conclusions.

Hypothesis testing

The model of scientific procedure involves the testing of preformulated hypotheses which have been derived from strict deductive reasoning or more general theoretical considerations. Certain logical operations must thus precede the collection of the data. If the hypothesis derives directly from these logical operations, and if the empirical data turn out to confirm the hypothesis, then the theory which engendered the hypothesis is supported. . . . [But] hypothesis testing, though a relatively severe criterion of the adequacy of one's theoretical reasoning, is far from foolproof.

Actual research affords a number of illustrations. In a study of self-images among adolescents, the hypothesis was advanced that upper-class adolescents would have higher self-esteem than lower-class adolescents. This hypothesis derived logically from a cogent body of theory. Mead had suggested that the self was a product of reflected appraisals, and Cooley had stressed that self-estimates were fundamentally determined by our assumptions concerning others' attitudes toward us. Since social class reflects societal prestige, it would follow that people who are generally well regarded and respected in society would have greater self-respect than those who are disdained. And the empirical data did, in fact, agree with the hypothesis; the upper-class adolescents did have higher self-esteem than the lower-class respondents. While the results were thus consistent with the theoretical reasoning of Mead and Cooley, they did not prove its correctness. Further analysis, in fact, suggested that this theory had little to do with the results – that the results were actually due to certain normative patterns of closeness of fathers to sons and fathers to daughters in the several social classes.[1] . . .

The second reason why hypothesis-testing cannot serve as the sole scientific procedure is this: that even if the hypothesis is confirmed in survey analysis, one's job is still not done. The possibility still remains that the relationship may be spurious, that is, may be due to extraneous variables. It is thus often necessary to control on certain variables to insure that there is an inherent link between the independent and dependent variables. In the experimental method, the 'block-booking' problem is overcome by insuring that the experimental and control groups are as alike as possible (either through matching or through random selection). The empirical support of an hypothesis in survey research represents weaker confirmation than hypotheses tested by means of experimentation. Some form of elaboration is thus almost always required in a theoretically based survey.

The third point is that much can be learned in survey analysis which is not based on the explicit testing of clearly stipulated pre-formulated hypotheses. Indeed, the strict and exclusive adherence to hypothesis-testing as the sole scientific model may seriously impoverish research. The wide range of knowledge which can be obtained through the various processes of elaboration, the flow of analysis, the 'pursuit of an idea,' and the assaying of evidence is largely cut off through strict adherence to the model of hypothesis-testing. Pure hypothesis-testing is a valuable research model and should be employed where appropriate, but research can be severely cramped if it is employed as the *sole* method of analysis.

Elaboration

At least as common in survey analysis is the process of elaborating the relationship between two variables by introducing a third variable into the analysis. The purpose is to 'explain' or to 'specify' the relationship, thus making it more meaningful or more exact. Elaboration helps to answer the questions of 'why' and 'under what circumstances.'

The basic format suggested in our discussion of analysis involves a relationship between two variables which is stratified according to the categories of a test factor. When this simple step is taken, an enormous amount of information is potentially available. The information which the table can yield, however, *depends entirely upon the perspective one brings to bear on it*. The data are unable to speak for themselves; they are only able to respond to the questions asked of them.

---

1 Morris Rosenberg, *Society and the Adolescent Self-Image* (Princeton, NJ: Princeton University Press, 1965), chapter 3.

Two errors commonly made in the elaboration of a two-variable table are these: one is to look at only one item of information in the table, the other to look at all the information at once. The first procedure is wasteful, the second confusing. A great deal of information can potentially be derived by introducing a third variable into the analysis, but the full exploitation of this information is possible only if one treats the various questions separately and asks some of the essential questions first. *Elaboration may thus properly be viewed as a sequence of steps.* How does the process of elaboration proceed?

Take the familiar and well-documented finding that working-class people are more likely to vote Democratic than those in the middle class. What questions might one pose of such a finding that could be answered by the introduction of a third variable? In principle, a surprisingly large number are susceptible of systematic investigation. . . .

Assume, for example, that one interpreted the relationship between class and voting in terms of a theory of economic interest: the higher classes vote Republican because they feel that the government will protect their economic interests, whereas the lower classes vote Democratic for the same reason. But suppose this relationship turns out to be strong in the East but weak in the West. Should economic self-interest play less of a role on the Pacific than on the Atlantic coast? One's interpretation is thereby *challenged* by the data and must either be defended in terms of special circumstances or must exert pressure for an alternative interpretation which will effectively accommodate these divergent results.

One might also examine conditional relationships in an effort to *confirm* the interpretation. Assume that one had interpreted the relationship in reference group terms – that voting derived from an identification with a class group and adherence to its political norms. One could thus expect the relationship of class to voting to be stronger among those who firmly identified with their class groups than among those whose identification was weaker. If such turned out to be the case, it would add strength to the interpretation; if not, it would tend to undermine it.

Conditional relationships might not change the interpretation but might *modify* it to some extent. Interpreting the relationship of class to vote as due to self-interest, one might find that the relationship is great among factory workers and owners but not among other people. One might then conclude that economic self-interest does operate *if the presence of economic power is highly visible*, as in the factory. The interpretation has not been changed, but modified.

Conditional relationships might also reveal *trends*. Assume one examined the relationship of class to vote, controlling on age. If the relationship grew weaker as the age level decreased, this might suggest a decreasing level of class consciousness in the population in recent generations. If the relationship increased, the conclusion would be the reverse.

The analyst might also be interested in conditions that *mute* or *amplify* the relationship. He would probably find, for example, that the relationship between social class and support of the Republican or Democratic Parties was weak in the South, though strong in the North. The factor muting the relationship in the South would be the power of race and tradition on vote which would submerge the class factor.

On the other hand, the investigator might find that the relationship was stronger in cities than in small towns. This finding might suggest that the intensive intra-class interaction characteristic of densely populated areas would foster class polarization and class consciousness, whereas this would be less true of thinly populated areas.

Similarly, one would expect no relationship between class and vote unless certain *necessary conditions* obtained. In some sections of the South, particularly in local elections, victory in the Democratic primary is virtually tantamount to election. If the Republican Party in these regions is virtually defunct, one would expect little association between class and Republican or Democratic vote. A necessary condition for this association is serious two-party competition.

These illustrations perhaps suffice to suggest the abundance of information inherent in conditional relationships. Few analysts would be interested in looking at all these questions, of course, but an awareness of the range may alert the analyst to seek useful information he might otherwise overlook. . . .

In the analysis of survey data, then, there are a number of steps, corresponding to a series of questions, which should be considered in penetrating more deeply into the relationship. The vein of research data is almost always richer than it appears to be on the surface, but it can only be of value if mined. The purpose of the foregoing discussion has been to make explicit some of the contributions to understanding which can be gained by introducing a third variable. To the extent that the analyst is more explicitly aware of these varied contributions, his chances of more fully exploiting his data are increased.

It is thus apparent that, in survey analysis, the two-variable relationship represents the start, not the completion, of the analysis. But the formal procedure of elaboration is also not the end of the analysis. As each of the varied types of information is gained in the process of elaboration, it may yield results which suggest further investigation. This is the 'flow of analysis.' As the research analyst investigates a particular idea, his attention is captured by data which suggest new ideas, which in turn exert pressure to examine new data, and so on. Any of the types of information acquired through elaboration may serve as a springboard for this process.

This type of analysis inevitably involves a close interplay of theory and data. The data suggest, stimulate, and generate the theory and the theory is restrained, controlled, and disciplined by the data. The separation of theory and research becomes impossible when guided by the flow of analysis procedure. . . .

In actual practice, much survey analysis involves the hot pursuit of an idea down paths and byways which have little to do with one's original hypotheses. In this case, the investigator displays a willingness to be led by his data along unexpected paths although he of course also gives direction to the analytic course. A reluctance to follow the lead of the findings may stultify and abort a good deal of promising research. . . .

The 'pursuit of an idea' often involves a complex interplay between theory and data – the data exercising pressure on the theorist to account for them, the consequent theory pointing the direction to the appropriate data for testing or elaborating the theory. This research strategy is possible only if one demonstrates a willingness to be led by the data but, at the same time, to direct it in accord with some interpretive or theoretical position.

PART FIVE

Critiques of quantification

INTRODUCTION

DISSATISFACTION WITH QUANTITATIVE APPROACHES to social research, where investigators appeared to treat people as if they were no different from material objects, and social processes as if they were systems of machinery, grew during the 1960s. The first of the readings in this section, by Julius Roth (reading 21) concerns the conditions under which data may be produced in large-scale social surveys. Through a series of case studies derived from his personal experience, Roth describes the cheating that can occur when 'hired hand' interviewers feel alienated from the aims of a research project. Roth feels that this makes the results of such research questionable.

Cicourel (reading 22) participated in the same wave of dissatisfaction with the social survey as Roth. Unlike Roth, though, who was an ethnographer, Cicourel was an important figure in the development of ethnomethodology, a general approach that was to lead to the qualitative method of conversation analysis (see readings 47 and 48). Though he raises similar concerns to Roth, he is interested also in much deeper issues of meaning and it is difficult to see how the problems he describes could be solved purely by better motivation of interviewers. In 1964, when Cicourel's piece was written, it was difficult to challenge the then-dominant quantitative orthodoxy in American sociology. His book *Method and Measurement in Sociology* was therefore presented in part as an attempt to improve survey research practice, so the piece reads now as somewhat ironical. In fact, Cicourel's critique of the fixed-choice question, and of survey procedures in general, appeared devastating to many readers and the book became a very popular methods text as a variety of qualitative alternatives gathered pace in the years that followed.

Not all researchers, however, were impressed with Cicourel's points. Marsh (reading 23) in an impassioned defence of the method, addresses his views head on, arguing that structured questionnaires and fixed-choice questions are not always used in social surveys, and that when they are, careful piloting can eliminate many of the problems of meaning involved. Marsh claims that alternative methods are subject to similar problems to those identified by Cicourel, and that the way forward is to recognize the limitations of all approaches to research, but also to recognize and build on strengths of particular techniques.

Houtkoop-Steenstra (reading 24) is a conversation analyst (see readings 47 and 48) who has studied the conduct of structured interviewing in microscopic detail. Her work thus demonstrates the application of a qualitative method to investigate and perhaps improve the properties of a quantitative method of data collection. She focuses on the various ways in which interviewers deviate from printed instructions to generate responses, which therefore cannot be considered valid. In the rest of the book from which this extract is taken, Houtkoop-Steenstra makes many suggestions for the improvement of structured interviewing procedures.

Reading 25 is an exchange from the *New York Review of Books* following a critical review of a large-scale social survey investigating the sexual practices of Americans (Laumann *et al.* 1994). The criticisms and the rebuttals centre on the issue of whether people will have told the truth, and the absence of any adequate checks on the possibility that lies were told. In the impassioned exchanges that follow the initial review, one critic (Burress) says 'I do hope but do not expect that social scientists will add this book review to their reading lists in quantitative methods.' Here it is.

DISCUSSION POINTS

- How representative is Roth's sample of research case studies of the wider popu-lation of research to which he wishes to generalize his results? Is his case strengthened by the finding of similar processes in studies of other kinds of workplace? To what extent do the considerations outlined by Hyman *et al.* (read-ing 10) address Roth's concerns?

- Do the methods for question design outlined by Moser and Kalton (reading 9) address the criticisms made by Cicourel of fixed-choice questions? (Consider, for example, the view that the criticisms might apply differently to factual and attitudinal questions.)

- How convincing is Marsh's depiction of qualitative alternatives to survey research? In what ways does she believe the problems identified by Cicourel can be overcome?

- How does the study by Houtkoop-Steenstra influence your evaluation of the arguments of Cicourel and Marsh? In other words, should the use of fixed-choice questions be abandoned, or improved by piloting exercises and other methods? How would you investigate a (learning-disabled) person's 'quality of life'?

- Surveys of sexual practices were done quite frequently in a number of 'developed' countries in the wake of the HIV/AIDS epidemic. It was hoped that a better understanding of people's sexual behaviour would help in preventing the spread of the virus. Having considered the exchanges in reading 25, how would you advise social researchers to generate useful information about this?

REFERENCE

Laumann, E.O., Gagnon, J.H., Michael, R.T. and Michaels, S. (1994) *The Social Organiza- tion of Sexual Practices in the United States,* Chicago: University of Chicago Press.

FURTHER READING

Best, J. (2001) *Damned Lies and Statistics: Untangling Numbers from the Media, Politicians and Activists,* Berkeley, Cal.: University of California Press.

Herrnstein, R. and Murray, C. (1994). *The Bell Curve: Intelligence and Class Struc- ture in American Life,* New York: The Free Press.

Hindess, B. (1973) *The Use of Official Statistics: A Critique of Positivism and Ethnomethodology,* London: Macmillan.

Jacoby, R. and Glauberman, N. (eds) (1995) *The Bell Curve Debate,* New York: Ran- dom House.

Marsh, C. (1973) 'Problems with surveys: method or epistemology?' *Sociology* 13 (2): 293–305.

Chapter 21

Julius A. Roth

HIRED HAND RESEARCH

From *The American Sociologist* 1 (4): 190–196 (1966).

Case I

AFTER IT BECAME OBVIOUS how tedious it was to write down numbers on pieces of paper which didn't even fulfill one's own sense of reality and which did not remind one of the goals of the project, we all in little ways started avoiding our work and cheating on the project. It began for example when we were supposed to be observing for hour and a half periods, an hour and a half on the ward and then an hour and a half afterwards to write up or dictate what we had observed, in terms of the category system which the project was supposed to be testing and in terms of a ward diary. We began cutting corners in time. We would arrive a little bit late and leave a little bit early. It began innocently enough, but soon boomeranged into a full cheating syndrome, where we would fake observations for some time slot which were never observed on the ward. Sam, for example, in one case, came onto the ward while I was still finishing up an assignment on a study patient and told me that he was supposed to observe for an hour and a half but that he wasn't going to stay because he couldn't stand it anymore. He said he wasn't going to tell anyone that he missed an assignment, but that he would simply write up a report on the basis of what he knew already about the ward and the patients. I was somewhat appalled by Sam's chicanery, and in this sense I was the last one to go. It was three or four weeks after this before I actually cheated in the same manner. . . .

In order to ensure the reliability of our coding, the research design called for an 'Inter-Rater Reliability Check' once every two months, in which each of the four of us would pair up with every other member of the team and be rated on our ability to code jointly the same interaction in terms of the same categories and dimensions.

We learned to loathe these checks; we knew that the coding system was inadequate in terms of reliability and that our choice of categories was optional, subjective, and largely according to our own sense of what an interaction is really about, rather than according to the rigid, stylized, and preconceived design into which we were supposed to make reality fit. We also knew, however, that our principal investigators insisted on an inter-rater reliability coefficient of .70 in order for the research to proceed. When the time came for another check, we met together to discuss and make certain agreements on how to bring our coding habits into conformity for the sake of achieving reliability. In these meetings we would confess our preferences for coding certain things in certain ways and agree on certain concessions to each other for the duration of the check. Depending on what other individual I was to be paired with, for example, I had a very good idea of how I could code in order to achieve nearly the same transcriptions. We didn't end it there. After each phase of a check, each pair of us would meet again to go over our transcriptions and compare our coding and if there were any gross discrepancies, we corrected them before sending them to the statistician for analysis. Needless to say, as soon as the reliability checks were over with, we each returned to a coding rationale which we as individuals required in order to do any coding at all – in order to maintain sanity.

Case II

There didn't appear to be too much concern with the possibility of inconsistency among the coders. Various coders used various methods to determine the code of an open-end question. Toward the end of the coding process, expediency became the key-note, leading to gross inconsistency. The most expedient method of coding a few of the trickier questions was to simply put down a '4' (This was the middle-of-the-road response on the one question that had the most variation.). If the responses were not clear or comprehensible, the coder had two alternatives: on the one hand, he could puzzle over it and ask for other opinions or, on the other hand, he could assign it an arbitrary number or forget the response entirely. . . .

The final problem leading to gross inconsistency was the factor of time. The supervisor made it clear that the code sheets had to be in to the computation center by Saturday. This meant that on Saturday morning and early afternoon the aim of the coders was to code the questionnaires as quickly as possible, and the crucial factor was speed, even at the expense of accuracy. The underlying thought was that there were so many questionnaires coded already (that were *assumed* to be coded consistently and correctly) that the inconsistencies in the remainder would balance themselves out and be of no great importance. I found myself adapting to this way of thinking, and after spending two or three hours there on Saturday morning, I joined in the game of 'let's get these damn things out already.' It did indeed became a game, with the shibboleth, for one particularly vague and troublesome question, 'Oh, give it a four.'

Case III

One of the questions on the interview schedule asked for five reasons why parents had put their child in an institution. I found most people can't think of five reasons. One or two – sometimes three. At first I tried pumping them for more reasons, but I never got any of them up to five. I didn't want (the director) to think I was goofing off on the probing, so I always filled in all five. . . .

Any reader with research experience can probably recall one or more cases in which he observed, suspected, or participated in some form of cheating, careless-ness, distortion, or cutting of corners in the collection or processing of research data. He probably thought of these instances as exceptions – an unfortunate lapse in ethical behavior or a failure of research directors to maintain proper controls. I would like to put forth the thesis that such behavior on the part of hired data-collectors and processors is not abnormal or exceptional, but rather is exactly the kind of behavior we should expect from people with their position in a production unit.

The cases I have presented do not constitute proof, of course. Even if I pre-sented ten or twenty more, my efforts could be dismissed as merely an unusually industrious effort to record professional dirty linen (or I might be accused of making them up!) and not at all representative of the many thousands of cases of hired researching carried out every year. Rather than multiply examples, I would like to take a different tack and examine the model we have been using in thinking about research operations and to suggest another model which I believe is more appropriate. . . .

When a researcher hires others to do the collecting and processing tasks of his research plan, we often assume that these assistants fit the 'dedicated scientist' ideal and will lend their efforts to the successful conduct of the over-all study by carrying out their assigned tasks to the best of their ability. As suggested by my examples, I doubt that hired assistants usually behave this way even when they are junior grade scholars themselves. It becomes more doubtful yet when they are even further removed from scholarly tradition and from the direct control of the research dir-ectors (e.g., part-time survey interviewers).

It seems to me that we can develop a more accurate expectation of the contribu-tion of the hired research worker who is required to work according to somebody else's plan by applying another model which has been worked out in some detail by sociologists – namely, the work behavior of the hired hand in a production organization. . . .

'Restriction of production' and deviation from work instructions is no longer regarded by students of the sociology of work as a moral issue or a form of social delinquency. Rather, it is the expected behavior of workers in a production organiza-tion. The only problem for an investigator of work practices is discovering the details of cutting corners, falsifying time sheets, defining work quotas, dodging supervision, and ignoring instructions in a given work setting.

There is no reason to believe that a hired hand in the scientific research business will behave any different from those in other areas of productive activity. It is far more reasonable to assume that their behavior will be similar. They want to make as much money as they can and may pad their account or time sheet if they are paid on that basis, but this type of behavior is a minor problem so far as the present discussion is concerned. They also want to avoid difficult, embarrassing, inconvenient, time-consuming situations as well as those activities which make no sense to them. (Thus, they fail to make some assigned observations or to ask some of the interview questions.) At the same time they want to give the right impression to their superiors – at least right enough so that their material will be accepted and they will be kept on the job. (Thus, they modify or fabricate portions of the reports in order to give the boss what he *seems* to want.) They do not want to 'look stupid' by asking too many questions, so they are likely to make a stab at what they think the boss wants – e.g., make a guess at a coding category rather than having it resolved through channels.

Even those who start out with the notion that this is an important piece or work which they must do right will succumb to the hired-hand mentality when they realize that their suggestions and criticisms are ignored, that their assignment does not allow for any imagination or creativity, that they will receive no credit for the final product, in short, that they have been hired to do somebody else's dirty work. When this realization has sunk in, they will no longer bother to be careful or accurate or precise. They will cut corners to save time and energy. They will fake parts of their reporting. They will not put themselves out for something in which they have no stake except in so far as extrinsic pressures force them to. Case No. I is an excerpt from the statement of a research worker who started out with enthusiasm and hard work and ended with sloppy work and cheating when she could no longer escape the fact that she was a mere flunky expected to do her duty whether or not it was meaningful. The coders in Case II soon gave up any effort to resolve the ambiguities of their coding operation and followed the easiest path acceptable to their supervisor. In this case, the supervisor himself made little effort to direct the data-processing toward supplying answers to meaningful research issues. We must remember that in many research operations the supervisors and directors themselves are hired hands carrying out the requests of a client or superior as expeditiously as possible. . . .

When the tasks of a research project are split up into small pieces to be assigned to hired hands, none of these data-collectors and processors will ever understand all the complexities and subtleties of the research issues in the same way as the person who conceived of the study. No amount of 'training' can take the place of the gradual development of research interests and formulations on the part of the planner. Since the director often cannot be sure what conceptions of the issues the hired hands have as a result of his explanations and 'training,' he must make dubious guesses about the meaning of much of the data they return to him. If he attempts to deal with this difficulty by narrowly defining the permissible behavior of each hired hand (e.g., demand that all questions on a schedule be asked in a set wording), he merely increases the alienation of the hired hand from his work and thus increases the likelihood of cutting corners and cheating. As he gains in quantity of data, he loses in validity and meaningfulness. . . .

There has been very little discussion in our journals and our books on research methods on the relationship of the hired hand to the data collected. Whatever discussion there *has* been can be found in the survey interview field where there have been some studies of the effect of such demographic factors as age, sex, and race, sometimes measured personality traits, on 'interviewer bias.' The nature of the interviewer's status in a research organization is seldom discussed in print. The problem of interviewer cheating, although a common subject of informal gossip, is seldom dealt with openly as a serious problem. . . .

Control measures can hope to block only the cruder, more obvious, and repeated forms of cheating. The postal card follow-up will catch the interviewer who does not bother to contact his respondents at all. Spot-check follow-up interviewing may eventually catch the interviewer who makes contacts, but fabricates demographic data (to fill a quota sample) or completes only part of the interview and fills in the rest in a stereotyped manner later on. (Even here, many of his interviews may be used before he is detected.) However, from the cases of hired hand interviewing which I am familiar with, I would say such crude cheating is not the most common form of cutting corners on the job. Far more common is the kind found in Case III where the interviewer makes his contact, obtains a fairly complete interview, but leaves partial gaps here and there because he found it time-consuming, embarrassing, or troublesome, felt threatened by the respondent, or simply felt uncertain about how the study director wanted certain lines of questioning developed. With a little imagination, such gaps can be filled in later on in a way that is very unlikely to be detected in a follow-up interview. If, for example, a supervisor in Case III had returned to the respondents and asked them whether the 'five reasons' listed on their interview form were accurate reflections of their opinion, probably most would have said yes, and the few who objected to one or two of the reasons could have been dismissed as the degree of change that one expects on re-interview. . . .

In their research methods texts, our students are told a great deal about the mechanics of research technique and little about the social process of researching. What little is said on the latter score consists largely of Pollyannaish statements about morale, honesty, and 'proper motivation.' It should be noted that appeals to morality and patriotism never reduced goldbricking and restriction of production in industry, even during the time of a world war. There is no reason to believe that analogous appeals to interviewers, graduate students, research assistants, and others who serve as hired hands will be any more effective. If we want to avoid the hired hand mentality, we must stop using people as hired hands. . . .

When reading a research report, we should pay close attention to the description of how the data was collected, processed, analyzed, interpreted, and written up with an eye to determining what part, if any, was played by hired hands. This will often be a difficult and highly tentative judgement, requiring much reading between the lines with the help of our knowledge of how our colleagues and we ourselves often operate. However, we can get hints from such things as the size of the staff, the nature of the relationship of the staff members, the manner in which the research plans were developed and applied, the organizational setting in which the research was done, mention made of assignment of tasks, and so on. If there is good reason to believe that significant parts of the research have been carried out by hired hands, this would, in my opinion, be a reason for discounting much or all of the results of the study.

Chapter 22

Aaron V. Cicourel

FIXED-CHOICE QUESTIONNAIRES

From *Method and Measurement in Sociology*, New York: Free Press (1964).

S OME ADVOCATES OF THE interview often point out that the question-naire with fixed-choice response categories precludes the possibility of obtaining unanticipated definitions of the situation which reveal the subject's private thoughts and feelings. While fixed-choice alternatives may be adequate and necessary for obtaining factual data, seeking information on social process by this means may force the subject to provide precise responses to events and issues about which he may be ignorant or vague. Fixed-choice alternatives may preclude obtaining meaningful information on social process if the interactional context is restricted by questions asked. This chapter will discuss the following:

1   Do fixed-choice questions become 'grids' through which our understanding of social process is distorted? The attaining of what kinds of information would be precluded by this method?
2   What would we have to know about language, cultural meanings, and the structure of social action to construct a successful questionnaire with fixed-choice answers?
3   What is the role of theory in coding and scaling fixed-choice responses? Our task will be to ask how the survey with fixed-choice questions achieves solutions to substantive research problems in spite of the lack of knowledge about basic theoretical issues which are presupposed in all field research.

Social process and fixed-choice questionnaires

There are many sources in the literature which show considerable consensus on how one goes about conducting a survey using fixed-choice questionnaires. The technical details do not differ significantly, nor do the formal descriptions of what should be done. Most likely to differ are the various unofficial ways in which surveys are actually conducted. Information on day-to-day problems in this kind of research is seldom available because the unofficial practices are 'buried' in the files of researchers, or in unpublished reports because space did not permit publication of such procedures. A list of variations from ideal procedures is impractical to compose and would probably dwarf the substantive results and discussion. Yet a general account, omitting the details, of how a survey is conducted obscures the subtle inferences and decisions required in each stage of the research. . . .

Can we assume that the interviewers, ethnological 'scouts,' coders, data analysts, and the director of social science research are all employing the same theoretical frame of reference and interpreting each event, respondent, etc., identically, that is, using the same meaning structures in different contexts with the same interpretive rules? . . . Standardized questions with fixed-choice answers provide a solution to the problem of meaning by simply avoiding it. . . .

A strong argument can be made for eliminating much of interviewer bias by the introduction of fixed-choice questionnaires. Standardized questions with a finite number of choices that are self-administered give the appearance of objectivity and lend themselves to translation into numerical representations. But what are the ideal conditions? Consider the following:

1   Every subject's response pattern would have to be predictable on explicit theoretical grounds before the instrument could test hypotheses. Every question would have to be formulated according to specific theoretical interests, indicating what would be required to accept or reject the hypothesis associated with it.

2   Preliminary interviewing with open-ended questions and pretests would constitute trial runs which would help modify both theory and operational procedures because of the questions and answers obtained and their coding rules.

3   The elements of social process would have to be known in sufficient detail to enable the researcher to use the questionnaire responses as 'meter' readings of intricate social interaction and meaning structures which produced the responses.

4   The question and response would have to reflect the kinds of typicality that the actor uses to mange his daily world, be couched in the everyday language he is familiar with, and evoke replies which are not altered by the idiosyncracies of occasional expressions, particular relevance structures, a pretense of agreement, or the particular biographical circumstances of the respondent, unless such properties are variable conditions in the research design.

5   The various clock-time slices which make up the final distribution of respondents' answers must correspond with some set of identical intervals of the actors' experiences. More precisely, the various types of respondents (determined in advance by their response pattern in mock-up tables), conceived as

equivalence classes (each type constitutes one class), would produce various responses to each question. Such a view presupposes identical ways of responding to the environments of objects projected by the questionnaire. The questionnaires presumably create a set of identical possible environments.

6   Each type of respondent would have to understand the meaning of the relevant questions identically, and somehow assign these meanings according to some existing common culture or 'rules' shared by all but where the differential responses become indicative of different hypothetical inner states (and hence differential perception and interpretation of the same stimuli) which can exist in the same common culture. Stated another way, in these identical environments there are stimuli which communicate invariant meanings, for different equivalence classes of respondents, but in these identical environments the differential assignment of meanings is determined according to the actor's hypothetical inner states.

7   The observer's theory would have to include a sub-theory of meaning structures, 'rules' governing their use, and show how different types of actors (with different hypothetical inner states) are likely to interpret the questions. This assumes an invariant language structure which links the perception of the environment to inner states and corresponds precisely to meaning structures used by the actor for interpreting the symbolic forms which constitute the questionnaire. The content of the message is invariant to the interpreter. The test of this assumption often consists of demonstrating to the reader that the respondents had no trouble filling out the questionnaire. To take this line of argument, the observer would have to show that the different types of respondents constitute equivalence classes with respect to their answers to the questions. This does not resolve the problem completely but does provide an operational test for the assumption that the content of each question is invariant to the respondent.

8   Fixed-choice questions supply the respondent with highly structured clues about their purpose and the answers expected. The 'forced' character of the responses severely restricts the possibility that the actor's perception and interpretation of the items will be problematic.

9   A detailed and analytic knowledge of common-sense meanings as used in everyday life becomes fundamental for the construction of fixed-choice questionnaires, but this knowledge does not guarantee that the content of the questions is invariant to the interpreter. Textbooks on methods merely urge or state flatly that the wording of the questions must be 'understandable' to the respondents and conform to their cultural or subcultural usage. But the textbooks and manuals say little about the structure of such everyday language and usage. The vocabulary used to tap the respondent's interpretations of different stimuli must be distinguished from the vocabulary employed by the social scientist for describing the actor's responses. Rules for translating the one into the other (and vice versa) are required. In order to predict the patterning in advance, some knowledge is required of how the hypothetical 'inner states' of the respondent are linked to the way he decodes the meaning of the question (its content) and how he decides the appropriate fixed-choice response. But the actor's vocabulary, with its common-sense meaning structures,

constitutes, in an important sense, a separate province of meaning from the hypothetical 'inner states' of the actor. This would be the case if the content of the message were invariant to the interpreter. . . .

The correspondence between the hypothetical world inferred from questionnaire items and actual behavior of the actor remains an open empirical problem. Questionnaire items which seek to measure values, attitudes, norms, and the like tend to ignore the emergent, innovational and problematic character of everyday life by imposing a deterministic 'grid' on it with its fixed-choice structure. . . .

Questionnaire items become 'frozen' clock-time slices of hypothetically defined situations. The fixed-choice questionnaire provides standardized propositions (stimuli), from the point of view of the researcher, but begs all of the relevant questions posed by language and meaning, treats the 'rules' or norms as self-evident, and eliminates the problem of situational definitions by a static conception of role-taking. Questionnaire responses are like the punched holes of an IBM card; the meanings and rules for their creation and interpretation are not to be found in them *per se* or in aggregates of them, but rather in their differential perceptions and interpretations which produced the researcher's decision in composing them and the respondent's perception and interpretation of the action scene in answering them. . . .

If some form of fixed-choice questionnaire items are ever to serve as useful operational definitions of sociological concepts, they will have to be constructed in such a way that the structure of everyday life experience and conduct is reflected in them. We must be able to demonstrate a correspondence between the structure of social action (cultural meanings, their assignment in situational contexts, the role-taking process) and the items intended as operational definitions thereof. Unless this correspondence is achieved, our findings will reflect our inadequate methods and not generate theoretically defensible propositions.

Chapter 23

Cathie Marsh

THE CRITICS OF SURVEYS

From *The Survey Method: The Contribution of Surveys to Sociological Explanation*, London: Allen and Unwin (1982).

. . .

THERE ARE THREE PROMINENT critics who have concerned themselves in different ways with measurement problems in surveys, Cicourel, Blumer and Phillips.

Cicourel, in the first chapter of *Method and Measurement* (1964), gives an extremely stringent set of rules for how variables should be constructed. Using the language of measurement derived from psychophysics, he argues that scientific models should be explicit axiomatic theories where the relations between the variables should have a functional form isomorphic to some mathematical system. As he quite correctly notes, explicit theories of this precision are never found in the social sciences. His criticism is directed against attempts to construct a scale with ordinal and interval properties from social data; you have to be able to prove that the thing that you are measuring has the properties that you are trying to measure, rather than just assume that it does. He calls this literal measurement as opposed to measurement by fiat. He rightly notes that some techniques of scaling impose unidimensionality rather than demonstrate its existence, but does not acknowledge the fact that there are other techniques which aim to test this very assumption. The reason why survey research fails to be scientific in his terms is not because his rules are ridiculously stringent, of course, but because social life is mediated through shared meanings.

Cicourel seems shocked to discover that social scientists, when they develop their scales and variables, are not merely reflecting the properties of social phenomena objectively and literally in their measures, but using a commonsense understanding of the meaning of this act or institution for the actors involved. There are several ways to approach these social meanings in a reliable fashion in a survey. There are some situations in which one can ask people for their reasons directly. There are some subjective variables which can be measured quite successfully. It is possible for outsiders to reliably agree on the meaningfulness of events. These solutions all call for careful and painstaking piloting, but Cicourel seems to imagine that the need for piloting proves his point that the social researcher cannot assume that the commonsense meanings are common to the subjects and the researcher.

This argument has had a popularity among social scientists that I have never been able to fully comprehend. This book is still the most popular book on the reading lists of methodology courses in British universities (Marsh 1979); my heart sinks when I try to imagine what students make of the rather tortured arguments. It is cited in support of the view that surveys have inherent positivistic flaws by those who would consider Cicourel's demand for rigorous measurement of this type even more positivistic. His remarks have force when directed to some attempts at deriving ordinal or interval scales from social data; they also have force with regard to the many surveys that are performed without adequate pretesting and piloting. Not all survey research is of this type, but even if it were, Cicourel would not be able to argue that it has to be that way. One single counter example would be enough to knock his card-house down.

Other critics have focused attention on the problem of interpreting the very 'obvious' variables that survey researchers use. One frequently cited critic is the symbolic interactionist, Herbert Blumer. In two key articles in the 1950s attacking contemporary views of social theory, he argued that until the variables that were being used in the theoretical endeavours were what he called 'generic' variables, nothing interesting would ensue (Blumer 1954 and 1956). Blumer held that we should not be trying to correlate observables, but showing the relationship of one basic attribute of social life to another. He cites as an example the concept of age. When we discover that age is related to some attitude, we need to know, not that age was defined as the answer to the question 'How old were you on your last birthday?', but rather whether the important thing about this correlation is the effect of stage in the life-cycle, generation membership, or epoch (Berger 1960). Blumer is convinced that survey variables will never be able to capture the 'intimate and inner-moving complex of meanings' which underly social processes, but Lazarsfeld or Rosenberg would have responded by suggesting either that the complex variables should be broken down into their components or that intervening variables should be introduced to delineate how any independent variable is producing its effect.

One important derivation of these arguments has been a criticism of the use of structured questionnaires. The first thing to say is that criticisms of questionnaires alone cannot damn surveys as a whole, for questionnaires are not the only systematic method of data collection. Anthropologists have investigated the existence of cultural universals by coding features of various societies (Murdock 1967). Sociologists of the media have made correlations between different factors coded from magazines (Funkhouser 1973). There have been studies of police behaviour where the unit of analysis was the police–citizen interaction and where the method of collecting the data was observation, not interview (Reiss 1971). In situations where it was not possible to conduct structured interviews, researchers have coded the information that they needed afterwards from tape-recordings of the interviews (Brown and Harris 1978). So the criticism of surveys that equates them with structured questionnaires is just ignorant. (However, if you have ever had to go through even a small number of tape-recorded interviews, transcribe them and then code them, you begin to realise why structured questions are so useful when they can be justified. This is why that is the most common way of collecting data.)

But it must be said that structured questionnaires are used too readily, and with insufficient thought; many, perhaps a majority, are inadequately designed and piloted, and, too often for comfort, are not an appropriate way of collecting the information that was required for the problem at hand. It is a damning reflection on survey research as currently practised that no book exists specifically to guide researchers through the pretesting and pilot stages of a survey.

There are huge difficulties with standardised question-wording, but we should note, in passing, the irony of surveys getting blamed for the difficulties that arise in asking questions which are sensitive to minor changes in wording; surveys have highlighted a problem that must exist in any form of data collection which relies upon the answers to questions, and it is quite mistaken to assume that anything less problematic ensues from more informal 'negotiated' interactions in a pub over a pint of beer. Many of the subtle meanings in different adverbial qualifiers, for example, have only been discovered through their use in survey research and through experimenting with different forms of wording in a split-ballot (Bartram and Yelding 1973), so there is no reason to suppose that a 'very' uttered in a pub is any less problematic. . . .

Research into the effects of different forms of question-wording has been pitifully meagre, until recently. Now researchers in both Britain (Kalton *et al.* 1978) and in the USA (Schuman and Presser 1981; Bradburn and Sudman 1979) are investigating these problems systematically. The results of this research . . . [show] the various ways in which the social context of the interview and the task required of the respondent have an impact on the type of responses that are given. This research will not enable us to remove these effects . . . but should improve our understanding of the interview as a process of social interaction and enable us to design interviews which achieve higher degrees of communication between the interviewer and the respondent. Reactivity is a fact of life in social research. We cannot get away from the problems by . . . blaming the respondent to the question when she makes a 'response error'.

Critics of interviews, however, have frequently gone much further than this in their criticism of structured questionnaires. Instead of conducting the painstaking research required to pin these problems down, some critics have instead proposed that we abandon this attempt to get at the social world, and indeed 'abandon method'. The development of the ideas in two books by Derek Phillips is a good case in point of this kind of thinking. In his earlier book, *Knowledge from What?* (1971), Phillips reviews some of the problems that have been shown to exist in communication in interviews. He reminds us that attributes of the interviewer can have their effect on responses given to this interviewer (although he is somewhat selective in his reporting of the literature, and does not review the findings of many who have concluded that interviewer characteristics are not an important source of difficulty in interviewing). Attributes of the subject may lead to problems, especially when the subject tries to please the interviewer, or is apprehensive about the likelihood of an evaluation of performance resulting from the responses given in interviews, or tends to agree to anything the interviewer says. Human beings need social approval, not just for themselves as people, but also for the views that they hold. The physical setting of the research can have important effects on responses, claims Phillips (although here again his evidence is weak and has not generally been borne out). And perhaps most importantly, respondents have expectations of what is required of them, and will try to get clues about what it is that the interviewer or researcher expects.

In this first book, Phillips argues quite plausibly that interviews are often used when they are not the most appropriate method of data collection, but he concedes that there are occasions when they are the best way of collecting information – when details of past activities, private activities, motives, beliefs, or attitudes are under study (a long list!). They generate data that is standardised, amenable to statistical treatment and can be generalised. If triangulated with other methods they have their uses. But by the time he wrote *Abandoning Method* (1973), a curious cocktail of Kuhn, Winch, Wittgenstein and Feyerabend was having an effect on him, and he concludes that social scientists, being no special breed of human beings, should stop trying to pretend that they have any peculiar claim to social knowledge, and should rely on the method of introspection, and try to look at the world 'through their own eyes' rather than through the scientific instruments which are currently clouding their vision. In effect we are back to the ridiculous idea that it is possible to perceive the world without the instruments of perception.

. . . In *Method and Measurement* . . . [Cicourel's] chapter on the use of fixed format questionnaires [states] 'Standardised questions with fixed-choice answers provide a solution to the problem of meaning simply by ignoring it'; survey researchers treat the meaning of events and situations as 'self-evident'. Some clearly do, but any reader who thinks this is true for the entire class of survey researchers should turn now to chapter 5 and read the account of the two years George Brown and his team spent designing scales which could assess the threat associated with events that happened in their subjects' lives.[1] Cicourel elaborates (1964: 109–11) nine rules which would need to apply before one could treat the results of fixed questions as meaningfully valid.

1   Every response would have to be explicable theoretically.
2   Pretests would have to have been done.
3   The social researcher would have to know the situation so well that the responses to questionnaire items could be read as indicators of a social process.
4   Question and response would have to use familiar language the meaning of which was not to be altered by context.
5   Clock time must agree with actor's experience of time.
6   Meanings of questions would have to be understood identically.
7   Researchers need a theory of meaning to show how (4) and (6) have been achieved.

[1 Editor's note: See Brown and Harris (1978).]

8   The forced nature of the questions would have to be removed.
9   It is not just enough to say that the words must be understandable but the meanings which respondents have must be translated to the social scientist's language by means of invariant correspondences.

There are two themes underlining these rules. The first is perfectly acceptable, namely, that all the small decisions about coding and grouping that are made in the course of the research should (a) be recorded and (b) be defended according to some theoretical rationale. To the extent that Cicourel can be read as arguing for a much greater discussion of these points of detail, his contribution could be very positive. But his insistence that the questions should be understood identically and not open to different interpretation according to 'particular relevance structures' is much more problematic. He is not just asking for unambiguous questions; every textbook that has ever been written on questionnaire design suggests that this is a good aim. When treating people's beliefs and attitudes, there is a very thin line dividing the meaning people endow social objects with and their feelings about them. When you ask people their attitudes to the EEC, they are *not* all really responding to the same stimulus, because they all have different associations with this object. The researcher will be keen to discover precisely how views of the EEC vary according to 'particular relevance structures', if I understand the term correctly. And one interesting method of eliciting the assumptions respondents make about events and institutions is to probe precisely what they mean by and associate with particular stimuli. Stressing the need for invariant meanings capable of being coded by explicit literal rules of correspondence is effectively saying that this type of research is simply impossible, until indeed the basic categories of daily life *have* been clarified and their numerical properties ordered axiomatically, whatever he says he is arguing.

Structured questionnaires are not the only way of collecting systematic information from a cross-section of cases, but they constitute a very popular way of doing so. They always run into difficulties with unanticipated definitions and responses, as Cicourel points out, so, to succeed, they rely on very careful piloting (for a painstaking example from the National Readership Survey, see Belson 1968). Neither do they have a monopoly on the problems of meaningfulness of social action. They have problems of their own which require more thought and research than they have been given to date. But discussions like this are cited in defence of the case that the problems are insurmountable. Certainly, Cicourel never went on to show how it could be done, or to elaborate a theory of meaning which could achieve his fourth and sixth rules.

References

Bartram, P. and Yelding, D. (1973) 'The development of an empirical method of selecting phrases used in verbal rating scales: a report on a recent experiment', *Journal of the Market Research Society*, 15 (3), July, pp. 156–9.

Belson, W.A. (1968) 'Respondent understanding of survey questions', *Polls*, 3 (4), pp. 1–10.

Berger, B. (1960) 'How long is a generation?', *British Journal of Sociology*, vol. xi, March, pp. 10–23.

Blumer, H. (1954) 'What is wrong with social theory?', *American Sociological Review*, 119, pp. 3–10.

—— (1956) 'Sociological analysis and the variable', *American Sociological Review*, 21, pp. 683–90.

Bradburn, N.M., Sudman, S. and associates (1979) *Improving Interview Method and Questionnaire Design: Response Effects to Threatening Questions in Survey Research*, San Francisco: Jossey-Bass.

Brown, G.W. and Harris, T. (1978) *The Social Origins of Depression: A Study of Psychiatric Disorder in Women*, London: Tavistock.

Cicourel, A.V. (1964) *Method and Measurement in Sociology*, Glencoe, Ill.: Free Press.

Funkhouser, G.R. (1973) 'The issues of the sixties', *Public Opinion Quarterly*, 37 (1), Spring, pp. 62–75.

Kalton, G., Collins, M. and Brook, L. (1978) 'Experiments in wording opinion questions', *Applied Statistics*, 27 (2), pp. 149–161.

Marsh, C. (1979) 'Social sciences methods bibliography: British Universities 1978', Cambridge: Social and Political Sciences Committee, University of Cambridge, mimeo.

Murdock, G.P. (1967) *Social Structure*, New York: Free Press.

Phillips, D.L. (1971) *Knowledge from What? Theories and Methods in Social Research*, Chicago: Rand McNally.

—— (1973) *Abandoning Method: Sociological Studies in Methodology*, London: Jossey-Bass.

Reiss, A.J. (1971) 'Systematic observation of natural social phenomena', in H. Costner (ed.), *Sociological Methodology*, San Francisco: Jossey-Bass, pp. 1–33.

Schuman, H. and Presser, S. (1981) *Questions and Answers*, New York: Academic Press.

Chapter 24

Hanneke Houtkoop-Steenstra

QUALITY OF LIFE ASSESSMENT INTERVIEWS

From *Interaction and the Standardised Survey Interview,* Cambridge: Cambridge University Press (2000).

IN THIS CHAPTER WE will study a number of Quality of Life assessment interviews with mildly learning-disabled persons in order to see how the interviewers deal with the scripted questions. . . . The focus in this chapter is on the ways the interviewers revise and repair scripted questions. I will show that the interviewers produce responses that are (at least) questionable in terms of validity. I will also show that the questionnaire that is used in these interviews does not suit the respondents of the survey. It fails because it creates interactional problems, and the interviewers' attempts to compensate for these problems lead to systematic biasing of the results . . .

Psychometrically valid questions

In the Quality of Life questionnaire under consideration, each item of the script consists of a question and three (sometimes four) response options from which the respondent is to choose the answer that matches his or her condition or situation. The format of the pen-and-paper questionnaire (held by the interviewer) looks like this:

Questions	Answer alternatives		record here
	3 points	2 points	1 point
1 Overall, would	Brings out the	Treats you like	Doesn't give –
you say that life	best in you?	everybody else?	you a chance?
2 How much fun	Lots	Some	Not much –
and enjoyment			
do you get out			
of life?			
–			
–			
–			
40			

Figure 24.1 Items from the Quality of Life questionnaire.

Each question is followed by response options, and the interviewer is supposed to read out the entire text. Note that the first option is always the most positive one; that is to say, it accumulates three points towards an end score, and a higher end score indicates higher quality of life.

The explicit instructions for the interviewer printed on the cover sheet of the questionnaire are 'When reading the items, pay close attention to the exact wording.' The questionnaire does attempt to be responsive to its target group, however, and acknowledges that cognitive difficulties may present themselves, which would require interviewers to paraphrase the question and to repeat it 'to ensure the respondent's understanding of the item content.' However, no instructions are given on how to do so. We shall see how this allowable paraphrasis and repetition comes out in practice.

Third-turn repair: presenting the scripted text as an optimistic yes–no question

Many of these respondents display that they do not understand the purpose of the question. When an interviewer reads out the scripted text, a respondent is expected to select one of the response options being presented to him or her. However, these respondents rarely follow this implicit response instruction.

How do the interviewers deal with this lack of understanding? . . . In the fragment below we find a situation in which the initial [question] + [three response options] is met with some non-appropriate material from the respondent. The interviewer then revises the original question into a yes–no question in which the 'yes' option is the most positive alternative:

Question 30
Overall, would you say that your life is:
Free?
Somewhat planned for you?
Cannot usually do what you want?

(5) Quality of Life interview

1	I.	right (0.2) ↑o:k (0.2) (w'd) ↑you ↓say that
2		your ↑li:fe is (0.5) ↑free
3		(0.8)
4		or do the ↑sta:ff sometimes ↓plan things for ↑you
5		(0.8)
6		or you ↑can't do what you want to d↓::o.
7		(0.8)
8	R.	(sometimes I) (0.2) I ↑shout an' (0.2)
9		(start screaming)
10	I.	↓o::hh ↑dea::r ↑do ↑you > ↑hehh hehh <
11		↓hehh (0.5) hh
12		(0.8)
13	R.	(ch- ch-) ↑come he↓::re (.) ⌈ ( )
14	I.	⌊ ↑ oh is that ↑y'r cat
15		(0.5)
16		y'r ↑cat's come ↑ho↓me
17		(0.5)
18		↑so can you usually ↑do what you ↓want to do
19		Ei-Eileen?
20	R.	↑ye:s (I can) ↑ye:s ( )

The interviewer delivers the scripted question and its response options in lines 1–6. Rather than choosing one of the three options, the respondent produces talk that does not explicitly choose among the alternatives. After both the interviewer and the respondent talk about the cat in lines 10–14, the interviewer re-asks the initial question and response options as a yes–no question: '↑so can you usually ↑do what you ↓ want to do Ei-Eileen?' in line 18–19. The interviewer chooses the optimistic version when rephrasing the question, which is then confirmed by the respondent: '↑ye:s (I can) ↑ ye:s ( ).' The interviewer then moves on to the next question. . . .

Interviewers reformulating unclear talk

. . . Interviewers use this method in instances where the respondent's post-question talk cannot be interpreted as an appropriate answer to the prior question. This method is also used when the respondent's answer does not clearly match one of the pre-coded response options. I refer to both types of talk as 'unclear talk' or 'non-answers,' and they will be marked in the fragments with an asterisk. Here is an example: . . .

Question 22
Who decides how you spend your money?
I do.
I do, with assistance from others.
Someone else decides.

(10) Quality of Life interview

1	I.	who decides how you spend your ↓ money?
2		(2.0)
3	R.	°well° =
4	I.	= d'you make your ↓own mind up?
5		(d') ↑staff help you or
6		(0.2)
7	R.	if I go out?
8	I.	yeh (0.8) (ts-)
9	R.*	( ) to Mc↑Donald's to: ( )
10		cup of tea an' that =
11	I.	= mhm
12	R.*	and e:r (0.2) ham↑burger
13	I.	yea:h
14	R.*	an' ↓chips
15	I.	m↑hm
16		(0.8)
17	R.*	and ( ) (↑they) comes out with (0.2)
18		( ) with a (saucepan)
19		(0.2)
20	I.	r(h)ight
21	R.*	(y'see) see ( ) for ↓tea
22		he said ↑right yes you can ↑'ave one
23	I.	↑right (0.2) so ↑you decide how you spend
24		your money =
25	R.	= yes
26	I.	yeh?
27		(2.0)
28	I.	°o↑k.°

In response to the question in line 1, 'Who decides how you spend your ↓money?' when going out, the respondent reports going to McDonald's and having tea, a hamburger and chips. The interviewer treats this talk as if the gist of it would make an appropriate answer to the question: '↑right (0.2) so ↑you decide how you spend your money' in line 23. This is confirmed by the respondent.

Note, as mentioned above, that the answer receipt in line 23 begins with a 'so,' which marks the utterance as a conclusion, and that the utterance is structured using declarative syntax. Declarative questions are treated by recipients as requests for confirmation and tend to be confirmed rather than disconfirmed.

Questions are structured in a declarative syntax when the speaker has good reason to believe the proposition is a fact. Therefore, the most likely response to a declarative question is an agreement/confirmation, as the question is built to occasion an agreeing response. In the rare case that a recipient disagrees with a declarative question, we might expect to find the disagreement put in a dispreferred turn format. In this set of data, however, the respondents never disagreed with a declarative question. When we look at declarative questions from a survey interview standpoint, we can say that they have the quality of being leading/directive questions. . . .

Why do interviewers choose the most positive answer in a situation in which it is unclear which answer the respondent really meant to give? It seems that the interviewers follow a procedural rule that says: select the most optimistic answer unless there are clear indications in the respondent's talk that another answer is more in accord with what the respondent means to report. The example below shows what happens in the rare case that the interviewer treats the talk as having such evidence:

Question 1
Overall, would you say that life:
Brings out the best in you?
Treats you like everybody else?
Doesn't give you a chance?

(20) Quality of Life interview

```
 1    I.      overall would you say ↑that ↓life brings
 2            ↑out (0.2) the ↓best in you
 3    R.      ↑yes
 4    I.      treats you like everybody ↓else =
 5    R.      = ↑yes:
 6    I.      or doesn't give a chance
 7    R.      eh:?
 8            (1.0)
 9    I.      what > do you think ↓that < (0.2) life (0.2)
10            brings out the best in ↑you
11            (0.5)
12          ⌈ or (   )
13    R.     ⌊ yeah the ↑best yeah yeah
14    I.      Right (0.5) so that's ↓your (0.2) your
15            answer ↑yeah ⌈ life >br< life brings
16    R.                  ⌊ ↑yes yes
17    I.      out the best in you does it?
18            ((some lines omitted))
19    I.      okay (0.2) so of those ↑three (0.2) you think
20            ↓life brings out the best it doesn't (0.2)
21            treat ↓you like everyone ↓else an ↑it (0.2)
22            it ↓doesn't (0.2) not give you a chance
23    R.      (hhh) =
24    I.      = yeah?
25            (2.0)
26    R.      °°(doesn't) give me a ↑chance°° .h ⌈ hh ((sniff))
27    I.                                         ⌊ okay
28            (1.0)
29            al↑right (0.5) next ↑one
```

The interviewer's pursuit of the response past the point at which the respondent has given a technically satisfactory response ('Yeah the ↑best yeah yeah') in line 13 eventually leads to a wholly contradictory response in line 26: '°°(doesn't)°° give me a ↑chance.' Which of these two answers is more genuine is, of course, not up to me to say, but what I want to point out is that the initial one (with which the interviewer would normally be satisfied) occurs in response to a projected no-problem question. . . .

Conclusion

Rather than providing the reader with quantitative information with regard to how often certain interactional procedures occur in this set of interviews and how they affect the final answer, I restrict myself to describing the procedures as such. I believe that I do not need numerical figures to say that this questionnaire is not an adequate instrument for validly assessing the quality of life of people with a learning disability. . . .

Chapter 25

R.C. Lewontin[1]

SEX, LIES, AND SOCIAL SCIENCE
(a book review with subsequent correspondence)

From *New York Review of Books* April 20th 1995, 24–29.

The Social Organization of Sexuality: Sexual Practices in the United States
by Edward O. Laumann, John H, Gagnon, Robert T. Michael, and Stuart Michaels.
University of Chicago Press, 718 pp. $49.95

. . .

THE FAMOUS STUDIES BY Alfred Kinsey and his collaborators in the 1940s and 1950s which have become part of everyday reference as 'The Kinsey Report,' the later research by Masters and Johnson, and the more popularly read work of Shere Hite,[2] are part of a long history of the science of 'sexology.' . . . The latest try at knowing who does what to whom, and how often, is the National Opinion Research Center's *The Social Organization of Sexuality* . . .

The problem for every sample survey is to know whether the answers are systematically untrue. Surveyed populations can lie in two ways. They can answer untruthfully, or they can fail to answer at all. This latter problem is known in the trade as 'non-response bias.' No matter how hard one tries, a significant portion of the sample that has been chosen will fail to respond, whether deliberately, through accident, lack of interest, or by force of circumstance.

---

1 Professor Lewontin notes that the material shown here is excerpted from a much longer article on methodological problems in sample surveys.
2 A.C. Kinsey, W.B. Pomeroy, and C.E. Martin, *Sexual Behavior in the Human Male* (Saunders, 1948); A.C. Kinsey, W.B. Pomeroy, C.E. Martin and P.H. Gebhard, *Sexual Behavior in the Human Female* (Saunders, 1953); W.H. Masters and V.E. Johnson, *Human Sexual Response* (Little Brown, 1966); S. Hite, *The Hite Report on Female Sexuality* (Knopf, 1979) and *The Hite Report on Male Sexuality* (Knopf, 1981).

It is almost always the case that those who do not respond are a non-random sample of those who are asked. Sometimes the problem is bad design. If you want to know how many women work outside the home you will not try to find out from a telephone survey that makes calls to people at home between nine AM and six PM. Much of the expertise of sample survey designers is precisely in knowing how to avoid such mistakes. The real problem is what to do about people who deliberately avoid answering the very questions you want to ask. Are people who refuse to cooperate with sex surveys more prudish than others, and therefore more conserva- tive than the population at large in their practices? Or are they more outrageous, yet sensitive to social disapprobation? Because they do not answer, and self-report is the only tool available, one can never know how serious the nonresponse bias may be. The best that can be done is to try to minimize the size of the non-responding population by nagging, reasoning, and bribing. The NHSLS team tried all these approaches and finally got a response of 79 percent (3,432 households) after repeated visits, telephone calls, videotapes, and bribes ranging from $10 to an occasional $100. The result was that there were now three sample populations, those who were cooperative from the start, those who were reluctant but finally gave in, and those who refused to the end.

From an analysis of the eager and the reluctant it was concluded that for most questions there was no difference between the two, but that still leaves in the air the unanswerable question about the sex lives of those who found $100 an insufficient payment for their true confessions. If I can believe even half of what I read in *The Social Organization of Sexuality*, my own sex life is conventional to the point of being old-fashioned and I wouldn't have cooperated for any price the NORC was likely to find in its budget.

Finally, we cannot avoid the main question, whether those who did respond, reluctantly or eagerly, told the truth. Far from avoiding the issue, the study team came back to this central question over and over, but their mode of answering it threatens the claim of sociology to be a science. At the outset they give the game away.

> In the absence of any means to validate directly the data collected in a survey of sexual behavior, these analyses assess data quality by checking for bias in the realized sample that might result from potential respondents' unwillingness to participate because of the subject matter, as well as by comparing results with other surveys. In every case, the results have greatly exceeded our expectations of what would be possible. They have gone a long way toward allaying our own concerns and skepticism. . . . [emphasis added].

In other words, people must be telling the truth because other people have said it before and they say the same thing even if reluctant to answer. That many people at many times have independently claimed to have been present at Satanic rituals or seen Our Lady descend at Fatima, and that some of these witnesses have been reluctant to testify at first, will presumably convince Professor Laumann and his colleagues of the reality of those events.

Again and again the problems of how we elicit the truth when both conscious and unconscious distortions may be suspected are dealt with disingenuously. Men and women were interviewed by women and men indiscriminately, and there was no attempt to match race of interviewer and race of the respondent.

> Will men and women respondents be affected in similar or different ways [by this mixing of sexes of interviewer and respondent]? Will people who have engaged in socially disapproved activities (e.g., same-gender sex, anal sex, prostitution, or extramarital sex relations) be equally likely to tell this to a male as to a female interviewer? At present, these questions remain unresolved empirically. . . . Although this issue is certainly important, . . . we did not expect the effect of gender matching to be especially large or substantively noteworthy. The experience and belief among NORC survey research professionals was that the quality of the interviewer was important but that it was not necessarily linked to gender or race.

In other words, they don't know and hope the problem will go away. While sex and race are 'master status' variables, 'organizing the pattern of social relationships,' apparently being interviewed about your sex life is not part of social relationships. Instead of investigating the problem, the team 'concentrated our time and money on recruiting and training the best interviewers we could find.' That meant three days of a 'large-scale' training session in Chicago.

Anyway, why should anyone lie on a questionnaire that was answered in a face-to-face interview with a total stranger? After all, complete confidentiality was observed. It is frightening to think that social science is in the hands of professionals who are so deaf to human nuance that they believe that people do not lie to themselves about the most freighted aspects of their own lives and that they have no interest in manipulating the impression that strangers have of them. Only such deafness can account for their acceptance, without the academic equivalent of a snicker, of the result of a NORC survey reporting that 45 percent of men between the ages of eighty and eighty-four still have sex with a partner.

It is not that the research team is totally unaware of sensitivities. In addition to about a hundred face-to-face interview questions, respondents were asked to fill out four short printed forms that were placed by them in sealed 'privacy' envelopes for later evaluation by someone other than the interviewer. Many of the questions were repetitions of questions asked in the personal interviews, following the common practice of checking on accuracy by asking the same question twice in different ways. Two matters were asked about, however, that were considered so jarring to the American psyche that the information was elicited only on the written forms: masturbation and total household income. Laumann et al. are not so deaf to American anxieties as it seemed.

There is, in fact, one way that the truth of the answers on a sex survey can be checked for internal consistency. A moment's reflection makes it clear that, discounting homosexual partners, the average number of sex partners reported by men must be equal to the average number reported by women. This is a variant on the economist Robert Solow's observation that the only law in economics is that the

number of sales must be equal to the number of purchases. Yet, in the NHSLS study;
and other studies like it, men report many more partners than women, roughly
75 percent more during the most recent five years of their lives. The reaction of the
authors to this discrepancy is startling. They list 'in no particular order' seven
possible explanations including that American men are having lots of sex out of the
country, or that a few women are having hundreds of partners (prostitutes are
probably underrepresented in an address sample, but prostitution was not regarded
as a 'master status' variable to be inquired about since presumably it is not a 'basic
concept of self-identity'). Our authors then say,

> We have not attempted to reconcile how much of the discrepancy that
> we observe can be explained by each of these seven logical possibilities,
> but we conjecture that the largest portion of the discrepancy rests with
> explanation 6.

Explanation 6 is that 'Either men may exaggerate or women may understate.' So, in
the single case where one can actually test the truth, the investigators themselves
think it most likely that people are telling themselves and others enormous lies. If
one takes the authors at their word, it would seem futile to take seriously the other
results of the study. The report that 5.3 percent of conventional Protestants, 3.3
percent of fundamentalists, 2.8 percent of Catholics, and 10.7 percent of the non-
religious have ever had a same-sex partner may show the effect of religion on
practice or it may be nothing but hypocrisy. What is billed as a study of 'Sexual
Practices in the United States' is, after all, a study of an indissoluble jumble of
practices, attitudes, personal myths and posturing.

The social scientist is in a difficult, if not impossible position. On the one
hand there is the temptation to see all of society as one's autobiography writ
large, surely not the path to general truth. On the other, there is the attempt to
be general and objective by pretending that one knows nothing about the
experience of being human, forcing the investigator to pretend that people usually
know and tell the truth about important issues, when we all know from our own
lives how impossible that is. How, then, can there be a 'social science'? The
answer, surely, is to be less ambitious and stop trying to make sociology into a
natural science although it is, indeed, the study of natural objects. There are some
things in the world that we will never know and many that we will never know
exactly. Each domain of phenomena has its characteristic grain of knowability.
Biology is not physics, because organisms are such complex physical objects, and
sociology is not biology because human societies are made by self-conscious
organisms. By pretending to a kind of knowledge that it cannot achieve, social
science can only engender the scorn of natural scientists and the cynicism of
humanists.

To the Editors:
We are puzzled by the review of our book, *The Social Organization of Sexuality* [NYR,
April 20], because it is professionally incompetent and motivated by such an evident
animus against the social sciences in general. . . .

The central premise of Lewontin's review is that people routinely and pervasively lie about sexual behavior – indeed, it would seem all aspects of their lives – and thus none of the data from our survey of 3,432 people can be taken seriously. But Lewontin relates no systematic empirical information to substantiate his claim. Rather, he relies on a set of rhetorical devices that tendentiously advance his assertions.

Lewontin opens the review with an argument based on a false analogy. He discusses at length the problems of credibility in autobiographical statements and then asserts the analogical equivalence of autobiography and the self-reports given in response to our questions. The reader by now is supposed to be thinking, 'I certainly would not tell anybody that I had sex with my spouse last night while clutching a yellow rubber ducky. I'd lie – at least about the rubber ducky.' But autobiography, by definition, involves the public disclosure of the identity of the person. This sets in train all the motivations to create a favorable self-image in the minds of others and perhaps some of the outcomes Lewontin asserts. In contrast, we went to great lengths to guarantee the privacy, confidentiality and anonymity of our respondents' answers as well as to provide a strong rationale for an individual to be candid and honest with us. We spent a great deal of time worrying about how we could check the reliability and honesty of our respondents' answers. While we readily admit that we were not always successful in securing full disclosure, his false analogy simply misses the point altogether.

Lewontin's next move is to provide an instance demonstrating the data's invalidity by discussing the large discrepancy between the average numbers of partners reported by men and women and the logical impossibility of such a situation assuming that they are recruiting their partners from a common pool. In the 52-page chapter devoted to the numbers of sex partners, we explicitly discuss (on p. 174) the undesirability of using averages (means) to summarize the central tendencies of distributions as skewed and narrowly concentrated (with long, unevenly distributed tails) as these are. In addition, we explore in considerable detail the reasons for this discrepancy. Lewontin argues that if we could not get this 'simple fact' right, it is evidence that all else is spurious. Error is a problem in all observations, how it is dealt with and its public recognition is the test of science. His decision to rest his case on this single issue without reference to its context forces us to conclude that he willfully misrepresented our analysis. . . .

Finally, we have Lewontin's discussion of our finding that 45 percent of men between the ages of 80 and 84 claim to have sex partners. He chuckles at our credulity in reporting such patent nonsense, being just one more instance of our hopeless gullibility of believing everything we are told by our respondents. Now this is a rather nice instance of his tendentious and misleading use of our data to support his central claim that everybody is lying about their sex lives. The survey in question, the General Social Survey (GSS), is a widely known, high-quality, regularly conducted survey that professionally knowledgeable people rely on for estimating social trends of various sorts. It is sponsored by the National Science Foundation and has been subjected to regular scientific peer review for some twenty years. To the professional social scientist, it is well known to be a household-based sample that excludes the *institutionalized* parts of the population. Any number of census and other highly regarded survey studies have also noted that, due to differential mortality and other factors, older women are progressively more likely to be living alone.

By age 70, about 70 percent of women report, in the GSS, no sex partners in the past year. Older men, in contrast, are far more likely to be living with someone – the sex ratio is increasingly in their favor so far as the surplus of older women to older men is concerned. It is therefore not at all surprising that noninstitutionalized men in their eighties – presumably healthy enough to be living on their own – would have a fair chance of reporting that they have a sex partner. We discuss at length in the book the different meanings of sexuality across age, time and social circumstance. We believe the answers are hardly likely to be crazed lies by sex-starved octogenarians who are posturing like teenagers for the edification of credulous social scientists.

The review is a pastiche of ill-informed personal opinion that makes unfounded claims of relevant scientific authority and expertise. Readers of *The New York Review of Books* deserve better.

Edward O. Laumann
John H. Gagnon
Robert T. Michael
Stuart Michaels

Department of Sociology
The University of Chicago
Chicago, Illinois

To the Editors:

In the course of Richard Lewontin's brilliant essay 'Sex, Lies, and Social Science' he remarks that if the study he reviewed is typical of American scientific sociology, then this discipline must be in 'deep trouble.' That's putting it mildly, American sociology has become a refuge for the academically challenged. Some universities have closed their sociology departments; many have decided the discipline merits little new money.

Yet mere stupidity cannot explain the analytic weaknesses of studies like the NORC sexuality project; nor do social scientists so very gainfully employed in such shops simply misunderstand the scientific enterprise. The difficulties with this research, like the larger troubles of sociology, are political. . . .

However, if Lewontin's exposé is just, he uses a meat cleaver where a scalpel would have served him better. Is quantifying social phenomena an inherent evil, as at points in his essay he seems to suggest? Lewontin surely wouldn't deny that the Census Bureau provides useful and necessary information. In principle, survey research has its uses, in revealing how people think about themselves. (I found it both interesting and cheering that 45 percent of men between the ages of 80 and 84 in the NORC study reported still having sex with a partner, even if the aged have confused fantasy with fact.) Method *per se* isn't the issue.

I wish Lewontin had put his attack in a larger historical context. From its origins in Social Darwinism and the Progressive movement, American sociology has struggled with the contrary claims of those afflicted with physics envy and researchers – whether deploying numbers or words – more engaged in the dilemmas of society. In that struggle, midwestern Protestant mandarins of positivist science often came into conflict with East Coast Jews who in turn wrestled with their own Marxist commitments; great quantitative researchers from abroad, like Paul Lazarsfeld at

Columbia, sought to disrupt the complacency of native bean counters. In the last twenty years, more interesting 'hard' sociological research has been done in medical, planning, and law schools, and better research on culture and society in the humanities departments, than in sociology departments. The *intellectual* enterprise of sociology is hardly represented by the dumbed-down study Lewontin rips apart.

What places like NORC command, like other reactionary enterprises, is money. To defend themselves, the minions of these institutions will undoubtedly attack Lewontin for being anti-empirical, which will miss exactly his point, that their brand of science represses trenchant social evidence. My word is that this repression is more than an academic evil. Sociology in its dumbed-down condition is emblematic of a society that doesn't want to know too much about itself.

Richard Sennett

New York University
New York City

R.C. Lewontin *replies*:

It should come as no surprise to the readers of *The New York Review* that the authors of *The Social Organization of Sexuality* did not like what I wrote. . . .

Our authors touch on the central methodological issue. It is their view that, although people may lie or exaggerate in autobiographies because they are trying to create a public persona, they will tell the truth in anonymous interviews; because there is no motivation to manipulate the impression that strangers have of us. Is it really true that quantitative sociologists are so divorced from introspection and so insensitive to social interactions that they take such a naive view of human behavior? . . .

First, Professor Laumann, people do not tell *themselves* the truth about their own lives. The need to create a satisfying narrative out of an inconsistent and often irrational and disappointing jumble of feelings and events leads each of us to write and rewrite our autobiographies inside our own heads, irrespective of whether anyone else is every privy to the story. Second, these stories, which we then mistake for the truth, become the basis for further conscious manipulation and manufacture when we have exchanges with other human beings. If the investigators at NORC really do not care what strangers think of them, then they are possessed of an insouciance and hauteur otherwise unknown in Western society. It is precisely in the interaction with strangers who are not part of their social network, and who will never intersect their lives again, that people feel most free to embroider their life stories, because they will never be caught out.

Laumann et al. try to minimize the impact of the observed discrepancy in the number of sexual partners reported by men and by women. There is an attempt at obfuscation in a remark by Laumann and his colleagues about averages not contain- ing as much information as more detailed frequency descriptions. True, but irrele- vant, because in their data men consistently report more partners across the entire frequency distribution. Anyway, Laumann et al. do not deny the discrepancy. Indeed it is they who brought it up and discussed it in the book, and it is they, not I, who offered as the most likely explanation that men 'exaggerate' and women 'minimize' their sexual promiscuity. Then they try to discount the impact of the discrepancy on the study as a whole. After all, it is just one false note, and we cannot expect perfection. People may lie or fantasize about how many sexual partners they have, but we can take everything else they say at face value.

But this neatly ignores the fact that this comparison provides the *only* internal check on consistency that the study allows. I nowhere claimed that 'all else is spurious,' but rather that we are left in the unfortunate position of not knowing what is true when our only test fails. . . .

While Laumann and his colleagues believe that men exaggerate while they are aged between eighteen and fifty-nine, they (backed by the peer review panels of the National Science Foundation) seem to have complete confidence in the frankness of octogenarians. Perhaps, as men contemplate their impending mortality, the dread of something after death makes lying about sex seem risky. We must, however, at least consider the alternative that affirming one's continued sexual prowess in great age is a form of whistling in the dark.

I have considerable sympathy for the position in which sociologists find themselves. They are asking about the most complex and difficult phenomena in the most complex and recalcitrant organisms, without that liberty to manipulate their objects of study which is enjoyed by natural scientists. . . .

Richard Sennett . . . is, of course, right when he insists that quantitative information is important in sociology. Data on birth, death, immigration, marriage, divorce, social class, neighborhood, causes of mortality and morbidity, occupations, wage rates, and many other variables are indispensable for sociological investigations. My 'meat cleaver' was never meant to sever those limbs from the body of knowledge. But it does not follow that collecting statistics, especially survey statistics with their utter ambiguity of interpretation, is sociology. . . . numbers can have no interpretation in themselves without a coherent narrative of social life. . . . Like it or not, there are a lot of questions that cannot be answered, and even more that cannot be answered exactly. There is nothing shameful in that admission.

To the Editors:
Professor Lewontin lobs grenades . . . with deadly effects on some of the fatter targets of social science method. Indeed, uncollaborated survey reports about sexual activity and other sensitive matters do deserve limited credence. Consequently our ignorance about private behavior is much greater than social scientists like to pretend. I do hope but do not expect that social scientists will add this book review to their reading lists in quantitative methods.

On a much smaller target, Professor Lewontin's aim is very slightly awry. Based on 1-to-1 mapping argument, he states that the average number of heterosexual partners of females should equal the average number for males. Well, actually not. One reason lies in the fact that members of the present cohort can have partners from earlier or later cohorts. As an artificial example, suppose there were equal numbers of males and females with equal life expectancy, each taking a single partner for life, but males mated with older females. Then because of young females not yet partnered, males would have a higher average ratio than females. (In fact, American males do report on average that they lose their virginity at lower ages than females.) Moreover, there are several other confounding influences: there are more females than males in the adult cohorts, females outlive males, and because of population growth newer cohorts are larger than older cohorts. Given that men claim 1.75 as many sex partners as women claim, Professor Lewontin and the books under review are probably correct to infer a severe reporting bias, but rigorous proof awaits a detailed quantitative argument.

And on a target of a middling size. I believe Professor Lewontin is too pessimistic about future possibilities for obtaining reasonably well-founded information about human behavior in private. There are many promising improvements in survey methods (admittedly, rather costly ones) that we have barely begun to try. Thus, while there is evidence that surveys of long term recollections are of limited value, diary and especially snapshot approaches are better (e.g. because they limit opportunities for self-deception). Also, we can sometimes gather data from multiple observers of a single private event (e.g. interviewing both sex partners separately). And we can set up experimental situations designed to bias responses one way or the other, (e.g. using an apparently opinionated interviewer) and see how far the responses can be manipulated.

At the same time we can develop more inside checks on survey data, like the sex partner ratio example discussed above. More usefully, we can develop outside checks, for example calibrated models that work back and forth between micro data about private behavior (e.g. unprotected intercourse) and observable data such as public consequences (e.g. births, abortions, and AIDS cases) or experimentally testable rates (e.g. conceptions per acts of unprotected intercourse). An existing practical example is the comparison of market survey data with eventual sales outcomes. . . . If and when we finally do find out how to ask the questions in ways that make the survey data consistent with the available public data, then I believe we will have a reasonable warrant to rely on the survey data.

David Burress

Research Economist
Institute for Public Policy and Business Research
University of Kansas
Lawrence, Kansas

R.C. Lewontin *replies:*
. . . Dr. Burress offers some suggestions for checking on the validity of survey responses, but they do not seem to help us. The idea that diaries will somehow reflect the truth of peoples' lives is extraordinary. Are diaries not meant for other eyes? Remember the Tolstoys who left their diaries open on each other's bedside tables. Even when diaries are only a form of talking to oneself, one may engage in an elaborate composition of a self-justificatory autobiography, much of it unconscious. Can he really demonstrate that diaries or even snapshots 'limit opportunities for self-deception.' Who took the picture and why? To what extent are our family records of smiling children and indulgent parents in the Piazza San Marco part of our construction of a wished for life? Burress does not tell us how the records of births, abortions, and AIDS can do more than tell us that some claims of virginity are not to be credited. It is important to distinguish acts that are public or leave public traces from those for which nothing but self-report is available. So, we know that people over-report church attendance because one can actually count the house, and nutritional surveys are notorious for their unreliability because it has been possible to paw through garbage to find out what people really

eat. But these examples raise the question of why it is worthwhile to do a sample survey in the first place, if the information can be obtained by direct observation. . . .

To the Editors:
Both Sennett and Lewontin focus on one particular piece of data reported by the NORC investigators as evidence for their accusations. This observation is that 45 percent of men between the ages of 80 and 85 report having sex with their partner. Both Sennett and Lewontin feel this is so obviously untrue that it calls into question the validity of the entire survey and the reports that were drawn from it.

Why do they think it is so obvious that this is a lie? Neither of them offers a single shred of empirical evidence that would support their doubt. They are in fact operating on the same unfortunate negative stereotype of aging that far too many Americans still hold – that aging is a period of sexlessness, silence and social irrelevance. In particular, sexuality in elderly men is viewed as either absent or, if present, with disgust as embodied in the phrase 'dirty old man.'

And yet part of the miracle of the dramatic increase in life expectancy that developed countries have witnessed in this century is that for many people old age is a much healthier condition than many of us could ever imagine. The 80- to 85-year-olds surveyed excluded those in institutions and therefore selected the healthiest of elderly men. Furthermore because of increased life expectancy of women compared to men at that age there are two to three times as many women as men, and active men are very much in demand. If Professors Lewontin or Sennett had chosen to heed their own admonitions and seek empirical support for their claims they might have checked the medical literature on sexual activity in the elderly. If they had done so they would have found that in one study of noninstitutionalized elderly men over 65 the prevalence of sexual activity was 73.8 percent in married men and 31.1 percent in unmarried men. Studies done at Duke University showed that 75 to 85 percent of men in their sixties and seventies maintained a continuing interest in sex. And an additional study of male veterans found, that even men in their nineties maintained sexual interest. Intercourse frequency declined from monthly in men in their sixties to less frequently but at least once a year for men in their seventies and older. And in up to 15 percent of elderly men followed longitudinally there was an increased level of sexual interest and activity at a certain point in old age such as after recovery from the grieving period of widowerhood. A recent study of 202 healthy upper middle-class men and women living in a residential retirement facility between the ages of 80 and 102 with a mean age of 86 found that 53 percent of the men had a sexual partner.

I hope that scholars who call for an alertness to problems of validity and accuracy in social science would consider their own biases before using unsupported stereotypes to criticize such a major piece of work as the NORC study.

Christine K. Cassel, M.D.

George Eisenberg Professor in Geriatrics
Professor of Medicine and Public Policy Studies
Studies University of Chicago
Chicago, Illinois

Richard Lewontin *replies:*

. . . My criticism of the NORC study certainly does not focus on the report of sexual activity by octogenarians, nor did I claim that it was sufficient to 'call into question the validity of the entire survey and the reports that were drawn from it.' [Dr. Cassel] has confused this issue with my discussion of the internal contradiction between the reports of men and women respondents. The data on old men was not part of the NORC study, but the result of one of their previous surveys, and it was mentioned because it illustrated the inconsistent standards of the NORC team, who claimed on the one hand that men between 18 and 65 exaggerated their sexual contacts, but, on the other, accepted the self-reports of 80 year olds.

Indeed, the empirical evidence that men between 80 and 85 lie about their sexual exploits is that younger men do. Or does Dr. Cassel share with Laumann et al. the view that only the young exaggerate? Nowhere in what I (or Sennett) wrote is there a single word that even suggests that aging is a 'period of silence and social irrelevance,' nor, for that matter, is the belief that old men exaggerate their sexual activity a claim for their 'sexlessness.' Dr. Cassel's citation of various studies from the 'medical literature' only illustrates again the lack of methodological care that characterizes the field. Unless, unknown to the rest of us, medical science has produced an electronic scanner or a blood test that will give an objective read-out of how many sex partners a man has had in the last year, studies like those cited by Cassel are just self-reports, offering nothing different than the NORC survey except smaller sample sizes, and less survey expertise. Calling it 'medical literature' is only a bit of propaganda meant to lend 'an air of verisimilitude to a bald and otherwise unconvincing narrative.' . . .

PART SIX

The limits of science

INTRODUCTION

SEVERAL OF THE READINGS in Part Five identified the attempt to transfer natural science methods to the study of the social world as the source of many of the difficulties faced by social researchers. Wallace (reading 4) is perhaps the strongest advocate of this in this book. Lewontin and Sennett (in reading 25) are perhaps the most explicit critics. Yet there have long existed critical accounts of the assumptions made by natural scientists about their methods, and these acquired a particular importance for social 'scientists' concerned to develop alternative approaches. Feyerabend (reading 26) and Kuhn (reading 27) are perhaps the best known of these philosophers of science. Their central contribution (whether they intended this or not) was to make relativism 'thinkable' for scientists, opening a door for a host of alternative perspectives in social research.

The title of Feyerabend's book, *Against Method*, is a provocative signal. He outlines an 'anarchistic methodology' in which the main principle is that 'anything goes' in science. Universal methodological principles only inhibit the creativity of the scientist whom Feyerabend (quoting Einstein) depicts as an 'unscrupulous opportunist'. The greatest developments in science, he claims, occurred when scientists decided to break methodological rules.

Kuhn, like Feyerabend, draws on the history of science to make his points, similarly challenging textbook accounts of scientific method. He deconstructs the distinction between 'myth' and scientific 'truth', saying that this is simply the product of hindsight. Scientific truth ('normal' science) is an agreement reached by scientists at a particular time and place, and scientific revolutions occur from time to time, replacing systems of 'truth' (or 'paradigms') that can no longer suppress discrepancies. Thus science is not a gradual process of accumulation, but a series of revolutions in which systems of thought replace one another at crisis points.

Swales (reading 28) is not a philosopher of science, but a linguist interested in the history of scientific writing. His account of the development of the research article illustrates the way early scientists constructed normal scientific practice. An essential aspect of such writing was to make it appear that facts spoke 'for themselves', and that the writing was an objective report of a scientific procedure, rather than one of several possible versions. A variety of linguistic techniques used in modern scientific papers, designed to promote reader's trust in the author, are outlined by Swales.

DISCUSSION POINTS

- Compare Feyerabend's depiction of scientific activity with Billig's (reading 1) account of methodology versus scholarship. What similarities and differences do you perceive between Billig's 'scholar' and Feyerabend's preferred way of doing science? Does Feyerabend really mean that *anything* goes? How might this translate into social research practice?
- Is Kuhn a relativist (believing that truth is relative to the perspective of the beholder), or is he a Popperian falsificationist (reading 5)? Can you identify different paradigms in your own subject discipline? Is there a 'normal science' paradigm in your own discipline at present?
- Examine a research report in a journal in your own subject discipline. Can you detect any of the features Swales mentions? Are there features designed to appeal to the particular discipline in which the article is located? To what extent do social researchers *construct* (rather than reveal) their 'truths' in their approach to writing?

FURTHER READING

Medawar P. (1991; first published 1963) 'Is the scientific paper a fraud?' in Medawar, P. (ed.) *The Threat and the Glory*, Oxford: Oxford University Press.

Nola, R. and Sankey, H. (2000) *After Popper, Kuhn and Feyerabend: Recent Issues in Theories of Scientific Method*, Dordrecht: Kluwer Academic.

Yearley, S. (1981) 'Textual persuasion: the role of social accounting in the construction of scientific arguments', *Philosophy of Science* 11: 409–435.

Chapter 26

Paul Feyerabend

AGAINST METHOD

From *Against Method,* London: New Left Review Editions (1975).

Science is an essentially anarchistic enterprise: theoretical anarchism is more humanitarian and more likely to encourage progress than its law-and-order alternatives.

THE FOLLOWING ESSAY IS written in the conviction that *anarchism*, while perhaps not the most attractive *political* philosophy, is certainly excellent medicine for *epistemology*, and for the *philosophy of science*.

The reason is not difficult to find.

'History generally, and the history of revolutions in particular, is always richer in content, more varied, more many-sided, more lively and subtle than even' the best historian and the best methodologist can imagine.[1] History is full of 'accidents and conjunctures and curious juxtapositions of events'[2] and it demonstrates to us the 'complexity of human change and the unpredictable character of the ultimate consequences of any given act or decision of men'.[3] Are we really to believe that the naive and simple-minded rules which methodologists take as their guide are capable of accounting for such a 'maze of interactions'?[4] And is it not clear that successful *participation* in a process of this kind is possible only for a ruthless opportunist who is

---

1 . . . V. I. Lenin, 'Left-Wing Communism – An Infantile Disorder', *Selected Works*, vol. 3, London, 1967, p. 401. Lenin is addressing parties and revolutionary vanguards rather than scientists and methodologists; the lesson, however, is the same, cf. footnote 5.

2 Herbert Butterfield, *The Whig Interpretation of History*, New York, 1965, p. 66.

3 ibid., p. 21.

4 ibid., p. 25. . . .

not tied to any particular philosophy and who adopts whatever procedure seems to fit the occasion?

This is indeed the conclusion that has been drawn by intelligent and thoughtful observers. 'Two very important practical conclusions follow from this [character of the historical process],' writes Lenin,[5] continuing the passage from which I have just quoted. 'First, that in order to fulfil its task, the revolutionary class [i.e. the class of those who want to change either a part of society such as science, or society as a whole] must be able to master *all* forms or aspects of social activity without exception [it must be able to understand, and to apply, not only one particular methodology, but any methodology, and any variation thereof it can imagine] . . .; second [it] must be ready to pass from one to another in the quickest and most unexpected manner.' 'The external conditions,' writes Einstein,[6] 'which are set for [the scientist] by the facts of experience do not permit him to let himself be too much restricted, in the construction of his conceptual world, by the adherence to an epistemological system. He therefore, must appear to the systematic epistemologist as a type of unscrupulous opportunist. . . .' A complex medium containing surprising and unforeseen developments demands complex procedures and defies analysis on the basis of rules which have been set up in advance and without regard to the ever-changing conditions of history.

Now it is, of course, possible to simplify the medium in which a scientist works by simplifying its main actors. The history of science, after all, does not just consist of facts and conclusions drawn from facts. It also contains ideas, interpretations of facts, problems created by conflicting interpretations, mistakes, and so on. On closer analysis we even find that science knows no 'bare facts' at all but that the 'facts' that enter our knowledge are already viewed in a certain way and are, therefore, essentially ideational. This being the case, the history of science will be as complex, chaotic, full of mistakes, and entertaining as the ideas it contains, and these ideas in turn will be as complex, chaotic, full of mistakes, and entertaining as are the minds of those who invented them. Conversely, a little brainwashing will go a long way in making the history of science duller, simpler, more uniform, more 'objective' and more easily accessible to treatment by strict and unchangeable rules.

Scientific education as we know it today has precisely this aim. It simplifies 'science' by simplifying its participants: first, a domain of research is defined. The domain is separated from the rest of history (physics, for example, is separated from metaphysics and from theology) and given a 'logic' of its own. A thorough training in such a 'logic' then conditions those working in the domain; it makes *their actions* more uniform and it freezes large parts of the *historical process* as well. Stable 'facts' arise and persevere despite the vicissitudes of history. An essential part of the training that makes such facts appear consists in the attempt to inhibit intuitions that might lead to a blurring of boundaries. A person's religion, for example, or his

---

5   ibid. We see here very clearly how a few substitutions can turn a political lesson into a lesson for *methodology*. This is not at all surprising. Methodology and politics are both means for moving from one historical stage to another. The only difference is that the standard methodologies disregard the fact that history constantly produces new features. We also see how an individual, such as Lenin, who is not intimidated by traditional boundaries and whose thought is not tied to the ideology of a profession, can give useful advice to everyone, philosophers of science included.

6   Albert Einstein, *Albert Einstein: Philosopher Scientist*, ed. P. A. Schilpp, New York, 1951, pp. 683f.

metaphysics, or his sense of humour (his *natural* sense of humour and not the inbred and always rather nasty kind of jocularity one finds in specialized professions) must not have the slightest connection with his scientific activity. His imagination is restrained, and even his language ceases to be his own. This is again reflected in the nature of scientific 'facts' which are experienced as being independent of opinion, belief, and cultural background.

It is thus *possible* to create a tradition that is held together by strict rules, and that is also successful to some extent. But is it *desirable* to support such a tradition to the exclusion of everything else? Should we transfer to it the sole rights for dealing in knowledge, so that any result that has been obtained by other methods is at once ruled out of court? This is the question I intend to ask in the present essay. And to this question my answer will be a firm and resounding NO.

There are two reasons why such an answer seems to be appropriate. The first reason is that the world which we want to explore is a largely unknown entity. We must, therefore, keep our options open and we must not restrict ourselves in advance. Epistemological prescriptions may look splendid when compared with other epistemological prescriptions, or with general principles – but who can guarantee that they are the best way to discover, not just a few isolated 'facts', but also some deep-lying secrets of nature? The second reason is that a scientific education as described above (and as practised in our schools) cannot be reconciled with a humanitarian attitude. It is in conflict 'with the cultivation of individuality which alone produces, or can produce, well-developed human beings'[7]; it 'maims by compression, like a Chinese lady's foot, every part of human nature which stands out prominently, and tends to make a person markedly different in outline'[8] from the ideals of rationality that happen to be fashionable in science, or in the philosophy of science. The attempt to increase liberty, to lead a full and rewarding life, and the corresponding attempt to discover the secrets of nature and of man entails, therefore, the rejection of all universal standards and of all rigid traditions. . . .

There are certainly some people to whom this is 'not so clear'. Let us, therefore, start with our outline of an anarchistic methodology and a corresponding anarchistic science. There is no need to fear that the diminished concern for law and order in science and society that characterizes an anarchism of this kind will lead to chaos. The human nervous system is too well organized for that. There may, of course, come a time when it will be necessary to give reason a temporary advantage and when it will be wise to defend its rules to the exclusion of everything else. I do not think that we are living in such a time today.

*

This is shown both by an examination of historical episodes and by an abstract analysis of the relation between idea and action. The only principle that does not inhibit progress is: anything goes.

The idea of a method that contains firm, unchanging, and absolutely binding principles for conducting the business of science meets considerable difficulty when

---

7 John Stuart Mill, 'On Liberty', *The Philosophy of John Stuart Mill*, ed. Marshall Cohen, New York, 1961, p. 258.
8 ibid., p. 265.

confronted with the results of historical research. We find then, that there is not a single rule, however plausible, and however firmly grounded in epistemology, that is not violated at some time or other. It becomes evident that such violations are not accidental events, they are not results of insufficient knowledge or of inattention which might have been avoided. On the contrary, we see that they are necessary for progress. Indeed, one of the most striking features of recent discussions in the history and philosophy of science is the realization that events and developments, . . . occurred only because some thinkers either *decided* not to be bound by certain 'obvious' methodological rules, or because they *unwittingly broke* them.

This liberal practice, I repeat, is not just a *fact* of the history of science. It is both reasonable and *absolutely necessary* for the growth of knowledge. More specifically, one can show the following: given any rule, however 'fundamental' or 'necessary' for science, there are always circumstances when it is advisable not only to ignore the rule, but to adopt its opposite. . . .

It is clear, then, that the idea of a fixed method, or of a fixed theory of rationality, rests on too naive a view of man and his social surroundings. To those who look at the rich material provided by history, and who are not intent on impoverishing it in order to please their lower instincts, their craving for intellectual security in the form of clarity, precision, 'objectivity', 'truth', it will become clear that there is only *one* principle that can be defended under *all* circumstances and in *all* stages of human development. It is the principle: *anything goes.*

Chapter 27

Thomas S. Kuhn

THE STRUCTURE OF SCIENTIFIC REVOLUTIONS

From *The Structure of Scientific Revolutions* (2nd edition), Chicago: University of Chicago Press (1970).

HISTORY, IF VIEWED AS a repository for more than anecdote or chronology, could produce a decisive transformation in the image of science by which we are now possessed. That image has previously been drawn, even by scientists themselves, mainly from the study of finished scientific achievements as these are recorded in the classics and, more recently, in the textbooks from which each new scientific generation learns to practice its trade. Inevitably, however, the aim of such books is persuasive and pedagogic; a concept of science drawn from them is no more likely to fit the enterprise that produced them than an image of a national culture drawn from a tourist brochure or a language text. This essay attempts to show that we have been misled by them in fundamental ways. Its aim is a sketch of the quite different concept of science that can emerge from the historical record of the research activity itself.

Even from history, however, that new concept will not be forthcoming if historical data continue to be sought and scrutinized mainly to answer questions posed by the unhistorical stereotype drawn from science texts. Those texts have, for example, often seemed to imply that the content of science is uniquely exemplified by the observations, laws, and theories described in their pages. Almost as regularly, the same books have been read as saying that scientific methods are simply the ones illustrated by the manipulative techniques used in gathering textbook data, together with the logical operations employed when relating those data to the textbook's theoretical generalizations. The result has been a concept of science with profound implications about its nature and development. . . .

In recent years, however, a few historians of science have been finding it more and more difficult to fulfil the functions that the concept of development-by-accumulation assigns to them. As chroniclers of an incremental process, they discover that additional research makes it harder, not easier, to answer questions like: When was oxygen discovered? Who first conceived of energy conservation? Increasingly, a few of them suspect that these are simply the wrong sorts of questions to ask. Perhaps science does not develop by the accumulation of individual discoveries and inventions. Simultaneously, these same historians confront growing difficulties in distinguishing the 'scientific' component of past observation and belief from what their predecessors had readily labeled 'error' and 'superstition.' The more carefully they study, say, Aristotelian dynamics, phlogistic chemistry, or caloric thermodynamics, the more certain they feel that those once current views of nature were, as a whole, neither less scientific nor more the product of human idiosyncrasy than those current today. If these out-of-date beliefs are to be called myths, then myths can be produced by the same sorts of methods and held for the same sorts of reasons that now lead to scientific knowledge. If, on the other hand, they are to be called science, then science has included bodies of belief quite incompatible with the ones we hold today. Given these alternatives, the historian must choose the latter. Out-of-date theories are not in principle unscientific because they have been discarded. That choice, however, makes it difficult to see scientific development as a process of accretion. The same historical research that displays the difficulties in isolating individual inventions and discoveries gives ground for profound doubts about the cumulative process through which these individual contributions to science were thought to have been compounded.

The result of all these doubts and difficulties is a historiographic revolution in the study of science, though one that is still in its early stages. Gradually, and often without entirely realizing they are doing so, historians of science have begun to ask new sorts of questions and to trace different, and often less than cumulative, developmental lines for the sciences. Rather than seeking the permanent contributions of an older science to our present vantage, they attempt to display the historical integrity of that science in its own time. They ask, for example, not about the relation of Galileo's views to those of modern science, but rather about the relationship between his views and those of his group, i.e., his teachers, contemporaries, and immediate successors in the sciences. Furthermore, they insist upon studying the opinions of that group and other similar ones from the viewpoint – usually very different from that of modern science – that gives those opinions the maximum internal coherence and the closest possible fit to nature. . . .

The early developmental stages of most sciences have been characterized by continual competition between a number of distinct views of nature, each partially derived from, and all roughly compatible with, the dictates of scientific observation and method. What differentiated these various schools was not one or another failure of method – they were all 'scientific'– but what we shall come to call their incommensurable ways of seeing the world and of practicing science in it. Observation and experience can and must drastically restrict the range of admissible scientific belief, else there would be no science. But they cannot alone determine a particular body of such belief. An apparently arbitrary element, compounded of personal and historical accident, is always a formative ingredient of the beliefs espoused by a given scientific community at a given time.

That element of arbitrariness does not, however, indicate that any scientific group could practice its trade without some set of received beliefs. Nor does it make less consequential the particular constellation to which the group, at a given time, is in fact committed. Effective research scarcely begins before a scientific community thinks it has acquired firm answers to questions like the following: What are the fundamental entities of which the universe is composed? How do these interact with each other and with the senses? What questions may legitimately be asked about such entities and what techniques employed in seeking solutions? At least in the mature sciences, answers (or full substitutes for answers) to questions like these are firmly embedded in the educational initiation that prepares and licenses the student for professional practice. Because that education is both rigorous and rigid, these answers come to exert a deep hold on the scientific mind. That they can do so does much to account both for the peculiar efficiency of the normal research activity and for the direction in which it proceeds at any given time. . . . Normal science, the activity in which most scientists inevitably spend almost all their time, is predicated on the assumption that the scientific community knows what the world is like. Much of the success of the enterprise derives from the community's willingness to defend that assumption, if necessary at considerable cost. Normal science, for example, often suppresses fundamental novelties because they are necessarily subversive of its basic commitments. Nevertheless, so long as those commitments retain an element of the arbitrary, the very nature of normal research ensures that novelty shall not be suppressed for very long. Sometimes a normal problem, one that ought to be solvable by known rules and procedures, resists the reiterated onslaught of the ablest members of the group within whose competence it falls. On other occasions a piece of equipment designed and constructed for the purpose of normal research fails to perform in the anticipated manner, revealing an anomaly that cannot, despite repeated effort, be aligned with professional expectation. In these and other ways besides, normal science repeatedly goes astray. And when it does – when, that is, the profession can no longer evade anomalies that subvert the existing tradition of scientific practice – then begin the extraordinary investigations that lead the profession at last to a new set of commitments, a new basis for the practice of science. The extraordinary episodes in which that shift of professional commitments occurs are the ones known in this essay as scientific revolutions. They are the tradition-shattering complements to the tradition-bound activity of normal science. . . .

In this essay, 'normal science' means research firmly based upon one or more past scientific achievements, achievements that some particular scientific community acknowledges for a time as supplying the foundation for its further practice. Today such achievements are recounted, though seldom in their original form, by science textbooks, elementary and advanced. These textbooks expound the body of accepted theory, illustrate many or all of its successful applications, and compare these applications with exemplary observations and experiments. Before such books became popular early in the nineteenth century (and until even more recently in the newly matured sciences), many of the famous classics of science fulfilled a similar function . . . Their achievement was sufficiently unprecedented to attract an enduring group of adherents away from competing modes of scientific activity. Simultaneously, it was sufficiently open-ended to leave all sorts of problems for the redefined group of practitioners to resolve.

Achievements that share these two characteristics I shall henceforth refer to as 'paradigms,' a term that relates closely to 'normal science.' By choosing it, I mean to suggest that some accepted examples of actual scientific practice – examples which include law, theory, application, and instrumentation together – provide models from which spring particular coherent traditions of scientific research.

. . . Discovery commences with the awareness of anomaly, i.e., with the recognition that nature has somehow violated the paradigm-induced expectations that govern normal science. It then continues with a more or less extended exploration of the area of anomaly. And it closes only when the paradigm theory has been adjusted so that the anomalous has become the expected. Assimilating a new sort of fact demands a more than additive adjustment of theory, and until that adjustment is completed – until the scientist has learned to see nature in a different way – the new fact is not quite a scientific fact at all. . . .

If an anomaly is to evoke crisis, it must usually be more than just an anomaly. There are always difficulties somewhere in the paradigm-nature fit; most of them are set right sooner or later, often by processes that could not have been foreseen. The scientist who pauses to examine every anomaly he notes will seldom get significant work done. . . .

When . . . an anomaly comes to seem more than just another puzzle of normal science, the transition to crisis and to extraordinary science has begun. The anomaly itself now comes to be more generally recognized as such by the profession. More and more attention is devoted to it by more and more of the field's most eminent men. If it still continues to resist, as it usually does not, many of them may come to view its resolution as *the* subject matter of their discipline. For them the field will no longer look quite the same as it had earlier. Part of its different appearance results simply from the new fixation point of scientific scrutiny. An even more important source of change is the divergent nature of the numerous partial solutions that concerted attention to the problem has made available. The early attacks upon the resistant problem will have followed the paradigm rules quite closely. But with continuing resistance, more and more of the attacks upon it will have involved some minor or not so minor articulation of the paradigm, no two of them quite alike, each partially successful, but none sufficiently so to be accepted as paradigm by the group. Through this proliferation of divergent articulations (more and more frequently they will come to be described as *ad hoc* adjustments), the rules of normal science become increasingly blurred. Though there still is a paradigm, few practitioners prove to be entirely agreed about what it is. Even formerly standard solutions of solved problems are called in question. . . .

The resulting transition to a new paradigm is scientific revolution . . . Confronted with anomaly or with crisis, scientists take a different attitude toward existing paradigms, and the nature of their research changes accordingly. The proliferation of competing articulations, the willingness to try anything, the expression of explicit discontent, the recourse to philosophy and to debate over fundamentals, all these are symptoms of a transition from normal to extraordinary research. It is upon their existence more than upon that of revolutions that the notion of normal science depends.

Chapter 28

John M. Swales

EPISODES IN THE HISTORY OF THE RESEARCH ARTICLE

From *Genre Analysis: English in Academic and Research Settings,* Cambridge: Cambridge University Press (1990).

THE SCIENTIFIC [RESEARCH ARTICLE] emerged, albeit in embryonic form, contemporaneously with the establishment of the first scientific periodical, *The Philosophical Transactions of the Royal Society,* in 1665. According to Ard (1983), the genre of the scientific article developed from the informative letters that scientists had always written to each other – and still do. Thus, many of the early contributions to the *Transactions* took the first person descriptive narrative form associated with letters, some even having the salutation 'Sir' at their outset. However, as the *Transactions* and subsequent journals began to assume a role of providing a regular arena for discussion, the new and recurring rhetorical situation that emerged led to the creation of a new genre increasingly distinct from its letter-writing origin. In Bazerman's words:

> By talking to each other in a specific format scientists were figuring out how to talk to each other and changed the format according to what they were figuring out.
>
> (Bazerman 1983: 1)

Another powerful force that shaped the early scientific article came from the existing tradition of published scientific treatises; most immediately, from the efforts of Robert Boyle and his fellow experimentalists in the decade preceding the appearance of the first issue of the *Transactions* to establish a proper foundation for scientific knowledge (Shapin 1984). According to Shapin, Boyle and his colleagues sought to transform claims and speculations into generally-accepted knowledge by way of the experimental *matter of fact*. In order to achieve this transformation, Boyle would appear to have developed a largely self-conscious and highly complex set of strategies. Some of these strategic elements are as follows:

a) The key apparatus for his pneumatic experiments was the air pump. At that time air pumps were very expensive, elaborate and temperamental; they were thus rare and well beyond the means of the great majority of potential users. Boyle presented his machine to the Royal Society to ease the problem of access and to pre-empt objections that might be based on traditional opposition to alchemical secrecy or to aristocratic aloofness. (Boyle was a son of the Earl of Cork.)

b) In Boyle's program of work the capacity of experiments to yield matters of fact depended less on getting the apparatus to do certain things than on securing the agreement of the relevant community that these things had, in fact, been done. He needed witnesses, the more the better and the better qualified the better. Experiments were performed before an audience at the Royal Society and members were encouraged to sign a register as witness that they had seen what they had seen.

c) Boyle also recognized that witnesses could be multiplied by encouraging others to replicate experiments. Although he strongly advocated this practice, he came soon enough to realize that many attempts at replication would fail.

d) According to Shapin, Boyle's most important way of trying to establish facts was by what Shapin calls *virtual witnessing*: 'the technology of virtual witnessing involves the production in a reader's mind of such an image of an experimental scene as obviates the necessity for either its direct witness or its replication' (1984: 491). Boyle set out to achieve this objective by a variety of methods:

   i) If there were to be illustrations of apparatus in his published work, Boyle was insistent that these should be realistic, exact and detailed.

   ii) He wrote deliberately elaborate and prolix accounts of his experiments so that the reader would be encouraged to believe that he was getting a full and honest account.

   iii) He offered his readers circumstantial accounts of *failed* experiments.

   iv) He deliberately avoided philosophical speculation.

   v) Boyle wrote very cautiously and made much use of what today have become known as 'hedges' (e.g. Lakoff 1972). As Boyle himself put it, 'in almost every one of the following essays I . . . speak so doubtingly, and use so often *perhaps, it seems, it is not improbable* and other such expressions, as argue a diffidence to the truth of the opinions I incline to . . .' (quoted by Shapin, 1984: 495).

e) A further important aspect of Boyle's contribution to the rhetoric of science was his attempts to regulate scientific disputes; in particular he insisted that disputes should be about findings and not about persons. In this way he stood out against the common *ad hominem* style of arguing at that time. As he elegantly puts it, 'I love to speak of persons with civility, though of things with freedom' (Shapin, 1984: 502).

Of course it is sometimes thought that the facts 'speak for themselves'; that is, a scientist's description of natural reality, if it is carefully and competently done, is simply a reflection of that reality. However, if this were to be the case, then Boyle's complex strategy would have been unnecessary. Rather, even the foregoing short summary of Shapin's analysis seems to show clearly enough how hard Boyle and his collaborators had to work to *make* a rhetoric – to *develop* a convincing style for the research report. It would appear that phenomena only acquire fact-like status by consensus and that consensus may not be achievable without rhetorical persuasion. The art of the matter, as far as the creation of facts is concerned, lies in deceiving the reader into thinking that there is no rhetoric, that research reporting is indeed 'writing degree zero' (Barthes 1975) and that the facts are indeed speaking for themselves. . . .

[There are] genre-specific conventions that constrain and shape the research article. Consequently, and despite appearances to the contrary, we find ourselves far away from a world in which it is expected that researchers will 'tell it as it hap- pened'. Despite the conventional sectioning of the research article, we are far away from a world in which the research itself is comparably compartmentalized. Despite an objective 'empiricist' repertoire, we are far away from a world in which power, allegiance and self-esteem play no part, however much they may seem absent from the frigid surface of RA discourse. And yet we find the research article, this key product of the knowledge-manufacturing industry, to be a remarkable phenomenon, so cunningly engineered by rhetorical machining that it somehow still gives an *impression* of being but a simple description of relatively untransmuted raw material. . . .

There are certain characteristics of RAs which, by and large, tend to occur and recur in samples drawn from an extensive range of disciplines. . . . RAs are rarely simple narratives of investigations. Instead, they are complexly distanced reconstructions of research activities, at least part of this reconstructive process deriving from a need to anticipate and discountenance negative reactions to the knowledge claims being advanced. And this need in turn explains the long-standing (Shapin 1984) and widespread use of 'hedges' as rhetorical devices both for project- ing honesty, modesty and proper caution in self-reports, and for diplomatically creating research space in areas heavily populated by other researchers.

On the other hand, the RA varies from one disciplinary sector to another in terms of degree of standardization and of the prevalence of a nominalized impersonal style (Smith 1982). In those areas of knowledge variously described as 'hard', 'exact' or 'physical', consensus on objectives, ground-rules and points of departure has led to textual products with regularized macro-structure and with rhetorics that follow identifiable role-models. In these fields, there is a perceivable inter-relationship between the RA as a peer-group intellectual object, the abstract nominal style, and the presence of authorial intrusion mainly in contexts thought to need persuasive support, or to need some revelation of the authors' individual cognitive processes. As is well known, certain groups in the social and behavior sciences have tried, with varying degrees of success, to adopt and adapt the hard science paradigm (cf. Bazerman 1987). Others, such as ethnographers of various persuasions, have not. These and many in the humanities tend to align their scholarly and research products to their preferred intellectual schools and scholarly traditions rather than to disciplines as such. In general, differences between the genres of articles, books, reviews, and so on are less marked in the humanities.

Finally, there are two principal corollaries of this variation – and one unexpected outcome. First, the more established the conventions, the more articulated the genre. Thus on a superficial level, the RA text becomes increasingly divided into standardized divisions ([Introduction, Methods, Results, Discussion] or a disciplinary variant); on a less obvious level, the more likely we will find that different sections will have different rhetorical features (e.g. Introductions in contrast to Methods). The second corollary is that as we move towards the diffuse end of the continuum the more necessary it becomes for authors to engage in acts of persuasion that will encourage the readerships to share particular visions of the research world. The surprise is that, on preliminary evidence at least, the major differences do not lie so much in Introductions and Discussions (where I believe most people would expect it) but rather in the Method and Results sections. Finally, there is perhaps an element of irony in a situation wherein social scientists are engaged in a cognitive and rhetorical upgrade of Method at a time when their mentors in the hard sciences are beginning, rhetorically at least, to downgrade its importance.

References

Ard, Josh (1983) 'The role of the author in scientific discourse.' Paper given at the annual American Applied Linguistics Meeting, Minneapolis, Minn., December, 1983.

Barthes, Roland (1975) *The Pleasure of the Text* (translated by R. Miller). New York: Hill.

Bazerman, Charles (1983) 'Reporting the experiment: the changing account of scientific doings in the *Philosophical Transactions of the Royal Society*, 1665–1800' (mimeo).

——(1987) 'Codifying the social scientific style: the APA publication manual as a behaviorist rhetoric.' In Nelson, Megill and McCloskey (eds.): 125–44.

Lakoff, G. (1972) 'Hedges: a study in meaning criteria and the logic of fuzzy concepts.' In *Papers from the Eighth Regional Meeting, Chicago Linguistic Society*, 183–228.

Nelson, J. S., A. Megill and D. N. McCloskey (eds) (1987) *The Rhetoric of the Human Sciences.* Madison, Wis.: Wisconsin University Press.

Shapin, Steven (1984) 'Pump and circumstance: Robert Boyle's literary technology.' *Social Studies of Science* 14:481–520.

Smith, Edward I. (1982) 'Writer–reader interactiveness in four genres of scientific English.' Unpublished PhD dissertation, University of Michigan, Ann Arbor.

PART SEVEN

Ethnography: the qualitative alternative

INTRODUCTION

THUS FAR, IT MAY seem as if quantitative research pre-dated qualitative research, which somehow emerged as an alternative after a Kuhnian-style (see reading 27) 'revolution' that occurred in the 1960s. While some important changes did occur around this time, such an interpretation does not do justice to the qualitative tradition, the historical roots of which lie much further back. Arguably these are in the work of anthropologists in the early part of the twentieth century practising a method (or, really, a collection of methods) that became known as ethnography. This part contains readings outlining the ethnographic method both in terms of research practice and at more philosophical levels.

Reading 29, by the philosopher Schutz, is an outline of one of several possible general frameworks available to qualitative researchers, and to ethnographers in particular. It was written as a response to another philosopher, Nagel, who argued that it was impossible to study the inner lives of people (their 'subjectivity') in an objective way, in part because one cannot experience another's subjectivity through sensory observation. Schutz departs from the 'naturalism' of Nagel (by which he means his attempt to transfer natural science methods to the study of the social world), claiming that important differences need to be acknowledged. The object of study in social research, unlike that in the natural sciences of physics or chemistry, is a human being who thinks and feels. Social scientists, therefore, must look into these thoughts and feelings. Schutz outlines a general approach for doing this based on a Weberian analysis of typical patterns of motivation and behaviour, about which he claims it is perfectly possible to be objective.

While ethnography is not the only method for gathering information about these matters, many ethnographers have derived inspiration from Schutz's writings. The readings that follow show ethnographers at work. Whyte (reading 30) in his method-ological appendix to the sociological classic *Street Corner Society*, a study of Ameri-can city dwellers in a run-down area done in the 1930s, describes what it was like to negotiate access. After some false starts, this is finally made possible by an encounter with an unusually helpful member of the social scene Whyte wants to study. Once 'in the field', though, an ethnographer commonly adopts a role. The extract from Junker (reading 31) outlines the kinds of information ethnographers commonly seek and the advantages and disadvantages of adopting different observer positions in trying to get such information. Secrecy, for example, may have certain advantages in minimizing people's reactions to the presence of the observer, but it can also limit what can be seen without giving the game away.

In 'Theoretical sampling' (reading 32), Glaser and Strauss outline an approach to deciding who to speak with next when doing an ethnographic research project, or which setting to observe, that is very different in purpose from that of the social survey researcher concerned with representativeness (see reading 8). Theoretical sampling is devoted to maximizing the possibility of generating theory (which Glaser and Strauss call 'grounded theory'). These authors illustrate the procedure with examples from their participant observation in hospitals treating people who die.

Once access has been gained, settings or people sampled and observations made, there is the issue of how to record what is seen and said. While the advent of mechanical recording devices (the tape recorder, the camcorder) has transformed certain areas of qualitative research practice, writing down a written account of observations is still an important aspect of data recording for many ethnographers. Lofland (reading 33) gives detailed advice on how to do this in ways that maximize the chances of this being usable once analysed. Importantly, Lofland advocates a separation between an account of what happened and of what the researcher thought about this.

Geertz, in reading 34, analyses ethnographic writing, pointing out that it is fre-quently devoted to persuading the reader that the writer was really 'there', though this may be done in different ways. This is done to persuade the reader to believe in the conclusions reported. Though ethnographic writing is a very different genre, this is not far from the purpose of the scientific research report analysed by Swales (reading 28), in so far as all research writing can be understood to involve the deployment of rhetorical skills.

Having gone through some key stages in doing an ethnographic project in readings 30–34 (gaining access, adopting a role, sampling settings and people, recording infor-mation and writing a report), it seems sensible to assess the value of what this approach can achieve. Hammersley (reading 35) has written extensively on the stand-ards that can be applied to the assessment of qualitative research studies, and here turns his mind to the products of ethnography. He outlines a variety of approaches to this, pointing out differences between 'methodists, realists, relativists, and instru-mentalists', all of whom start from differing philosophical positions. His own position he describes as 'subtle realism', in which the relation between claims and evidence for those claims is crucial.

The final reading in this part is a debate about the relative merits of observation and interviews (both of which are used by ethnographers). This relates to a problem encountered in reading 11 on the measurement of attitudes, and in reading 25 on discovering facts about sexual behaviour: what people say may not be what they do. Clearly Becker and Geer believe ethnographic participant observation (which in their case includes informal chats with people) is superior to interviewing alone, since people can lie in interviews. Trow, however, argues against this point, noting that people can say things in the privacy of an interview that they would never reveal in a more public setting. Becker and Geer then respond to Trow's points.

DISCUSSION POINTS

- How is it possible to be objective about studying subjectivity?
- How would you gain access to do research on the following groups of people and settings? What kinds of 'gatekeeper' would you encounter? What difficulties could there be? (the police; a school class; a public library; people engaged in illegal dog fighting; a football team; a family; a friendship).
- What are the different ways in which secret observation can be done? What advantages and disadvantages are there to this? (Try applying these questions to the groups/settings listed above.)
- How do theoretical sampling and random sampling (reading 8) differ? What are the advantages and disadvantages of each?
- Lofland advocates that researchers writing field notes keep detailed, 'concrete' descriptions of events (facts) separately from the 'analytic memos' in which researchers reflect on, or interpret, what has happened. Think back to reading 5, in which Cook and Campbell discuss the view that all 'facts' are produced by underlying theoretical assumptions. Does this technique of Lofland's overcome this problem? If not, what might?
- Use Geertz's analysis of ethnographic writing style to analyse the account by Whyte in this part of the book. How does Whyte persuade us that he has 'been there'?
- What are the four approaches to validity outlined by Hammersley? What are the advantages and disadvantages of his 'subtle realist' position?
- Outline and compare the contribution that (a) interviews alone and (b) participant observation might make to a study of the groups and settings listed in the second discussion point above.

FURTHER READING

Atkinson, P., Coffey, A., Delamont, S., Lofland, J. and Lofland L. (eds.) (2001) *Handbook of Ethnography*, London: Sage.

Becker, H.S. (1970) *Sociological Work: Method and Substance*, Chicago, Ill.: Aldine.

Burgess, R. (1984) *In the Field: An Introduction to Field Research*, London: George Allen and Unwin.

Denzin, N.K. (1997) *Interpretive Ethnography: Ethnographic Practice for the 21st Century,* Thousand Oaks, Cal.: Sage.

Geertz, C. (1993) *The Interpretation of Cultures,* London: Fontana Press (first published 1973).

Hammersley, M. and Atkinson, P. (1995) *Ethnography: Principles in Practice,* London: Routledge. (2nd edition.)

—— (1992), *What's Wrong With Ethnography: Methodological Explorations,* London: Routledge.

Hammersley, M. (1983) *Reading Ethnographic Research: A Critical Guide,* London: Longman.

Malinowski, B. (1967) *A Diary in the Strict Sense of the Term,* New York: Harcourt, Brace and World.

Mead, M. (1943; first published 1928) *Coming of Age in Samoa: A Study of Adolescence and Sex in Primitive Societies,* Harmondsworth: Penguin.

Webb, E.J., Campbell, D.T., Schwartz, R.D. and Sechrest. L. (1966) *Unobtrusive Measures: Non-reactive Research in the Social Sciences,* Chicago: Rand McNally.

Wolcott, H.F. (1999) *Ethnography: A Way of Seeing,* Walnut Creek, Cal.: AltaMira Press.

Chapter 29

Alfred Schutz

CONCEPT AND THEORY FORMATION IN THE SOCIAL SCIENCES

From Emmet, D. and MacIntyre, A. (eds.) *Sociological Theory and Philosophical Analysis*, London: Macmillan (1970), pp. 1–19 (first published 1953).

. . .

I SHALL HERE CONCENTRATE on Professor Nagel's[1] criticism of the claim made by Max Weber and his school that the social sciences seek to 'understand' social phenomena in terms of 'meaningful' categories of human experience and that, therefore, the 'causal functional' approach of the natural sciences is not applicable in social inquiry. This school, as Dr Nagel sees it, maintains that all socially significant human behaviour is an expression of motivated psychic states, that in consequence the social scientist cannot be satisfied with viewing social processes simply as concatenations of 'externally related' events, and that the establishment of correlations or even of universal relations of concomitance cannot be his ultimate goal. On the contrary, he must construct 'ideal types' or 'models of motivations' in terms of which he seeks to 'understand' overt social behaviour by imputing springs of action to the actors involved in it. If I understand Professor Nagel's criticism correctly, he maintains:

1   That these springs of action are not accessible to sensory observation. It follows and has frequently been stated that the social scientist must imaginatively identify himself with the participants and view the situation which they

---

1 Published in the volume *Science, Language and Human Rights* (American Philosophical Association, Eastern Division, I, Philadelphia, 1952) pp. 43–86 (referred to as 'SLH').

face as the actors themselves view it. Surely, however, we need not undergo other men's psychic experiences in order to know that they have them or in order to predict their overt behaviour.

2   That the imputation of emotions, attitudes, and purposes as an explanation of overt behaviour is a twofold hypothesis: it assumes that the agents participating in some social phenomenon are in certain psychological states; and it assumes also definite relations of concomitance between such states, and between such states and overt behaviour. Yet none of the psychological states which we imagine the subjects of our study to possess may in reality be theirs, and even if our imputations should be correct none of the overt actions which allegedly issue from those states may appear to us understandable or reasonable.

3   That we do not 'understand' the nature and operations of human motives and their issuance in overt behaviour more adequately than the 'external' causal relations. If by meaningful explanation we assert merely that a particular action is an instance of a pattern of behaviour which human beings exhibit under a variety of circumstances and that, since some of the relevant circumstances are realised in the given situation, a person can be expected to manifest a certain form of that pattern, then there is no sharp gulf separating such explanations from those involving merely 'external' knowledge of causal connections. It is possible to gain knowledge of the actions of men on the evidence supplied by their overt behaviour just as it is possible to discover and know the atomic constitution of water on the evidence supplied by the physical and chemical behaviour of that substance. Hence the rejection of a purely 'objective' or 'behaviouristic' social science by the proponents of 'meaningful connections' as the goal of social sciences is unwarranted.

Since I shall have to disagree with Nagel's findings on several questions of a fundamental nature, I might be permitted to start with a brief summary of the no less important points on which I find myself happily in full agreement with them. I agree with Professor Nagel that all empirical knowledge involves discovery through processes of controlled inference, and that it must be statable in propositional form and capable of being verified by anyone who is prepared to make the effort to do so through observation – although I do not believe, as Professor Nagel does, that this observation has to be sensory in the precise meaning of this term. Moreover, I agree with him that 'theory' means in all empirical sciences the explicit formulation of determinate relations between a set of variables in terms of which a fairly extensive class of empirically ascertainable regularities can be explained. Furthermore, I agree whole-heartedly with his statement that neither the fact that these regularities have in the social sciences a rather narrowly restricted universality, nor the fact that they permit prediction only to a rather limited extent, constitutes a basic difference between the social and the natural sciences, since many branches of the latter show the same features. As I shall try to show later on, it seems to me that Professor Nagel misunderstands Max Weber's postulate of subjective interpretation. Nevertheless, he is right in stating that method which would require that the individual scientific observer identify himself with the social agent observed in order to understand the motives of the latter, or a method which would refer the selection of the facts observed and their interpretation to the private value system of the particular observer, would merely lead to an uncontrollable private and subjective image in the mind of this particular student of human affairs, but never to a scientific theory. But I do not know of any social scientist of stature who ever advocated such a concept of subjectivity as that criticised by Professor Nagel. Most certainly this was not the position of Max Weber.

I also think that our authors are prevented from grasping the point of vital concern to social scientists by their basic philosophy of sensationalistic empiricism or logical positivism, which identifies experience with sensory observation and which assumes that the only alternative to controllable and, therefore, objective sensory observation is that of subjective and, therefore, uncontrollable and unverifiable introspection. This is certainly not the place to renew the age-old controversy relating to the hidden pre-suppositions and implied metaphysical assumptions of this basic philosophy. On the other hand, in order to account for my own position, I should have to treat at length certain principles of phenomenology. Instead of doing so, I propose to defend a few rather simple propositions:

1   The primary goal of the social sciences is to obtain organised knowledge of social reality. By the term 'social reality' I wish to be understood the sum total of objects and occurrences within the social cultural world as experienced by the commonsense thinking of men living their daily lives among their fellow-men, connected with them in manifold relations of interaction. It is the world of cultural objects and social institutions into which we are all born, within which we have to find our bearings, and with which we have to come to terms. From the outset, we, the actors on the social scene, experience the world we live in as a world both of nature and of culture, not as a private but as an inter-subjective one, that is, as a world common to all of us, either actually given or potentially accessible to everyone; and this involves intercommunication and language.

2   All forms of naturalism and logical empiricism simply take for granted this social reality, which is the proper object of the social sciences. Intersubjectivity, interaction, inter-communication and language are simply presupposed as the unclarified foundation of these theories. They assume, as it were, that the social scientist has already solved his fundamental problem, before scientific enquiry starts. . . .

3   The identification of experience with sensory observation in general and of the experience of overt action in particular (and that is what Nagel proposes) excludes several dimensions of social reality from all possible inquiry.

  (a)   Even an ideally refined behaviourism can, as has been pointed out for instance by George H. Mead,[2] merely explain the behaviour of the observed, not of the observing behaviourist.

  (b)   The same overt behaviour (say a tribal pageant as it can be captured by the movie camera) may have an entirely different meaning to the performers. What interests the social scientist is merely whether it is a war dance, a barter trade, the reception of a friendly ambassador, or something else of this sort.

2 *Mind, Self and Society* (Chicago, 1937).

(c)   Moreover the concept of human action in terms of commonsense think-
       ing and of the social sciences includes what may be called 'negative
       actions', i.e. intentional refraining from acting,[3] which, of course, escapes
       sensory observation. Not to sell certain merchandise at a given price is
       doubtless as economic an action as to sell it.

(d)   Furthermore, as W.I. Thomas has shown,[4] social reality contains elements
       of beliefs and convictions which are real because they are so defined by
       the participants and which escape sensory observation. To the inhabit-
       ants of Salem in the seventeenth century, witchcraft was not a delusion
       but an element of their social reality and is as such open to investigation
       by the social scientist.

(e)   Finally, and this is the most important point, the postulate of sensory
       observation of overt human behaviour takes as a model a particular and
       relatively small sector of the social world, namely, situations in which
       the acting individual is given to the observer in what is commonly called
       a face-to-face relationship. But there are many other dimensions of the
       social world in which situations of this kind do not prevail. If we put a
       letter in the mail box we assume that anonymous fellow-men, called
       postmen, will perform a series of manipulations, unknown and
       unobservable to us, with the effect that the addressee, possibly also
       unkown to us, will receive the message and react in a way which also
       escapes our sensory observation; and the result of all this is that we
       receive the book we have ordered. Or if I read an editorial stating that
       France fears the rearmament of Germany, I know perfectly well what
       this statement means without knowing the editorialist and even without
       knowing a Frenchman or a German, let alone without observing their
       overt behaviour.

In terms of commonsense thinking in everyday life men have knowledge of
these various dimensions of the social world in which they live. To be sure, this
knowledge is not only fragmentary since it is restricted principally to certain sectors
of this world, it is also frequently inconsistent in itself and shows all degrees of
clarity and distinctness from full insight or 'knowledge-about,' as James[5] called it,
through 'knowledge of acquaintance' or mere familiarity, to blind belief in things
just taken for granted. In this respect there are considerable differences from individual to individual and from social group to social group. Yet, in spite of all these
inadequacies, commonsense knowledge of everyday life is sufficient for coming to
terms with fellow-men, cultural objects, social institutions – in brief, with social
reality. This is so, because the world (the natural and the social one) is from the
outset an intersubjective world and because . . . our knowledge of it is in various ways
socialised. Moreover, the social world is experienced from the outset as a meaning-

---

3 See Max Weber, *The Theory of Social and Economic Organisation*, trans. A.M. Henderson and Talcott
   Parsons (New York, 1947) p. 88.
4 See W.I. Thomas, *Social Behaviour and Personality*, ed. E. H. Volkart (New York, 1951) p. 81.
5 *Principles of Psychology*, i 221 f.

ful one. The Other's body is not experienced as an organism but as a fellow-man, its overt behaviour not as an occurrence in the time of the outer-world, but as our fellow-man's action. We normally 'know' what the Other does, for what reason he does it, why he does it at this particular time and in these particular circumstances. That means that we experience our fellow-man's action in terms of his motives and goals. And in the same way, we experience cultural objects in terms of the human action of which they are the result. A tool, for example, is not experienced as a thing in the outer world (which of course it is also) but in terms of the purpose for which it was designed by more or less anonymous fellow-men and its possible use by others. . . .

There is an essential difference in the structure of the thought objects or mental constructs formed by the social sciences and those formed by the natural sciences. It is up to the natural scientist and to him alone to define, in accordance with the procedural rules of his science, his observational field, and to determine the facts, data and events within it which are relevant for his problem or scientific purpose at hand. Neither are those facts and events preselected, nor is the observational field preinterpreted. The world of nature, as explored by the natural scientist, does not 'mean' anything to molecules, atoms and electrons. But the observational field of the social scientist – social reality – has a specific meaning and relevance structure for the human beings living, acting and thinking within it. By a series of commonsense constructs they have preselected and preinterpreted this world which they experience as the reality of their daily lives. It is these thought objects of theirs which determine their behaviour by motivating it. The thought objects constructed by the social scientist, in order to grasp this social reality, have to be founded upon the thought objects constructed by the commonsense thinking of men, living their daily life within their social world. Thus, the constructs of the social sciences are, so to speak, constructs of the second degree, that is, constructs of the constructs made by the actors on the social scene, whose behaviour the social scientist has to observe and to explain in accordance with the procedural rules of his science.

Thus, the exploration of the general principles according to which man in daily life organises his experiences, and especially those of the social world, is the first task of the methodology of the social sciences. . . . The most serious question which the methodology of the social sciences has to answer is: How is it possible to form objective concepts and an objectively verifiable theory of subjective meaning-structures? The basic insight that the concepts formed by the social scientist are constructs of the constructs formed in commonsense thinking by the actors on the social scene offers an answer. The scientific constructs formed on the second level, in accordance with the procedural rules valid for all empirical sciences, are objective ideal typical constructs and, as such, of a different kind from those developed on the first level of commonsense thinking which they have to supersede. They are theoretical systems embodying general hypotheses. . . . This device has been used by social scientists concerned with theory long before this concept was formulated by Max Weber and developed by his school.

. . . Let us briefly consider the particular attitudes of the theoretical social scientist to the social world, in contradistinction to that of the actor on the social scene. The theoretical scientist – *qua* scientist, not *qua* human being (which he is, too) – is not involved in the observed situation, which is to him not of practical but merely of cognitive interest. The system of relevances governing commonsense interpretation in daily life originates in the biographical situation of the observer. By making up his mind to become a scientist, the social scientist has replaced his personal biographical situation by what I shall call, following Felix Kaufmann,[6] a scientific situation. The problems with which he has to deal might be quite unproblematic for the human being within the world and vice versa. Any scientific problem is determined by the actual state of the respective science, and its solution has to be achieved in accordance with the procedural rules governing this science, which among other things warrant the control and verification of the solution offered. The scientific problem, once established, alone determines what is relevant for the scientist as well as the conceptual frame of reference to be used by him. This and nothing else, it seems to me, is what Max Weber means when he postulates the objectivity of the social sciences, their detachment from value patterns which govern or might govern the behaviour of the actors on the social scene. . . .

6 *Methodology of the Social Sciences*, (New York, 1941), pp. 52 and 251.

Chapter 30

William Foote Whyte

FIRST EFFORTS

From *Street Corner Society: The Social Structure of an Italian Slum,* (3rd edition) Chicago: University of Chicago Press (3rd, edition (1981; first published 1943).

. . .

WHEN I BEGAN MY work, I had had no training in sociology or anthropology. I thought of myself as an economist and naturally looked first toward the matters that we had taken up in economics courses, such as economics of slum housing. At the time I was sitting in on a course in slums and housing in the Sociology Department at Harvard. As a term project I took on a study of one block in Cornerville. To legitimize this effort, I got in touch with a private agency that concerned itself in housing matters and offered to turn over to them the results of my survey. With that backing, I began knocking on doors, looking into flats, and talking to the tenants about the living conditions. This brought me into contact with Cornerville people, but it would be hard now to devise a more inappropriate way of beginning a study such as I was eventually to make. I felt ill at ease at this intrusion, and I am sure so did the people. I wound up the block study as rapidly as I could and wrote it off as a total loss as far as gaining a real entry into the district.

Shortly thereafter I made another false start – if so tentative an effort may even be called a start. At the time I was completely baffled at the problem of finding my way into the district. Cornerville was right before me and yet so far away. I could walk freely up and down its streets, and I had even made my way into some of the flats, and yet I was still a stranger in a world completely unknown to me.

At this time I met a young economics instructor at Harvard who impressed me with his self-assurance and his knowledge of Eastern City. He had once been attached to a settlement house, and he talked glibly about his associations with the tough young men and women of the district. He also described how he would occasionally drop in on some drinking place in the area and strike up an acquaintance with a girl, buy her a drink, and then encourage her to tell him her life-story. He claimed that the women so encountered were appreciative of this opportunity and that it involved no further obligation.

This approach seemed at least as plausible as anything I had been able to think of. I resolved to try it out. I picked on the Regal Hotel, which was on the edge of Cornerville. With some trepidation I climbed the stairs to the bar and entertainment area and looked around. There I encountered a situation for which my adviser had not prepared me. There were women present all right, but none of them was alone. Some were there in couples, and there were two or three pairs of women together. I pondered this situation briefly. I had little confidence in my skill at picking up one female, and it seemed inadvisable to tackle two at the same time. Still, I was determined not to admit defeat without a struggle. I looked around me again and now noticed a threesome: one man and two women. It occurred to me that here was a maldistribution of females which I might be able to rectify. I approached the group and opened with something like this: 'Pardon me. Would you mind if I joined you?' There was a moment of silence while the man stared at me. He then offered to throw me downstairs. I assured him that this would not be necessary and demonstrated as much by walking right out of there without any assistance.

I subsequently learned that hardly anyone from Cornerville ever went into the Regal Hotel. If my efforts there had been crowned with success, they would no doubt have led somewhere but certainly not to Cornerville.

For my next effort I sought out the local settlement houses. They were open to the public. You could walk right into them, and – though I would not have phrased it this way at the time – they were manned by middle-class people like myself. I realized even then that to study Cornerville I would have to go well beyond the settlement house, but perhaps the social workers could help me to get started.

As I look back on it now, the settlement house also seems a very unpromising place from which to begin such a study. If I had it to do over again, I would probably make my first approach through a local politician or perhaps through the Catholic church, although I am not myself Catholic. John Howard, who worked with me later, made his entry very successfully through the church, and he, too, was not a Catholic – although his wife was.

However that may be, the settlement house proved the right place for me at this time, for it was here that I met Doc. I had talked to a number of the social workers about my plans and hopes to get acquainted with the people and study the district. They listened with varying degrees of interest. If they had suggestions to make, I have forgotten them now except for one. Somehow, in spite of the vagueness of my own explanations, the head of girls' work in the Norton Street House understood what I needed. She began describing Doc to me. He was, she said, a very intelligent and talented person who had at one time been fairly active in the house but had dropped out, so that he hardly ever came in any more. Perhaps he could understand what I wanted, and he must have the contacts that I needed. She said she frequently encountered him as she walked to and from the house and sometimes stopped to chat with him. If I wished, she would make an appointment for me to see him in the house one evening. This at last seemed right. I jumped at the chance. As I came into the district that evening, it was with a feeling that here I had my big chance to get started. Somehow Doc must accept me and be willing to work with me.

In a sense, my study began on the evening of February 4, 1937, when the social worker called me in to meet Doc. She showed us into her office and then left so that we could talk. Doc waited quietly for me to begin, as he sank down into a chair. I found him a man of medium height and spare build. His hair was a light brown, quite a contrast to the more typical black Italian hair. It was thinning around the temples. His cheeks were sunken. His eyes were a light blue and seemed to have a penetrating gaze.

I began by asking him if the social worker had told him about what I was trying to do.

'No, she just told me that you wanted to meet me and that I should like to meet you.'

Then I went into a long explanation which, unfortunately, I omitted from my notes. As I remember it, I said that I had been interested in congested city districts in my college study but had felt very remote from them. I hoped to study the problems in such a district. I felt I could do very little as an outsider. Only if I could get to know the people and learn their problems first hand would I be able to gain the understanding I needed.

Doc heard me out without any change of expression, so that I had no way of predicting his reaction. When I was finished, he asked: 'Do you want to see the high life or the low life?'

'I want to see all that I can. I want to get as complete a picture of the community as possible.'

'Well, any nights you want to see anything, I'll take you around. I can take you to the joints – gambling joints – I can take you around to the street corners. Just remember that you're my friend. That's all they need to know. I know these places, and, if I tell them that you're my friend, nobody will bother you. You just tell me what you want to see, and we'll arrange it.'

The proposal was so perfect that I was at a loss for a moment as to how to respond to it. We talked a while longer, as I sought to get some pointers as to how I should behave in his company. He warned me that I might have to take the risk of getting arrested in a raid on a gambling joint but added that this was not serious. I only had to give a false name and then would get bailed out by the man that ran the place, paying only a five-dollar fine. I agreed to take this chance. I asked him whether I should gamble with the others in the gambling joints. He said it was unnecessary and, for a greenhorn like myself, very inadvisable.

At last I was able to express my appreciation. 'You know, the first steps of getting to know a community are the hardest. I could see things going with you that I wouldn't see for years otherwise.'

'That's right. You tell me what you want to see, and we'll arrange it. When you want some information, I'll ask for it, and you listen. When you want to find out their philosophy of life, I'll start an argument and get it for you. If there's something else you want to get, I'll stage an act for you. Not a scrap, you know, but just tell me what you want, and I'll get it for you.'

'That's swell. I couldn't ask for anything better. Now I'm going to try to fit in all right, but, if at any time you see I'm getting off on the wrong foot, I want you to tell me about it.'

'Now we're being too dramatic. You won't have any trouble. You come in as my friend. When you come in like that, at first everybody will treat you with respect. You can take a lot of liberties, and nobody will kick. After a while when they get to know you they will treat you like anybody else – you know, they say familiarity breeds contempt. But you'll never have any trouble. There's just one thing to watch out for. Don't spring [treat] people. Don't be too free with your money.'

'You mean they'll think I'm a sucker?'

'Yes, and you don't want to buy your way in.'

We talked a little about how and when we might get together. Then he asked me a question. 'You want to write something about this?'

'Yes, eventually.'

'Do you want to change things?'

'Well – yes. I don't see how anybody could come down here where it is so crowded, people haven't got any money or any work to do, and not want to have some things changed. But I think a fellow should do the thing he is best fitted for. I don't want to be a reformer, and I'm not cut out to be a politician. I just want to understand these things as best I can and write them up, and if that has any influence . . .'

'I think you can change things that way. Mostly that is the way things are changed, by writing about them.'

That was our beginning. At the time I found it hard to believe that I could move in as easily as Doc had said with his sponsorship. But that indeed was the way it turned out. . . .

Chapter 31

Buford H. Junker

THE FIELD WORK SITUATION
Social roles for observation

From *Fieldwork: An Introduction to the Social Sciences,* Chicago: University of Chicago Press (1960).

. . .

THE FIELD WORKER, IN order to initiate his observations, first goes about learning how to enter the social situation and get along with the persons he intends to observe. He may receive some guidance from a more experienced field worker or some help from the literature on his kind of situation, or perhaps he simply generalizes from his earlier experiences in responding to everyday social cues. And then, if all goes well, he engages in a rather curious task. In effect, he learns all the fundamentals of the social situation as he enters and survives in it – he 'learns the social organization' before he completely and explicitly *knows* what he has learned.

Since the field worker deals primarily in communications (interactions in which all kinds of information are exchanged, by voice, social gesture, conveyance of feelings, or even by artifact, such as a document), his first concern is with the kinds of distinctions people make in selecting what to communicate and to whom to communicate it. He therefore pays attention to the two dimensions that are simultaneously in use: (1) that which categorizes information-in-society and (2) that which categorizes the social roles of communicants (especially his own social role).

Since information-in-society is evaluated in ways that vary from one situation to another, the field worker develops sensitivity to the many kinds of distinctions people may make over a range from public to private. (Insensitivity, or inability to take the role of the other and sufficiently accept his values to facilitate communication, will not be rewarded in the situation of observation and may even be punished, just as rudeness is in everyday life.) Even though parts of the range may not find explicit or detailed representation in the data-about-society he publishes, all these distinctions are latent in every social situation and hence affect what can be communicated to him. This range may be indicated by the general labels and descriptions which follow:

Public. 'What everybody knows and can talk about.' One form of this is 'the news,' either as it appears in a newspaper or other public record or as it turns up in whatever people are interested in and 'talk about openly.' Field workers sometimes call the information received at this level the 'community norms,' the 'logics' or 'ideologies,' the 'apologia,' etc. (Even children may recognize it, as in satirizing 'teacher-talk.') But what may appear to be evaluated as 'public' within a situation may also be regarded as 'confidential' or 'secret' vis-à-vis outsiders, and in that event the field worker's sensitivity to such a basic fact about the social organization under study will help him avoid blunders.

Confidential. What is 'told in confidence.' One form of this is the statement made 'not for attribution,' which means that if it is ever used in a field worker's published report, it is to be so presented as to protect the giver's anonymity.

Secret. What is known to members of an in-group who avoid letting it be known to any outsider, since its exclusive possession is important to the in-group's solidarity and continued existence. As such it cannot be reported by a social science field worker, but it can be imparted in a scientific communication as information received and reported, like information at the confidential level, in such a manner as to protect the anonymity not only of the giver but of the in-group itself. One form of this is information obtained in a secret society, or in the 'inner fraternity' of a profession, or in a suppressed group presenting some opposition to authority (slaves, convicts, adolescents, etc.).

Private. What is personal to an individual and can be told only with certain kinds of help from others (such as a psychotherapist, who receives private information in accounts of dreams, free associations, and other kinds of private symbolic behavior). One or another form of this is presented to the field worker continuously, instant by instant, as he goes about his field work – the unconscious gesture, the 'Freudian slip,' the style of dress or room furnishing, the multitude of personal choices people make in everything they do. How these phenomena are to be recorded or ignored and what account of them is to be given in a social science publication are questions whose solution from scientific and ethical value positions must also take account of the possible consequences of current and later evaluations made by the persons concerned. In that regard, private information must be treated by the field worker with the same respect he owes to secret, confidential, and even public information, if he wants to survive in the field and also wants his social science to thrive. . . .

Here, referring to Figure 31.1, I shall set forth my own conceptions of four theoretical social roles for field work. These range from the polar ideal type of complete participant to that of complete observer, and I shall now summarize what I believe is known from field work on field work, about the social positions (vis-à-vis the people observed) and activities of field workers taking these roles.

I *Complete Participant.* In this role, the observer's activities as such are wholly concealed. The field worker is or becomes a complete member of an in-group, thus sharing secret information guarded from outsiders. The field worker's freedom to

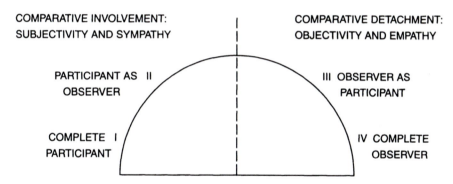

Figure 31.1 Theoretical social roles for field work.

observe outside the in-group system of relationships may be severely limited, and such a role tends to block perception of the workings of the reciprocal relations between the in-group and the larger social system, nor is it easy to switch from this to another role permitting observation of the details of the larger system. When the complete participant emerges, so to speak, to report as a social scientist, he may expect to be evaluated by some persons as something of a spy and he must also be prepared to cope with difficult problems of ethics and professional responsibility, not to mention problems of identity and self-conception.

This role may be suitable, and scientifically even absolutely necessary, in those social situations in which the people make sharp and clear evaluations about the information a field worker might seek: that is, they try to maintain a maximum of categorical difference between what is public, confidential, secret, and private, and one might expect that just as the in-group severely limits what may be made public to those in the larger system, so they would also set up barriers to the field worker's penetration into the secret level if he were an outsider to begin with. If the in-group is the kind that takes in converts, a rather prolonged period of indoctrination and testing may have been instituted, and this may be the mode by which the field worker chooses or is led to become a complete participant. Alternatively, if the field worker has always been a member of the in-group, at least until he left it physically or intellectually long enough to become indoctrinated either as a social scientist or as one serving social science purposes, his problems may be less those of getting in and staying in and more those of getting out. Such problems are likely to include maintaining sufficient detachment intellectually and reporting with the objectivity and empathy his scientific audience will demand. If he escapes the problems of a spy, he takes on those of a traitor.

II *Participant as Observer*. In this role, the field worker's observer activities are *not* wholly concealed, but are 'kept under wraps' as it were, or subordinated to activities as participant, activities which give the people in the situation their main bases for evaluating the field worker in his role. This role may limit access to some kinds of information, perhaps especially at the secret level: precisely how he 'rates' as a pseudo-'Member of the Wedding' will affect the field worker's ability to communicate below the level of public information. In his reporting, the social scientist who uses this position finds he must gear his responsibilities to the degree of secrecy (or confidentiality) of the information he was allowed by the people to obtain, under the implicit bargain which won him acceptance more as participant ('good friend') than as an observer ('snooping stranger').

III *Observer as Participant*. This is the role in which the observer activities as such are made publicly known at the outset, are more or less publicly sponsored by people in the situation studied, and are intentionally *not* 'kept under wraps.' The role may provide access to a wide range of information, and even secrets may be given to the field worker when he becomes known for keeping them, as well as for guarding confidential information. In this role the social scientist might conceivably achieve maximum freedom to gather information but only at the price of accepting maximum constraints upon his reporting. In a given situation, this combination of freedom and responsibility is likely to hinge upon the previous behavior of social scientists who have conditioned the people in it. Hence the question of professional ethics may be more critical for this position than for other roles. If the people find it possible to accept the field worker as a person with a scientific mandate and a publicly accorded right to receive information at all four levels from public to private, they are very likely to expect that the 'contract' as it developed during the field inquiry will be honored at the time of reporting. One constraint, for example, will require the scientific reporter to maintain the people's distinctions between public, confidential, and so on. The consequences of this for the necessary publication of a scientific contribution to knowledge may well deserve some thought in advance of conducting field work in and through this role. The latter may have advantages for some scientific problems and not for others.

IV *Complete Observer*. This describes a range of roles in which, at one extreme, the observer hides behind a one-way mirror, perhaps equipped with sound film facilities, and at the other extreme, his activities are completely public in a special kind of theoretical group where there are, by consensus, 'no secrets' and 'nothing sacred.' Such a group is not found naturally in society, so far as I know, but its form and functioning may be approximated in small experimental groups in which the observer has a formal role, as in situations created in a group dynamics laboratory. At the latter kind of extreme, all levels of information are theoretically equally accessible to all participants and hence an observer would become instead a kind of complete participant – though different from what is implied by such full participation in a natural group.

In less extreme form, this role may be thought of as taken by the field worker at rest or reflecting or as taken in a similar sort of vicarious activity by a learner who may usefully think of himself as there but not involved, as a participant but not really participating, etc. Of course, in these forms it is strictly an imaginary role, not evaluated by the people in the situation being studied, but of some use to the development of the beginner's self-concept as a social scientist, perhaps.

The role of complete observer is more imaginary than real or possible, although, as noted, it may be approximated in a laboratory or simulated in reflection, and its actualization would require the existence in society of a group, with provision for such a person, and with such a state of perfect communication, such a void of secrets, that is so rare as to have escaped observation. It might be argued that such a group is present when one is in a colleague group of psychiatrists or field workers which accepts a member playing this role, but it seems highly likely that this would soon reform itself into a proper in-group and such would change the role of the observer to that of complete participant with all that it implies.

In Figure 31.1, and in these definitions, it is made to appear that the four roles can be sharply distinguished and that the field worker will find himself cast in one and only one position, with its opportunities and limitations as indicated. But the practicing field worker may well find his position and activities shifting through time from one to another of these theoretical points, even as he continues observing the same human organization. Indeed, as hinted in the foregoing, imaginary role-taking is part of the process by which the field worker, in periods of reflection, can estimate where events have taken him and can speculate upon whether a change in his tactics has a chance of success or whether the cues being received indicate that the wisest course is consistency in the same role. In some studies of communities or other large organizations that require field work over a relatively long period of time, and in the early stages of reconnaissance, the first activities of the field worker may be in the role of complete observer, but after a while, as he interacts with more and more people, he moves into the observer-as-participant role and later still, perhaps, into the participant-as-observer role. Looking at events from the field worker's point of view, he finds himself oscillating along this range, day by day or even moment to moment, and, from the viewpoints of individuals with whom he interacts, for some he is more participant than observer, for others he remains more observer than participant, and there may even be many individuals in complex situations who are not at all aware of him as in any way extraordinary but who might regard him as queer or threatening if they saw him as an observer. In not interacting with these, the field worker may retain some activities of the complete observer role, but in his relations with others his activities inevitably take on some of the variable meanings attached to participating both by him and by the others. . . .

Chapter 32

Barney G. Glaser and Anselm L. Strauss

THEORETICAL SAMPLING

From *The Discovery of Grounded Theory: Strategies for Qualitative Research,* Chicago: Aldine (1967).

THEORETICAL SAMPLING IS THE process of data collection for generating theory whereby the analyst jointly collects, codes, and analyzes his data and decides what data to collect next and where to find them, in order to develop his theory as it emerges. This process of data collection is *controlled* by the emerging theory. . . . The initial decisions for theoretical collection of data are based only on a general sociological perspective and on a general subject or problem area (such as . . . what happens to students in medical school that turns them into doctors). The initial decisions are not based on a preconceived theoretical framework.

The sociologist may begin the research with a partial framework of 'local' concepts, designating a few principal or gross features of the structure and processes in the situations that he will study. For example, he knows before studying a hospital that there will be doctors, nurses, and aides, and wards and admission procedures. These concepts give him a beginning foothold on his research. Of course, he does not know the relevancy of these concepts to his problem – this problem must emerge – nor are they likely to become part of the core explanatory categories of his theory. His categories are more likely to be concepts about the problem itself, not its situation. Also, he discovers that some anticipated 'local' concepts may remain unused in the situations relevant to his problem – doctors may, for the problem, be called therapists – and he discovers many more structural and processional 'local' concepts than he could have anticipated before his research.

The sociologist should also be sufficiently *theoretically sensitive* so that he can conceptualize and formulate a theory as it emerges from the data. Once started, theoretical sensitivity is forever in continual development. It is developed as over many years the sociologist thinks in theoretical terms about what he knows, and as he queries many different theories on such questions as ' "What does the theory do? How is it conceived? What is its general position? What kinds of models does it use?" Theoretical sensitivity of a sociologist has two other characteristics. First, it involves his personal and temperamental bent. Second, it involves the sociologist's ability to have theoretical insight into his area of research, combined with an ability to make something of his insights.

These sources of developing theoretical sensitivity continually build up in the sociologist an armamentarium of categories and hypotheses on substantive and formal levels. This theory that exists within a sociologist can be used in generating his specific theory if, after study of the data, the fit and relevance to the data are emergent. A discovered, grounded theory, then, will tend to combine mostly con- cepts and hypotheses that have emerged from the data with some existing ones that are clearly useful. . . .

Potential theoretical sensitivity is lost when the sociologist commits himself exclusively to one specific preconceived theory (e.g., formal organization) for then he becomes doctrinaire and can no longer 'see around' either his pet theory or any other. He becomes insensitive, or even defensive, toward the kinds of questions that cast doubt on his theory; he is preoccupied with testing, modifying and seeing everything from this one angle. For this person, theory will seldom truly emerge from data. In the few instances where theory does emerge, the preconceived theory is likely to be readily dropped or forgotten because it now seems irrelevant to the data.

Beyond the decisions concerning initial collection of data, further collection cannot be planned in advance of the emerging theory (as is done so carefully in research designed for verification and description). The emerging theory points to the next steps – the sociologist does not know them until he is guided by emerging gaps in his theory and by research questions suggested by previous answers.

The basic question in theoretical sampling (in either substantive or formal theory) is: what groups or subgroups does one turn to next in data collection? And for what theoretical purpose? In short, how does the sociologist select multiple comparison groups? The possibilities of multiple comparisons are infinite, and so groups must be chosen according to theoretical criteria. . . .

Our main purpose is to generate theory, not to establish verifications with the 'facts.' We trust that these criteria will also appear to create a more systematic, relevant, impersonal control over data collection than do the preplanned, routin- ized, arbitrary criteria based on the existing structural limits of everyday group boundaries. The latter criteria are used in studies designed to get the facts and test hypotheses. One reason for emphasizing this difference in control is immediately apparent. The criteria of theoretical sampling are designed to be applied in the on- going joint collection and analysis of data associated with the generation of theory. Therefore, they are continually tailored to fit the data and are applied judiciously at the right point and moment in the analysis. The analyst can continually adjust his control of data collection to ensure the data's relevance to the impersonal criteria of his emerging theory.

By contrast, data collected according to a preplanned routine are more likely to force the analyst into irrelevant directions and harmful pitfalls. He may discover unanticipated contingencies in his respondents, in the library and in the field, but is unable to adjust his collection procedures or even redesign his whole project. In accordance with conventional practice, the researcher is admonished to stick to his prescribed research design, no matter how poor the data. If he varies his task to meet these unanticipated contingencies, readers may judge that his facts have been contaminated by his personal violation of the preconceived impersonal rules. Thus he is controlled by his impersonal rules and has no control over the relevancy of his data, even as he sees it go astray . . .

How to select groups

Part of the sociologist's decision about which groups to select is the problem of *how* to go about choosing particular groups for theoretically relevant data collection. First, he must remember that he is an active sampler of theoretically relevant data, not an ethnogapher trying to get the fullest data on a group, with or without a preplanned research design. As an active sampler of data, he must continually analyze the data to see where the next theoretical question will take him. He must then systematically calculate where a given order of events is – or is not – likely to take place. If ongoing events do not give him theoretical relevance, he must be prepared to manipulate events by words or actions in order to see what will happen.

The following memo from our research for *Awareness of Dying* describes how the active search for data occurs as the researcher asks himself the next theoretically relevant question, which, in turn, directs him to seek particular groups for study:

> Visits to the various medical services were scheduled as follows: I wished first to look at services that minimized patient awareness (and so first looked at a premature baby service and then at a neurosurgical service where patients were frequently comatose). I wished next to look at dying in a situation where expectancy of staff and often of patients was great and dying was quick, so I observed on an Intensive Care Unit. Then I wished to observe on a service where staff expectations of terminality were great but where the patient's might or might not be, and where dying tended to be slow. So I looked next at a cancer service. I wished then to look at conditions where death was unexpected and rapid, and so looked at an emergency service. While we were looking at some different types of services, we also observed the above types of service at other types of hospitals. So our scheduling of types of service was directed by a general conceptual scheme – which included hypotheses about awareness, expectedness and rate of dying – as well as by a developing conceptual structure including matters not at first envisioned. Sometimes we returned to services after the initial two or three or four weeks of continuous observation, in order to check upon items which needed checking or had been missed in the initial period.

And in connection with cross-national comparisons, here is another research memo which shows how groups are selected:

The emphasis is upon extending the comparisons made in America in theoretically relevant ways. The probability of fruitful comparisons is increased very greatly by choosing different and widely contrasting countries. That is, the major unit of comparison is the country, not the type of hospital. The other major unit of comparison, as we have seen in our own hospitals, is the type of hospital service, since what ensues around the terminal patient depends on how he dies and under what circumstances. In each country, therefore, I shall attempt to maximize the kinds of dying situations which I would see. I know, for instance, that in some Asian countries many hospitals consist of only one large ward, and this means that I will have to visit hospitals in contrasting regions of the countries. But in the cities, even in Asia, the same hospital may have differing services; and, as in Malaya, there will be hospitals for Chinese and hospitals for mixed ethnic groups right within the same city.

The selection of hospitals and services at which I would observe overseas will be guided, as in the current terminal study, by the conceptual framework developed to date. I will want to observe at hospitals, to begin with, where [four important] structural conditions we have noted are different than in America. I will observe, where possible, in hospitals (or on wards) where all four conditions are maximally different from the usual American conditions; also where three are different, where two are different, and one. I shall also choose wards or services which will maximize some of the specific conditions studied in the United States: namely, wards where dying is predominantly expected by staff and others where dying is relatively unexpected; wards where patients tend to know they are dying, and ones where they do not; wards where dying tends to be slow, and wards where predominant mode of dying tends to be relatively rapid. I hope to observe on various of those wards patients who are of high as well as low social value, and will try to visit locales where conditions are such that very many patients tend to be of low social value, as well as where there would tend to be many patients of high social value.

. . .

Theoretical saturation

. . . The sociologist must continually judge how many groups he should sample for each theoretical point. The criterion for judging when to stop sampling the different groups pertinent to a category is the category's *theoretical saturation. Saturation* means that no additional data are being found whereby the sociologist can develop properties of the category. As he sees similar instances over and over again the researcher becomes empirically confident that a category is saturated. He goes out of his way to look for groups that stretch diversity of data as far as possible, just to make certain that saturation is based on the widest possible range of data on the category.

Theoretical and statistical sampling

It is important to contrast theoretical sampling based on the saturation of categories with statistical (random) sampling. Their differences should be kept clearly in mind for both designing research and judging its credibility. Theoretical sampling is done in order to discover categories and their properties, and to suggest the interrelationships into a theory. Statistical sampling is done to obtain accurate evidence on distributions of people among categories to be used in descriptions or verifications. Thus, in each type of research the 'adequate sample' that we should look for (as researchers and readers of research) is very different.

The adequate theoretical sample is judged on the basis of how widely and diversely the analyst chose his groups for saturating categories according to the type of theory he wished to develop. The adequate statistical sample, on the other hand, is judged on the basis of techniques of random and stratified sampling used in relation to the social structure of a group or groups sampled. The inadequate theoretical sample is easily spotted, since the theory associated with it is usually thin and not well integrated, and has too many obvious unexplained exceptions. The inadequate statistical sample is often more difficult to spot; usually it must be pointed out by specialists in methodology, since other researchers tend to accept technical sophistication uncritically. . . .

Another important difference between theoretical and statistical sampling is that the sociologist must learn when to stop using the former. Learning this skill takes time, analysis and flexibility, since making the theoretically sensitive judgment about saturaton is never precise. The researcher's judgment becomes confidently clear only toward the close of his joint collection and analysis, when considerable saturation of categories in many groups to the limits of his data has occurred, so that his theory is approaching stable integration and dense development of properties.

By contrast, in statistical sampling the sociologist must continue with data collection no matter how much saturation he perceives. In his case, the notion of saturation is irrelevant to the study. Even though he becomes aware of what his findings will be, and knows he is collecting the same thing over and over to the point of boredom, he must continue because the rules of accurate evidence require the fullest coverage to achieve the most accurate count. . . .

Conclusion

Theoretical sampling, then, by providing constant direction to research, gives the sociologist momentum, purpose and confidence in his enterprise. He develops strong confidence in his categories, since they have emerged from the data and are constantly being selectively reformulated by them. The categories, therefore, will fit the data, be understood both to sociologists and to laymen who are knowledgeable in the area, and make the theory usable for theoretical advance as well as for practical application. The sociologist will find that theoretical sampling, as an active, purposeful, searching way of collecting data, is exciting, invigorating and vital. This point is especially important when one considers the boring, dull, and stultifying effects on creativity of the methods involving separate and routine data collection, coding and analysis which are used frequently in descriptive and verificatory studies. Conventional field research is also exciting work but, as we have detailed, it lacks the more extensive commitment to discovery of theory displayed by research utilizing theoretical sampling. . . .

Chapter 33

John Lofland

FIELD NOTES

From *Analyzing Social Settings: A Guide to Qualitative Observation*, Belmont, Cal.: Wadsworth (1971).

. . .

FOR BETTER OR WORSE, the human mind forgets massively and quickly. The people under study forget massively and quickly, too. In order, then, to have any kind of an edge on the participants in articulating and understanding their world, it is necessary to have some means to overcome forgetting. Writing is such a device. Without the sustained writing down of what has gone on, the observer is in hardly a better position to analyze and comprehend the working of a world than are the members themselves. Writing, in the form of continued notes with which the forgotten past can be summoned into the present, is an absolutely necessary if not sufficient condition for comprehending the objects of observation. Aside from getting along in the setting, the fundamental concrete task of the observer is the taking of field notes. Whether or not he performs this task is perhaps the most important determinant of later bringing off a qualitative analysis. Field notes provide the observer's *raison d'être*. If he is not doing them, he might as well not be in the setting. . . .

What goes in?

What do field notes consist of? At the most general level they are a more or less chronological log of what is happening, to and in the setting and to and in the observer. Beyond this general statement, the following materials typically and properly appear in field notes.

Running Description. For the most part, they consist of a running description of events, people, things heard and overheard, conversations among people, conversations with people. Each new physical setting and person encountered merits a description. Changes in the physical setting or persons should also be recorded. Since one is likely to encounter the same physical settings and persons again and again, such descriptions need not be repeated, only augmented as changes occur. Observers often draw maps into their field notes, indicating the approximate layouts of locations and the physical placement of persons in scenes, indicating also gross movements of persons through a period of observation.

Since the notes will be heavily chronological, records can be kept of approximate times at which various events occurred.

The writing of running descriptions can be guided by at least two rules of thumb.

Be concrete. Rather than summarizing or employing abstract adjectives and adverbs, attempt to be behavioristic and concrete. Attempt to stay at the lowest possible level of inference. Avoid, as much as possible, employing the participants' descriptive and interpretative terms as one's own descriptive and interpretative terms. If person *A* thought person *B* was happy, joyous, depressed, or whatever, today, report this as the imputation of person *A*. Try to capture person *B's* raw behavioral emissions, leaving aside for that moment any final judgment as to *B's* 'true state' or the 'true meaning' of his behavior. The participant's belief as to the 'true meaning' of objects, events and people are thus recorded as being just that.

Recall distinctions. Truman Capote has alleged his ability to recall verbatim several hours of conversation. Such an ability is strikingly unusual. More typically, people recall some things verbatim and many other things only in general. Whether or not one is giving a verbatim account should be indicated in one's field notes. One might consider adopting notations such as those employed by Anselm Strauss *et al.* in their study of a mental hospital: 'Verbal material recorded within quotations signified exact recall; verbal material within apostrophes indicated a lesser degree of certainty or paraphrasing and verbal material with no markings meant reasonable recall but not quotation' (Strauss, Schatzman, Bucher, Ehrlich and Sabshin, 1964: 29).

Previously Forgotten, Now Recalled. As observation periods mount up, one finds himself recalling – often at odd moments – items of information he now remembers that he has not previously entered into the field notes. An occurrence previously seen as insignificant, or simply forgotten, presents itself in consciousness as meriting of record. Summoning it up as best one can, enter the item's date, content, context, and the like into the current day's notes.

Analytic Ideas and Inferences. If one is working at it at all, ideas will begin to occur about how things are patterned in this setting; how present occurrences are examples of some sociological or other concept; how things 'really seem to work around here'; and the like. Some of these ideas may seem obvious and trivial; some may seem far fetched and wild; and many may seem in between. *Put all of them into the field notes.*

The only proviso about putting them in is to be sure to mark them off as being analytic ideas and inferences. This can be done with various characters that appear on a typewriter key board – especially brackets [ ].

When one eventually withdraws from the setting and concentrates upon performing analysis he should thus have more than only raw field material. The period of concerted analysis is greatly facilitated if during the field work itself one is also assembling a background, a foundation of possible lines of analysis and interpretation.

Analytic ideas are likely to be of three varieties. (1) Ideas about the master theme or themes of the study. 'What will be the main notions around which all this minutiae is going to be organized?' (2) 'Middle-level' chunks of analysis. 'Although the topic could not carry the entire analysis, here seems to be developing a set of materials in the field notes that hang together in the following way . . . taking up perhaps ten to twenty pages in the final report.' 'Relative to this topic, I want to consider . . .' (3) Minute pieces of analysis. 'Here is a neat little thing that will perhaps work out in this way . . . taking a few pages to write up in the final report.'

One is very likely to have many more of these memos on analytic directions included in his field notes than he will ever include in the final report. But, by building a foundation of memos and tentative pieces of and directions for analysis, the analytic period will be much less traumatic. Analysis becomes a matter of selecting from and working out analytic themes that already exist. (This is in decided contrast to the pure field note grubber who has no ideas and faces the trauma of inventing analysis during the subsequent period of writing the report. Such people tend not to write the reports or to write highly undisciplined description.)

Personal Impressions and Feelings. The field notes are not only for recording the setting; they are for 'recording' the observer as well. The observer has his personal opinions of people; he has emotional responses to being an observer and to the setting itself. He can feel discouraged, joyous, rejected, loved, etc. In order to give himself some distance on himself, the observer should also be recording whatever aspect of his emotional life is involved in the setting. If he feels embarrassed, put down, looked upon with particular favor, if he falls in love, hates someone, has an affair, or whatever, this private diary should be keeping track of such facts. Such keeping track can serve at least two important functions. (1) In being at least privately honest with oneself about one's feelings toward objects, events, and people, one may find that some of the participants *also* feel quite similar things and that one's private emotional response was more widespread, thus providing a clue for analysis. In feeling, for instance, that some person in the setting is getting screwed by a turn of events, and getting privately angry over it, one may also discover later that many other people privately felt the same way. And a fact of this kind may lead into important analytic trails. (2) Periodically, one will review his notes, and during analysis one will work with them intensively. A concurrent record of one's emotional state at various past times, might, months later and away from the setting in a cooler frame of mind, allow one to scrutinize one's notes for obvious biases he might have had. One becomes more able to give the benefit of the doubt in cases where one was perhaps too involved or uninvolved in some incident. This running record of one's opinions, impressions, emotions, and the like should, of course, also be labeled as such in the notes.

Notes for Further Information. Any given day's observations are likely to be incomplete. An account of an incident may lack adequate description of given persons' behavior or their conscious intentions. The event, or whatever, may only be sketchily known. A well-described incident may lead one to want to look for further occurrences of events of that kind. In other words, a given day's notes raise a series of observational questions. It is reasonable to make note of these as one is writing up the notes. One can then review the notes and assemble all these queries as reminders of questions unobtrusively to ask of particular people or of things to look for. . . .

Reference

Strauss, Anselm, Leonard Schatzman, Rue Bucher, Danuta Ehrlich, and Melvin Sabshin, *Psychiatric Ideologies and Institutions*, New York: Free Press, 1964.

Chapter 34

Clifford Geertz

BEING THERE

From *Works and Lives: The Anthropologist as Author*, Stanford, Cal.: Stanford University Press (1988).

. . .

THE ABILITY OF ANTHROPOLOGISTS to get us to take what they say seriously has less to do with either a factual look or an air of conceptual elegance than it has with their capacity to convince us that what they say is a result of their having actually penetrated (or, if you prefer, been penetrated by) another form of life, of having, one way or another, truly 'been there.' And that, persuading us that this offstage miracle has occurred, is where the writing comes in. . . .

A good place to look in looking at ethnographies is at beginnings – at the scene-setting, task-describing, self-presenting opening pages. So let me take, then, to indicate more clearly what I am talking about, two examples, one from a classic ethnography deservedly regarded as a model study, calm and magisterial, and one from a quite recent one, also very well done, that breathes the air of the nervous present.

The classic work is Raymond Firth's *We, the Tikopia*, first published in 1936. After two introductions, one by Malinowski, which says Firth's book 'strengthens our conviction that cultural anthropology need not be a jumble of slogans or labels, a factory of impressionistic short-cuts, or guesswork reconstructions [but rather] a social science – I almost feel tempted to say, the science among social studies,' and one by Firth, which stresses the necessity of 'lengthy personal contact with the people [one studies]' and apologizes for the fact that 'this account represents not the

field-work of yesterday but that of seven years ago,' the book itself begins its first
chapter, 'In Primitive Polynesia':

In the cool of the early morning, just before sunrise, the bow of the
Southern Cross headed towards the eastern horizon, on which a tiny dark
blue outline was faintly visible. Slowly it grew into a rugged mountain
mass, standing up sheer from the ocean; then as we approached within a
few miles it revealed around its base a narrow ring of low, flat land, thick
with vegetation. The sullen grey day with its lowering clouds strengthened my grim impression of a solitary peak, wild and stormy, upthrust in
a waste of waters.

In an hour or so we were close inshore and could see canoes coming
round from the south, outside the reef, on which the tide was low. The
outrigger-fitted craft drew near, the men in them bare to the waist,
girdled with bark-cloth, large fans stuck in the backs of their belts,
tortoise-shell rings or rolls of leaf in the ear-lobes and nose, bearded,
and with long hair flowing loosely over their shoulders. Some plied the
rough heavy paddles, some had finely plaited pandanus-leaf mats resting
on the thwarts beside them, some had large clubs or spears in their
hands. The ship anchored on a short cable in the open bay off the coral
reef. Almost before the chain was down the natives began to scramble
aboard, coming over the side by any means that offered, shouting
fiercely to each other and to us in a tongue of which not a word was
understood by the Mota-speaking folk of the mission vessel. I wondered
how such turbulent human material could ever be induced to submit to
scientific study.

Vahihaloa, my 'boy,' looked over the side from the upper deck, 'My
word, me fright too much,' he said with a quavering laugh; 'me tink this
fella man he savvy kaikai me.' *Kaikai* is the pidgin-English term for 'eat.'
For the first time, perhaps, he began to doubt the wisdom of having left
what was to him the civilization of Tulagi, the seat of Government four
hundred miles away, in order to stay with me for a year in this far-off
spot among such wild-looking savages. Feeling none too certain myself
of the reception that awaited us – though I knew that it would stop short
of cannibalism – I reassured him, and we began to get out the stores.
Later we went ashore in one of the canoes. As we came to the edge of
the reef our craft halted on account of the falling tide. We slipped
overboard on to the coral rock and began to wade ashore hand in hand
with our hosts, like children at a party, exchanging smiles in lieu of
anything more intelligible or tangible at the moment. We were surrounded by crowds of naked chattering youngsters, with their pleasant
light-brown velvet skins and straight hair, so different from the Melane-
sians we had left behind. They darted about splashing like a shoal of fish,
some of them falling bodily into pools in their enthusiasm. At last the
long wade ended, we climbed up the steeply shelving beach, crossed the
soft, dry sand strewn with the brown needles of the Casuarina trees – a
home-like touch; it was like a pine avenue – and were led to an old chief,

clad with great dignity in a white coat and a loin-cloth, who awaited us on his stool under a large shady tree.[1]

There can be little doubt from this that Firth was, in every sense of the word, 'there.' All the fine detail, marshaled with Dickensian exuberance and Conradian fatality – the blue mass, lowering clouds, excited jabberings, velvet skins, shelved beach, needle carpet, enstooled chief – conduce to a conviction that what follows, five hundred pages of resolutely objectified description of social customs – the Tikopia do this, the Tikopia believe that – can be taken as fact. Firth's anxieties about inducing 'such turbulent human material . . . to admit to scientific study' turned out to be as overdrawn as those of his 'boy' that he would be eaten.

But they also never quite disappeared. The 'this happened to me' accents reappear periodically; the text is nervously signed and re-signed throughout. To its last line, Firth struggles with his relation to what he has written, still seeing it in field-method terms. 'The greatest need,' that last line goes, 'in the social sciences to-day is for a more refined methodology, as objective and dispassionate as possible, in which, while the assumptions due to the conditioning and personal interest of the investigator must influence his findings, that bias shall be consciously faced, the possibility of other initial assumptions be realized and allowance be made for the implications of each in the course of the analysis' (p. 488). At deeper levels his anxieties and those of his 'boy' may not in fact have been so entirely different. 'I give this somewhat egoistic recital,' he writes apologetically after reviewing his field techniques, his language abilities, his mode of life on the island, and so forth, 'not because I think that anthropology should be made light reading . . . but because some account of the relations of the anthropologist to his people is relevant to the nature of his results. It is an index to their social digestion – some folk cannot stomach an outsider, others absorb him easily' (p. 11).

The recent text whose opening pages I want to instance as displaying the authorial uneasiness that arises from having to produce scientific texts from bio-graphical experiences is *The Death Rituals of Rural Greece*, by a young ethnographer, Loring Danforth. Like many of his generation, weaned on *Positivismuskritik* and anti-colonialism, Danforth seems more concerned that he will swallow his subjects than that they will swallow him, but the problem is still seen to be essentially epistemo-logical. I quote, with a good deal of ellipsis, from his introduction, called 'Self and Other':

> Anthropology inevitably involves an encounter with the Other. All too often, however, the ethnographic distance that separates the reader of anthropological texts and the anthropologist himself from the Other is rigidly maintained and at times even artificially exaggerated. In many cases this distancing leads to an exclusive focus on the Other as primi-tive, bizarre, and exotic. The gap between a familiar 'we' and an exotic 'they' is a major obstacle to a meaningful understanding of the Other, an obstacle that can only be overcome through some form of participation in the world of the Other.

---

1 R. Firth, *We, the Tikopia* (London, 1936), pp. 1–2.

The maintenance of this ethnographic distance has resulted in . . . the parochialization or the folklorization of the anthropological inquiry into death. Rather than confronting the universal significance of death, anthropologists have often trivialized death by concerning themselves with the exotic, curious, and at times violent ritual practices that accompany death in many societies . . . If, however, it is possible to reduce the distance between the anthropologist and the Other, to bridge the gap between 'us' and 'them,' then the goal of a truly humanistic anthropology can be achieved. . . . [This] desire to collapse the distance between Self and Other which prompted [my] adoption of this [approach] springs from my fieldwork. Whenever I observed death rituals in rural Greece, I was acutely aware of a paradoxical sense of simultaneous distance and closeness, otherness and oneness. . . . To my eyes funeral laments, black mourning dress, and exhumation rites *were* exotic. Yet . . . I was conscious at all times that it is not just Others who die. I was aware that my friends and relatives will die, that I will die, that death comes to all, Self and Other alike.

Over the course of my fieldwork these 'exotic' rites became meaningful, even attractive alternatives to the experience of death as I had known it. As I sat by the body of a man who had died several hours earlier and listened to his wife, his sisters, and his daughters lament his death, I imagined these rites being performed and these laments being sung at the death of my relatives, at my own death. . . . When the brother of the deceased entered the room, the women . . . began to sing a lament about two brothers who were violently separated as they sat clinging to each other in the branches of a tree that was being swept away by a raging torrent. I thought of my own brother and cried. The distance between Self and Other had grown small indeed.[2]

There are of course great differences in these two scene-settings and self-locatings: one a realistic novel model (Trollope in the South Seas), the other a philosophical meditation model (Heidegger in Greece); one a scientist worry about being insufficiently detached, the other a humanistic worry about being insufficiently engaged. Rhetorical expansiveness in 1936, rhetorical earnestness in 1982. But there are even greater similarities, all of them deriving from a common *topos* – the delicate but successful establishment of a familiar sensibility, much like our own, in an intriguing but unfamiliar place, not at all like our own. Firth's coming-into-the-country drama ends with his encounter, a royal audience almost, with the chief. After that, one knows they will come to understand one another, all will be well. Danforth's haunted reflections on Otherness end with his echoic mourning, more fantasy than empathy. After that, one knows the gap will be bridged, communion is

2 L. Danforth, *The Death Rituals of Rural Greece* (Princeton, N.J., 1982), pp. 5–7. For a similar modern or post-modern complaint about 'the anthropology of death,' growing out of a personal experience, the accidental death of his wife, in the field, see R. Rosaldo, 'Grief and a Headhunter's Rage. On the Cultural Force of Emotions,' in E. Bruner, ed., *Text, Play, and Story, 1983 Proceedings of the American Ethnological Society* (Washington, D.C. 1984), pp. 178–95.

at hand. Ethnographers need to convince us (as these two quite effectively do) not merely that they themselves have truly 'been there,' but (as they also do, if rather less obviously) that had we been there we should have seen what they saw, felt what they felt, concluded what they concluded. . . .

Chapter 35

Martyn Hammersley

SOME REFLECTIONS ON
ETHNOGRAPHY AND VALIDITY

From *Qualitative Studies in Education* 5 (3): 195–203 (1991).

. . .

THIS PAPER WILL SKETCH four philosophical positions that have been, and still are, influential among ethnographers, looking particularly at their implications for the question of the criteria by which we should assess ethnographic studies. I will suggest that none of these positions is satisfactory, and will outline the direction in which I think we have the best hope of finding a solution.

One of the most common rationales for ethnographic or qualitative research rests on a rejection of what is seen as the positivist idea that the truth can be discovered by applying the method of the natural sciences to the study of the social world. This rejection is usually based on the claim that social phenomena are different in character from physical phenomena. And what is recommended in place of a reliance on scientific method is closeness to, if not participation in, the reality being studied; that reality being thought of as a culture or at least a cultural situation. So ethnographers long have sought to justify their approach on the grounds that it enables them to get closer to social phenomena and thereby facilitates a superior understanding to that provided by other methods. . . .

Central to this ethnographic critique and self-justification is a rejection of what I will call 'methodism' (commitment to scientific method as *the* source of knowledge) in favor of the belief that knowledge of social phenomena can be gained only by direct experience, a view I will refer to as 'ethnographic realism.' The heart of this realism is the idea that there are independent and unknown realities that can come to be known by the researcher getting into direct contact with them, for example through participant observation or depth interviewing. . . .

. . . While ethnographers often have seen and have presented themselves as advocating realism against the methodism of positivism, many have tended in practice to draw on both realist and methodist ideas. In addition to emphasizing the importance of getting close to reality, they also have appealed often to the use of various methods – triangulation, respondent validation, theoretical sampling, analytic induction, and so forth – in seeking to establish the validity of their claims. In general, realism has been used to urge the superiority of ethnography against quantitative method, while methodism has been employed to defend it against criticism that it is impressionistic and therefore unscientific, being no different from common-sense perspectives on the world.

. . . A third epistemological idea is found in the character of ethnographers' accounts of the people they study. Here the approach is what increasingly is referred to as 'constructivism.' This involves a rejection of the idea that people simply respond to a fixed reality. Rather, they interpret the stimuli they experience and act on those stimuli to change them; and different groups and individuals interpret and act in different ways, thereby producing multiple realities or diverse cultures that are valid in their own terms. . . .

Increasingly, constructivism has been taken to imply a relativism of some kind or another . . . Relativism leads to a rather different view of validity than is characteristic of either methodism or realism. The idea of validity as correspondence with an independent reality clearly is not appropriate, since it is denied that there is any such reality. But neither is the idea accepted that validity can be guaranteed by following scientific method; instead, there are multiple methods producing different but equally valid results. The belief that there may be multiple, contradictory (or at least incommensurable) truths is the hallmark of relativism. Validity is here defined in terms of consensus within a community, that consensus being based on values, purposes, and interests; and no knowledge claims are accepted as universally valid.

The final philosophical position I shall discuss that has been influential in ethnographic thinking is instrumentalism. This often portrays itself as rejecting epistemology in favor of a down-to-earth concern with the usefulness of the products of research. Versions of instrumentalism can be found in pragmatism, especially in the writings of William James, but also in some interpretations of Marxism that portray revolutionary action as bringing reality into line with theory and thereby vindicating that theory . . . and some versions of feminism . . . In some cases instrumentalism seems to lead to little more than an attempt to turn ethnography away from what is seen as an aping of the language of science to the use of representational forms that are more able to capture the reality of social life (Eisner 1988). At the other extreme, an approach is advocated in which research is viewed as a form of direct political action. . . .

I am not implying that among ethnographers there are methodists, realists, relativists, and instrumentalists. The situation is much less clear-cut. One will find traces of more than one, if not of all four, of these tendencies in the methodological thinking and practice of many ethnographers. Nor do I want to suggest that we are doomed to a choice among the four positions I have outlined. In my judgement, none of them is satisfactory as it stands, and I shall draw on elements from all of them to try to construct a more convincing position.

My starting point is an acceptance from realism of the correspondence theory of truth, the idea that one goal of ethnographic (and other forms of) research is to produce accurate representations of phenomena that largely are independent of the researcher and of the research process. It seems to me that none of the other positions can avoid relying implicitly on such a concept of truth. . . .

The correspondence theory of truth, taken from realism, is my starting point. However, this does not imply that I accept the other elements of ethnographic realism. I do not believe that the correspondence between knowledge and reality is necessarily to be maximized by bringing the researcher into close contact with the phenomenon to be understood. Validity is not a function of the closeness of researcher and researched. The argument that we can obtain knowledge through contact with reality seems to be based on what might be called an impression view of the inquiry process, in which by 'being there,' by participating in a situation or culture, the nature of that situation or culture is impressed upon the researcher. A little reflection, I think, is enough to convince us that this is not so. While closeness may provide us with information that would not otherwise be available, as ethnographers themselves have recognized, it also can lead to bias through the process of over-rapport or 'going native.' Furthermore, the impression theory fails to recognize that what we experience is not what is there but, rather, the effects of what is there on us, those effects being the product of considerable physiological and cultural processing. We have to try to construct a view of what is there; the latter does not simply impress itself upon us. Even the most apparently direct experiences we have of the world are constructions, albeit subconscious ones, rather than simple impressions. . . .

Another important implication of the point of view I am advocating is that there is not a single valid description of a situation or culture. Descriptions do not *capture* reality; at best they simply represent those aspects of it that are relevant to the purposes motivating the inquiry. Multiple valid descriptions and explanations of the same phenomenon are always available. To this extent, I agree with the relativists, but I must stress that I do not accept that there can be multiple, *contradictory*, yet valid accounts of the same phenomenon.

In relation to methodism, I reject the idea that method can provide guaranteed access to the truth, or even that methodological prescriptions can or should control research practice. There are no *guarantees* of validity of any kind, and there is an inevitable element of practical decision-making involved in research, as in any other activity. Decisions about research strategy have to be taken in light of the context of the research: the nature of what is being investigated, the resources available, and so forth. However, this is not to say that methodological guidelines are of no value. Indeed, the development of methodological knowledge provides an essential basis for the improvement of research; it represents the collective refinement of our thinking about the goals and means of inquiry. The point is simply that, as with any other sort of theory, its contribution to practice is valuable but limited.

For the sake of a name, I shall call my position 'subtle realism,' to contrast it both with the naive realism to be found in some ethnographic methodology and with the other views I have outlined. Clearly, on this view, validity still means the degree of correspondence between a claim and the phenomena to which it relates; that is, whether the features of the phenomena match what is claimed. However, there is no guaranteed way of producing valid knowledge, either by following methodological prescriptions or by getting into contact with reality. And this raises the question: at what point should we stop in offering or demanding evidence for a claim?

For me, the point at which we should stop providing or asking for further evidence depends on our judgement in particular cases about what we can take as beyond reasonable doubt and what relevant others will take to be beyond reasonable doubt. And any such judgement subsequently may be questioned by those others, or even by us should we revise our views about the validity of our assumptions. What is essential to research, on this view, is a dialogue in which there is a search for common ground and an attempt to work back from this to resolve disagreements, plus a willingness to revise views about previously accepted assumptions and adjust our beliefs accordingly. What research offers from this perspective is not knowledge that can be taken to be valid because it is based on a certain foundation, but rather knowledge that can reasonably be assumed to be (on average) less likely to be invalid than information from other sources. This is because the kind of dialogue I have outlined functions to expose and eliminate errors.

In constructing the position that I have called 'subtle realism,' I have drawn hardly at all, up to now, on instrumentalism. Indeed, I reject the instrumentalist substitution of goodness of effect for truth . . . However, I do believe that this position is important for its challenge to the idea sometimes (but by no means always) associated with the other views: that research simply is concerned with producing knowledge for posterity. . . .

I believe that research must be guided by a criterion of relevance, albeit a somewhat different one than that advanced by instrumentalists. In my view, research should be aimed at producing knowledge that contributes to the problem-solving capacities of some group of people, perhaps even of everyone. Of course, by contrast with instrumentalism's pragmatic maxim, this is a relatively weak criterion. There are two reasons for this. First, there is an ineradicable element of uncertainty surrounding judgements about what knowledge will make such a contribution, an uncertainty that stems from the contingent relationship between knowledge and the outcomes of action based on it that I have noted. Second, in my view, the contribution that inquiry of any kind can make to practice is usually quite small. I do not believe that research is a key ingredient that can transform practice in such a way as to bring about some radical improvement in human life. Achieving any such improvement always is difficult, and (at best) research can play only a minor role in bringing it about. . . .

I do not believe that philosophical reflection about research is of value in itself or is a substitute for research. Neither philosophy nor research is foundational for the other. At the same time, it seems to me that researchers do have an obligation to examine the philosophical assumptions on which they operate, at least now and again, to reflect on those that seem questionable, and to seek to resolve any inconsistencies they find among them. And the issues considered in this paper have profound implications, since they concern not just the means by which we do research but also its goals.

Reference

Eisner, E. W. (1988) 'The primacy of experience and the politics of method.' *Educational Researcher*, 17 (5), 15–20.

Chapter 36

Howard S. Becker and Blanche Geer
(and a subsequent exchange with
Martin Trow)

PARTICIPANT OBSERVATION AND

INTERVIEWING

A comparison

From McCall, G. and Simmons, J.L. (eds.), *Issues in Participant Observation*, New York: Addison-Wesley (1969).

. . .

W E WANT, IN THIS paper, to compare the results of intensive field work with what might be regarded as the first step in the other direction along this continuum: the detailed and conversational interview (often referred to as the unstructured or undirected interview). In this kind of interview, the interviewer explores many facets of his interviewee's concerns, treating subjects as they come up in conversation, pursuing interesting leads, allowing his imagination and ingenuity full rein as he tries to develop new hypotheses and test them in the course of the interview.

In the course of our current participant observation among medical students, we have thought a good deal about the kinds of things we were discovering which might ordinarily be missed or misunderstood in such an interview. We have no intention of denigrating the interview or even such less precise modes of data gathering as the questionnaire, for there can always be good reasons of practicality, economy, or research design for their use. We simply wish to make explicit the difference in data gathered by one or the other method and to suggest the differing uses to which they can legitimately be put. In general, the shortcomings we attribute to the interview exist when it is used as a source of information about events that have occurred elsewhere and are described to us by informants. Our criticisms are not relevant when analysis is restricted to interpretation of the interviewee's conduct *during the interview*, in which case the researcher has in fact observed the behavior he is talking about. . . .

Learning the native language

Any social group, to the extent that it is a distinctive unit, will have to some degree a culture differing from that of other groups, a somewhat different set of common understandings around which action is organized, and these differences will find expression in a language whose nuances are peculiar to that group and fully under-stood only by its members. Members of churches speak differently from members of informal tavern groups; more importantly, members of any particular church or tavern group have cultures, and languages in which they are expressed, which differ somewhat from those of other groups of the same general type. So, although we speak one language and share in many ways in one culture, we cannot assume that we understand precisely what another person, speaking as a member of such a group, means by any particular word. In interviewing members of groups other than our own, then, we are in somewhat the same position as the anthropologist who must learn a primitive language with the important difference that . . . we often do not understand that we do not understand and are thus likely to make errors in interpreting what is said to us. In the case of gross misunderstandings the give and take of conversation may quickly reveal our mistakes, so that the interviewee can correct us; this presumably is one of the chief mechanisms through which the anthropologist acquires a new tongue. But in speaking American English with an interviewee who is, after all, much like us, we may mistakenly assume that we have understood him and the error be small enough that it will not disrupt communica-tion to the point where a correction will be in order.

The interview provides little opportunity of rectifying errors of this kind where they go unrecognized. In contrast, participant observation provides a situation in which the meanings of words can be learned with great precision through study of their use in context, exploration through continuous interviewing of their implica-tions and nuances, and the use of them oneself under the scrutiny of capable speakers of the language. . . .

Matters interviewees are unable or unwilling to talk about

Frequently, people do not tell an interviewer all the things he might want to know. This may be because they do not want to, feeling that to speak of some particular subject would be impolitic, impolite, or insensitive, because they do not think to and because the interviewer does not have enough information to inquire into the matter, or because they are not able to. The first case – the problem of 'resistance' – is well known and a considerable lore has developed about how to cope with it. It is more difficult to deal with the last two possibilities for the interviewee is not likely to reveal, or the interviewer to become aware, that significant omissions are being made. Many events occur in the life of a social group and the experience of an individual so regularly and uninterruptedly, or so quietly and unnoticed, that people are hardly aware of them, and do not think to comment on them to an interviewer; or they may never have become aware of them at all and be unable to answer even direct questions. Other events may be so unfamiliar that people find it difficult to put into words their vague feelings about what has happened. If an interviewee, for any of these reasons, cannot or will not discuss a certain topic, the researcher will find gaps in his information on matters about which he wants to know and will perhaps fail to become aware of other problems and areas of interest that such discussion might have opened up for him.

This is much less likely to happen when the researcher spends much time with the people he studies as they go about their daily activities, for he can see the very things which might not be reported in an interview. Further, should he desire to question people about matters they cannot or prefer not to talk about, he is able to point to specific incidents which either force them to face the issue (in the case of resistance) or make clear what he means (in the case of unfamiliarity). Finally, he can become aware of the full meaning of such hints as are given on subjects people are unwilling to speak openly about and of such inarticulate statements as people are able to make about subjects they cannot clearly formulate, because he frequently knows of these things through his observation and can connect his knowledge with these half-communications.

Researchers working with interview materials, while they are often conscious of these problems, cannot cope with them so well. If they are to deal with matters of this kind it must be by inference. They can only make an educated guess about the things which go unspoken in the interview; it may be a very good guess, but it must be a guess. They can employ various tactics to explore for material they feel is there but unspoken, but even when these are fruitful they do not create sensitivity to those problems of which even the interviewer is not aware. . . .

Things people see through distorting lenses

In many of the social relationships we observe, the parties to the relation will have differing ideas as to what ought to go on in it, and frequently as to what does in fact go on in it. These differences in perception will naturally affect what they report in an interview. A man in a subordinate position in an organization in which subordinates believe that their superiors are 'out to get them' will interpret many incidents in this light though the incidents themselves may not seem, either to the other party in the interaction or to the observer, to indicate such malevolence. Any such mythology will distort people's view of events to such a degree that they will report as fact things which have not occurred, but which seem to them to have occurred. Students, for example, frequently invent sets of rules to govern their relations with teachers, and, although the teacher may never have heard of such rules, regard the teachers as malicious when they 'disobey' them. The point is that things may be reported in an interview through such a distorting lens, and the interviewer may have no way of knowing what is fact and what is distortion of this kind; participant observation makes it possible to check . . . description against fact and, noting discrepancies, become aware of systematic distortions made by the person under study; such distortions are less likely to be discovered by interviewing alone. This point, let us repeat, is only relevant when the interview is used as a source of information about situations and events the researcher himself has not seen. It is not relevant when it is the person's behavior in the interview itself that is under analysis.

Inference, process and context

. . . The difficulties in analyzing change and process on the basis of interview material are particularly important because it is precisely in discussing changes in themselves and their surroundings that interviewees are least likely or able to give an accurate account of events. Changes in the social environment and in the self inevitably produce transformations of perspective, and it is characteristic of such transformations that the person finds it difficult or impossible to remember his former actions, outlook, or feelings. Reinterpreting things from his new perspective, he cannot give an accurate account of the past, for the concepts in which he thinks about it have changed and with them his perceptions and memories. Similarly, a person in the midst of such change may find it difficult to describe what is happening, for he has not developed a perspective or concepts which would allow him to think and talk about these things coherently. . . .

Participant observation does not have so many difficulties of this sort. One can observe actual changes in behavior over a period of time and note the events which precede and follow them. Similarly, one can carry on a conversation running over weeks and months with the people he is studying and thus become aware of shifts in perspective as they occur. In short, attention can be focused both on what has happened and on what the person says about what has happened. Some inference as to actual steps in the process or mechanisms involved is still required, but the amount of inference necessary is considerably reduced. Again, accuracy is increased and the possibility of new discoveries being made is likewise increased, as the observer becomes aware of more phenomena requiring explanation.

The participant observer is both more aware of these problems of inference and more equipped to deal with them because he operates, when gathering data, in a social context rich in cues and information of all kinds. Because he sees and hears the people he studies in many situations of the kind that normally occur for them, rather than just in an isolated and formal interview, he builds an evergrowing fund of impressions, many of them at the subliminal level, which give him an extensive base for the interpretation and analytic use of any particular datum. This wealth of information and impression sensitizes him to subtleties which might pass unnoticed in an interview and forces him to raise continually new and different questions, which he brings to and tries to answer in succeeding observations.

The biggest difference in the two methods, then, may be not so much that participant observation provides the opportunity for avoiding the errors we have discussed, but that it does this by providing a rich experiential context which causes him to become aware of incongruous or unexplained facts, makes him sensitive to their possible implications and connections with other observed facts, and thus pushes him continually to revise and adapt his theoretical orientation and specific problems in the direction of greater relevance to the phenomena under study. Though this kind of context and its attendant benefits cannot be reproduced in interviewing (and the same degree of sensitivity and sense of problem produced in the interviewer), interviewers can profit from an awareness of those limitations of their method suggested by this comparison and perhaps improve their batting average by taking account of them.

Comment on 'Participant observation and interviewing: a comparison'
MARTIN TROW

Insofar as the paper by Becker and Geer says: 'Participant observation is a very useful way of collecting data, and here are some illustrations to show how useful we found it in one study,' I can take no issue with them. On the contrary, I profited from their discussion of the method and their illustrations of its use.

But, unfortunately, Becker and Geer say a good deal more than that. In their first paragraph they assert that participant observation, by virtue of its intrinsic qualities, 'gives us more information about the event under study than data gathered by any other sociological method.' And since this is true, 'it provides us with a yardstick against which to measure the completeness of data gathered in other ways. . . .'

It is with this assertion, that a given method of collecting data – *any* method – has an inherent superiority over others by virtue of its special qualities and divorced from the nature of the problem studied, that I take sharp issue. The alternative view, and I would have thought this the view most widely accepted by social scientists, is that different kinds of information about man and society are gathered most fully and economically in diferent ways, and that the problem under investigation properly dictates the methods of investigation. If this is so, then we certainly can use other methods of investigation as 'yardsticks' against which to measure the adequacy of participant observation for the collection of certain kinds of data. And my impression is that most of the problems social scientists are studying seem to call for data gathered in other ways than through participant observation. Moreover, most of the problems investigated call for data collected in several different ways, whether in fact they are or not. This view seems to me implied in the commonly used metaphor of the social scientist's 'kit of tools' to which he turns to find the methods and techniques most useful to the problem at hand. Becker and Geer's argument sounds to me very much like a doctor arguing that the scalpel is a better instrument than the forceps – and since this is so we must measure the forceps' cutting power against that of the scalpel. . . .

The first thing that struck me on reading this paper is its oddly parochial view of the range and variety of sociological problems. To state flatly that participant observation 'gives us more information about the event under study than . . . any other sociological method' is to assume that all 'events' are directly apprehensible by participant observers. But what are some of the 'events' that sociologists study? Is a national political campaign such an 'event'? Is a long-range shift in interracial attitudes an 'event'? Is an important change in medical education and its aggregate of consequences an 'event'? Are variations in suicide rates in different social groups and categories an 'event'? If we exclude these phenomena from the definition of the term 'event' then we exclude most of sociology. If we define 'event' broadly enough to include the greater part of what sociologists study, then we find that most of our problems require for their investigation data of kinds that cannot be supplied by the participant observer alone. . . .

Every cobbler thinks leather is the only thing. Most social scientists, including the present writer, have their favorite research methods with which they are familiar and have some skill in using. And I suspect we mostly choose to investigate problems that seem vulnerable to attack through these methods. But we should at least try to be less parochial than cobblers. Let us be done with the arguments of 'participant observation' *versus* interviewing – as we have largely dispensed with the arguments for psychology *versus* sociology – and get on with the business of attacking our problems with the widest array of conceptual and methodological tools that we possess and they demand. This does not preclude discussion and debate regarding the relative usefulness of different methods for the study of specific problems or types of problems. But that is very different from the assertion of the general and inherent superiority of one method over another on the basis of some intrinsic qualities it presumably possesses.

'Participant observation and interviewing': a rejoinder

HOWARD S. BECKER AND BLANCHE GEER

We read Martin Trow's 'Comment' on our 'Participant observation and interviewing: a comparison' with interest and profit. An unfortunate ambiguity in key terms led Trow to misinterpret our position radically. We would like to clear up the confusion briefly and also to discuss a few interesting questions raised in this argument.

Trow believes us to have said that participant observation is the best method for gathering data for all sociological problems under all circumstances. We did not say this and, in fact, we fully subscribe to his view 'that different kinds of information about man and society are gathered most fully and economically in different ways, and that the problem under investigation properly dictates the methods of investigation'. We did say, and now reiterate, that participant observation gives us the most complete information about social events and can thus be used as a yardstick to suggest what kinds of data escape us when we use other methods. This means, simply, that, if we see an event occur, see the events preceding and following it, and talk to various participants about it, we have more information than if we only have the description which one or more persons could give us. . . .

We intended to refer only to specific and limited events which are observable, not to include in the term such large and complex aggregates of specific events as national political campaigns. Naturally, such events are not 'directly apprehensible' by an observer. But to restate our position, the individual events of absorbing information about an election, discussing it with others, and deciding which way to vote are amenable to observation. It is the information that one gets about these events, and then combines in order to arrive at generalizations, which one might want to examine for completeness by the yardstick of participant observation. . . .

PART EIGHT

Qualitative interviewing

INTRODUCTION

LOOSELY STRUCTURED INTERVIEWING IS perhaps the most often used method for gathering qualitative data. It seems to make intuitive sense that if you want to find out about something you should go and ask some people about their experience of it. In this respect, the qualitative interview is rather like the semi-automatic resort to hurriedly put-together fixed-choice questions when inexperienced researchers decide they want to 'do a survey'. One of the messages of this book is that nothing should be done on a semi-automatic basis in social research. In the case of interviews, careful thought needs to be given to the potential of other methods before deciding to use them. Better, and more viable alternatives often exist.

Having said that, interviews are good for some research problems, and social researchers need to know how to use and think about them. The first reading (number 37 by Jones) focuses on how to do 'depth' interviews, contrasting these with the kind of 'formal questionnaire' discussed in readings 9–11. Jones firmly places herself in the Schutzian position (reading 29) of researchers concerned to explore subjectivity. Additionally, she distances herself from the model of the research process outlined by Wallace (reading 4) in which hypotheses are specified at the outset, instead characterizing qualitative research using interviews as exploratory.

The humanist commitment of Jones to understanding people on their own terms is taken a step further by Oakley (reading 38). She argues against both the 'mechanical' approach of structured interviewing and the 'non-directive' approach of some qualitative interviewing, in which nothing is revealed by the researcher for fear of creating 'bias'. Instead, Oakley argues (from a feminist position), researchers ought to tell interviewees about their own experiences so that the encounter becomes a mutually co-operative event. She says that the level of trust and commitment that this is then likely to generate will result in more authentic information than otherwise, as there is less likelihood of a false front being presented to the researcher. A later commentary by Malseed is then included, in which Oakley's characterization of textbook accounts of survey research interviewing is questioned and then responded to by Oakley.

Kitzinger's account (reading 39) of focus groups explores the potential that this form of group discussion has for adding a dimension that is normally absent in the one-to-one interview: the interaction between participants. Focus groups are 'artificial' in the same sense as interviews, so could be said to suffer from some of the problems identified by Becker and Geer (reading 36). But they help a little in providing a more naturalistic environment, since people are influenced in what they can say and do by the presence of others, who they may meet again in their everyday lives. This limits the possibilities for fantasy reports about actions and events, but it can also help the researcher treat the event as an opportunity for semi-naturalistic observation in its own right, rather than simply a resource for gathering reported experience. In fact, this 'topicalization' of interview data is in line with discourse and conversation analytic approaches to interview data (readings 47–48, 52, 55; see also Seale (1998)).

DISCUSSION POINTS

- Is Jones's characterization of quantitative survey research practice accurate? (See readings in earlier parts of the book describing this.)
- How would you do a qualitative interviewing study of a group of people like you (e.g. other students, other researchers) in a study of their experience of things which you have also experienced (e.g. being a student, being a researcher)? Would you adopt the non-directive 'psycho-analytic' style in which you do not reveal your own experience? Or would you tell your respondents about your own experience, and get involved with helping them out in problems they may have? What are the advantages and disadvantages of the approach you choose and the approach you reject?
- Imagine you are doing a research project on bullying in schools. What would a focus group reveal about this, as opposed to an observational study of children in school settings?

REFERENCE

Seale, C.F. (1998) 'Qualitative interviewing', in Seale, C.F. (ed.) *Researching Society and Culture*, London: Sage.

FURTHER READING

Deutscher, I. (1969/70) 'Asking questions and listening to answers', *Sociological Focus* 3 (2): 13–32.

Devault, M.L. (1990) 'Talking and listening from women's standpoint: feminist strategies for interviewing and analysis', *Social Problems* 37: 96–116.

Gubrium, J.F. and Holstein, J.A. (2002) *Handbook of Interview Research*, Thousand Oaks, Cal.: Sage.

Holstein, J.A. and Gubrium, J.F. (1995). *The Active Interview*, Thousand Oaks, Cal.: Sage.

Krueger, R. (1988) *Focus Groups: A Practical Guide for Applied Research*, London: Sage. (2nd edition, 1994)

Kvale, S. (1996). *Interviews: An Introduction to Qualitative Research Interviewing*, Thousand Oaks, Cal.: Sage.

Merton, R.K., Fiske, M. and Kendall, P. (1990) (2nd edition) *The Focused Interview*, London: The Free Press (Macmillan).

Mishler, E.G. (1986). *Research Interviewing: Context and Narrative*, Cambridge, Mass.: Harvard University Press.

Morgan, D. (1988) *Focus Groups as Qualitative Research*, London: Sage.

Morgan, D.L., (ed.) (1993). *Successful Focus Groups: Advancing the State of the Art*, London: Sage.

Personal Narratives Group (ed.) (1989) *Interpreting Women's Lives: Feminist Theory and Personal Narratives*, Bloomington: Indiana University Press.

Silverman, D. (1998) 'The quality of qualitative health research: the open-ended interview and its alternatives', *Social Sciences in Health* 4 (2): 104–117.

Spradley, J.P. (1979) *The Ethnographic Interview*, New York: Holt, Rinehart and Winston.

Chapter 37

Sue Jones

DEPTH INTERVIEWING

From Walker, R. (ed.), *Applied Qualitative Research*, Aldershot: Gower (1985).

. . .

IN CHARACTERISING WHAT THEY do, I have heard different researchers use the label 'depth interview' to cover many different approaches. These have ranged from the supposedly totally 'non-directive' to that where the main difference from the formal questionnaire interview seems to be that the interviewer does not have a typed sheet of paper, varies the exact wording of the questions and perhaps asks more 'probe' questions than is usual in a formal questionnaire. Between these two extremes is an abyss of practice and therefore theory about the purpose and nature of the qualitative interview.

There is, of course, a considerable literature on the theoretical bases for qualitative methodology to which justice cannot be done here. To summarise my own theoretical starting point: it comes from a particular 'model of man' which sees human beings not as organisms responding, Pavlovian fashion, to some external stimulus, nor inexorably driven by internal needs and instincts, nor as 'cultural dopes', but as persons, who *construct* the meaning and significance of their realities. They do so by bringing to bear upon events a complex personal framework of beliefs and values, which they have developed over their lives to categorise, characterise, explain and predict the events in their worlds. It is a framework which, in a social world, is shared in some parts with some others but one in which the points of commonality cannot be assumed as self-evidently, non-problematically, 'given'. In order to understand *why* persons act as they do we need to understand the meaning and significance they give to their actions. The depth interview is one way – not the only way and often used most appropriately in conjunction with other ways – of doing so. For to understand other persons' constructions of reality we would do well to ask them (rather than assume we can know merely by observing their overt behaviour) and to ask them in such a way that they can tell us in their terms (rather than those imposed rigidly and *a priori* by ourselves) and in a depth which addresses the rich context that is the substance of their meanings (rather than through isolated fragments squeezed onto a few lines of paper).

Structure and ambiguity

The above leads naturally to consideration of one central issue in the conduct of depth interviews, that of the degree of structure in the interview. It is an issue I have found to be of recurring concern among those just starting to do qualitative research, reflected in such questions as: How non-directive can I, ought I to be? Do I always ask open-ended questions? Can I never disagree with the respondents? Qualitative research methodologies seek to learn about the social world in ways which do not rigidly structure the direction of enquiry and learning within simplifying, acontextual, *a priori* definitions. Thus, interviews in which interviewers have prepared a long list of questions which they are determined to ask, come what may, over a period of say an hour and a half, are not depth interviews. This is so even if the researchers are contingent enough to alter the exact wording and order of their questions and even if the questions all centre around the same broad topic. For in this way the interviewers have already predicted, in detail, what is relevant and meaningful to their respondents about the research topic; and in doing this they have significantly prestructured the direction of enquiry within their own frame of reference in ways that give little time and space for their respondents to elaborate their own. They are additionally likely to be so anxious to cover all their questions that even if they hear something they know they ought to follow up, they do not. Often they will not hear such crucial clues anyway.

Yet the issue of structure is not straightforward. There is no such thing as a totally unstructured interview and the term is over-used and often carelessly used. . . .

The crucial point is that there is no such thing as presuppositionless research. . . . The process of interviewing is one in which researchers are continually making choices, based on their research interests and prior theories, about which data they want to pick up and explore further with respondents and those which they do not. The making of these choices is the imposition of some structure.

Yet although we are tied to our own frameworks, we are not totally tied up by them. If we ask more questions arising from what we hear at the time than we have predetermined we will ask, if we hold on to, modify, elaborate and sometimes abandon our prior schemes in a contingent response to what our respondents are telling us is significant in the research topic, then we are some way to achieving the complex balance between restricting structure and restricting ambiguity.

The problem of ambiguity is illustrated by the 'non-directive' style of interviewing, where researchers encourage interviewees to ramble in any direction they choose and give no indication of what they themselves are interested in. 'Non-directive' interviews are anything but non-directive. What one person will say to another depends on what he or she assumes the other is 'up to' in the situation. If the respondents have no clear idea of what the researchers' interests and intentions are, they are less likely to feel unconstrained than constrained by the need to put energy into guessing what these are. Furthermore, the level of ambiguity means not only that the interviewees do not know 'what questions the researchers are asking' but also, and therefore, that the researchers do not know what questions the respondents are answering. In short, researchers are more likely to get good data, and know what data they are getting, if the interviewees are told at the outset what the research topic is, even if initially in relatively broad terms, and why the topic is of interest.

Interviewer bias?

The issue of structure is closely related to that of 'interviewer bias'. Many of those who come to qualitative methods in policy-related research come from a quantitative tradition in which the need to avoid interviewer bias is usually regarded as crucial. It is a concern bound to ideas, for example, of reliability and replication. In qualitative research the notion of some kind of impersonal, machine-like investigator is recognised as a chimera. An interview is a complicated, shifting, social *process* occurring between two individual human beings, which can never be exactly replicated. We cannot get at some 'objective truth' that would be there if only the effects of interpersonal interaction could be removed. . . .

There cannot be definitive rules about the use of open-ended questions, leading and loaded questions, disagreement with respondents, and so on. Such choices must depend on the understanding researchers have of the person they are with and the kind of relationship they have developed in the encounter. Some relationships may allow, without destroying trust and comfort, much more of the to-and-fro of debate and discussion between two human beings than others. What is crucial is that researchers choose their actions with a self-conscious awareness of why they are making them, what the effects are likely to be upon that relationship – and indeed whether their own theories and values are getting in the way of understanding those of the respondents.

A social interaction

. . . If we as researchers want to obtain good data it would be better that the persons we are interviewing trust us enough to believe that we will not use the data against them, or that we will not regard their opinions as foolish; that they are not trying very hard to please; or are not so untouched by us as individuals and the process of being interviewed that they produce a well-rehearsed script that tells very little about what actually concerns and moves them; or that they do not see an opportunity to manipulate us to suit certain personal ends of which we are unaware, and so on. Thus, the stress in much that is said about interviewing is on the need to assure respondents of confidentiality, on using and developing the social skills (verbal and non-verbal) which we have all used at some time or other to convince others that we want to hear what they have to say, take it seriously, and are indeed hearing them.

We do need to pay attention to the crucial non-verbal data – of posture, gesture, voice intonation, facial expression, eye contact, and so on – by which we can communicate, for example, interest, encouragement, warmth and caring, on the one hand, or boredom, disapproval, coldness and indifference on the other. We need not only to ask questions in such a way that the others are encouraged to answer and elaborate further, in their terms, but also to give them enough time and space to do so. We also of course do need to listen – to hear what seems to be significant to the respondents in the research topic and explore this further, to be aware of the data that tell us we have misread significance and should change the line of probing. We need to know how to judge when we are getting data that are off the track of what we are interested in, be very sure that we are not just making this judgement on the basis of our own preconceptions and missing data that are relevant to the research topic as construed by the respondents; and then how to bring them back gently. We need to check meaning when we are not sure that we have understood, and not assume too quickly that we have understood. And just as we need to think very carefully about the types of people we are going to interview, the likely range of their experiences and possible responses, and adapt our approach and self-presentation appropriately, so we need to adapt our style to the particular person we are with (that is, the individual, not the 'type') and to the shifts and developments during the interaction.

These are essential skills that have to be thought about and practised, and if researchers do not develop such skills the likelihood of overcoming some of the problems outlined earlier is significantly reduced. . . .

Chapter 38

Ann Oakley (and a subsequent exchange with Joanna Malseed)

INTERVIEWING WOMEN
A contradiction in terms

From Roberts, H. (ed.), *Doing Feminist Research*, London: Routledge (1981) and Malseed, J., 'Straw men: a note on Ann Oakley's treatment of textbook prescriptions for interviewing,' *Sociology* 21(4): 629–631 (1987).

. . .

I SHALL ARGUE IN this chapter that social science researchers' awareness of those aspects of interviewing which are 'legitimate' and 'illegitimate' from the viewpoint of inclusion in research reports reflect their embeddedness in a particular research protocol. This protocol assumes a predominantly masculine model of sociology and society. The relative undervaluation of women's models has led to an unreal theoretical characterisation of the interview as a means of gathering sociological data which cannot and does not work in practice. This lack of fit between the theory and practice of interviewing is especially likely to come to the fore when a feminist interviewer is interviewing women (who may or may not be feminists).

Interviewing: a masculine paradigm?

. . . The paradigm of the social research interview prompted in the methodology textbooks emphasise[s] (a) its status as a mechanical instrument of data-collection; (b) its function as a specialised form of conversation in which one person asks the questions and another gives the answers; (c) its characterisation of interviewees as essentially passive individuals, and (d) its reduction of interviewers to a question asking and rapport-promoting role. Actually, two separate typifications of the interviewer are prominent in the literature, though the disjunction between the two is never commented on. In one . . . the interviewer must treat the interviewee as an object or data-producing machine which, when handled correctly will function properly; the interviewer herself/himself has the same status from the point of view of the person/people, institution or corporation conducting the research. Both interviewer and interviewee are thus depersonalised participants in the research process.

The second typification of interviewers in the methodology literature is that of the interviewer as psychoanalyst. The interviewer's relationship to the interviewee is hierarchical and it is the body of expertise possessed by the interviewer that allows the interview to be successfully conducted. Most crucial in this exercise is the interviewer's use of non-directive comments and probes to encourage a free association of ideas which reveals whatever truth the research has been set up to uncover. Indeed, the term 'nondirective interview' is derived directly from the language of psychotherapy and carries the logic of interviewer-impersonality to its extreme. . . .

It seems clear that both psychoanalytic and mechanical typifications of the interviewer and, indeed, the entire paradigmatic representation of 'proper' interviews in the methodology textbooks, owe a great deal more to a masculine social and sociological vantage point than to a feminine one. For example, the paradigm of the 'proper' interview appeals to such values as objectivity, detachment, hierarchy and 'science' as an important cultural activity which takes priority over people's more individualised concerns. Thus the errors of poor interviewing comprise subjectivity, involvement, the 'fiction' of equality and an undue concern with the ways in which people are not statistically comparable. This polarity of 'proper' and 'improper' interviewing is an almost classical representation of the widespread gender stereotyping which has been shown, in countless studies, to occur in modern industrial civilisations. . . . Women are characterised as sensitive, intuitive, incapable of objectivity and emotional detachment and as immersed in the business of making and sustaining personal relationships. Men are thought superior through their capacity for rationality and scientific objectivity and are thus seen to be possessed of an instrumental orientation in their relationships with others. Women are the exploited, the abused; they are unable to exploit others through the 'natural' weakness of altruism – a quality which is also their strength as wives, mothers and housewives. Conversely, men find it easy to exploit, although it is most important that any exploitation be justified in the name of some broad political or economic ideology ('the end justifies the means'). . . . It is no accident that the methodology textbooks (with one notable exception) (Moser 1958) refer to the interviewer as male. Although not all interviewees are referred to as female, there are a number of references to 'housewives' as the kind of people interviewers are most likely to meet in the course of their work. . . .

Women interviewing women: or objectifying your sister

Before I became an interviewer I had read what the textbooks said interviewing ought to be. However, I found it very difficult to realise the prescription in practice, in a number of ways which I describe below. It was these practical difficulties which led me to take a new look at the textbook paradigm. In the rest of this chapter the case I want to make is that when a feminist interviews women: (1) use of prescribed interviewing practice is morally indefensible; (2) general and irreconcilable contradictions at the heart of the textbook paradigm are exposed; and (3) it becomes clear that, in most cases, the goal of finding out about people through interviewing is best achieved when the relationship of interviewer and interviewee is non-hierarchical and when the interviewer is prepared to invest his or her own personal identity in the relationship.

Before arguing the general case I will briefly mention some relevant aspects of my own interviewing experience. I have interviewed several hundred women over a period of some ten years, but it was the most recent research project, one concerned with the transition to motherhood, that particularly highlighted problems in the conventional interviewing recipe. Salient features of this research were that it involved repeated interviewing of a sample of women during a critical phase in their lives (in fact 55 women were interviewed four times; twice in pregnancy and twice afterwards and the average total period of interviewing was 9.4 hours.) It included for some my attendance at the most critical point in this phase: the birth of the baby. The research was preceded by nine months of participant observation chiefly in the hospital setting of interactions between mothers or mothers-to-be and medical people. . . .

My difficulties in interviewing women were of two main kinds. First, they asked me a great many questions. Second, repeated interviewing over this kind of period and involving the intensely personal experiences of pregnancy, birth and motherhood, established a rationale of personal involvement I found it problematic and ultimately unhelpful to avoid. . . .

I set out to convey to the people whose cooperation I was seeking the fact that I did not intend to exploit either them or the information they gave me. For instance, if the interview clashed with the demands of house-work and motherhood I offered to, and often did, help with the work that had to be done. When asking the women's permission to record the interview, I said that no one but me would ever listen to the tapes; in mentioning the possibility of publications arising out of the research I told them that their names and personal details would be changed and I would, if they wished, send them details of any such publications, and so forth. The attitude I conveyed could have had some influence in encouraging the women to regard me as a friend rather than purely as a data-gatherer.

The pilot interviews, together with my previous experience of interviewing women, led me to decide that when I was asked questions I would answer them. The practice I followed was to answer all personal questions and questions about the research as fully as was required. For example, when two women asked if I had read their hospital case notes I said I had, and when one of them went on to ask what reason was given in these notes for her forceps delivery, I told her what the notes said. On the emotive issue of whether I experienced childbirth as painful (a common topic of conversation) I told them that I did find it so but that in my view it was worth it to get a baby at the end. Advice questions I also answered fully but made it clear when I was using my own experiences of motherhood as the basis for advice. I also referred women requesting advice to the antenatal and childbearing advice literature or to health visitors, GPs, etc. when appropriate – though the women usually made it clear that it was my opinion in particular they were soliciting. When asked for information I gave it if I could or, again, referred the questioner to an appropriate medical or non-medical authority. Again, the way I responded to inter- viewee's questions probably encouraged them to regard me as more than an instru- ment of data-collection.

Dissecting my practice of interviewing further, there were three principal reasons why I decided not to follow the textbook code of ethics with regard to interviewing women. First, I did not regard it as reasonable to adopt a purely exploitative attitude to interviewees as sources of data. My involvement in the women's movement in the early 1970s and the rebirth of feminism in an academic context had led me, along with many others, to re-assess society and sociology as masculine paradigms and to want to bring about change in the traditional cultural and academic treatment of women. 'Sisterhood', a somewhat nebulous and prob- lematic, but nevertheless important, concept, certainly demanded that women re- evaluate the basis of their relationships with one another.

The dilemma of a feminist interviewer interviewing women could be summar- ised by considering the practical application of some of the strategies recommended in the textbooks for meeting interviewee's questions. For example, these advise that such questions as 'Which hole does the baby come out of?' 'Does an epidural ever paralyse women?' and 'Why is it dangerous to leave a small baby alone in the house?' should be met with such responses from the interviewer as 'I guess I haven't thought enough about it to give a good answer right now,' or 'a head-shaking gesture which suggests "that's a hard one"' (Goode and Hatt 1952 [. . .]). Also recommended is laughing off the request with the remark that 'my job at the moment is to get opinions, not to have them' (Selltiz *et al.* 1965 [. . .]).

A second reason for departing from conventional interviewing ethics was that I regarded sociological research as an essential way of giving the subjective situation of women greater visibility not only in sociology, but, more importantly, in society, than it has traditionally had. Interviewing women was, then, a strategy for docu- menting women's own accounts of their lives. What *was* important was not taken- for-granted sociological assumptions about the role of the interviewer but a new awareness of the interviewer as an instrument for promoting a sociology for women – that is, as a tool for making possible the articulated and recorded commentary of women on the very personal business of being female in a patriarchal capitalist society. Note that the formulation of the interviewer role has changed dramatically from being a data-collecting instrument for researchers to being a data-collecting instrument for those whose lives are being researched. Such a reformulation is enhanced where the interviewer is also the researcher. It is not coincidental that in the methodological literature the paradigm of the research process is essentially disjunctive, i.e. researcher and interviewer functions are typically performed by different individuals.

A third reason why I undertook the childbirth research with a degree of scepti- cism about how far traditional percepts of interviewing could, or should, be applied in practice was because I had found, in my previous interviewing experiences, that an attitude of refusing to answer questions or offer any kind of personal feedback was not helpful in terms of the traditional goal of promoting 'rapport'. A different role, that could be termed 'no intimacy without reciprocity', seemed especially important in longitudinal in-depth interviewing. Without feeling that the interviewing process offered some personal satisfaction to them, interviewees would not be prepared to continue after the first interview. This involves being sensitive not only to those questions that are asked (by either party) but to those that are not asked. The interviewee's definition of the interview is important.

The success of this method cannot, of course, be judged from the evidence I have given so far. On the question of the rapport established in the Transition to Motherhood research I offer the following cameo:

> A.O.: 'Did you have any questions you wanted to ask but didn't when you last went to the hospital?'
>
> M.C.: 'Er, I don't know how to put this really. After sexual intercourse I had some bleeding, three times, only a few drops and I didn't tell the hospital because I didn't know how to put it to them. It worried me first off, as soon as I saw it I cried. I don't know if I'd be able to tell them. You see, I've also got a sore down there and a discharge and you know I wash there lots of times a day. You think I should tell the hospital; I could never speak to my own doctor about it. You see I feel like this but I can talk to you about it and I can talk to my sister about it.'

More generally the quality and depth of the information given to me by the women I interviewed can be assessed in *Becoming a Mother* (Oakley 1979), the book arising out of the research which is based almost exclusively on interviewee accounts.

So far as interviewees' reactions to being interviewed are concerned, I asked them at the end of the last interview the question, 'Do you feel that being involved in this research – my coming to see you – has affected your experience of becoming a mother in any way?' Table 38.1 shows the answers.

Table 38.1 'Has the research affected your experience of becoming a mother?' (percentages)

No	27
Yes:	73
Thought about it more	30
Found it reassuring	25
A relief to talk	25
Changed attitudes/behaviour	7

* Percentages do not add up to 100% because some women gave more than one answer.

Nearly three-quarters of the women said that being interviewed had affected them and the three most common forms this influence took were in leading them to reflect on their experiences more than they would otherwise have done; in reducing the level of their anxiety and/or in reassuring them of their normality; and in giving a valuable outlet for the verbalisation of feelings. None of those who thought being interviewed had affected them regarded this affect as negative. There were many references to the 'therapeutic' effect of talking: 'getting it out of your system'. (It was generally felt that husbands, mothers, friends, etc., did not provide a sufficiently sympathetic or interested audience for a detailed recounting of the experiences and difficulties of becoming a mother.) It is perhaps important to note here that one of the main conclusions of the research was that there is a considerable discrepancy between the expectations and the reality of the different aspects of motherhood – pregnancy, childbirth, the emotional relationship of mother and child, the work of childrearing. A dominant metaphor used by interviewees to describe their reactions to this hiatus was 'shock'. In this sense, a process of emotional recovery is endemic in the normal transition to motherhood and there is a general need for some kind of 'therapeutic lisener' that is not met within the usual circle of family and friends. . . .

An anthropologist has to 'get inside the culture'; participant observation means 'that . . . the observer participates in the daily life of the people under study, either openly in the role of researcher or covertly in some disguised role' (Becker and Geer 1957, p. 28). A feminist interviewing women is by definition both 'inside' the culture and participating in that which she is observing. However, in these respects the behaviour of a feminist interviewer/researcher is not extraordinary. Although (Stanley and Wise 1979, pp. 359–361)

> descriptions of the research process in the social sciences often suggest that the motivation for carrying out substantive work lies in theoretical concerns . . . the research process appears a very orderly and coherent process indeed. . . . The personal tends to be carefully removed from public statements; these are full of rational argument [and] careful discussion of academic points. [It can equally easily be seen that] all research is 'grounded', because no researcher can separate herself from personhood and thus from deriving second order constructs from experience.

A feminist methodology of social science requires that this rationale of research be described and discussed not only in feminist research but in social science research in general. It requires, further, that the mythology of 'hygienic' research with its accompanying mystification of the researcher and the researched as objective instruments of data production be replaced by the recognition that personal involvement is more than dangerous bias – it is the condition under which people come to know each other and to admit others into their lives.

References

Becker, H.S. and Geer, B. (1957) 'Participant observation and interviewing: a comparison?', *Human Organisation*, vol. xvi, pp. 28–32.

Goode, W.J. and Hatt, P.K. (1952) *Methods in Social Research*, McGraw Hill, New York.

Moser, C.A. (1958) *Survey Methods in Social Investigation*, Heinemann, London.

Oakley, A. (1979) *Becoming a Mother*, Martin Robertson, Oxford.

Selltiz, C., Jahoda, M., Deutsch, M. and Cook, S.W. (1965) *Research Methods in Social Relations*, Methuen, London.

Stanley, L. and Wise, S. (1979) 'Feminist research, feminist consciousness and experiences of sexism', *Women's Studies International Quarterly*, vol. 2, no. 3, pp. 359–379.

Straw men: a note on Ann Oakley's treatment of textbook prescriptions for interviewing

JOANNA MALSEED

. . . Is Oakley's representation of the textbooks' prescriptions entirely accurate and fair to her sources? The textbooks explain that the nature of the research problem should determine the type of interviewing used. For some research problems a formal, structured interview with interviewer detachment and interviewee passivity provides an appropriate method of data collection. However, for some research problems, particularly those investigating subjective phenomena – such as perceptions, feelings and attitudes, as in Oakley's research – the textbooks describe an alternative less structured, less formal method of data collection. Some examples of this are:

> To overcome the limitations of the structured interview, the researcher must resort to the unstructured interview . . . The unstructured interview assumes a variety of forms, (b)ut all offer, in contrast to the structured type, considerable freedom in the questioning procedure; at times the question-and-answer sessions approach the informality of ordinary conversations. Moreover, they emphasize the informant's world of meaning and utilize the informant's categories rather than the scientist's . . .
>
> (Sjoberg and Nett 1968:211)

. . .

> (F)or some research problems, a still more flexible approach than that provided by a standardised interview with open-ended questions is appropriate . . . They are commonly used for a more intensive study of perceptions, attitudes, motivations, etc., than a standardised interview . . . This type of interview is inherently more flexible . . . in which neither the exact questions the interviewer asks, nor the response the subject is permitted to make are pre-determined . . . Obviously this approach is impossible in a questionnaire
>
> (Selltiz et al. 1965:263)

However, Oakley's references to the textbooks' accounts of interviewing methods fail to explore fully the implications for data collection of the textbook recommendations at the informal end of the scale. The more active role of interviewees and personal involvement of the interviewer with interviewees outlined by Oakley would feature inevitably under the conditions of informal interviewing described in the texts as appropriate for research into complex, subjective phenomena.

The non-hierarchical, interactive interview relationships which occurred in Oakley's interviewing do not constitute a lack of fit between textbook interviewing theory and her practice, but accord with the textbooks' outline of appropriate methods for research into subjective phenomena. Thus, Oakley's dissatisfaction with the textbooks' accounts of interviewing techniques is less the result of their inadequacies and the consequent need for an alternative methodology, and more the result of her inadequate exploration of their implications for the interview relationship and data collection.

References

Selltiz, C., Jahoda, M., Deutsch, M. and Cook, S.W. 1965. *Research Methods in Social Relations*, London: Methuen.
Sjoberg, G. and Nett, R. 1968. *A Methodology for Social Research*. New York: Harper and Row.

Comment on Malseed
ANN OAKLEY

. . . The main point made, that the traditional methodology textbooks do recognize something called the 'informal' interview, would seem to me to prove the point I contended in the original article. The textbooks discuss first something called the 'formal' interview, and then go on to allow for the fact that sometimes, as when subjective issues are being probed, it may be more appropriate to conduct the interview less formally. (This is, not coincidentally nor irrelevantly, considered less reliable.) But acknowledging the existence of informal interviews does not detract from the fact that *normally* interviewing is/should be formal, structured, and designed to conceal the interviewer's personal identity. The one is a deviation from the other. Subjective material is a deviation from the objective, and thus calls for a modification of normal methods of enquiry.

Moreover, the extent to which an interview is structured tells us nothing about the extent to which it has been characterized by mutuality. The interviewing experiences I described in my article . . . cannot be accommodated to the 'deviation from normal' model recognized by the textbooks, because what they speak to is the division between public and private which leads to the very dichotomy we set up between 'objective' and 'subjective' experiences. . . .

Chapter 39

Jenny Kitzinger

THE METHODOLOGY OF FOCUS GROUPS
The importance of interaction between research participants

From *Sociology of Health and Illness* 16 (1): 104–121 (1994).

Introduction

FOCUS GROUPS ARE GROUP discussions organised to explore a specific set of issues such as people's views and experiences of contraception . . ., drink-driving . . ., nutrition . . . or mental illness. . . . The group is 'focused' in the sense that it involves some kind of collective activity – such as viewing a film, examining a single health education message or simply debating a particular set of questions. Crucially, focus groups are distinguished from the broader category of group inter-views by 'the explicit use of the group interaction' as research data (see Merton *et al.* 1956 and Morgan 1988: 12). . . .

However, group work has not been systematically developed as a research technique within social science in general and although group interviews have often implicitly informed research they are rarely acknowledged as part of the process . . . Even when group work is explicitly included as part of the research it is often simply employed as a convenient way to illustrate a theory generated by other methods or as a cost-effective technique for interviewing several people at once. Reading some such reports it is hard to believe that there was ever more than one person in the room at the same time. This criticism even applies to many studies which explicitly identify their methodology as 'focus group discussion' – in spite of the fact that the distinguishing feature of focus groups is supposed to be the use of interaction as part of the research data. Reviewing over 40 published reports of 'focus group studies' I could not find a single one concentrating on the conversation between participants and very few that even included any quotations from more than one participant at a time. This article attempts to redress the balance through a detailed examination of the interactions between the research participants on the AIDS Media Research Project. . . .

Perceiving the research session as a forum within which ideas could be clarified rather than simply as a 'natural event' influenced the ways in which we chose to run the groups. Sessions were conducted in a relaxed fashion with minimal intervention from the facilitator – at least at first. This allowed the facilitator to 'find her feet' and permitted the research participants to set the priorities. However, the researcher was never passive. Trying to maximise interaction between participants could lead to a more interventionist style: urging debate to continue beyond the stage it might otherwise have ended, challenging people's taken for granted reality and encouraging them to discuss the inconsistencies both between participants and within their own thinking. . . .

The fact that group participants provide an audience for each other encourages a greater variety of communication that is often evident within more traditional methods of data collection. During the course of the AIDS project group participants argued, boasted, made faces at each other, told stories and on one occasion, sang songs. Group work is characterised by teasing, joking and the kind of acting out that goes on among peers. For example, some participants acted out the 'look' of an 'AIDS carrier' (contorting their faces, squinting and shaking) and others took evident delight in swapping information about the vast quantities of saliva one would need to drink before running any risk of infection. (You'd need to swallow 'six gallons', 'eight gallons', 'ten gallons' or 'bathe in it while covered in open sores'.) Brainstorming and loose word association was a frequent feature of the research sessions. In several groups any attempt to address the risks HIV poses to gay men were drowned out by a ritual period of outcry against homosexuality:

> ITM Benders, poufs
> ITM Bent bastards
> ITM Bent shops
> ITM they're poufs, I mean I don't know how a man could have sex with another man it's . . .
> ITM It's disgusting [. . .]
> ITM Ah, Yuk!

A certain amount of similar 'brain-storming' accompanied discussion of the idea that 'AIDS comes from Africa':

> ITF Look at all the famine over there, all the disease coming off the dead cows and all that, they die and all that
> ITM Dirtiness
> ITM Filthy
> ITF Blackness
> JK   Blackness? what about it?
> ITM It's black
> ITF Black, Blackness, its black, that's what I mean its dirty
> ITM It's just disgusting. [Young people in intermediate treatment]

These sorts of interactions can make groups seem unruly (both at the time and when attempting to analyse the data) but such 'undisciplined' outbursts are not irrelevant or simply obstructive to the collection of data about what people 'know'. On the contrary, the enthusiasm with which some people acted out 'the look of an AIDS carrier' vividly demonstrates the voyeuristic fascination of 'the Face of AIDS' and the way in which some media images are reproduced, reinforced and reiterated through social interaction. The relish with which people swapped information about the vast quantities of saliva needed to pose any risk of infection highlights the potency of the 'yuk' factor in helping them to recall certain 'facts' about AIDS and suggest the potential of harnessing peer communication. The outcry provoked by any mention of homosexuality and the loose word-association about 'blackness' reveal an essential element in how people think about AIDS among gay men or in Africa. They form part of why some people believe that gay men (and lesbians) are inherently vulnerable to HIV or why they so readily accept that Africa is a hotbed of HIV infection (Kitzinger and Miller 1992). Tapping into such variety of communication is important because people's knowledge and attitudes are not entirely encapsulated in reasoned responses to direct questions. Everyday forms of communication such as anecdotes, jokes or loose word association may tell us *as much*, if not *more*, about what people 'know'. In this sense focus groups 'reach the parts that other methods cannot reach' – revealing dimensions of understanding that often remain untapped by the more conventional one-to-one interview or questionnaire. . . .

There are 10 main advantages to be gained from the interaction between participants. Such interaction:

- highlights the *respondents'* attitudes, priorities, language and framework of understanding
- encourages a great variety of communication from participants – tapping into a wide range and form of understanding
- helps to identify group norms
- provides insight into the operation of group/social processes in the articulation of knowledge (e.g. through the examination of what information is censured or muted within the group)
- can encourage open conversation about embarrassing subjects and facilitate the expression of ideas and experiences that might be left underdeveloped in an interview

Through detailed attention to the interaction between different members of the group a researcher can:

- explore difference between group participants in situ with them and, because, participants reflect upon each other's ideas, ensure that the data is organic/ interconnected.
- use the conflict between participants in order to clarify why people believe what they do. Examine the questions that people ask one another in order to reveal their underlying assumptions and theoretical frameworks.
- explore the arguments people use against each other, identify the factors

which influence individuals to change their minds and document how facts and stories operate in practice – what ideological work they do.

• analyse how particular forms of speech facilitate or inhibit peer communication, clarify or confuse the issue (in ways directly relevant to improving communication). . . .

We are none of us self-contained, isolated, static entities; we are part of complex and overlapping social, familial and collegiate networks. Our personal behaviour is not cut off from public discourses and our actions do not happen in a cultural vacuum whether that is negotiating safer sex, sharing needles, attending for a smear test or going 'queer bashing'. We learn about the 'meaning' of AIDS, (or sex, or health or food or cigarettes) through talking with and observing other people, through conversations at home or at work; and we act (or fail to act) on that knowledge in a social context. When researchers want to explore people's understandings, or to influence them, it makes sense to employ methods which actively encourage the examination of these social processes in action.

References

Kitzinger, J. and Miller, D. (1992) 'African AIDS: the media and audience beliefs.' In Aggleton, P., Davies, P. and Hart, G., *AIDS: Rights, Risk and Reason*. London: Falmer Press, 28–52.

Merton, R. *et al.* (1956) *The Focused Interview: A Report of the Bureau of Applied Social Research.* Columbia University.

Morgan, D. (1988) *Focus Groups as Qualitative Research*. London: Sage.

PART NINE

Other sources of qualitative data

INTRODUCTION

ONE OF THE MORE pleasant discoveries of my career as a researcher has been that almost anything can be thought of as data. For example, the other day I was advising a student who wanted to do a study of 'mixed race' marriages. She was going to interview some participants in such marriages but was worried about whether this would tell her very much. She was particularly interested in asking them how they negotiated food preferences if different cultural traditions were involved. I suggested that she do a survey of the objects in the kitchens in these homes (the contents of cupboards, the fridge, etc.). I supposed she could combine this with asking them about where an item came from, who used it and for what, so that the original plan of interviewing them was not lost, but the data on what objects were there could reveal something. This is what anthropologists do when they study 'material culture'.

The readings in this section consider the uses of some other forms of research data. The first, reading 40 by Collier and Collier, explores the potential for photographs and film. Interestingly, these researchers also take family meals as an example where photographs can reveal a great deal about the cultural patterning of family life, though here it is pictures of family meals rather than the contents of cupboards that are the key resource. Reading 41 concerns the uses of a variety of documents. Plummer notes the research uses of many, including diaries, letters, photograph albums, documentary films, tombstones and suicide notes. Clearly, there are more that he does not mention (websites, advertisements, minutes of meetings, newspaper reports, medical records, press releases – the list is endless). All of these can be, and have been, used by researchers studying particular social and cultural processes.

Archives of statistical data have been available to social researchers for some time now for secondary analysis (see readings 16 and 17). Increasingly, qualitative data archives are being established too. Hammersley's account (reading 42) raises prospects and problems for this form of secondary analysis. He considers, too, the potential of archives for checking the conclusions of original researchers. On both counts he sees considerable problems as well as some potential.

Hamman (reading 43) discusses the use of on-line chat rooms as a site for ethnographic work. He is particularly concerned with the analysis of differences between face-to-face interviewing and internet interviewing, noting that the distance and anonymity of internet interviewing means that people are more likely to admit to acts that they find too embarrassing to discuss face-to-face, but that the reliance on written messages allows much scope for misunderstanding.

DISCUSSION POINTS

- Collier and Collier suggest that the analyst should look at visual materials 'until their character is clear.' They say that 'The ideal analysis process allows the data to lead to its own conclusions' and they claim that 'Photographic data are the closest approximation to primary experience that we can gather.' How objective are photographs? Are some ways of taking photographs more objective than others?
- People usually say a research project starts with questions and then proceeds by gathering data to answer the questions. This exercise encourages you to think of the research questions last: in fact, it is how a lot of research projects actually get done. Follow these steps in sequence: (1) think of a documentary source of data; (2) imagine a social research project that would use it as data; (3) what research questions could this answer?
- Compare Hammersley's observations about the issues involved in doing secondary analysis of archived qualitative data with those raised by Kiecolt and Nathan (reading 16) and Dale *et al.* (reading 17) with regard to archived statistical data. What similarities and differences are there?
- How could you treat the internet as a site for observation rather than interviewing? Find the website of a large, profit-oriented business organization and compare it with the website of a pressure group, or a university. What does the organization and design of the website tell you about the structures of power and authority within these organizations?

FURTHER READING

Bateson, G. and Mead, M. (1942) *Balinese Character: A Photographic Analysis*, New York: New York Academy of Sciences.
Hill, M.R. (1993) *Archival Strategies and Techniques*, Thousand Oaks, Cal.: Sage.
Hine, C. (2000); *Virtual Ethnography*, London: Sage.
Jones, S. (1999); *Doing Internet Research: Critical Issues and Methods for Examining the Net*, Thousand Oaks, Cal.: Sage.

Kress, G. and van Leeuwen, T. (1996) *Reading Images: The Grammar of Visual Design*, London and New York: Routledge.

Mann, C. and Stewart, F. (2000) *Internet Communication and Qualitative Research: A Handbook for Researching Online*, London: Sage.

Pink, S. (2001) *Doing Visual Ethnography: Images, Media and Representation in Research*, London: Sage.

Scott, J. (1990) *A Matter of Record*, Cambridge: Polity Press.

Chapter 40

John Collier, Jr. and Malcolm Collier

PRINCIPLES OF VISUAL RESEARCH

From *Visual Anthropology: Photography as a Research Method,* Albuquerque: University of New Mexico Press (1986).

. . .

Basic considerations in visual research

AN ELEMENTARY REALITY IS that total documentation is almost always impossible, and if such saturated recording were attempted we would become engulfed in an overload of complex details from which it might be impossible to reconstruct a contextual view. A whole view is the product of a breadth of samples that allows us comprehend the whole through systematic analysis of those carefully selected parts. A good selection process provides a sufficient reflection of cultural circumstance from which to establish a reliable perspective. Analysis may also require sampling within the data if we are not to be overwhelmed with the mass of detail and complexities often present in visual records. . . .

Researchable visual data

The most beautiful and technically superb photograph is useless in visual research if it does not conform to the needs of systematized observation. For this reason we need to review what can be seen and researched in photographs. . . .

The significance of what we find in analysis is shaped by the context established by systematic recording during fieldwork. As an example, a study could be made of family structure in a confining class or caste-defined society. A systematized record-ing of family gatherings throughout the social organization in comparable circum-stances (meals, ceremonials, work, etc.) could supply a profile of family structure through comparison of family behavior in comparable situations. We would be careful to obtain records of the same range of phenomena in each circumstance, such as proxemic relationships, the functional identity of all participants, physical setting, the temporal sequences of behavior and events, as well as a variety of other categories of information.

An unusable study of the same subject would contain family scenes in which visual identity and spatial relationships would be unclear and temporal order jum-bled. Imagery might be obscured by shadows, soft focus, and angles of view that miss crucial information or are inconsistent from situation to situation. Such a collection of data would be as limited in value as a mass of archeological artifacts dumped on the floor of a lab with no information regarding the locations in which they were found. Like misplaced artifacts, these images might still be aesthetically satisfying but they would not be a reliable source of knowledge. This criticism should not discourage 'extra sensory' or 'artistic' recordings made to gather the overtones of cultural circumstance, but it should emphasize that such records be made within the setting of a larger research process that can provide the necessary contextual rela-tionships to allow photographs to become meaningful.

Impressionistic and ragged recording is not the only danger of unsystematized field observation. A conscientious fieldworker might attempt mechanistically to record every detail of environment and cultural content, creating a further form of uncomputable data in which we would become overloaded with disorganized detail. The danger of this approach is illustrated by Mark Twain's description of a river pilot cursed with an unselective memory in which trivial detail overwhelmed the more important elements: 'Such a memory as that is a great misfortune. To it, all occurrences are of the same size. Its possessor cannot distinguish an interesting circumstance from an uninteresting one' (Twain 1917: 112). The purpose of sys-tematic fieldwork and analysis is to provide the researcher with information that is significant and exclude that which is not. In this manner the complexity of the real world is put into a form from which meaningful conclusions can be made.

[Editor's note: At this point in the original text three photographs were shown portraying, first, an evening meal in a home in Vicos, Peru; second, supper in a Spanish American home in New Mexico; and, third, breakfast in the home of an advertising executive's family in Westport, Connecticut.]

The range of photographic observation

The question raised in making intelligible observations is how fluent should be your sense of evidence in order to gather meaningful data? There are a number of elements to consider.

. . . A less rigid approach to recording can draw upon the unexpected and spontaneous happening. An overly structured approach could edit out holistic and circumstantial relationships of great importance. An example comes from the work of Samuel Barrett, who produced a series of film records of California Indian technology. Barrett's film crew included anthropology students whose ethnographic interests went beyond the reconstruction of traditional craft methods. Eventually there was a conflict over Barrett's structured approach. This confrontation took place in an empty lot in Santa Rosa, California, where an elderly Pomo woman demonstrated basketmaking. In the background were junked cars, political posters, and urban mess. The students tried to include this modern context, but Barrett refused to shift the camera focus from the details of basket manufacture. In the perceptions of the young anthropologists, the ethnographic significance was that Pomo baskets were still being made, even in a cluttered city lot. In the students' eyes, Barrett was framing out this significant data (Robert Wharton and David Peri, personal communication). . . .

Designs for analysis

In our classes a rude beginning to analysis is experienced when students are pre-sented with a strewn pile of beach pebbles on a white sheet of paper. Faced with the assignment 'analyze this data, this pebble community,' students tend to take one or the other of two extreme approaches. One is to observe the pebbles as a cosmology, the second is to reorganize the pebbles in orderly categories of color, size, shape. What can be learned from each approach? What conclusions might each support? We begin our discussion of research design in analysis with this example.

A cosmological approach would reveal the distribution pattern formed by the pebbles. Smaller and more mobile pebbles might be strewn at a greater distance than the large, less mobile ones. The distribution might then be seen as a function of the characteristics of different pebbles. *Mapping* the location of the pebbles might be an act that could clarify the precise position of each 'artifact.'

A typological approach that breaks the pebbles into different categories would reveal statistical content about the pebble 'community' with no visually patterned relationships. It would tell us what was there but not how. Once the pebbles have been removed from their authentic position the contextual order would be lost and the associational relationships could not be considered. Similar confusions can occur in handling photographic data when the contextual information and spatial/temporal relationships are lost.

Like good fieldwork, analysis also should include a phase of free discovery. . . . Open-ended viewing may yield important findings or at least define new, unanticipated directions for more structured analysis. In this phase we yield our-selves to the reality of our data. Photographic data are the closest approximation to primary experience that we can gather, and we want to carry this photographic authenticity from the field into analysis. Frequently, the analysis of visual records is a dialogue between researcher and images, a two way communication similar to fieldwork.

But as in fieldwork if we do not have a cumulative scheme that directs our analytic explorations we can become locked into endless circles of confusing detail from which we may never emerge. Sometimes these disorganized processes can be traced to inadequacies in the field recording, but usually the cause lies in a lack of coherent command of research procedure and techniques during analysis. Just as in fieldwork we must move from open response to directed activities, so in analysis we must move from visual impressions to systematized procedures for handling visual data.

The ideal analysis process allows the data to lead to its own conclusions through a dynamic interplay between open and structured procedures. As one example, we can begin the analysis of a home inventory with an immersion in the images of the home environment that can give a sense of direct interaction with the details and functions of the habitation. These first impressions reflect all the skills of intuitive discovery and intellectual speculation and can also help us develop *categories* for more structured counting, measuring, and comparing procedures. These are often in the form of questions: 'How does this home serve as place of relaxation and renewal? How does the home serve as a place for socializing? As a place of retreat?' The photographs can be inventoried to provide specific information on these questions. If the sample is large, this process will produce statistical findings that may lead us to define better our initial perceptions or, equally possible, to decide where they are faulty.

In this manner analysis involves a two-part question: 'What do I see?' and 'How do I know?' or better 'What can be seen and identified in the visual record that gives me that impression?' Deliberate combinations of open and structured procedures during analysis enable us to discover with our full capacities of perception while defining and checking those perceptions through careful reference to specific visual evidence. In some respects this is an art process, but it is guarded from remaining impressionistic by scientific procedures. . . .

These principles suggest a basic design sequence for analysis of all visual records, including film and video as well as photographs. You begin by looking at the film or photographs repeatedly until their character is clear. In this stage film and video are viewed uncut in proper chronological order. Photographs are arranged in temporal or spatial orders that approximate the original circumstance in which they were made. The open immersion may take weeks.

The next stage will usually involve some sort of inventory or logging process in which the content of scenes or photographs is broken into categories of behavior, actions, material content, and spatial arrangement that are then noted in some standardized form or code. The purpose is one of becoming familiar with even the mundane content of the visual records and identifying the location of data within the total sample.

After this step it is common to engage in focused analysis, shaped by initial research questions and new propositions discovered during earlier stages of the analysis. At this point one might carefully compare one living room with another, measure the distance between participants in different interactions, count how many times the teacher looks at a particular child, track people through time, or carry out other specific analytic activities. It is now that one might do micro-analysis, examining every frame of film in a particular sequence, counting every item in every photograph of every room. The detailed information that is gathered in this stage is useful because it fits within a larger framework.

In the end you must formulate conclusions. We have found that dynamic conclusions are usually best produced through a final review of all the film or all the photographs. This clears your mind of minutiae and places important details in their larger context, preserving the lively character of photographic evidence that is the most important aspect of visual anthropology.

Reference

Twain, Mark (1917) *Life on the Mississippi*. New York: Harper and Brothers Publishers.

Chapter 41

Ken Plummer

ON THE DIVERSITY OF LIFE
DOCUMENTS

From *Documents of Life*, Thousand Oaks, Cal.: Sage (2000, first published 1983)

. . . any research procedure which can tell us something about the subjective orientation of human actors has a claim to scholarly consideration.

(Blumer 1979, p. xxiii)

THE WORLD IS CRAMMED full of personal documents. People keep diaries, send letters, take photos, write memos, tell biographies, scrawl graffiti, publish their memories, write letters to the papers, leave suicide notes, inscribe memorials on tombstones, shoot films, paint pictures, make music and try to record their personal dreams. All of these expressions of personal life are hurled out into the world by the millions and can be of interest to anyone who cares to seek them out. They are all in the broadest sense 'documents of life', and the aim of this chapter is to explore a little of this diversity. . . .

The diary

For Allport (1942, p. 95), the diary is the document of life *par excellence*, chronicling as it does the immediately contemporaneous flow of public and private events that are significant to the diarist. The word 'contemporary' is very crucial here, for each diary entry – unlike life histories – is sedimented into a particular moment in time: they do not emerge 'all at once' as reflections on the past, but day by day strive to record an ever-changing present. . . .

There are three apparent forms of diary research that social scientists could use. . . . The first is simply for the sociologist to ask informants to keep diaries. Thus

Maas and Kuypers (1974) as part of a statistical, longitudinal study of adjustments to old age in the lives of 142 upper-class San Franciscans asked a number of their respondents to keep diaries for a week. Their study is subsequently richly documented with extracts from these diaries. . . .

Closely allied to this approach is the gathering of 'logs' and 'time budgets'. Sorokin pioneered this method when he asked informants to keep detailed 'time-budget schedules' showing just how they allocated their time during a day (Sorokin and Berger 1938). . . . But perhaps the most celebrated use is that of Oscar Lewis.

Lewis's particular method focused on a few specific families in Mexico, and the analysis of a 'day' in each of their lives. Of course his actual familiarity with each family was in no way limited to a day – nothing of value could possibly be gained from that. He 'spent hundreds of hours with them in their homes, ate with them, joined in their fiestas and dances, listened to their troubles, and discussed with them the history of their lives' (Lewis 1959, p. 5). But in the end he decided that it would be analytically more valuable, for both humanistic and scientific purposes, to focus upon 'the day' as a unit of study. Thus each family – Martinez, Gomez, Gutierez, Sanchez and Castro – is first presented as a 'cast of characters' and then followed through one arbitrarily chosen but not untypical day of their life. Lewis believed that a study of a day had at least a threefold value: practically, it was small enough to allow for intensive observation, quantitatively it permitted controlled comparisons across family units, and qualitatively it encouraged a sensitivity to the subtlety, immediacy and wholeness of life.

A third type of diary study has been dubbed 'the diary–diary interview method'. Here, Zimmerman and Wieder (1975), in the course of examining the Californian counter-culture, found considerable difficulties in observing the full daily pattern of activities of their subjects. In place of observation they instituted a method in which respondents were paid a fee of $10 to keep a full diary for seven days. . . .

Of particular interest in their method is not just the rich documentation they gained about seven days of a person's life, but the fact that the person is subsequently interviewed step by step on each facet of the diary that has been presented.

The above three forms of diary – the requested, the log and the 'diary–diary interview' – all entail the social scientist soliciting diaries and are comparable to the social scientist soliciting life histories. But just as the life historian could also turn to pre-existing biographies to analyse, so the diary researcher could turn to pre-existing diaries.

The letter

Letters remain a relatively rare document of life in the social sciences. Without doubt, the most thoroughgoing use of letters is still to be found in Thomas and Znaniecki's *Polish Peasant* where on discovering that there was extensive correspondence between Poles and Polish emigrés to America, an advertisement was placed in a Chicago journal offering to pay between 10 to 20 cents for each letter received. Through this method they were able to gain many hundreds of letters. . . . Thomas and Znaniecki suggest that the letters perform five main functions corresponding to five main types of letters. These are:

1   Ceremonial letters – 'sent on such familial occurrences as normally require the presence of all the members of the family – weddings, christenings, funerals, Christmas, New Year, Easter. These letters are substitutes for ceremonial speeches.'
2   Informing letters – providing 'a detailed narration of the life of the absent member of the family group'.
3   Sentimental letters – which have 'the task of reviving the feelings in the individual, independently of any ceremonial occasion'.
4   Literary letters – which have a central aesthetic function, and
5   Business letters – (cf. Thomas and Znaniecki 1958).

The letters are used inductively to arrive at a more general characterisation of peasant society, particularly its subjective aspects. . . .

Many insights can be gained from the study of letters, yet these materials are only rarely to be found in social science. And in good part this may simply be due to the obvious fact that such letters are increasingly hard to come by – letter-writing appears to be a dying art, and even when letters are sent they are most commonly thrown away rather than stored and collected. . . . Nevertheless, even when such letters are available, social scientists are likely to remain suspicious of their value. . . . Every letter speaks not just of the writer's world, but also of the writer's perceptions of the recipient. The kind of story told shifts with the person who will read it – witness the different letters produced by Robert Burns to his mistress, his friends, his wife on the same day. The social scientist then should view a letter as an interactive product, always inquiring into the recipient's role. . . .

The photograph

If diaries and letters became central life documents (as least in the middle classes) during the nineteenth century, they have now been rapidly overtaken by photography. Born at approximately the same time as sociology, photography has gone on to become many things: the democratiser of personal documents (in family albums and holiday shots for all), a major new genre of art, the embodiment of individualism (in the rise of photographic portraiture), a mode of refusing experience, a strategy for conveying immortality upon experience, and last but not least, a form of surveillance and control (cf. Sontag 1978). Millions of photographs are produced by lay person and professional alike each year, but still sociology remains relatively unscathed by it. It is true that in the earliest days of the *American Journal of Sociology*, photographs were a regular feature in connection with its muck-raking, reformist articles: between 1896 and 1916 thirty-one articles used 244 photographs (see Stasz 1979). Likewise many of the early Chicago studies – Thrasher's *The Gang*, for example – included an array of photographs. But in the main sociologists have not taken much interest in what should now be viewed as a major tool for investigation; the lead has primarily come from anthropologists (and in particular the pioneering work of Gregory Bateson and Margaret Mead (1942) . . . It was only during the 1970s that a small group of American sociologists became concerned about its use, organised exhibitions of their photographic work, and coined the term 'visual sociology'.

There are many ways in which photography could be put to work for sociology. Curry and Clark (1977) suggest it may serve as an illustration, as visual information or as source material for analysis, whilst Wagner (1979, pp. 16–19) suggests five modes of photographic research: as interview stimuli, for systematic recordings of social phenomena, for sustained content analysis, for 'native' image making and for 'narrative visual theory'.

Perhaps the most obvious use to date is that of the photograph as documentation – an essentially descriptive task where the photo is designed simply to illustrate a text. . . . [In other work] the photos are fully linked in with the text. They do not merely illustrate: they integrate. The model for this kind of work is revealed in the classic 1930s' study of average – and thereby poor – white families of tenant farmers in the Southern States of America: *Let Us Now Praise Famous Men* by James Agee and Walker Evans. Here Agee, no sociologist, spent time absorbed in the lives of the tenant families whilst Evans . . . produces the first volume of the study with photographs of places, objects and people. As Agee says, 'The photographs are not illustrative. They, and the text, are co-equal, mutually independent, and fully collaborative' (p. xiii). . . .

A few sociologists have taken this further through 'narrative visual theory', where the 'implicit elements of social theory are clearly acknowledged' (Wagner 1979, p. 18). Here the photos are systematically selected through a tacit theory – Jackson looks at prison life (1977, 1978), and Harper looks at tramps (1978). They come close to being ethnographies which instead of relying upon the written word become organised through visual imagery. In this view, the task is to theorise through photography (cf. Becker 1974).

A further way in which photos may be used by social scientists is as a resource for further explanations. Thus Thompson (1974) was able to interview respondents through photos of the My Lai massacre, and in Banish's work on *City Families* (1976) the technique was to combine interview with photography. This researcher first visited selected families in order to take photographs of them as they wished to see themselves and then returned both to talk about the photographs, to ask which was their favourite and to interview them about their hopes and aspirations in life. The study is composed of the preferred photographs on one page matched with the interviews and observations on the opposite page. Of added interest in this study is the range of families studied and the contrasts drawn between the families of two cities: London and Chicago.

From this comes one of the most apparent methods for using photographs in social science: to ask the respondent for a look at their family albums (cf. Musello 1979). In a most striking way, all manner of details about childhood relationships, friendship, family rituals and family history are highlighted. . . .

Film

If social scientists have only occasionally considered the benefits of photography to their work, most have never countenanced the significance of film. . . . Documentary film makers have provided historians with much fodder for analysis but it is anthropologists who have been most adept at exploiting this medium to date. At the start of the century, ethnographers started to film various tribal peoples engaged in social rituals – Spencer, in 1901, filmed Australian aborigines in kangaroo dances and rain ceremonies, while in 1914 Curtis filmed the Kwakiutl Indians. But the birth of the documentary film is commonly agreed to be Robert Flaherty's (1922) *Nanook of the North* about Eskimo life. Flaherty, a compassionate romantic appalled by the dehumanisation of modern technology (cf. Calder-Marshall 1963), lived in Eskimo country for eleven years, and shot his film under the most adverse conditions on the life of one specific individual – Nanook. In this film he reveals the constant struggle for life in a hostile environment. . . .

Film is now accepted as an integral part of the anthropologist's armoury of tools. This is far from the case in sociology. There have been a few attempts, such as Morin's work with Rouch on Parisians talking about the summer of 1960 (the Algerian War dominated) in *Chronicles of a Summer*, but in the main sociologists have either ignored the medium or used the documentaries created by film makers, like those of Frederick Wiseman.

Frederick Wiseman's films perhaps come closest to embodying sociological concerns: most deal directly with the ways in which individuals throughout their hierarchies cope (or fail to) with the day-to-day pressures of social institutions. As he puts it:

> What I'm aiming at is a series on American institutions, using the word 'institutions' to cover a series of activities that take place in a limited geographical area with a more or less consistent group of people being involved. I want to use film technology to have a look at places like high schools, hospitals, prisons, and police, which seems to be very fresh material for film; I want to get away from the typical documentary where you follow one charming person or one Hollywood star around. I want to make films where the institutions will be the star but will also reflect larger issues in general society.
>
> (in Rosenthal 1971, p. 69)

Hence his 'documents' treat not 'lives' but 'institutions' – the police in *Law and Order* (1969), hospitals for the criminally insane in *The Titicut Follies* (1969), army life in *Basic Training* (1971) as well as films on *Welfare, High School* and *Hospital*. For Wiseman, it is blindingly obvious that all such films are 'subjective' documents – how could it be otherwise? Yet they are 'fair': honest, worked at, not driven by ideological commitment, desirous of showing that people are much the same in their daily struggles and 'very suspicious of people who can make . . . glib classifications, whatever that classification may be, and wherever it may fall politically' (Wiseman 1971, p. 325). These concerns – for disciplined subjectivity and humanistic impartiality – are the hallmarks of life documents.

A miscellanea

So far I have produced a simple catalogue of life documents, but the listing could go on. Some researchers, for example, have made use of the inscriptions on tombstones (Warner 1959 and Woltemade 1976, cited in Curry and Clarke 1977), while others have scrutinised suicide notes showing how they provide 'an unsolicited account of the victim's thoughts and emotions regarding his intended act, and often, what he felt was responsible for it' (Schwartz and Jacobs 1979, pp. 156–67). . . .

What a person owns, or fails to own, can serve both as a useful indicator of lifestyle and, when combined with an interview especially, can act as a remarkable memory jogger. To grasp the significance of this, conduct a little experiment on yourself. Simply move around your house or room, inspecting each item you have purchased or have been given as a present. Ponder the circumstances in your life that led to you getting this 'possession' – your interests and friends, where you were at the time, what's happened to it since, your feelings towards it then and now. A bookcase or a record collection is a goldmine of biographical incidents – many items may have been acquired randomly and have little history, but many others will speak to hugely complex stories. Rummaging through attics can be particularly rewarding and, on occasions, as Hughes has shown, dustbins are not without a tale to tell (cf. Webb *et al.* 1966, p. 41).

A classic illustration of this concern is the systematic examination of the possessions of fourteen poor families living in a Mexico City slum, by Oscar Lewis (1970). As he puts it:

> The inquiry opens up a mine of interesting questions. What proportions of their income do poor people spend on furniture, on clothing, on religious objects, on luxury items, on medicines? How much of what they buy is new? How much second hand? To what extent do they depend on gifts or hand me downs? How do families in poverty finance their purchases? Where do they do their shopping? How wide are their choices? What is the physical condition of their possessions? How long do they manage to hold on to them? I was able to obtain rather detailed information on all these matters.
>
> (Lewis 1970, p. 442)

His analysis considers thirteen categories of possession and does provide a number of interesting insights. For instance, all the poor families had at least one shelf for religious ornaments, but this was the only category of possessions where the poorer families had spent more than the better off. . . .

Conclusion

Imagine another research text that huddled together in one chapter an outline of surveys, questionnaires, interviews, attitude scaling, participant observation and a few other common research techniques! The result would be laughable: we know too much about these methods for them to be discussed in such brief terms – most frequently whole volumes would be devoted to each method. Yet in this chapter I have been deliberately wide-ranging: from photography and film through diaries and . . . letters. My intent, therefore, was not to be comprehensive but merely suggestive. For here are a whole battery of research tools, widely ignored and neglected in both research texts and courses, which have enormous potential for exploring concrete social experience in humanistic fashion. . . .

References

Agee, J., and Evans, W. (1965) *Let Us Now Praise Famous Men: Three Tenant Families* (London: Peter Owen).

Allport, G.W. (1942) *The Use of Personal Documents in Psychological Science* (New York: Social Science Research Council).

Banish, R. (1976) *City Families: Chicago and London* (New York: Pantheon).

Bateson, G., and Mead, M. (1942) *Balinese Character* (New York: New York Academy of Science, vol. II).

Becker, H.S. (1974) 'Photography and sociology', *Studies in the Anthropology of Visual Communication*, vol. 5, pp. 3–26.

Blumer, H. (1979) 'Introduction to the *Transaction* edition', in *Critiques of Research in the Social Sciences: An Appraisal of Thomas and Znaniecki's The Polish Peasant in Europe and America* (New Brunswick, NJ: Transaction Books).

Calder-Marshall, A. (1963) *The Innocent Eye: The Life of R. J. Flaherty* (London: W.H. Allen).

Curry, T., and Clarke, A.C. (1977) *Introducing Visual Sociology* (Dubuque: Kendall/Hunt).

Harper, D. (1978) 'At home on the rails: ethics in a photographic research project', *Qualitative Sociology*, vol. 1, pp. 61–77.

Jackson, B. (1977) *Killing Time: Life in the Arkansas Penitentiary* (New York: Cornell University Press).

—— (1978) 'Killing time: life in the Arkansas Penitentiary', *Qualitative Sociology*, vol. 1, pp. 21–32.

Lewis, O. (1959) *Five Families* (New York: Basic Books).

—— (1970) *A Death in the Sanchez Family* (London: Secker & Warburg).

Maas, S. and Kuypers, J.A. (1974) *From Thirty to Seventy: a 40 Year Longitudinal Study of Adult Life Styles and Personality* (London: Jossey-Bass).

Musello, C. (1979) 'Family photography', in J. Wagner (1979) pp. 101–18.

Rosenthal, A. (1971) *The New Documentary in Action: A Casebook in Film Making* (Berkeley, Cal.: University of California Press).

Schwartz, H., and Jacobs, J. (1979) *Qualitative Sociology: A Method to the Madness* (London: Collier-Macmillan).

Sontag, S. (1978) *On Photography* (Harmondsworth: Penguin).

Sorokin, P., and Berger, C. (1938) *Time Budgets of Human Behaviour* (Cambridge, Mass.: Harvard University Press).

Stasz, C. (1979) 'Texts, images and display conventions in sociology', *Qualitative Sociology*, vol. 2, no. 1 (May), pp. 29–44.

Thomas, W.I., and Znaniecki, F. (1958) *The Polish Peasant in Europe and America* (New York: Dover Publications); original editions published 1918–20.

Thompson, K.S., and Dinitz, S. (1974) 'Reactions to My Lai: a visual verbal comparison', *Sociology and Social Research*, vol. 58, pp. 122–9.

Wagner, J. (ed.) (1979) *Images of Information: Still Photography in the Social Sciences* (Beverly Hills, Cal.: Sage).

Webb, E.J., Campbell, D.T., Schwartz, R.D. and Sechrest, L. (1966) *Unobtrusive Measures: Non-reactive Research in the Social Sciences* (Chicago: Rand McNally).

Wiseman, F. (1971) 'Interview with Wiseman', in G. Roy Levin, *Documentary Explorations*, pp. 313–328 (New York: Doubleday).

Zimmerman, D.H., and Wieder, D.L. (1977) 'The diary diary-interview method', *Urban Life*, vol. 5, no. 4 (January), pp. 479–697.

Chapter 42

Martyn Hammersley

QUALITATIVE DATA ARCHIVING
Some reflections on its prospects and problems

From *Sociology* 31 (1): 131–142 (1997).

T HE SHARING OF DATA by social scientists has been a growing trend in recent years, especially in the United States; and it has encompassed not just quantitative but also ethnographic and other forms of qualitative or textual data (Sieber 1981). An important part of this is the creation of data archives. Quantitative data archives began to be established many years ago – for example the ESRC Data Archive (originally the SSRC Survey Archive) was set up at the University of Essex in 1969. No equivalent archive has existed in Britain for qualitative data, but the establishment of QUALIDATA offers the prospect of more systematic and extensive archiving of these data in the future.[1]

There are two main functions that the archiving of research data can serve. First, it provides a means by which the findings of studies can be checked by other researchers through reanalysis of the original data. Second, it offers a bank of data that can be used for secondary analysis; enabling researchers either to supplement their own primary data or to carry out free-standing historical, comparative or meta analysis on the basis of data from a range of studies.

I want to consider these two uses of archived qualitative data and some of their implications, both for those depositing data and for users. These two functions offer considerable potential for the future development of qualitative research, but neither is unproblematic.

---

1 There has long been archiving of some kinds of qualitative data, for example by the Mass Observation archive at the University of Sussex and by the Oral History archive at the University of Essex. QUALIDATA is a development out of the latter; but it is primarily a clearing-house for archivable data, it does not provide archive facilities itself. For further information see Corti *et al.* 1995.

Checking findings through re-analysis

The way that archiving can facilitate assessment of the validity of findings needs to be viewed against the background of the role that such assessment ought to play in social science. It is a generally recognised requirement of scientific practice that the findings of any study be checked. The importance of this is highlighted by the emphasis on the role of the research community in the production of knowledge that is central to several otherwise very different philosophies of science, for instance those of Popper (1959: 44–8), Polanyi (1962) and Kuhn (1970). . . .

In my view, the starting point for all assessment of research findings is an examination of the likely validity of the arguments presented by a researcher; in terms of plausibility, how far they are compatible with what is already taken to be known about the types of (or actual) phenomena concerned; and credibility, the likelihood of error in the evidence offered and how well that evidence supports that claims made.

Given that such assessment of research findings is essential to science, there is an obligation placed on researchers to provide the information necessary for it to take place. However, at present this process of assessment does not operate very effectively in many areas of the social sciences; perhaps especially not in the case of qualitative inquiries. Research reports often do not provide all the information that is required in order to determine the truth or falsity of the findings. . . .

Lincoln and Guba (1985) . . . argue that for the findings of qualitative research to be trustworthy it must be possible for an auditor to retrace the path of the researcher, checking the premises on which each step of the analysis depended. In other words, the researcher must provide an audit trail . . . [comprising] not just the raw data (fieldnotes, audio- and video-recordings, documents, etc.) but also methodological and theoretical notes produced in the course of the research, and even the researcher's diary or personal log. An obvious implication of this is that in order to be able to facilitate the assessment of studies, archives may need to be more than just depositories for data, considerable ancillary material might also be required.

However, the auditing analogy is potentially misleading. . . . One reason for this is that research is not founded on data whose meaning and validity are given. The concept of research auditing seems to rely on epistemological foundationalism. From this point of view, research involves deduction from data to conclusions, and assessment of it simply requires that each step in the process be checked. Yet, as Popper, among others, has emphasised, what is crucial for the testing of knowledge claims is not how those claims were produced but their cogency in the light of the evidence. While it is true that as part of any assessment we must address threats to the credibility of the evidence, and therefore need information about how the research was done, an exhaustive account of the research process is not required. . . . In other words, there is an important difference between the trajectory of a research project and the arguments presented in the research report(s) it produces. The availability of archive materials may constitute an important additional resource that can be drawn on when assessing research reports, but that material cannot validate the findings of the research in the way that the auditing analogy suggests. . . .

Archived data as a basis for secondary analysis

Let me turn now to the other main function of qualitative data archiving: the facilitation of secondary analysis. It does seem extraordinary that there has been very little effort to preserve the mass of data that has been produced by qualitative researchers in the social sciences over the past 20 or 30 years (Thompson 1991). By now a great deal of this has probably been lost, and much of the rest may be beyond recovery.

This is a matter for considerable regret. Social historians often express disappointment that data are not available about the experiences of whole categories of people and about many types of activity in the past. To take an example from my own field, education, we have relatively little information about the precise form that teaching took in different types of school in the early part of this century. In general, all we have are evaluative, prescriptive or fictional accounts. Of course, for much of this century we can still call on oral histories. But often these are not able to provide the detail or quality of data required. Only with the emergence of ethnographic studies in the late 1960s and 1970s did concrete data about classroom interaction start to be collected, sometimes in audio- or even video-recorded form. But unless these data are archived, historians of the future will be in much the same position as we are today.

Secondary data analysis is not only of value in relation to historical study of the past, of course. Indeed, it could be that with the increased resistance to being researched which is emerging in some areas, as a result of the intensification of work and greater bureaucratic control in many public and private organisations, secondary analysis of qualitative data will become more common in contemporary sociological analysis. There are other reasons for the importance of secondary analysis as well. One of the criticisms frequently directed at qualitative research is that its findings are not generalisable to populations of wide practical or political significance, and this arises from the fact that studies usually focus on relatively small numbers of cases. Data archiving could offer a partial remedy for this too. Researchers may be able to use data from other studies dealing with the same population to assess the generalisability of their findings in relevant respects.

Equally important, archiving opens up the possibility of wide ranging comparative analysis. The comparative dimension is given considerable emphasis within qualitative research methodology. It is central both to theory development and to theory testing. However, very often, particular studies have not been able to collect data on a sufficient number of cases to make comparative analysis fully effective. Archived data may enable us to overcome this, especially since analysis of large amounts of qualitative data can now be facilitated by the use of sophisticated software for searching and exploring relationships within and across texts.

At the same time, we should not underestimate the difficulties involved in this use of archived data. . . . More fundamentally, there are potential misconceptions about the idea of a data bank. As I noted earlier, there are no data that are simply empirical givens, nor would it ever be possible to gather together all the data on which any particular study had originally been based. Etymologically, the term 'datum' means 'what is taken as given': it does not refer to facts that are free of theoretical presuppositions lying around in research sites waiting to be 'collected'. It is now widely recognised that, however apparently concrete data are, they are in an important sense constructed. Indeed, ethnographic or qualitative data, perhaps more than other kinds, involve an informal or intuitive element. It is a central assumption of much qualitative research that in order to understand behaviour one must learn the culture which informs it. And most researchers believe that cultures cannot be exhaustively formulated in explicit terms, for example as a set of algorithmic rules.

This intuitive component in qualitative research is sometimes referred to as 'headnotes', by comparison with the written fieldnotes that often form much of the documentary base for ethnographic research (Sanjek 1990). What is involved is a kind of culture *habitus* that a researcher acquires over time in fieldwork. Its role is illustrated by the fact that social anthropologists have often found it impossible to analyse colleagues' fieldnotes without going into the field themselves. Reporting his experience of using the fieldnotes of a fellow anthropologist who had died, Frederick Barth comments:

> My repeated attempts at writing up this material were most frustrating. Lacking any kind of connected analysis from Robert Pehrson's hand, I found it impossible to work systematically with the notes . . . I finally decided that the failure might be caused by the lack of adequate political and ecological data and that in any case the only hope of success lay in being able to visit the area.
>
> (quoted in Bond 1990: 276)

What this points to is that there is a difference between how ethnographers read the fieldnotes they have produced themselves and how someone else will read them. The fieldworker interprets them against the background of all that he or she tacitly knows about the setting as a result of first-hand experience, a background that may not be available to those without that experience. And much the same problem arises with other sorts of data, even with listening to audio-tapes and watching video-recordings that someone else has produced.

There are limits, then, to the usability of others' data. Where data are produced on the basis of different cultural assumptions, theoretical presuppositions, etc., they cannot be treated as if they represented a common currency, with material from different studies simply being added together. Even where the original researcher and the secondary analyst share the same perspective, there will almost certainly be relevant data missing. And to the extent that the user has different purposes to the original researcher, gaps in the data will become larger and more significant. . . .

References

Bond, G.C. (1990) 'Fieldnotes: research in past occurrences', in R. Sanjek (ed.) *Fieldnotes*. New York, Cornell University Press.

Corti, L., Foster, J. and Thompson, P. (1995) 'Archiving qualitative research data'. *Social Research Update* 10, Department of Sociology, University of Surrey.

Kuhn, T.S. (1970) *The Structure of Scientific Revolutions* (2nd edition). Chicago: University of Chicago Press.

Lincoln, Y. S. and Guba, E. G. (1985) *Naturalistic Inquiry*. Beverly Hills, Cal.: Sage.

Polanyi, M. (1962) 'The republic of science', *Minerva* 1/1: 54–73.

Popper, K.R. (1959) *The Logic of Scientific Discovery*. London: Hutchinson.

Sanjek, R. (ed.) (1990) *Fieldnotes: The Makings of Anthropology*. Ithaca, New York: Cornell University Press.

Sieber, J.E. (ed.) (1981) *Sharing Social Science Data*. Newbury Park: Sage.

Thompson, P. (1991) 'Report from a feasibility study for a qualitative data archival resource centre'. University of Essex.

Chapter 43

Robin Hamman

THE APPLICATION OF ETHNOGRAPHIC METHODOLOGY IN THE STUDY OF CYBERSEX

From *Cybersociology* 1, www.socio.demon.co.uk/magazine/plummer.html

IN RECENT YEARS ACADEMIC researchers have written extensively about computer mediated communication (CMC). A significant amount of this research has looked at the ways in which people use text based CMC to chat with each other in real time on the Internet and on socially oriented online services such as America Online (AOL) and CompuServe. In these studies, researchers have found that text based virtual environments (chat rooms, IRC chat channels, and MUDs) are places where users can experiment with identity and gender (re)construction . . . form new friendships . . ., and join together with other users in the building of virtual communities. . . . Most of the existing social scientific research of the online world has been ethnographic. Given the prevalence of ethnographic methodology in the study of social phenomenon in text based virtual environments, it is surprising that its use in cyberspace has yet to be analysed in any great detail. . . .

Researchers who have used ethnographic methods in cyberspace have been confronted with several problems that are different from the ones they are likely to encounter in research off-line. These problems are: locating the parameters of the population of study, whether or not to depend on online interviews, and the frequent misinterpretations caused by the absence of physical cues and gestures in text based virtual environments.

Parameters of population

We know that the use of the Internet and online services such as AOL is growing rapidly, and that the language of these virtual inhabitants is almost always English.

We also know that the use of these technologies requires not just literacy, but computer literacy. On AOL, there are methods of obtaining data on the number of people using a specific chat room and of determining the total number of chat rooms at a given point in time. On AOL, there is also a way to access a 'profile', a personal biography stating characteristics such as age and gender as well as listing hobbies and other interests, for chat room participants who wish to make their personal details public.

Unfortunately, our data on the parameters of the population of online chat room users is limited to the above. We don't know the age, race, or gender of chat room users unless they make that information available to us. We don't know how many people, over an extended period of time, use online chat rooms. There is no data telling us how long each individual user spends engaged in online chat and we don't know at which times they are likely to come and go. In fact most of the demographic information that we do have about users of online chat rooms is self-reported and unverifiable. Online services I have contacted are unwilling to supply academic researchers with demographic data since data of this type is a closely guarded trade secret which could be used by competitors if it were made public.

Online interviews?

An important question faced by researchers of online chat rooms is whether to depend solely upon online interviews and observations in the gathering of data. Sherry Turkle . . . (1995: 324) chooses not to use online interviews in her research unless she has additonally met that person in real life. . . . Others suggest that there are certain advantages to interviewing people in their own environment. According to Hammersley and Atkinson, 'interviewing them [respondents] on their own territory . . . is the best strategy. It allows them to relax much more than they would in less familiar surroundings.' (Hammersley and Atkinson 1995: 150 brackets added) . . . In fact, most of my respondents admit that they would not talk with me about cybersex (and the other issues it brings up such as solitary masturbation) if I were to interview them face to face. In contrast to this, in the online interviews that I completed, I found that nearly all respondents were almost immediately willing to speak about very intimate details of their sex lives.

Another problem with face to face interviews is locating suitable respondents away from the location where cybersex chat occurs. I did attempt to use other interviewing strategies before settling on the use of online interviews. These included attending a computer user group meeting and speaking with people at cyber-cafes, both of which failed because I was unable to locate users who reported that they had previously engaged in cybersex. A similar problem with attempting to undertake face to face interviews with members of this population is that, due to the geographically disperse nature of computer networks, respondents may be physically located far from the researcher. To locate people who have cybersex in online chat rooms, and in order for them to feel comfortable enough to speak about such activities, online interviews are a necessity.

Narrow-bandwidth communication and misinterpretations in cyberspace

Stone makes an important distinction between face to face communication and computer mediated communication (CMC), explaining that 'Reality is wide-bandwidth, because people who communicate face to face in real time use multiple modes simultaneously – speech, gestures, facial expression, the entire gamut of semiotics . . . Computer conferencing is narrow-bandwidth, because communication is restricted to lines of text on a screen.' (Stone 1995: 93) In narrow-bandwidth computer mediated communications, information important for understanding is missing, making 'ferocious misunderstandings over simple textual utterances' frequent. (Stone 1995: 175) The ease with which misinterpretations of language can occur in text based CMC is of methodological concern as well as of concern to the users of chat rooms who must confront it every time they go online. . . . Online interviews may be a good way to elicit sensitive data and to gain access to online research populations, but researchers must be keenly aware that misinterpretations of language are frequent in the narrow bandwidth of text based cyberspaces.

References

Hammersley, Martyn and Paul Atkinson. *Ethnography: Principles in Practice*. London: Routledge, 1995 (2nd edition).

Stone, Allucquere Rosanne. *The War of Desire and Technology at the Close of the Mechanical Age*. London: Massachusetts Institute of Technology Press, 1995.

Turkle, Sherry. *Life on the Screen: Identity in the Age of the Internet*. New York: Simon and Schuster, 1995.

PART TEN

Analysing qualitative data

INTRODUCTION

THERE ARE SOME QUITE specialized ways of analysing qualitative data (conversation and discourse analysis, semiotic analysis) that will be explored in this and later parts of this book. I often find that students doing qualitative projects feel obliged to identify and name the analytic method that they use; without this they feel they have no firm justification for the approach they have adopted. So they end up saying they are doing 'discourse analysis' when really they have just looked at a text and identified themes of interest. These days, sociology students (my discipline) don't like to say they have done 'content analysis' because this has been associated with quantitative methods by some of their lecturers, and they have discovered that this could be seen as 'positivist' and therefore a bad thing. Some insecure researchers feel this obligation to name their analytic method too. I often see researchers claiming to have done 'phenomenological analysis' or 'grounded theory' when in reality, once again, they have just done what the students do: looked for interesting themes, usually in some text they have generated.

Perhaps this phenomenon is due to the fact that people lack confidence in using their everyday intelligence to look for interesting things in qualitative material. I would like to propose a name for this very common activity of looking for interesting things in qualitative data: 'qualitative content analysis' (although 'interpretive analysis' could be an alternative). I think it describes what most qualitative analysts seem to do most of the time. This part contains readings that will show you what is involved. At the heart of it often lies the operation of coding, described here by Strauss and Corbin in reading 44. What they call 'open coding' is here presented by them in the context of a book about how to discover 'grounded theory'. You should know, though, that doing open coding is only one part of doing grounded theory (for example, it involves theoretical sampling as well – see reading 32), so don't make the mistake of claiming to have 'done' grounded theory just because you coded your data. These authors show that coding is basically a form of categorizing, labelling or indexing interesting things in research materials. A good coding scheme relates data to litera-ture review and is the bridge between research materials ('data') and theoretical points.

Gibbs (reading 45) describes the use of computer software (in this case, NVIVO) to code and retrieve segments of text or other data. His account is useful, showing a range of things that can be coded, including formal features of a text (for example, metaphors) as well as content. Computers are of immense use in the rapid sorting and ordering of research materials for a variety of analytic purposes but, as Gibbs makes clear, they do not do the analysis by themselves.

Kelle's article (reading 46) begins by discussing an associated worry that com-puters might somehow take over the analytic process from the researcher. Kelle is helpful in demonstrating that the procedures carried out by computers are, at root, those which have been followed by scholars in a variety of disciplines for many years. Indexing and cross-referencing (forms of coding) need not be associated with any particular approach (such as grounded theory). Computers simply facilitate these operations. In this section, too, are two readings in which a highly specialised approach to qualitative data analysis is described: conversation analysis (CA). The work of Harvey Sacks, explained here by Silverman (reading 47) is seminal here. Sacks, through Silverman, demonstrates that this is basically an observational method that, for reasons similar to those of Becker and Geer (reading 36), rejects the use of reported experience in interviews as research data. Conversation analysts make detailed transcriptions of talk in order to understand the 'machinery' with which talk gets 'done'. Studies using CA have been helpful in illuminating a variety of important social processes that involve verbal communication, including medical consultations and court cases. Reading 24 is an example of CA at work, applied to talk in research interviews.

Peräkylä (reading 48) demonstrates the concern of conversation analysts to address scientific standards of validity and reliability, contrasting the capacity of CA to deal with this with that of ethnography. This is because the approach involves showing to the reader all of the data on which claims are based. Although only very short extracts of talk are therefore analysed, Peräkylä does not regard this as a barrier to generalization.

DISCUSSION POINTS

- Find some text (for example, a newspaper article, an interview transcript) and develop two coding schemes for it. The first should identify interesting content (for example, the main points made by the speaker or writer). The second should identify interesting forms (for example, metaphors, comparisons, hesitations). If each coding scheme were to be applied to a collection of similar texts, what might each of the two exercises tell you about a social or cultural process?

- What is a 'negative case' and why would a researcher want to find one?
- Some people say that software for qualitative data analysis, and the 'coding and retrieval' approach is really only suitable if you are doing grounded theory. Do you agree? If not, how could researchers employing other analytic approaches (for example, conversation analysis) use such software?
- What are the relative advantages and disadvantages of ethnographic field notes see reading 33) and conversation analytic transcriptions (see also reading 24)?
- Conversation analysis is empirical, behaviourist, objective and concerned with reliability, validity and generalizability. Does this make it 'scientific' in the way that Wallace (reading 4) or Cook and Campbell (readings 5 and 6) would recognize?

FURTHER READING

Becker, H.S. (1986) *Writing for Social Scientists*, Chicago: University of Chicago Press.

Coffey, A. and Atkinson, P. (1996) *Making Sense of Qualitative Data Analysis: Complementary Strategies*, Thousand Oaks, Cal.: Sage.

Have, P. ten (1998) *Doing Conversation Analysis: A Practical Guide*, London: Sage.

Hutchby I. and Wooffitt, R. (1998) *Conversation Analysis: Principles, Practices and Applications*, Cambridge: Polity Press.

Kelle, U. (ed.) (1995) *Computer-Aided Qualitative Data Analysis: Theory Methods and Practice*, London: Sage.

Kvale, S. (ed.) (1989) *Issues of Validity in Qualitative Research*, Lund: Studentlitteratur.

Miles, M. and Huberman, A. (1994) *Qualitative Data Analysis: An Expanded Sourcebook*, Thousand Oaks, Cal.: Sage.

Seale C.F. (2002) 'Computer-assisted analysis of qualitative interview data', in Gubrium, J.F. and Holstein, J.A. (eds) *Handbook of Interview Research*, Thousand Oaks, Cal.: Sage.

Seale, C.F. and Silverman, D. (1997) 'Ensuring rigour in qualitative research', *European Journal of Public Health* 7: 379–384.

Silverman, D. (2001) *Interpreting Qualitative Data: Methods for Analysing Talk, Text and Interaction*, London: Sage.

Strauss, A.L. (1987) *Qualitative Analysis for Social Scientists*, Cambridge: Cambridge University Press.

Wetherell, M., Taylor, S. and Yates, S. (2001) *Discourse as Data*, London and New York: Sage.

Wetherell, M., Taylor, S. and Yates, S. (2001) *Discourse Theory and Practice: A Reader*, London: Sage.

Wolcott, H. (1990) *Writing Up Qualitative Research*, Newbury Park, Cal.: Sage.

Chapter 44

Anselm L. Strauss and Juliet Corbin

OPEN CODING

From *Basics of Qualitative Research: Grounded Theory Procedures and Techniques,* Newbury Park, Cal.: Sage (1990).

Definition of terms

Concepts: Conceptual labels placed on discrete happenings, events, and other instances of phenomena.

Category: A classification of concepts. This classification is discovered when concepts are compared one against another and appear to pertain to a similar phenomenon. Thus the concepts are grouped together under a higher order, more abstract concept called a category.

Coding: The process of analyzing data.

Open Coding: The process of breaking down, examining, comparing, conceptualizing, and categorizing data. . . .

Open coding is the part of analysis that pertains specifically to the naming and categorizing of phenomena through close examination of data. Without this first basic analytical step, the rest of the analysis and communication that follows could not take place. During open coding the data are broken down into discrete parts, closely examined, compared for similarities and differences, and questions are asked about the phenomena as reflected in the data. Through this process, one's own and others' assumptions about phenomena are questioned or explored, leading to new discoveries. . . .

Labeling phenomena

. . . Concepts are the basic units of analysis in the grounded theory method. One can count 'raw' data, but one can't relate or talk about them easily. **Therefore, conceptualizing our data becomes the first step in analysis**. By breaking down and conceptualizing we mean taking apart an observation, a sentence, a paragraph, and giving each discrete incident, idea, or event, a name, something that stands for or represents a phenomenon. Just how do we do this? We ask questions about each one, like: What is this? What does it represent? We compare incident with incident as we go along so that similar phenomena can be given the same name. Otherwise, we would wind up with too many names and very confused!

Let's stop here and take an example. Suppose you are in a fairly expensive but popular restaurant. The restaurant is built on three levels. On the first level is a bar, on the second a small dining area, and on the third, the main dining area and the kitchen. The kitchen is open, so you can see what is going on. Wine, liqueurs, and appropriate glasses in which to serve them are also available on this third level. While waiting for your dinner, you notice a lady in red. She appears to be just standing there in the kitchen, but your common sense tells you that a restaurant wouldn't pay a lady in red just to stand there, especially in a busy kitchen. Your curiosity is piqued, so you decide to do an inductive analysis to see if you can determine just what her job is. (Once a grounded theorist, always a grounded theorist.)

You notice that she is intently looking around the kitchen area, **a work site**, focusing here and then there, taking a mental note of what is going on. *You ask, yourself, what is she doing here? Then you label it* **watching**. Watching what? **Kitchen work**.

Next, someone comes up and asks her a question. She answers. This act is different than watching, so *you code it* as **information passing**.

She seems to notice everything. You call this **attentiveness**.

Our lady in red walks up to someone and tells him something. Since this incident also involves information that is passed on, *you also label it*, **information passing**.

Although standing in the midst of all this activity, she doesn't seem to disrupt it. *To describe this phenomenon* you use the term **unintrusiveness**.

She turns and walks quickly and quietly, **efficiency**, into the dining area, and proceeds to **watch**, the activity here also.

She seems to be keeping track of everyone and everything, **monitoring**. But monitoring what? Being an astute observer you notice that she is monitoring the **quality** of the service, how the waiter interacts and responds to the customer; the **timing of service**, how much transpires between seating a customer, their ordering, the delivery of food; and **customer response and satisfaction** with the service.

A waiter comes with an order for a large party, she moves in to help him, **providing assistance**.

The woman looks like she knows what she is doing and is competent at it, **experienced**.

She walks over to a wall near the kitchen and looks at what appears to be a schedule, **information gathering**.

The maitre d' comes down and they talk for a few moments and look around the room for empty tables and judge at what point in the meal the seated customers seem to be: the two are **conferring**.

This example should be sufficient for you to comprehend what we mean by labeling phenomena. It is not unusual for beginning researchers to summarize rather than *conceptualize* data. That is, they merely repeat briefly the gist of the phrase or sentence, but still in a descriptive way. For instance, instead of using a term such as 'conferring' to describe the last incident, they might say something like 'sat and talked to the maitre d'.' Or, use terms such as: 'read the schedule,' 'moved to the dining room,' and 'didn't disrupt.' To invent such phrases doesn't give you a concept to work with. You can see just from this initial coding session that conceptually it is more effective to work with a term such as 'information gathering' rather than 'reading the schedule,' because one might be able to label ten different happenings or events as **information gathering** – her asking a question of one of the chefs, checking on the number of clean glasses, calling a supplier, and so forth.

Discovering categories

In the course of our research, we may come up with dozens, even hundreds of conceptual labels. . . . These concepts also have to be grouped, like with like, otherwise we would wind up in a plight similar to that of the old lady in the shoe with so many children (concepts) we wouldn't know what to do (and that is exactly how students sometimes feel at this point).

Once we have identified particular phenomena in data, we can begin to group our concepts around them. This is done to reduce the number of units with which we have to work. The process of grouping concepts that seem to pertain to the same phenomena is called *categorizing*. . . . The phenomenon represented by a category is given a conceptual name, however this name should be more abstract than that given to the concepts grouped under it. Categories have conceptual power because they are able to pull together around them other groups of concepts or subcategories.

We still haven't answered our question about the nature of the job of our lady in red, so let us return to our example, and talk about categories at the same time. There are different ways to approach the categorization process. Thus we can take each concept as we go along with our labeling process, and ask to what class of phenomenon does it seem to pertain, and is it similar or different from the one before or after? Or, we can step back and look at the entire observation with many concepts in mind and say: what does this seem to be about? Using either method, we should reach the same conclusion. We shall illustrate the second approach only, our purpose not being to talk now about various ways of categorizing but to clarify *what* is entailed in the process of categorizing.

As an example, we might take the concept **monitoring** and ask: Why is she monitoring the traffic flow? the customer satisfaction? the quality of service? and the timing? Is it for the same or for a different purpose than the watching that she's doing in the kitchen? Or the conferring she is doing with the maitre d? What does being experienced have to do with the monitoring? Here we might conclude that monitoring, conferring, and watching all seem to pertain to the same thing – **work** that she is engaging in to **assess and maintain the flow of work**. It is a special kind of work however – preparing and bringing food to a table in a restaurant. We can label all concepts pertaining to work as: **types of work for assessing and maintaining work flow**. But, the concept **experience** doesn't quite fit under this heading. If we compare it with unintrusiveness and attentiveness, it is similar. Thus the three can be grouped under the heading of *attributes* or qualities. But attributes and qualities of what? Answer: A person good at assessing and maintaining the flow of work. But this long phrase is far too cumbersome, so we must give her job a better name. Since the job seems to have to do with keeping the flow of work going in a restaurant, and since the work pertains to food, we might call her a **food orchestrator**. Then, attentiveness, unintrusiveness, and experience become 'attributes of' or 'conditions' for a good restaurant food orchestrator. Attributes or conditions refer to a different, but related class of phenomena. So, we now have a category (Food Orchestrator) and two subcategories (Types of work for Assessing and Maintaining Work Flow; also Conditions for being a good Food Orchestrator). Remember that at the beginning of this chapter we gave a definition of 'category'. We suggest you go back and read it again in light of the preceding paragraphs.

Now the lady's actual job title will of course not be 'restaurant food orchestrator' but that's close enough for us. She is no longer the mysterious lady in red. In our minds we have classified her by giving her a job title, and we know a little about her tasks and the attributes that it takes to do them. (Indeed, many a study has originated with just these kinds of casual observations or conversations, which become more serious, intense, and systematic when the observer or listener decides: 'This is really worth studying, or at least could be great fun.') If we were doing a real grounded theory study, we couldn't stop here just with the initial observations and coding. (Although if your purpose is just to pull out themes, then you could pretty much stop here). You want more than just a listing of concepts or even a grouping of them. Categories, after all, have to be analytically developed by the researcher. . . .

Chapter 45

Graham R. Gibbs

SEARCHING FOR TEXT

From *Qualitative Data Analysis: Explorations with NVivo*, Buckingham: Open University Press (2002).

MUCH OF THE ACTIVITY in qualitative analysis consists of looking for things in the text. A lot of the time there is no substitute for reading and thinking. No computer can interpret the text, only people can do that. However, humans have their limits too. We can quickly get bored and sloppy with repetitive tasks, such as looking for the occurrences of specific words or phrases. The chances are that this will result in biases in the way that we code text and hence biases in the conclusions we draw from the analysis. Fortunately, computers, dumb though they are, do not suffer from boredom. When asked to find some text or a particular combination of coded text, they will find every occurrence exactly as specified. Computer searching is no substitute for reading and thinking, but it can help with completeness and reliability, both in examining the text and in the analysis.

What to search the text for

Most of the use of text searching comes down to two things: coding and checking for completeness. Coding can be done by reading the documents and marking or coding sections of text. One common approach here is simply to start reading the documents and try to tease out coding and analytic ideas. As each occurs, you can create a new node[1] (perhaps as an in vivo one, based on the respondent's terms) or

[1 Editor's footnote: A 'node' is a term used by the makers of NVivo to indicate the location of analytic categories, such as codes.]

code the text at an existing node if it is another example of something you have already coded. Thus a key action is the search for similar passages of text that can be coded at established nodes. This is where computer searching can help. Often the passages already coded will contain terms, words or passages that might occur elsewhere. Put these terms into the text search facility and the software will quickly find all the further occurrences. Clearly this does not mean you have now found all the passages that can be coded at that node. There may be relevant passages that do not contain the terms you have searched for or the respondent might be using equivalent terms, synonyms of the terms you have searched for. Some of these you might pick up in the new passages found in the initial search operation, and these can then in turn be used as new search terms.

As well as failing to find some relevant passages, the search may find passages that aren't in fact relevant at all. These contain the search terms but are not in fact relevant to the node in question. Sometimes this is because they are about the same subject but express a different or opposite view. In that case you might consider creating some new nodes for them. In other cases, there is no link at all with the original node idea and you will have to uncode these passages. Thus each result of a search operation needs you, the human, to read through what is found and assess its meaning and relevance to the concepts you are working on. The computer will help you find all the relevant passages, but it can't ensure that it finds *only* relevant material.

Although, by default, searching in NVivo will create a new node with all the found text passages coded at that node, you don't have to keep it. At any time you can delete nodes. You can therefore use searching simply as a way of getting to know your data. Search for terms that arise out of your theoretical hunches and then inspect the passages found in the original documents.

A second important use for text searching is as a way of checking the completeness and validity of coding. Searching on nodes is a particularly important way of checking hypotheses in qualitative research. This often amounts to searching for what are known as negative cases: occurrences, patterns or phenomena that don't fit the pattern or theory we think we have discovered. If after exhaustive examination of the data we can only find a few (or better, no) negative cases then we can be more confident that our hypothesis has some validity and some grounding in the data. (However, note that in qualitative analysis the discovery of negative cases does not mean we simply reject the hypothesis. We are more likely to modify it to take into account the negative case). Using nodes to search for negative cases means relying on the fact that no significant examples have been missed in the coding at that node. Again the fallibility of the human researcher is a limitation. Qualitative texts tend to be voluminous – and reading them, looking for examples to code and all the time remaining unbiased is hard work. It is easy to miss key examples of text that should be coded at your developing node because you are not expecting to find it in this case or because it does not take the form you are looking for. It is just these examples that are likely to constitute the negative cases that are so important in validity checking. Computers are not affected by these problems. A computer search can therefore be a way of ensuring that there are no obvious examples of text (using terms and passages you know about or can think of) that should be coded at the node in question. Useful though this is, it is important not to get carried away here. The computer can never do all the work for you. There will always be examples of text that won't fit any text search pattern and will only be discovered by a careful reading of the documents. . . .

An example can be seen in Figure 45.1, which shows the result of searching in a project containing six documents, four interviews, a memo and the minutes of a committee meeting. The four interviews have been made into a set and some text has been coded at the node 'Used contacts network'. To find out what the older interviewees had said about using a contacts network you might carry out a Boolean search to find all the text coded at the node 'Used contacts network' in interviews with the older respondents – that is to say, a Boolean search for the node 'Used contacts network' and the attribute 'Age ≥ 45' with scope the set of all interview documents. The text found would be just that coded at the node in the documents John, Harry and June. Coded text in the document Cttee. Mins. would be omitted as the document is not in the search scope, and coded text in the interview with Pauline would be omitted because she is less than 45 years old (the document has

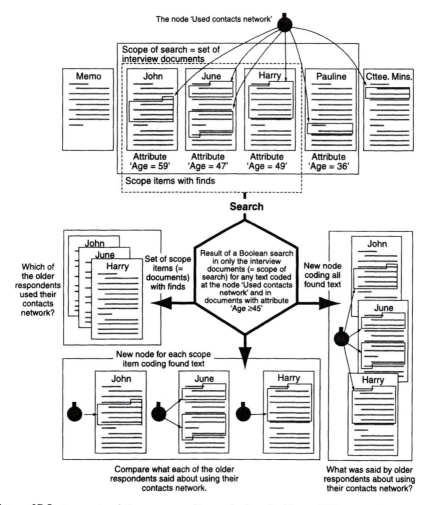

Figure 45.1 Example of the ways results can be handled in an NVivo search.

the attribute 'Age = 36'). If you had selected the option to handle the results by creating a new node then just the four passages marked in grey (= coded at the node 'Used contacts network') in the documents John, Harry and June would be coded at the new node created. If you opted to create a new set with the finds then a set consisting of the three documents John, Harry and June would be created. . . .

In the search illustrated in Figure 45.1, you might want to note in the memo that all the passages returned discussed using networks of work colleagues and former work colleagues. You might have a hunch that this was different for younger people looking for work, who might tend to use networks of friends, neighbours and relatives more often.

Metaphors and accounts

There has been a great expansion in recent decades in analysis of the use of language and what it can tell us about respondents and the society and culture they inhabit. This exploration of narrative focuses not just on what people say, but how they say it. Shared expressions and shared vocabulary can tell us a lot about how social groups see themselves and how they account for their experiences. Two good examples of this, where the text search facility might help, are the use of metaphor and the giving of accounts.

Metaphor is the use of imagery as a kind of rhetorical device. Very few people have the ability and imagination of Shakespeare to create new metaphors. Most of us, most of the time, use standard metaphors that reflect the milieux and culture we live in. As analysts, we can investigate how the metaphors are structured, how they are used and how others understand them. Sometimes metaphor is used because people find it difficult to express themselves without their use or because there is an emotional content to what they are saying that is easier to convey metaphorically – for example, 'getting hitched' instead of getting married and 'passing away' instead of dying. In other cases it is just an example of a shared common term. Examples of this in the Job Search project were when a respondent referred to looking for work as 'shopping' for jobs or when another referred to the unemployed as being 'in a mess'. On the other hand, in some cases the use of specific metaphors reflects shared ideas and concepts among the narrower group to which the respondents belong and is characteristic of the specific cultural domain. There wasn't much evidence of this among the interviewees in the Job Search project, perhaps because they could not really be considered a community or social group. Being unemployed is a very individual and isolating experience for most people.

In contrast, there were some good examples of account giving. As you might expect in the unemployed, explaining why they were without a job was a major concern of many of the respondents. The examination of accounts can be traced back at least to the work of Mills (1940) who described them as containing vocabularies of motive, and they are also examples of what Austin referred to as 'doing things with words' (Austin 1962). Account giving is the specific use of narrative where people try to account for, justify, excuse, legitimate and so on their actions or their situation. There are two principal types of account: excuses, where people try to mitigate or relieve questionable action or conduct perhaps by appeal to accident, forces outside their control or lack of information; and justifications, where people try to neutralize or attach positive value to questionable actions or conduct. Account giving is exactly what I had noticed when I spotted the frequent use of the term 'luck' by the Job Search respondents to explain who did and did not get jobs.

In both the case of metaphors and accounts the text search facility can both alert you to the use of certain terms and give a good indication of how common the usage is. I put the string 'luck–lucky–unlucky' in the Text Search dialog window. . . . The report suggested that five out of the nine respondents used the terms – a significant proportion of the interviewees. On reading the paragraphs in which the terms occurred, I could see that respondents were mainly trying to account for why they were unemployed or how others managed to get jobs. However, this is just the start of an investigation of account giving by unemployed people. It is necessary to check what other kind of accounts people were giving. Again, some reading is required, but this can be complemented by searching when some new terms are discovered. For example, some respondents used the term 'fortunate' in their speeches picked up by the search for 'luck'. This could be added to the search string. It would also be interesting to know if anything distinguished the five respondents who used the term 'luck'. They weren't distinguished by gender. However, there was a hint that maybe the older people were more likely to use the term 'luck'.

The use of the text search facility is summarized in Table 45.1. . . .

Table 45.1 Using the text search facility creatively and to enhance validity

1	Spread finds to paragraphs (or many characters either side of find) and review finds, adding and subtracting from the coding as appropriate.
2	Carry out a search and then read the finds to become familiar with the data.
3	Look for further relevant words and terms in the passages that are found.
4	Merge the results of new searches with relevant previous nodes created from searches.
5	Construct a glossary of terms to search for. Add to these using a thesaurus or your own knowledge. Keep the glossary in a memo.
6	Look for certain types of language use such as metaphor, and investigate contrasts between different subsets of the project data such as young and old respondents. Use change of scope to do this.
7	Use searching to look for negative cases, those that don't fit your assumed hypothesis.
8	Check by searching to see if a theme you think is dominant really is. It may occur less often than you imagined.
9	Use searching to try and achieve completeness in your coding, to ensure that all occurrences of the theme have actually been coded.
10	Use search on your memos to help keep control of your analysis.

References

Austin, J.L. (1962) *How to Do Things with Words*, Cambridge, Mass.: Harvard University Press.

Mills, C. Wright (1940) 'Situated actions and vocabularies of motive,' *American Sociological Review* 5: 904–913.

Chapter 46

Udo Kelle

THEORY BUILDING IN QUALITATIVE RESEARCH AND COMPUTER PROGRAMS FOR THE MANAGEMENT OF TEXTUAL DATA

From *Sociological Research Online* 2, 2: http://www.soc.surrey.ac.uk/socresonline

IN THEIR ARTICLE *Qualitative Data Analysis: Technologies and Representations*, Coffey, Holbrook and Atkinson (1996) have expressed their concerns that the increasing use of specific computer software could lead researchers to adopt a new orthodoxy of qualitative analysis. The authors argue that this would go strictly against current postmodernist and poststructuralist trends within ethnography which foster the acceptance and celebration of diversity. The article by Coffey and colleagues represents the most recent in a series of concerned warnings regarding potential methodological dangers of computer-aided qualitative data analysis software . . . Since the advent of such software, many qualitative researchers . . . have felt unease about the prospect that the use of computers could alienate the researcher from their data and enforce analysis strategies that go against the methodological and theoretical orientations qualitative researchers see as the hallmark of their work. . . . The idea that a computer could become a kind of Frankenstein's monster and finally turn against its human creators is. . . . a firm part of modern mythology. Reservations of qualitative researchers against computer-aided methods of data analysis at least partly reflected the distance of these scholars from the mainstream methodology of quantitative survey and experimental research where, during the 1960s and 1970s, the computer became an indispensible aid.

A closer look at the philosophical and epistemological roots of interpretive research makes clear that a certain caution against computer technology is justified with regard to the nature of the process of hermeneutic *Verstehen*. Philosophical approaches which play an important role within qualitative research, such as Phenomenology, the Oxford Philosophy of Language and continental Hermeneutical

Philosophy . . . had always stressed that ambiguity and context-relatedness have to be regarded as central characteristics of everyday language use. Following this argument – which has been further elaborated by contemporary postmodernist approaches (Denzin and Lincoln 1994: pp. 10f.) – it is impossible to make sense of written or spoken messages in everyday contexts – an operation which forms the core of hermeneutic *Verstehen* – without a 'tacit knowledge' which cannot easily (if at all!) be formalized. Contrary to that, the application of a 'Turing machine' (which represents the most general concept of an information processing machine) to a certain domain requires the formulation of exact and precisely stated rules which are completely context-free and contain no ambiguities. Thus, the attempt to apply the logic of a Turing machine to the domain of human understanding can be regarded as problematic. . . .

[But] the danger of methodological biases and distortion arising from the use of certain software packages for qualitative research may be overemphasized, as far as basic tasks of textual data management usually performed by this software are concerned. . . . 'Coding and retrieval' represents an 'open technology' which can be creatively used in various contexts of hermeneutic work. The connection between certain data archiving strategies on the one hand and certain methodologies (especially 'Grounded Theory') on the other is far more loose than often assumed. . . .

The general limitations of a Turing machine with regard to the understanding of the ambiguities and context-relatedness of everyday language have already been discussed. Nevertheless, there are a variety of mechanic data organization procedures which play a role in qualitative research. These procedures which refer to the necessity of the analyst to identify similarities, differences and relations between different text passages, can be mechanized and thus be performed with the help of an electronic data processing machine. In order to be able to retrieve text segments from different parts of the text corpus, an organizing scheme must be constructed. In principle two possibilities are available for the construction of such a scheme which have been widely used for hundreds or even thousands of years by scholars who work with text in the historical sciences, philology, literary criticism, theology, and, nowadays, the social sciences: (1) the construction of indexes and (2) the inclusion of cross references into the text.

We are all familiar with *indexes* (or 'registers', or 'concordances') of various kinds; the widest applied form of an index is certainly an author and subject index in a book. An electronic index is usually constructed by storing index words together with the 'addresses' of text passages. Such an address may contain the beginning and the end, in terms of line numbers, of a certain text passage to which the index word refers. Software programs which are based on these principles have been called 'code-and-retrieve' programs. . . .

Electronic *cross references* can be constructed with the help of so-called 'hyperlinks'. By pressing a 'button' the user of a textual database can jump between the text passages which are linked together. With the advent of hypertext and hypermedia technology it has often been forgotten that their main underlying principles have been widely known and applied for hundreds of years. One can easily see this by opening an ordinary King James Bible where a multitude of 'hyperlinks' are displayed on the margins of every page. By using these links a 'bible user' can, for example, jump between a teaching of Jesus in one of the Gospels and a passage of the Old Testament to which Jesus refers in this teaching.

Such straightforward techniques of data management should not at all be considered trivial. Instead, they have a far-reaching methodological significance. The comparison of text passages ('synopsis'), for example, helped to develop the most widely accepted theory about the origin of the four gospels. Coffey and her colleagues assume a convergence between methodological approaches and the prefered technique of data organization, thereby assuming that 'indexing' or 'coding' is nearer to an 'orthodox, grounded theory oriented' style of analysis while 'cross-referencing' through 'hyperlinks' would be more adequate for a 'postmodernist' approach which celebrates diversity. Looking at biblical exegesis as a field of hermeneutics, where extended experiences with such techniques have been collected, one will not find very much evidence that confirms such assumptions: techniques of indexing or cross referencing are used simultaneously by all interpreters, regardless whether they are more 'orthodox' and 'dogmatic' or more 'liberal', that means whether they take into account or not the polyvocality and diversity of biblical authors, their intentions and their diverse cultural backgrounds. And those (mostly historical) connections that can be found between data management techniques and hermeneutical schools which really exist point to the fact that 'indexing' (or 'coding') is extremely well suited to be used as a weapon against orthodoxy. Techniques of indexing and coding were used extensively in the 18th and 19th century (and are still used) by such biblical scholars who wish to challenge claims of biblical inerrancy and infallibility. But, needless to say, also biblical literalists and fundamentalists make use of synopses, thereby denying inconsistencies between text passages by means of complicated and devious interpretations.

Reasons for the preference of indexing over cross referencing by the developers of the first software programs for qualitative analysis may be far more simple than Coffey and her colleagues assume: if a certain text is structured for the first time, indexing is much easier than the use of cross references. Let us assume that the analyst finds a text passage 'B' which contains a similarity or a substantive relation to a text passage 'A'. To now define a cross reference or the 'hyperlink' between 'A' and 'B', 'A' has to be found in the text corpus, which is much more simple if 'A' has been previously indexed. . . .

'Code-and-retrieve' methods are useful for any researcher who wants to compare text segments coming from different sources and refer to a common topic, regardless of whether he or she is affiliated to the methodology of Grounded Theory or not. The comparison of text segments is conducted in different hermeneutic sciences, such as sociology, history, theology etc. Consequently, there should be no reason for an exclusive methodological link between Grounded Theory on the one hand and computer software for qualitative data administration on the other hand. . . .

In user's guides and methodological writings software is not only regarded as an instrument for data archiving and management but also as a tool for data analysis. Therefore, a methodological underpinning is needed. At present, proponents of the Grounded Theory approach belong to those very few authors who try to describe in detail the analytical procedures applied in qualitative research. Novices in qualitative research often welcome such detailed accounts of analysis procedures which help to overcome uncertainties caused by the often bemoaned lack of explicitness of qualitative research procedures. One reason for this lack of explicitness certainly lies in the difficulty of formalizing the interpretive and hermeneutic analysis of text, and, therefore, many scholars prefer to address interpretive analysis as an artistic endeavour rather than as a 'method' (Eisner 1981). The obvious fact that interpretive analysis in ethnography and qualitative sociology contains ineliminable subjective elements has not only always raised the suspicion of adherents of quantitative mainstream methodology but also inspired the shift of many colleagues towards 'postmodernist' and 'deconstructionist' approaches. At present, Grounded Theory seems to be almost the only approach which can meet the desire of others who look for a concrete and applicable methodology of qualitative analysis. But a closer look at the concepts and procedures of Grounded Theory makes clear that Glaser, Strauss and Corbin provide the researcher with a variety of useful heuristics, rules of thumb and a methodological terminology rather than with a set of precise methodological rules (or 'algorithms'). Consequently, concerns about a new orthodoxy of qualitative analysis based on Grounded Theory seem to lack solid ground. . . .

If coding is done within a hypothetico-deductive (H-D) research strategy (eg. in the context of 'quantitative content analysis') it is obvious that codes must represent the theoretical categories applied to the field under study. If a quantitative content analyst wants to find out whether newspapers with a 'liberal party affiliation' express a more positive attitude towards certain social policy measures than newspapers with a 'conservative party affiliation', s/he is well advised to operationalize these categories in a proper way and to code newspapers according to the party affiliation of their staff. But, as Charmaz points out:

> Qualitative coding is not the same as quantitative coding. The term itself provides a case in point in which the language may obscure meaning and method. Quantitative coding requires preconceived, logically deduced codes into which the data are placed. Qualitative coding, in contrast, means creating categories from interpretation of the data. Rather than relying on preconceived categories and standardized procedures, qualitative coding has its own distinctive structure, logic and purpose.
>
> (Charmaz 1983: p. 111)

In qualitative analysis, codes are often used not to denote facts but to 'break up' the data (Strauss and Corbin 1990: pp. 61ff.). Such codes represent 'perspectives' of the researcher rather than clear-cut empirical contentful categories (cf. Becker and Geer 1960: p. 280). According to Becker and Geer, these perspectives and the 'areas to which they apply' are only 'tentatively identified' when the coding begins. Coding is then done by going 'through the summarized incidents, marking each incident with a number or numbers that stand for the various areas to which it appears to be relevant'. Consequently, the coding of text does not serve to condense relevant information and to decide whether a certain person or event falls under a certain class of events or persons, but simply to make sure 'that all relevant data can be brought to bear on a point'. Here, the function of coding is restricted to sign-posting: codes are stored together with the 'address' of a certain text passage and, drawing on this information, the researcher can locate all the possible information provided by the textual data on the relevant topic. . . .

Conclusion

In recent discussions about software use in qualitative research the danger of a 'Frankenstein's monster' methodology, which alienates the researcher from his or her data or which leads to a 'new orthodoxy' in qualitative research has often been over-emphasized. Theoretical and methodological concepts of developers and users of computer software for textual data managemant are much more diverse and heterogenous than is often assumed. Frequent references to the methodology of Grounded Theory in their methodological writings may be due to the fact that (1) developers often look for a methodological underpinning for rather mundane tech-niques of data management and draw on grounded theory as an established 'brand name' in qualitative research, that (2) proponents of the Grounded Theory approach belong to those very few authors who try to describe in detail many of the folklore techniques widely applied in different qualitative approaches, especially the indexing (adressed within the Grounded Theory approach with the somewhat misleading term 'coding') and comparison of text passages is such a folklore technique which has been used for centuries in different hermeneutic sciences. This technique is applicable in various methodological contexts where different text passages that relate to a similar topic are compared. Consequently, indexing and comparing text segments ('coding' and 'retrieval' with the help of a computer) can be and has been applied not only in projects with a Grounded Theory background, but also by researchers who employ methods of discourse analysis or critical ethnography. . . . Software programs are tools to mechanize clerical tasks of ordering and archiving texts used in the hermeneutic sciences now for hundreds of years. To be clear about this issue we should address these programs as software for 'data administration and archiving' rather than as tools for 'data analysis'. . . .

References

Becker, H. and Geer, B. (1960) 'Participant observation: the analysis of qualitative field data' in R.N. Adams and J.J. Preiss (eds) *Human Organization Research: Field Relations and Techniques*. Homewood, Ill.: Dorsey Press.

Charmaz, K. (1983) 'The grounded theory method: an explication and interpretation' in R.M. Emerson (ed.) *Contemporary Field Research: A Collection of Writings*. Prospect Heights: Waveland Press.

Coffey, A, Holbrook, B. and Atkinson, P. (1996) 'Qualitative data analysis: technologies and representations', *Sociological Research Online*, vol. 1, no. 1, http://www.socresonline.org.uk/socresonline/1/1/4.html

Eisner, E. (1981) 'On the differences between scientific and artistic approaches to qualitative research', *Educational Researcher*, vol. 10, pp. 5–9.

Glaser, B. and Strauss, A. (1967) *The Discovery of Grounded Theory: Strategies for Qualitative Research*. New York: Aldine de Gruyter.

Strauss, A. and Corbin, J. (1990) *Basics of Qualitative Research: Grounded Theory Procedures and Techniques*. Thousand Oaks: Sage.

Chapter 47

David Silverman

HARVEY SACKS
Social science and conversation analysis

From *Harvey Sacks: Social Science and Conversation Analysis*, Cambridge: Polity (1998).

. . .

Seven methodological rules

1 Gather observational data

SACKS'S WORK IS ALWAYS driven by data. Rather than sit in his armchair and construct grand theories about society, he preferred, like the early eth-nographers, to 'get his hands dirty' with some data. As we have seen, this was not because he was necessarily fascinated by such data in themselves. Instead, it was because any data raised for him basic questions about the machinery of interaction. As he commented: 'We are trying to find the machinery. In order to do so we have to get access to its products' (Sacks 1984: 26–7).

Wanting 'access' to the 'products' of this machinery meant that Sacks rejected the use of hypothetical examples as a helpful method of social science. This was not because such examples might not be compelling. Rather the problem is that, pre-cisely because such examples make sense, they conceal the sense-making abilities of both scientists and their audiences (*LC2*: 419).

Equally, interview data gathered by the researcher is not necessarily helpful. This is because the interview method *generates* categories instead of looking at how categories are ordinarily deployed. As Sacks argues: 'the trouble with [interview studies] is that they're using informants; that is, they're asking questions of their subjects. That means that they're studying the categories that Members use . . . they are not investigating their categories by attempting to find them in the activities in which they're employed' (*LC1*: 27).

By contrast to both interview-based and hypothetical data, Sacks stressed, like the ethnographers of his time, the potential of observation. As he put it: 'I want to encourage the sense that interesting aspects of the world, that are as yet unknown, are accessible to observation' (*LC2*: 420). These 'interesting aspects of the world' may be very far away from what an everyday perspective finds interesting. So, from Sacks's point of view, we turn to observational data 'as a basis for theorizing' about things we could never imagine: 'Thus we can start with things that are not currently imaginable, by showing that they happened' (1984: 25; see also *LC2*: 420).

2 Making recordings

'The kind of phenomena I deal with are always transcriptions of actual occurrences in their actual sequence' (Sacks 1984: 25): while the earlier ethnographers had generally relied on recording their observations through fieldnotes, why did Sacks prefer to use an audio-recorder? Sacks's answer is that we cannot rely on our recollections of conversations. Certainly, depending on our memory, we can usually summarize what different people said. But it is simply impossible to remember (or even to note at the time) such matters as pauses, overlaps, inbreaths and the like.

Now whether you think these kinds of things are important will depend on what you can show with or without them. Indeed, you may not even be convinced that conversation itself is a particularly interesting topic. But at least by studying tapes of conversations, you are able to focus on the 'actual details' of one aspect of social life. As Sacks put it:

> My research is about conversation only in this incidental way, that conversation is something that we can get the actual happenings of on tape and transcribe them more or less, and therefore have something to begin with. If you can't deal with the actual detail of actual events then you can't have a science of social life.
>
> (*LC2*: 26)

Tapes and transcripts also offer more than just 'something to begin with'. In the first place, they are a public record, available to the scientific community, in a way that fieldnotes are not. Second, they can be replayed and transcriptions can be improved and analyses take off on a different tack unlimited by the original transcript. As Sacks told his students:

> I started to play around with tape recorded conversations, for the single virtue that I could replay them; that I could type them out somewhat, and study them extendedly, who knew how long it might take . . . It wasn't from any large interest in language, or from some theoretical formulation of what should be studied, but simply by virtue of that; I could get my hands on it, and I could study it again and again. And also,

consequentially, others could look at what I had studied, and make of it what they could, if they wanted to disagree with me.

(LC1: 622)

A third advantage of detailed transcripts is that, if you want to, you can inspect sequences of utterances without being limited to the extracts chosen by the first researcher. For it is in these sequences, rather than in single turns of talk, that we make sense of conversation. As Sacks points out: 'having available for any given utterance other utterances around it, is extremely important for determining what was said. If you have available only the snatch of talk that you're now transcribing, you're in tough shape for determining what it is' *(LC1: 729)*.

3 Being behaviourist

A popular activity in everyday life is to wonder about people's motives. Indeed, in the case of talk-shows, the motives of the rich, famous or just plain unlucky or deviant become a central topic. Yet, in many respects, social science has picked up this habit, taking as its task the revelation of other people's 'motives' and 'experiences'. Elsewhere, I have noted this 'Romantic' tendency in social science (Silverman 1993; Atkinson and Silverman 1997).

Even in the 1960s, Sacks seemed fully aware of these issues. His kind of social science always turned away from the insides of people's heads and towards their observable activities. In this sense, Sacks was a self-proclaimed behaviourist who announced that his task was to elucidate how members did whatever they did. As he put it:

> For Members, activities are observables. They see activities. They see persons doing intimacy, they see persons lying, etc. . . . And that poses for us the task of being *behaviourists* in this sense: finding how it is that people can produce sets of actions that provide that others can see such things.
>
> *(LC1: 119)*

As examples of such 'sets of actions', Sacks offers 'describing' and 'questioning'. These are interesting examples because each may be seen as a *resource* for social scientists as when ethnographers 'describe' cultures and 'question' informants. However, Sacks wants to make both activities a *topic* by examining them as forms of behaviour which, through some methods awaiting inspection, are produced and recognized.

4 Members' methods

It follows that how societal members (including social researchers) 'see' particular activities is, for Sacks, the central research question. In this respect, together with Garfinkel (1967), he offers a unique perspective in social science which 'seeks to describe methods persons use in doing social life' (Sacks 1984: 21).

When researchers 'describe' and 'question', the problem is that they are tacitly using members' methods. If we are to study such methods, it is, therefore, crucial that we don't take for granted what it is we appear to be 'seeing'. As Sacks says: 'In setting up what it is that seems to have happened, preparatory to solving the [research] problem, do not let your notion of what could conceivably happen decide for you what must have happened' (LC1: 115). Here Sacks is telling us that our 'notion of what could conceivably happen' is likely to be drawn from our unexamined knowledge as members. Instead, we need to proceed more cautiously by examining the methods members use to produce activities as observable and reportable.

Put at its simplest, researchers must be very careful how they use categories. For instance, Sacks quotes from two linguists who appear to have no problem characterizing particular (invented) utterances as 'simple', 'complex', 'casual' or 'ceremonial'. For Sacks, such rapid characterizations of data assume 'that we can know that without an analysis of what it is [they] are doing' (LC1: 429). Such an analysis needs to locate particular utterances in sequence of talk (LC1: 430, 622). So an ethnographer who reports that she or he heard someone tell a 'story' only raises a further question: how the ethnographer (and presumably the members of the group studied) heard an activity as a 'story'.

For Sacks an account only becomes a 'story' when displayed and monitored as such by teller and recipient: 'We want to see: Is the fact that someone is telling a story something that matters to the teller and the hearer? How can it matter, and why does it matter, and of course when does it matter?' (LC2: 223). So the category 'story' must be treated as what Sacks calls 'a candidate name' and we are only interested in what has happened as a 'story' if we can show how an activity is produced as a 'story'.

5 Concepts in social science

At this point, the experienced researcher might respond that Sacks has characterized conventional research as over-naive. In particular, most researchers are aware of the danger of assuming any one-to-one correspondence between their categories and the aspects of 'reality' which they purport to describe. Instead, following Weber (1949), many researchers claim that they are simply using hypothetical constructs (or 'ideal types') which are only to be judged in relation to whether they are *useful*, not whether they are '*accurate*' or '*true*'.

However, Sacks was aware of this argument. As he notes:

> It is a very conventional way to proceed in the social sciences to propose that the machinery you use to analyze some data you have is acceptable if it is not intendedly the analysis of real phenomena. That is, you can have machinery which is a 'valid hypothetical construct', and it can analyze something for you.
>
> (LC1: 315)

By contrast, the 'machinery' in which Sacks is interested is not a set of 'hypothetical constructs'. Instead, Sacks's ambitious claim is throughout 'to be dealing with the real world' (LC1: 316). The 'machinery' he sets out, then, is not to be seen as a set of more or less useful categories but the *actual* categories and mechanisms that members use. In this sense, he points out: 'I intend that the machinery I use to explain some phenomenon, to characterize how it gets done, is just as *real* as the thing I started out to explain' (*LC1*: 315, emphasis added).

6 Locating the machinery

Let me try to clarify the nature of the machinery in which Sacks is interested. As Sacks argues in the quotation above, the machinery is what allows some 'phenomenon' to 'get done'. In this sense, social research must seek to construct the *machinery* that would produce any naturally occurring event. As Sacks puts it:

> The kind of phenomena we are dealing with are always transcriptions of actual occurrences, in their actual sequence. And I take it our business is to try to construct the machinery that would produce these occurrences. That is, we find and name some objects, and find and name some rules for using those objects.
>
> (*LC1*: 113)

The implication is that Sacks is interested in 'occurrences' only in so far as they can be studied as outcomes of particular members' methods. Take the case of a telephone call. The interest is not specifically in the mundane contents of the call. So it is unlikely that Sacks's analytic purposes could be satisfied by, say, listing the topics people are talking about. Instead, Sacks is interested in such calls 'as really one machine product. That is to say, it's not this conversation that we're really interested in, but we can begin to see machinery that produces this as a series of moves' (*LC2*: 169).

Sacks's language of 'machinery' and 'production' fits his rejection of over-rationalistic models of human action. So, for instance, people don't intend to grab the floor in order to tell a story, yet somehow they do it. This also means that, for Sacks, it is an error to assume that the machinery is somehow rationally designed to achieve certain ends or products. Instead, Sacks argues:

> Most of the things that we [other social scientists, laypeople] treat as products, i.e. the achieved orderliness of the world of some sort, are *byproducts*. That is, there is machinery that produces orderly events, but most of the events that we come across that are orderly are not specifically the product of a machine designed to produce them, but are off-shoots of a machine designed to do something else or nothing in particular.
>
> (*LC2*: 240)

So it is a gross error to assume that Sacks uses the term 'machinery' to identify some all-determining apparatus like, say, 'culture'. Admittedly, his references to 'machinery' and sometimes to 'the technology of conversation' (*LC2*: 339) do seem to imply that he is working with a deterministic model. This may be why Goffman (1981: 17) criticized what he took to be Sacks's perspective of a 'systems engineer'.

And there does seem evidence for this in certain parts of his lectures where Sacks seems to imply a very mechanical model. For instance, he describes interactions 'as being spewed out by machinery, the machinery being what we're trying to find; where, in order to find it we've got to get a whole bunch of its products' (LC2: 169).

However, a fuller reading of the lectures shows, by contrast, that Sacks is consistently interested in how members *use* the machinery. As he puts it: 'the idea is to take singular sequences of conversation and tear them apart in such a way as to find rules, techniques, procedures, methods, maxims [which] can be used to generate the orderly features we find in the conversations we examine' (LC2: 339).

Bearing in mind Sacks's insistence that his machinery 'is just as real as the thing I started out to explain' (LC1: 315), the rules, procedures and so on that Sacks identifies here are members' rules and procedures used by members to 'generate . . . orderly features'. For instance, Sacks argues that members, just like analysts, treat 'the positioning of an utterance' as 'a resource for finding what it's talking to' (LC2: 427) and, thereby, use that positioning to display an understanding of something (as an invitation, a question, and so on).

7 Building a data analysis

How do we actually go about inspecting some data in order to identify the locally employed machinery used to produce them? Sacks offers an important warning that apparently simple phenomena may need complex explanations. As he puts it: 'There is no necessary fit between the complexity or simplicity of the apparatus you need to construct some object, and the face-value complexity or simplicity of the object. Just because something seems 'pretty routine', we cannot assume that it is not difficult to explain. As Sacks points out: 'the activities that molecules are able to engage in quickly, routinely, have not been described [even] by enormously brilliant scientists' (LC1: 115).

Now replace molecules with a social activity like issuing invitations. The aim then is 'to build a method which will provide for some utterance as a "recognizable invitation" ' (LC1: 300). Moreover, 'since invitations stand in alternation to rejection', we need to be able 'to discriminate between the two'. What our analysis is looking for is a method that will

> provide for the recognizability of 'invitation' for some cases and for the recognizability of 'rejection' for others. And if we get a method, then we ought to be able to use it to generate other cases than this one; where, then, the ones that we generate ought to be equally recognizable as invitations or rejections.
>
> (LC1: 301)

. . . It should not be assumed that Sacks is merely seeking understandings of discrete or isolated activities like invitations. On the contrary, his investigation of a particular piece of data is always intended as part of a cumulative enterprise where one finding leads to another: 'recurrently it happens that some piece of data is analyzed, and when you're analyzing something else you find that the machinery built and tested to analyze one thing is now important for this other thing. That permits you to tie things together' (*LC*1: 316).

So the overall aim is to 'tie things together'. But, contrary to Goffman, this does not mean that we can ever lose sight of the fact that we are trying to identify a machinery built *in situ* to produce a particular data-set: 'the core point is that when you introduce a piece of machinery, that piece of machinery in the first instance [is] introduced where it, itself, analyzes the things of which it's built' (*LC*1: 316).

Moreover, even when you set out this way and, as sometimes happens, discover that you cannot explain your original problem, this does not mean that you should be discouraged or assume that 'you've got nothing'. In fact: 'You may have learned an enormous amount, as you've fitted various pieces of machinery together, [learned] about what they're doing, about other data' (*LC*1: 316).

So, somewhat reassuringly, Sacks reminds us that our original research problem may be forced to change. And, providing the analytic thrust remains, this need not be a problem because we can then go on to discover new, perhaps even 'deeper' things. . . .

References

Atkinson, J.M. and Heritage, J. (eds) (1984) *Structures of Social Action: Studies in Conversation Analysis*. Cambridge: Cambridge University Press.

Atkinson, P. and Silverman, D. (1997) 'Kundera's *Immortality*: the interview society and the invention of self.' *Qualitative Inquiry*, 3(3), 304–325.

Garfinkel, E. (1967) *Studies in Ethnomethodology*, Englewood Cliffs: Prentice Hall.

Goffman, E. (1981) *Forms of Talk*. Oxford: Blackwell.

Sacks, H. (1984) 'Notes on methodology.' In Atkinson and Heritage 1984, 21–7. Based on transcripts of several lectures.

—— (1992) *Lectures on Conversation*, ed. Gail Jefferson, introduction by Emanuel Schegloff. 2 vols, Oxford: Blackwell. Abbreviated as *LC* in the text. Combined in one paperback volume 1995.

Silverman, D. (1993) *Interpreting Qualitative Data: Strategies for Analysing Talk, Text and Interaction*. London: Sage.

Weber, M. (1949) *Methodology of the Social Sciences*. New York: Free Press.

Chapter 48

Anssi Peräkylä

RELIABILITY AND VALIDITY IN RESEARCH BASED ON TAPES AND TRANSCRIPTS

From Silverman, D. (ed.), *Qualitative Research: Theory, Method and Practice*, London: Sage (1997).

. . .

THE AIM OF ALL conversation analytic studies (both on ordinary conversation and on institutional interaction) is to produce descriptions of recurrent patterns of social interaction and language use. CA is particularly rigorous in its requirement of an empirical grounding for any descriptions to be accepted as valid. In this respect, CA differs from some other forms of discourse analysis (Fairclough 1992; Parker 1992) which emphasize more the 'openness' of any language use to different interpretations and hence underline more the active contribution of the researcher in 'constructing' the descriptions that she or he produces about language use.

Reliability

. . . Working with tapes and transcripts eliminates at one stroke many of the problems that ethnographers have with the unspecified accuracy of field notes and with the limited public access to them. . . . Tape recordings and transcripts based on them can provide for highly detailed and publicly accessible representations of social interaction. Therefore, Kirk and Miller's suggestion that in qualitative research 'issues of reliability have received little attention' (1986: 42) does not apply to conversation analytic research. CA claims part of its justification on the basis of being free of many shortcomings in reliability characteristic of other forms of qualitative research, especially ethnography.

Although tape-recorded data have intrinsic strength in terms of accuracy and public access, special attention needs to be paid to the *inclusiveness* of such data. Video or audio recordings of specific events (such as telephone conversations, medical consultations or public meetings) may entail a loss of some aspects of social interaction, including (a) medium- and long-span temporal processes, (b) ambulatory events and (c) impact of texts and other 'non-conversational' modalities of action. The potential loss can be prevented with appropriate arrangements in the data collection. . . . However, it also needs to be pointed out that *conversation analytic studies do not aim at describing all aspects of social organization.* (This is, of course, true concerning any other methodology as well.) The organization of verbal interaction in face to face encounters and telephone conversations is the domain in which adequate conversation analytic studies can rightly claim superior reliability, and this is indeed the home base of CA methodology. In studies that focus primarily on other aspects of social organization (such as textual, pictorial or technological realities) other methods may be more suitable. . . .

The technical quality of recordings is a decisive issue: if something is lost from sight or remains inaudible in the tapes, there is no way of recovering it. It may be extremely frustrating to have some badly recorded sections of events that at a later stage of the research turn out to be of primary importance for the analysis. This kind of frustration can be minimized by already at the planning stage of the research paying enough attention both to the quality of the equipment and to the arrangements of recording. . . .

The adequacy of transcripts is equally important: even though in a proper analysis of data the tapes need to be listened to and watched, at least the selection of what is analysed in detail is usually done on the basis of the transcripts only. The quality of transcripts in research on naturally occurring interaction seems to vary greatly. Not only are the details of intonation and prosody sometimes omitted, but what is more problematic, whole utterances (especially in multi-party situations) can be missing from transcripts in studies that otherwise have been seriously and adequately designed and conducted.

Transcription is a skill that can only be acquired through long enough training. It is extremely useful if an experienced transcriber can supervise a beginner. This is most easily done by the more experienced one correcting some of the beginner's transcripts. In fact, the correction of transcripts is useful for anybody preparing transcripts: another researcher can always hear some of the things that one has not noticed. Correction by colleagues also enhances a culture of shared practices in measuring pauses, intonation, and so on.

It is advisable to include many aspects of vocal expression in the initial transcripts (for conversation analytic transcription conventions developed by Gail Jefferson, see Atkinson and Heritage, 1984: ix–xvi). A rich transcript is a resource of analysis; at the time of transcribing, the researcher cannot know which of the details will turn out to be important for the analysis. After the analysis has been accomplished and the results are published, however, some of the special notation not used in the analysis can be left out. 'Simplified' transcripts can make the reception of the analysis easier, especially if the audience is not specialized in conversation analysis.

In sum, reliability of observations in conversation analytic research (as in any other empirical method) can only be achieved through serious effort. The method

itself does not guarantee reliability. In conversation analytic studies, proper attention needs to be paid to the selection and technical quality of recordings as well as to
the adequacy of the transcripts.

Validity in conversation analytic research

. . . In discussions about validity, especially in the context of quantitative research,
there is an underlying background assumption about a separation between the 'raw'
observations and the issues that these observations stand for or represent. Responses
to questionnaires, for example, can be more or less valid representations of underlying social phenomena, such as the respondents' attitudes or values. Conversation
analysis is in stark contrast to this kind of approach: the core of its very aim is to
investigate talk-in-interaction, not as 'a screen on which are projected other processes', but as a phenomenon in its own right (Schegloff 1992: xviii). This commitment to naturalistic description of the interaction order (Goffman, 1983) and the
social action taking place within that order (cf. also Sacks, 1984) gives a distinctive
shape to the issues of validation in conversation analysis.

The transparence of analytic claims

. . . The results of (good) conversation analytic research exhibit in a positive manner, what Kirk and Miller (1986: 22) called *apparent validity*: once you have read
them, you are convinced that they are transparently true. A conversational activity
called 'fishing' may serve as an example. Anita Pomerantz showed in a paper published in 1980 how participants in a conversation can indirectly 'fish' for information
from one another by telling what they themselves know. Descriptions of events
displaying their producer's 'limited access' to the relevant facts may work as a device
for inviting the other party to disclose his/her authorized version of the same issues
(assuming of course, that the other party is in a position of having privileged access
to the relevant facts). Such dynamics are at work in cases like the following:

```
(1)        B:   Hello::,
           A:   HI:::.
           B:   Oh:hi:: 'ow are you Agne::s,
     →     A:   Fi:ne. Yer line's been busy.
           B:   Yeuh my fu (hh)- .hh my father's wife called me
                ..hh So when she calls me::, .hh I can always talk
                for a long time. Cuz she e'n afford it'n I can't.
                hhhh heh .ehhhhhh
                (Pomerantz 1980: 195)
```

In Extract 1 above, the description based on a limited access to relevant facts
given by A (marked with an arrow) works as what Pomerantz called 'a fishing
device', successfully eliciting B's insider's report in the next turn. By telling her
observations about the line having been busy, A makes it relevant for B to disclose to
whom she was talking.

The description of an activity like 'fishing' tends to 'ring a bell' as soon as anyone stops to think about it. 'Fishing' is something in which everybody has participated in different roles. But until Pomerantz's article, this activity has not been described formally. The results of Pomerantz's analysis are very simple. Her argument is transparently true, or, in Kirk and Miller's (1986) terms, it has a genuine 'apparent validity'. . . .

Validation through 'next turn'

As Sacks *et al.* pointed out, research on talk-in-interaction has an inherent method-ological resource that research on written texts lacks: 'Regularly . . . a turn's talk will display its speaker's understanding of a prior turn's talk, and whatever other talk it marks itself as directed to' (1974: 728). In other words, in the unfolding of the interaction, the interactants display to one another their interpretations of what is going on, especially of what was going on in the immediately preceding turn of talk (Atkinson and Heritage 1984). From this fact arises a fundamental validation procedure that is used in all conversation analytic research:

> But while understandings of other turn's talk are displayed to co-participants, they are available as well to professional analysts, who are thereby afforded a proof criterion . . . for the analysis of what a turn's talk is occupied with.
>
> (Sacks *et al.* 1974: 729)

At the beginning of this chapter, it was pointed out that conversation analysis differs from those forms of discourse analysis which emphasize the open-endedness of the meaning of all linguistic expressions. Now we can see the reason for this: even though the meaning of any expression, if considered in isolation is extremely open-ended, any utterance that is produced in talk-in-interaction will be locally inter-preted by the participants of that interaction. In the first place, their interpretation is displayed in the next actions after the utterance. Hence, any interpretations that conversation analysts may suggest can be subjected to the 'proof procedure' outlined by Sacks et al.: the next turn will show whether the interactants themselves treat the utterance in ways that are in accordance with the analyst's interpretation.

Therefore in Extract 1 shown above, the utterance produced by B in lines 5–8 provides a proof procedure for the interpretation suggested by Pomerantz concern-ing A's turn in line 4. (What Pomerantz suggested was that 'telling my side' [what A did in line 4] can operate as a 'fishing device', which indirectly elicits an authorita-tive version of the events from the interlocutor.) And as we see, Pomerantz's interpretation passes the test: in lines 5–8, B gives her first-hand account of what had happened.

In much everyday conversation analytic work, things are not as nice and simple as in Extract 1: the next turns may be ambiguous in relation to the action performed in the preceding turn. However, the 'proof procedure' provided by the next turn remains the primordial criterion of validity that must be used as much as possible in all conversation analytic work. . . .

Generalizability of conversation analytic findings

. . . Due to their work-intensive character, most conversation analytic studies are necessarily based on relatively small databases. How widely can the results, derived from relatively small samples, be generalized?

This character of the problem is closely dependent on the type of conversation analytic research. In studies of ordinary conversation, the baseline assumption is that the results are or should be generalizable to the whole domain of ordinary conversations, and to a certain extent even across linguistic and cultural boundaries. Even though it may be that the most primordial conversational practices and structures such as turn-taking or adjacency pairs – are almost universal, there are others, such as openings of telephone calls . . . which show considerable variation in different cultures. This variation can only be tackled through gradual accumulation of studies on ordinary conversation in different cultures and social milieus. . . .

However, the question of generalizability can also be approached from a different direction. The concept of *possibility* is a key to this. *Social practices that are possible*, that is, *possibilities of language use*, are the central objects of all conversation analytic case studies on interaction in particular institutional settings. The possibility of various practices can be considered generalizable even if the practices are not actualized in similar ways across different settings. For example, in my study on AIDS counselling in a London teaching hospital (Peräkylä, 1995), the research objects were specific questioning practices used by the counsellors and their clients. . . .

As possibilities, the practices that I analysed are very likely to be generalizable. There is no reason to think that they could not be made possible by any competent member of (at least any Western) society. In this sense, this study produced generalizable results. The results were not generalizable as descriptions of what other counsellors or other professionals do with their clients; but they were generalizable as descriptions of what any counsellor or other professional, with his or her clients, *can* do, given that he or she has the same array of interactional competencies as the participants of the AIDS counselling sessions have. . . .

References

Atkinson, J.M. and Heritage, J. (eds) (1984) *Structures of Social Action. Studies in Conversation Analysis*. Cambridge: Cambridge University Press.

Fairclough, N. (1992) *Discourse and Social Change*. Cambridge: Polity.

Goffman, E. (1983) 'The interaction order', *American Sociological Review*, 48 (1): 1–17.

Kirk, J. and Miller, M.L. (1986) *Reliability and Validity in Qualitative Research*. London: Sage.

Parker, I. (1992) *Discourse Dynamics: Critical Analysis for Social and Individual Psychology*. London: Routledge.

Peräkylä, A. (1995) *AIDS, Counselling: Institutional Interaction and Clinical Practice*. Cambridge: Cambridge University Press.

Pomerantz. A. (1980) 'Telling my side: "Limited access" as a "fishing device"'. *Sociological Inquiry*. 50: 186 98.

Sacks, H. (1984) 'Notes on methodology', in J.M. Atkinson and J. Heritage (eds). *Structures of*

Social Action: Studies in Conversation Analysis. Cambridge: Cambridge University Press, pp. 21–27.

Sacks, H. Schegloff, E.A. and Jefferson, G. (1974) 'A simplest systematics for the organization of turn-taking for conversation', *Language*, 50 696–735.

Schegloff, E.A. (1992) 'Introduction', in H. Sacks, *Lectures on Conversation*, vol. I, ed G. Jefferson. Oxford: Blackwell, pp. ix–lxii.

PART ELEVEN

Structuralism, post-structuralism and the linguistic turn

INTRODUCTION

THE MOVE FROM STRUCTURALISM to post-structuralism in social and literary theory exercised a considerable influence over a range of disciplines, including those to which social and cultural researchers relate. The readings in this section seek to demonstrate what these terms mean, and to show their implications for research practice. Perhaps most importantly, these theoretical (and to some extent philosophical) shifts were associated with an increased interest in the ways in which language (both words and images) constructs, rather than simply reflects or reports on, reality. This, then, has been called the 'linguistic turn', and a number of practical research techniques have arisen from this, including some forms of discourse analysis.

Structuralists seek to identify the underlying structures that produce meaning in texts, thus sharing with Durkheim (reading 3) a concern to discover universal laws or rules that govern phenomena. Lévi-Strauss (reading 49) analysed myth with this in mind, and in this reading seeks to explain why myths, though apparently a story form where anything might happen, in fact share an underlying similarity across different regions of the world. He demonstrates this in an analysis of the Oedipus myth.

Lévi-Strauss developed his ideas having studied those of the linguist Saussure, regarded as the founder of semiotics, or the science of signs. Signs may be words, or they may be pictures, or a host of other things (hairstyles, items of clothing, etc.). The essential point that Saussure made is that signs acquire their meaning through their relationship with other signs rather than sitting in a fixed relationship with reality. Thus wearing a Hawaiian shirt in the 1960s 'meant' something different from wearing one in the 1990s. Leiss *et al.* (reading 50), drawing on both Saussure and Barthes (an author who applied semiotic method to the study of popular culture), show how the structuralist method of semiotics can be applied to the study of advertisements, outlining both the strengths and weaknesses of this form of analysis.

Almost as soon as it appeared, structuralism attracted criticism and this developed into an alternative known as 'post-structuralism'. While post-structuralists accept the basic Saussurian view that the meaning of signs is relational, they depart from the structuralist search for universal underlying rules that govern the production of meaning. Instead, they are much more interested in exploring the diversity of interpretations that can be placed on a single text. Hall's account of the ideas of the post-structuralist theorist Foucault (reading 51) reveals Foucault's additional interest in relations of power, a concern that made his work particularly relevant to sociologists, historians and political analysts. Crucially, Foucault was interested in discourse, by which he meant something much broader than mere language. This was to provide an important influence on the development of 'discourse analysis'.

In psychology discourse analysis (DA) has developed as a qualitative alternative to quantitative method. Potter and Wetherell (reading 52) contrast quantitative approaches to attitude measurement (see also reading 11) with a discourse analytic approach which sees 'attitudes' as being fluid, changeable and constructed for the purposes of the moment, rather than being underlying traits determining behaviour. While Potter and Wetherell begin to show how a discourse analyst would approach a text or transcript, the next reading by Fairclough and Wodak (reading 53) provides considerably more detail in their analysis of an interview with a politician (Thatcher). These authors see themselves as practising a variant of DA known as 'critical' DA, or CDA, called this because of the political engagement of its practitioners. In this respect, CDA practitioners mirror Foucault's interest in power relations.

Linguistics is a discipline that has also contributed much to the development of discourse analysis. Widdowson, who is a linguist, reviewing books by three CDA practitioners (reading 54), is highly critical of the approach. Instead of providing an objective analysis CDA practitioners, claims Widdowson, impose their own biased readings without regard for negative instances that might contradict their line.

This part of the book ends with an example of narrative analysis by Riessman (reading 55). This approach shares much with DA (and CDA), reflecting an interest in the ways in which speakers (and writers) use language to construct particular versions of the world. In narrative analysis the focus is generally on the way speakers deploy story-telling devices (such as plot compression, or episodes reporting concrete details of events) for persuasive effect.

DISCUSSION POINTS

- Take a series of newspaper articles describing different instances of the same thing (for example, car crash stories). What regular features underly this form of reporting? Do the same for some well-known fairy stories (e.g. Snow White; Sleeping Beauty; Cinderella).
- Leiss et al. list various weaknesses of semiotic analysis as well as outlining its

strengths. Elsewhere in their book they argue that combining a semiotic approach with that of content analysis (see reading 14 for one version of this) represents a good compromise. How would you study advertisements using both these methods? Do you agree that the advantages of one approach remedy the disadvantages of the other?

- If, as Foucault argues, knowledge is a particular construction of the world, part of a 'regime of truth', or 'discourse' that is historically specific to particular groupings of people or institutional interests, how might we evaluate the claims made by social researchers in their research reports?

- Examine Potter and Wetherell's critique of Marsh's approach to the measurement of attitudes. How does this compare with Cicourel's criticisms of fixed choice questions (reading 22)? How does the discourse analytic approach to attitudes differ from that of Marsh and of Oppenheim (reading 11)?

- Choose a political speech by a politician with whose views you are broadly sympathetic. How has the speaker made the speech persuasive? How might someone arguing the opposite point of view use the same rhetorical techniques?

- Do Widdowson's criticisms of CDA hold true for the analysis of the Thatcher interview provided by Fairclough and Wodak (reading 53)? How does the approach outlined by Fairclough and Wodak compare with the way a conversation analyst might have approached this interview (see readings 47 and 48)? Would a CA approach overcome the problems that Widdowson identifies? What discursive techniques does Widdowson employ to make his text persuasive?

- Is narrative analysis different from CDA or DA? If so, how?

FURTHER READING

Barthes, R. (1966) 'Introduction to the structural analysis of narratives', in Sontag, S. (ed.) A Barthes Reader, New York: Vintage, 1993.

—— (1977) Elements of Semiology, New York: Hill and Wang.

—— (1986) Mythologies, London: Paladin.

Burman, E. and Parker I. (eds) (1993) Discourse Analytic Research: Repertoires and Readings of Texts in Action, London: Routledge.

Czarniawska, Barbara (1997) A Narrative Approach to Organization Studies, Thousand Oak, Cal.: Sage.

Eco, U. (1976) A Theory of Semiotics, Bloomington: Indiana University Press.

Foucault, M. (1992) The Order of Things: An Archaeology of the Human Sciences, (first published 1970), London: Routledge.

Gee, J.P. (1999) An Introduction to Discourse Analysis, London: Taylor and Francis.

Hawkes, T. (1977) Structuralism and Semiotics, London: Routledge.

Kendall, G. and Wickham G. (1998) Using Focault's Methods, London: Sage.

Labov, W. (1997) 'Some further steps in narrative analysis', Journal of Narrative and Life History. Available online at http://www.ling.upenn.edu/~labov/sfs.html.

Riessman, C.K. (1993) Narrative Analysis, Newbury Park, Cal.: Sage.

Chapter 49

Claude Lévi-Strauss

THE STRUCTURAL STUDY OF MYTH

From *Structural Anthropology*, vol. 1, translated by C. Jacobson and B.G. Schoepf, London: Penguin (1993, first published 1963).

. . .

IN ORDER TO UNDERSTAND what a myth really is, must we choose between platitude and sophism? Some claim that human societies merely express, through their mythology, fundamental feelings common to the whole of mankind, such as love, hate, or revenge or that they try to provide some kind of explanations for phenomena which they cannot otherwise understand – astronomical, meteorological, and the like. But why should these societies do it in such elaborate and devious ways, when all of them are also acquainted with empirical explanations? On the other hand, psychoanalysts and many anthropologists have shifted the problems away from the natural or cosmological toward the sociological and psychological fields. But then the interpretation becomes too easy: If a given mythology confers prominence on a certain figure, let us say an evil grandmother, it will be claimed that in such a society grandmothers are actually evil and that mythology reflects the social structure and the social relations; but should the actual data be conflicting, it would be as readily claimed that the purpose of mythology is to provide an outlet for repressed feelings. Whatever the situation, a clever dialectic will always find a way to pretend that a meaning has been found.

Mythology confronts the student with a situation which at first sight appears contradictory. On the one hand it would seem that in the course of a myth anything is likely to happen. There is no logic, no continuity. Any characteristic can be attributed to any subject; every conceivable relation can be found. With myth, everything becomes possible. But on the other hand, this apparent arbitrariness is belied by the astounding similarity between myths collected in widely different regions. Therefore the problem: If the content of a myth is contingent, how are we going to explain the fact that myths throughout the world are so similar?

It is precisely this awareness of a basic antinomy pertaining to the nature of myth that may lead us toward its solution. For the contradiction which we face is very similar to that which in earlier times brought considerable worry to the first philosophers concerned with linguistic problems; linguistics could only begin to evolve as a science after this contradiction had been overcome. Ancient philosophers reasoned about language the way we do about mythology. On the one hand, they did notice that in a given language certain sequences of sounds were associated with definite meanings, and they earnestly aimed at discovering a reason for the linkage between those *sounds* and that *meaning*. Their attempt, however, was thwarted from the very beginning by the fact that the same sounds were equally present in other languages although the meaning they conveyed was entirely different. The contradiction was surmounted only by the discovery that it is the combination of sounds, not the sounds themselves, which provides the significant data. . . .

To invite the mythologist to compare his precarious situation with that of the linguist in the prescientific stage is not enough. As a matter of fact we may thus be led only from one difficulty to another. There is a very good reason why myth cannot simply be treated as language if its specific problems are to be solved; myth *is* language: to be known, myth has to be told; it is a part of human speech. In order to preserve its specificity we must be able to show that it is both the same thing as language, and also something different from it. Here, too, the past experience of linguists may help us. For language itself can be analyzed into things which are at the same time similar and yet different. This is precisely what is expressed in Saussure's distinction between *langue* and *parole*, one being the structural side of language, the other the statistical aspect of it, *langue* belonging to a reversible time, *parole* being nonreversible. If those two levels already exist in language, then a third one can conceivably be isolated. . . .

To sum up the discussion at this point, we have so far made the following claims: (1) If there is a meaning to be found in mythology, it cannot reside in the isolated elements which enter into the composition of a myth, but only in the way those elements are combined. (2) Although myth belongs to the same category as language, being, as a matter of fact, only part of it, language in myth exhibits specific properties. (3) Those properties are only to be found *above* the ordinary linguistic level, that is, they exhibit more complex features than those which are to be found in any other kind of linguistic expression. . . .

The true constituent units of a myth are not the isolated relations [of its elements] but *bundles of such relations*, and it is only as bundles that these relations can be put to use and combined so as to produce a meaning. Relations pertaining to the same bundle may appear diachronically at remote intervals, but when we have succeeded in grouping them together we have reorganized our myth according to a time referent of a new nature, corresponding to the prerequisite of the initial hypothesis, namely a two-dimensional time referent which is simultaneously diachronic and synchronic, and which accordingly integrates the characteristics of *langue* on the one hand, and those of *parole* on the other. . . .

[A] comparison may help to explain what we have in mind.

Let us first suppose that archaeologists of the future coming from another planet would one day, when all human life had disappeared from the earth, excavate one of our libraries. Even if they were at first ignorant of our writing, they might succeed in deciphering it – an undertaking which would require, at some early stage, the discovery that the alphabet, as we are in the habit of printing it, should be read from left to right and from top to bottom. However, they would soon discover that a whole category of books did not fit the usual pattern – these would be the orchestra scores on the shelves of the music division. But after trying, without success, to decipher staffs one after the other, from the upper down to the lower, they would probably notice that the same patterns of notes recurred at intervals, either in full or in part, or that some patterns were strongly reminiscent of earlier ones. Hence the hypothesis: What if patterns showing affinity, instead of being considered in succession, were to be treated as one complex pattern and read as a whole? By getting at what we call *harmony*, they would then see that an orchestra score, to be meaningful, must be read diachronically along one axis – that is, page after page, and from left to right – and synchronically along the other axis, all the notes written vertically making up one gross constituent unit, that is, one bundle of relations. . . .

Now for a concrete example of the method we propose. We shall use the Oedipus myth, which is well known to everyone. . . . The myth will be treated as an orchestra score would be if it were unwittingly considered as a unilinear series; our task is to re-establish the correct arrangement. Say, for instance, we were confronted with a sequence of the type: 1,2,4,7,8,2,3,4,6,8,1,4,5,7,8,1,2,5,7,3,4, 5,6,8 . . ., the assignment being to put all the 1's together, all the 2's, the 3's, etc.; the result is a chart:

1	2		4				7	8
	2	3	4			6		8
1			4	5			7	8
1	2			5			7	
		3	4	5	6			8

We shall attempt to perform the same kind of operation on the Oedipus myth, trying out several arrangements of the mythemes until we find one which is in harmony with the principles enumerated above. Let us suppose, for the sake of argument, that the best arrangement is [that on p. 338] (although it might certainly be improved with the help of a specialist in Greek mythology).

We thus find ourselves confronted with four vertical columns, each of which includes several relations belonging to the same bundle. Were we to *tell* the myth, we would disregard the columns and read the rows from left to right and from top to bottom. But if we want to *understand* the myth, then we will have to disregard one half of the diachronic dimension (top to bottom) and read from left to right, column after column, each one being considered as a unit.

All the relations belonging to the same column exhibit one common feature which it is our task to discover. For instance, all the events grouped in the first column on the left have something to do with blood relations which are over-emphasized, that is, are more intimate than they should be. Let us say, then, that the first column has as its common feature the *overrating of blood relations*. It is obvious

Cadmos seeks his sister Europa, ravished by Zeus			
		Cadmos kills the dragon	
	The Spartoi kill one another		
			Labdacos (Laios' father) = *lame* (?)
	Oedipus kills his father, Laios		Laios (Oedipus' father) = *left-sided* (?)
		Oedipus kills the Sphinx	
			Oedipus = *swollen-foot* (?)
Oedipus marries his mother, Jocasta			
	Eteocles kills his brother, Polynices		
Antigone buries her brother, Polynices, despite prohibition			

that the second column expresses the same thing, but inverted: *underrating of blood relations*. The third column refers to monsters being slain. As to the fourth, a few words of clarification are needed. The remarkable connotation of the surnames in Oedipus' father-line has often been noticed. However, linguists usually disregard it, since to them the only way to define the meaning of a term is to investigate all the contexts in which it appears, and personal names, precisely because they are used as such, are not accompanied by any context. With the method we propose to follow the objection disappears, since the myth itself provides its own context. The significance is no longer to be sought in the eventual meaning of each name, but in the fact that all the names have a common feature: All the hypothetical meanings (which may well remain hypothetical) refer to *difficulties in walking straight and standing upright*.

What then is the relationship between the two columns on the right? Column three refers to monsters. The dragon is a chthonian[1] being which has to be killed in

[1 Editor's footnote: chthonion, autochthonion: springing from, or dwelling in, the soil/earth.]

order that mankind be born from the Earth; the Sphinx is a monster unwilling to permit men to live. The last unit reproduces the first one, which has to do with the *autochthonous origin* of mankind. Since the monsters are overcome by men, we may thus say that the common feature of the third column is *denial of the autochthonous origin of man*.

This immediately helps us to understand the meaning of the fourth column. In mythology it is a universal characteristic of men born from the Earth that at the moment they emerge from the depth they either cannot walk or they walk clumsily. This is the case of the chthonian beings in the mythology of the Pueblo: Muyingwu, who leads the emergence, and the chthonian Shumaikoli are lame ('bleeding-foot,' 'sore-foot'). The same happens to the Koskimo of the Kwakiutl after they have been swallowed by the chthonian monster, Tsiakish: When they returned to the surface of the earth 'they limped forward or tripped side-ways.' Thus the common feature of the fourth column is *the persistence of the autochthonous origin of man*. It follows that column four is to column three as column one is to column two. The inability to connect two kinds of relationships is overcome (or rather replaced) by the assertion that contradictory relationships are identical inasmuch as they are both self-contradictory in a similar way. Although this is still a provisional formulation of the structure of mythical thought, it is sufficient at this stage.

Turning back to the Oedipus myth, we may now see what it means. The myth has to do with the inability, for a culture which holds the belief that mankind is autochthonous (see, for instance, Pausanias, VIII, xxix, 4: plants provide a *model* for humans), to find a satisfactory transition between this theory and the knowledge that human beings are actually born from the union of man and woman. Although the problem obviously cannot be solved, the Oedipus myth provides a kind of logical tool which relates the original problem – born from one or born from two? – to the derivative problem: born from different or born from same? By a correlation of this type, the overrating of blood relations is to the underrating of blood relations as the attempt to escape autochthony is to the impossibility to succeed in it. Although experience contradicts theory, social life validates cosmology by its similarity of structure. Hence cosmology is true. . . .

Three final remarks may serve as conclusion.

First, the question has often been raised why myths, and more generally oral literature, are so much addicted to duplication, triplication, or quadruplication of the same sequence. If our hypotheses are accepted, the answer is obvious: The function of repetition is to render the structure of the myth apparent. For we have seen that the synchronic-diachronic structure of the myth permits us to organize it into diachronic sequences (the rows in our tables) which should be read synchronic-ally (the columns). Thus, a myth exhibits a 'slated' structure, which comes to the surface, so to speak, through the process of repetition.

However, the slates are not absolutely identical. And since the purpose of myth is to provide a logical model capable of overcoming a contradiction (an impossible achievement if, as it happens, the contradiction is real), a theoretically infinite number of slates will be generated, each one slightly different from the others. Thus, myth grows spiral-wise until the intellectual impulse which has produced it is exhausted. Its *growth* is a continuous process, whereas its *structure* remains dis-continuous. If this is the case, we should assume that it closely corresponds, in the realm of the spoken word, to a crystal in the realm of physical matter. This analogy may help us to better understand the relationship of myth to both *langue* on the one hand and *parole* on the other. Myth is an intermediary entity between a statistical aggregate of molecules and the molecular structure itself.

Prevalent attempts to explain alleged differences between the so-called primitive mind and scientific thought have resorted to qualitative differences between the working processes of the mind in both cases, while assuming that the entities which they were studying remained very much the same. If our interpretation is correct, we are led toward a completely different view – namely, that the kind of logic in mythical thought is as rigorous as that of modern science, and that the difference lies, not in the quality of the intellectual process, but in the nature of the things to which it is applied. This is well in agreement with the situation known to prevail in the field of technology: What makes a steel ax superior to a stone ax is not that the first one is better made than the second. They are equally well made, but steel is quite different from stone. In the same way we may be able to show that the same logical processes operate in myth as in science, and that man has always been thinking equally well; the improvement lies, not in an alleged progress of man's mind, but in the discovery of new areas to which it may apply its unchanged and unchanging powers.

Chapter 50

William Leiss, Stephen Kline and Sut Jhally

SEMIOLOGY AND THE STUDY OF ADVERTISING

From *Social Communication in Advertising: Persons, Products and Images of Well-Being*, London: Methuen (1986).

. . .

SEMIOLOGY (OR SEMIOTICS) IS a method for examining textual material that emerged from linguistics and from literary and cultural analysis, rather than from the tradition of social science research. It can be used to study many kinds of social phenomena; anything in which meaning is thought to inhere can be investigated from this standpoint. The Swiss linguist Ferdinand De Saussure (1966), who was especially interested in the internal structures of linguistic systems, applied the term 'semiology' to what he described as 'the science of signs.' From the outset, semiologists have concentrated on relationships among the parts of a message or communication system, for, they contend, it is only through the interaction of component parts that meaning is formed. . . . We shall confine ourselves to outlining the reasons why semiology is especially appropriate to the study of contemporary advertising and some of the basic concepts of the method (describing how, according to semiology, we derive meaning from advertising). . . .

The growing preponderance of visuals in ads has enhanced the ambiguity of meaning embedded in message structures. Earlier advertising usually states its message quite explicitly through the medium of written text (even if the most outrageous claims were made in the process), but starting in the mid-1920s visual representation became more common, and the relationship between text and visual image became complementary – that is, the text explained the visual. In the postwar period, and especially since the early 1960s, the functions of text moved away from explaining the visual and toward a more cryptic form, in which text appeared as a kind of 'key' to the visual.

In all, the effect was to make the commercial message more ambiguous; a 'reading' of it depended on relating elements in the ad's internal structure to each other, as well as drawing in references from the external world. 'Decoding' what is happening in these more complicated message structures requires the use of a method – such as semiology – sensitive to these nuances. . . .

Advertising draws deeply from the predispositions, hopes, and concerns of its audiences, but it reformulates them to suit its own purposes, not reflecting meaning but rather *reconstituting* it. Looking at advertisements today is a bit like walking through a carnival hall of mirrors, where the elements of our ordinary lives are magnified and exaggerated but are still recognizable.

And this is why semiology is so appropriate, for it is about trying to answer some very basic questions concerning meaning: 'How is meaning reconstituted both by advertisers and viewers of messages?' More simply: 'How do ads work?' Semiology is the study of signs. Signs are things that have a meaning, that communicate messages to people. As such, almost anything can perform as a sign – an object, book, film, person, building, song, or ad. In other words, anything that has a meaning is a sign. Here we will confine our remarks to the advertisement as sign, and, more particularly, to the product in the ad. The question we wish to pose is: 'How does the product come to have meaning?' . . .

Semiology originates in a discussion of signs, or more specifically of a 'system of signs.' A sign within a system of meaning may be separated into two components: 'the signifier' and 'the signified.' The signifier is the material vehicle of meaning; the signified actually 'is' the meaning. The signifier is its 'concrete' dimension; the signified is its 'abstract' side. While we can separate the two for analytical purposes, in reality they are inseparable.

Roland Barthes gives the example of roses, which in most western cultures signify romantic or passionate love. The 'meaning' of roses in our cultural setting is thus tied up with the idea of passion. In analytical terms, then, we have three elements in the communicative process: (1) the signifier – roses; (2) the signified – passion; (3) the sign – their unity as 'passionified roses.' One of semiology's most important points is the distinction between the signifier and the sign; they are not the same, although they appear to be the same. Nothing inherent in roses limits their meaning to passion alone. In another culture, or in another system of meaning, roses could signify something totally different, perhaps even the opposite of passion. The rose as signifier without the signified is empty of meaning. The rose as sign is full of meaning. In advertising, the creators of messages try to turn signifiers (goods), with which audiences may have little or no familiarity, into meaningful signs that, they hope, will prompt consumers to respond with appropriate behaviour.

Many aspects of our daily lives have a long and complex history within specific cultural processes, and it is often difficult to show how signs have arisen as meaningful constructions. For example, just how did roses come to have the meaning they do? It turns out to be easier to pose these questions about things that are explicitly designed to supply us with meanings, such as advertisements. . . . How, then, do ads communicate the meanings associated with products?

One of the best semiological analyses is Judith Williamson's *Decoding Advertise-*

ments (1978). She uses ads from the French perfume manufacturer Chanel to illustrate her arguments. Her point of reference is seemingly a very simple ad: the face of a woman (the French fashion model/actress Catherine Deneuve) is shown with a picture of the product (a bottle of Chanel No. 5) in the corner of the image. To the question, What is the meaning of this ad? we might answer: It tells us that Chanel No. 5 is chic, sophisticated, and elegant; that by wearing it we would be adding something to our character which is the epitome of 'Frenchness,' specifically, glamour and flawless beauty.

Breaking this down in semiological terms, we have the signifier – the actual bottle of perfume; the signified – French chic, glamour, beauty, and sophistication (represented by Catherine Deneuve); their unity in the sign – 'Chanel No. 5' *is* French chic, glamour, beauty, and sophistication.

Assuming that this is the meaning of the ad to us, the question becomes: How did we arrive at this conclusion? Nothing in the ad explicitly states this. The semiological approach, however, suggests that the meaning of an ad does not float on the surface just waiting to be internalized by the viewer, but is built up out of the ways that different signs are organized and related to each other, both within the ad and through external references to wider belief systems. More specifically, for advertising to create meaning, the reader or the viewer has to do some 'work.' Because the meaning is not lying there on the page, one has to make an effort to grasp it. There are three steps to the process.

First, the meaning of one sign is transferred to another. In Williamson's example, the meaning of 'Catherine Deneuve' (herself a sign meaning French chic) is transferred to the product. No line of argument links the two, and the transferral depends on their juxtaposition within the structure of the ad. There are many ways this transfer can take place: between persons and objects as here; between social situations and objects; between objects and objects; and, finally, between feelings and objects.

Second, this transfer of significance is not completed within the ad: we must make the connection ourselves. For instance, nowhere is it stated that 'Chanel No. 5' is like 'Catherine Deneuve.' This meaning does not exist until we complete the transfer. . . . Williamson stresses that a sign is only capable of being transferred or of replacing something if it has a meaning in the first place for the reader or viewer. The transference requires our active participation: 'There is a space, a gap left where the speaker should be; and one of the peculiar features of advertising is that we are drawn in to fill that gap, so that we become both listener and speaker, subject and object' (Williamson 1978: 13–14).

Meaning is not 'received' in a unidirectional flow from elsewhere: the audience creates and re-creates it. It works not at us but through us. The ad is a mediator between creator and reader, standing at the confluence of the double symbolic process in the marketplace, where producers of goods attempt to construct one set of meanings, and where consumers use these meanings (along with meanings drawn from other sources) in the construction of their own lifestyles. This is the process of internal transference:

> We are given two signifiers and required to make a 'signified' by exchanging them. The fact that we have to make this exchange, to do the

linking work which is not *done* in the ad, but which is only made possible by its form, draws us into the transformational space between the units of the ad. Its meaning only exists in this space: the field of transaction; and it is here that we operate – we are this space.

(Williamson 1978: 44)

Third, in order for the transfer to take place, the first object must already have a meaning to be transferred – it must already be significant to the audience. We must already know what Catherine Deneuve 'stands for,' what she means within the world of glamour, or there would be no significance to transfer. . . .

As a method for the study of advertising, semiology suffers from a number of related weaknesses. First, it is heavily dependent upon the skill of the individual analyst. In the hands of someone like Roland Barthes or Judith Williamson, it is a creative tool that allows one to reach the deeper levels of meaning-construction in ads. A less skilful practitioner, however, can do little more than state the obvious in a complex and often pretentious manner. As a result, in these types of studies there is little chance to establish consistency or reliability – that is, a sufficient level of agreement among analysts on what is found in a message.

Second, because the semiological approach stresses individual readings of messages, it does not lend itself to quantification of results: it is impossible to base an overall sense of constructed meanings on the examination of a large number of messages. What insights may be extracted from this approach must remain impressionistic.

Third, semiology cannot be applied with equal success to all kinds of ads. For example, Williamson does not take a random sample of ads and then apply the semiological method to them, but seems to choose ads specifically to illustrate her points. Because such a procedure courts the danger of self-confirming results, the conclusions should, strictly speaking, be confined to those instances alone and not generalized to the entire range of advertising. . . .

References

Barthes, Roland (1973) *Mythologies*. London: Paladin.
De Saussure, Ferdinand (1966) *Course in General Linguistics*. New York: McGraw-Hill.
Williamson, Judith (1978) *Decoding Advertisements*. London: Marion Boyars.

Chapter 51

Stuart Hall

FOUCAULT AND DISCOURSE

From *Representation: Cultural Representation and Signifying Practices,* London: Sage (1997).

. . .

FOUCAULT'S PROJECT WAS STILL to some degree indebted to Saussure and Barthes while in other ways departing radically from them. Foucault's work was much more historically grounded, more attentive to historical specificities, than the semiotic approach. The particular objects of Foucault's attention were the various disciplines of knowledge in the human and social sciences – what he called 'the subjectifying social sciences'. These had acquired an increasingly prominent and influential role in modern culture and were, in many instances, considered to be the discourses which, like religion in earlier times, could give us the 'truth' about knowledge. . . .

He moved away from an approach like that of Saussure and Barthes, based on 'the domain of signifying structure', towards one based on analysing what he called 'relations of force, strategic developments and tactics':

> Here I believe one's point of reference should not be to the great model of language (*langue*) and signs, but to that of war and battle. The history which bears and determines us has the form of a war rather than that of a language relations of power not relations of meaning . . .
> (Foucault 1980: pp. 114–115)

. . . The first point to note, then, is the shift of attention in Foucault from 'language' to 'discourse'. He studied not language, but *discourse* as a system of representation.

Normally, the term 'discourse' is used as a linguistic concept. It simply means passages of connected writing or speech. Michel Foucault, however, gave it a different meaning. What interested him were the rules and practices that produced meaningful statements and regulated discourse in different historical periods. By 'discourse', Foucault meant 'a group of statements which provide a language for talking about – a way of representing the knowledge about – a particular topic at a particular historical moment. . . . Discourse is about the production of knowledge through language. But . . . since all social practices entail *meaning*, and meanings shape and influence what we do – our conduct – all practices have a discursive aspect' (Hall 1992: 291). It is important to note that the concept of *discourse* in this usage is not purely a 'linguistic' concept. It is about language *and* practice. It attempts to overcome the traditional distinction between what one *says* (language) and what one *does* (practice). Discourse, Foucault argues, constructs the topic. It defines and produces the objects of our knowledge. It governs the way that a topic can be meaningfully talked about and reasoned about. It also influences how ideas are put into practice and used to regulate the conduct of others. Just as a discourse 'rules in' certain ways of talking about a topic, defining an acceptable and intelligible way to talk, write, or conduct oneself, so also, by definition, it 'rules out', limits and restricts other ways of talking, of conducting ourselves in relation to the topic or constructing knowledge about it. Discourse, Foucault argued, never consists of one statement, one text, one action or one source. The same discourse, characteristic of the way of thinking or the state of knowledge at any one time (what Foucault called the *episteme*), will appear across a range of texts, and as forms of conduct, at a number of different institutional sites within society. However, whenever these discursive events 'refer to the same object, share the same style and . . . support a strategy . . . a common institutional, administrative or political drift and pattern' (Cousins and Hussain 1984: 84–5), then they are said by Foucault to belong to the same *discursive formation*.

Meaning and meaningful practice is therefore constructed within discourse. Like the semioticians, Foucault was a 'constructionist'. However, unlike them, he was concerned with the production of knowledge and meaning, not through language but through discourse. There were therefore similarities, but also substantive differences between these two versions.

The idea that 'discourse produces the objects of knowledge' and that nothing which is meaningful exists *outside discourse*, is at first sight a disconcerting proposition, which seems to run right against the grain of common-sense thinking. It is worth spending a moment to explore this idea further. Is Foucault saying – as some of his critics have charged – that *nothing exists outside of discourse*? In fact, Foucault does *not* deny that things can have a real, material existence in the world. What he does argue is that '*nothing has any meaning outside of discourse*' (Foucault 1972). As Laclau and Mouffe put it, 'we use [the term discourse] to emphasize the fact that every social configuration is *meaningful*' (1990: 100). The concept of discourse is not about whether things exist but about where meaning comes from. . . .

This idea that physical things and actions exist, but they only take on meaning and become objects of knowledge within discourse, is at the heart of the *constructionist* theory of meaning and representation. Foucault argues that since we can only have a knowledge of things if they have a meaning, it is discourse – not the things-in-themselves – which produces knowledge. Subjects like 'madness', 'punishment' and 'sexuality' only exist meaningfully *within* the discourses about them. Thus, the study of the discourses of madness, punishment or sexuality would have to include the following elements:

1   statements about 'madness', 'punishment' or 'sexuality' which give us a certain kind of knowledge about these things;
2   the rules which prescribe certain ways of talking about these topics and exclude other ways – which govern what is 'sayable' or 'thinkable' about insanity, punishment or sexuality, at a particular historical moment;
3   'subjects' who in some ways personify the discourse – the madman, the hysterical woman, the criminal, the deviant, the sexually perverse person; with the attributes we would expect these subjects to have, given the way knowledge about the topic was constructed at that time;
4   how this knowledge about the topic acquires authority, a sense of embodying the 'truth' about it; constituting the 'truth of the matter', at a historical moment;
5   the practices within institutions for dealing with the subjects – medical treatment for the insane, punishment regimes for the guilty, moral discipline for the sexually deviant – whose conduct is being regulated and organized according to those ideas;
6   acknowledgement that a different discourse or *episteme* will arise at a later historical moment, supplanting the existing one, opening up a new *discursive formation*, and producing, in its turn, new conceptions of 'madness' or 'punishment' or 'sexuality', new discourses with the power and authority, the 'truth', to regulate social practices in new ways.

The main point to get hold of here is the way discourse, representation, knowledge and 'truth' are radically *historicized* by Foucault, in contrast to the rather ahistorical tendency in semiotics. Things meant something and were 'true', he argued, *only within a specific historical context*. Foucault did not believe that the same phenomena would be found across different historical periods. He thought that, in each period, discourse produced forms of knowledge, objects, subjects and practices of knowledge, which differed radically from period to period, with no necessary continuity between them.

Thus, for Foucault, for example, mental illness was not an objective fact, which remained the same in all historical periods, and meant the same thing in all cultures. It was only *within* a definite discursive formation that the object, 'madness', could appear at all as a meaningful or intelligible construct. It was 'constituted by all that was said, in all the statements that named it, divided it up, described it, explained it, traced its development, indicated its various correlations, judged it, and possibly gave it speech by articulating, in its name, discourses that were to be taken as its own' (1972, p. 32). And it was only after a certain definition of 'madness' was put into practice, that the appropriate subject – 'the madman' as current medical and psychiatric knowledge defined 'him' – could appear. . . .

Knowledge linked to power, not only assumes the authority of 'the truth' but has the power to *make itself true*. All knowledge, once applied in the real world, has real effects, and in that sense at least, 'becomes true'. Knowledge, once used to regulate the conduct of others, entails constraint, regulation and the disciplining of practices. Thus, 'There is no power relation without the correlative constitution of a field of knowledge, nor any knowledge that does not presuppose and constitute at the same time, power relations' (Foucault 1977; 27).

According to Foucault, what we think we 'know' in a particular period about, say, crime has a bearing on how we regulate, control and punish criminals. Knowledge does not operate in a void. It is put to work, through certain technologies and strategies of application, in specific situations, historical contexts and institutional regimes. To study punishment, you must study how the combination of discourse and power – power/knowledge – has produced a certain conception of crime and the criminal, has had certain real effects both for criminal and for the punisher, and how these have been set into practice in certain historically specific prison regimes.

This led Foucault to speak, not of the 'Truth' of knowledge in the absolute sense – a Truth which remained so, whatever the period, setting, context – but of a discursive formation sustaining a *regime of truth*. Thus, it may or may not be true that single parenting inevitably leads to delinquency and crime. But if everyone believes it to be so, and punishes single parents accordingly, this will have real consequences for both parents and children and will become 'true' in terms of its real effects, even if in some absolute sense it has never been conclusively proven. In the human and social sciences, Foucault argued:

> Truth isn't outside power. . . . Truth is a thing of this world; it is produced only by virtue of multiple forms of constraint. And it induces regular effects of power. Each society has its regime of truth, its 'general politics' of truth; that is, the types of discourse which it accepts and makes function as true, the mechanisms and instances which enable one to distinguish true and false statements, the means by which each is sanctioned . . . the status of those who are charged with saying what counts as true.
>
> (Foucault 1980: 131)

. . . Foucault is concerned with the production of knowledge and meaning through discourse. Foucault does indeed analyse particular texts and representations, as the semioticians did. But he is more inclined to analyse the whole *discursive formation* to which a text or a practice belongs. His concern is with knowledge provided by the human and social sciences, which organizes conduct, understanding, practice and belief, the regulation of bodies as well as whole populations. Although his work is clearly done in the wake of, and profoundly influenced by, the 'turn to language' which marked the *constructionist* approach to representation, his definition of *discourse* is much broader than language, and includes many other elements of practice and institutional regulation which Saussure's approach, with its linguistic focus, excluded. Foucault is always much more historically specific, seeing forms of power/knowledge as always rooted in particular contexts and histories. Above all, for Foucault, the production of knowledge is always crossed with questions of power and the body; and this greatly expands the scope of what is involved in representation.

The major critique levelled against his work is that he tends to absorb too much into 'discourse', and this has the effect of encouraging his followers to neglect the influence of the material, economic and structural factors in the operation of power/knowledge. Some critics also find his rejection of any criterion of 'truth' in the human sciences in favour of the idea of a 'regime of truth' and the will-to-power (the will to make things 'true') vulnerable to the charge of relativism. Nevertheless, there is little doubt about the major impact which his work has had on contemporary theories of representation and meaning.

References

Cousins, M. and Hussain, A. (1984) *Michel Foucault*, Basingstoke, Macmillan.

Foucault, M. (1972) *The Archaeology of Knowledge*, London, Tavistock.

—— (1977) *Discipline and Punish*, London, Tavistock.

—— (1980) *Power/Knowledge*, Brighton, Harvester.

Hall, S. (1992) 'The West and the Rest', in Hall, S. and Gieben, B. (eds) *Formations of Modernity*, Cambridge, Polity Press/The Open University.

Laclau, E. and Mouffe, C. (1990) 'Post-Marxism without apologies' in Laclau, E., *New Reflections on the Revolution of our Time*, London, Verso.

Chapter 52

Jonathan Potter and Margaret Wetherell

UNFOLDING DISCOURSE ANALYSIS

From *Discourse and Social Psychology: Beyond Attidues and Behaviour*, London: Sage (1987).

. . .

WHAT IS REQUIRED IS an analysis of discourse which focuses on variability and the construction of accounts. However, before making any more moves we must illustrate in more detail how a discourse analyst approaches accounts. This goal can be attained by demonstrating how we would deal with one of the most fundamental social psychological notions: attitudes. Our approach to attitudes should reveal that distinctiveness of the discourse position and put some flesh on the notion of variability in accounts along with the idea that accounts are constructed to have specific consequences . . .

Traditional approaches to attitudes and racism

In 1976 a British researcher, Alan Marsh, asked a random sample of 1,785 people to express their attitude to 'coloured immigrants' by placing a mark on a scale which ran from 'completely sympathetic', through to, 'no feelings about them either way', to 'completely unsympathetic'. In McGuire's (1988), terms the object of thought would be the 'coloured immigrants', while the dimension of judgement would consist of the 'sympathy' which the respondent can offer or refuse. Marsh's survey resembles myriads of other surveys, the techniques he used are extremely common in attitude research. Having collected his responses, Marsh went on to split his scale up 'logically' into categories. These are labelled 'very hostile', 'hostile', 'neutral' and so on (see Table 52.1).

Table 52.1 Distribution of sympathetic and unsympathetic feelings towards coloured immigrants

Completely unsympathetic		No feelings about them either way				Completely sympathetic
0	1–20	21–45	46–55	56–79	80–99	100
12%	13%	17%	25%	20%	10%	3%
Very hostile	Hostile	Unsympathetic	Neutral	Sympathetic	Positive	Very positive

Notes: in sample: unweighted = 1,785, weighted = 1,482; 'don't know' (excluded = 4%).

Source: Marsh 1976.

From the point of view of a discourse analyst, there are a number of interesting points to be made about the kind of practical research procedures illustrated by Marsh's scale; we will concentrate on three issues.

First, there are obvious problems with the status of 'coloured immigrants' as an object of thought. One way of looking at the term 'coloured immigrants' would be as a simple category label for a group of people, in fact those people who fit the descriptions 'coloured' and 'immigrant'. However, things are a lot more complex than this. For example, there is no clear-cut neutral way of deciding how to apply the category 'coloured immigrant'. That is, there are no objective criteria for category membership. . . .

The proper application of 'coloured' is dependent on unstated theories of race and biology. But modern theories of genetics and population give no support to the idea that 'races' of people can be distinguished in terms of unambiguous, underlying physical, and ultimately genetic, differences (Husband 1982). In addition, 'immigrant' means (in the dictionary sense) a person who comes into a foreign country as a settler. Yet Marsh (1976) does not address the problem of splitting 'coloured immigrants' from 'coloured residents', and it is clear that he takes the term 'coloured immigrant' as a bland descriptive category covering both these groups. In fact this is reflected in the very title of his article, which is called 'Who hates the Blacks' not 'Who hates those people who are both recent settlers in Britain and black defined'. His terminology is not neutral. If you have lived in a country for the whole of your life you might be concerned if people start calling you an immigrant – a term often used to connote aliens or outsiders. . . .

A second problem arises when we examine the transformations which Marsh makes to his subjects' responses. If we look at Table 52.1 we can see that Marsh has transformed one dimension, running from 'completely unsympathetic' to 'completely sympathetic', into a more complex set of labels: 'very hostile', 'hostile', 'unsympathetic' etc. There is no coherent justification for making transformations of this kind. For example, it is probably wrong to suggest respondents mean the same thing by the words 'very hostile' and 'completely unsympathetic'. For one thing, the term hostility is often used to imply an *active* disposition, while if someone lacks sympathy, they are *without* a certain kind of active disposition. By making this transformation the analyst is riding roughshod over subtle distinctions that may play a crucial role in the participants' discourse, and certainly in their methods of making sense of the survey questions.

A third problem also concerns translation: in this case the researchers' translation of participants' responses into the underlying theoretical category of attitude. The aim of attitude scales is not merely to show how people fill in these scales, but to identify attitudes. That is, to identify where on a specific dimension a person locates an object of thought; in the current example, where the respondents locate 'coloured immigrants' on the dimension of 'sympathy'. The crucial assumption of attitude researchers is that there is something enduring within people which the scale is measuring – the attitude.

Discourse analysis points to many difficulties with this. We need to ask, for instance, whether people filling in an attitude scale are performing a neutral act of describing or expressing an internal mental state, their attitude or whether they are engaged in producing a specific linguistic formulation turned to the context at hand. From the discourse analytic perspective, given different purposes or a different context a very different 'attitude' may be espoused. Put another way, if a certain attitude is expressed on one occasion it should not necessarily lead us to expect that the same attitude will be expressed on another. Instead there may be systematic variations in what is said, which cast doubt on the enduring homogeneous nature of the supposed internal mental attitude.

How, then, should we deal with these three problems which are by no means unique to Marsh: first, the meaning of interpretation given to the terms in the attitude scale; second, the translation between participants' discourse and analysts' categories; and third, the treatment of linguistic products as transparent indicators of underlying objects or dispositions. More generally, what might a study of participants' discourse tell us about phenomena traditionally understood in terms of attitudes? The time has come to get down to the nitty-gritty of accounts and perform our own analysis.

Discourses of immigration

In the remainder of this chapter we will indicate how a discourse analyst might go about researching attitudes to constructed categories such as 'coloured immigrants'. . . . All the accounts we shall analyze have been extracted from open-ended interviews with white, middle-class New Zealanders. . . .

The goals of our analysis will obviously differ from those determining traditional attitude research. Broadly speaking, discourse analysts are interested in the different ways in which texts are organized, and the consequences of using some organizations rather than others. So our aim will be to look at the different forms taken by evaluative discourse about minority groups, and the effects of these forms. At the same time, the analysis will try to avoid the three problems we identified as endemic in traditional attitude research, namely presupposing the existence of the 'attitudinal object', making translations from unexplicated participants' discourse to unexplicated analysts' discourse, and treating utterances as indicators of the presence of enduring, underlying attitudes. We shall try to show why the concept of an enduring attitude is theoretically redundant.

Context

Perhaps the first thing which becomes apparent when embarking on this task is the sheer complexity of working with extended sequences of talk rather than the brief isolated utterances which make up responses to attitude questionnaires. Take the following interview extract for example.

> 1   *Respondent.* I'm not anti them at all you know
>
> (Benton: 26).

We do not have any trouble in reading this as a relatively positive statement of the speaker's position on 'them' – in this case, in the New Zealand context, 'Polynesian immigrants'. In attitude terms, the 'object of thought' is 'Polynesian immigrants', the 'dimension of judgment' lies from pro to anti, and the position espoused is pro. Following standard attitude theory, we would treat this speaker as possessing a specific attitude. If they had to fill in Marsh's questionnaire they might endorse the 'sympathetic' end of the scale – or so the traditional account would have it.

Yet, when we look at more of this sequence, the simplicity starts to fall away. Here is the entire turn of talk from which Extract One was taken.

> 2   *Respondent.* I'm not anti them at all you know, I, if they're willing to get on and be like us; but if they're just going to come here, just to be able to use our social welfares and stuff like that, then why don't they stay home?
>
> (Benton: 26).

There are a number of interesting features here which immediately question our first interpretation. To begin with, the 'pro immigrants' claim is made contingent on immigrants exhibiting a willingness 'to be like us'. Thus we can no longer read it as an unqualified expression of sympathy. . . . Even a small amount of additional information about context can throw into question what, at first, appears to be a reasonable interpretation of a person's utterance. The discourse has an action orientation; it is constructed in such a way that particular tasks – in this case blaming and disclaiming responsibility for the obnoxious effects of this blaming – are facilitated.

These points have important implications for attitude scale research. If the person filling in the scale is viewed as merely *describing* or *expressing* their attitude, things seem quite clear-cut. Yet, if we start to view their response as a discursive act, which it always is, things become murkier, because there is a great deal of scope to perform different kinds of acts when filling in the scale. For example, a person might fill in the scale to perform the task of disclaiming by marking the 'sympathetic' pole; or they might perform the task of blaming by marking the 'unsympathetic' pole. They might hesitate because they see themselves as sympathetic and unsympathetic at the same time – 'I'm not anti but . . .'. Two people putting the same mark on the scale could well be doing very different things with their discourse. If the opinion pollster is coordinating an interview rather than requiring paper and pen responses the person might offer the whole utterance to the pollster and how it emerges, in terms of the category scales, will depend on the pollsters current method of scaling.

One way we could proceed, given this line of argument, is to suggest that attitude measurement might survive in its present form if it became a more subtle business, more sensitive to the different acts performed. We should note, however, that this continues to assume that there is such a thing as 'an attitude' or an enduring, underlying state expressed in talk and behaviour. This position becomes extremely difficult to maintain when we look at the variations which appear in participants' accounts.

Variability

The following example is typical of the sort of variation in accounts which has now been documented in a wide swathe of different kinds of discourse. These two extracts are taken from subsequent pages of the interview transcript.

> 3   *Respondent.* What I would li . . . rather see is that, sure, bring them ['Polynesian immigrants'] into New Zealand, right, try and train them in a skill, and encourage them to go back again (Pond: 17).
>
> 4   *Respondent.* I think that if we encouraged more Polynesians and Maoris to be skilled people they would want to stay here, they're not um as uh nomadic as New Zealanders are (*Interviewer*, Haha.) so I think that would be better
>
> (Pond: 18).

The contradiction is stark. In Extract Three the respondent states that they would like Polynesian immigrants to be trained in New Zealand and then to return to the Pacific Islands. In Extract Four the respondent claims it would be better if Polynesians were encouraged to become skilled and then stay in New Zealand. What are we to make of this variability? The problem is particularly acute for the attitude researcher because of the conflict between versions. An attempt to recover the person's 'underlying attitude' is not going to get very far.

The discourse analyst's response is rather different from the attitude researcher. We do not intend to use the discourse as a pathway to entities or phenomena lying 'beyond' the text. Discourse analysis does not take for granted that accounts reflect underlying attitudes or dispositions and therefore we do not expect that an individual's discourse will be consistent and coherent. Rather, the focus is on the discourse *itself*: how it is organized and what it is doing. Orderliness in discourse will be viewed as a product of the orderly *functions* to which discourse is put . . .

Constitution

In traditional attitude theory, the attitude is considered to be separate from the 'object of thought'. The entire logic of attitude measurement, where a scale is used to compare different people's attitudes to the same object, is based upon this. If the object is not the same for different people there is no sense in comparing attitudes and the notion ceases to have utility. However, when we come to look at the detail of people's accounts this separation becomes virtually impossible to sustain. Far from the object of thought being a simple already present entity, the object is formulated and constructed in discourse in the course of doing evaluation.

Take the following extract, for example, which is part of an answer to a question about Polynesian crime.

> 7 *Respondent.* Then again, it's a problem of their racial integration. They've got a big racial minority coming in now and so they've got to get used to the way of life and, er, perhaps rape is accepted over in Samoa and Polynesia, but not in Auckland. They've got to learn that. And the problem's that a lot of people coming in with mental disease I think it is, because there is a lot of interbreeding in those islan . . . islands. And that brings a big, high increase of retards and then people who come over here, retards perhaps and they//
>
> *Interviewer.* // and that causes problems?
> *Respondent.* And that's pretty general I know
> (Johnston: 20–1).

In this passage the speaker is not just giving his views *about* 'Polynesian immigrants', he is formulating the very nature of the Polynesian immigrant. That is, he is not working with a neutral description of an object and then saying how he feels about it; he is constructing a *version* of the object. It is in this way evaluation is displayed. His version of the object carries off his evaluation. Polynesian immigrants are floridly depicted as a group who are involved in rapes and are carriers of 'mental disease'. It is implied they are from a culture which cannot control its desires properly, something they will have to learn to do before settling in New Zealand. . . .

In summary, a brief analysis of some extracts from interviews has highlighted the importance of a number of phenomena which have been relatively neglected in traditional attitude research. We stressed first the importance of examining context. Contextual information gives the researcher a much fuller understanding of the detailed and delicate organization of accounts. In addition, an understanding of this organization clarifies the action orientation of talk and its involvement in acts such as blaming and disclaiming.

The second phenomenon we illustrated was variability. A high degree of variation in accounts is a central prediction of the discourse approach: widely different kinds of accounts will be produced to do different things. On the other hand, considerable consistency must be predicted if participants are producing their language in the light of sets of attitudes which are stable across different contexts.

Variability of the kind seen in detailed studies of discourse is thus a considerable embarrassment to traditional attitude theories.

The third phenomena we noted was the construction of the attitudinal object in discourse. The customary view is that attitudes are about distinct entities. Attitudes to immigrants, for instance, should concern an existing out-there-in-the-world group of people. Yet when we examined actual discourse this simple 'word and object' view of attitudes became unworkable. It is clear that the attitudinal object can be constituted in alternative ways, and the person's evaluation is directed at these *specific* formulations rather than some abstract and idealized object.

In response to these difficulties, the discourse approach shifts the focus from a search for underlying entities – attitudes – which generate talk and behaviour to a detailed examination of how evaluative expressions are produced in discourse. Two central and novel questions become dramatized. How is participants' language constructed, and what are the consequences of different types of construction? Whether at the end of this examination space is found for some modified notion of attitudes is, as yet, unclear. All we have done . . . is indicate how an analyst might begin to address these questions. However, we hope we have given an initial demonstration of some of the limitations of traditional research and the promise of discourse analysis.

References

Husband, C. (1982) 'Introduction: "Race", the continuity of a concept', in C. Husband (ed.), *'Race' in Britain: Continuity and Change*. London: Hutchinson.

McGuire, W.J. (1985) 'Attitudes and attitude change', in G. Lindzey and E. Aronson (eds), *Handbook of Social Psychology* (3rd edition) vol. 2. New York: Random House.

Marsh, A. (1976) 'Who hates the blacks?', *New Society*, 23 September, 649–652.

Chapter 53

Norman Fairclough and Ruth Wodak

CRITICAL DISCOURSE ANALYSIS

From van Dijk, T. (ed.), *Discourse Studies: A Multidisciplinary Introduction*, Vol. 2, London: Sage (1997).

LIKE OTHER APPROACHES TO discourse analysis, critical discourse analysis (henceforth CDA) analyses real and often extended instances of social interaction which take a linguistic form, or a partially linguistic form. The critical approach is distinctive in its view of (a) the relationship between language and society, and (b) the relationship between analysis and the practices analysed. Let us take these in turn.

CDA sees discourse – language use in speech and writing – as a form of 'social practice'. Describing discourse as social practice implies a dialectical relationship between a particular discursive event and the situation(s), institution(s) and social structure(s) which frame it. A dialectical relationship is a two-way relationship: the discursive event is shaped by situations, institutions and social structures, but it also shapes them. To put the same point in a different way, discourse is socially *constitutive* as well as socially shaped: it constitutes situations, objects of knowledge, and the social identities of and relationships between people and groups of people. It is constitutive both in the sense that it helps to sustain and reproduce the social status quo, and in the sense that it contributes to transforming it. Since discourse is so socially influential, it gives rise to important issues of power. Discursive practices may have major ideological effects: that is, they can help produce and reproduce unequal power relations between (for instance) social classes, women and men, and ethnic/cultural majorities and minorities through the ways in which they represent things and position people. So discourse may, for example, be racist, or sexist, and try to pass off assumptions (often falsifying ones) about any aspect of social life as mere common sense. Both the ideological loading of particular ways of using language and the relations of power which underlie them are often unclear to people. CDA aims to make more visible these opaque aspects of discourse.

CDA sees itself not as dispassionate and objective social science, but as engaged and committed. It is a form of intervention in social practice and social relationships: many analysts are politically active against racism, or as feminists, or within the peace movement, and so forth. But CDA is not an exception to the normal objectivity of social science: social science is inherently tied into politics and formulations of policy, as for instance Foucault's (1971, 1979) work convincingly demonstrated. What is distinctive about CDA is both that it intervenes on the side of dominated and oppressed groups and against dominating groups, and that it openly declares the emancipatory interests that motivate it. The political interests and uses of social scientific research are usually less explicit. This certainly does not imply that CDA is less scholarly than other research: standards of careful, rigorous and systematic analysis apply with equal force to CDA as to other approaches. . . .

CDA in action

Our aim in this section is to give an example of CDA. We shall work with a version of CDA based upon eight principles of theory or method, and we shall show how each affects the practice of CDA through an analysis – necessarily partial – of the following extract from a radio interview with Margaret Thatcher, former Prime Minister of Britain.[1] . . .

1	*MC:*	Prime Minister you were at Oxford in the nineteen
		forties and after the war Britain would embark on a
		period of relative prosperity for all the like of which it
		had hardly known but today there are three and a
5		quarter million unemployed and e:m
		Britain's economic performance by one measurement
		has fallen to the rank of that of Italy now can you
		imagine yourself back at the University today what
		must seem to be the chances in Britain and the
10		prospects for all now
	MT:	they are very different worlds you're talking about
		because the first thing that struck me very forcibly as
		you were speaking of those days was that now we do
		enjoy a standard of living which was undreamed
15		of then and I can remember Rab Butler saying after
		we returned to power in about 1951–52 that if we played
		our cards right the standard of living within twenty
		five years would be twice as high as it was then and

1   The interview was conducted by Michael Charlton, and was broadcast on BBC Radio 3 on 17 December 1985. For a fuller analysis, see Chapter 7 of Fairclough (1989).

em he was just about right and it was remarkable
20 because it was something that we had never thought
of now I don't think now one would necessarily think
wholly in material terms indeed I think it's wrong to
think in material terms because really the kind of
country you want is made up by the strength of its
25 people and I think we're returning to my vision of
Britain as a younger person and I was always brought
up with the idea look Britain is a country whose
people think for themselves act for themselves can act
on their own initiative they don't have to be told
30 don't like to be pushed around are self-reliant and
then over and above that they're always responsible
for their families and something else it was a kind of
em I think it was Barrie who said do as you would be
done by e: you act to others as you'd like them to act
35 towards you and so you do something for the
community now I think if you were looking at
another country you would say what makes a country
strong it is its people do they run their industries well
are their human relations good e: do they respect law
40 and order are their families strong all of those kind of
things
    [and you know it's just way beyond economics
MC: [but you know people still   people still ask
though e: where is she going now General de Gaulle
45 had a vision of France e: a certain idea of France as he
put it e: you have fought three major battles in this
country the Falkland Islands e:m against the miners
and local councils and against public expenditure and
people I think would like to hear what this vision you
50 have of Britain is it must be a powerful one what is it
that inspires your action
MT: I wonder if I perhaps I can answer best by saying how
I see what government should do and if government
really believes in people what people should do I
55 believe that government should be very strong to do
those things which only government can do it has to
be strong to have defence because the kind of Britain I
see would always defend its freedom and always be a
reliable ally so you've got to be strong to your own
60 people and other countries have got to know that you
stand by your word then you turn to internal security
and yes you HAVE got to be strong on law and order
and do the things that only governments can do but
there it's part government and part people because
65 you CAN'T have law and order observed unless it's

in partnership with people then you have to be strong
to uphold the value of the currency and only
governments can do that by sound finance and then
you have to create the framework for a good

70   education system and social security and at that point
you have to say over to people people are inventive
creative and so you expect PEOPLE to create thriving
industries thriving services yes you expect people
each and every one from whatever their background

75   to have a chance to rise to whatever level their own
abilities can take them yes you expect people of all
sorts of background and almost whatever their
income level to be able to have a chance of owning
some property tremendously important the

80   ownership of property of a house gives you some
independence gives you a stake in the future you're
concerned about your children

MC: but could ⎡ you sum this vision up

MT: ⎣ (   ) you said my vision

85   please let me just go on and then that isn't enough
if you're interested in the future yes you will
probably save you'll probably want a little bit of
independent income of your own and so constantly
thinking about the future so it's very much a Britain

90   whose people are independent of government but
aware that the government has to be strong to do
those things which only governments can do

MC: but can you sum it up in a in a in a phrase or two the
aim is to achieve what or to restore what in Britain

95   when clearly risking a lot and winning in a place like
the Falkland Islands is just as important in your
philosophy ⎡ for Britain as as

MT: ⎣ I think

MC: restoring sound money reducing the money supply in

100   the Bank of England

MT: but of course it showed that we were reliable in the
defence of freedom and when part of Britain we: was
invaded of course we went we believed in defence of
freedom we were reliable I think if I could try to sum

105   it up in a phrase and that's always I suppose most
difficult of all I would say really restoring the very
best of the British character to its former
preeminence.

MC: but this has meant something called Thatcherism now

110   is that a description you accept as something quite
distinct from traditional conservatism in this country

MT: no it is traditional conservatism

       MC: but it's radical and populist and therefore not
                  conservative
115 *MT:*   it is radical because at the time when I took over we
                  needed to be radical e: it is populist I wouldn't call it
                  populist I would say that many of the things which
                  I've said strike a chord in the hearts of ordinary
                  people why because they're British because their
120   character IS independent because they DON'T like to
                  be shoved around coz they ARE prepared to take
                  responsibility because they DO expect to be loyal
                  to their friends and loyal allies that's why you call it
                  populist. I say it strikes a chord in the hearts of
125   people I know because it struck a chord in my heart
                  many many years ago

1 CDA addresses social problems

. . . A critical discourse analysis of the extract above might be seen as a contribution to the analysis of Thatcherism. . . . It could help develop a critical awareness of the discursive strategies of Thatcherism which might be one resource in struggles against it. . . .

    Thatcherism as an ideological project for building a new hegemony can be seen as an attempt to restructure political discourse by combining diverse existing discourses together in a new way. This is evident in the extract above. There is a characteristic combination of elements of traditional conservative discourse (the focus on law and order, the family, and strong government, for example *do they respect law and order are their families strong*) and elements of a liberal political discourse and economic discourse (the focus on the independence of the individual, for example *because their character IS independent because they DON'T like to be shoved around coz they ARE prepared to take responsibility*; and on the individual entrepreneur as the dynamo of the economy, for example *you expect PEOPLE to create thriving industries thriving services*).

    These are mixed with elements from discourses of ordinary life and ordinary experience which give Thatcher's discourse the populist quality referred to by the interviewer – for example, the expressions *stand by your word, shoved around*, and *strikes a chord in [people's] hearts*. This novel combination of discourses is associated with distinctive representations of social reality and distinctive constructions of social and political relations and identities (see below). It achieved a dominant position in the field of political discourse, though it is arguable to what extent it became hegemonic in the sense of winning widespread acceptance.

2 Power relations are discursive

CDA highlights the substantively linguistic and discursive nature of social relations of power in contemporary societies. This is partly a matter of how power relations are exercised and negotiated in discourse. One issue that receives a great deal of attention is power relations between the media and politics . . . Close analysis of power relations in political interviews in the media can cast some light on this issue. On the face of it, interviewers exercise a lot of power over politicians in interviews: interviewers generally control the way in which interviews begin and end, the topics which are dealt with and the angles from which they are tackled, the time given to politicians to answer questions, and so forth. In the case of the Thatcher interview, Michael Charlton's questions do set and attempt to police an agenda (see for instance lines 83, 93–94). However, politicians do not by any means always comply with interviewers' attempts to control interviews, and there is often a struggle for control. Charlton for instance in line 83 tries to bring Thatcher back to the question he asked in lines 49–51, but she interrupts his attempt at policing her talk, and carries on with what is effectively a short political speech. The fact that Thatcher makes speeches in her answers to Charlton's questions – or perhaps better, interprets Charlton's questions as opportunities to make speeches rather than requiring answers – points to another dimension of power relations in discourse. Thatcher tries to exercise what we might call rhetorical power, . . . This power – in so far as it is effective – is primarily power over the radio audience, but it is also germane to power relations between Thatcher and Charlton in that it circumvents and marginalizes Charlton's power as interviewer. Thatcher's rhetorical power is realized for instance in the large-scale linguistic devices which organize her contributions, such as the triple parallel structure of lines 56–67 (*it has to be strong to have defence*, 56–7; *you HAVE got to be strong on law and order*, 62; *you have to be strong to uphold the value of the currency*, 66–7). . . .

3 Discourse constitutes society and culture

We can only make sense of the salience of discourse in contemporary social processes and power relations by recognizing that discourse constitutes society and culture, as well as being constituted by them. Their relationship, that is, is a dialectical one. This entails that every instance of language use makes its own small contribution to reproducing and/or transforming society and culture, including power relations. That is the power of discourse; that is why it is worth struggling over.

. . . Lines 11–21 of the example incorporate a narrative which gives a very different representation of history to the one in the interviewer's question: the latter's contrast between prosperous past and depressed present is restructured as a past Conservative government creating present prosperity. . . .

Notice also the vague and shifting meanings of the pronoun *we* (lines 13–25, 101–104) in Thatcher's talk. *We* is sometimes what is traditionally called 'inclusive' (it includes the audience and the general population, for example *we do enjoy a standard of living which was undreamed of then*, 13–14), and sometimes 'exclusive' (for example, *after we returned to power*, 15–16, where *we* refers just to the Conservative Party). In other cases, it could be taken as either (for example, *if we played our cards right*, 16–17; *we went we believed in defence of freedom we were reliable*, 103–104). Even if we take the first of these examples as exclusive, it is still unclear who the *we* identifies; is it the Conservative Party, or the government? Also, calling *we* 'inclusive' is rather misleading, for while *we* in for instance *we do enjoy a standard of living which was undreamed of then* does identify the whole community, it constructs the community in a way which excludes those who have not achieved prosperity. Similarly, *we went we believed in defence of freedom we were reliable*, on an 'inclusive' reading, may leave those who opposed the Falklands adventure feeling excluded from the general community. The pronoun *you* is used in a similarly strategic and manipulative way on lines 59–88. We are not suggesting that Thatcher or her aides are consciously planning to use *we* and *you* in these ways, though reflexive awareness of language is increasing among politicians. Rather, there are broader intended strategic objectives for political discourse (such as building a popular base for political positions, mobilizing people behind policy decisions) which are realized in ways of using language that are likely themselves to be unintended. . . .

4 Discourse does ideological work

. . . In our example, the political and economic strategies of Thatcherism are an explicit topic, and are clearly formulated, notably in lines 52–92, including the central idea of strong government intervention to create conditions in which markets can operate freely. But Thatcher's formulation is actually built around a contrast between government and people which we would see as ideological: it covers over the fact that the 'people' who dominate the creation of 'thriving industries' and so forth are mainly the transnational corporations, and it can help to legitimize existing relations of economic and political domination. It is a common feature of Thatcherite populist discourse. The opposition between government and people is quite explicit here, but ideologies are typically more implicit. They attach for instance to key words which evoke but leave implicit sets of ideological assumptions – such as *freedom, law and order* or *sound finance*. Notice also *thriving industries thriving services*. This is another instance of the list structure discussed above, though it is a short list with just two items. *Thriving industries* is a common collocation, but *thriving services* is an innovation of an ideologically potent sort: to achieve a coherent meaning for the list one needs to assume that services can be evaluated on the same basis as industries, a truly Thatcherite assumption which the listener however is left to infer. . . .

5 Discourse is historical

. . . Discourses are always connected to other discourses which were produced earlier, as well as those which are produced synchronically and subsequently. In this respect, we include intertextuality as well as sociocultural knowledge within our concept of context. Thus, Thatcher's speech relates to what she and her government have said earlier, to other speeches and proclamations, to certain laws which have been decided upon, to reporting in the media, as well as to certain actions which were undertaken.

This becomes very clear if we consider allusions which occur in the text and which presuppose certain worlds of knowledge, and particular intertextual experience, on the part of the listeners. For example, to be able to understand and analyse Thatcher's responses profoundly and in depth, we would have to know what the situation in Britain in the *nineteen forties* (1–2) was like, who Rab Butler (15) or Barrie (33) were, what kind of *vision* de Gaulle had (44–5), why the war in the

Falkland Islands was important and what kind of symbolic meaning it connotes (58), etc. It becomes even more difficult when Thatcher alludes to *traditional conservatism* (111) and to what is meant by this term within the Thatcherite tendency in contrast to other meanings. . . .

6 The link between text and society is mediated

. . . The Charlton–Thatcher interview was one of a series of in-depth interviews with prominent figures in public life. Its conventions are those of a 'celebrity interview'. Questions probe the personality and outlook of the interviewee, and answers are expected to be frank and revelatory. Audience members are constructed as overhearers listening in on a potentially quite intense interaction between interviewer and interviewee. The programme should at once be educative and entertaining. However, while Charlton is working according to these ground rules, Thatcher is not. She treats the encounter as a political interview. As politicians commonly do, she therefore uses the interview as an occasion for political speech making, constructing the audience rather than the interviewer as addressee, not answering the questions, and avoiding the liberal intellectual discourse of the questions in favour of a populist discourse. The interaction thus has rather a complex character generically: there is a tension between the participants in terms of which media genre is oriented to (celebrity interview versus political interview), and Thatcher's recourse to political interview entails a further tension between media practices and the rhetorical practices of political discourse. . . .

7 Discourse analysis is interpretative and explanatory

Discourse can be interpreted in very different ways, due to the audience and the amount of context information which is included . . . How much contextual knowledge do we need for an interpretation? Are the critical readings provided by CDA privileged, better, or just more justifiable? For example, the meaning of *you have to say over to people people are inventive creative and so you expect PEOPLE to create thriving industries thriving services yes you expect* (lines 72–73) is certainly opaque. Who is meant by *people*: all British subjects, government included or excluded? Human beings *per se*, or people in the sense of citizens, of the German *Volk*? People who vote Conservative, who are ideologically committed to Thatcherism, or everybody? The group is not clearly defined, which allows readers to include or exclude themselves according to their own ideologies and beliefs. If we continue in the text, it becomes clearer that these *people* have to be able to influence the growth of industries and services in a positive way (*thriving*). But only powerful people are able to do this – elites, managers and politicians. If that is the case, the use of *people* is certainly misleading; it suggests participation where there is none. It mystifies the influence ordinary men and women might have on decisions of the government, an influence which they actually do not have and never would have. This piece of text exemplifies a contradiction which only a CDA might deconstruct and in doing so show the different implications of different readings for social action. . . .

8 Discourse is a form of social action

We stated at the beginning of our chapter that the principal aim of CDA was to uncover opaqueness and power relationships. CDA is a socially committed scientific paradigm, and some scholars are also active in various political groups. In contrast to many scholars, critical linguists make explicit interests which otherwise often remain covered.

The Thatcher example we have analysed arguably has such applicability in political struggles. But there exist also other examples of important applications of CDA. . . .

One important area is sexist language use. Guidelines for nonsexist language use have been produced in many countries (Wodak *et al.*, 1987). Such guidelines serve to make women visible in language, and thus also socially, in institutions. Different discourse with and about women can slowly lead to changes in consciousness. . . .

Conclusion

We suggested earlier in the chapter that late modern society is characterized by enhanced reflexivity, and that a critical orientation towards discourse in ordinary life is one manifestation of modern reflexivity. A key issue for critical discourse analysts is how the analyses which they produce in academic institutions relate to this critical activity in ordinary life. There is no absolute divide between the two: critical discourse analysts necessarily draw upon everyday critical activities (associated for instance with gender relations, patriarchy and feminism) including analysts' own involvement in and experience of them, and these activities may be informed by academic analysis (as feminism has been). Yet critical discourse analysis is obviously not just a replication of everyday critique: it can draw upon social theories and theories of language, and methodologies for language analysis, which are not generally available, and has resources for systematic and in-depth investigations which go beyond ordinary experience. . . .

References

Fairclough, N. (1989) *Language and Power*. London: Longman.

Foucault, M. (1971) *L'Ordre du discours*. Paris: Gallimard.

—— (1979) *Discipline and Punish: The Birth of Prison*. Harmondsworth: Penguin.

Wodak, R., Moosmüller, S., Doleschal, U. and Feistritzer, G. (1987) *Das Sprachverhalten von Frau und Mann*. Vienna: Ministry for Social Affairs.

Chapter 54

H.G. Widdowson

THE THEORY AND PRACTICE OF CRITICAL DISCOURSE ANALYSIS

From *Applied Linguistics* 19(1): 136–151 (1998).

C. R. Caldas-Coulthard and M. Coulthard (eds.): *Texts and Practices. Readings in Critical Discourse Analysis*. Routledge 1996
N. Fairclough: *Critical Discourse Analysis*. Longman 1995
R. Hodge and G. Kress: *Language as Ideology, 2nd Edition*. Routledge 1993

WHAT IS MOST PLAINLY distinctive about critical discourse analysis (henceforth CDA) is its sense of responsibility and its commitment to social justice. This is linguistics with a conscience and a cause, one which seeks to reveal how language is used and abused in the exercise of power and the suppression of human rights. In a grossly unequal world where the poor and the oppressed are subject to discrimination and exploitation such a cause is obviously a just and urgent one which warrants support. And it has struck a chord, playing as it does on the academic conscience with its worries about its relevance to social life. CDA has inspired a reconsideration of the purposes of language description, and it has pursued its own purposes with vigour, acting upon its own definition of discourse as a mode of social action.

The significance of a scholarly enquiry can be judged, in part at least, by its yield of publications, and in this respect CDA is very important indeed. Its practitioners have been very productive, and the books referred to here are only a small sample of what has appeared in print over the past ten years or so. These are of special note, however, in that they can be taken as an authoritative representation of the state of the art in CDA, for all those who have been most prominent in promoting it figure here as authors. We might accordingly expect that if we are looking for enlightenment about the principles of this highly influential approach to linguistic analysis, these books are likely to provide it. . . .

Over and over again, in all three of these books, there is the insistence that you cannot read significance straight off from the text, but that it is a matter of relating texts to their conditions of production and consumption. But what they say is not what they do. Fairclough in the introduction of his own collection of papers admits:

> The principle that textual analysis should be combined with analysis of practices of production and consumption has not been adequately oper-ationalized in the papers collected here. (p. 9)

But this is not a minor matter to be mentioned in passing. If these discursive practices have not been adequately taken into account, the textual analyses are correspondingly inadequate, precisely because they are dissociated from the con-textual conditions which lend them pragmatic significance. This admission would seem to invalidate the whole critical operation. And in practice, it is not just a matter of these conditions being inadequately taken into account; they are not taken into account at all. The producers and consumers of texts are never consulted. Thus, no attempt is ever made to establish empirically what writers might have intended by their texts. Their intentions are vicariously inferred from the analysis itself, by reference to what the analyst assumes in advance to be the writer's ideological position. Nor is there any consultation with the readers for whom texts are designed. Their understanding is assigned to them by proxy, which in effect means that the analysis use the linguistic features of the text selectively to confirm their own prejudice.

The following can be taken as an example of the tactic. Van Dijk's contribution to critical discourse theory in *Texts and Practices* is a paper about the way power is exercised by controlling access to different discourses. There is nothing contentions about the general point; indeed it seems obvious that it is of the very nature of any society to establish self-enclosed communities where access to the defining discourse is controlled by conditions of membership and where solidarity necessarily carries implications of power. It can be argued that if all discourse communities were equally accessible, the difference between insiders and outsiders would disappear, and with it any basis for defining such communities as distinct, or of talking about social structure at all.

What is relevant to CDA is how the texts of a particular community exemplify and exercise this control of access. Van Dijk takes an example from the *Sun*. This is an article with the headline:

Britain invaded by an army of illegals

Van Dijk notes that the metaphor here explicitly signals where the paper stands on the issue of immigration, and confirms its right-wing position. Nobody, I imagine, would want to quarrel with that. However, there are features of the text following the headline which, on the face of it, are not consistent with this bias.

Britain is being swamped by a tide of illegal immigrants so desperate for
a job that they will work for a pittance . . . slaving behind bars, cleaning
hotel rooms and working in kitchens . . .

Van Dijk notes that such expressions seem to be 'a suggestion of commiseration with
the immigrants'. But this is inconvenient for his case. So he interprets the phrase
working for a pittance as implying that 'since immigrants will do any job for any wage,
they compete with white British workers' (p. 99), and makes no comment at all on
the expressions *so desperate for a job* or *slaving behind bars*. One would have thought
that the second of these in particular might call for some comment. The term *slaving*
(with its cognates *slave* and *slavery*) has intertextual echoes with the discredited
discourse of overt racism which the newspaper would presumably wish to avoid.
And is there not an ironic ambiguity here in the term *behind bars*, with its implication
of imprisonment? It could, after all, be easily avoided (*serving/toiling in bars*). Might
one not say that there is textual evidence therefore that the *Sun* is not so rabidly
racist as might at first appear, that these phrases are perhaps unwitting liberal chinks
in its rightist armour? And if not, why not? The answer is, of course, that Van Dijk is
looking only for textual confirmation of a bias he has attributed to the source of his
text in advance. Everything that appears in the *Sun* is necessarily racist. So in effect,
what Van Dijk is doing here is controlling our access to this text by imposing his own
discourse upon it.

One might, of course, object that I am trying to place too much prominence on
a phrase or two. But (as we have it on the authority of Kress) this is just what critical
discourse analysis is meant to do: scanning texts for traces which might otherwise
escape notice. There is, after all, little point in its telling us what is all too apparent
anyway. It is the subtlety of covert significance we are looking for, and this might be
found lurking in the slightest linguistic nuance. Thus, employing this process of
critical scanning I have here drawn attention to a particular collocation (*slaving
behind bars*) as a possible trace of colonial conscience, and so of a less racist attitude
than is evident in the rest of the text. This may seem unlikely on the face of it, but
we are not looking at the face of it, but at what lies beneath.

Furthermore, I can here also claim the authority of Fairclough for my analysis.
For he too gives particular weight to the occurrence of a single collocation in
comments he makes (in extending a previous analysis in Downing 1990) on a text
fragment from a South African newspaper about a black student demonstration and
its suppression by the police. The fragment reads:

Exactly how and why a student protest became a killer riot may not be
known until the conclusion of an elaborate enquiry that will be carried
out by Justice Petrus Cillie, Judge President of the Transvaal.

'The key expression,' Fairclough tells us 'is of course, *killer riot*.' Why 'of course'?
Because the collocation, he claims, carries the implication that black Africans are
barbarous, and so marks the text as expressing a position favourable to the white
authorities. His analysis reads as follows:

Riot, as I have suggested, places the responsibility on the students, and

> *killer* implies not just the production of fatalities on this occasion (*fatal riot* would have done that), but the involvement in the riot (and therefore the existence among the students) of those whose nature is to kill (which is the reputation of 'killer whales', and which is implied in locutions like 'he's a killer', 'killer on the loose'). (p. 196)

The implication inferred here is based entirely on the assumption that the collocate of *killer* always denotes something 'whose nature is to kill'. But is this in fact the case? Fairclough consults a concordance to find out and comes up with the following finding:

> There are two instances of *killer dust*, one each of *killer earthquake, killer hurricane, killer rabbit*, and *killer sub*. All of these involve the notion of that whose nature or function is to kill.

He then adds: 'There is also one instance of *killer instinct*' (p. 213).

So why, one wonders, was this last instance simply added as an aside, and not included with the others. Perhaps it is too obvious a counter-example. But there are counter-examples too among those collocations which *are* offered as evidence. By what stretch of the imagination can it be said that it is of the very nature or function of dust to kill? And rabbits? *Killer rabbits* is a comic collocation which exists only in the fantasy world of Monty Python. How can we take any analysis seriously which is based on such a distortion of data, and which slips counter evidence into an aside where it might escape notice? The fact is, at least as revealed by the corpus referred to, there is no collocational evidence at all for Fairclough's interpretation of *killer riot* as the 'key expression' in this passage. Actually a more convincing candidate for key status would be *elaborate*, which Fairclough chooses to ignore entirely. For a glance at a concordance here will reveal that it commonly collocates with *too* and is predominantly used in a pejorative sense: on collocational evidence, you do not generally commend an inquiry by calling it elaborate. So the use of the word in this text could be taken to imply a certain scepticism, and to position the writer in opposition to the authorities. Fairclough does not of course, point to this possible implication. It does not suit his case, so he suppresses it, and conviction carries the day.

If this were just an occasional lapse or aberration, it would not matter much. But this disregard of inconvenient textual features seems to be endemic in the critical approach. . . . The procedures of ideological exposure by expedient analysis which characterize the practices of CDA can, of course, be taken up to further *any* cause, right wing as well as left, evil as well as good. They are the familiar tactics of polemic and propaganda, and they have a long history in human affairs. In this respect they are not revolutionary at all. If you have the conviction and commitment, you will always find your witch.

And to be critical about discourse is to be aware of this: to be aware of the essential instability of language and the necessary indeterminacy of all meaning which must always give rise to a plurality of possible interpretations of text. And this means that to foreclose on any interpretation must be to impose a significance which you are disposed to find. And here, I think, is the central problem with CDA, and the reason why it is so influential while being so obviously defective. It carries conviction because it espouses just causes, and this is disarming, of course: It conditions the reader into acceptance. If you can persuade people by an appeal to moral conscience, you do not *need* good arguments. But such persuasion deflects attention from questions of validity. It thus inhibits intellectual enquiry and ultimately undermines its integrity in the interests of expediency. The work that appears in these books exemplifies a whole range of problems about the analysis and interpretation of text, which it persistently fails to examine. Indeed the overall impression that is given is that there *are* no problems of any note. In this respect what is distinctive about Critical Discourse Analysis is that it is resolutely uncritical of its own discursive practices.

Reference

Downing, J. 1990. 'US media discourse in South Africa: the development of a situation model.' *Discourse and Society* 1/1: 39–60.

Chapter 55

Catherine Kohler Riessman

STRATEGIC USES OF NARRATIVE IN THE PRESENTATION OF SELF AND ILLNESS
A research note

From *Social Science and Medicine* 30(11): 1195–1200 (1990).

. . .

IN THE RESEARCH INTERVIEW as in the rest of social life, language is the major cultural resource that participants draw on to jointly create reality, a process that qualitative studies are ideally suited to uncovering. Narrative retelling in interviews is a vivid instance of this. A teller convinces a listener who wasn't there that certain events 'happened', that the teller was affected by them. A particular self is constituted through these narratives, occasioned by the presence of a listener, her questions and comments. Typically, the moral character of the protagonist is sustained.

This paper analyzes how one narrator, 'Burt' – a recently separated working class man with advanced multiple sclerosis – projects a definition of himself as husband, father and worker. . . . The self that Burt projects is a very favorable one, and the narratives attest to his resilience. He does not allow himself to be defined as a cuckold, as the rejected spouse (yet his wife left him for another man after he became disabled), nor does he portray himself as an inadequate parent or worker (yet his adolescent son left home and he is no longer able to hold down a job). By effectively narrating his experience, in the context of cultural understandings about sickness, he is able to project a strong masculine identity, even in the face of behavior that violates common sense definitions of masculinity. A close analysis of his narrative account, and especially its narrative structure, reveals how he accomplishes this reality.

This paper also has a methodological purpose – to show how narrative analysis is done. This method is particularly well suited to studying the presentation of self in everyday life, for storifying experience is a naturalistic form for telling others about ourselves. Unlike traditional qualitative methods, this approach does not fragment the text into discrete content categories for coding purposes but, instead, identifies longer stretches of talk that take the form of narrative – a discourse organized around time and consequential events in a 'world' recreated by the narrator. The approach assumes interviewees structure their replies in the ways they do for strategic reasons – to effectively communicate 'what happened' – and, consequently, determining the organization of the discourse is an important analytic task. To enable this, a full taped transcription of the interview is made, the analyst identifies the boundaries of narrative segments, noting their contexts, and parses these texts to display the underlying structure. . . . Along with this structural analysis, narratives are interpreted, both as individual units and in relation to one another, by identifying thematic and linguistic connections between the narrative segments. Taken together, they constitute a teller's 'narrative reconstruction'[1] or 'account'[2] of his or her lived experience. . . .

'I was a good husband'

Burt moves to control the interviewer's impression of him early in their interaction. He says he took the initiative and filed for divorce, adding 'it wasn't my fault that she just packed up and left one day and that was the end of it.' He elaborates this definition of the situation – that he is not to blame – by moving back in time and staging a narrative, beginning with a preface.

> Well, I can go back to 1975 when I first found out I had MS. And when she was told by the doctor that it eventually would cripple me, put me in a wheelchair. Seems like back in 1975 that she seemed to drift apart from me, that she didn't accept the disease.

Although the two events – his diagnosis and his divorce – are not temporally related (the diagnosis occurred 9 years before he began to live apart from his wife), he has effectively linked them. As he later elaborates, MS is responsible for the divorce, not anything he did. She didn't 'accept the disease', where he implies he has. In this preface, Burt has projected a definition of the situation, making an 'explicit claim to be a person of a particular kind'. He has also made a moral demand upon the interviewer, obligating her 'to value and treat him in the manner that persons of his kind have a right to expect'.[3]

The divorce narrative formally begins after a series of moves. The interviewer asks a closed ended question (which spouse was primarily responsible for the decision to separate) that Burt responds to, saying that none of the fixed responses

1 Williams G. 'The genesis of chronic illness; narrative reconstruction. *Social.' Hlth Illn.* 6, 175, 1984.
2 Scott M.B. and Lyman S.M. 'Accounts.' *Am. Sociol. Rev.* 46, 46. 1968.
3 Goffman E. *The Presentation of Self In Everyday Life.* pp. 9–10. Anchor Press, Doubleday, New York, 1959.

'actually apply'. To borrow from Young, he breaks into the framework of the realm of the research interview, flouting its conventions.[4] . . . She responds by creating a 'slot' in the interaction for a narrative ('Tell me, then, in your own words'). Into this enclave, he inserts a long story, portions of which are reproduced in transcript 1.

Transcript 1

01	OK, when she left in February
02	we tried to get back together in May . . . [tells of going to see her in motel and asking her to 'come home' and she said 'I'm not coming home.'] . . .
03	That night (p) about twelve o'clock
04	there was a call (p) and it was her
05	and Susan [daughter] picked the phone up
06	and she had been drinking
07	and she said she wanted to come home
08	so Susan went down to the motel and picked her up . . .
10	brought her down here
11	she slept here that night
12	she came into my room
13	gave me a big hug and a big kiss
14	said 'I'm glad to be back'
15	I said 'I'm glad you're back'
16	I says 'We have all missed you.'
17	The following day
18	she seemed like she had a split personality
19	seemed like she changed into a different person.
20	She got up in the morning
21	I came out and sat in the chair here an'
22	she went back to the same routine that she had done before she (p) decided to move out.
23	She's telling me that I'm gonna be put in a nursing home
24	. . . she's going sell the house.
25	And I said 'hey, look, no, nothin' is gonna change
26	it's not gonna be any different than before we were married.
27	Now if you want to stay here you can, you know,
28	you gonna be – act the same way you were before you left.'
29	So she just packed up and left.

Notation system:

(p) = pause of 3 seconds or longer,
– = break off of word.

Stories, more than other forms of discourse, effectively pull the listener into the teller's point of view. They re-present a slice of life, often by dramatizing and

---

4 Young K. 'Narrative embodiments: enclaves of the self in the realm of medicine.' In *Texts of Identity* (edited by Shotter J. and Gergen K.J.), pp. 152–165. Sage, Newbury Park, Cal., 1989.

re-enacting a particular interaction, thereby providing 'proof' of how it was. They draw the listener so deeply into the teller's experience that often a kind of intersubjective agreement about 'how it was' is reached. To borrow from Goffman, they can also function in interaction as 'defensive practices,' saving the definition of the situation that a teller has projected.[3]

Through the story in Transcript 1, Burt makes the claim that he was a devoted husband. He provides an illustrative instance of how he was willing to forgive, thus laying full responsibility for the divorce on his wife. This supportive story sustains a positive identity in the face of physical disability and loss. The story also reaffirms his central position, as a man, in the hierarchy of the family. Despite his confinement to a wheelchair, the point of the story is that he stood up to his wife, refusing to allow himself to be defined as incompetent.

Looking briefly at the form of the story, we see that it has many of the structural features of this genre of narrative as outlined by Labov.[5] It orients the listener to time and place (lines 1, 3, 17), contains a core plot or complicating action (lines 4, 7, 11–16, 20, 22) which is resolved by the protagonist's actions (lines 25–29), and the story includes the narrator's evaluation of the events (lines 6, 18–19). Climactic points in the plot are dramatized (lines 14–16 and 25–28), an especially effective device for building tension and drawing a listener in. The evaluative clauses (the 'soul' of the narrative for they convey quality of mind and the attitude of the narrator) are especially significant in this story because they convey Burt's understanding that it was her 'illness', not his, that was the problem – her drinking and her 'split personality'.

Yet the story leaves us with many questions unanswered. For instance, did Burt and his wife have sexual relations on the night they got back together? The plot as he develops it skips over this topic (perhaps because he is interacting with a woman interviewer), just as his narrative account more generally leaves out any mention of the effect of his disease on the sexual aspect of their marriage. Although we have no way of knowing what 'really' happened MS can result in sexual impairment. And we know from elsewhere in the interview[6] that Burt's wife took a lover toward the end of the marriage. Yet narratives are always edited versions of reality, not objective and impartial descriptions of it and interviewees always make choices about what to divulge. In this case, the ambiguity about intimacy functions to uphold the definition of the divorce situation that Burt has projected from the start. Goffman[3] alerts us to attend to the impression that Burt has composed of himself, one that takes as its central thread his marital devotion and masculine competence. . . .

Conclusion

I have used narrative analysis to show how a physically disabled man sustains a positive impression of himself – a portrait that contrasts sharply with some of the

5 Labov W. and Waletzky J. 'Narrative analysis: oral versions of personal experience.' In *Essays on the Verbal and Visual Arts. Proceedings of the 1966 Annual Spring meeting of the American Ethnological Society* (edited by Helm J.). University of Washington Press, Seattle, Wash., 1967.
6 For a fuller version of this man's narrative account, see Riessman C. K. 'Life events, meaning and narrative: the case of infidelity and divorce.' *Soc. Sci. Med.* 29, 743–751, 1989.

'realities' of his condition and how he might be viewed, given outward signs and other 'facts' about his divorce. To do this, he creates enclaves in the structured interview to assert a self, with the narrative retelling healing some of the discontinu-ities and contradictions in the nature of this self. The thematic material, while quite ancillary to the manifest purpose of the interview, can be inserted and sustained because it observes the convention of narrative in conversation. By retelling con-sequential events and elaborating on their meanings, he guides the impression that he gives, sustaining a reality, and a self, one that is sealed inside the narrative.[4]

As a whole, this man's narrative reconstruction of a biography disrupted by illness preserves key aspects of his masculinity – his adequacy as husband, father and worker. Although chronic illness has interfered with his life plan in each domain, the narrator creates a social self that is competent, controlled and feelingful. This is not a portrait of a man who is denying the severity of his illness, or the sadness of his divorce, but neither is it a portrait of victimization and dependency. . . .

Telling narratives is a major way that individuals make sense of disruptive events in their lives. Beyond making meaning, examining the story told and the story listened to can illuminate the performance aspects of language – how we create our realities and ourselves through the strategic choices we make in social interaction.

PART TWELVE

Reflexivity and representation

INTRODUCTION

THE READINGS IN THIS book are not arranged entirely in a chronological sequence, but it is fair to say that concerns about reflexivity have increased in recent years, social researchers being relatively more confident in their authority in past times. In part, concern with the legitimacy with which social researchers can claim a right for their 'truths' to be heard has intensified because of the growth of interest in analysing how language constructs particular versions of the world. Because social researchers themselves communicate in language (usually in writing), a developed sensitivity to the persuasive and rhetorical aspects of language almost inevitably would come to be applied to research reports themselves. But a concern with reflexivity (that is to say, reflecting on one's own research practice) pre-dates the linguistic turn and this is exemplified in the extract from Gouldner (reading 56), who makes a powerful argument for sociologists to become more self-critical.

Taking up this concern, Clifford (reading 57) presents a classic statement in which the linguistic turn is brought to bear on the reporting practices of social research (in his case, anthropological writing). He employs the oxymoron 'true fiction' to convey the tension that exists between scientific and literary approaches to social research writing. Associated with this is a concern with the political legitimacy of anthropological knowledge, where a history of association with colonialism must be addressed. This requires a reassessment of the relationship between researchers and the people they research.

Research reports, though, are not the only form of research writing. Atkinson (reading 58), continuing the concern with reflexivity, considers the constructed nature of various attempts to transcribe speech, noting that social researchers have often done a considerable amount of 'tidying up' when presenting informants' speeches so that this editing work encourages a partial version of speakers. The textual depiction of non-standard language forms can serve to denigrate the character of speakers from minority groups.

Turning to the issue of relations between researchers and the people researched, Rosaldo (reading 59) tells a story from his field-work experience in the Philippines. His emotions on experiencing a personal tragedy, in which his wife died in an accident, helped him understand where the kind of rage that led his informants to episodes of head hunting might come from. He contrasts this insight from shared experience with the rather laughable attempts he had made earlier to explain to the head hunters that their actions might be explainable by 'exchange theory'. It was only when he had a similar experience that he could understand their behaviour, and he regarded the detachment provided by the usual conventions of social research to be a barrier to such understanding.

Concern with the constructed nature of research writing has led some to experiment with new ways of reporting. Richardson in reading 60 uses a poem to convey the perspective of an interviewee. She claims that this is more free from the distorting, singular reading that a conventional social research report would impose, allowing readers a freer play of interpretations. Thus the author of the research text is 'de-centred'.

The ethnographic critique of ethnography, represented by authors like Clifford, has had a different impact on different research workers. Brewer (reading 61) seeks to defend and reinstate the authority of the author rather than to seek ways of abandoning such authority in the manner of Richardson. He argues that the deconstruction of ethnographic texts carried out by authors such as Geertz (reading 34) and Clifford should be used to generate principles for the construction of such texts rather than abandoning the enterprise.

DISCUSSION POINTS

- Gouldner, arguing that sociologists ought to become more aware of the assumptions that determine their vision of the world, assumes that all sociologists are 'men' and all people are potentially 'brothers'. Women don't get mentioned. Does this suggest that Gouldner was a person lacking in insight, or that any social researcher trying to be reflexive will be judged as limited by later generations? If the latter is the case, where does this leave the general project of reflexivity? What could its purpose be?

- If ethnographic writing is neither an attempt to report the truth, nor a fictional account, then what is it? Consider this question in relation to a particular research report.

- Do the transcription conventions of conversation analysis (see readings 24 and 48) suffer from the problems Atkinson identifies? Are some transcription methods better than others? In what ways might field notes (see reading 33) raise similar issues to those identified by Atkinson?

- Compare Rosaldo's account with that of Oakley (reading 38). What similarities and differences do you see? How similar were the experiences of Oakley to those

of the women she interviewed, and those of Rosaldo to the experiences of Ilongot
people?

- Is Richardson's approach to research writing, using poetry, better than conventional research reporting?
- Can Brewer's recommendations for good ethnographic research writing be usefully employed to assess the quality of Richardson's report? Which approach
  (Richardson's or Brewer's) do you feel is most valuable?

FURTHER READING

Atkinson, P. (1990) *The Ethnographic Imagination: Textual Constructions of Reality*,
London: Routledge.

Coffey, A., Holbrook, B. and Atkinson, P. (1996) 'Qualitative data analysis: technologies and representations', *Sociological Research On-line* 1, http://www.soc.sur-
rey.ac.uk/socresonline

Crapanzano, V. (1980) *Tuhami: Portrait of a Moroccan*, Chicago, Ill.: University of
Chicago Press.

Lynch, M. (2000) 'Against reflexivity as an academic virtue and source of privileged
knowledge', *Theory Culture and Society* 17(3): 26–54.

Mishler, E., (1991); 'Representing discourse: the rhetoric of transcription', *Journal of
Narrative and Life History* 1(4): 225–280.

Snow, D.A. and Morrill, C. (1993) 'Reflections on anthropology's ethnographic crisis
of faith', *Contemporary Sociology* 22: 8–11.

Van Maanen, J. (1988) *Tales of the Field: On Writing Ethnography*, Chicago, Ill.:
University of Chicago Press.

——(1995) *Representation in Ethnography*, Thousand Oaks, Cal.: Sage.

Woolgar, S. (ed.) (1988) *Knowledge and Reflexivity: New Frontiers in the Sociology
of Knowledge*, London: Sage.

Chapter 56

Alvin W. Gouldner

TOWARD A REFLEXIVE SOCIOLOGY

From *The Coming Crisis of Western Sociology,* London: Heinemann (1972).

. . .

SOCIOLOGISTS ARE NO MORE ready than other men to cast a cold eye on their own doings. No more than others are they ready, willing, or able to tell us what they are really doing and to distinguish this firmly from what they *should* be doing. Professional courtesy stifles intellectual curiosity; guild interests frown upon the washing of dirty linen in public; the teeth of piety bite the tongue of truth. Yet, first and foremost, a Reflexive Sociology is concerned with what sociologists want to do and with what, in fact, they actually do in the world.

The intellectual development of sociology during the last two decades or so, especially the growth of the sociologies of occupations and of science, is, when fused with the larger perspectives of the older sociology of knowledge, one promising basis for the development of a Reflexive Sociology. We have already seen some of the first stirrings of a Reflexive Sociology, in one form or another. Indeed, I believe we have already also seen the emergence of defensive reactions that, in effect, seek to contain the impact of a Reflexive Sociology by defining it as just one other technical speciality within sociology.

What sociologists now most require from a Reflexive Sociology, however, is not just one more specialization, not just another topic for panel meetings at professional conventions, and not just another burbling little stream of technical reports about the sociological profession's origins, educational characteristics, patterns of productivity, political preferences, communication networks, nor even about its fads, foibles, and phonies. For there are ways and ways of conducting and reporting such studies. There are ways that do not touch and quicken us but may, instead, deaden us to the disorders we bear; by allowing us to talk about them with a ventriloquist's voice, they only create an illusion of self-confrontation that serves to disguise a new form of self-celebration. The historical mission of a Reflexive Sociology as I conceive it, however, would be to *transform* the sociologist, to penetrate deeply into his daily life and work, enriching them with new sensitivities, and to raise the sociologist's self-awareness to a new historical level.

To the extent that it succeeds in this, and in order to succeed in it, a Reflexive Sociology is and would need to be a radical sociology. Radical, because it would recognize that knowledge of the world cannot be advanced apart from the sociologist's knowledge of himself and his position in the social world, or apart from his efforts to change these. Radical, because it seeks to transform as well as to know the alien world outside the sociologist as well the alien world inside of him. Radical, because it would accept the fact that the roots of sociology pass through the sociologist as a total man, and that the question he must confront, therefore, is not merely how to *work* but how to *live*.

The historical mission of a Reflexive Sociology is to transcend sociology as it now exists. In deepening our understanding of our own sociological selves and of our position in the world, we can, I believe, simultaneously help to produce a new breed of sociologists who can also better understand other men and their social worlds. A Reflexive Sociology means that we sociologists must – at the very least – acquire the ingrained *habit* of viewing our own beliefs as we now view those held by others.

It will be difficult for many sociologists to accept that we presently know little or nothing about ourselves or other sociologists or, in point of fact, that we know little about how one piece of social research, or one sociologist, comes to be esteemed while another is disparaged or ignored. The temptation is great to conceal our ignorance of this process behind a glib affirmation of the proprieties and to pretend that there is no one here but us scientists. In other words, one of the basic reasons we deceive ourselves and lie to others is because we are moral men. Sociologists, like other men, confuse the moral answer with the empirical and, indeed, often prefer it to the empirical. Much of our noble talk about the importance of 'truth for its own sake' is often a tacit way of saying that we want the truth about *others*, at whatever cost it may be to *them*. A Reflexive Sociology, however, implies that sociologists must surrender the assumption, as wrongheaded as it is human, that others believe out of need while we believe – only or primarily – because of the dictates of logic and evidence.

A systematic and dogged insistence upon seeing ourselves as we see others would, I have suggested, transform not only our view of ourselves but also our view of others. We would increasingly recognize the depth of our kinship with those whom we study. They would no longer be viewable as alien others or as mere objects for our superior technique and insight; they could, instead, be seen as brother sociologists, each attempting with his varying degree of skill, energy, and talent to understand social reality. In this respect, all men are basically akin to those whom we usually acknowledge as professional 'colleagues,' who are no less diversified in their talents and competence. With the development of a Reflexive Sociology that avoids becoming molded into just another technical specialty, such rigor as sociology attains may be blended with a touch of mercy, and such skills as sociologists possess may come to yield not only information but perhaps even a modest measure of wisdom.

The development of a Reflexive Sociology, in sum, requires that sociologists cease acting as if they thought of subjects and objects, sociologists who study and 'laymen' who are studied, as two distinct breeds of men. There is only one breed of man. But so long as we are without a Reflexive Sociology, we will act upon the tacit dualistic premise that there are two, regardless of how monistic our professions of methodological faith.

I conceive of Reflexive Sociology as requiring an empirical dimension which might foster a large variety of researches about sociology and sociologists, their occupational roles, their career 'hangups,' their establishments, power systems, subcultures, and their place in the larger social world. Indeed, my emphasis on the empirical character of a Reflexive Sociology and my insistence that the method-ological morality of social science not be confused with the description of its social system and cultures, may seem to express a Positivistic bias. Yet while I believe that a Reflexive Sociology must have an empirical dimension, I do not conceive of this as providing a factual basis that determines the character of its guiding theory. Which is to say that I do not conceive of the theory of a Reflexive Sociology merely as an induction from researches or from 'facts.' And more important, I do not conceive of these researches or their factual output as being 'value-free,' for I would hope that their originating motives and terminating consequences would embody and advance certain specific *values*. A Reflexive Sociology would be a moral sociology. . . .

Conventional Positivism premises that the self is treacherous and that, so long as it remains in contact with the information system, its primary effect is to bias or distort it. It is assumed, therefore, that the way to defend the information system is to insulate it from the scholar's self by generating distance and by stressing impersonal detachment from the objects studied. From the standpoint of a Reflexive Sociology, however, the assumption that the self can be sealed off from information systems is mythological. The assumption that the self affects the information system solely in a distorting manner is one-sided: it fails to see that the self may also be a source both of valid insight that enriches study and of motivation that energizes it. A Reflexive Sociology looks, therefore, to the deepening of the self's capacity to recognize that it views certain information as hostile, to recognize the various dodges that it uses to deny, ignore, or camouflage information that is hostile to it, and to the strengthening of its capacity to accept and to use hostile information. In short, what Reflexive Sociology seeks is not an insulation but a *transformation* of the sociologist's self, and hence of his praxis in the world.

A Reflexive Sociology, then, is not characterized by *what* it studies. It is dis-tinguished neither by the persons and the problems studied nor even by the tech-niques and instruments used in studying them. It is characterized, rather, by the *relationship* it establishes between being a sociologist and being a person, between the role and the man performing it. A Reflexive Sociology embodies a critique of the conventional conception of segregated scholarly roles and has a vision of an alternative. It aims at transforming the sociologist's relation to his work. . . .

Chapter 57

James Clifford

PARTIAL TRUTHS

From Introduction to Clifford, J. and Marcus, G.E. *Writing Culture: The Poetics and Politics of Ethnography*, Berkeley: University of California Press (1986).

. . .

WRITING HAS EMERGED AS central to what anthropologists do both in the field and thereafter. The fact that it has not until recently been portrayed or seriously discussed reflects the persistence of an ideology claiming transparency of representation and immediacy of experience. Writing reduced to method: keeping good field notes, making accurate maps, 'writing up' results.

The essays collected here assert that this ideology has crumbled. They see culture as composed of seriously contested codes and representations; they assume that the poetic and the political are inseparable, that science is in, not above, historical and linguistic processes. They assume that academic and literary genres interpenetrate and that the writing of cultural descriptions is properly experimental and ethical. Their focus on text making and rhetoric serves to highlight the constructed, artificial nature of cultural accounts. It undermines overly transparent modes of authority, and it draws attention to the historical predicament of ethnography, the fact that it is always caught up in the invention, not the representation, of cultures. . . .

Ethnography is actively situated *between* powerful systems of meaning. It poses its questions at the boundaries of civilizations, cultures, classes, races, and genders. Ethnography decodes and recodes, telling the grounds of collective order and diversity, inclusion and exclusion. It describes processes of innovation and structuration, and is itself part of these processes. . . .

'Literary' approaches have recently enjoyed some popularity in the human sciences. In anthropology influential writers such as Clifford Geertz, Victor Turner, Mary Douglas, Claude Lévi-Strauss, Jean Duvignaud, and Edmund Leach, to mention only a few, have shown an interest in literary theory and practice. In their quite different ways they have blurred the boundary separating art from science. Nor is theirs a new attraction. Malinowski's authorial identifications (Conrad, Frazer) are well known. Margaret Mead, Edward Sapir, and Ruth Benedict saw themselves as both anthropologists and literary artists. In Paris surrealism and professional ethnography regularly exchanged both ideas and personnel. But until recently literary influences have been held at a distance from the 'rigorous' core of the discipline. Sapir and Benedict had, after all, to hide their poetry from the scientific gaze of Franz Boas. And though ethnographers have often been called novelists manqué (especially those who write a little too well), the notion that literary procedures pervade any work of cultural representation is a recent idea in the discipline. To a growing number, however, the 'literariness' of anthropology – and especially of ethnography – appears as much more than a matter of good writing or distinctive style. Literary processes – metaphor, figuration, narrative – affect the ways cultural phenomena are registered, from the first jotted 'observations,' to the completed book, to the ways these configurations 'make sense' in determined acts of reading.

It has long been asserted that scientific anthropology is also an 'art,' that ethnographies have literary qualities. We often hear that an author writes with style, that certain descriptions are vivid or convincing (should not every accurate description be convincing?). A work is deemed evocative or artfully composed in addition to being factual; expressive, rhetorical functions are conceived as decorative or merely as ways to present an objective analysis or description more effectively. Thus the facts of the matter may be kept separate, at least in principle, from their means of communication. But the literary or rhetorical dimensions of ethnography can no longer be so easily compartmentalized. They are active at every level of cultural science. Indeed, the very notion of a 'literary' approach to a discipline, 'anthropology,' is seriously misleading. . . .

To call ethnographies fictions may raise empiricist hackles. But the word as commonly used in recent textual theory has lost its connotation of falsehood, of something merely opposed to truth. It suggests the partiality of cultural and historical truths, the ways they are systematic and exclusive. Ethnographic writings can properly be called fictions in the sense of 'something made or fashioned,' the principal burden of the word's Latin root, *fingere*. But it is important to preserve the meaning not merely of making, but also of making up, of inventing things not actually real. (*Fingere*, in some of its uses, implied a degree of falsehood.) Interpretive social scientists have recently come to view good ethnographies as 'true fictions,' but usually at the cost of weakening the oxymoron, reducing it to the banal claim that all truths are constructed. The essays collected here keep the oxymoron sharp. For example, Vincent Crapanzano portrays ethnographers as tricksters, promising, like Hermes, not to lie, but never undertaking to tell the whole truth either. Their rhetoric empowers *and* subverts their message. Other essays reinforce the point by stressing that cultural fictions are based on systematic, and contestable, *exclusions*. These may involve silencing incongruent voices ('Two Crows denies it!') or deploying a consistent manner of quoting, 'speaking for,' translating the reality of others. Purportedly irrelevant personal or historical circumstances will also be

excluded (one cannot tell all). Moreover, the maker (but why only one?) of ethnographic texts cannot avoid expressive tropes, figures, and allegories that select and
impose meaning as they translate it. In this view, more Nietzschean than realist or
hermeneutic, all constructed truths are made possible by powerful 'lies' of exclusion and rhetoric. Even the best ethnographic texts – serious, true fictions – are
systems, or economies, of truth. Power and history work through them, in ways
their authors cannot fully control. . . .

Ethnographers are more and more like the Cree hunter who (the story goes)
came to Montreal to testify in court concerning the fate of his hunting lands in the
new James Bay hydroelectric scheme. He would describe his way of life. But when
administered the oath he hesitated: 'I'm not sure I can tell the truth. . . . I can only
tell what I know.' . . .

Different rules of the game for ethnography are now emerging in many parts of
the world. An outsider studying Native American cultures may expect, perhaps as a
requirement for continuing research, to testify in support of land claim litigation.
And a variety of formal restrictions are now placed on field work by indigenous
governments at national and local levels. These condition in new ways what can,
and especially cannot, be said about particular peoples. A new figure has entered
the scene, the 'indigenous ethnographer' (Fahim 1982; Ohnuki-Tierney 1984).
Insiders studying their own cultures offer new angles of vision and depths of
understanding. Their accounts are empowered and restricted in unique ways. The
diverse post- and neo-colonial rules for ethnographic practice do not necessarily
encourage 'better' cultural accounts. The criteria for judging a good account have
never been settled and are changing. But what has emerged from all these ideological shifts, rule changes, and new compromises is the fact that a series of
historical pressures have begun to reposition anthropology with respect to its
'objects' of study. Anthropology no longer speaks with automatic authority for
others defined as unable to speak for themselves ('primitive,' 'pre-literate,' 'without history'). Other groups can less easily be distanced in special, almost always
past or passing, times – represented as if they were not involved in the present
world systems that implicate ethnographers along with the peoples they study.
'Cultures' do not hold still for their portraits. Attempts to make them do so always
involve simplification and exclusion, selection of a temporal focus, the construction
of a particular self-other relationship, and the imposition or negotiation of a power
relationship.

The critique of colonialism in the postwar period – an undermining of 'The
West's' ability to represent other societies – has been reinforced by an important
process of theorizing about the limits of representation itself. . . .

In a related polemic against 'Orientalism' Edward Said (1978) identifies persist-
ent tropes by which Europeans and Americans have visualized Eastern and Arab
cultures. The Orient functions as a theater, a stage on which a performance is
repeated, to be seen from a privileged standpoint. For Said, the Orient is 'textual-
ized'; its multiple, divergent stories and existential predicaments are coherently
woven as a body of signs susceptible of virtuoso reading. This Orient, occulted and
fragile, is brought lovingly to light, salvaged in the work of the outside scholar. The
effect of domination in such spatial/temporal deployments (not limited, of course,
to Orientalism proper) is that they confer on the other a discrete identity, while also

providing the knowing observer with a standpoint from which to see without being seen, to read without interruption. . . .

A major consequence of the historical and theoretical movements traced in this Introduction has been to dislodge the ground from which persons and groups securely represent others. A conceptual shift, 'tectonic' in its implications, has taken place. We ground things, now, on a moving earth. There is no longer any place of overview (mountaintop) from which to map human ways of life, no Archimedian point from which to represent the world. Mountains are in constant motion. So are islands: for one cannot occupy, unambiguously, a bounded cultural world from which to journey out and analyze other cultures. Human ways of life increasingly influence, dominate, parody, translate, and subvert one another. Cultural analysis is always enmeshed in global movements of difference and power. However one defines it, and the phrase is here used loosely, a 'world system' now links the planet's societies in a common historical process. . . .

One launches a controversial collection like this with some trepidation, hoping it will be seriously engaged – not simply rejected, for example, as another attack on science or an incitement to relativism. Rejections of this kind should at least make clear why close analysis of one of the principal things ethnographers do – that is, write – should not be central to evaluation of the results of scientific research. The authors in this volume do not suggest that one cultural account is as good as any other. If they espoused so trivial and self-refuting a relativism, they would not have gone to the trouble of writing detailed, committed, critical studies.

Other, more subtle, objections have recently been raised to the literary, theoretical reflexivity represented here. Textual, epistemological questions are sometimes thought to be paralyzing, abstract, dangerously solipsistic – in short, a barrier to the task of writing 'grounded' or 'unified' cultural and historical studies. In practice, however, such questions do not necessarily inhibit those who entertain them from producing truthful, realistic accounts. All of the essays collected here point toward new, better modes of writing. One need not agree with their particular standards to take seriously the fact that in ethnography, as in literary and historical studies, what counts as 'realist' is now a matter of both theoretical debate and practical experimentation.

The writing and reading of ethnography are overdetermined by forces ultimately beyond the control of either an author or an interpretive community. These contingencies – of language, rhetoric, power, and history – must now be openly confronted in the process of writing. They can no longer be evaded. But the confrontation raises thorny problems of verification: how are the truths of cultural accounts evaluated? Who has the authority to separate science from art? realism from fantasy? knowledge from ideology? Of course such separations will continue to be maintained, and redrawn; but their changing poetic and political grounds will be less easily ignored. In cultural studies at least, we can no longer know the whole truth, or even claim to approach it. The rigorous partiality I have been stressing here may be a source of pessimism for some readers. But is there not a liberation, too, in recognizing that no one can write about others any longer as if they were discrete *objects or texts*? And may not the vision of a complex, problematic, partial ethnography lead, not to its abandonment, but to more subtle, concrete ways of writing and reading, to new conceptions of culture as interactive and historical? Most of the essays in this volume, for all their trenchant critiques, are optimistic about ethnographic writing. The problems they raise are incitements, not barriers.

These essays will be accused of having gone too far: poetry will again be banned from the city, power from the halls of science. And extreme self-consciousness certainly has its dangers – of irony, of elitism, of solipsism, of putting the whole world in quotation marks. But I trust that readers who signal these dangers will do so (like some of the essays below) *after* they have confronted the changing history, rhetoric, and politics of established representational forms. In the wake of semiotics, post-structuralism, hermeneutics, and deconstruction there has been considerable talk about a return to plain speaking and to realism. But to return to realism one must first have left it! Moreover, to recognize the poetic dimensions of ethnography does not require that one give up facts and accurate accounting for the supposed free play of poetry. 'Poetry' is not limited to romantic or modernist subjectivism: it can be historical, precise, objective. And of course it is just as conventional and institutionally determined as 'prose.' Ethnography is hybrid textual activity: it traverses genres and disciplines. The essays in this volume do not claim ethnography is 'only literature.' They do insist it is always writing.

References

Fahim, Hussein, (ed.) (1982) *Indigenous Anthropology in Non-Western Countries*. Durham, NC: Carolina Academic Press.

Ohnuki-Tierney, Emiko (1984) ' "Native" anthropologists.' *American Ethnologist* 11, 3: 584–86.

Said, Edward (1978) *Orientalism*, New York: Pantheon.

Chapter 58

Paul Atkinson

TRANSCRIPTIONS

From *Understanding Ethnographic Texts,* London: Sage (1992).

. . .

TEXTUAL CONVENTIONS EXERT A powerful influence on the representation of informants' or other social actors' own words. The naive might
think that there is no problem in the factual reporting of what people say. The
author has no need to engage in the kind of invention required of the playwright or
novelist. The ethnographer, after all, has no need to contrive plausible dialogue or
monologue in order to convey actors' speech. The ethnographic author *has* their
speech (noted or recorded). Surely, the task is merely to select and reproduce
extracts of the original talk in order to report those data faithfully. Clifford refers to
this as *transcription*. It is a broader set of activities than just the technical work of
'transcribing' audio-tapes. Transcription also implies writing down 'already formulated, fixed discourse or lore' (Clifford 1990: p. 57). It includes much classical
anthropological fieldwork, such as 'taking dictation, recording the myth or magical
spell' (Clifford 1990: 51), as well as the recording of interviews and other spoken
social action. Here is clearly illustrated the problem of 'readability.' Informants
cannot 'speak for themselves.' In order to give an impression of it we have to select,
edit, and *represent* their spoken narratives. Moreover, the more *comprehensible* and
readable the reported speech, the less 'authentic' it must be. The less the ethnographer intervenes, the more delicately he or she transcribes, the *less* readable
becomes the reported speech. Clifford (1990) suggests that in contrast to 'inscription,' transcription implies a different power relationship between fieldworker and
informant: 'The authority of the researcher who brings passing, usually oral, experience into permanent writing is decentred' (p. 58). This contrast is misleading,

however, for it overlooks the textual work ethnographers bring to bear in making recorded speech readable.

In practice the reporting of informants' talk is as dependent on textual convention as any other element of the text. Any and every method for rendering spoken language is found to be conventional. There is no such thing as a 'natural' mechanism for the representation of speech. Orthography, punctuation, type-setting – these are all textual methods through which speech is reconstructed and rendered accessible to the knowledgeable reader. In fact, ethnographers have used a very wide range of styles to represent their data. Each has its effects on the reader. Each may be used – consciously or unconsciously – to convey different interpretative connotations. The different conventions may allow the author to construct informants in quite different ways. The representation of speech, moreover, helps to impart particular qualities and characteristics.

It is often claimed as a strength of ethnographic and other qualitative research that social actors may be allowed to 'speak for themselves.' And indeed it is a noticeable feature of many ethnographic texts: they are often sprinkled liberally with direct quotations from actors. Sometimes entire texts comprise personal accounts. The cognate genre of the life-history is, of course, especially dependent on the subject's own narratives. In such contexts the accounts and quotations may be thought of as 'data.' But they are inescapably dependent on textual conventions that are in turn implicative of writers' and readers' interpretations.

Nonetheless, one must be careful not to rely uncritically on the 'authenticity' of the modern recording. The verbatim record, for instance, is normally transcribed, and the transcription itself depends on the *conventional* representation of speech. The ethnographer of talk must use textual conventions and representations to convey the data to his or her reader. Just as the representation of talk in fictional writing is dependent on certain textual (including typographical) conventions, so the construction of scholarly transcripts depends on conventional typographical resources. They are themselves matters of interpretation, and *can* be thoroughly implicated in the writer's preoccupations and presuppositions, 'readability,' 'accessibility,' and the like. Moreover, the representation of speech can be used to convey the status and character of the speaker. The choice of conventions is thus a choice about the representation of persons as social and moral actors in the text.

Some ethnographers have constructed their accounts almost exclusively through the first-person narratives of their informants. The strategy can be a powerful one. In the hands of a skillful author, the resulting text can have the appearance of a vivid and privileged reconstruction of the speaker's experience. A social world may be conveyed dramatically through the voice of the informant. A variety of narrative accounts can provide a shifting point of view: a kaleidoscope of contrasting or complementary perspectives is provided through a variety of voices.

Oscar Lewis, in his accounts of everyday life in the 'culture of poverty' of Mexico City or Puerto Rico, is a classic exponent. He reconstructed the Spanish speech of his informants into extended, highly readable first-person narratives in English. Books like *The Children of Sanchez* (1961) or *La Vida* (1965) are composed out of juxtaposed accounts by family members, each of whom provides a different view of a shared life-world. Lewis's first-person narratives are successful in several ways. The books are among the most widely read works of cultural anthropology.

Many readers will have been left with lasting impressions of poverty in the tenement and the slum. The vivid accounts did more to convey Lewis's idea about the culture of poverty than any extended analytic exposition could ever have done. Lewis's overt anthropological interventions in the books are restricted to rather brief introductory essays. The rest is devoted to the lengthy narratives in which the various characters 'speak for themselves.'

This is not the reality, however. (I do not mean that Lewis practices deception). The characters who speak for themselves in Lewis's texts, do so in voices and in narratives that are highly contrived and reconstructed by Lewis himself. The narratives are edited into coherent, extended texts. No one person – whatever his or her cultural origins – ever spoke such narratives with that assurance and precision. In Lewis's hands what must of necessity have been fragmentary and repetitious become seamlessly smooth. His narrators do not stumble and falter; they do not lose the thread; they do not break off to change the subject or do something more pressing than talk to the ethnographer. They all turn out to be extraordinarily adroit storytellers. The reader's attention will be held equally by each of the narratives.

In practice, of course, we know that Oscar Lewis took considerable liberties in constructing 'their' accounts. The editorial hand has exercised considerable licence, and the role of the anthropologist has been a *creative* one. In one sense, the work of the anthropologist is visible to all attentive readers, quite apart from any explicit statement on his part. We can tell that the books are contrivances. The careful juxtaposition of the accounts is transparently artful. The narratives are clearly reconstructed: they are too lengthy and too 'literary' to be the actual transcripts of single tellings. They bear none of the tell-tale signs of spontaneous speech. They are too 'smooth'; everyday speech is less fluent, less grammatical, and less readable.

Crapanzano (1986) constructs his account in a way very similar to Lewis's method. His book consists very largely of first-person narratives by white South Africans, in what is an undeniably arresting set of accounts from a politically dominant but culturally muted group. The work has been categorized as an example of contemporary 'multivocal' ethnography: Crapanzano grants the informants their individual 'voices,' rather than subsuming them all under his own authorial jurisdiction. In practice Crapanzano does not simply report and juxtapose those voices. He exercises a great deal of tacit and invisible authorial work in collating, editing and rewriting the personal narratives. The original contexts of their production (such as the interviews and conversations with Crapanzano) are lost to view. Each character is assembled by Crapanzano out of the fragments of narrative available to him, and then freed to address the reader directly, to the accompaniment of occasional asides from Crapanzano. His or her words are fashioned into highly coherent and cogent narratives. Like Lewis before him Crapanzano thus invests his characters with particular kinds of 'voices.' Each of the Afrikaners, in his or her own way, confronts the reader as an individual hero or heroine in his or her own life-world. This is an *accomplishment* of the authorial activity of the anthropologist. Character is 'inscribed,' but speech is 'transcribed.'

Oscar Lewis and Vincent Crapanzano represent one end of a spectrum, and one response to a recurrent dilemma. To what extent should the ethnographer exercise editorial control in order to render the informants' words more coherent and more readable? It is a problem faced by all qualitative researchers who ever wish to quote their informants. If we quote a completely unvarnished version (not that *that* is ever entirely possible), then it may be so difficult to read (because so fragmentary, so far from standard discourse, so full of hesitations and similar phenomena) that the sense of the utterances is all but lost to view. If we adopt the Oscar Lewis solution, then we run the danger of misrepresenting the original speech and rendering it implausibly fluent.

The author who renders the spoken accounts in well-turned prose, elegantly grammatical and without hesitations, is engaged in a task of textual conversion. The *spoken* narrative is translated into the conventions and appearances of *written* discourse. What *reads* like spontaneously natural speech is a highly conventionalized reconstruction or representation. The use of more-or-less standard punctuation or the textual devices of layout (starting each new conversational turn on a fresh line, using punctuation marks) are devices so familiar we remain unaware of them. The average reader will only become aware of the conventions when – as in many modern works – they are not adhered to in the 'normal' manner. The ethnographer draws on the same discursive and textual mechanisms in contriving 'natural' speech.

The other extreme is to represent the 'original' speech in such a way that preserves features of spontaneous speech. In order to do so, of course, the social scientist must again use highly contrived conventional methods. Whereas the first strategy just outlined assimilates the spoken account to the 'common' stock of textual representations, the second draws on highly specialized techniques. In recent years the interests of sociologists and anthropologists have converged with those of cognate disciplines to focus on the detailed examination of naturally occurring language. The particular intellectual commitments of conversation analysis, discourse analysis, narrative analysis, folklore (ethnopoetics), and the like differ in their respective emphases. Nevertheless, they share much common ground in the detailed treatment of spoken language.

Despite the considerable detail in which extracts of language are represented in transcriptions, the latter are not, of course, 'literal' transcriptions. They are conventional. Moreover, the particular use of the relevant conventions is a matter of interpretation, and may be intended to encourage specific responses and interpretations on the part of the reader. For instance, one of the best known sociolinguists to have directed attention to spoken language is William Labov. Labov's pioneering work on Black English Vernacular is rightly famous not only among linguists, but also among sociologists and educational researchers. His account of the 'logic of non-standard English' (1969) is a much-cited and often-anthologised demonstration of how non-standard dialect may be used to express coherently logical thought-processes. The analysis rests heavily on the speech of one respondent, 'Larry.' In the course of an interview Larry provides a vigorous account of 'what happens to you after you die.' Labov reads the relevant extract as a taut, idiomatic expression of a series of propositions. He also contrasts Larry's talk with that of a speaker of standard English, proposing that not only are the differences merely stylistic but also the non-standard English conveys *more* information and a more cogent argument.

What is less well known, perhaps, is the perceptive commentary on Labov's work by Cooper (1984). He persuasively argues that Labov himself has allowed his preconceptions and interests to colour the analysis – even to the extent of biassing his punctuation of Larry's speech! It is, of course, obvious on reflection that any punctuation of reported speech is a conventionalized imposition on the stream of utterances. It is at best a rough-and-ready representation of patterns of intonation, amplitude, tempo, and pausing. Since the utterances of natural speech rarely correspond to the grammatical constructions of 'correct' written language, the use of standard punctuation markers is a matter of interpretation. Cooper suggests that Labov inadvertently prejudges his analysis of standard and non-standard English. He punctuates Larry's speech in a very 'sympathetic' manner, so enhancing the apparent cogency of Larry's argument (which he further graces with a translation into more explicit logical propositions). The argument is, then, that we can strongly influence the apparent character of our informants in the eyes of readers by our choice of textual conventions. By choice of punctuation a narrative can be made more or less readable, more or less coherent, more or less strange to the reader.

The same sort of argument can be extended from punctuation to spelling. If we do not use strict phonetic transcription (poorly understood by most social scientists), then we are faced with all sorts of decisions about orthography. To what extent do we use standard orthography to represent variations of accent and style? There is not space to enter into this complex topic here, but a few problems and dilemmas can be noted. First, in the absence of an 'etic' transcription, the actual interpretation of the written form depends on (a) the accent of the *reader* and/or (b) the reader's prior knowledge of the reported speaker's accent. Secondly, there are frequently arbitrary boundaries to be drawn between 'standard' and 'non-standard' spelling. In everyday speech there are many fine gradations between a clear, unambiguous 'I don't know' and 'I dunno' (not to mention semantically equivalent utterances one might have to represent as something like 'A-u-know'). But where does one draw the line? A more or less continuous variation is translated into discrete categories. If one represents a great deal of speech in non-standard spellings, then the reader will likely find it barely intelligible – though it may be comprehensible in its original spoken form. Further, an over-liberal use of non-standard spellings can create a negative typification of the character in the text.

The latter is an obvious danger precisely when we are dealing with ethnic minorities and other non-standard dialect/accent users. We severely distort things if we 'transcribe' them apparently speaking with Received Pronunciation. Equally, however, we may on many occasions find it necessary to avoid the embarrassing effect associated with some fictional forms, such as the representation of Southern Black American that creates the 'Uncle Remus' image, London working-class speech in Dickens, the representation of 'stage Irish,' and so on. Apparently when Oscar Hammerstein adapted Bizet's opera *Carmen* to make *Carmen Jones*, set in a U.S. parachute factory rather than a Seville cigarette factory, and among black boxers rather than Spanish toreadors, he introduced a good deal of 'stage' black American speech. Carmen ends her seductive *habanera* with 'If I love you, dat's de end of you,' and the fighter Husky Miller begins his version of the Toreador Song with 'Stan' up an' fight until you hear de bell.'

A careless representation of 'otherness' can readily lead the writer into what Preston (1982, 1985) calls the 'Li'l Abner Syndrome.' Preston shows how some sociolinguists, folklorists, and others use conventions of orthography to produce the textual equivalents of dialect forms. Common examples are the use of forms such as *sez, wuz, wun*. When Hammerstein rewrote *Carmen*, he included *fewcher* for *future* –

quite gratuitously. Preston suggests that such forms 'serve mainly to denigrate the speaker so represented by making him or her appear boorish, uneducated, rustic, gangsterish, and so on' (1985: 328). He goes so far as to propose that virtually all respellings 'share in this defamation of character' (328).

The sustained representation of non-standard forms or regional/class accents is one way in which the 'subjects' of the reported speech may be represented as 'other' than, different from the reader *and* the ethnographer. Irrespective of the actual individuals, the implied author and reader of most texts share the speech and the written style of the literate intelligentsia. An affinity between the reader and the reported narrator may be implied by the 'standardization' of the speech, however. The life-histories and narratives that Oscar Lewis created were not reported in (translated) representations of working-class dialect or accent. The effect is, perhaps, to universalize their reported experiences; they may, too, be invested with greater gravitas and dignity in the eyes of the average reader. Short of unreadable 'etic' representations, therefore, the ethnographer who would have his or her informants 'speak for themselves' is faced with a number of decisions. Some degree of arbitrary imposition is necessary, and these decisions will have implications for just how those social actors are constructed in the text. The reflective ethnographer will need to be sensitive to the ways in which his or her representation of speech establishes the speaking subjects as 'Others' in a dialogue of difference, or assimilates them to a complicity of identity with ethnographer and reader. . . .

References

Clifford, J. (1990) 'Notes on (field)notes.' In R. Sanjek (ed.), *Fieldnotes: The Makings of Anthropology* (pp. 47–70). Ithaca, NY: Cornell University Press.

Cooper, D.E. (1984) 'Labov, Larry and Charles.' *Oxford Review of Education, 10*, 177–192.

Crapanzano, V. (1986) *Waiting: The Whites of South Africa*. London: Paladin.

Labov, W. (1969) *The Logic of Non-standard English*. Washington, DC: Center for Applied Linguistics.

Lewis, O. (1961) *The Children of Sanchez: Autobiography of a Mexican Family*. New York: Random House.

—— (1965) *La Vida: A Puerto Rican Family in the Culture of Poverty – San Juan and New York*. New York: Random House.

Preston, D.R. (1982) 'Ritin fowlklower daun 'rong: folklorists' failures in phonology.' *Journal of American Folklore, 95*, 304–326.

—— (1985) 'The Li'l Abner syndrome: written representations of speech.' *American Speech, 60*, 328–336.

Chapter 59

Renato Rosaldo

GRIEF AND A HEADHUNTER'S RAGE

From *Culture and Truth: The Remaking of Social Analysis,* London: Routledge (1989).

IF YOU ASK AN older Ilongot man of northern Luzon, Philippines, why he cuts off human heads, his answer is brief, and one on which no anthropologist can readily elaborate: He says that rage, born of grief, impels him to kill his fellow human beings. He claims that he needs a place 'to carry his anger.' The act of severing and tossing away the victim's head enables him, he says, to vent and, he hopes, throw away the anger of his bereavement. Although the anthropologist's job is to make other cultures intelligible, more questions fail to reveal any further explanation of this man's pithy statement. To him, grief, rage, and headhunting go together in a self-evident manner. Either you understand it or you don't. And, in fact, for the longest time I simply did not.

In what follows, I want to talk about how to talk about the cultural force of emotions. The *emotional force* of a death, for example, derives less from an abstract brute fact than from a particular intimate relation's permanent rupture. It refers to the kinds of feelings one experiences on learning, for example, that the child just run over by a car is one's own and not a stranger's. Rather than speaking of death in general, one must consider the subject's position within a field of social relations in order to grasp one's emotional experience.

My effort to show the force of a simple statement taken literally goes against anthropology's classic norms, which prefer to explicate culture through the gradual thickening of symbolic webs of meaning. By and large, cultural analysts use not *force* but such terms as *thick description, multi-vocality, polysemy, richness,* and *texture.* The notion of force, among other things, opens to question the common anthropological assumption that the greatest human import resides in the densest forest of symbols and that analytical detail, or 'cultural depth,' equals enhanced explanation of a culture, or 'cultural elaboration.' Do people always in fact describe most thickly what matters most to them?

The rage in Ilongot grief

Let me pause a moment to introduce the Ilongots, among whom my wife, Michelle Rosaldo, and I lived and conducted field research for thirty months (1967–69, 1974). They number about 3,500 and reside in an upland area some 90 miles northeast of Manila, Philippines. They subsist by hunting deer and wild pig and by cultivating rain-fed gardens (swiddens) with rice, sweet potatoes, manioc, and vegetables. Their (bilateral) kin relations are reckoned through men and women. After marriage, parents and their married daughters live in the same or adjacent households. The largest unit within the society, a largely territorial descent group called the *bertan*, becomes manifest primarily in the context of feuding. For them-selves, their neighbors, and their ethnographers, head-hunting stands out as the Ilongots' most salient cultural practice.

When Ilongots told me, as they often did, how the rage in bereavement could impel men to headhunt, I brushed aside their one-line accounts as too simple, thin, opaque, implausible, stereotypical, or otherwise unsatisfying. Probably I naively equated grief with sadness. Certainly no personal experience allowed me to imagine the powerful rage Ilongots claimed to find in bereavement. My own inability to conceive the force of anger in grief led me to seek out another level of analysis that could provide a deeper explanation for older men's desire to headhunt.

Not until some fourteen years after first recording the terse Ilongot statement about grief and a headhunter's rage did I begin to grasp its overwhelming force. For years I thought that more verbal elaboration (which was not forthcoming) or another analytical level (which remained elusive) could better explain older men's motives for headhunting. Only after being repositioned through a devastating loss of my own could I better grasp that Ilongot older men mean precisely what they say when they describe the anger in bereavement as the source of their desire to cut off human heads. Taken at face value and granted its full weight, their statement reveals much about what compels these older men to headhunt.

In my efforts to find a 'deeper' explanation for headhunting, I explored exchange theory, perhaps because it had informed so many classic ethnographies. One day in 1974, I explained the anthropologist's exchange model to an older Ilongot man named Insan. What did he think, I asked, of the idea that headhunting resulted from the way that one death (the beheaded victim's) canceled another (the next of kin). He looked puzzled, so I went on to say that the victim of a beheading was exchanged for the death of one's own kin, thereby balancing the books, so to speak. Insan reflected a moment and replied that he imagined somebody could think such a thing (a safe bet, since I just had), but that he and other Ilongots did not think any such thing. Nor was there any indirect evidence for my exchange theory in ritual, boast, song, or casual conversation.

In retrospect, then, these efforts to impose exchange theory on one aspect of Ilongot behavior appear feeble. Suppose I had discovered what I sought? Although the notion of balancing the ledger does have a certain elegant coherence, one wonders how such bookish dogma could inspire any man to take another man's life at the risk of his own. My life experience had not as yet provided the means to imagine the rage that can come with devastating loss. . . .

How I found the rage in grief

One burden of this introduction concerns the claim that it took some fourteen years for me to grasp what Ilongots had told me about grief, rage, and headhunting. During all those years I was not yet in a position to comprehend the force of anger possible in bereavement, and now I am. Introducing myself into this account requires a certain hesitation both because of the discipline's taboo and because of its increasingly frequent violation by essays laced with trendy amalgams of continental philosophy and autobiographical snippets. If classic ethnography's vice was the slippage from the ideal of detachment to actual indifference, that of present-day reflexivity is the tendency for the self-absorbed Self to lose sight altogether of the culturally different Other. Despite the risks involved, as the ethnographer I must enter the discussion at this point to elucidate certain issues of method.

The key concept in what follows is that of the positioned (and repositioned) subject. In routine interpretive procedure, according to the methodology of hermeneutics, one can say that ethnographers reposition themselves as they go about understanding other cultures. Ethnographers begin research with a set of questions, revise them throughout the course of inquiry, and in the end emerge with different questions than they started with. One's surprise at the answer to a question, in other words, requires one to revise the question until lessening surprises or diminishing returns indicate a stopping point. This interpretive approach has been most influentially articulated within anthropology by Clifford Geertz.

Interpretive method usually rests on the axiom that gifted ethnographers learn their trade by preparing themselves as broadly as possible. To follow the meandering course of ethnographic inquiry, field-workers require wide-ranging theoretical capacities and finely tuned sensibilities. After all, one cannot predict beforehand what one will encounter in the field. One influential anthropologist, Clyde Kluckhohn, even went so far as to recommend a double initiation: first, the ordeal of psychoanalysis, and then that of fieldwork. All too often, however, this view is extended until certain prerequisites of field research appear to guarantee an authoritative ethnography. Eclectic book knowledge and a range of life experiences, along with edifying reading and self awareness, supposedly vanquish the twin vices of ignorance and insensitivity.

Although the doctrine of preparation, knowledge, and sensibility contains much to admire, one should work to undermine the false comfort that it can convey. At what point can people say that they have completed their learning or their life experience? The problem with taking this mode of preparing the ethnographer too much to heart is that it can lend a false air of security, an authoritative claim to certitude and finality that our analyses cannot have. All interpretations are provisional; they are made by positioned subjects who are prepared to know certain things and not others. Even when knowledgeable, sensitive, fluent in the language, and able to move easily in an alien cultural world, good ethnographers still have their limits, and their analyses always are incomplete. Thus, I began to fathom the force of what Ilongots had been telling me about their losses through my own loss, and not through any systematic preparation for field research.

My preparation for understanding serious loss began in 1970 with the death of my brother, shortly after his twenty-seventh birthday. By experiencing this ordeal with my mother and father, I gained a measure of insight into the trauma of a parent's losing a child. This insight informed my account, partially described earlier, of an Ilongot man's reactions to the death of his seventh child. At the same time, my bereavement was so much less than that of my parents that I could not then imagine the overwhelming force of rage possible in such grief. My former position is probably similar to that of many in the discipline. One should recognize that ethnographic knowledge tends to have the strengths and limitations given by the relative youth of field-workers who, for the most part, have not suffered serious losses and could have, for example, no personal knowledge of how devastating the loss of a long-term partner can be for the survivor.

In 1981 Michelle Rosaldo and I began field research among the Ifugaos of northern Luzon, Philippines. On October 11 of that year, she was walking along a trail with two Ifugao companions when she lost her footing and fell to her death some 65 feet down a sheer precipice into a swollen river below. Immediately on finding her body I became enraged. How could she abandon me? How could she have been so stupid as to fall? I tried to cry. I sobbed, but rage blocked the tears. Less than a month later I described this moment in my journal: 'I felt like in a nightmare, the whole world around me expanding and contracting, visually and viscerally heaving. Going down I find a group of men, maybe seven or eight, standing still, silent, and I heave and sob, but no tears.' An earlier experience, on the fourth anniversary of my brother's death, had taught me to recognize heaving sobs without tears as a form of anger. This anger, in a number of forms, has swept over me on many occasions since then, lasting hours and even days at a time. Such feelings can be aroused by rituals, but more often they emerge from unexpected reminders (not unlike the Ilongots' unnerving encounter with their dead uncle's voice on the tape recorder).

Lest there be any misunderstanding, bereavement should not be reduced to anger, neither for myself nor for anyone else. Powerful visceral emotional states swept over me, at times separately and at other times together. I experienced the deep cutting pain of sorrow almost beyond endurance, the cadaverous cold of realizing the finality of death, the trembling beginning in my abdomen and spreading through my body, the mournful keening that started without my willing, and frequent tearful sobbing. My present purpose of revising earlier understandings of Ilongot headhunting, and not a general view of bereavement, thus focuses on anger rather than on other emotions in grief.

Writings in English especially need to emphasize the rage in grief. Although grief therapists routinely encourage awareness of anger among the bereaved, upper-middle-class Anglo-American culture tends to ignore the rage devastating losses can bring. Paradoxically, this culture's conventional wisdom usually denies the anger in grief at the same time that therapists encourage members of the invisible community of the bereaved to talk in detail about how angry their losses make them feel. My brother's death in combination with what I learned about anger from Ilongots (for them, an emotional state more publicly celebrated than denied) allowed me immediately to recognize the experience of rage.

Ilongot anger and my own overlap, rather like two circles, partially overlaid and partially separate. They are not identical. Alongside striking similarities, significant differences in tone, cultural form, and human consequences distinguish the 'anger' animating our respective ways of grieving. My vivid fantasies, for example, about a life insurance agent who refused to recognize Michelle's death as job-related did not lead me to kill him, cut off his head, and celebrate afterward. In so speaking, I am illustrating the discipline's methodological caution against the reckless attribution of one's own categories and experiences to members of another culture. Such warnings against facile notions of universal human nature can, however, be carried too far and harden into the equally pernicious doctrine that, my own group aside, everything human is alien to me. One hopes to achieve a balance between recognizing wide-ranging human differences and the modest truism that any two human groups must have certain things in common.

Only a week before completing the initial draft of an earlier version of this introduction, I rediscovered my journal entry, written some six weeks after Michelle's death, in which I made a vow to myself about how I would return to writing anthropology, if I ever did so, 'by writing Grief and a Headhunter's Rage . . .' My journal went on to reflect more broadly on death, rage, and headhunting by speaking of my 'wish for the Ilongot solution; they are much more in touch with reality than Christians. So, I need a place to carry my anger – and can we say a solution of the imagination is better than theirs? And can we condemn them when we napalm villages? Is our rationale so much sounder than theirs?' All this was written in despair and rage.

Not until some fifteen months after Michelle's death was I again able to begin writing anthropology. Writing the initial version of 'Grief and a Headhunter's Rage' was in fact cathartic, though perhaps not in the way one would imagine. Rather than following after the completed composition, the catharsis occurred beforehand. When the initial version of this introduction was most acutely on my mind, during the month before actually beginning to write, I felt diffusely depressed and ill with a fever. Then one day an almost literal fog lifted and words began to flow. It seemed less as if I were doing the writing than that the words were writing themselves through me.

My use of personal experience serves as a vehicle for making the quality and intensity of the rage in Ilongot grief more readily accessible to readers than certain more detached modes of composition. At the same time, by invoking personal experience as an analytical category one risks easy dismissal. Unsympathetic readers could reduce this introduction to an act of mourning or a mere report on my discovery of the anger possible in bereavement. Frankly, this introduction is both and more. An act of mourning, a personal report, *and* a critical analysis of anthropological method, it simultaneously encompasses a number of distinguishable processes, no one of which cancels out the others. Similarly, I argue that ritual in general and Ilongot headhunting in particular form the intersection of multiple coexisting social processes. Aside from revising the ethnographic record, the paramount claim made here concerns how my own mourning and consequent reflection on Ilongot bereavement, rage, and headhunting raise methodological issues of general concern in anthropology and the human sciences. . . .

Ethnographies that eliminate intense emotions not only distort their descriptions but also remove potentially key variables from their explanations.

. . .

This book argues that a sea change in cultural studies has eroded once-dominant conceptions of truth and objectivity. The truth of objectivism – absolute, universal, and timeless – has lost its monopoly status. It now competes, on more nearly equal terms, with the truths of case studies that are embedded in local contexts, shaped by local interests, and colored by local perceptions. The agenda for social analysis has shifted to include not only eternal verities and lawlike generalizations but also political processes, social changes, and human differences. Such terms as *objectivity*, *neutrality*, and *impartiality* refer to subject positions once endowed with great institutional authority, but they are arguably neither more nor less valid than those of more engaged, yet equally perceptive, knowledgeable social actors. Social analysis must now grapple with the realization that its objects of analysis are also analyzing subjects who critically interrogate ethnographers – their writings, their ethics, and their politics.

Chapter 60

Laurel Richardson

THE CONSEQUENCES OF POETIC REPRESENTATION

From Ellis, C. and Flaherty, M. (eds.), *Investigating Subjectivity*, Thousand Oaks, Cal.: Sage (1992).

O NE EVENING, AS PART of a larger project on unmarried mothers, I interviewed Louisa May. I transcribed the tape into 36 pages of text and then fashioned that text into a three-page poem, using *only* her words, her tone, and her diction but relying on poetic devices such as repetition, off-rhyme, meter, and pauses to convey her narrative. Poetic representation plays with connotative structures and literary devices to convey meanings; poetry commends itself to multiple and open readings in ways conventional sociological prose does not.

For sociological readers, the poem may seem to omit 'data' that they want to know. But this is Louisa May's narrative, not the sociologist's. She does not choose, for example, to talk about her educational level or her employment. The questions the poem raises for readers about Louisa May thus reflect their own particular subtexts, not universal texts. If they wonder, for example, how Louisa May supports herself, are they tapping into stereotypes about 'unwed mothers'? If they feel they cannot understand her unless they know about her schooling, are they telling us something about their own relationship to education, its meaning in their own lives? More generally, have the concepts of sociology been so reified that even interpretivists cannot believe they 'know' about a person's life without refracting it through a sociologically prescribed lens?

Here is 'Louisa May's story of her life,' a transcript masquerading as a poem/a poem masquerading as a transcript.

LOUISA MAY'S STORY OF HER LIFE

i

The most important thing
to say   is that
I grew up in the South.
Being Southern shapes
aspirations   shapes
what you think you are
and what you think you're going to be.

> *(When I hear myself, my Ladybird*
> *kind of accent on tape. I think. OH Lord,*
> *You're from Tennessee.)*

No one ever suggested to me
that anything
might happen *with* my life.

I grew up poor in a rented house
in a very normal sort of way
on a very normal sort of street
with some very nice middle-class friends

> *(Some still to this day)*

and so I thought I'd have a lot of children.

I lived outside.

Unhappy home. Stable family, till it fell apart.
The first divorce in Milfrount County.

So, that's how that was worked out.

ii

Well, one thing that happens
growing up in the South
is that you leave. I
always knew I would

I would leave.
> *(I don't know what to say . . .*
> *I don't know what's germane.)*

My high school sweetheart and I married,
went north to college.
          I got pregnant and miscarried,
and I lost the child.

(As I see it now it was a marriage
situation which got increasingly horrendous
where I was under the most stress
and strain without any sense
of how to extricate myself.)

It was purely chance
that I got a job here,
and Robert didn't.
I was mildly happy.

After 14 years of marriage,
That was the break.

We divorced.

A normal sort of life.

iii

So, the Doctor said, 'You're pregnant.'
I was 41. John and I
had had a happy kind of relationship,
not a serious one.
But beside himself with fear and anger,
awful, rageful, vengeful, horrid,
Jody Mae's father said,
'Get an Abortion.'

I told him,
'I would never marry you.
I would never marry you.
I would never.

'I am going to have this child.
I am going to.
I am. I am.

Just Go Away!'

But he wouldn't. He painted the nursery.
He slept on the floor. He went to therapy.
We went to LaMaze.

(We ceased having a sexual relationship directly
after I had gotten pregnant and that has never again
entered the situation.)

He lives 100 miles away now.
He visits every weekend.
He sleeps on the floor.
We all vacation together.
We go camping.

I am not interested in a split-family,
her father taking her on Sundays.
I'm not interested in doing so.

So, little Jody Mae always has had a situation which is normal.

Mother — bless her — the word 'married' never crossed her lips.

> *(I do resent mother's stroke. Other mothers have their mother.)*

So, it never occurs to me really that we are unusual in any way.

No, our life really is very normal. I own my house.
I live on a perfectly ordinary middle-class street.
So, that's the way that was worked out.

iv

She has his name. If she wasn't going to have a father,
I thought she should have a father, so to speak.

We both adore her.
John says Jody Mae saved his life.

OH, I do fear that something will change —

v

> *(Is this helpful?)*

This is the happiest time in my life.

I am an entirely different person.

With no husband in the home there is less tension.
And I'm not talking about abnormal families here.
Just normal circumstances. Everyone comes home tired.

I left the South a long time ago.
I had no idea how I would do it.

So, that's the way that worked out.

> *(I've talked so much my throat hurts.)*

. . . Representing the sociological as poetry is one way of decentering the unreflex-
ive 'self' to create a position for experiencing the self as a sociological knower/
constructor — not just talking about it, but doing it. In writing the Other, we can
(re)write the Self. That is the moral of this story.

I am indebted to Louisa May.
And that's the way
   this has turned
Out.

Chapter 61

John D. Brewer

THE ETHNOGRAPHIC CRITIQUE OF ETHNOGRAPHY

From *Sociology* 28(1): 231–244 (1994).

A S PART OF THE anthropological critique of ethnography, attention was given to how the great anthropologists of the past artfully constructed in their texts the impression of special insight and knowledge. Ethnographic texts in anthropology were thus deconstructed and shown to be social artefacts, as Anderson also showed for texts in natural science (1978). One of the devices by which anthropologists constructed their privileged status and created this false distinction between 'ethnographer' and 'native', was by means of what Woolgar calls exoticism (1988: 27–29). The more strange the culture being represented, the more the reader has to rely on the ethnographer's accounts; readers lack their own descriptions with which they can challenge those of the ethnographer.

While early ethnographic studies in sociology by the Chicago School had much the same quality because they focused on social worlds on the margins of modern industrial capitalism, of which mainstream society had little experience, this device can rarely work in sociology now that these margins are so well mapped and encountered. Ethnographic texts in sociology are thus more skillfully managed, imaginative and artful productions than those in anthropology. They are also more open to dispute as readers challenge the findings based on their own common sense experience of the setting.

As Atkinson shows in his deconstruction of ethnographic texts in sociology (1990), writers skillfully construct their integrity and establish the authority of the data by such means as: self-displays by the author to assert special knowledge and status; establishing the authenticity of the ethnographer's first-hand attendance and participation in the setting, and thus by extension also their account of it; providing guidelines or frames for a 'reasonable' way of reading the data; the use of various textual formats and writing styles to emphasise both the facticity of the account and graphic features of the setting; and providing 'voices in the text', by which the people observed are allowed to speak (via lengthy and judicious extracts from fieldwork notes or recorded talk) in order to validate the authenticity of the eth-nographer's description.

In this way, Atkinson identifies the social processes involved in the production of ethnographic texts. This is consistent with the general reflexivity project, in which ethnographers are encouraged to adopt a critical attitude toward their work (in writing-up as well as at other stages of research). He argues that ethnographers must be aware of these processes in writing texts if they are to be reflexive . . .

In defence of ethnography

In the hands of these ethnographers, ethnography appears to be like the Emperor at last stripped of clothes; the claims to special insight or privileged status finally shown as illusionary. However, what they attempt, on the whole, is the reconstruction rather than destruction of ethnography. Even Atkinson, whose work can be seen as the most deconstructionist, can be read as requesting simply that ethnographers do not neglect the reflexivity enterprise when writing their texts. . . . I contend that their critique offers guidelines for good ethnographic practice rather than ruling out ethnographic data completely: instructions to the Emperor as to where to find a good tailor rather than a sentence to perpetual nakedness.

With ethnographic research there are no statistical tests which others can use to check independently the researcher's interpretations and descriptions. The con-fidence which others have thus depends upon evaluations of the ethnographer's integrity and good practice. The injunctions for good practice which follow from the ethnography are clear. . . . In doing and writing up ethnographic research, eth-nographers should:

1   Establish the wider relevance of the setting and the topic, and clearly identify the grounds on which empirical generalisations are made, such as by establish-ing the representativeness of the setting, its general features, or its function as a special case study with a broader bearing.
2   Identify the features of the topic that they are addressing in the study and those left unresearched, and discuss why these choices have been made and what implications follow from these decisions for the research findings.
3   Identify the theoretical framework they are operating within, and the broader values and commitments (political, religious, theoretical and so on) they bring to their work.
4   Establish their integrity as researcher and author, by outlining:

   (i)   the grounds on which knowledge claims are being justified (length of fieldwork, the special access negotiated, discussing the extent of the trust and rapport developed with respondents, and so on);
   (ii)   their background and experience in the setting and topic;

    (iii)   their experiences during all stages of the research, especially mentioning the constraints imposed therein;

    (iv)   the strengths and weaknesses of their research design and strategy.

5   Establish the authority of the data, by:

    (i)   discussing the problems that arose during all stages of the research;

    (ii)   outlining the grounds on which they developed the categorisation system used to interpret the data, identifying clearly whether this is an indigenous one, used by respondents themselves, or an analyst-constructed one; and if the latter, the grounds which support this;

    (iii)   discussing rival explanations and alternative ways of organising the data;

    (iv)   providing sufficient data extracts in the text to allow readers to evaluate the inferences drawn from them and the interpretations made of them;

    (v)   discussing power relations within the research, between researcher(s) and subjects and within the research team, in order to establish the effects of class, gender, race and religion on the practice and writing up of the research.

6   Show the complexity of the data, avoiding the suggestion there is a simple fit between the social world under scrutiny and the ethnographic representation of it, by:

    (i)   discussing negative cases which fall outside the general patterns and categories employed to structure the ethnographic description, which often serve to exemplify and support positive cases;

    (ii)   showing the multiple and often contradictory descriptions proffered by respondents themselves;

    (iii)   stressing the contextual nature of respondents' accounts and descriptions, and identifying the features which help to structure them.

The ethnographic imagination

We need to be mindful of one more requirement if ethnographic data are to be recognised as having authority. No matter how good the practice of an ethnographer, and irrespective of their reflexivity, ethnographic data require for their authority that the reader adopt a particular perspective toward ethnography which we might call the ethnographic imagination. Atkinson (1990) uses the term to describe the creative and artful abilities of writers of ethnographic texts, but readers also need to take an imaginative leap before they can recognise the authority of the data.

    The adoption of the ethnographic imagination is not suggested as a means to ensure that readers are necessarily sympathetic to ethnographic data, or that they make allowances for this sort of research which they would not for others. Nor is it a device to ensure readers overlook bad ethnographic practice and the weaknesses of the data. Rather, it calls for an openness in people's attitude toward ethnographic data in which their reliability, usefulness and import is not immediately dismissed out of hand; that readers accept that ethnographic data have strengths rather than focusing entirely on their limitations – a readiness to see the Emperor clothed rather than naked.

The ethnographic imagination has three dimensions, which are predicated on the injunctions for good ethnographic practice:

1   The belief that fragments of recorded talk, extracts from fieldwork notes, and reports of observed actions can reliably represent a social world which cannot be completely described in the restricted spatial confines of an ethnographic text, so long as the ethnographer has been reflexive and thereby established his or her integrity and the authority of the data.

2   The belief that small-scale, micro events in everyday life have at least common features with the broader social world, such that general processes permeate down to and are in part reproduced at the level of people's everyday lives. Thus, microscopic events can illustrate features of broader social processes, so long as the ethnographer sets out the grounds on which these empirical generalisations are made.

3   The belief that people make sense of their everyday lives, and offer accounts and descriptions thereof, involving a complex reasoning process, which must be analysed if that social world is to be understood in the round, rather than being ignored or accepted at face value . . .

Some readers of ethnographic texts will always dispute the data because they are resistant to adopting the ethnographic imagination, wishing for other forms of empirical evidence and testing. They can interpret data and arguments differently in the light of other value systems, theoretical frameworks, viewpoints and experiences. Their objections cannot be satisfied through appeals to good practice because these are epistemological rather than technical differences. Thus, no set of guidelines or conditions will ever be sufficient to rule out alternative explanations. At best an ethnographer (like all social scientists) can only persuade the reader to agree that the explanation is a plausible one, but not that it is the *only* plausible one. However, critics who dispute an argument's plausibility are duty bound to offer the grounds on which it is implausible. The thrust of this paper is to claim that it is insufficient for critics now to do so merely by reference to the fact that it is based on ethnographic data; by following guidelines such as the above, ethnography can be made more systematic and less easily dismissed.

References

Anderson, D. (1978) 'Some organisational features of the local production of a plausible text'. *The Philosophy of the Social Sciences* 8: 113–35.

Atkinson, P. (1990) *The Ethnographic Imagination*. London: Routledge.

Woolgar, S. (1988) 'Reflexivity is the ethnographer of the text' in S. Woolgar (ed.), *Knowledge and Reflexivity*. London: Sage.

PART THIRTEEN

Postmodernism

INTRODUCTION

MANY HAVE FELT THAT the considerations that accompanied increased reflexivity mean that there is a crisis of legitimation and representation in social research and the human sciences generally. Postmodernism is a term that seeks to embrace this crisis, and incorporate social researchers in new forms of intellectual activity. The readings in this part of the book all suggest ways in which this might be done. Bauman's statement about this shift (reading 62) takes the form of a distinction between intellectuals (for which read 'social researchers') who act as 'legislators', whom he identifies with a modernist stance on matters like objectivity, universality and social control, and 'interpreters' who occupy a more relativist stance, seeing their role as one of facilitating and deepening the level of 'conversations' between groups.

Sarup's account of the ideas of Lyotard (reading 63) takes us closer to an understanding of the postmodernist position. Lyotard, claims Sarup, distinguishes between the 'denotative' language game of 'epic' science legitimated by the state, and narrative knowledge, where issues of truth merge with those of beauty and justice in stories that promote social bonds. Importantly, scientific truths depend on narrative methods to establish their credibility and authority.

Frank's discussion of the issues involved when researchers get interested in suffering brings the generalized discussions of Bauman and Lyotard to the level of research practice. Specifically, Frank is concerned with the relations between researchers and their subjects, starting from his own standpoint as one who has experienced the suffering of illness. Drawing on the ideas of Levinas, he criticizes research practice which seeks to form an extra-local, generalizable form of knowledge through the categorization of different forms of suffering. This, he claims, does violence to the experience of suffering. Such an approach censors experiences that do not fit into the master text.

Frank's own research practice aims to amplify the voices of ill people by allowing them to tell their stories from more prominent vantage points, so that professionals and others with power can hear these stories more fully.

The postmodern alternative to modernist aspirations to extra-local knowledge raises issues for discussions of the validity of social research. Lather (reading 65) seeks to ground a postmodern approach to validity in the conduct of particular research studies that serve as exemplars. She argues for a commitment to disruption of scientific categories through research practice. One of her examples is the writing practice of Richardson (for which see reading 60), which she feels demonstrates an appropriate form of 'disruptive excess'.

Schwandt continues the discussion of validity that arises from an acceptance of the postmodern critique of science. Like others in this part of the book, Schwandt wants to go beyond objectivism and the adoption of a 'third-person' viewpoint, characteristic of both the quantitative tradition and qualitative, interpretivist alternatives. Collaborative inquiry that enhances the practical reasoning and critical intelligence of participants while 'decentring' the authority of the researcher is preferable. This is a more democratic mode of research practice and essentially substitutes for theoretical explanation the goal of practical emancipation.

DISCUSSION POINTS

- Bauman says that postmodernism does not supersede or invalidate modernism. What kind of social research practice, then, is desirable?
- Compare Bauman and Lyotard's ideas about legislators, scientific knowledge, interpreters and narrative knowledge. What parallels do you see?
- Frank's discussion begins from his own experience of suffering. Rosaldo's research practice (reading 59) also involves an account of his own suffering and an exploration of its relevance for his research practice. What differences do you see between Rosaldo and Frank? For example, would Rosaldo concur with Frank's critique of 'extra-local' knowledge? How do Frank's ideas about the role of research fit in with the conceptual distinctions set up by Bauman and Lyotard?
- The piece by Lather is, for me, the most uncomfortably jargon-ridden writing in this book. I found it almost impossible to edit so that it made sense to me and even now I can only relate to parts of it because of the difficulty of the language. How was it for you? Can you summarize her arguments? What consequences might they have for research practice? Should we give up on difficult writing, or carry on trying to understand the message?
- Imagine that you are researching (a) the activities of a pressure group seeking justice for asylum seekers and (b) the activities of a fascist group. For each of these, consider how you would apply the emancipatory research practice recommended by Schwandt. In each case, how would you know whether you had achieved a study that, in his terms, was a good study?

FURTHER READING

Denzin, N.K. and Lincoln, Y.S. (1994) *Handbook of Qualitative Research*, Thousand Oak, Cal.: Sage (see particularly sections written by the editors)

—— (2000) *Handbook of Qualitative Research*, Thousand Oak, Cal.: Sage, 2nd edition (see particularly sections written by the editors)

Dickens, D.R. and Fontana, A. (1994) (eds) *Postmodernism and Social Inquiry*, London: University College London Press.

Docherty, T. (ed.) (1993) *Postmodernism: A Reader*, London: Harvester Wheatsheaf.

Game, A. (1991) *Undoing the Social: Towards a Deconstructive Sociology*, Buckingham: Open University Press.

Lyotard, J-F. (1984), *The Postmodern Condition: A Report on Knowledge*, Manchester: Manchester University Press.

Scheurich, J. (1999) *Research Method in the Postmodern*, Brighton: Falmer Press.

Smart, B. (1993) *Postmodernity*, London: Routledge.

Chapter 62

Zygmunt Bauman

INTELLECTUALS
From modern legislators to post-modern interpreters

From *Legislators and Interpreters,* Cambridge: Polity (1987).

W HEN IT WAS COINED in the early years of the present century, the word 'intellectuals' was an attempt to recapture and reassert that societal centrality and those global concerns which had been associated with the production and dissemination of knowledge during the age of Enlightenment. The word was addressed to a motley collection of novelists, poets, artists, journalists, scientists and other public figures who felt it their moral responsibility, and their collective right, to interfere directly with the political process through influencing the minds of the nation and moulding the actions of its political leaders. . . .

It makes no sense to compose a list of professions whose members are intellectuals, or draw a line inside professional hierarchy above which the intellectuals are located. In any place and at any time 'the intellectuals' are constituted as a combined effect of mobilization and self-recruitment. The intentional meaning of 'being an intellectual' is to rise above the partial preoccupation of one's own profession or artistic *genre* and engage with the global issues of truth, judgement and taste of the time. The line dividing 'intellectuals' and 'non-intellectuals' is drawn and redrawn by decisions to join in a particular mode of activity. . . .

In referring to intellectual practices, the opposition between the terms modern and post-modern stands for differences in understanding the nature of the world, and the social world in particular, and in understanding the related nature, and purpose, of intellectual work.

The typically modern view of the world is one of an essentially orderly totality; the presence of a pattern of uneven distribution of probabilities allows a sort of explanation of the events which – if correct – is simultaneously a tool of prediction and (if required resources are available) of control. Control ('mastery over nature', 'planning' or 'designing' of society) is well nigh synonymously associated with ordering action, understood as the manipulation of probabilities (rendering some events more likely, others less likely). Effectivity of control depends on the adequacy of knowledge of the 'natural' order. Such adequate knowledge is, in principle, attainable. Effectivity of control and correctness of knowledge are tightly related (the second explains the first, the first corroborates the second), whether in laboratory experiment or societal practice. Between themselves, they supply criteria to classify existing practices as superior or inferior. Such classification is – again in principle – objective, that is, publicly testable and demonstrable each time the above-mentioned criteria are applied. Practices which cannot be objectively justified (for example, practices which legitimize themselves by reference to habits or opinions binding in a particular locality or particular time) are inferior as they distort knowledge and limit effectivity of control. Moving up the hierarchy of practices measured by the control/knowledge syndrome, means also moving toward universality and away from 'parochial', 'particularistic', 'localized' practices.

The typically post-modern view of the world is, in principle, one of an unlimited number of models of order, each one generated by a relatively autonomous set of practices. Order does not precede practices and hence cannot serve as an outside measure of their validity. Each of the many models of order makes sense solely in terms of the practices which validate it. In each case, validation brings in criteria which are developed within a particular tradition; they are upheld by the habits and beliefs of a 'community of meanings' and admit of no other tests of legitimacy. Criteria described above as 'typically modern' are no exception to this general rule; they are ultimately validated by one of the many possible 'local traditions', and their historical fate depends on the fortunes of the tradition in which they reside. There are no criteria for evaluating local practices which are situated outside traditions, outside 'localities'. Systems of knowledge may only be evaluated from 'inside' their respective traditions. If, from the modern point of view, relativism of knowledge was a problem to be struggled against and eventually overcome in theory and in practice, from the post-modern point of view relativity of knowledge (that is, its 'embeddedness' in its own communally supported tradition) is a lasting feature of the world.

The typically modern strategy of intellectual work is one best characterized by the metaphor of the 'legislator' role. It consists of making authoritative statements which arbitrate in controversies of opinions and which select those opinions which, having been selected, become correct and binding. The authority to arbitrate is in this case legitimized by superior (objective) knowledge to which intellectuals have a better access than the non-intellectual part of society. Access to such knowledge is better thanks to procedural rules which assure the attainment of truth, the arrival at valid moral judgement, and the selection of proper artistic taste. Such procedural rules have a universal validity, as do the products of their application. The employment of such procedural rules makes the intellectual professions (scientists, moral philosophers, aesthetes) collective owners of knowledge of direct and crucial relevance to the maintenance and perfection of the social order. The condition of this being so is the work of the 'intellectuals proper' – meta-professionals, so to speak – to be responsible for the formulation of procedural rules and to control their correct application. Like the knowledge they produce, intellectuals are not bound by localized, communal traditions. They are, together with their knowledge, extra-territorial. This gives them the right and the duty to validate (or invalidate) beliefs which may be held in various sections of society. Indeed, as Popper observed, falsifying poorly founded, or unfounded views is what the procedural rules are best at.

The typically post-modern strategy of intellectual work is one best character-ized by the metaphor of the 'interpreter' role. It consists of translating statements, made within one communally based tradition, so that they can be understood within the system of knowledge based on another tradition. Instead of being orientated towards selecting the best social order, this strategy is aimed at facilitating com-munication between autonomous (sovereign) participants. It is concerned with pre-venting the distortion of meaning in the process of communication. For this pur-pose, it promotes the need to penetrate deeply the alien system of knowledge from which the translation is to be made (for example, Geertz's 'thick description'), and the need to maintain the delicate balance between the two conversing traditions necessary for the message to be both undistorted (regarding the meaning invested by the sender) and understood (by the recipient). It is vitally important to note that the post-modern strategy does not imply the elimination of the modern one; on the contrary, it cannot be conceived without the continuation of the latter. While the post-modern strategy entails the abandonment of the universalistic am-bitions of the intellectuals' own tradition, it does not abandon the universalistic ambitions of the intellectuals towards their own tradition; here, they retain their meta-professional authority, legislating about the procedural rules which allow them to arbitrate controversies of opinion and make statements intended as binding. . . .

One last remark is in order. In no way am I implying that the post-modern mode constitutes an advance over the modern one, that the two may be arranged in a progressive sequence in any of the possible meanings of the notoriously confusing idea of 'progress'. Moreover, I do not believe that modernity, as a type of intel-lectual mode, has been conclusively superseded by the advent of post-modernity, or that the latter has refuted the validity of the first (if one can refute anything taking a consistently post-modern stance). I am merely interested in understanding the social conditions under which the appearance of the two modes has been possible; and the factors responsible for their changing fortunes. . . .

Chapter 63

Madan Sarup

POSTMODERNISM

From *An Introductory Guide to Post-structuralism and Postmodernism*, Hemel Hempstead: Harvester Wheatsheaf (1993).

. . .

THE TERM POSTMODERNISM ORIGINATED among artists and critics in New York in the 1960s and was taken up by European theorists in the 1970s. One of them, Jean-François Lyotard, in a famous book entitled *The Postmodern Condition*, attacked the legitimating myths of the modern age ('the grand narratives'), the progressive liberation of humanity through science, and the idea that philosophy can restore unity to learning and develop universally valid knowledge for humanity. Postmodern theory became identified with the critique of universal knowledge and foundationalism. Lyotard believes that we can no longer talk about a totalizing idea of reason for there is no reason, only reasons.

. . . Many commentators stress that postmodernists espouse a model which emphasizes not depth but surface. They are highly critical of structuralism and Marxism and are antagonistic to any theory that 'goes beyond' the manifest to the latent. . . . There are continual references to eclecticism, reflexivity, self-referentiality, quotation, artifice, randomness, anarchy, fragmentation, pastiche and allegory. Moreover, with the development of postmodernism in recent years, there has been a move to 'textualize' everything: history, philosophy, jurisprudence, sociology and other disciplines are treated as so many optional 'kinds of writing' or discourses. . . .

I will focus on Lyotard's reflections on science, the changing nature of knowledge in computerized societies, the differences between narrative knowledge and scientific knowledge, the ways in which knowledge is legitimated and sold, and the social changes that may take place in the future. . . . Lyotard is a post-structuralist who adopts a postmodernist stance. . . .

In *The Postmodern Condition* Lyotard argues that during the last forty years the leading sciences and technologies have become increasingly concerned with language: theories of linguistics, problems of communication and cybernetics, computers and their languages, problems of translation, information storage and data banks.

The technological transformations are having a considerable impact on knowledge. The miniaturization and commercialization of machines are already changing the way in which learning is acquired, classified, made available and exploited.

Lyotard believes that the nature of knowledge cannot survive unchanged within this context of general transformation. The status of knowledge is altered as societies enter what is known as the postmodern age. He predicts that anything in the constituted body of knowledge that is not translatable into quantities of information will be abandoned and the direction of new research will be dictated by the possibility of its eventual results being translatable into computer language. The old principle that the acquisition of knowledge is indissociable from the training of minds, or even of individuals, is becoming obsolete. Knowledge is already ceasing to be an end in itself. It is and will be produced in order to be sold. . . .

For Lyotard knowledge is a question of competence that goes beyond the simple determination and application of the criterion of truth, extending to the determination of criteria of efficiency (technical qualification), of justice and/or happiness (ethical wisdom), of beauty (auditory or visual sensibility), etc. Knowledge is what makes someone capable of forming not only 'good' denotative utterances but also 'good' prescriptive and 'good' evaluative utterances. But how are they to be assessed? They are judged to be good if they conform to the relevant criteria (of justice, beauty, truth and efficiency) accepted in the social circle of the 'knower's' interlocutors.

It is important to mention here that Lyotard, who has been greatly influenced by Wittgenstein's notion of language games, makes the following observations. Each of the various categories of utterance can be defined in terms of rules specifying their properties and the uses to which they can be put. The rules of language games do not carry within themselves their own legitimation, but are objects of a contract, explicit or not, between players; if there are no rules, there is no game. Every utterance is thought of as a 'move' in a game. Messages have quite different forms and effects depending on whether they are, for example, denotatives, prescriptions, evaluatives, performatives, etc.

Lyotard believes that language games are incommensurable. He distinguishes the denotative game (in which what is relevant is the true/false distinction) from the prescriptive game (in which the just/unjust distinction pertains) and from the technical game (in which the criterion is the efficient/inefficient distinction). It seems to me that Lyotard sees between tricksters. . . .

Narrative knowledge and scientific knowledge

Scientific knowledge does not represent the totality of knowledge; it has always existed in competition and conflict with another kind of knowledge which Lyotard calls narrative. In traditional societies there is a pre-eminence of the narrative form. Narratives (popular stories, myths, legends and tales) bestow legitimacy upon social institutions, or represent positive or negative models of integration into established institutions. Narratives determine criteria of competence and/or illustrate how they are to be applied. They thus define what has the right to be said and done in the culture in question.

In traditional societies a narrative tradition is also the tradition of the criterion defining a threefold competence – 'know-how', 'knowing how to speak' and 'knowing how to hear' – through which the community's relationship to itself and its environment is played out. In the narrative form statements about truth, justice and beauty are often woven together. What is transmitted through these narratives is the set of rules that constitute the social bond.

Lyotard discusses the retreat of the claims of narrative or story-telling knowledge in the face of those of the abstract, denotative or logical and cognitive procedures generally associated with science. In the science language game the sender is supposed to be able to provide proof of what s/he says, and on the other hand s/he is supposed to be able to refute any opposing or contradictory statements concerning the same referent. Scientific rules underlie what nineteenth-century science calls verification, and twentieth-century science falsification. They allow a horizon of consensus to be brought to the debate between partners (the sender and the addressee). Not every consensus is a sign of truth, but it is presumed that the truth of a statement necessarily draws a consensus. Now, scientists need an addressee, a partner who can verify their statements and in turn become the sender. Equals are needed and must be created.

Didactics is what ensures that this reproduction takes place. Its first presupposition is that the student does not know what the sender knows; obviously this is why s/he has something to learn. Its second presupposition is that the student can learn what the sender knows and become an expert whose competence is equal to that of the teacher. As the students improve their skills, experts can confide in them what they do not know but are trying to learn. In this way students are introduced to the game of producing scientific knowledge. In scientific knowledge any already accepted statement can always be challenged. Any new statement that contradicts a previously approved statement regarding the same referent can be accepted as valid only if it refutes the previous statement.

The main difference between scientific knowledge and narrative knowledge is that scientific knowledge requires that one language game, denotation, be retained and all others be excluded. Both science and non-scientific (narrative) knowledge are equally necessary. Both are composed of sets of statements; the statements are 'moves' made by the players within the framework of generally applicable rules. These rules are specific to each particular kind of knowledge, and the 'moves' judged to be 'good' in one cannot be the same as those judged 'good' in another (unless it happens that way by chance). It is therefore impossible to judge the existence or validity of narrative knowledge on the basis of scientific knowledge or vice versa: the relevant criteria are different.

Lyotard argues that narrative knowledge certifies itself without having recourse to argumentation and proof. Scientists, however, question the validity of narrative statements and conclude that they are never subject to argumentation or proof. Narratives are classified by the scientist as belonging to a different mentality: savage, primitive, underdeveloped, backward, alienated, composed of opinions, customs, authority, prejudice, ignorance, ideology. Narratives are fables, myths, legends fit only for women and children.

Here there is an interesting twist in Lyotard's argument. He says that scientific knowledge cannot know and make known that it is the true knowledge without resorting to the other, narrative kind of knowledge, which from its point of view is no knowledge at all. In short, there is a recurrence of the narrative in the scientific.

The state spends large amounts of money to enable science to pass itself off as an epic. The state's own credibility is based on that epic, which it uses to obtain the public consent its decision-makers need. Science, in other words, is governed by the demand of legitimation. . . .

Chapter 64

Arthur W. Frank

CAN WE RESEARCH SUFFERING?

From *Qualitative Health Research* 11 (3): 353–362 (2001).

. . .

I **PROPOSE THAT RESEARCH** has a problem encountering suffering, and in its evasions of suffering, research can create more suffering for ill people. I begin with my own suffering. Just more than 6 years ago after an annual follow-up examination for cancer, my chest X ray showed lymph nodes on my lung and diaphragm. I was used to false positives on these tests, but then a computed tomography scan showed more nodes than the X ray had. . . . I was surprised, afraid, and I suffered. . . . I would learn from a later biopsy that I was sick but not with cancer. The sickness I had – an inflammation of the lymph system called sarcoidosis – would never have been diagnosed if I had not been followed for cancer. Sarcoidosis can be a very serious disease, but my case had no effect on how I felt. I called it my virtual illness.

During the month between getting the bad news of the irregular chest X ray and receiving the good news about the biopsy, my paradoxical condition was to enjoy very good health in the verified presence of serious illness. I experienced the suffering of illness without experiencing any disease. My bizarre confluence of circumstances turned that month into a controlled experiment in pure suffering. . . .

Let me tell a story that begins to suggest why suffering is so difficult to define and to research. As part of the preoperative routine before my biopsy surgery, I was interviewed by a nurse who asked me, at the end of her inventory of required questions, how my wife and I were coping with my possible cancer. I told her that we had a new baby, my wife was still recovering from a difficult pregnancy and birth, and we were doing very badly indeed. Her reply confirmed my worst suspicions about medical pretenses to caring and also taught me much about suffering. 'You have to talk to each other,' she admonished as she closed her clipboard and left. End of interview; no follow-up was offered. Of course she was right; we certainly needed to talk to each other. But our suffering was why we could not talk. Our suffering was what we could not say. We feared saying what we felt, and we feared our words could never convey what we felt but would reduce those feelings to complaints and specific concerns. 'Don't you know,' I wanted to shout to that nurse as she walked away, 'it's what your patients can't say.' . . .

The medical model, so potent against what can be located, identified, and acted upon, is equally impotent against suffering that resists location, identification, and action. As an organized enterprise, medicine's war against suffering is like Napoleon's invasion of Russia; the enemy continues to withdraw while the conquering army becomes increasingly hungry, flea- and frostbitten, homesick, and depressed. The problem – which I hope my contrasting illness experiences illustrate – is that suffering has no necessary connection to illness. Illness is only one occasion for suffering. Individual medical professionals certainly engage their patients' suffering and can diminish it, but I suggest that they do so by working outside the biomedical model. My present concern, however, is not medical professionals but researchers.

My case that qualitative health research has difficulty encountering suffering begins with a critique presented by Dorothy Smith (1999), describing the rhetorical form of sociological texts. The book she refers to happens to be about soccer violence, but 'the young men' she talks about could just as well be the sample in a study of some disease:

> At the beginning of the book, they describe the young men they studied as the 'dramatis personae.' The metaphor expresses exactly the sociological relation created in the text. Respondents have the appearance of free agents. They have the appearance of speaking with their own voices. But, in fact, the sociologists' script prescribes how they appear and what they say. The sociologists speak through their dramatis personae. Standpoint has effectively been conceptually shifted from that of the young men with whom they talked, and whose viewpoint they wanted to make central, back to the standpoint of the discourse locating the reading subject in the relations of ruling.
>
> (p. 67)

This passage troubles me because it describes work I have done myself, work I have refereed and reviewed, and work I have supervised.

Smith (1999) describes how 'theory is deployed to pick out and tailor extracts from the original events to appear conceptually reconstructed or as fragments of speech or writing sustaining the discursive project' (p. 141). What is wrong with such work begins with the respondents who are thus fragmented and reconstructed. During a session at the 1998 meeting of the American Sociological Association, I invited a friend in the audience, Shelly Diamond, to respond to a discussion about the ethics of such conceptual reconstruction of respondents. She spoke eloquently about how disrespected she felt when she read the research reports that included her responses to an interview study concerning her particular illness. What insulted her was the fragmentation of her story described by Smith. Bits of her story were made to reappear as instances validating whatever point the social scientist was making in that particular chapter. The literal integrity of her story was sacrificed to generate the apparent integrity of the social scientist's narrative. If only the feelings of respondents were at stake, the issue would be serious enough but not, I think, as serious as it is.

Many qualitative researchers would reply to Smith (1999) that what she calls the script is not the sociologist's creation – as Smith claims it is – but is inductively derived from the respondents themselves. Researchers seek to reassure themselves of this by taking the script back to the respondents to verify that they recognize it as theirs, thus guaranteeing that it is not being imposed on them. For all that gesture has to recommend it, I believe it fails to understand what is crucial for Smith. If the sociological text that respondents are being asked to approve is, as Smith contends, an extension of the relations of ruling in which those respondents are already embedded, then their approval might signal their resignation to the inescapability of those ruling relations: They offer not assent but capitulation to the authority of social science . . .

I can now return to Smith's (1999) complex sentence, quoted above: 'Standpoint has been conceptually shifted from that of [the respondents] . . . back to the standpoint of the discourse locating the reading subject in the relations of ruling' (p. 67). As part of their organization of local settings, texts organize how they themselves are read. The reader – whether medical professional or patient – is required to adopt the extralocal perspective from which the text makes sense. Through the dominance of this perspective, Smith writes, 'The stylistics of universality are preserved against the threat of fragmentation and disorder' (p. 153). This threat – and I will speak later about suffering as a prime example of such threats – is that the problematic of the local situation might challenge the organizing effect of the text. Texts that meet such challenges must do more than tell local readers what actions to undertake. Texts must also alter the standpoint of local readers, who are taught by the text to dismiss such challenges. The stylistics of universality endow readers with the extralocal relevances of ruling relations. Such relevances dictate ignoring what is now merely local, such as suffering. . . .

The problem for ill people is ruling relations' insistence that all can be spoken; the nurse who said that my wife and I must talk to each other expressed this insistence. Research is one practice – psychotherapy is often another – in which ruling relations demand that all be spoken. Such research organizes suffering by making it reappear as categories that may all be valid enough for what can be spoken, but they refuse to acknowledge that aspects of suffering remain unspeakable. Suffering, the mute embodied sense of absence, both eludes extralocal categories and threatens the standpoint of discourse that supports those categories. Suffering threatens discourse because discourse cannot assimilate it to extralocal demands. When expressions of suffering break into discourse, the reader is returned to his or her own contingent embodiment in all its locality. When one's own body is attended to, the textual spell of the extralocal is broken . . .

I propose that the problem of suffering is not how we know it but how we encounter it. I follow the philosopher Emmanuel Levinas (1985, 1989, 1998) in understanding suffering as a call; to encounter one who suffers is to feel called to respond. As I understand Levinas, even the substantive noun *suffering* should be suspect. The only reality is the face – the embodied humanity – of the person who suffers. Levinas teaches, perhaps more clearly than anyone, that this responsibility to recognize and respond to suffering is emphatically not to pretend to know the other's suffering. As Robbins (1999) writes, for Levinas, the other 'is not under a category. He is the one to whom I speak' (p. 10). To place the other under a category is, for Levinas, a form of symbolic violence against the other. A claim to know the other's suffering takes away part of that other's integrity. An appropriate Levinasian model of response to suffering would seem to be Job's friends during the 7 days and nights while they sit with him in silence, before they begin to interrogate him.

A researcher might respond to Levinas, 'What do you want from me?' The task of research is to specify the conditions that cause suffering so that these conditions can be changed to lessen suffering. The task of the researcher is not to sit in silence with Job but to find out how he got onto the dung heap so that others can be kept off similar dung heaps. Research seeks to find what resources Job may need to get himself off his dung heap. Research can claim that it is empathic and compassionate, whereas Levinas's emphasis on the absolute alterity of the other – the unknowable nature of the other's suffering – seems distant, even cold. For all Levinas's talk of responsibility for the other, he seems to create a greater distance from that other's situation and the possibility of changing it.

This response to Levinas would make sense if one accepts its fundamental premise. This premise is given ironic expression by Jean Baudrillard (1998), writing about the logic of consumer society in which every desire is assured of finding a corresponding object that can bring satisfaction. Failures of satisfaction can never be acknowledged. 'All the things [that] do not fit into this positive vision,' Baudrillard writes, 'are rejected, censored by satisfaction itself . . . and no longer finding any possible outlet, crystallize into a gigantic fund of anxiety' (p. 177). . . .

Ruling relations provide assurance, from their extralocal omniscient site, that local needs are being met and there is no reason not to feel satisfied. All the things that do not fit this assurance are, as Baudrillard (1998) said, censored; the text allows no space for their presence. Smith (1999) makes the same point when she writes, 'The dialogue interior to the text offers no purchase to the challenge offered by counter-examples' (p. 152) and later when she describes 'the power of a theoretical text to insulate the discourse against subversive voices' (p. 155). Suffering is the subversive voice in the biomedical discourse; it is central among all the things that do not fit. Social science and biomedical discourse perpetuate this censoring when they reduce suffering's embodied locality to extralocal categories that organize responses. Clinicians informed by such discourse respond not to the person who suffers but to the person viewed as an instance of a type of suffering that the text has taught the professional to recognize.

Any concluding prescriptions of new ways of doing qualitative health research risk becoming more extralocal organizing of your local practice, but we all need some principles through which we can reflect on our practices. Smith (1999) offers one especially clear guideline when she writes, 'The aim is not to explain people's behavior but to be able to explain to them/ourselves the socially organized powers in which their/our lives are embedded and to which their/our activities contribute' (p. 8). Too much research on illness rewrites their and/or our lives as behavior to be explained: coping, giving and receiving support, denial, adherence (the more politically correct name for the old compliance), even grieving all become behaviors to be explained as functional and adaptive with reference to clinically normative standards. Smith advocates a different aim: not explaining respondents' behavior to experts but explaining social systems to respondents so they can understand the powers in which their lives are embedded.

A complementary aim of research, less ambitious social scientifically and closer to my own previous work, is to use academic privileges of publication and platform to amplify the voices of the ill themselves, offering them previously unrecognized connections and a sense of community. Insofar as my work does employ organizing categories, I have sought to construct categories that do not explain ill people's experiences and their stories. The aim of mapping stories is to allow ill people to connect their stories to others and perhaps to recognize what stories they have not yet told. A complementary aim is to offer professionals an enhanced sense of the different stories people tell; to get them to think less about these stories and more with these stories (Frank 1995). Sometimes, thinking with the story means listening to silence, to the story that resists becoming a narrative. . . .

References

Baudrillard, J. (1998) *The Consumer Society*. London: Sage.

Frank, A.W. (1995) *The Wounded Storyteller: Body, Illness, and Ethics*. Chicago: University of Chicago Press.

Levinas, E. (1985) *Ethics and Infinity*. Pittsburgh: Duquesne University Press.

—— (1989) *The Levinas Reader* (S. Hand, ed.). Cambridge, Mass.: Blackwell.

—— (1998) *Entre Nous: Thinking-of-the-other*. New York: Columbia University Press.

Robbins, J. (1999) *Altered Reading: Levinas and Literature*. Chicago: University of Chicago Press.

Smith, D.E. (1987) *The Everyday World as Problematic: A Feminist Sociology*. Toronto: University of Toronto Press.

—— (1999) *Reading the Social: Critique, Theory, and Investigations*. Toronto: University of Toronto Press.

Chapter 65

Patti Lather

FERTILE OBSESSION
Validity after poststructuralism

From *Sociological Quarterly* 34 (4): 673–693 (1993).

[P]ost-modernism involves the development of new rhetories of science, new stories of knowledge 'after truth' . . . The postmodern world is without guarantees, without 'method' . . . All we can do is invent. We must construct and exemplify the rhetorics of the future . . . through . . . endless stories. Like this one.

Tomlinson (1989), 44, 57

Validity as an incitement to discourse

POISED AT THE END of the twentieth century, the human sciences are in search of a discourse to help chart the journey from the present to the future. Withering critiques of realism, universalism and individualism take us into the millennium . . . Conferences are held to explore the End of Science, others argue for science as rhetoric . . ., narrative . . . and/or social practice . . . Regardless of terms, each is part of some move 'to grow up in our attitudes toward science' in an antifoundational era characterized by the loss of certainties and absolute frames of reference . . .

This article comes out of such ferment and is written against 'the merely deconstructive and the endlessly prefatory' (Borgmann 1992: 2). Believing that 'science is a performance' (Fine 1986: 148), my effort is to anticipate a generative methodology that registers a possibility and marks a provisional space in which a different science might take form. Seeking answers to such a project in inquiry as it is lived, the article works at the edges of what is currently available in moving toward a science with more to answer to in terms of the complexities of language and the world.

In pursuit of a less comfortable social science, I continue my seeming obsession with the topic of validity: the conditions of the legitimation of knowledge in contemporary postpositivism. Over the last decade or so of postpositivism, the boundaries surrounding the issue of research legitimation have been constructed from many angles: naturalistic and constructivist . . ., discourse theory . . ., ethnographic authority . . .; poststructuralism . . .; forms of validity appropriate to an emancipatory interest. . . . Long interested in how the core but changing concept of validity is shaped across the proliferation of 'paradigms' that so characterizes post-positivism (Lather 1991b), my thoughts on validity are on the move again. While extending my earlier work toward counter-practices of authority that are adequate to emancipatory interests (Lather 1986a, 1986b), my primary desire here is to rethink validity in light of antifoundational discourse theory. Rather than jettisoning 'validity' as the term of choice, I retain the term in order to both circulate and break with the signs that code it. What I mean by the term, then, is all of the baggage that it carries plus, in a doubled-movement, what it means to rupture validity as a regime of truth. . . .

'Where, after the metanarratives, can legitimacy reside?' Lyotard asks (1984: xxv). This article addresses Lyotard's question via a dispersion, circulation, and proliferation of counter-practices of authority that take the crisis of representation into account. What are the antifoundational possibilities outside the limits of the normative framings of validity in the human sciences? What might open-ended and context sensitive validity criteria look like? Why is validity the site of such attraction? How much of this obsession with legitimation/validity issues in research methodology is part of the disciplinary nature of our society of confession and conscience? This paper is situated at the nexus of such doubled questions. Fragmenting and colliding both hegemonic and oppositional codes, my goal is to reinscribe validity in a way that uses the antifoundational problematic to loosen the master code of positivism that continues to so shape even postpositivism (Scheurich 1991). My task is to do so in a way that refuses over-simple answers to intractable questions.

The masks of methodology

. . . Post-epistemic concerns reframe validity as multiple, partial, endlessly deferred. They construct a site of development for a *validity of transgression* that runs counter to the standard *validity of correspondence*: a nonreferential validity interested in how discourse does its work, where transgression is defined as 'the game of limits . . . at the border of disciplines, and across the line of taboo' (Pefanis 1991: 85; see, also, Foucault 1977).

In the discourses of the social sciences, validity has always been the problem, not the solution (Cronbach and Meehl 1955). Across such qualitative practices as member checks and peer debriefing (Lincoln and Guba 1985), triangulation (Denzin 1989), and catalytic validity (Lather 1986b), various postpositivist efforts have been made to resolve the problem without exhausting it, constantly providing answers to and freeing itself from the problem, but always partially, temporarily. More recently and more attuned to discourse theory, Mishler's (1990) reformulation traces the irrelevance of standard approaches to validity through various postpositivist efforts to rearticulate it. Reframing validity as 'problematic in a deep theoretical sense, rather than as a technical problem' (p. 417), Mishler surveys some 'candidate exemplars' for generating new practices of validation that do not rely on a correspondence model of truth or assumptions of transparent narration. . . . To not revert to the dominant foundational, formulaic and readily available codes of validity requires the invention of counter discourse/practices of legitimation.

Like Woolgar (1988), my own position is that the most useful stories about science are those which interrogate representation, 'a reflexive exploration of our own practices of representation' (p. 98). This entails taking a position regarding the contested bodies of thought and practice which shape inquiry in the human sciences, negotiating the complex heterogeneity of discourses and practices. This ability to establish and maintain an acceptable dialogue with readers about ' "how to go about reality construction"' (Goldknopf, quoted in Conrad 1990: 101) involves making decisions about which discursive policy to follow, which 'regime of truth' to locate one's work within, which mask of methodology to assume. What follows is, in effect, a call for a kind of validity after poststructuralism in which legitimation depends on a researcher's ability to explore the resources of different contemporary inquiry problematics and, perhaps, even contribute to 'an "unjamming" effect in relation to the closed truths of the past, thereby freeing up the present for new forms of thought and practice' (Bennett 1990: 277).

Counter-practices of authority

The following is a dispersion, circulation, and proliferation of counter-practices of authority which takes the crisis of representation into account. In creating a nomadic and dispersed validity, I employ a strategy of excess and categorical scandal in the hope of both imploding ideas of policing social science and working against the inscription of another 'regime of truth.' Rather than the usual couching of validity in terms of disciplinary maintenance, disciplining the disciplines, my goal is to open new lines of discussion about changed conditions and possibilities for a critical social science (Fay 1987) and the discourse theories that so problematize that project. Rather than prescriptions for establishing validity in postpositivist empirical work, like Walter Benjamin, I offer 'a forthrightly personal and deliberately ephemeral antithesis' (Werkmeister 1982, p. 114) to more conventional and prescriptive discourse-practices of validity.

Frame 1:. . . ironic validity: . . . James Agee and Walker Evans's (1988) *Let Us Now Praise Famous Men*, originally published in 1941 and recently claimed as a postmodern text (Rabinowitz 1992: Quinby 1991), illustrates what I mean by ironic validity. Documenting the devastation of rural America by the economic disasters of the 1930's through the study of three white tenant farm families, the text is prefaced by Evans's uncaptioned photographs which set the stage for the focus on the politics of knowing and being known. Agee's text, which serves somewhat as one long caption for the photographs, foregrounds the insufficiencies of language via prose that is meandering, incantational, and deeply inscribed by musical forms. Beginning with three vignettes and concluding with multiple endings, Agee presents his awkwardness and hesitancies where his anxiety about 'his relationship to his subjects becomes an anxiety about the form of the book' (Rabinowitz 1992: 160). Both seeking and refusing a center, he combines documentary and autobiography to describe with 'words which are "not words"' (p. 161) as he moves from representations of the tenant families to the disclosure of his own subjectivity. Agee's 'self-indulgent, confessional narrative of middle-class seeing' is both redeemed and problematized by Evans's photographs which resist narrative, sentimentality and sensationalism while still 'reveal[ing] the ways differences can be organized and contained' (p. 163). . . .

Endlessly shifting the location of the unknowable and ironically using researcher power to undercut practices of representation, Agee and Evans create a text that is dense with the absence of referential finalities. Foregrounding the production of meaning-effects, they, nonetheless, construct a text of such specificity that the human cost of economics run amuck is made 'visible' in ways that are amplified in flesh.

Refusing closure and turning the analytical categories of the human sciences against themselves, Agee and Evans enact the struggle of an 'I' to become an 'eye' that both inscribes and interrupts normalizing power/knowledge (Quinby 1991). Fifty years after its original publication, their self-scrutinizing, non-normalizing production of knowledge is generative of research practices that, by taking the crisis of representation into account, create texts that are both double without being paralyzed and implode controlling codes.

Frame 2: . . . neo-pragmatic validity: . . . A recent dissertation on African-American women and leadership positions to higher education gives some feel for the parameters of [neo-pragmatic] validity (Woodbrooks 1991). Woodbrooks's study was 'designed to generate more interactive and contextual ways of knowing' (p. 93) with a particular focus on openness to counter-interpretations. 'The overarching goal of the methodology is to present a series of fruitful interruptions that demonstrate the multiplicity of meaning-making and interpretation.' (p. 94).

In analyzing interview data, Woodbrooks made extensive use of two familiar qualitative practices of validity, member checks and peer debriefing (Lincoln and Guba 1985). Using both to purposefully locate herself in the contradictory borderland between feminist emancipatory and poststructural positions, she attempted to interrupt her role as the Great Interpreter, 'to shake, disrupt, and shift' her feminist critical investments (Woodbrooks 1991: 103). Peer debriefing and member checks, both coherent within present forms of intelligibility, were used to critique her initial analysis of the data, her 'perceptions of some broadly defined themes that emerged as I coded the transcripts' (p. 132). Reanalyzing the data and her original analysis, Woodbrooks then sent a second draft out to participants and phoned for responses. This resulted in a textual strategy that juxtaposed the voices of the white female researcher with those of the African-American female participants.

In her textual strategy, Woodbrooks first tells a realist tale which backgrounds the researcher's shaping influence and foregrounds participant voices. She interrupts this with a critical tale that foregrounds how her theoretical investments shaped her analysis of the data. Finally, in a third-person voice, she tells a deconstructive tale which draws on participant reactions to the critical tale. Here, she probes her own desire, 'suspicious of . . . the hegemony [of] feminism' (p. 140) in her analysis which marginalized both African-American identity as a source of pride and strength (ascribing it totally to gender) and participant concerns with male/female relations. 'This strategy [of feminist consciousness-raising] perpetuates feminism as a white middle class project and trivializes the deep emotional ties that black women share with black men' (p. 200).

Holding up to scrutiny her own complicity, Woodbrooks creates a research design that moves her toward unlearning her own privilege and displacing the colonizing gaze. Foregrounding the availability of multiple discourses and how they can be used to decenter the researcher as the master of truth and justice, she enacts her knowledge of language games as she assumes responsibility for the rules and effects of her investments. Such a strategy refines our sensitivity to differences, introduces dissensus into consensus, and legitimates via fostering heterogeneity. Woodbrooks' expanded use of the familiar techniques of member checks and peer debriefing, a using of what is already available 'rather than hoping for something else to come along or to create utopia from thin air' (Kulchyski 1992: 192), results in a search for instabilities and a foregrounding of the multiplicity of language games.

Frame 3: . . . rhizomatic validity: . . . To probe what rhizomatic validity might mean in the context of an empirical study, I draw from the work of an Australian dissertation student, Erica Lenore McWilliam. In a study of student needs talk in pre-service teacher education, McWilliam (1992; in press) developed a research design that involved 1) an initial reflexive phase where researcher theoretical and political investments were put under scrutiny by moving back and forth among various contestatory discourses in a way that resituated the researcher away from the 'transformative intellectual' come to 'save' the oppressed; 2) an empirical phase that focused on student-teacher constructions of teacher work; and 3) a final reciprocal phase designed as reflection in action and an extended co-theorizing process that contested and reconstructed the researcher's reading of the phase II data. Each stage paid particular attention to discrepant data, the facts unfit to fit categorical schemes in a way that both uses and collides poststructuralism and feminist emancipatory discourses. Of note are McWilliam's learnings that research practices which inter-rupt researcher privilege must be more about constructing 'an interrogative researcher text . . . a questioning text.' Such a text overtly 'signals tentativeness and partiality' in decentering expert authority and moving toward practices of co-theorizing (1992: 271). Paying particular attention to the tendencies of much advo-cacy research toward inaccessible language and 'intellectual bullying' of the researched (in press), she attempts to create the conditions in which it becomes possible for both researcher and researched to rethink their attitudes and practices. . . .

Frame 4: voluptuous validity/situated validity: . . . An example . . . is Richardson's (1992) essay about her larger interview study of unmarried mothers. 'Consciously self-revelatory' in probing the lived experience of the researcher (p. 125), Richard-son cheekily hopes that she has not 'ventured beyond Improper' as she 'breache[s] sociological writing expectations by writing sociology as poetry' (p. 126). First presenting 'a transcript masquerading as a poem/a poem masquerading as a tran-script' (p. 127), her primary goal is 'to create a position for experiencing the self as a sociological knower/constructor – not just talking about it, but doing it' (p. 136). Speaking autobiographically in order to provide 'an opportunity to rethink socio-logical representation' (p. 133), Richardson writes of her need to break out of the 'dreary' writing of ' "straight" sociological prose' (p. 131). The part of her that had written poetry for eight years is called on to 'provide a new strategy for resolving those horrid postmodernist writing dilemmas' (p. 131). Deliberately choosing a transcript from a woman quite different from herself in order to encounter the 'postmodernist issues of "authorship"/authority/appropriation,' she works toward a text that is 'bounded and unbounded, closed and open' (p. 132). . . .

Richardson exemplifies a disruptive excess which brings ethics and epis-temology together in self-conscious partiality, an embodied positionality and a tentativeness which leaves space for others to enter, for the joining of partial voices. Authority comes from engagement and reflexivity in a way that exceeds Lyotardian paralogy via practices of textual representation that, by hegemonic standards, 'go too far' with the politics of uncertainty. This effect is achieved by blurring the lines between the genres of poetry and social science reporting. Theorizing out of auto-biography where her 'leaky' practice collapses the private/public distinction, Rich-ardson is mother, wife, scholar, and poet in her desire to move toward some way of doing science more in keeping with her feminist-poststructuralism.

Offered as more problem than solution, my scandalous categories and the exemplars I have recruited as provocateurs of validity after poststructuralism are performances of a transgressive validity that works off spaces already in the making. Situated in the crisis of authority that has occurred across knowledge systems, my challenge has been to make productive use of the dilemma of being left to work from traditions of research legitimacy and discourses of validity that appear no longer adequate to the task. Between the no longer and the not yet lies the possibil-ity of what was impossible under traditional regimes of truth in the social sciences: a deconstructive problematic that aims not to govern a practice but to theorize it, deprive it of its innocence, disrupt the ideological effects by which it reproduces itself, pose as a problem what has been offered as a solution (Rooney 1989). Derrida terms this 'a "science of the possibility of science" . . . a nonlinear, multiple, and dissimulated space . . . Thus we discover a science whose object is not "truth," but the constitution and annulment of its own text and the subject inscribed there' (Sollers 1983: 137, 179). . . .

References

Agee, James and Walker Evans (1988) *Let Us Now Praise Famous Men.* Boston: Houghton Mifflin.

Bennett, Tony (1990) *Outside Literature.* London: Routledge.

Borgmann, Albert (1992) *Crossing the Postmodern Divide.* Chicago: University of Chicago Press.

Conrad, Charles (1990) 'Rhetoric and the display of organizational ethnographies.' Pp. 95–106 in *Communication Yearbook 13*, edited by James Anderson. Newbury Park: Sage.

Cronbach, Lee and P. Meehl (1955) 'Construct validity in psychological tests.' *Psychological Bulletin* 52: 281, 302.

Denzin, Norman K. (1989) *The Research Act*, 3rd edition, Englewood Cliffs, NJ: Prentice-Hall.

Fay, Brian (1987) *Critical Social Science.* Ithaca: Cornell University Press.

Fine, Arthur (1986) *The Shaky Game: Einstein, Realism and the Quantum Theory.* Chicago: University of Chicago Press.

Foucault, Michel (1977) *Language, Counter-memory, Practice*, edited by Donald Bouchard, Ithaca: Cornell University Press.

Kulchyski, Peter (1992) 'Primitive subversions: totalization and resistance in native Canadian politics.' *Cultural Critique* 21 (Spring): 171–196.

Lather, Patti (1986a) 'Research as praxis.' *Harvard Educational Review* 56(3): 257–277.

—— (1986b) 'Issues of validity in openly ideological research: between a rock and a soft place.' *Interchange* 17(4): 63–84.

—— (1991) *Within/Against: Feminist Research in Education*. Geelong. Australia: Deakin University Monograph Series.

Lincoln, Yvonna and Egon Guba (1985) *Naturalistic Inquiry*. Newbury Park: Sage.

Lyotard, Jean-François (1984) *The Postmodern Condition: A Report on Knowledge*, translated by G Bennington and B. Massumi, Minneapolis: University of Minnesota Press.

McWilliam, Erica Lenore (1992) *In Broken Images: A Postpositivist Analysis of Student Needs Talk in Pre-service Teacher Education*. Unpublished dissertation. The University of Queensland.

Mishler, Elliot (1990) 'Validation in inquiry guided research: the role of exemplars in narrative studies.' *Harvard Educational Review* 60(4): 415–442.

Petanis, Julian (1991) *Heterology and the Postmodern: Bataille, Baudrillard, and Lyotard*. Durham: Duke University Press.

Quinby, Lee (1991) *Freedom, Foucault, and the Subject of America*. Boston: Northeastern University Press.

Rabinowitz, Paula (1992) 'Voyeurism and class consciousness: James Agee and Walker Evans. Let us now praise famous men.' *Cultural Critique* 21 (Spring): 143–170.

Richardson, Laurel (1992) 'The consequences of poetic representation: writing the Other, rewriting the self.' Pp. 125–140 in *Windows on Lived Experience*, edited by Carolyn Ellis and M. Flaherty. Newbury Park, Cal.: Sage.

Rooney, Ellen (1989) *Seductive Reasoning: Pluralism as the Problematic of Contemporary Literary Theory*. Ithaca: Cornell University Press.

Scheurich, Jim (1991) 'The paradigmatic transgressions of validity.' Paper presented at the annual conference of the *Journal of Curriculum Theorizing*, Dayton, Ohio, October.

Sollers, Philippe (1983) *Writing and the Experience of Limits*, edited by D. Hayman, translated by P. Barnard and D. Hayman. New York: Columbia University Press.

Woodbrooks, Catherine (1991) 'The construction of identity through the presentation of self: black women candidates interviewing for administrative positions at a research university.' Unpublished dissertation, Ohio State University.

Woolgar, Steve (1988) *Science: The Very Idea*, London: Tavistock.

Chapter 66

Thomas A. Schwandt

FAREWELL TO CRITERIOLOGY

From *Qualitative Inquiry* 2 (1): 58–72 (1996).

I**N TROLLOPE'S** *The Last Chronicle of Barset*, two aging clergymen muse regretfully on the changes wrought by High Victorianism on the ecclesiastical vocation. 'In the old days,' says one, 'there wasn't so much fuss, and there was a lot more reality.' Today, as social inquirers face the challenges of postmodernism, postfoundationalism, and the like in what Baynes, Bohman, and McCarthy (1987) characterize as the period 'after philosophy,' they are likely to feel at times much like these clergymen. The epistemology of logical positivism has proven to be untenable. The firm conviction that the social-political world was simply 'out there' waiting to be discovered and described has been exposed as a convenient fiction. The belief that social science would achieve paradigm takeoff by imitating the aims and methods of the natural sciences has been shown to be wishful thinking at best. . . .

The logical positivists and their successors, the logical empiricists, argued that it was only by means of applying logical (and empirical) criteria that we are able to distinguish genuine, objective knowledge from mere belief. Their epistemology sought to realize the Cartesian dream of knowledge as the outcome of a rational individual's act of applying necessary and sufficient tests of truth. They were unwavering in their commitment both to the power of reason and to the certainty of empirical data. . . .

The period characterized as 'after philosophy' in both philosophy and social science comprises a broad set of criticisms of the foregoing foundationalist picture of social scientific inquiry. There are two central themes in this set of criticisms. First, the object of social science inquiry is both a linguistic and a social construction, and hence, because this object is represented in social scientific discourse it is partially constituted by this discourse. Stated somewhat differently, social scientific knowledge is not presuppositionless but is instead shaped by moral and political values and concerns. Second, as we abandon the modern attempts to model our practice on the natural sciences, we turn to social practice and practical philosophy. This turn toward practical philosophy takes up several ideas. It means (a) that conceptions of the aim of social inquiry are now being shaped not by the demand for a 'neutral, objectifying science of human life and action' (Taylor 1987: 472) or for *episteme* but by the search for a better understanding of *praxis*; (b) that the kind of investigation required here must attend to both ethical and political concerns . . . and (c) that the rationality of everyday life (and the rationality of social scientific practice itself) is regarded as intrinsically dialogical and communicative. . . .

Before sketching that conception further, it is necessary to review an approach to social inquiry that appears to take seriously this turn to human action but does so only in a limited way. An abiding concern for the life world – that is, for various kinds of social practices and ways of life as they are actually experienced (or lived, felt, and undergone) by participants in those practices or life ways – has, of course, long been the interest of interpretive approaches to social science. By *interpretive* here I mean those ways of conceiving of sociological and anthropological investigations that draw on the German *Verstehen* tradition and the phenomenology of Alfred Schutz. These are social inquiries that we label ethnographic, qualitative, interpretive, phenomenological, field based, case based, and so forth. Yet these inquiries, for the most part, cling to objectivating approaches in investigating lived reality. In other words, interpretivist studies generally have not abandoned the third-person point of view. They continue to be predicated on the assumption of research *on* human action and formulating social theory *about* human action.

To be sure, these approaches advocate entering the world of human actors via participant observation and attending carefully and with open-mindedness and open-heartedness . . . to the ways in which participants define their situations. Yet these actions on the part of the interpretive inquirer are largely strategic and methodological moves designed to facilitate access to respondents' ways of meaning making. Interpretive inquirers are advised to remain 'marginal natives' never relinquishing an analytical distance from subjects or respondents. As the British ethnographers Hammersley and Atkinson (1983) remind us,

> From the perspective of the 'marginal' reflexive ethnographer, there can be no question of total commitment, 'surrender,' or 'becoming' [the 'other']. There must always remain some part held back, some social and intellectual 'distance.' For it is in the 'space' created by this distance that the analytic work of the ethnographer gets done. Without that distance, without such analytic space, the ethnography can be little more than the autobiographical account of personal conversion. This would be an interesting and valuable document, but not an ethnographic study.
>
> (p. 102)

Hammersley and Atkinson overstate the case a bit here. One can never 'become' the other. Critics of the ethnographic marginal native posture are not arguing that the alternative to keeping oneself at a distance from the other is to deny the alterity of the other – to assume we are all the same. What they are saying is that the marginal native posture is a kind of disengagement correlative of objectification. And such objectification of the other deprives it of its normative force for the investigator (Taylor 1989).

Traditional interpretive social inquiry remains largely descriptive, objectifying, and theory focused – descriptive in that it offers careful documentation of human action and life ways but does not engage in normative critique, theory focused because it aims ultimately at empirical, explanatory theories of that action. . . .

Social inquiry as practical philosophy

In contrast to these traditional interpretive approaches, social inquiry as a kind of practical philosophy is both descriptive and normative. It is not a form of inquiry *on* human action as much as it is inquiry *with* human actors. It aims less (or not at all) at developing social theory about action but rather is concerned with 'improving the rationality of a particular practice by enabling practitioners to refine the rationality of the practice for themselves' (Carr 1995: 118). Various forms of action inquiry, collaborative inquiry, and critical feminist inquiry seem generally to embrace this view. Other characteristics of social inquiry as practical philosophy include the following.

First, inquirers seek to establish a dialogical relationship of openness with participants in the inquiry. . . .

Second, inquirers view the participants in an inquiry (e.g., managers, administrators, teachers, laborers) as themselves engaged in performing a practical art. . . .

Third, the aim of such inquiry is not to replace practitioners' commonsense knowledge of their respective and joint practices with allegedly more sophisticated, theoretical, scientific knowledge but to encourage practitioners to critically reflect on and reappraise their commonsense knowledge. . . .

Finally, social inquiry as dialogical, practical reasoning (or practical philosophy, if you will) is in part continuous with the project of modernity. It does not so much seek to overcome modernity as it does to give it new meaning. We retain the Enlightenment insight regarding the importance of self-clarity about our nature as knowing agents or actors as a way to become rationally empowered to transform ourselves. But we seek to adopt a better and more critically defensible notion of what this entails by criticizing the foundationalist Enlightenment narrative in which that ideal took shape.

If we make this turn toward social inquiry as practical philosophy, how then are we to judge the goodness of this undertaking and its product? We must seek an answer to this question in an alternative to the traditional project of criteriology. Criteriological solutions are incompatible with social inquiry as a form of practical philosophy that arises from postfoundationalist epistemology. . . . Rather than use the term 'criteria,' which typically appears in the phrase 'epistemic criteria' and, further, connotes efforts to develop and test propositions in a language from which all perspective, bias, and so forth have been removed, I suggest we use some different terms to speak of ways in which we criticize and judge the practice of social inquiry as practical philosophy. I prefer to speak of a 'guiding ideal' that shapes the aim of the practice and a set of 'enabling conditions' that characterize its practice. . . .

The guiding ideal that informs the aim of the practice of social inquiry as practical philosophy is quite opposed to the guiding ideal that informs traditional social scientific inquiry. Taylor (1985) reminds us that the 'adoption of a framework for explanation [in sociopolitical] inquiry carries with it the adoption of the value-slope implicit in it' (p. 75). The value slope of traditional social scientific inquiry is theory-centered, value-neutral, atomistic, disengaged instrumental reason (although, of course, traditional social science claimed to have no value slope whatsoever). By contrast, the value slope of social inquiry as practical philosophy is democracy, understood as a moral ideal, not a set of formal procedures. . . .

I have characterized the practice of social inquiry as practical philosophy in terms of the ways it unfolds and in terms of the ideal that informs or guides it. Left unsaid thus far is how we are to evaluate the outcomes of this engagement and how we are to locate it in the spectrum of *professional* social inquiry. Before addressing these concerns, it is necessary to note that the entire undertaking of social inquiry as thus far defined ought to have the effect of decentering the cultural authority of the professional practice of social scientific inquiry. If rational behavior in social inquiry is not equated with *scientific* rationalism – that is, with the possession of some special method or criteria for discriminating genuine knowledge from mere belief – but is founded instead in the ordinary actions of everyday people as they struggle to come to terms with conflicting views and opinions, then professional social inquiry cannot claim special status based on special knowledge. . . . We can point to three kinds of considerations that might be used to evaluate the goodness of the product or outcome of social inquiry as practical philosophy.

The first consideration . . . is that social inquiry ought to generate knowledge that complements or supplements rather than displaces lay probing of social problems. . . .

Second, the outcome of social inquiry as practical philosophy can be judged in terms of whether the social inquirer or inquiry team is successful at enhancing or cultivating *critical* intelligence in parties to the research encounter. . . . Critical intelligence is not simply the ability to understand strategies and implement procedures but also the willingness and ability to debate the value of various ends of a practice. The social inquirer ought to teach in such a way as to encourage the development of this capacity for critical intelligence.

Third, as a contributor to the discourse on social science, the social inquirer qua practical philosopher can be evaluated on the success to which his or her reports of the inquiry enable the training or calibration of human judgment. The crucial issue in practical philosophy is the application of general principles to particular cases. As Aristotle explained, moral and political life requires a sort of knowledge that can be acquired only through guided experience. This kind of knowledge is practical wisdom . . . There can be no scientific theory of practical wisdom or judgment. That is, we will not be able to state rules in propositional form that will direct us in linking the general to the particular or the theoretical to the practical. But we can calibrate or train that kind of determining judgment through the study of particular cases. Hence the social inquirer as practical philosopher must endeavor to prepare accounts of cases that are useful in training the capacity for practical wisdom. . . .

Although the foundational, criteriological project of epistemology is now bankrupt, that does not mean we can forgo the issue of defining, acting on, and justifying a choice about the proper aim of social inquiry. Saying farewell to criteriology means abandoning the pursuit of autonomous, indisputable criteria for distinguishing legitimate from not so legitimate social scientific knowledge. Saying farewell to criteriology means not that we have resolved this quest for criteria but that we have gotten over it or gone beyond it. What once was the critical problem of the correct criteria becomes the problem of how to cultivate practical reasoning. And for tentative answers to this redefined problem, we do not look to following procedures or defining or specifying the right criteria but to the practices, consequences, and outcomes of our ways of deliberating. The greatest danger to this proposal is not relativism but cynicism, the disbelief in shared values that comprise dialogical, interpretive, democratic communities of inquirers intent on improving their practices.

References

Baynes, K., Bohman, J. and McCarthy, T. (eds). (1987) *After Philosophy: End or Transformation?* Cambridge, Mass.: MIT Press.

Carr, W. (1995) *For Education: Towards Critical Educational Inquiry.* Philadelphia: Open University Press.

Hammersley, M. and Atkinson, P. (1983) *Ethnography: Principles in Practice.* London Tavistock.

Taylor, C. (1985) *Philosophy and the Human Sciences: Philosophical Papers* (vol. 2). Cambridge: Cambridge University Press.

—— (1987) 'Overcoming epistemology'. In K. Baynes, J. Bohman and T. McCarthy (eds), *After Philosophy: End or Transformation?* (pp. 459–488). Cambridge, Mass.: Massachusetts Institute of Technology Press.

—— (1989) *Sources of the Self.* Cambridge, Mass.: Harvard University Press.

PART FOURTEEN

Political and ethical aspects of research practice

INTRODUCTION

INEVITABLY THE CRISIS OF legitimation that has accompanied dissatisfaction with modernist justifications for social research leads us to consider the political position of researchers and intellectuals in general. Part Thirteen of the book already touched on different views about this, but it would be a mistake to imagine that discussion of the role of political and other values in social research began with postmodernism. The sociologist Max Weber (reading 67) presented views on this in the early part of the twentieth century, using the figure of the 'teacher' to stand for researcher or intellectual. For Weber's 'student' we might substitute 'user of research'. Thus translated, Weber can be understood as arguing that politics is out of place in a social research project. Weber is firmly committed to increasing the stock of knowledge about society rather than promoting particular forms of social organization. Such knowledge is likely to be relevant to people in opposing camps (he uses the example of the Catholic and the Freemason), the value of this being in the capacity of the social researcher to present uncomfortable facts that *both* may have to confront.

The relationships that may exist between policy-makers and research knowledge are outlined by Weiss (reading 68), who begins by dismissing the idea that the mere existence of knowledge ensures that it will be used. However, even where research has been commissioned with the explicit goal of informing specific decisions, it does not always get used in this way. Instead, research is diffused into the worlds of policy-makers in a variety of less direct ways, some of which reflect its selective use in the strategic bargaining that goes on when policies are negotiated.

The extracts from research ethics guidelines of two social research organizations make for an interesting comparison, as these conceive of relations with funding bodies in different ways. The British Sociological Association (BSA) emphasizes both obligations to sponsors and the need to demonstrate independence from sponsors' interests. The Council of American Survey Research Organizations (CASRO) envisages a less independent relationship, whereby the interests of sponsors predominate over those of the general public. This reflects the differing institutional positions of the two organizations, on the one hand speaking for a subject discipline located in universities, on the other speaking for commercial organizations.

Relationships with policy-makers and research funders are clearly important for social researchers, but relationships with research participants are equally so, and similarly subject to issues that relate to values. The rest of the readings in this section consider this. Meyer's account of action research (reading 70) outlines a participative approach to research inquiry whereby researchers facilitate a simultaneous contribution to both knowledge and social change in a democratic mode of research organization.

Harding (reading 71) and Maynard (reading 72) outline feminist positions in social research practice. Harding makes clear that this is largely an epistemological debate, not a discussion of methods of, for example, collecting information. A feminist researcher, therefore, is particularly concerned with how research questions are formulated, wanting these to arise from the position and perspective of women rather than the position of men. The goal is to produce knowledge that assists in the emancipation of women. Maynard relates these considerations to the argument (seen, for example, in Oakley (reading 38)) that a feminist method is inevitably qualitative. While an appropriate stance in the early 1980s, Maynard feels that this by the time she is writing (1994) this is outmoded, as statistical information can often be helpful in exploring matters that concern women. Maynard also discusses feminist standpoint epistemology and feminist postmodernism as more recent perspectives that have imbued feminist social research practice.

Rather similar debates have been proceeding in research on racism, as Back and Solomos (reading 73) demonstrate. Early work, such as that of Rex, emphasized academic autonomy and objectivity; this contrasts with later work that emphasized the role of researchers in using action research to promote anti-racist initiatives. Back and Solomos contrast their own research practice with both of these; first, they were interested in understanding the perspectives of the powerful as much as those of the powerless; second, they are aware that claiming to be objective is an asset in gaining acceptance of their findings, even though they themselves understand their research to be 'partial'. They decide to deploy the image of themselves as value free where it appears to be useful in gaining credibility for their findings.

Hammersley's piece (reading 74) arose in the context of a discussion of feminist methodology, but might equally be applied to race research or other issues that involve the negotiation of value positions. He considers the issue of power imbalances between researchers and researched as well as the idea that social research ought to be devoted to emancipating particular groups. In rejecting political conceptions of social research, he returns us to the position outlined by Weber (reading 67) at the start of this section.

DISCUSSION POINTS

- Compare the positions of Schwandt (reading 66) and Weber on the relationship each feels should obtain between researchers (in the case of Weber, substitute this term for 'teachers') and democratic ideals. Revisit the last discussion point on page 410 and answer it in terms of Weber's recommendations.

- Public policy-makers often want evidence on which to base their policies. Examine a recent announcement of government policy in an area such as crime, health care, foreign affairs or education. This may involve examining recent news articles. How has social research contributed to this (if at all)? If this is not evident to you, what kind of social research might have been relevant in formulating the policy? Which of the meanings of research utilization outlined by Weiss are relevant to understanding how this policy was formulated?

- The BSA plans to substitute the word 'professionally' for 'as objectively as possible' in its recommendation for how social researchers should conduct inquiry sponsored by other organizations (see editor's footnote to the first part of reading 69). This word change reflects recent shifts in the discussion of objectivity as a desirable goal in social research. Do you agree with this change of wording? What issues are at stake here?

- Meyer suggests that action research can help health care practitioners improve the quality of their service. Outline an action research project that would benefit users of health services.

- Towards the end of her article Harding raises the issue of whether male researchers can be considered suitable as feminist researchers. What are the arguments for and against this?

- Both Harding and Maynard observe that the issue of whether there is a feminist *method* (as opposed to a feminist epistemology) is questionable, pointing to differences between their position and that of Oakley, who advocated a particular form of qualitative interviewing (reading 38). What are your views on this?

- Back and Solomos contrast a value-free stance with a politically partial position in research on race. They are unhappy with the first of these and uncomfortable with the second. They want to recognize that their research is 'partial' but also to make it 'persuasive.' What strategy do they suggest for dealing with this? Is their position ethically defensible? Are there alternative solutions to the dilemma they identify?

- Is Hammersley's characterization of the feminist position on hierarchy and emancipation an accurate reflection of the view of Oakley (reading 38), Harding (reading 71) and Maynard (reading 72)? Do you agree with his views?

FURTHER READING

Asad, T. (ed.) (1973) *Anthropology and the Colonial Encounter*, London: Ithaca Press.

Becker, H.S. (1967) 'Whose side are we on?' *Social Problems* 14: 239–248.

Finch, J. (1984) ' "It's great to have someone to talk to": ethics and politics of interviewing women', in Bell, C. and Roberts, H. (eds) *Social Researching: Politics, Problems, Practice*, London: Routledge.

Harding, S. (1986) *The Science Question and Feminism*, Bloomington: Indiana University Press.

Harding, S. (ed.) (1987) *Feminism and Methodology*, Milton Keynes: Open University Press.

Homan, R. (1991) *The Ethics of Social Research*, London: Longman.

Majchrzak, A. (1984) *Methods for Policy Research*, Thousand Oaks, Cal.: Sage

Mauthner, M., Birch, M., Jessop, J. and Miller, T. (eds) (2002) *Ethics in Qualitative Research*, London: Sage.

Reason, P. and Bradbury, H. (2002) *Handbook of Action Research: Participative Inquiry and Practice*, London and Thousand Oaks, Cal.: Sage.

Reinharz, S. (1992) *Feminist Methods in Social Research*, Oxford: Oxford University Press.

Scheurich, J.J. and Young, M. (1997) 'Coloring epistemologies: are our research epistemologies racially biased?' *Educational Researcher* 26 (4): 4–16.

Stanfield, J.H. and Dennis, R.M. (1993) *Race and Ethnicity in Research Methods*, Newbury Park, Cal.: Sage.

Tanesini, A. (1991) *An Introduction to Feminist Epistemologies*, London: Blackwell.

Chapter 67

Max Weber

SCIENCE AS A VOCATION

From Gerth, H. and Mills, C.W. (eds.) *From Max Weber,* Oxford: Oxford University Press (1949).

. . .

L ET US CONSIDER THE disciplines close to me: sociology, history, eco-nomics, political science, and those types of cultural philosophy that make it their task to interpret these sciences. It is said, and I agree, that politics is out of place in the lecture-room. It does not belong there on the part of the students. . . . Neither does politics, however, belong in the lecture-room on the part of the docents,[1] and when the docent is scientifically concerned with politics, it belongs there least of all.

To take a practical political stand is one thing, and to analyze political structures and party positions is another. When speaking in a political meeting about dem-ocracy, one does not hide one's personal standpoint; indeed, to come out clearly and take a stand is one's damned duty. The words one uses in such a meeting are not means of scientific analysis but means of canvassing votes and winning over others. They are not plow-shares to loosen the soil of contemplative thought; they are swords against the enemies: such words are weapons. It would be an outrage, however, to use words in this fashion in a lecture or in the lecture-room. If, for instance, 'democracy' is under discussion, one considers its various forms, analyzes them in the way they function, determines what results for the conditions of life the one form has as compared with the other. Then one confronts the forms of dem-ocracy with non-democratic forms of political order and endeavors to come to a position where the student may find the point from which, in terms of his ultimate ideals, he can take a stand. But the true teacher will beware of imposing from the

[1 Editor's footnote: 'docent'=teacher or lecturer.]

platform any political position upon the student, whether it is expressed or suggested. 'To let the facts speak for themselves' is the most unfair way of putting over a political position to the student.

Why should we abstain from doing this? I state in advance that some highly esteemed colleagues are of the opinion that it is not possible to carry through this self-restraint and that, even if it were possible, it would be a whim to avoid declaring oneself. Now one cannot demonstrate scientifically what the duty of an academic teacher is. One can only demand of the teacher that he have the intellectual integrity to see that it is one thing to state facts, to determine mathematical or logical relations or the internal structure of cultural values, while it is another thing to answer questions of the *value* of culture and its individual contents and the question of how one should act in the cultural community and in political associations. These are quite heterogeneous problems. If he asks further why he should not deal with both types of problems in the lecture-room, the answer is: because the prophet and the demagogue do not belong on the academic platform.

To the prophet and the demagogue, it is said: 'Go your ways out into the streets and speak openly to the world,' that is, speak where criticism is possible. In the lecture-room we stand opposite our audience, and it has to remain silent. I deem it irresponsible to exploit the circumstance that for the sake of their career the students have to attend a teacher's course while there is nobody present to oppose him with criticism. The task of the teacher is to serve the students with his knowledge and scientific experience and not to imprint upon them his personal political views. It is certainly possible that the individual teacher will not entirely succeed in eliminating his personal sympathies. He is then exposed to the sharpest criticism in the forum of his own conscience. And this deficiency does not prove anything; other errors are also possible, for instance, erroneous statements of fact, and yet they prove nothing against the duty of searching for the truth. I also reject this in the very interest of science. I am ready to prove from the works of our historians that whenever the man of science introduces his personal value judgment, a full understanding of the facts *ceases*. . . .

I ask only: How should a devout Catholic, on the one hand, and a Freemason, on the other, in a course on the forms of church and state or on religious history ever be brought to evaluate these subjects alike? This is out of the question. And yet the academic teacher must desire and must demand of himself to serve the one as well as the other by his knowledge and methods. Now you will rightly say that the devout Catholic will never accept the view of the factors operative in bringing about Christianity which a teacher who is free of his dogmatic presuppositions presents to him. Certainly! The difference, however, lies in the following: Science 'free from presuppositions,' in the sense of a rejection of religious bonds, does not know of the 'miracle' and the 'revelation.' If it did, science would be unfaithful to its own 'presuppositions.' The believer knows both, miracle and revelation. And science 'free from presuppositions' expects from him no less – and no more – than acknowledgment that *if* the process can be explained without those supernatural interventions, which an empirical explanation has to eliminate as causal factors, the process has to be explained the way science attempts to do. And the believer can do this without being disloyal to his faith.

But has the contribution of science no meaning at all for a man who does not care to know facts as such and to whom only the practical standpoint matters? Perhaps science nevertheless contributes something.

The primary task of a useful teacher is to teach his students to recognize 'inconvenient' facts – I mean facts that are inconvenient for their party opinions. And for every party opinion there are facts that are extremely inconvenient, for my own opinion no less than for others. I believe the teacher accomplishes more than a mere intellectual task if he compels his audience to accustom itself to the existence of such facts. I would be so immodest as even to apply the expression 'moral achievement,' though perhaps this may sound too grandiose for something that should go without saying. . . .

Chapter 68

Carol H. Weiss

THE MANY MEANINGS OF RESEARCH UTILIZATION

From *Public Administration Review* 39 (5): 426–431 (1979).

. . .

THE USE OF SOCIAL science research in the sphere of public policy is an extraordinarily complex phenomenon. . . . Here I will try to extract seven different meanings that have been associated with the concept.

The knowledge-driven model

The first image of research utilization is probably the most venerable in the literature and derives from the natural sciences. It assumes the following sequence of events: basic research → applied research → development → application. The notion is that basic research discloses some opportunity that may have relevance for public policy; applied research is conducted to define and test the findings of basic research for practical action; if all goes well, appropriate technologies are developed to implement the findings; whereupon application occurs. . . .

The assumption is that the sheer fact that knowledge exists presses it towards development and use. . . . In the social sciences few examples can be found. The reasons appear to be several. Social science knowledge is not apt to be so compelling or authoritative as to drive inevitably towards implementation. Social science knowledge does not readily lend itself to conversion into replicable technologies, either material or social. Perhaps most important, unless a social condition has been consensually defined as a pressing social problem, and unless the condition has become fully politicized and debated, and the parameters of potential action agreed upon, there is little likelihood that policy-making bodies will be receptive to the results of social science research. . . .

Problem-solving model

The most common concept of research utilization involves the direct application of the results of a specific social science study to a pending decision. The expectation is that research provides empirical evidence and conclusions that help to solve a policy problem. The model is again a linear one, but the steps are different from those in the knowledge-driven model. Here the decision drives the application of research. A problem exists and a decision has to be made; information or understanding is lacking either to generate a solution to the problem or to select among alternative solutions; research provides the missing knowledge. With the gap filled, a decision is reached.

Implicit in this model is a sense that there is a consensus on goals. It is assumed that policy-makers and researchers tend to agree on what the desired end state shall be. The main contribution of social science research is to help identify and select appropriate means to reach the goal. . . .

Even a cursory review of the fate of social science research, including policy research on government-defined issues, suggests that these kinds of expectations are wildly optimistic. Occasional studies have a direct effect on decisions, but usually on relatively low-level, narrow-gauge decisions. Most studies appear to come and go without leaving any discernible mark on the direction or substance of policy. It probably takes an extraordinary concatenation of circumstances for research to influence policy decisions directly. . . .

However, the problem-solving model remains the prevailing imagery of research utilization. Its prevalence probably accounts for much of the disillusionment about the contribution of social science research to social policy. Because people expect research use to occur through the sequence of stages posited by this model, they become discouraged when events do not take the expected course. However, there are other ways in which social science research can be 'used' in policy-making.

Interactive model

Another way that social science research can enter the decision arena is as part of an interactive search for knowledge. Those engaged in developing policy seek information not only from social scientists but from a variety of sources – administrators, practitioners, politicians, planners, journalists, clients, interest groups, aides, friends, and social scientists, too. The process is not one of linear order from research to decision but a disorderly set of interconnections and back-and-forthness that defies neat diagrams. . . .

In this model, the use of research is only one part of a complicated process that also uses experience, political insight, pressure, social technologies and judgement. It has applicability not only to face-to-face settings but also to the multiple ways in which intelligence is gathered through intermediaries and brought to bear. It describes a familiar process by which decision-makers inform themselves of the range of knowledge and opinion in a policy area.

Political model

Often the constellation of interests around a policy issue predetermines the positions that decision-makers take. Or debate has gone on over a period of years and opinions have hardened. At this point, decision-makers are not likely to be receptive to new evidence from social science research. For reasons of interest, ideology, or intellect, they have taken a stand that research is not likely to shake.

In such cases, research can still be used. It becomes ammunition for the side that finds its conclusions congenial and supportive. Partisans flourish the evidence in an attempt to neutralize opponents, convince waverers and bolster supporters. . . . When research is available to all participants in the policy process, research as political ammunition can be a worthy model of utilization.

Tactical model

There are occasions when social science research is used for purposes that have little relation to the substance of the research. It is not the content of the findings that is invoked but the sheer fact that research is being done. For example, government agencies confronted with demands for action may respond by saying, 'Yes, we know that's an important need. We're doing research on it right now.' Research becomes proof of their responsiveness. Faced with unwelcome demands, they may use research as a tactic for delaying action ('We are waiting until the research is completed'). . . .

Enlightenment model

Perhaps the way in which social science research most frequently enters the policy arena is through the process that has come to be called 'enlightenment' (Crawford and Biderman 1969; Janowitz 1972). Here it is not the findings of a single study nor even of a body of related studies that directly affect policy. Rather it is the concepts and theoretical perspectives that social science research has engendered that permeate the policy-making process.

There is no assumption in this model that decision-makers seek out social science research when faced with a policy issue or even that they are receptive to, or aware of, specific research conclusions. The imagery is that of social science generalizations and orientations percolating through informed publics and coming to shape the way in which people think about social issues. Social science research diffuses circuitously through manifold channels – professional journals, the mass media, conversations with colleagues – and over time the variables it deals with and the generalizations it offers provide decision-makers with ways of making sense out of a complex world.

Rarely will policy-makers be able to cite the findings of a specific study that influenced their decisions, but they have a sense that social science research has given them a backdrop of ideas and orientations that has had important consequences. . . . Research sensitizes decision-makers to new issues and helps turn what were non-problems into policy problems. . . . Conversely, research may convert existing problems into non-problems, for example, marijuana use. Research can drastically revise the way that policy-makers define issues, such as acceptable rates of unemployment, the facets of the issue they view as susceptible to alteration, and the alternative measures they consider. It helps to change the parameters within which policy solutions are sought. In the long run, along with other influences, it often redefines the policy agenda. . . .

Research as part of the intellectual enterprise of the society

A final view of research utilization looks upon social science research as one of the intellectual pursuits of a society. It is not so much an independent variable whose effects on policy remain to be determined as it is another of the dependent variables, collateral with policy – and with philosophy, journalism, history, law and criticism. Like policy, social science research responds to the currents of thought, the fads and fancies, of the period. Social science and policy interact, influencing each other and being influenced by the larger fashions of social thought.

It is often emerging policy interest in a social issue that leads to the appropriation of funds for social science research in the first place, and only with the availability of funds are social scientists attracted to study of the issue. Early studies may accept the parameters set by the policy discussion, limiting investigation to those aspects of the issue that have engaged official attention. Later, as social science research widens its horizons, it may contribute to reconceptualization of the issue by policy-makers. Meanwhile, both the policy and research colloquies may respond, consciously or unconsciously, to concerns sweeping through intellectual and popular thought ('citizen participation', 'local control', spiralling inflation, individual privacy). In this view, research is one part of the interconnected intellectual enterprise.

These, then, are some of the meanings that 'the use of social science research' can carry. Probably all of them are applicable in some situations. Certainly none of them represents a fully satisfactory answer to the question of how a polity best mobilizes its research resources to inform public action. . . .

References

Crawford, E.T. and Biderman, A.D. (1969) 'The functions of policy-oriented social science' in E. Crawford and A. Biderman (eds), *Social Scientists and International Affairs* (New York: Wiley), pp. 233–243.

Janowitz, M. (1972) 'Professionalization of sociology', *American Journal of Sociology*, vol. 78, pp. 105–135.

Chapter 69

British Sociological Association (BSA) and Council for American Survey Research Organizations (CASRO)

RESEARCH ETHICS
Two statements

From www.britsoc.org.uk/about/ethic.htm (2002)
and www.casro.org/codeofstandards.cfm (2002).

Statement of Ethical Practice (BSA)

STYLES OF SOCIOLOGICAL WORK are diverse and subject to change, not least because sociologists work within a wide variety of settings. Sociologists, in carrying out their work, inevitably face ethical, and sometimes legal, dilemmas which arise out of competing obligations and conflicts of interest.

The following statement aims to alert the members of the Association to issues that raise ethical concerns and to indicate potential problems and conflicts of interest that might arise in the course of their professional activities.

While they are not exhaustive, the statement points to a set of obligations to which members should normally adhere as principles for guiding their conduct. Departures from the principles should be the result of deliberation and not ignorance.

The strength of this statement and its binding force rest ultimately on active discussion, reflection, and continued use by sociologists. In addition, the statement will help to communicate the professional position of sociologists to others, especially those involved in or affected by the activities of sociologists.

The statement is meant, primarily, to inform members' ethical judgements rather than to impose on them an external set of standards. The purpose is to make members aware of the ethical issues that may arise in their work, and to encourage them to educate themselves and their colleagues to behave ethically.

The statement does not, therefore, provide a set of recipes for resolving ethical choices or dilemmas, but recognises that often it will be necessary to make such choices on the basis of principles and values, and the (often conflicting) interests of those involved. . . .

Relations with and responsibilities towards sponsors and/or funders

A common interest exists between sponsor, funder and sociologist as long as the aim of the social inquiry is to advance knowledge, although such knowledge may only be of limited benefit to the sponsor and the funder. That relationship is best served if the atmosphere is conducive to high professional standards.

Members should attempt to ensure that sponsors and/or funders appreciate the obligations that sociologists have not only to them, but also to society at large, research participants and professional colleagues and the sociological community. The relationship between sponsors or funders and social researchers should be such as to enable social inquiry to be undertaken as objectively as possible.[1]

Research should be undertaken with a view to providing information or explanation rather than being constrained to reach particular conclusions or prescribe particular courses of action.

1   Clarifying obligations, roles and rights

(a)   Members should clarify in advance the respective obligations of funders and researchers where possible in the form of a written contract. They should refer the sponsor or funder to the relevant parts of the professional code to which they adhere. Members should also be careful not to promise or imply acceptance of conditions which are contrary to their professional ethics or competing commitments.

Where some or all of those involved in the research are also acting as sponsors and/or funders of research the potential for conflict between the different roles and interests should also be made clear to them.

(b)   Members should also recognise their own general or specific obligations to the sponsors whether contractually defined or only the subject of informal and often unwritten agreements. They should be honest and candid about their qualifications and expertise, the limitations, advantages and disadvantages of the various methods of analysis and data, and acknowledge the necessity for discretion with confidential information obtained from sponsors.

They should also try not to conceal factors which are likely to affect satisfactory conditions or the completion of a proposed research project or contract.

2   Pre-empting outcomes and negotiations about research

(a)   Members should not accept contractual conditions that are contingent

[1 Editor's footnote: In March 2002 the Association produced draft guidelines in which 'as objectively as possible' would be replaced by 'professionally.']

upon a particular outcome or set of findings from a proposed inquiry. A conflict of obligations may also occur if the funder requires particular methods to be used.

(b)   Members should try to clarify, before signing the contract, that they are entitled to be able to disclose the source of their funds, its personnel, the aims of the institution, and the purposes of the project.

(c)   Members should also try to clarify their right to publish and spread the results of their research.

(d)   Members have an obligation to ensure sponsors grasp the implications of the choice between alternative research methods.

3   Guarding privileged information and negotiating problematic sponsorship

(a)   Members are frequently furnished with information by the funder who may legitimately require it to be kept confidential. Methods and procedures that have been utilised to produce published data should not, however, be kept confidential unless otherwise agreed.

(b)   When negotiating sponsorships members should be aware of the requirements of the law with respect to the ownership of and rights of access to data.

(c)   In some political, social and cultural contexts some sources of funding and sponsorship may be contentious. Candour and frankness about the source of funding may create problems of access or co-operation for the social researcher but concealment may have serious consequences for colleagues, the discipline and research participants. The emphasis should be on maximum openness.

(d)   Where sponsors and funders also act directly or indirectly as gatekeepers and control access to participants, researchers should not devolve their responsibility to protect the participants' interests onto the gatekeeper. Members should be wary of inadvertently disturbing the relationship between participants and gatekeepers since that will continue long after the researcher has left.

4   Obligations to sponsors and/or funders during the research process

(a)   Members have a responsibility to notify the sponsor and/or funder of any proposed departure from the terms of reference of the proposed change in the nature of the contracted research.

(b)   A research study should not be undertaken on the basis of resources known from the start to be inadequate, whether the work is of a sociological or inter-disciplinary kind.

(c)   When financial support or sponsorship has been accepted, members must make every reasonable effort to complete the proposed research on schedule, including reports to the funding source.

(d)   Members should be prepared to take comments from sponsors or funders or research participants.

(e)   Members should, wherever possible, spread their research findings.

(f)   Members should normally avoid restrictions on their freedom to publish or otherwise broadcast research findings.

Code of Standards and Ethics for Survey Research (CASRO)

Introduction

This Code of Standards and Ethics for Survey Research sets forth the agreed upon rules of ethical conduct for Survey Research Organizations. Acceptance of this Code is mandatory for all CASRO Members.

. . . This Code is not intended to be, nor should it be, an immutable document. Circumstances may arise that are not covered by this Code or that may call for modification of some aspect of this Code. The Standards Committee and the Board of Directors of CASRO will evaluate these circumstances as they arise and, if appropriate, revise the Code. The Code, therefore, is a living document that seeks to be responsive to the changing world of Survey Research. To continue to be contemporary, CASRO advocates ongoing, two-way communication with Members, Respondents, Clients, Outside Contractors, Consultants and Interviewers. . . .

Responsibilities to clients

A   Relationships between a Survey Research Organization and Clients for whom the surveys are conducted should be of such a nature that they foster confidence and mutual respect. They must be characterized by honesty and confidentiality.

B   The following specific approaches describe in more detail the responsibilities of Research Organizations in this relationship:

1   A Survey Research Organization must assist its Clients in the design of effective and efficient studies that are to be carried out by the Research Company. If the Survey Research Organization questions whether a study design will provide the information necessary to serve the Client's purposes, it must make its reservations known.

2   A Research Organization must conduct the study in the manner agreed upon. However, if it becomes apparent in the course of the study that changes in the plans should be made, the Research Organization must make its views known to the Client promptly.

3   A Research Organization has an obligation to allow its Clients to verify that work performed meets all contracted specifications and to examine all operations of the Research Organization that are relevant to the proper execution of the project in the manner set forth. While Clients are encouraged to examine questionnaires or other records to maintain open access to the research process, the Survey Research Organization must continue to protect the confidentiality and privacy of survey Respondents.

4   When more than one Client contributes to the cost of a project specially

commissioned with the Research Organization, each Client concerned shall be informed that there are other Participants (but not necessarily their identity).

5   Research Organizations will hold confidential all information that they obtain about a Client's general business operations, and about matters connected with research projects that they conduct for a Client.

6   For research findings obtained by the agency that are the property of the Client, the Research Organization may make no public release or revelation of findings without expressed, prior approval from the Client.

C   Bribery in any form and in any amount is unacceptable and is a violation of a Research Organization's fundamental, ethical obligations. A Research Organization and/or its principals, officers and employees should never give gifts to Clients in the form of cash. To the extent permitted by applicable laws and regulations, a Research Organization may provide nominal gifts to Clients and may entertain Clients, as long as the cost of such entertainment is modest in amount and incidental in nature. . . .

Chapter 70

Julienne Meyer

WHAT IS ACTION RESEARCH?

From 'Using qualitative methods in health related action research,' *British Medical Journal* 320: 178–181 (2000).

A CTION RESEARCH IS NOT easily defined. It is a style of research rather than a specific method. First used in 1946 by Kurt Lewin, a social scientist concerned with intergroup relations and minority problems in the United States, the term is now identified with research in which the researchers work explicitly with and for people rather than undertake research on them.[1] Its strength lies in its focus on generating solutions to practical problems and its ability to empower practitioners – getting them to engage with research and subsequent 'development' or implementation activities. Practitioners can choose to research their own practice, or an outside researcher can be engaged to help them identify problems, seek and implement practical solutions, and systematically monitor and reflect on the process and outcomes of change.

Most definitions of action research incorporate three important elements: its participatory character; its democratic impulse; and its simultaneous contribution to social science and social change.

Participation is fundamental to action research: it is an approach which demands that participants perceive the need to change and are willing to play an active part in the research and the change process. All research requires willing subjects, but the level of commitment required in an action research study goes beyond simply agreeing to answer questions or be observed. The clear cut demarcation between

---

1 Reason P. and Rowan J. *Human Inquiry: A Sourcebook of New Paradigm Research*, Chichester: Wiley, 1981.

'researcher' and 'researched' that is found in other types of research may not be so apparent in action research. The research design must be continually negotiated with participants, and researchers need to agree an ethical code of practice with the participants. This is especially important as participation in the research, and in the process of change, can be threatening. Conflicts may arise in the course of the research: outside researchers working with practitioners must obtain their trust and agree rules on the control of data and their use and on how potential conflict will be resolved within the project. The way in which such rules are agreed demonstrates a second important feature of action research – namely, its democratic impulse.

'Democracy' in action research usually requires participants to be seen as equals. The researcher works as a facilitator of change, consulting with participants not only on the action process but also on how it will be evaluated. One benefit of this is that it can make the research process and outcomes more meaningful to practitioners, by rooting them in the reality of day to day practice.

Throughout the study, findings are fed back to participants for validation and to inform decisions about the next stage of the study. This formative style of research is thus responsive to events as they naturally occur in the field and frequently entails collaborative spirals of planning, acting, observing, reflecting, and replanning. . . . An action researcher needs to be able to work across traditional boundaries . . . and juggle different, sometimes competing, agendas. This requires excellent interpersonal skills as well as research ability.

There is increasing concern about the 'theory-practice' gap; practitioners have to rely on their intuition and experience since traditional scientific knowledge . . . often does not seem to fit the uniqueness of the situation. Action research is seen as one way of dealing with this because, by drawing on practitioners' intuition and experience, it can generate findings that are meaningful and useful to them. . . .

In considering the contribution of action research to knowledge, it is important to note that generalisations made from action research studies differ from those made on the basis of more conventional forms of research. To some extent, reports of action research studies rely on readers to underwrite the account of the research by drawing on their own knowledge of human situations. It is therefore important, when reporting action research, to describe the work in its rich contextual detail. The researcher strives to include the participants' perspective on the data by feeding back findings to participants and incorporating their responses as new data in the final report. In addition, the onus is on the researcher to make his or her own values and beliefs explicit in the account of the research so that any biases are evident. This can be facilitated by writing self reflective field notes during the research.

The strength of action research is its ability to influence practice positively while simultaneously gathering data to share with a wider audience. However, change is problematic, and although action research lends itself well to the discovery of solutions, its success should not be judged solely in terms of the size of change achieved or the immediate implementation of solutions. Instead, success can often be viewed in relation to what has been learnt from the experience of undertaking the work. For instance, a study which set out to explore the care of older people in accident and emergency departments did not result in much change in the course of the study.[2] However, the lessons learnt from the research were reviewed in the context of national policy and research and carefully fed back to those working in the [institution]; as a result, changes have already been made within the organisation to act on the study's recommendations. Some positive changes were achieved in the course of the study (for example, the introduction of specialist discharge posts in accident and emergency departments), but the study also shed light on continuing gaps in care and issues that needed to be improved in future developments. Participants identified that the role of the 'action researcher' had enabled greater understanding and communication between two services (the accident and emergency department and the department of medicine for elderly people) and that this had left both better equipped for future joint working. In other words, the solutions emerged from the process of undertaking the research. . . .

2 Meyer J. and Bridges J. *An Action Research Study into the Organisation of Care of Older People in the Accident and Emergency Department.* London: City University, 1998.

Chapter 71

Sandra Harding

IS THERE A FEMINIST METHOD?

From *Feminism and Methodology*, Bloomington, Ind. and Buckingham: Indiana University Press and Open University Press (1987).

O VER THE LAST TWO decades feminist inquirers have raised fundamental challenges to the ways social science has analyzed women, men, and social life. From the beginning, issues about method, methodology, and epistemology have been intertwined with discussions of how best to correct the partial and distorted accounts in the traditional analyses. Is there a distinctive feminist method of inquiry? How does feminist methodology challenge – or complement – traditional methodologies? On what grounds would one defend the assumptions and procedures of feminist researchers? Questions such as these have generated important controversies within feminist theory and politics, as well as curiosity and anticipation in the traditional discourses.

The most frequently asked question has been the first one: is there a distinctive feminist method of inquiry? However, it has been hard to get a clear focus on the kind of answer to this question that we should seek. My point here is to argue against the idea of a distinctive feminist method of research. I do so on the grounds that preoccupation with method mystifies what have been the most interesting aspects of feminist research processes. Moreover, I think that it is really a different concern that motivates and is expressed through most formulations of the method question: what is it that makes some of the most influential feminist-inspired biological and social science research of recent years so powerful? I shall first try to disentangle some of the issues about method, methodology, and epistemology. Then I turn to review briefly (or to introduce, depending on the reader) the problems with thinking that attempting to 'add women' to existing social science analyses does all that should be done in response to feminist criticisms. Finally, I shall draw attention to three distinctive characteristics of those feminist analyses that go beyond the additive approaches. I shall try to show why we should not choose to think of these as methods of research, though they clearly have significant implications for our evaluations of research methods.

Method, methodology, epistemology

One reason it is difficult to find a satisfactory answer to questions about a distinctive feminist method is that discussions of method (techniques for gathering evidence) and methodology (a theory and analysis of how research should proceed) have been intertwined with each other and with epistemological issues (issues about an adequate theory of knowledge or justificatory strategy) in both the traditional and feminist discourses. This claim is a complex one and we shall sort out its components. But the point here is simply that 'method' is often used to refer to all three aspects of research. Consequently, it is not at all clear what one is supposed to be looking for when trying to identify a distinctive 'feminist method of research.' This lack of clarity permits critics to avoid facing up to what *is* distinctive about the best feminist social inquiry. It also makes it difficult to recognize what one must do to advance feminist inquiry.

A research *method* is a technique for (or way of proceeding in) gathering evidence. One could reasonably argue that all evidence-gathering techniques fall into one of the following three categories: listening to (or interrogating) informants, observing behavior, or examining historical traces and records. In this sense, there are only three methods of social inquiry. As the essays in this collection show, feminist researchers use just about any and all of the methods, in this concrete sense of the term, that traditional androcentric researchers have used. Of course, precisely how they carry out these methods of evidence gathering is often strikingly different. For example, they listen carefully to how women informants think about their lives and men's lives, and critically to how traditional social scientists conceptualize women's and men's lives. They observe behaviors of women and men that traditional social scientists have not thought significant. They seek examples of newly recognized patterns in historical data.

There is both less and more going on in these cases than new methods of research. The 'less' is that it seems to introduce a false sense of unity to all the different 'little things' feminist researchers do with familiar methods to conceptualize these as 'new feminist research methods.' However, the 'more' is that it is new methodologies and new epistemologies that are requiring these new uses of familiar research techniques. If what is meant by a 'method of research' is just this most concrete sense of the term, it would undervalue the transformations feminist analyses require to characterize these in terms only of the discovery of distinctive methods of research.

That social scientists tend to think about methodological issues primarily in terms of methods of inquiry (for example, in 'methods courses' in psychology, sociology, etc.) is a problem. That is, it is primarily when they are talking about concrete techniques of evidence gathering that they raise methodological issues. No doubt it is this habit that tempts social scientists to seek a unique method of inquiry as the explanation for what is unusual about feminist analyses. On the other hand, it is also a problem that philosophers use such terms as 'scientific method' and 'the method of science' when they are really referring to issues of methodology and epistemology. They, too, are tempted to seek whatever is unique about feminist research in a new 'method of inquiry.'

A *methodology* is a theory and analysis of how research does or should proceed; it includes accounts of how 'the general structure of theory finds its application in particular scientific disciplines.'[1] For example, discussions of how functionalism (or Marxist political economy, or phenomenology) should be or is applied in particular research areas are methodological analyses. Feminist researchers have argued that traditional theories have been applied in ways that make it difficult to understand women's participation in social life, or to understand men's activities as gendered (vs. as representing 'the human'). They have produced feminist versions of trad-itional theories. Thus we can find examples of feminist methodologies in discussions of how phenomenological approaches can be used to begin to understand women's worlds, or of how Marxist political economy can be used to explain the causes of women's continuing exploitation in the household or in wage labor. But these sometimes heroic efforts raise questions about whether even feminist applications of these theories can succeed in producing complete and undistorted accounts of gender and of women's activities. And they also raise epistemological issues.

An *epistemology* is a theory of knowledge. It answers questions about who can be a 'knower' (can women?); what tests beliefs must pass in order to be legitimated as knowledge (only tests against men's experiences and observations?); what kinds of things can be known (can 'subjective truths' count as knowledge?), and so forth. Sociologists of knowledge characterize epistemologies as strategies for justifying beliefs: appeals to the authority of God, of custom and tradition, of 'common sense,' of observation, of reason, and of masculine authority are examples of familiar justificatory strategies. Feminists have argued that traditional epistemologies, whether intentionally or unintentionally, systematically exclude the possibility that women could be 'knowers' or *agents of knowledge*; they claim that the voice of science is a masculine one; that history is written from only the point of view of men (of the dominant class and race); that the subject of a traditional sociological sentence is always assumed to be a man. They have proposed alternative theories of knowledge that legitimate women as knowers. . . . These issues, too, are often referred to as issues about method. Epistemological issues certainly have crucial implications for how general theoretical structures can and should be applied in particular disciplines and for the choice of methods of research. But I think that it is misleading and confusing to refer to these, too, as issues about method.

In summary, there are important connections between epistemologies, meth-odologies, and research methods. But I am arguing that it is *not* by looking at research methods that one will be able to identify the distinctive features of the best of feminist research. . . .

---

1 Peter Caws, 'Scientific method,' in *The Encyclopedia of Philosophy*, ed. Paul Edwards (New York: Macmillan, 1967), p. 339.

What's new in feminist analyses?

Let us ask about the history of feminist inquiry the kind of question Thomas Kuhn posed about the history of science.[2] He asked what the point would be of a philosophy of science for which the history of science failed to provide supporting evidence. We can ask what the point would be of elaborating a theory of the distinctive nature of feminist inquiry that excluded the best feminist social science research from satisfying its criteria. Some of the proposals for a feminist method have this unfortunate consequence. Formulating this question directs one to attempt to identify the characteristics that distinguish the most illuminating examples of feminist research.

I shall suggest three such features. By no means do I intend for this list to be exhaustive. We are able to recognize these features only after examples of them have been produced and found fruitful. As research continues, we will surely identify additional characteristics that expand our understandings of what makes feminist accounts explanatorily so powerful. No doubt we will also revise our understandings of the significance of the three to which I draw attention. My point is not to provide a definitive *answer* to the title question of this section, but to show that this historical approach is the best strategy if we wish to account for the distinctive power of feminist research. While these features have consequences for the selection of research methods, there is no good reason to call them methods.

New empirical and theoretical resources: women's experiences

Critics argue that traditional social science has begun its analyses only in men's experiences. That is, it has asked only the questions about social life that appear problematic from within the social experiences that are characteristic for men (white, Western, bourgeois men, that is). It has unconsciously followed a 'logic of discovery' which we could formulate in the following way: Ask only those questions about nature and social life which (white, Western, bourgeois) men want answered. How can 'we humans' achieve greater autonomy? What is the appropriate legal policy toward rapists and raped women which leaves intact the normal standards of masculine sexual behavior? On the one hand, many phenomena which appear problematic from the perspective of men's characteristic experiences do not appear problematic at all from the perspective of women's experiences. (The above two issues, for example, do not characteristically arise from women's experiences.) On the other hand, women experience many phenomena which they think *do* need explanation. Why do men find child care and housework so distasteful? Why do women's life opportunities tend to be constricted exactly at the moments traditional history marks as the most progressive? Why is it hard to detect black women's ideals of womanhood in studies of black families? Why is men's sexuality so 'driven,' so defined in terms of power? Why is risking death said to represent the distinctively human act but giving birth regarded as merely natural? Reflection on

2 Thomas S. Kuhn, *The Structure of Scientific Revolutions*, 2nd edition (Chicago: University of Chicago Press, 1970).

how social phenomena get defined as problems in need of explanation in the first place quickly reveals that there is no such thing as a problem without a person (or groups of them) who have this problem: a problem is always a problem *for* someone or other. Recognition of this fact, and its implications for the structure of the scientific enterprise, quickly brings feminist approaches to inquiry into conflict with traditional understandings in many ways.

The traditional philosophy of science argues that the origin of scientific problems or hypotheses is irrelevant to the 'goodness' of the results of research. It doesn't matter where one's problems or hypotheses come from – from gazing into crystal balls, from sun worshipping, from observing the world around us, or from critical discussion with the most brilliant thinkers. There is no logic for these 'contexts of discovery,' though many have tried to find one. Instead, it is in the 'context of justification,' where hypotheses are tested, that we should seek the 'logic of scientific inquiry.' It is in this testing process that we should look for science's distinctive virtues (for its 'method'). But the feminist challenges reveal that the questions that are asked – and, even more significantly, those that are not asked – are at least as determinative of the adequacy of our total picture as are any answers that we can discover. Defining what is in need of scientific explanation only from the perspective of bourgeois, white men's experiences leads to partial and even perverse understandings of social life. One distinctive feature of feminist research is that it generates its problematics from the perspective of women's experiences. It also uses these experiences as a significant indicator of the 'reality' against which hypotheses are tested. . . .

Finally, the questions an oppressed group wants answered are rarely requests for so-called pure truth. Instead, they are queries about how to change its conditions; how its world is shaped by forces beyond it; how to win over, defeat, or neutralize those forces arrayed against its emancipation, growth, or development; and so forth. Consequently, feminist research projects originate primarily not in any old 'women's experiences,' but in women's experiences in political struggles. (Kate Millett and others remind us that the bedroom and the kitchen are as much the site of political struggle as are the board room or the polling place.[3]) It may be that it is only through such struggles that one can come to understand oneself and the social world.

New purposes of social science: for women

If one begins inquiry with what appears problematic from the perspective of women's experiences, one is led to design research *for* women. That is, the goal of this inquiry is to provide for women explanations of social phenomena that they want and need, rather than providing for welfare departments, manufacturers, advertisers, psychiatrists, the medical establishment, or the judicial system answers to questions that they have. The questions about women that men have wanted answered have all too often arisen from desires to pacify, control, exploit, or manipulate women. Traditional social research has been *for men*. In the best of

---

3 Kate Millett, *Sexual Politics* (New York: Doubleday and Co. 1969).

feminist research, the purposes of research and analysis are not separable from the origins of research problems.

New subject matter of inquiry: locating the researcher in the same critical plane as the overt subject matter

There are a number of ways we could characterize the distinctive subject matter of feminist social analysis. While studying women is not new, studying them from the perspective of their own experiences so that women can understand themselves and the world can claim virtually no history at all. It is also novel to study gender. The idea of a systematic social construction of masculinity and femininity that is little, if at all, constrained by biology, is very recent. Moreover, feminist inquiry joins other 'underclass' approaches in insisting on the importance of studying ourselves and 'studying up,' instead of 'studying down.' While employers have often commissioned studies of how to make workers happy with less power and pay, workers have rarely been in a position to undertake or commission studies of anything at all, let alone how to make employers happy with less power and profit. Similarly, psychiatrists have endlessly studied what they regard as women's peculiar mental and behavioral characteristics, but women have only recently begun to study the bizarre mental and behavioral characteristics of psychiatrists. If we want to understand how our daily experience arrives in the forms it does, it makes sense to examine critically the sources of social power.

The best feminist analysis goes beyond these innovations in subject matter in a crucial way: it insists that the inquirer her/himself be placed in the same critical plane as the overt subject matter, thereby recovering the entire research process for scrutiny in the results of research. That is, the class, race, culture, and gender assumptions, beliefs, and behaviors of the researcher her/himself must be placed within the frame of the picture that she/he attempts to paint. This does not mean that the first half of a research report should engage in soul searching (though a little soul searching by researchers now and then can't be all bad!). Instead, as we will see, we are often explicitly told by the researcher what her/his gender, race, class, culture is, and sometimes how she/he suspects this has shaped the research project – though of course we are free to arrive at contrary hypotheses about the influence of the researcher's presence on her/his analysis. Thus the researcher appears to us not as an invisible, anonymous voice of authority, but as a real, historical individual with concrete, specific desires and interests.

This requirement is no idle attempt to 'do good' by the standards of imagined critics in classes, races, cultures (or of a gender) other than that of the researcher. Instead, it is a response to the recognition that the cultural beliefs and behaviors of feminist researchers shape the results of their analyses no less than do those of sexist and androcentric researchers. We need to avoid the 'objectivist' stance that attempts to make the researcher's cultural beliefs and practices invisible while simultaneously skewering the research object's beliefs and practices to the display board. Only in this way can we hope to produce understandings and explanations which are free (or, at least, more free) of distortion from the unexamined beliefs and behaviors of social scientists themselves. Another way to put this point is that the beliefs and behaviors of the researcher are part of the empirical evidence for (or against) the claims advanced in the results of research. *This* evidence too must be open to critical scrutiny no less than what is traditionally defined as relevant evidence. Introducing this 'subjective' element into the analysis in fact increases the objectivity of the research and decreases the 'objectivism' which hides this kind of evidence from the public. This kind of relationship between the researcher and the object of research is usually discussed under the heading of the 'reflexivity of social science.' I refer to it here as a new subject matter of inquiry to emphasize the unusual strength of this form of the reflexivity recommendation. The reader will want to ask if and how this strong form of the reflexivity recommendation can be found in the following analyses. How is it implicitly directing inquiry? How might it have shaped some of these research projects yet more strongly?

To summarize my argument, it is features such as these three – not a 'feminist method' – which are responsible for producing the best of the new feminist research and scholarship. They can be thought of as methodological features because they show us how to apply the general structure of scientific theory to research on women and gender. They can also be thought of as epistemological ones because they imply theories of knowledge different from the traditional ones. Clearly the extraordinary explanatory power of the results of feminist research in the social sciences is due to feminist-inspired challenges to the grand theories and the background assumptions of traditional social inquiry.

Two final issues

Before concluding this essay, I want to warn the reader against two inferences one should resist drawing from the analysis above. It is sometimes falsely supposed that in using women's experiences rather than men's as an empirical and theoretical resource, feminism espouses a kind of relativism. It is sometimes also falsely imagined that men cannot make important contributions to feminist research and scholarship. The two issues are related to each other.

First, we should note that on the account I gave above, women's and men's experiences are not equally reliable guides to the production of complete and undistorted social research. Feminist inquirers are never saying that sexist and antisexist claims are equally plausible – for example, that it's equally plausible to regard women as incapable of the highest kind of moral judgment (as men have claimed) and as exercising a different but equally 'high' kind of moral judgment (as Carol Gilligan argues). The reader can identify innumerable additional directly contradictory claims in the reports of feminist challenges to traditional social analyses which follow. Feminist researchers are arguing that women's and men's characteristic social experiences provide different but not equal grounds for reliable knowledge claims. . . . We all – men as well as women – should prefer women's experiences to men's as reliable bases for knowledge claims. . . .

The second faulty inference one might be tempted to make is that men cannot make important contributions to feminist research and scholarship. If the problems feminist inquiry addresses must arise from women's experiences, if feminist social science is to be for women, and if the inquirer is to be in the same critical plane as subject matters (which are often about women and gender), how could men do feminist social science? This vexing question has gained increasing attention as more and more men are, in fact, teaching in women's studies programs and producing analyses of women and gender.

On the one hand, there are clearly important contributions to the history of feminist thought which have been made by men. John Stuart Mill, Karl Marx, and Friedrich Engels are just the most obvious of these thinkers. Their writings are certainly controversial and, at best, imperfect; but so, too, are the writings of the most insightful women thinkers of these periods or, for that matter, in the present day. Moreover, there have always been women willing and able to produce sexist and misogynistic thought – Marabel Morgan and Phyllis Schlafly are just two of such recent writers. Obviously, neither the ability nor the willingness to contribute to feminist understanding are sex-linked traits!

Moreover, significant contributions to *other* emancipation movements have been made by thinkers who were not themselves members of the group to be emancipated. Marx and Engels were not members of the proletariat. There are whites in our own nation as well as in South Africa and other racist regimes who have been willing and able to think in antiracist ways – indeed, they have been lynched, exiled, and banned for their antiracist writings. Gentiles in Europe and the United States have argued for and suffered because of their defenses of Jewish freedoms. So it would be historically unusual if the list of contributors to women's emancipation alone excluded by fiat all members of the 'oppressor group' from its ranks.

On the other hand, surely women, like members of these other exploited groups, are wise to look especially critically at analyses produced by members of the oppressor group. Are women's experiences used as the test of adequacy of the problems, concepts, hypotheses, research design, collection, and interpretation of data? (Must the 'women's experience' from which feminist problematics arise be the experience of the investigator her/himself?) Is the research project *for* women rather than for men and the institutions men control? Does the researcher or theorist place himself in the same class, race, culture, and gender-sensitive critical plane as his subjects of study?

Once we ask these questions, we can see many research projects which are particularly suitable for men sympathetic to feminism to conduct. . . . There are some areas of masculine behavior and thought to which male researchers have easier and perhaps better access than do women researchers: primarily male settings and ones from which women are systematically excluded, such as board rooms, military settings, or locker rooms. They can bring a feminist perspective to bear on certain aspects of some relationships that is valuable in different ways from the perspective women would bring to such relationships. I am thinking here of the 'phallic critique' men could provide of friendships between men, or of relationships between fathers and sons, or between male lovers. How do these feel lacking to their participants? How do they contrast with the characteristics of friendships between women, and so forth?

In addition to the scholarly or scientific benefits which could accrue from such studies, this kind of self-critical research by men makes a kind of political contribution to the emancipation of women which inquiries *by women* cannot achieve. Just as courageous whites can set an example for other whites, and can use for antiracist ends the great power institutional racism bestows on even the most antiracist of whites, so too can men make an important but different kind of contribution to women's emancipation. If men are trained by sexist institutions to value masculine authority more highly, then some courageous men can take advantage of that evil and use their masculine authority to resocialize men. . . .

In spite of these arguments to the contrary, it is easy to understand why many feminists take a skeptical attitude toward a man's claim to be doing feminist research or providing an adequate account of gender or women's activities. Of course it is important to discourage men from thinking they can take over feminist research the way they do everything else which becomes significant in the public world – citing only other male researchers, doing little to alleviate the exploitation of their female colleagues or the women in their lives whose work makes their eminence possible, and so forth.

My own preference is to argue that the designation 'feminist' can apply to men who satisfy whatever standards women must satisfy to earn the label. To maximally increase our understanding, research must satisfy the three criteria discussed earlier. The issue here is not so much one of the right to claim a label as it is of the prerequisites for producing less partial and distorted descriptions, explanations, and understandings. . . .

Chapter 72

Mary Maynard

METHODS, PRACTICE AND EPISTEMOLOGY
The debate about feminism and research

From Maynard, M. and Purvis, J. (eds.), *Researching Women's Lives from a Feminist Perspective,* London: Taylor and Francis (1994).

. . .

The debate about methods

. . .

THE IDEA THAT FEMINISM has a method of conducting social research which is specific to it . . . is one which continues to be espoused. These arguments advocated and defended a qualitative approach to understanding women's lives as against quantitative methods of enquiry. The arguments were rooted in a critique of what were perceived to be the dominant modes of doing research which were regarded as inhibiting a sociological understanding of women's experiences. Quantitative research (particularly surveys and questionnaires) was seen to represent a 'masculinist' form of knowing, where the emphasis was on the detachment of the researcher and the collection and measurement of 'objective' social facts through a (supposedly) value-free form of data collection. By contrast, the use of qualitative methods, which focus more on the subjective experiences and meanings of those being researched, was regarded as more appropriate to the kinds of knowledge that feminists wished to make available, as well as being more in keeping with the politics of doing research as a feminist. Semi-structured or unstructured interviewing has been the research technique most often associated with this stance, although this can, of course, produce both quantitative and qualitative data. . . .

This position was particularly important at a time when feminist research was in its infancy and when women's lives and experiences were still largely invisible.

What was most usefully required then was an approach to research which maximized the ability to explore experience, rather than impose externally defined structures on women's lives. Thus feminists emphasized the importance of listening to, recording and understanding women's own descriptions and accounts. This strategy enabled researchers to extend knowledge of areas such as schooling and paid work, previously understood mainly from a male perspective. It also facilitated the development of new, woman-oriented fields of research, for example violence towards women, sexuality, childbirth and domesticity. At its heart was the tenet that feminist research must begin with an open-ended exploration of women's experiences, since only from that vantage point is it possible to see how their world is organized and the extent to which it differs from that of men.

With hindsight, however, it can be seen that this approach, which proved so beneficial to feminists in their early work, gradually developed into something of an unproblematized orthodoxy against which the political correctness, or otherwise, of *all* feminist research could be judged. It began to be assumed that *only* qualitative methods, especially the in-depth face-to-face interview, could really count in feminist terms and generate useful knowledge. Despite the fact that a number of feminist commentators *did* advocate the use of a range of research techniques and several deployed survey material and the statistical analysis of data to very effective critical ends, the tendency to equate feminist work with a qualitative approach has persisted. . . .

In rejecting quantification, feminists have overlooked the contribution that research involving enumeration has made to our knowledge and understanding of women's experiences. Further, the *political* potential of such work must not be underestimated. The significance of violence in women's lives, for example, is underlined by studies showing the extent and severity of its incidence. Issues such as the feminization of poverty and women's lack of progress in achieving equality, on a number of dimensions, with men in paid work also benefit from work which demonstrates the problem numerically. This is not to argue that only work of this kind is useful or of interest. Such a position would be absurd. It is, however, to suggest that the time has come for some rethinking in terms of what are regarded as acceptable methods for feminists engaged in empirical research. . . . It is no longer tenable for the old orthodoxy to remain.

Feminism and research practice

If the arguments for the existence of a distinctive feminist method can be dismissed, what other grounds might there be for defining research as feminist? Another way in which feminists have answered this question is to turn to issues of methodology, which involves the theory and analysis of how research should proceed, how research questions might best be addressed and the criteria against which research findings might be evaluated. In doing so, feminists have tended to concentrate attention on two main areas of concern, the position from which distinctively feminist research questions might be asked and the political and ethical issues involved in the research process. . . . Many of those who have written about feminist research practice have indicated that a theoretical perspective, acknowledging the pervasive influence of gender divisions on social life, is one of its most important defining characteristics. . . . A second way in which an understanding of the feminist research process has developed, and a consequence of gender-conscious theory and politics, is in the modifications which have been made to existing techniques. . . . Feminists have rejected the inevitability of a power hierarchy between researcher and researched. Instead, they have argued for the significance of a genuine, rather than an instrumental rapport between them. This, it has been claimed, encourages a non-exploitative relationship, where the person being studied is not treated simply as a source of data. Research becomes a means of sharing information and, rather than being seen as a source of bias, the personal involvement of the interviewer is an important element in establishing trust and thus obtaining good quality information. . . .

A final way in which feminist research practice might be said to be distinctive has been in its insistence on its political nature and potential to bring about change in women's lives. . . .

Epistemology and the nature of feminist knowledge

The feminist concern with epistemology has centred on the questions 'who knows what, about whom and how is this knowledge legitimized?' . . . One writer whose work in this area is well known is Sandra Harding. In Harding's view there are three stages in the development of feminist epistemology. The first of these, 'feminist empiricism', argues that it is possible to remove sexist and other biases from the processes of research, particularly when problems for study are initially being identified and defined, in the belief that, once these have been eliminated, value-neutral work will be produced.[1] Harding regards this as an attempt to reform 'bad' science, simply by 'adding' women into existing frameworks, rather than questioning the prejudiced assumptions that are constitutive of science *per se*. The second stage, and the one in which we are currently located, according to Harding, is that of the 'feminist standpoint'. Here the argument is that understanding women's lives from a committed feminist exploration of their experiences of oppression produces more complete and less distorted knowledge than that produced by men. Women lead lives that have significantly different contours and patterns to those of men, and their subjugated position provides the possibility of more complete and less perverse understandings. Thus, adopting a feminist standpoint can reveal the existence of forms of human relationships which may not be visible from the position of the 'ruling gender'.

In addition to 'feminist empiricism' and 'feminist standpoint' Harding suggests that there is a third epistemological position, that of feminist postmodernism. This, along with other variants of postmodernism, is critical of universalistic grand theories and rejects the existence of an authentic self. Its focus instead is on fragmentation, multiple subjectivities, pluralities and flux. Harding clearly does not regard these three stages of feminist epistemology as being absolutely distinct and she argues at one point, for instance, that the empiricism and standpoint positions are

1 Harding (1986).

locked into dialogue with each other. Further, although she refers to the latter as 'transitional' she is also uneasy about any postmodern alternatives. While apparently agreeing with the postmodern critique of science as a doomed project, she also sees problems in adopting it wholeheartedly, because of the way in which it deconstructs and demeans gender as an issue. Thus, feminists cannot afford to give up the standpoint approach because it is 'central to transferring the power to change social relations from the "haves" to the "have-nots"'[2] Postmodernism, in contrast, provides a vision of the future by deconstructing the possibilities as to what this might mean.

The idea of a 'feminist standpoint' has gained currency, although there are variations on precisely what this involves. Harding herself identifies the standpoint position as a 'successor science'. She argues that objectivity should involve the critical scrutiny of *all* evidence marshalled as part of the research process. Conventional notions of objectivity are 'weak' because they include the researchers' hidden and unexplicated cultural agendas and assumptions.[3] 'Strong' objectivity, as represented by the feminist standpoint, includes the systematic examination of such background beliefs. It thus 'avoids damaging forms of relativism . . . and transforms the reflexivity of research from a problem into a scientific resource'.[4]

This idea of a successor science has been challenged by Stanley and Wise. They draw attention to 'silences' in Harding's work, particularly the lack of any real consideration of Black feminist and lesbian feminist points of view and argue that, rather than there being one standpoint, there are a range of different but equally valid ones.[5] Harding has recently attempted to overcome this problem and, in *Whose Science? Whose Knowledge?*, has included a section on 'others' (rather an unfortunate term suggesting deviation from some 'proper' norm). However, she does not deal with Stanley and Wise's central point; once the existence of several feminist standpoints is admitted, then it becomes impossible to talk about 'strong' objectivity as a means of establishing superior or 'better' knowledge because there will, necessarily, be contested truth claims arising from the contextually grounded knowledge of the different standpoints. Stanley and Wise reject the idea of a successor science which, they say, still retains the implication that there is a social reality 'out there' that research can discover. Such 'foundationalism' is based on an insistence that 'truth' exists independently of the knower. They argue instead for a 'feminist fractured foundationalist epistemology'.[6] Whilst not disputing the existence of 'truth' and a material reality, judgments about them are always relative to the context within which such knowledge is produced.[7]

Those who defend the 'standpoint position', or one of its variants, deny that it signifies a collapse into total relativism, arguing, albeit sometimes for different reasons, that it occupies middle ground[8] in what is, conventionally and mistakenly, perceived as a foundationalism versus relativism dichotomy. There is still, however,

2 Ibid., p. 195.
3 Harding (1991), p. 149.
4 Ibid., p. 164.
5 Stanley and Wise (1990), p. 28.
6 Stanley and Wise (1993).
7 Stanley and Wise (1990), p. 41.
8 Ibid.; Harding (1991), p. 138.

the problem of the differing accounts which may emerge from different standpoints. While Stanley and Wise do not seem to regard this as an issue and write positively about such pluralism, others see difficulties.[9] Although it may be tempting to regard each standpoint as equally valid, this may be difficult when the power relations between women themselves differ. Things become particularly problematic, for example, when one standpoint contains elements or assumptions which are racist or heterosexist in nature. Another issue relates to whether it is the standpoint of the individual or the group which is being referred to and what the relationship between them might be. Neither is it clear whether it is the standpoints of feminists or of women more generally which are to be the focus of attention. The terms 'feminist' and 'women's' are often used interchangeably in the literature and, although a feminist approach is almost definitionally one which starts out from women's experiences, most women are not feminists and would not necessarily agree with accounts of the social world generated from a feminist stance.[10]

The 'standpoint' debate is an important one for the ways in which it systematically sets out the specific characteristics of a feminist epistemology and shows how these have relevance for a number of issues (relativism and objectivity, for instance) which are continually debated within sociology more generally. As has been seen, however, there are still areas of contention so that the notion of standpoint is not as definitive as the term itself might imply. Other matters also pertinent to the debate will be addressed in the more general discussions which follows.

Methods, research practice and epistemology: linking the terms of debate

The above sections have considered some of the significant arguments and developments in the debate about the constitutive features of feminist research. The focus of this debate seems to have changed over the years. Initially concerned with the rather narrow issue of method, it then broadened out to include different aspects of research practice. Recently, interest has been more epistemological in nature. One reason for this has been feminists' involvement in discussions about postmodernism which involves questioning many conventional notions about the nature of science, the legitimacy of theory and the status of empirical research.[11]

Although there is no one particular model of what feminist research should be like, recurrent themes appear throughout the literature. There is the focus on women's experiences, for example, and the concern for ethical questions which guide research practices. Feminists are concerned with the role of the researcher in the research, and with countering the scientist philosophy and practice which is often associated with it. Although these themes, along with others, may not be specific to feminist work, the ways that they are treated (informed as they are by feminist theorizing about gender and feminist politics more generally), together

9 Ramazanoglu (1989).
10 Ibid.
11 Flax (1987); Nicholson (1990).

with the manner in which they are combined, mean that it is possible to identify specific feminist research practices and epistemological positions.

There is a problem, however, in linking some of the arguments made at an epistemological level with what happens, or should happen, in terms of research practice and the use of particular research techniques. The discussion about feminist methods, for instance, which tends to have polarized qualitative versus quantitative approaches, is clearly at odds with the critique of the inhibiting effect of dualistic categorization that has been mounted by some feminists in the debate on epistemology. The methods literature has, thus, tended to reproduce the binary oppositions that have been criticized elsewhere, although there is now a move to advocate the importance of quantitative work, as indicated previously. Yet it is difficult to see how some of the issues currently at the forefront of epistemological concerns could really be empirically explored in anything other than qualitative work. The concern with the body and emotions as legitimate sources of knowledge, for example, with reflexivity and the critique of subject/object polarizations seem more appropriate to, and have more affinity with, research which employs relatively open-ended strategies. In many ways this should not surprise us. After all, as we have already seen, it was largely because of philosophical critiques of science and positivism that feminists developed their antipathy to quantification. But this now poses something of a problem because, despite feminists' disclaimers, the epistemological discussions still point to the overall legitimacy of qualitative studies, while researchers themselves are attempting to rehabilitate approaches that involve measurement and counting. This seems to indicate that arguments about what constitutes knowledge and discussions about methods of doing research are moving in opposite directions.

There is also divergence between the abstract analytical philosophizing which characterizes the literature on epistemology, particularly in its postmodernist form, and the more concrete language of that on methods and methodology. Can the former be translated into the practicalities of the latter? Whilst feminist postmodernism usefully directs attention to the fractured nature of womanhood, the possibilities of multiple identities and the dangers of totalizing theory, taken to their logical conclusions many of its precepts are inimical to the principles, never mind the practice, of undertaking empirical research. There are two main reasons for this. The first is that the social world is pictured as so fragmented, so individualistic, so totally in a state of flux that any attempt to present a more structured alternative, which, by its very nature, much social research does, is regarded as, a priori, mistaken. Not only is the task impossible, it is also seen as ill-conceived. A second reason is that the kind of research currently identified with the social sciences (be it surveys, interviews etc) is associated with precisely that modernist Enlightenment tradition which postmodernism is trying to transcend. Whilst analyses of discourse and text are possible from within a postmodern perspective, anything which focuses on the materiality of human existence is virtually impossible, unless analyzed in terms of discourse and text. This does not mean, of course, that a postmodern approach has nothing to offer feminists. What it does mean is that because it contains radically different assumptions from those of other epistemological positions it has, potentially, different things to offer. . . .

. . . Two things are at issue here. The first relates to the problem of political intervention. If one major goal of feminist research is to challenge patriarchal structures and bring about some kind of social change, however conceived, then the postmodern approach, which eshews generalizations and emphasizes deconstruction, can only have a limited role in that endeavour. The second is the development of another kind of orthodoxy among feminists which advocates the postmodern approach as *the* way forward and appears dismissive of other kinds of work.[12] Not only does such a stance attempt to undermine other feminist positions, it also refutes the pragmatism which has been argued for in feminist research.[13] One element which is missing in most discussions of such work is the nature of the *external* constraints which are frequently faced. Not least of these are lack of time, money and other resources, in addition to the requirements imposed by funding bodies. That such facts intrude into and colour the research undertaken needs to be acknowledged. To the hard pressed researcher, being asked to reflect on intractable epistemological concerns can sometimes appear to be something of a dispensable luxury. . . .

A final matter here concerns objectivity. Ramazanoglu has explained this in terms of how to produce scientific knowledge about meanings and social relationships, when people understand and experience these differently. This is a problem that feminism shares with sociology more generally, although, as already discussed, some have advocated a feminist notion of 'strong' objectivity, while others have dismissed it as a problem altogether. But perhaps the issue is not so much about objectivity (with its positivistic connotations of facticity), nor of value-neutrality (and the supposed null effect of the researcher on her research), as about the soundness and reliability of feminist research. Feminist work needs to be rigorous if it is to be regarded as intellectually compelling, politically persuasive, policy-relevant and meaningful to anyone other than feminists themselves. At the moment, it appears that this is more easily dealt with on a practical level than on an epistemological one. At the very least this call for rigour involves being clear about one's theoretical assumptions, the nature of the research process, the criteria against which 'good' knowledge can be judged and the strategies used for interpretation and analysis. In feminist work the suggestion is that all of these things are made available for scrutiny, comment and (re)negotiation, as part of the process through which standards are evaluated and judged. . . .

References

Flax, J. (1987) 'Postmodernism and gender relations in feminist theory', *Signs*, vol. 12, no. 4, pp. 621–643 (reprinted in Nicholson, L.J. (ed.) *Feminism/Postmodernism*, London, Routledge, 1991, pp. 39–63).

Harding, S. (1986) *The Science Question in Feminism*, Milton Keynes, Open University Press.

—— (1991) *Whose Science? Whose Knowledge? Thinking from Women's Lives*, Milton Keynes, Open University Press.

Hekman, S. (1990) *Gender and Knowledge*, Cambridge, Polity Press.

12 For example, Hekman (1990).
13 Kelly *et al.* (1992); Stanley and Wise (1990).

Kelly, L., Regan, L. and Burton, S. (1992) 'Defending the indefensible? Quantitative methods and feminist research', in Hinds, H., Phoenix, A. and Stacey, J. (eds) *Working Out: New Directions for Women's Studies*, London, Falmer Press.

Nicholson, L. (ed.) (1990) *Feminism/Postmodernism*, London, Routledge.

Ramazanoglu, C. (1989) 'Improving on sociology: the problems of taking a feminist standpoint', *Sociology*, vol. 23, no. 3, pp. 427–442.

Stanley, L. and Wise, S. (1990) 'Method, methodology and epistemology in feminist research processes', in Stanley, L. (ed.) *Feminist Praxis: Research, Theory and Epistemology in Feminist Sociology*, London, Routledge.

—— (1993) *Breaking Out Again*, London, Routledge.

Chapter 73

Les Back and John Solomos

DOING RESEARCH, WRITING POLITICS
The dilemmas of political intervention in research on racism

From *Economy and Society* 22(2): 178–199 (1993).

. . .

WITHIN THE SOCIOLOGY OF race in Britain a range of positions have been suggested *vis à vis* the relationship between research and politics. In this section we want to review two positions, ranging from the parameters of academic inquiry suggested by John Rex to the politicized research advocated by Gideon Ben-Tovim and his colleagues. We start, however, with those researchers who in a variety of ways have defended race relations research as being autonomous from direct political action.

Value free academics and the yardstick of justice

Within Britain the debate over the ethics of race relations research has in many ways followed the developments in the United States. The issue much debated in America was why academic research was being carried out on race relations, the relation of such research to the controlling arms of the state, and the role of white social scientists in such research . . . In the British context this debate was echoed in debates that occurred at the Institute of Race Relations . . . and by the development of fundamental criticisms of race relations research in radical black journals . . . More recently the focus of the criticisms has been on the objectives which research on race should have; for example, whether the main focus of research should be on minority communities and their cultural and family networks, or on the institutions of white racism. In addition the politicization of race issues over the past two decades has raised a number of complex ethical and political dilemmas which confront any researcher working in the field. In this kind of context researchers have found it necessary to give some account of the place and function of race relations research. This is what we refer to as *speaking positions.*

Much of the early research on race relations in Britain . . . emphasized the need for such work to be seen as autonomous from ideological and political commitments, or at best having only a tangential link with existing debates about racism. Another version of this approach does not eschew the need to look at the political or policy aspects of race relations, but argues that the only way to influence legislative and administrative branches of government is not through political analysis but through the presentation of factual statistical information about discrimination in such areas as housing, employment and social services. . . . The end result of this approach may be said to be an emphasis on race research as either a neutral academic discipline or uncommitted policy research which aims to present policy-makers with the facts on which they could base new policy initiatives.

A more complex variation on the academic autonomy argument is found in various writings by John Rex (Rex 1973, 1979, 1981). Rex's position is much more sophisticated than the work mentioned above. . . . Rex argues that biases can be found in much of the race relations literature in Britain. He notes, for example, the tendency in the literature to assume that various inadequacies in the culture or family life of West Indian and Asian immigrants are responsible for the social problems brought about by racism, unemployment, low wages, menial occupations, poor housing and bad schools. While accepting, however, the reality of this tendency to 'blame the victim', he argues forcefully against the reduction of social science research on race to the demands of special interests, whether it be those of the policy-makers or those of the black communities or political activists themselves. Rex maintains that there is a need to defend academic inquiry which is more than a neutral study of the 'facts' of racial disadvantage but does not fall into the trap of political rhetoric. . . .

Rex claims that by setting up theoretical 'yardsticks' against which reality can be measured, an account of social reality can be offered which is superior to what he identifies as myth and utopia. Thus in this context political and moral choices are quite separate from sociological analysis. His position can be summed up in the following passage:

> it is all too common today for sociologists to assert that their sociology is critical, non-value-free or reflexive, and having done so to abandon any attempt to conform to the sorts of standards of reasoning and proof which are characteristic of scientific thought.
>
> (1979: 314)

. . . While Rex maintains that his work is 'reflexive' there is little account of how the research on Handsworth was actually conducted. There are only a few glimpses of the relationship between the researchers and their informants within the book. . . .

Part of the agenda of doing research on the politics of racism must be a continual process of self-critical awareness and a sensitivity that research can have both intended and unintended political consequences. For this reason alone it is incumbent on researchers to make public the methods, values and assumptions on which their work is based. While Rex offers an eloquent defence of his own epistemology there exist glaring absences on these issues in his empirical and theoretical writing. We are left with a legacy of research that is both politically naive and methodologically problematic.

'The citizen as social scientist': action research and political participation

More recent work within the politics of race has attempted to advocate explicitly a direct relationship between research and political interventions. A clear example of this is the study by Gideon Ben-Tovim, John Gabriel, Ian Law and Kathleen Stredder on the *The Local Politics of Race*. This book is a radical departure from the perspectives outlined above, and represents a position that has attracted some attention in recent debates.

Ben-Tovim *et al.* argue for a mutual crossing of research and political action. In this situation researchers should be activists and activists should be researchers, and research should be placed in the forefront of political action. . . . Thus they argue for an approach to research which is intimately involved with pressure group politics. They criticize two academic traditions within the analysis of racism, i.e. the sociology of race relations and academic Marxism. They argue that research needs to be consciously politicized and that to defend the 'value free' stance is merely to defend the status quo. . . .

They also claim that academic Marxism has been equally guilty of absolving itself from political struggles. Thus critical writing on racism has gained itself a respectable academic niche where individual careers are advanced by hijacking a moral high ground. Marxism, like the sociology of race relations, takes a stance which is remote and not engaged with political struggles. Ben-Tovim *et al.* claim that both of these genres end up legitimating the very thing they set out to undermine:

> Race relations research which appears ostensibly committed to anti-racism or the elimination of racial discrimination but which is not explicitly designed to effect any change in those directions, effectively serves to maintain if not to endorse the status quo and sometimes, albeit unwittingly, to legitimate further inequalities.
>
> (ibid.: 9)

Their critique of academic writing on race relations is powerful and they raise important issues for debate. However, there are some important tensions within their speaking positions and a good deal is left unsaid on the subject of exactly how their research was harnessed to political engagements and struggles.

The Local Politics of Race is didactic without giving a full account of the way the research was conducted. . . . The authors talk about research on racism as if it was external to themselves and as if their own personal biographies and the biography of the project are not important. Equally their political position offers anti-racism as a placard, something to stand behind. We are given an image of a political context where there are 'us organizations', who are outside the local state (voluntary/community organizations, political parties) and who are the organs of change, and 'them organizations' (intransigent officers and bureaucrats and reactionaries). Political research is then placed squarely within the 'us organization' category. . . .

Such a perspective would be tantamount to saying that the researcher can become a kind of representative of the oppressed group, or spokesperson. Our doubts about this do not exist because we see ourselves as outside the political domain, or because we hold to some notion of value-free research, but result rather from our uncertainty about the utility of reducing all the voices of oppressed groups and their allies to a single voice. . . .

Researching the local politics of race in Birmingham

While we share Ben-Tovim et al.'s criticisms of politically disengaged scholarship we find their ultimate position which places them as advocates deeply problematic. In this sense the 'insiderism' which pervades their writing is open to question. It is important here also to point towards a key difference between their work and the approach we have adopted in our study of the local politics of race in Birmingham. Ben-Tovim et al. did not get access to the officers and bureaucrats within the local authorities which they studied. In a sense, this meant that they could only focus on those groups who were pressurizing the council from outside. In our work in Birmingham we have sought and gained access to those actors within the local state who are in positions of influence. This is a critical difference as we will show in what follows.

From the outset of our research we have sought to avoid the trap of a speaking position which ultimately can be reduced to a form of advocacy. We have preferred an approach which is concerned with understanding the ideologies and practices of those people who are in influential positions within Birmingham City Council. At least initially we adopted a position which shifted the focus of analysis from the study of the powerless to an analysis of those who influenced and determined race policy and political outcomes in Birmingham. We set out to examine the processes whereby the structures of racial inequality were maintained, and the role of white and black political actors in political action aimed at ameliorating these inequalities.

In particular, we wanted to assess the impact that the growth of black political participation was having on the political context. However, in approaching this issue we were concerned to locate the phenomenon of black political participation within the wider structures and processes of local politics in the city. . . .

We are trying to think through strategies whereby we can feed back our research findings into the authority in a way which will be beneficial to those who are working for racial justice within the city. Again we are consulting with relevant people within the organization in an attempt to construct a political strategy in which our research can have some impact on the local authority. In developing our strategy we are again being directed towards a position which is in contrast to the speaking position we advocated at the beginning of this paper. A political activist put it this way:

I think because you are outside the organization and are a third party, your research can be seen as an objective third party. If it had been conducted from within the race unit they would have immediately accused us of making it a put up job. I really believe that your document can affect what happens in this city and our attempts to strive for greater equality.

. . . We find ourselves in the dilemma where we are rejecting a 'value free' perspective we still have to show why our account of a variety of versions of events is a plausible explanation of processes and events. While we recognize that accounts provided by research are partial this does not absolve us of the need to provide an analysis which is persuasive.

The lesson that we have learned in the process of doing research and writing politics in Birmingham is that it is difficult to sustain one ethical position in all contexts. This begs the question of the utility of establishing or advocating unitary speaking positions. In the course of doing research it is sometimes necessary to defend spurious speaking/writing positions. While we see no easy way for research on racism that is not in some way political, we have also found it strategically appropriate to adopt other speaking positions in an attempt to pre-empt accusations of partiality and invalidity. The crucial issue seems to be the context and the nature of the audience. Clearly, we have doubts about John Rex's notion of a 'value free academic', but there are circumstances where a 'value free' position can be strategically useful.

If we are arguing for 'committed anti-racism' and an articulation between political action and research, we need to give our rhetoric a history so that more effective strategies can be thought through. What the current literature gives us are 'claims', forms of 'credentialism' and 'rhetoric', but not concrete examples of how an anti-racist project can effect change through research. We are arguing that the project is important but, as yet, the strategies are unclear. There is a danger of constructing an elaborate form of credentialism where one simply identifies oneself as doing 'anti-racist research'. What we have learned from our experience in Birmingham is that it is infinitely more complex than any simple abstract statement of anti-racist intent. The necessities of political struggle often demand a more flexible approach than is allowed for in the credentialism which pervades the debate. . . .

References

Ben-Tovim, G., Gabriel, J., Law, I. and Stredder, K. (1986) *The Local Politics of Race*, London: Macmillan.

Rex, J. (1973) 'The future of race relations research in Britain: sociological research and the politics of racial justice', *Race* xiv(4): 481–488.

—— (1979) 'Sociology, theory, typologies, value stand points and research', in J. Rex and S. Tomlinson, *Colonial Immigrants in a British City: A Class Analysis*, London: Routledge and Kegan Paul.

—— (1981) 'A working paradigm for race relations research', *Ethnic and Racial Studies* 4(1): 1–25.

Chapter 74

Martyn Hammersley

HIERARCHY AND EMANCIPATION

From 'On feminist methodology' in: *The Politics of Social Research*, London: Sage (1995).

. . .

Hierarchy

THERE HAS BEEN MUCH discussion within ethnographic methodology about the variety of roles that a participant observer can play, and about variations in the role of the interviewer. In large part the concern has been how to avoid disturbing what is being investigated, but ethnographers have not been unaware of the ethical issues involved, including their obligations to the people they study . . . Few, if any, researchers in the qualitative or ethnographic tradition would argue that the researcher can, or should try to, act as a neutral and uninvolved observer, even though they would not usually advocate commitment to a particular group within the field of investigation and active intervention on the part of that group. Similarly, the idea that the researcher's own values should be made explicit is also to be found in the non-feminist literature (most notably Weber 1949; Myrdal 1970). And, again, the advocacy and practice of collaborative research involving the people studied in the research process has emerged in a number of fields. . . .

There are three feminist arguments against hierarchy in the research relationship, appealing to ethical, methodological and tactical considerations respectively. Let me begin by considering the idea that hierarchy should be eliminated from the research process because there is an ethical requirement that women researchers always treat other women as equals not as subordinates. One obvious problem here is the assumption that feminists only study women. Some feminists have pointed to the importance of 'studying up', of researching the powerful (Harding 1987: 8), and this inevitably means studying men. However, the problem is more general than this: since the lives of women and men are so closely interrelated it would be very difficult to study women alone. The only way to do this would be to restrict one's focus to women's experiences, but this may not tell us much about the world that produced those experiences. And where men are included as sources of data, hierarchy probably cannot or should not be eliminated from the research process. The men may impose a hierarchy and, whether they do or not, presumably feminist researchers must exploit whatever resources they have to exert control over the relationship, on the grounds that in present circumstances the only choice is between being dominant or being dominated. This implies an important qualification to the feminist commitment to non-hierarchical research techniques. And it is worth adding that there are some women in powerful social positions in dealing with whom feminists may also be forced into hierarchical relationships, one way or the other.

Over and above this practical issue, though, I want to question the desirability of the principle of non-hierarchical relationships, if by that is meant equality of control over the research process between researchers and researched (which seems logically to imply the abolition of the distinction between the two). One of the problems with many feminist discussions of this issue is that the concept of hierarchy which is employed is one-dimensional and zero-sum: it implies control that is all-pervasive and that is always exercised by one person or group at the expense of others. On this view, the only alternatives are domination by either one side or the other, or equality/democracy. Yet, power is rarely all-encompassing, it is more usually restricted to particular domains, especially in large societies with complex divisions of labour (Giddens 1973). Thus, conventional researchers do not claim the right to control the lives of the people they study in some all-enveloping sense. The control they seek is restricted to the particular research project. They claim the right to define the research topic, to decide to a large extent how and what data are to be collected, to do the analysis and to write the research report. This does not even represent a claim to total control over the research process itself. Researchers do not, and could not, demand access to all settings, insist on interviewing anyone whom they desire to interview, or require the divulging of all relevant information. More importantly, the research they do is usually a small and marginal part of the lives of the people being studied. The control researchers seek to exercise is more limited than, say, that claimed by employers over employed or professionals over clients. If the researcher-researched relationship is a form of domination then these other relationships are also, and to a much greater degree.

What seems to be implicit in some feminist methodologists' opposition to hierarchical relationships, then, is a rejection of all inequalities in power and authority. But we must ask whether this is a reasonable goal. Could it be achieved? Is even its approximation desirable? Even if we take democracy as an omni-relevant ideal, does it not involve some people making decisions on behalf of others, acting as their democratic representatives? Every decision could not be made by a plebiscite. And is democracy always the best way of making decisions? At the very least these issues need discussion.

Following on from this, we must ask whether researchers' exercise of control over the research process is necessarily, or even typically, against the interests of others, including those of the people studied. This is only obviously so if it is assumed that 'having a say' in decisions, all decisions, is an overriding interest in every circumstance. And it is not clear to me why we should assume that this is the case. As far as research is concerned, advocacy of this view often seems to be based on the assumption that research findings are simply an expression of opinion by the researcher, and that her opinion is no better than that of any other woman. On this assumption the greater likelihood of the researcher's 'opinion' being published as against those of the women studied represents dominance by the one over the other. However, the premiss on which this argument is based is false. Research necessarily and legitimately involves a claim to intellectual authority, albeit of a circumscribed kind. That authority amounts to the idea that the findings of research are, on average, less likely to be in error than information from other sources. And this stems from the operation of the research community in subjecting research findings to scrutiny and thereby detecting and correcting errors.

While I accept that everyone has the right to come to their own opinions on any issue, I do not believe that this implies that we must treat everyone's opinions as equally likely to be true, and therefore equally worthy of attention. Nor do I believe that we do this or could do this in everyday life. This is not to say that only research findings are of value as a source of information. For example, we also tend to privilege sources of information based on first-hand experience as against second-hand reports, and justifiably so. Nor is it to say that research findings should be accepted at face value. The point is simply that it is rational to give them more attention than the opinions of people who have no distinctive access to relevant information. In short, research is not the only source of intellectual authority and its authority is limited and does not automatically imply validity, but research does inevitably involve a claim to authority. . . .

The second rationale for the abolition of hierarchy, indeed of any asymmetry in the researcher-researched relationship, is methodological in character: it is suggested that data deriving from hierarchical relationships will be distorted by that context and therefore be invalid. Once again, this seems to me to rest on an assumption which is unsound. If we were to assume that data took the form exclusively of accounts from informants, so that the only barrier to valid research findings was how full and accurate informants were prepared to make their accounts, then this argument would have some plausibility. Presumably, the more informants are treated as part of the research team, the more they are committed to its goals, the better the information they are likely to provide; though even in this case they will have other commitments which may well interfere with the quality of the data, and the danger of reactivity is likely to be increased. However, what we have here is an extremely restricted view of the nature of social science data. It is unreasonable to assume that the only data available consist of the information about the social world provided in the accounts of informants. Indeed, these accounts are not sufficient in themselves because we cannot assume that informants understand the wider social forces which lead them to behave in the ways that they do, that they are always reliable observers, or even that they will always know their own motives. Informants' accounts can and should be examined not just for what they tell us about the phenomena to which they refer but also for what we can infer from them about the informants themselves. Furthermore, many data are observational in character, consisting not of what people tell the researcher but of her/his observations of what they do.

Once we recognise this variation in the character of data, the role of the researcher becomes much more active, involving the piecing together of information from a diversity of sources; and this information is always subject to a variety of forms of potential error. It seems to me that one should use whatever information is available, but in all cases must examine its context with a view to assessing likely sources and directions of error. The idea that there is some single ideal or authentic situation in which data are necessarily error-free and that data from other situations must be rejected is false.

The final argument against hierarchy is the idea that if research has the practical goal of bringing about female emancipation, then the women studied need to be involved in the research if they are to be mobilised effectively. This argument depends on acceptance of that practical goal, and this will be my focus in the next section.

In summary, then, the choice is not between a hierarchical and an egalitarian/democratic form of relationship between researcher and researched. This dichotomy does not capture the relevant complexity of human relationships. Even feminists are not able to implement non-hierarchical relationships in all their research because this is at odds with the nature of the surrounding society. But even more importantly, there are serious questions about the wisdom of attempts to abandon the differentiation of role between researcher and researched. In my judgment, research inevitably involves a claim to intellectual authority (albeit of a severely limited kind) and a corresponding obligation on the part of the researcher to try to ensure the validity of the findings.

Furthermore, from an ethical point of view, the question of how much, and how, one should intervene in the lives of the people one is studying, and whether and in what respects they should be incorporated into the research process, is difficult to decide in general, in ethical or in methodological terms. What is appropriate depends in part on who one is and whom one is studying, in what aspect and for what purpose. This has been recognised by some feminists. Smart (1984), for example, reports that she could not employ a collaborative orientation in studying male solicitors. And Clegg (1975) suggests that collaborative methods are inappropriate for feminists studying men. Even collaborative research by women with other women is not always easy to sustain, as Acker et al. (1982) illustrate. They report a number of problems, including the demand from some of the women for the researchers to provide more of their own sociological analysis (p. 42). And Finch notes the danger that feminist researchers interviewing informants 'woman to woman' could be exploitative because information is elicited which would not otherwise be obtained and that could be used 'against the collective interests of women' (Finch 1984: 83). Finally, Stacey (1988: 22) asks whether the appearance of greater respect for and equality with research subjects in the ethnographic approach 'masks a deeper, more dangerous, form of exploitation'.

In my view, the proper relationship between researcher and researched is not something which can be legislated by methodology, feminist or otherwise. It will depend on the specifies of particular research investigations. Furthermore, we should avoid naive contrasts between the dilemmas and inequalities involved in the research process and some idealised conception of 'authentic, related [personhood]' (Stacey 1988: 23). The rest of life is full of dilemmas and inequalities, even more than research, and while ideals are important they should not be applied irrespective of circumstance. In short, advocacy of a non-hierarchical relationship between researcher and researched rests on some doubtful ideas about the social world and the relationship of research to it.

Emancipation as goal and criterion

The idea that scientific inquiry should be concerned with changing the world, not just describing it, goes back to Marx and beyond. . . . There have also been those who have argued that truth should be defined and/or judged in terms of practical efficacy of one kind or another. For instance, William James reformulated Peirce's pragmatic maxim in this direction (see Bird 1986); and some Marxists and critical theorists have adopted a similar instrumentalism, framed in terms of a contribution to emancipation (see, for example, Habermas 1968). Once again, then, we should recognise that what feminists are proposing is to be found in the non-feminist literature; and some of the problems with these ideas are well known.

I want to argue against both aspects of the emancipatory model of inquiry; the idea that changing the world should be the immediate goal of research, and that its success in this respect is the most important criterion by which it should be judged. It seems to me that the concept of emancipatory inquiry is based on a simplistic notion of practice (political and social). This is conceived as struggle for emancipation from oppression in a world that is neatly divided into oppressors and oppressed. As slogans, the terms 'oppression' and 'emancipation' may be appealing, but as analytic concepts they are problematic. For one thing, there is no single type or source of oppression. It is now widely recognised that 'racial', ethnic and sexual oppression cannot be reduced to class oppression. Nor can other types of oppression be reduced, directly or indirectly, to sexual oppression. Given this, we find that many people will be classed as both oppressors and oppressed from different points of view. At the very least, this introduces a considerable degree of complexity into the application of the oppressor-oppressed model. This problem has been highlighted by black feminists who have challenged the neglect of racism by white feminists (Davis 1981; Carby 1982). And, of course, even black women living in Western societies may be regarded as part of the oppressor group when the focus includes international exploitation.

There are also problems involved in the very concept of oppression, as Geuss has pointed out in a discussion of critical theory:

> It seems unrealistic under present conditions of human life to assume that any and every preference human agents might have can be satisfied, or to assume that all conflict between the preferences of different agents will be peacefully and rationally resolved. Some frustration – even some

imposed frustration – of some human preferences must be legitimate and unexceptionable. (Geuss 1981: 16)

In addition, the concept of oppression involves the assumption that we can identify what are real or genuine needs relatively easily. Yet . . . the identification of needs is not a matter of simple description. Rather, it is a reconstruction on the basis of what we feel and know, and what others say and do, and may well involve dealing with inconsistencies and disagreements. As a result, the needs ascribed to a group may not match the beliefs of many of its members. How do we smooth out the contradictions in what people say and do about their needs? How do we deal with inconsistencies and disagreements in our own orientations? How do we decide what are genuine desires, and what desires are against a person's own interests (or against those of others)? Geuss comments that 'To speak of an agent's "interests" is to speak of the way that agent's particular desires could be rationally integrated into a coherent "good life"' (Geuss 1981: 47–48). This highlights the danger of defining the 'real needs' of an oppressed group falsely. Worse still, the question arises: are there not likely to be several alternative rational reconstructions, especially since such judgments depend on value and factual assumptions? If so, there is room for genuine disagreement about needs and interests. . . .

These problems with 'oppression', and with the associated concepts of 'needs' and 'interests', also create difficulties for the notion of 'emancipation'. If oppression is not an all or nothing matter, is not restricted to a single dimension, and is a matter of judgment which is open to reasonable dissensus, it is not clear that it can be overcome in the form of the total, once and for all release from constraint which the term 'emancipation' implies. In Marxism these problems are obscured by a view of practice that portrays it as a historical process which brings reality into line with theory, that theory itself being a product of, and legitimated in terms of, its position and role in history. According to this view, desire and social obligation are miraculously harmonised as contradictions between subjectivity and objectivity, fact and value are resolved by the historical dialectic . . . Marx argued that the triumph of the proletariat would abolish all oppression because the proletariat is the universal class. Most feminists would probably doubt whether a successful proletarian revolution would lead to women's emancipation; and not without reason. But the argument works the other way too: as some feminists recognise, there is no good reason for assuming that women's emancipation (if such a concept is viable, given the problems outlined above) would abolish 'racial', ethnic, class and other forms of oppression. Indeed, it is possible that it could worsen them. Historicism, whether in Marxist or feminist form, is not convincing in my judgment (Hammersley 1992: ch. 6). However, without it the concept of emancipation becomes highly problematic. In its absence negative critique can be little more than negativism for the sake of it.

I am not denying the existence or illegitimacy of inequalities between the sexes, including power differences. Nor am I suggesting that feminist politics must stop until the analytical problems outlined here have been resolved. I am simply pointing to important problems whose resolution may require considerable rethinking: and this is (at least in part) the responsibility of researchers. And one result of such rethinking should be a less instrumentalist view of the relationship between 'theory' and 'practice'. Once we recognise the complexities of practice, it should become clear that research cannot play the commanding role it is given by some interpretations of the idea of research as directed towards bringing about female emancipation.

The other issue I want to raise about the emancipatory conception of inquiry concerns the idea that truth is to be judged in terms of a pragmatic criterion: in terms of its contribution to emancipation. It is fairly obvious, I think, that in practice it is not uncommon for successful action to be based on some false assumptions (this is fortunate, since otherwise humanity would not have survived). Equally, it is quite possible for action based on sound assumptions to fail; for example, because of contingencies which could not have been anticipated. Truth and effectiveness are in my view different values that, while not completely unrelated, have no *necessary* connection. And this has important implications for the nature of research and for its relationship to practice. Since its value cannot be judged entirely in terms of practical success, the research process must be given some autonomy from practical concerns if researchers are to be able to assess the validity of their products effectively. And this argument runs counter to the claim, to be found in some versions of feminist methodology, that any inquiry which is not directed in some relatively immediate way to bringing about emancipation is illegitimate. . . .

It seems to me that there is a case for institutionalised inquiry that is not geared to the immediate requirements of any single political or social practice. Such inquiry would produce knowledge that is potentially of relevance to a wide range of practices. Of course, by its very nature inquiry of this kind could not be specifically directed to pragmatic goals and could not be judged primarily in pragmatic terms, though it *would* need to be judged in terms of public relevance (Hammersley 1992). It is on some such view of inquiry that scholarship, science and universities have long relied. In my judgment that view needs to be defended against those who, for whatever reason and whatever their values, wish to tie inquiry to their own practical goals. . . .

References

Acker, J., Barry, K. and Esseveld, J. (1982) 'Objectivity and truth: problems in doing feminist research', *Women's Studies International Forum*, 6, 4: 423–435.

Bell, C. and Roberts, H. (eds) (1984) *Social Researching: politics, problems, practice*, London, Routledge and Kegan Paul.

Bird, G. (1986) *William James*, London, Routledge and Kegan Paul.

Carby, H. (1982) 'White woman listen! Black feminism and the boundaries of sisterhood', in Centre for Contemporary Cultural Studies (ed.), *The Empire Strikes Back: race and racism in 70s Britain*, London, Hutchinson.

Clegg, S. (1975) 'Feminist methodology – fact or fiction', *Quality and Quantity*, 19: 83–97.

Davis, A. (1981) *Women, Race and Class*, New York, Random House.

Finch, J. (1984) ' "It's great to have someone to talk to": the ethics and politics of interviewing women', in Bell and Roberts (eds) 1984.

Geuss, R. (1981) *The Idea of Critical Theory*, Cambridge, Cambridge University Press.

Giddens, A. (1973) *Class Structure of the Advanced Societies*, London, Hutchinson.

Habermas, J. (1968) *Knowledge and Interest*, English trans, Cambridge, Polity Press, 1987.

Hammersley, M. (1992) *What's Wrong with Ethnography?*, London, Routledge.

Harding, S. (ed.) (1987) *Feminism and Methodology*, Bloomington, Indiana University Press.

Myrdal, G. (1970) *Objectivity in Social Research*, London: Duckworth.

Smart, C. (1984) *The Ties that Bind: law, marriage and the reproduction of patriarchal relations*, London, Routledge and Kegan Paul.

Stacey, J. (1988) 'Can there be a feminist ethnography?', *Women's Studies International Forum*, 11, 1: 21–27.

Weber, M. (1949) *The Methodology of the Social Sciences*, New York: Free Press.

PART FIFTEEN

Paradigm disputes and resolutions

INTRODUCTION

I T SHOULD BE CLEAR by now that social research methodology is a highly contested field, in which a variety of styles and positions co-exist in sometimes uneasy tension. Occasionally 'paradigm wars' break out between advocates of different approaches. Equally, peace-makers may seek resolutions. This section contains instances of both.

The exchange reproduced in reading 75 is between Whyte, author of the classic work of sociological ethnography *Street Corner Society* (see reading 30), and his critics. The dispute involves a clash between the broadly realist and modernist version of qualitative method that Whyte represents, and the postmodern perspective embraced by Denzin and Richardson (see also reading 60). The starting point for this was the publication of a re-study by Boelen of the setting Whyte had originally studied, purporting to have found factual errors in his account. Expecting to resolve things by an appeal to 'the facts', Whyte was surprised to learn that the rules about facts had apparently changed. Richardson's response to Whyte's defence of his method is, in part, to invoke the kind of criticism that Frank (reading 64) makes of social science and its relationship with research participants: it diminishes participants' lives. Denzin criticizes Whyte's commitments to realism and positivism (as he sees it), and suggests that fact and fiction are not easily distinguished. Whyte's view is to dismiss these critics as representing a passing fad. The various parties to this dispute appear to be talking past each other.

Smith and Heshusius (reading 76) present an example of paradigm dispute between quantitative and qualitative traditions. They claim that pragmatic attempts *to combine the two* in research practice mean that an important debate gets 'closed down'. Like Harding (reading 71), these authors distinguish between method and methodology calling the latter the 'logic of justification'. They argue that it is at this second level that preserving the distinction matters. Essentially, an anti-foundationalist, idealist research practice should not be mixed up with one that founds claims to ultimate validity in the application of procedures whose justification depends on a realist epistemology. In a telling phrase that perhaps explains the incapacity of Denzin and Richardson to engage in productive dialogue with Whyte, these authors state: 'An appeal that one must accept a particular result because it is based on the facts will have little impact on one who believes there can be no uninterpreted facts.'

Bryman's piece (reading 77) attempts to detach issues of method from epistemological discussions. He outlines a series of practical ways in which quantitative and qualitative styles can be combined, characterizing Smith and Heshusius as 'doctrinaire and restrictive'. This is followed by a reading from Oakley (reading 78) who, in the 1980s, shifted her position away from one that was exclusively committed to qualitative interviewing (reading 38). Her piece describes the use of a randomized controlled trial (RCT) to assess experimentally the effectiveness of a health intervention, in the light of ethical considerations of relevance to feminist research practice. She ends by quoting another author (Keller) approvingly, suggesting that the objective standards of science, as reflected in RCTs, are helpful in rescuing the arbitration of truth from the political domain.

The final reading (number 79) of this book is by Cain and Finch. In it they argue that a commitment to research studies and the collection, or production, of 'data' is of profound importance. They seek to reconcile the perception that facts are never neutral and that research is never value-free with a commitment to objectivity and scholarly values. In advocating the kind of craft skills that Mills (reading 2) described, they also find themselves arguing for the reintegration of numerical skills in an essentially qualitative and interpretive research enterprise. At the same time, the uncritical embrace of an 'anything goes' mentality of the sort often induced by a thoughtless reading of Feyerabend (reading 26) is roundly dismissed. Ultimately, Cain and Finch argue, social research is a personal and a professional responsibility.

DISCUSSION POINTS

- Outline a study of street corner society that would be compatible with the principles of Denzin and Richardson. How would it differ from the one done by Whyte?
- Smith and Heshusius say that the quantitative–qualitative debate is one between fundamentally opposed philosophical positions (idealism and realism). Their characterization of disputes over facts exactly parallels the dispute between Whyte and his critics (reading 75). Yet neither Whyte nor his critics were quantitative researchers. What varieties of philosophical position underlie the qualitative research enterprise? Should you have to decide whether you are a realist or an idealist before doing a qualitative research project?
- Is Bryman's account of Smith and Heshusius an accurate representation of their position? Is his own pragmatic position on combining quantitative and

qualitative approaches a viable alternative to theirs? What might be lost and gained by engaging in such mixed-method research practice?

- The quotation at the end of Oakley's article suggests that modern science can be emancipatory, providing an objective arbitration of truth that is free from ideology. By implication, the experimental design of the RCT can provide such arbitration and emancipation. What are the problems involved in using RCTs in social research practice? Think of a research project that you have done, or that you have recently read. What role might an RCT have played in this context?
- How effectively do you think Cain and Finch reconcile the perspectives that they discuss? What problems have they overlooked?

FURTHER READING

Bryman, A. (1988) *Quantity and Quality in Social Research*, London: Unwin Hyman.

Fielding, N. and Fielding J.L. (1986) *Linking Data*, London: Sage.

Glassner, B. and Moreno, J.D. (eds) *The Qualitative–Quantitative Distinction in the Social Sciences*, Dordrecht: Kluwer.

Guba, E.G. and Lincoln, Y.S. (1994) 'Competing paradigms in qualitative research', in Denzin, N.K. and Lincoln, Y.S. (eds) *Handbook of Qualitative Research*, Thousand Oaks, Cal.: Sage, 105–117.

Hammersley, M. (1992) 'The paradigm wars: reports from the front', *British Journal of Sociology of Education* 13(1): 131–143.

Jayaratne, T.E. (1983) 'The value of quantitative methodology for feminist research', in Bowles, G. and Duelli Klein, R. (eds) *Theories of Women's Studies*, London: Routledge and Kegan Paul.

Jick, T.D. (1979) 'Mixing qualitative and quantitative methods: triangulation in action', *Administrative Science Quarterly* 24: 602–611.

Rossman, G.B. and Wilson, B.L. (1994) 'Numbers and words revisited: being "shamelessly eclectic"', *Quality and Quantity* 28: 315–327.

Sieber, S. (1979) 'The integration of fieldwork and survey methods', *American Journal of Sociology* 78 (6): 1135–1159.

Chapter 75

William Foote Whyte, Laurel Richardson and Norman K. Denzin

QUALITATIVE SOCIOLOGY AND DECONSTRUCTIONISM
An exchange

From Denzin, N.K., 'The facts and fictions of qualitative inquiry,' *Qualitative Inquiry* 2 (2): 230–241 (1996); Richardson, L., 'Ethnographic trouble,' *Qualitative Inquiry* 2 (2): 227–229 (1996); Whyte, W.F., 'Qualitative sociology and deconstructionism,' *Qualitative Inquiry* 2 (2): 220–226 (1996a); Whyte, W.F., 'Facts, interpretations, and ethics in qualitative Inquiry,' *Qualitative Inquiry* 2 (2): 242–244 (1996b).

1 Qualitative sociology and deconstructionism – William Foote Whyte

TO WHAT EXTENT CAN we consider a report of qualitative research as factual? I thought I knew the answer to that question until the recent surge of interest in critical epistemology, deconstructionism, and postpositivism. I had to face these new trends when the *Journal of Contemporary Ethnography* (1992) ran a special issue to evaluate *Street Corner Society* (*SCS*) (1981).

That issue arose out of a study submitted by W.A. Marianne Boelen (1992) to the journal. She had gone back to the North End of Boston on several occasions 30 to 45 years after I left it in 1940, had interviewed some of the people I knew and some others, and had written an interpretation quite different from mine. That issue contained my rejoinder and discussions of the controversy by three behavioral scientists, anthropologist Arthur Vidich (1992) and sociologists Laurel Richardson (1992) and Norman Denzin (1992).

When I received Boelen's (1992) 57-page paper, I was inclined simply to report that my field notes told a different story, but then I remembered Derek Freeman's attack on Margaret Mead, through what he claimed to be a restudy of a community Mead had studied years earlier. The Harvard University Press had lent credibility to the attack by publishing Freeman's book (1983). When that book appeared, Margaret Mead was dead. I had the advantage of being able to defend myself.

I sent a copy of the 1992 Boelen attack to my former corner boy assistant and long-time collaborator, Angelo Ralph Orlandella. He wrote a critique of the Boelen article. The editors decided to print it along with my rejoinder.

I had assumed that the assignment of the behavioral science critics was to rule whether my account or Boelen's (1992) was more likely to be an accurate description and interpretation of the North End in the late 1930s, but none of them took a position on that issue. Vidich (1992) simply stated that 'readers may draw their own conclusions about the issues raised in these essays' (p. 80).

Richardson (1992) and Denzin (1992) bypassed that issue, claiming that the nature of the critical game had changed since I did the study. As Richardson put it:

> The core of this postfoundational climate is *doubt* that any discourse has a privileged place, any text an authoritative 'corner' on the truth.
>
> (p. 104)

Denzin called me a 'positivist-social realist' (1992: 130) and stated that

> today, social realism is under attack. It is now seen as but one narrative strategy for telling stories about the world out there
>
> (p. 126)

> As the 20th century is now in its last decade, it is appropriate to ask if we any longer want this kind of social science that Whyte produced and Boelen, in her own negative way endorses?
>
> (p. 131)

In 1994, Denzin returned to this case with a further commentary, under the heading of 'Different tellings.'

> In a recent article, W.A. Marianne Boelen (1992) criticizes William Foote Whyte's classic study of *Street Corner Society* (1943) on several grounds. She notes that Whyle did not know Italian, was not an insider to the group studied, did not understand the importance of the family in Italian group life, and, as a consequence, seriously misrepresented many of the facts in 'Cornerville' society. Whyte (1992) has disputed Boelen's charges, but they linger, especially in light of Doc's (Whyte's key informant) estrangement from Whyte. But unnoticed is the fact that no permanent telling of a story can be given. There are only always different versions of different, not the same, stories when the same site is studied.
>
> (p. 506)

Criteria for evaluation of a research report

How should one evaluate a research report on a field study? First, we should recognize certain standard rules for scholarly writing. Then we can apply those rules to the studies we are seeking to evaluate: in this case, the Boelen (1992) essay first and then the critical judgments of the behavioral science critics – especially Richardson (1992) and Denzin (1992).

1. *The author should make clear the sources from which data are gathered to support the conclusions drawn.* Boelen (1992) drew her conclusions on the basis of personal interviews with 17 people, more or less. That imprecision is necessary because she mentions particular individuals and then also uses collective terms; 'the Nortons' and 'the restaurant family.' When I knew them, the Nortons consisted of 13 young men; she mentions two of them by the pseudonyms I gave them: Frank Bonelli and Nutsy. There is no indication that she interviewed any others of that group. She does not specify what members of the restaurant family she interviewed.

2. *The author should be open to contrary evidence.* Boelen (1992) writes that she sent the draft of her article to all her informants, with a request for them to tell her if they agreed with everything she wrote. She claims that every informant agreed with every conclusion. Can we believe that all informants not only read the 57-page paper but then also stated that they agreed with everything she wrote? Significantly, one of her informants she does not mention was Angelo Ralph Orlandella (Sam Franco in *SCS*, 1993). He read her preliminary outline for the article, along with a letter asking him to endorse her conclusions. Thinking Boelen was a friend of mine, he did not want to offend her so he simply failed to respond – until he later wrote for the special issue (1992, pp. 69–79).

3. *Quotations should not be drawn out of context, thus distorting what the original author meant.* I had written in *SCS* (1981) that I had completed the manuscript while in Boston and had not made any basic changes in my Chicago period (1940–1942). Boelen (1992) believes that I shaped *SCS* (1981) to meet the standards of the Chicago sociology department. To support that charge, she quotes the following passage from *SCS* (1981). I had written that, after arriving in Chicago, I had 'immersed myself in the sociological (slum) literature' (p. 356). She neglects to report the rest of that sentence and the one that follows. I went on to state that

> I became convinced that most of it was worthless and misleading. It seemed to me it would detract from the task at hand if I were required to clear away the garbage before getting into my story.
>
> (p. 356)

4. *The presumed facts presented should be checked as thoroughly as reasonably possible.* Boelen (1992) makes many easily demonstrated factual errors. Throughout her article, she refers to 'Easter City' – I had called it 'Eastern City.'

Boelen (1992) claims that Italian was the language spoken by the corner boys and that my command of Italian was not good enough to guide me accurately. She underestimates my knowledge of Italian at that time, but that should not be the point at issue. In fact, among the many corner groups I knew, I never heard any Italian spoken except for an occasional swear word. All of the men I knew had either been born in Boston or had arrived here at an early age and then had gone through school in this city. . . .[1]

To evaluate the Boelen (1992) critique, we should distinguish between physical and social facts, on one hand, and interpretations of the themes of a research report,

[1 Editor's note: A number of other factual errors made by Boelen are edited out here.]

on the other. Physical and social facts can be directly observed or otherwise documented. Interpretations cannot be proved or otherwise documented. To evaluate Boelen's interpretations, we have to consider the credibility of the author in terms of her performance in data gathering and critical analysis of her own data in this case. . . .

Because the Boelen (1992) article is full of factual errors and other deficiencies in meeting scholarly standards, should readers consider seriously the interpretations she makes of my behavior and that of others? Nevertheless, because some well-recognized scholars, such as Richardson and Denzin, do take seriously the issues she raised, I should focus my attention on their conception of positivism, postpositivism, and the other deconstructionist arguments that they make.

Positivism and social science

Am I a positivist? I have always resisted such attempts to characterize myself. Even though some positivists strictly avoid doing any applied research, so that their values do not contaminate what they write, that label does not describe me.

Denzin (1992) calls me a *social realist*. Because that is not a well-recognized sociological label, I have to interpret what it implies.

If a social realist is one who believes that social phenomena are real, that certainly describes me. But, in that sense, what does *real* mean?

I believe it is essential to distinguish between objective and subjective phenomena. Objective phenomena can be observed, subjective phenomena can only be inferred from the actions of people and from what they say about what motivated them, and upon what others report and interpret about their behavior.

In social science reporting, that involves distinguishing between description and interpretation. Regarding description, in my critique of Boelen, I have focused particularly on points on which she was mistaken regarding certain social . . . and physical facts.

In his further discussion of my exchange with Boelen, Denzin (1994) fails to recognize the distinction between description and interpretation. For example, he says that doubts of my version of events linger in light of Doc's estrangement from Whyte. That is clearly an interpretive statement, for which there is only inferential evidence. . . . I am arguing that, in scientific reporting, interpretation should be distinguished from description – of social and physical facts.

Both Richardson (1992) and Denzin (1992) subscribe to the Denzin (1994) statement that no permanent telling of a story can be provided. Even when the same site is studied, there are only different versions of different stories.

If we accept that statement, we are denying the possibility of building a behavioral science. There will always be different interpretations of the same scene by different interpreters of that scene, but it is of vital importance to distinguish interpretations from objectively observable physical and social facts. The different tellings should be recognized as interpretations, which may or may not seem reasonable but for which no absolute proof can be given. If we ground our research on observable physical and social facts, the field is wide open for scientific development.

The physical and social facts are only a small part of a research report, but, if the author is wrong about a number of these facts, that should raise serious questions about the interpretations the author makes about the scene studied. Interpretations can never be demonstrated to be right or wrong, but they become more or less credible according to whether the author has gotten the facts straight. . . .

References

Adler, P.A. and Adler, P. (ed.) (1992) 'SCS revisited' [Special issue]. *Journal of Contemporary Ethnography*, 21.

Boelen, W.A.M. (1992) 'SCS: Cornerville revisited.' *Journal of Contemporary Ethnography*, 21, 11–51.

Denzin, N. (1992) 'Whose Cornerville is it anyway?' *Journal of Contemporary Ethnography*, 21, 120–132.

Denzin, N. (1994) The art and politics of interpretation. In D. Lincoln & Y.S. Lincoln (Eds.), *Handbook of qualitative research* (pp. 500–515). Thousand Oaks, CA: Sage.

Freeman, D. (1983) *Margaret Mead and Samoa: The Making and Unmaking of an Anthropological Myth.* Cambridge, Mass.: Harvard University Press.

Richardson, L. (1992) 'Trash on the corner: ethics and technography.' *Journal of Contemporary Ethnography*, 21, 103–119.

Vidich, A.J. (1992) 'Boston's North End: an American epic.' *Journal of Contemporary Ethnography*, 21, 80–102.

Whyte, W.F. (1943) *Street Corner Society*. Chicago: University of Chicago Press.

—— (1955) *Street Corner Society* (2nd edition). Chicago: University of Chicago Press.

—— (1981) *Street Corner Society* (3rd edition). Chicago: University of Chicago Press.

—— (1993) *Street Corner Society* (4th edition). Chicago: University of Chicago Press.

2 Ethnographic trouble – Laurel Richardson

'Trash on the corner' (Richardson 1992) was my contribution to the symposium on *Street Corner Society* (Whyte 1981) that William Foote Whyte refers to in this journal . . . In 'Trash' I wrote about ethics, fact/fiction, and W.A. Marianne Boelen's missed opportunity to write about the women of 'Cornerville'. I wrote about my concerns for the players – Whyte, Boelen, the informant (Doc), and other members of the Norton Gang. Whyte responded to W.A. Marianne Boelen (1992), Norman Denzin (1992), and myself (1992), though, as a modernist ethnographer. He deployed an informant to back him and discredit Boelen's claims (as he does again here). He read my article as a critique of his science, not as an opportunity to engage in a contemporary conversation about literary intrusions into science writing and the ethical and human consequences of doing ethnographic research.

. . . Whyte is still trying to prove that he is a scientist who told the truth. I regret that contemporary ethnography does not catch his imagination, that he views poststructuralism as an attack upon himself and his life. . . .

My critique of Whyte that appears in 'Trash' (1992), I now think, has hit him at two levels. By asking, for example, how he could quote Doc verbatim when he didn't tape-record him, I obliquely challenge the science-truth of his work; and by pointing out the literary licenses he must have taken to construct a narrative, I have joined forces, in his mind, I think, with Boelen. But, in addition to the science problem in *Street Corner Society* (1981), I confront Whyte with an irreconcilable human problem: Whyte's text has diminished the informant Doc's life. . . .

References

Boelen, W.A.M. (1992) '*SCS*: Cornerville revisited.' *Journal of Contemporary Ethnography*, 21, 11–51.

Denzin, N. (1992) 'Whose Cornerville is it anyway?' *Journal of Contemporary Ethnography*, 21, 120–132.

Richardson, L. (1992) 'Trash on the corner: ethics and ethnography.' *Journal of Contemporary Ethnography*, 21, 80–102.

Whyte, W.F. (1981) *Street Corner Society* (3rd edition). Chicago: University of Chicago Press.

3 The facts and fictions of qualitative inquiry – Norman K. Denzin

Written in ethnography's first moment, in the genre of social realism, *SCS* is a canonical text that embodies the standards and criteria of traditional ethnographic inquiry. Seen (and told) primarily through two pairs of eyes, those of Doc, and Whyte, the young fieldworker, *SCS* tells the story of the social organization of an Italian community in Boston in the late 1930s. Adhering to the standards of classic anthropology, *SCS* positions itself as an objective text . . . Whyte is the outsider who became a quasi-knowledgeable insider through the use of an informant. This informant allowed him to gain knowledge about the rituals and rules that gave order to this small community. *SCS* is a monument to this small society, an ethnographic museum wherein this culture is reproduced and staged as a sacred, unchanging image that is not to be touched or tampered with (see Rosaldo 1989: 43).

Whyte's project is the one of behaviorial, positivistic, empirical science, a project that advances, one step at a time, building on the solid foundation of certain facts. This model of inquiry separates facts from fictions, from statements that cannot be verified. Facts, which may be physical, or social, are things that can be directly observed and correctly described. Facts are objective. They are different from interpretations, which are subjective and hence cannot be proven but only made more or less credible, if the author got the facts straight.

In presenting the results of inquiry, the researcher should follow certain standard rules. Facts must always be verified. The sources of facts must be revealed. Contradictory facts should be taken into account, and quotes should never be taken out of context. Arguments should be based on objective facts, not on pure interpretation, which is nonverifiable. How facts are produced is not clear nor is it clear how the description of a fact can avoid an interpretation. . . .

Whyte seems to equate science with logical empiricism, a belief system that distrusts philosophical and moral inquiry, and believes in a disinterested social science observer who applies rational rules to research. Deconstructionists question these rules and engage in moral inquiry. The chief rhetorical accomplishment of logical empiricism, now called behavioral science, is its attempt to ideologically separate moral discourse from empirical inquiry (Schwandt 1996). This is what Whyte attempts. He reduces the deconstructionist position to 'standards of judgment which shift with the changing trends of literary criticism' (1993: 371).

This is a questionable epistemology. During the 1980s sociology turned its back on the methodological controversies surrounding positivism, postpositivism, critical theory, and constructivism that were sweeping across neighboring social science fields (see Denzin and Lincoln 1994; Guba and Lincoln 1994). These controversies challenged the presuppositions of objective social science as well as traditional ways of bringing authority to that research, including the use of such terms as reliability and validity. The postpositivists (and others) came to reject the ontological, epistemological, and methodological presuppositions Whyte endorses. Gone were beliefs in ontological realism and objectivist epistemologies. The notion of knowledge as accumulation was replaced by a more relative, constructionist position (Guba and Lincoln 1994: 114). The concept of a fact was no longer taken for granted.

Fishkin (1985: 207) observes that 'during the last two decades the line between fact and fiction has grown more and more blurred.' A decade later, Mitchell and Charmaz (1995) argue, 'ethnographers and fiction writers rely on similar writing practices to tell their tales' (p. 1). Whyte writes from an earlier age when these distinctions were not blurred. He notes, in the fourth edition to SCS (1993, p. 366), that 'when I began my SCS research [1936], I wanted to contribute to building a science of society. . . . I based my own framework on a basic distinction between the objective (what is out there to be observed) and the subjective (how the observer or others interpret the observed phenomena).' For Whyte, there is a clear difference between fact and fiction. The differences are not to be minimized, for when they are, we are left with only rhetoric. This argument, of course, ignores the fact that science writing is a form of rhetorical persuasion. . . .

Fact and fiction have not always been so confused. Fishkin argues (1985, p. 207) that from the middle of the 19th century through the 1920s the journalist and the imaginative writer were held to different standards. Journalists worked with verifiable facts, and readers could expect stories to be factually accurate. Imaginative writers, novelists, told truths that were not necessarily factually accurate, but they adhered to esthetic standards of good storytelling. Ethnography enters this same terrain, and ethnographers such as William Foote Whyte learned how to objectively report the facts of the social situations they studied. Like good journalism, good ethnography reported the facts of life to a scientific, and at times public, community. So the duties and practices of sociologists and journalists were separated.

All of this held steady from the 1920s through the 1960s. There were three different professional groups, each producing different but often parallel tellings about society: journalists, novelists, and social science ethnographers. Then the lines between journalism, imaginative writing, and ethnography began to again blur. . . .

I have no desire to reproduce arguments that maintain distinctions between fictional (literary) and nonfictional (journalism, ethnography) texts. Such efforts inevitably resort to canon pointing and the use of essentializing categories. . . . I oppose all hierarchical categories, including those that distinguish literary and nonliterary, fictional and nonfictional textual forms. These categories, which are socially and politically constructed, work against the creation of an expansive, complex public discourse wherein multiple narrative forms circulate and inform one another . . . If all is narrative, then it can be argued that narrative techniques are neither fictional nor factual, they are merely formal 'methods used in making sense of all kinds of situations' (Eason 1982: 143). Truth is socially established by the norms that operate for each form, or genre.

So, qualitative inquiry in the sixth moment is more than the invention of new forms of textuality or the criticism of older writing styles. . . . Deconstructionists seek a resistance form of writing, utopian and dystopian texts that intervene in the world, producing material changes in the lives of people. . . .

References

Denzin, N.K. and Lincoln, Y.S. (1994) 'Introduction: entering the field of qualitative research.' In N.K. Denzin and Y.S. Lincoln (eds.), *Handbook of Qualitative Research* (pp. 1–17). Thousand Oaks, Cal.: Sage.

Eason, D. (1982) 'New Journalism, metaphor and culture.' *Journal of Popular Culture*, 15, 142–149.

Fishkin, S.F. (1985) 'From fact to fiction: journalism and imaginative writing in America.' Baltimore, Md: Johns Hopkins University Press.

Guba, E.E. and Lincoln, Y.S. (1994) 'Competing paradigms in qualitative research.' In N.K. Denzin and Y.S. Lincoln (eds), *Handbook of Qualitative Research* (pp. 105–117). Thousand Oaks, Cal.: Sage.

Rosaldo, R. (1989) *Culture and Truth*. Boston: Beacon.

Schwandt, T.A. (1996) 'Farewell to criteriology.' *Qualitative Inquiry*, 2, 58–72.

Whyte, W.F. (1993) *Street Corner Society* (4th edition). Chicago: University of Chicago Press.

4 Facts, interpretations, and ethics in qualitative inquiry – William Foote Whyte

In responding to Norman K. Denzin, I challenged him on several points. He does not reply to those challenges except in a very roundabout way through an essay on the 'sixth moment of qualitative inquiry.' If I were to undertake a serious study of the evolution of qualitative sociology in relation to journalism and deconstructionism, I would find the Denzin essay and footnotes an invaluable resource. Because I continue to believe that deconstructionism is a fad, which will pass away as behavioral scientists come to recognize that it leads nowhere, I am not inclined to participate in that line of research. . . .

[In answer to Richardson] has any individual been seriously damaged by what I wrote about him? I have never heard of such a case.

Such ethical questions should be the concern of all of us, but that concern should be balanced by the assessment of the contribution the book has made to the behavioral sciences.

Chapter 76

John K. Smith and Lous Heshusius

CLOSING DOWN THE CONVERSATION
The end of the quantitative–qualitative debate among educational inquirers

From *Educational Researcher* 15: 4–12 (1986).

A RECENT TREND IN the literature concerning quantitative versus qualitative approaches to research indicates two things about the nature of this debate. First, many inquirers now accept the idea that there are two different, equally legitimate, approaches to inquiry. Second, many inquirers also feel that whatever differences may exist between the two perspectives, they do not, in the final analysis, really matter very much. In other words, . . . many inquirers now seem to think that the profession has reached a stage of, if not synthesis, then certainly compatibility and cooperation between the two approaches. The demand that an inquirer be 'either/or' has been replaced by the injunction to employ both approaches in combination or to 'draw on both styles at appropriate times and in appropriate amounts' (Cronbach *et al.* 1980: 223).

The contention of this paper is that the claim of compatibility, let alone one of synthesis, cannot be sustained. Moreover, this hasty and unjustified 'leap to compatibility' has the unfortunate effect of 'closing down' an important and interesting conversation. . . .

Why was the original paradigmatic debate so rapidly transformed into a discussion of variations in techniques? Two factors are important: (a) a confusion over the definition of method and (b) an uncritical dependence on the idea that inquiry is a matter of 'what works.'

Method can be characterized in at least two ways. The most commonly encountered meaning is method as procedures or techniques. In this case the term invokes the kinds of 'how to-do-it' discussions long found in introductory textbooks on quantitative inquiry and, more recently, in a number of basic textbooks on qualitative inquiry (see, e.g., Goetz and LeCompte, 1984; Miles and Huberman,

1984b). The second characterization of method is as 'logic of justification.' In a sense common to continental European social philosophy, the focus here is not on techniques but on the elaboration of logical issues and, ultimately, on the justifications that inform practice. The term is used in this sense in the work of Durkheim (1983), Weber (1949), and, more recently, . . . Giddens (1976). This conceptualization involves such basic questions as, What is the nature of social and educational reality? What is the relationship of the investigator to what is investigated? and How is truth to be defined?

The important issue, then, is how one characterization of method relates to the other in the case of each approach. These relationships can be posed as a question: What does the logic of justification attendant to each perspective have to say about the practices one engages in in each case and vice versa? The point is that method as logic of justification, involving as it does basic philosophical assumptions, informs method as technique, and the two terms cannot be used interchangeably. To examine this situation we must first reaffirm the fact that major differences exist between the two perspectives at the level of logic of justification.

At the level of applying *specific individual procedures*, however, there are some relatively uninteresting questions about the differences between the two perspectives. In this case one frequently sees questions such as, Can quantitative inquirers supplement their controlled instrumentation with open-ended observation in naturalistic settings? or, Can qualitative inquirers supplement naturalistic observation with the quantification of events? The answer to these types of questions is yes. In both cases, but especially for qualitative inquiry, the logic of justification does not impose detailed boundaries that determine *every single aspect* of practice. Researchers of a realist orientation are not prohibited from using a certain practice normally associated with qualitative inquiry and vice versa. Thus, if the issue of quantitative-qualitative were confined to this level, one could grant that authors such as Cronbach *et al.* (1980), Miles and Huberman (1984a) and Reichardt and Cook (1979) are correct in their claim that the two approaches can be 'mixed.'

However, acceptance of this point cannot lead to the conclusion, at least implicitly made by many people, that the two perspectives are compatible or complementary. For quantitative inquiry and now, erroneously as it turns out, for the compatibility phase of qualitative inquiry, certain *sets* of practices, as opposed to particular, individual ones, are thought necessary to establish major conditions of inquiry such as the validity and reliability of studies. Since achieving these major conditions for either perspective is thought of as depending on the proper application of ordered practices, we can examine these concepts as 'linkage' points between method as logic of justification and method as 'how-to-do-it.' The crucial issue, however, is that how one characterizes these conditions depends not on the techniques employed, but rather on the logic of justification one accepts. That is the meaning assigned to the term *valid*, as in the statement, 'this study is internally valid,' is taken not from the practices involved but rather from how truth is defined. The epistemological position constrains how the condition is conceptualized and, by extension, directs the particular set of techniques that must be performed to achieve that condition (that is, as shall soon be noted, if any procedures can be so privileged for qualitative inquiry).

Clearly, if the two perspectives define truth differently, not only must each

accept a different conceptualization of validity, each must hold to a different interpretation of the place of procedures in the claim to validity. For the quantitative
approach, in which truth is defined as correspondence, the label valid announces
results that reflect or correspond to how things really are out there in the world.
Moreover, a judgment of validity in this case is conferred only when proper methods
or sets of techniques are employed. In fact, procedures properly applied, in that they
ensure objectivity and so on, lead to results that are thought to be compelling.
Rejection of such results may provoke the criticism that one is being irrational or
stubbornly subjective. For quantitative inquiry, a logic of justification that is epistemologically foundational leads to the position that certain sets of techniques are
epistemologically privileged in that their correct application is necessary to achieve
validity or to discover how things really are out there. Accordingly, for quantitative
inquiry, techniques stand separate from and prior to the conduct of any particular
piece of research.

From the perspective of qualitative inquiry, this line of reasoning is unacceptable. The assumptions or logic of justification in this case are not foundationalist and,
by extension, do not allow that certain sets of procedures are epistemologically
privileged. The idealist-oriented assumptions of reality as mind-dependent, no separation of facts and values, truth as agreement, and so on, are antifoundational; they
undermine the prospect of independent access to an independently existing reality
and, in so doing, undermine the possibility of certitude. Since reality is mind-
dependent, a description can only be matched to other descriptions and not to an
unconceptualized reality. . . . Since meaning is taken within context (that of the
subjects, the investigator, those who read the investigation, and so on) and the
process is hermeneutical, on what basis does one choose from among descriptions?
In other words, if all we have are various interpretations that are the realities of
various people based on their various interests, values, and purposes, what meaning
must be given to *valid* and how does one judge an interpretation valid or invalid?

Within the qualitative paradigm, valid is a label applied to an interpretation or
description with which one agrees. The ultimate basis for such agreement is that the
interpreters share, or come to share after an open dialogue and justification, similar
values and interests. As Taylor (1971) puts it,

> Ultimately, a good explanation is one which makes sense of the behavior;
> but then to appreciate a good explanation one has to agree on what
> makes good sense; what makes good sense is a function of one's read-
> ings; and these in turn are based on the kind of sense one understands.
>
> (p. 14)

There is a circularity to this interpretive process (the hermeneutical process can
have no definite beginning or ending points) that one cannot break out of, even by
methodological prescriptions.

Whereas the foundationalist assumptions of quantitative inquiry allow that
proper procedures will prevent this circularity (allow for certitude), such is not the
case for qualitative inquiry. The antifoundational assumptions mean that procedures
are related to the context of a particular inquiry and what it makes sense to do in
that particular context. Of course, what makes sense in any particular situation

depends on the kind of sense one understands. One may be interested in how a researcher did a study and agree with the strategies employed, or argue that others should have been employed. However, this is different from the claim that certain procedures are necessary to establish a correspondence of our words with an independently existing reality. Qualitative inquiry does not stipulate that certain things must be done or that validity is a matter of techniques properly applied.

Quite simply, a confusion of method as logic of justification with method as 'how-to-do-it' has allowed people to draw, even if only implicitly, an erroneous conclusion. That certain individual procedures can be mixed does not mean there are no differences of consequence. If one extends the different sets of assumptions to their logical implications, it is clear that the two perspectives part company over major issues such as the conceptualization given such basic conditions as validity and reliability, the place of techniques in the inquiry process, and the interpretation of research results. Quantitative inquiry aspires to certitude, to the idea that our descriptions can match actual conditions in the world and that we can know when this matching occurs and when it does not. This certitude is achieved primarily through an adherence to proper techniques. For the qualitative perspective, inquiry is a never-ending process (hermeneutical) of interpreting the interpretations of others. All that can be done is to match descriptions to other descriptions, choosing to honor some as valid because they 'make sense,' given one's interests and purposes. There is no rule book of procedures to follow.

Finally, the claim of compatibility is based not only on confusion over the definition of method, but also on the idea that research is a matter of what works. This idea, expressed in different forms, is present in many discussions of qualitative-quantitative inquiry. For example, this is in essence what Miles and Huberman (1984a) mean when they say that 'epistemological purity doesn't get research done' (p. 21) and what Reichardt and Cook (1979) mean with the comment that one should mix the approaches in order to 'satisfy the demands of evaluation research in the most efficacious manner possible' (p. 27). Although this idea is appealing, in that it calls up the image of researchers using whatever is necessary to solve serious educational problems, on closer examination it is also an oversimplification.

The problem is that what works, no matter how it is expressed, really tells us nothing about the process of inquiry and the interpretation of its results. Putnam's (1981) discussion of the phrase 'science seeks the truth' illustrates this point. According to Putnam, this is an empty statement in the absence of knowing

> . . . what [people] consider a rational way to pursue inquiry, what their standards of objectivity are, when they consider it rational to terminate an inquiry, [and] what grounds they will regard as providing good reason for accepting one verdict or another on whatever sort of questions they may be interested in.
>
> (p. 129)

In other words, 'truth is not the bottom line' (p. 130), because it derives its standing from the goals one accepts for inquiry, the criteria to be applied, and so on.

Similarly, the idea that research decisions can be made on the basis of what works is not the bottom line. These decisions depend on the goals one holds for inquiry, the criteria (if any) employed for judgments, and so on. If one holds that inquiry is a matter of matching statements to actual conditions, what works will differ from what works if one finds inquiry to be interpretations of the interpret-ations of others. It may be argued that this problem does not arise, because *all* inquiry is based on criteria such as scope, fruitfulness, simplicity, and accuracy. However, as Kuhn (1977) noted, these criteria are value terms and may be inter-preted differently, depending on the situation or context. As he said, 'Individually the criteria are imprecise: individuals may legitimately differ about their application to concrete cases' (p. 322). In the end, what works is not a firm foundation to stand on. What works depends on the kind of work one wants inquiry to do, which in turn depends on the paradigm within which one is working. . . .

Why does it matter that the conversation is being closed down? This question can be answered on two levels. On an abstract level, the conversation is important because ultimately it involves one of the most provocative and widespread intel-lectual challenges of our time: What is to be made of the issue of objectivism versus relativism? On a practical level, and of course very much related to the abstract issue, the conversation provokes some fundamental issues concerning the practice of inquiry, the evaluations of and interpretations given to the results of inquiry, and so on.

At a more practical level, to close down the conversation is to avoid numerous important considerations. Clearly, the interpretation given to the practices and results of research differs, depending on the logic of justification one accepts. The phrases 'research has shown . . .' and 'the results of research indicate . . .' are subject to different interpretations, given different paradigms. For quantitative inquiry, these phrases are claims to an accurate reflection of reality of the claim of certitude that one has discovered how some bit of the social world really is. For qualitative inquiry, these phrases announce an interpretation that, to the extent that it finds agreement, becomes reality for those people as it is at any given time and place. The former expresses certitude: the latter presents a description constrained by values and interests to be compared with other descriptions constrained by other values and interests.

Given these differences, on what basis can researchers justify their work to the public, and for that matter, to themselves? Do researchers, as is commonly held, deserve a hearing because method places them above the subjectivity common to everyday discourse and thus allows them to speak of things as they really are? Qualitative inquiry, based on the point that reality is made rather than found, must challenge this idea. Very little within this perspective would permit researchers to claim 'epistemological privilege' and, accordingly, to claim that they have a special right to be heard or that they deserve an overriding voice in the conversation. Perhaps research, in an allusion to Oakeshott (1975), is nothing more or less than another voice in the conversation – one that stands alongside those of others. Whether one finds this characterization acceptable or unacceptable is at present unimportant; the point is that the quantitative-qualitative debate raises serious ques-tions about the meaning of research results. . . .

Given the fundamental difference in the approach to disagreement, if a quantita-tive inquirer disagrees with a qualitative inquirer, is it even possible for them to talk to each other? The answer, for the present anyway, is a qualified no. An appeal that one must accept a particular result because it is based on the facts will have little impact on one who believes there can be no uninterpreted facts of the case. On the other hand, the idea that facts are value-laden and that there is no court of appeal beyond dialogue and persuasion will at the very least seem unscientific and insufficient to a quantitative inquirer. In the end, the two sides may be close to speaking different languages – a neutral scientific or value-free language versus a value-laden language of everyday discourse. Since it is not clear at present what kind of *via media* could be worked out between the two languages, it is all the more important that we make every effort to keep the conversation open. In any event, all of the issues that surrounded Weber's unresolved question, 'How can there be an objective science – one not distorted by our value judgments – of the value-charged productions of men?' (Aron 1967: 193), are again brought to the foreground by the quantitative-qualitative debate. . . .

To avoid the conversation is to avoid issues at the core of the research enterprise and, for that matter, at the core of our contemporary intellectual, practical, and moral lives. Moreover, since these issues are crucial to who we are and what we do as researchers, this is not something to be turned over to philosophers with the hope they will eventually solve our problems. Put quite simply, to close down the conversation by making the unjustified claims of compatibility and cooperation is the wrong move at the wrong time.

References

Aron, R. (1967) *Main Currents in Sociological Thought 2* (R. Howard and H. Weaver, trans.). New York: Penguin Books.

Cronbach, L. *et al.* (1980) *Toward Reform of Program Evaluation*. San Francisco: Jossey-Bass.

Durkheim, E. (1938) *Rules of the Sociological Method* (S. Solovay and J. Mueller, trans., and G. Catlin, ed.). Chicago: University of Chicago Press.

Giddens, A. (1976) *New Rules of the Sociological Method*. New York: Basic Books.

Goetz, J. and LeCompte, M. (1984) *Ethnography and Qualitative Design in Educational Research*. New York: Academic Press.

Kuhn, T. (1977) *The Essential Tension*. Chicago: University of Chicago Press.

Miles, M. and Huberman, A. (1984a) 'Drawing valid meaning from qualitative data: toward a shared craft.' *Educational Researcher*, 13, 20–30.

—— (1984b) *Qualitative Data Analysis*. Beverly Hills: Sage.

Oakeshott, M. (1975) 'The voice of poetry in the conversation of mankind.' In M. Oakeshott, *Rationalism in Politics*, New York: Methuen.

Putnam, H. (1981) *Reason, Truth, and History*. Cambridge: Cambridge University Press.

Reichardt, C. and Cook, T. (1979) 'Beyond qualitative versus quantitative methods.' In T. Cook and C. Reichardt (eds), *Qualitative and Quantitative Methods in Evaluation Research*, Beverly Hills: Sage.

Taylor, C. (1971) 'Interpretation and the sciences of man.' *Review of Metaphysics*, 25, 3–51.

Weber, M. (1949) *The Methodology the Social Sciences* (E. Shils and E. Finch, eds. and trans.). Glencoe: Free Press.

Chapter 77

Alan Bryman

QUANTITATIVE AND QUALITATIVE RESEARCH
Further reflections on their integration

From *Mixing Methods: Qualitative and Quantitative Research*, Aldershot: Avebury (1992).

INTEREST IN THE DIFFERENCES between quantitative research and qualitative research (or the alternative labels with which these approaches are often served), continues unabated, . . . though there is considerable disagreement over certain fundamental issues such as the possibility of integrating them. Moreover, a number of different terms have been employed to describe approaches to social research that seem to correspond closely to the quantitative/qualitative contrast. Table 77.1 attempts to identify some of the major labels that have been used to refer to approaches to research which correspond to quantitative and qualitative research.

As noted in Bryman (1988), discussions of the two approaches operate at different levels of analysis and discourse. Fundamentally, these can be reduced to

Table 77.1 Quantitative and qualitative research: alternative labels

Quantitative	Qualitative	Authors
Rationalistic	Naturalistic	Guba and Lincoln (1982)
Inquiry from the outside	Inquiry from the inside	Evered and Louis (1981)
Functionalist	Interpretive	Burrell and Morgan (1979)
Positivist	Constructivist	Guba (1990)
Positivist	Naturalistic-ethnographic	Hoshmand (1989)

two forms. Some writers prefer to identify quantitative and qualitative research (or their synonyms) as distinctive epistemological positions and hence divergent approaches to what is and should count as valid knowledge (for example, Smith and Heshusius 1986). Such writers sometimes use the term 'paradigm' to refer to each of the two positions though they do not always use it in the sense that Kuhn (1970) implied. . . . The conception of quantitative and qualitative research as each under-pinned by a distinct epistemological position has implications for the question of whether they can genuinely be combined or whether they are irreconcilable.

The view taken here is that quantitative and qualitative research represent distinctive approaches to social research. Each approach is associated with a certain cluster of methods of data collection; quantitative research is strongly associated with social survey techniques like structured interviewing and self-administered questionnaires, experiments, structured observation, content analysis, the analysis of official statistics and the like. Qualitative research is typically associated with participant observation, semi- and unstructured interviewing, focus groups, the qualitative examination of texts, and various language-based techniques like conver-sation and discourse analysis.

It is true that certain epistemological and theoretical positions have influenced the character of both quantitative and qualitative research. The former has clearly been influenced by the natural science model of research, and its positivist form in particular. Qualitative research has been influenced by an epistemological position that rejects the appropriateness of a natural science approach to the study of humans; this position finds its expression in such theoretical strands as phenomenology and symbolic interactionism. These epistemological precursors have influenced the con-cerns of the two research approaches: the concern in quantitative research about causality, measurement, generalizability etc., can be traced back to its natural science roots; the concern in qualitative research for the point of view of the individuals being studied, the detailed elucidation of context, the sensitivity to process, etc., can be attributed to its epistemological roots (Bryman 1988). But this is not to say that quantitative and qualitative research are forever rooted to their original epistemo-logical positions. Instead, the two approaches to research can have and do have an independence from their epistemological beginnings. As general approaches to social research, each has its own strengths and weaknesses as an approach to the conduct of social research. It is these strengths and weaknesses that lie behind the rationale for integrating them.

Approaches to integrating quantitative and qualitative research

In Bryman (1988: chapter 6), a number of different ways in which quantitative and qualitative research have been combined in published research were outlined. The following is a simple summary of the approaches that were identified.

1 The logic of 'triangulation'

The findings from one type of study can be checked against the findings deriving from the other type. For example, the results of a qualitative investigation might be checked against a quantitative study. The aim is generally to enhance the validity of findings.

2 Qualitative research facilitates quantitative research

Qualitative research may: help to provide background information on context and subjects; act as a source of hypotheses; and aid scale construction.

3 Quantitative research facilitates qualitative research

Usually, this means quantitative research helping with the choice of subjects for a qualitative investigation.

4 Quantitative and qualitative research are combined in order to provide a general picture

Quantitative research may be employed to plug the gaps in a qualitative study which arise because, for example, the researcher cannot be in more than one place at any one time. Alternatively, it may be that not all issues are amenable solely to a quantitative investigation or solely to a qualitative one.

5 Structure and process

Quantitative research is especially efficient at getting to the 'structural' features of social life, while qualitative studies are usually stronger in terms of 'processual' aspects. These strengths can be brought together in a single study.

6 Researchers' and subjects' perspectives

Quantitative research is usually driven by the researcher's concerns, whereas qualitative research takes the subject's perspective as the point of departure. These emphases may be brought together in a single study.

7 The problem of generality

The addition of some quantitative evidence may help to mitigate the fact that it is often not possible to generalize (in a statistical sense) the findings deriving from qualitative research.

8 Qualitative research may facilitate the interpretation of relationships between variables

Quantitative research readily allows the researcher to establish relationships among variables, but is often weak when it comes to exploring the reasons for those relationships. A qualitative study can be used to help explain the factors underlying the broad relationships that are established.

9 The relationship between 'macro' and 'micro' levels

Employing both quantitative and qualitative research may provide a means of bridging the macro-micro gulf. Quantitative research can often tap large-scale, structural features of social life, while qualitative research tends to address small-scale, behavioural aspects. When research seeks to explore both levels, integrating quantitative and qualitative research may be necessary.

10 Stages in the research process

Quantitative and qualitative research may be appropriate to different stages of a longitudinal study.

11 Hybrids

The chief example tends to be when qualitative research is conducted within a quasi-experimental (i.e. quantitative) research design.

It is unlikely that this list can be considered truly exhaustive, though it does represent a fairly comprehensive catalogue. Moreover, any piece of research can exhibit more than one of these approaches to integration. . . .

There seems to be a growth in the number of studies combining quantitative and qualitative research and it is possible that such research will become increasingly common. It may even be the case that such investigations will come to be seen as the yardstick for good research. But we should appreciate not only that a combined strategy must be appropriate to the research problem, but also that the presence of the additional research approach (be it quantitative or qualitative) must be more than cosmetic. When properly combined, one approach enhances the other. However, if integrated research became increasingly popular, it is possible that some investigations which combine quantitative and qualitative research would be undertaken in such a way that it is difficult to detect what advantages have accrued or even what advantages the investigator anticipated. In other words, we must not get into a frame of thinking whereby research is regarded as almost by definition superior if it combines quantitative and qualitative elements. The tendency for many researchers to be trained in or inclined towards just one approach may in fact militate against the successful integration of the two research styles, even when there was a clear case for integrating them. . . .

Quantitative and qualitative research are different, otherwise there would be no point in even discussing the possibility of combining them. They each have distinctive characteristics that make the possibility of combining them especially attractive. It is also clear each has been influenced by theoretical and epistemological concerns and issues, such as the acceptance or rejection of a natural science approach to social research, but this does not mean that they are forever tied to these concerns and issues. The view taken here is that the depiction of quantitative and qualitative research (and the alternative labels described in Table 77.1) as distinct epistemologies or paradigms that cannot be reconciled is both inaccurate, since they have achieved a certain degree of independence from their epistemological foundations, and unduly restrictive. . . . In the end, I am convinced that awareness of the advantages of integrating quantitative and qualitative research will be so overwhelming that the doctrinaire and restrictive views of writers who deprecate the virtues and accomplishments of combined research (e.g. Smith and Heshusius 1986) will be gradually eroded.

References

Bryman, A. (1988) *Quantity and Quality in Social Research*. London: Unwin Hyman.

Burrell, G. and Morgan, G. (1979) *Sociological Paradigms and Organizational Analysis*. London: Heinemann.

Evered, R. and Louis, M.R. (1981) 'Alternative perspectives in the organizational sciences: "inquiry from the inside" and "inquiry from the outside"'. *Academy of Management Review*, 6, pp. 385–395.

Guba, E.G. (1990) 'The alternative paradigm dialog'. In E.G. Guba (ed.) *The Paradigm Dialog*. Newbury Park: Sage.

Guba, E.G. and Lincoln, Y.S. (1982) 'Epistemological and methodological bases of naturalistic inquiry'. *Educational Communication and Technology Journal*, 30, pp. 233–252.

Hoshmand, L.S.T. (1989) 'Alternative research paradigms: a review and teaching proposal'. *The Counseling Psychologist*, 17, pp. 3–79.

Kuhn, T.S. (1970) *The Structure of Scientific Revolutions*, 2nd edition. Chicago: University of Chicago Press.

Smith, J.K. and Heshusius, L. (1986) 'Closing down the conversation: the end of the quantitative–qualitative debate among educational inquirers'. *Educational Researcher*, 15, pp. 4–12.

Chapter 78

Ann Oakley

WHO'S AFRAID OF THE RANDOMIZED CONTROLLED TRIAL?

Some dilemmas of the scientific method and 'good' research practice

From *Women and Health* 15(4): 25–59 (1959).

THIS CHAPTER FOCUSES ON the nature and uses of the methodology of the randomized controlled trial (RCT) in the light of recent critiques of science, including the feminist concern with the social structure of science as representing an inherently sexist, racist, classist and culturally coercive practice and form of knowledge. Using the example of one specific RCT aimed at promoting women's health, the paper outlines some of the dilemmas thus raised for the pursuit of 'good' research practice. The particular viewpoint from which the paper is written is that of a feminist sociologist who has been responsible for designing and carrying out a randomized trial in the field of prenatal health care. While the focus of the paper is on the use of the methodology of random allocation in health research, it is important to note that it has also been used in other areas of experimental research within the social sciences, for instance in psychology in the evaluation of educational interventions . . . and in the assessment of professional social work services . . . Although the study discussed in this paper and some of the other data drawn on are British, the issues highlighted are of general relevance to all communities where importance is attached to the goal of researching and promoting women's health in the broadest sense.

Origins and problems of the RCT as a tool for researching women's health

. . . The RCT is essentially an experimental test ('trial') of a particular treatment/ approach (or set of treatments/ approaches) comparing two or more groups of subjects who are allocated to these groups at random, i.e., according to the play of chance. Conclusions about the effectiveness of treatments based on an RCT rest upon two issues – an assessment of *significance* and a judgement about *causation*. Tests of statistical significance are used to determine whether any observed difference between trial groups is due to sampling variability or is evidence of a 'real' difference. If a difference is significant in this sense, then, as Schwartz and colleagues put it in their classic text *Clinical Trials* (1980: 7), 'a judgement of causation allows us to attribute it to the difference between (the) two treatments. This is only possible if the two groups are strictly comparable in all respects apart from the treatments given. Providing two such comparable groups is another statistical problem the correct solution of which is obtained by randomization.' It is important to note that the prerequisite for any RCT is *uncertainty* about the effects of a particular treatment. If something is known to work (and to be acceptable and without harmful effects) then there is no reason to put it to the test in the form of a trial. It is, however, this very issue of certainty/uncertainty that constitutes one of the central problems of the contemporary debate about RCTs. People can be certain that something (e.g., streptomycin, social workers) *is* effective but have no 'real' basis for their certainty; conversely, unless they are able to admit uncertainty, 'real' knowledge can never be gained.

The RCT has been increasingly promoted over the last twenty years as *the* major evaluative tool within medicine. Over the same period a new critical perspective has emerged towards what counts as 'knowledge' and the methods and techniques appropriate to its accumulation. Sources of this critique include the radical science movement . . . the emergence of 'ethnomethodology' within sociology . . . and the broad consensus located within the women's movement about the 'masculinist' orientation of much scientific activity. . . . Over the last twenty years, feminists have increasingly criticized the ways in which the construction of what counts as 'knowledge' omits women's perspectives and experiences and is embedded with masculinist values. . . . But, although feminist researchers have taken to task in recent years many methodologies both in the natural and 'unnatural' sciences, there has been virtually no discussion to date of this particular, increasingly advocated approach.

The notion of 'feminist' research as discussed in this paper is taken to mean research that relates to an understanding of women's position as that of an oppressed social group, and which adopts a critical perspective towards intellectual traditions rendering women either invisible and/or subject to *a priori* categorizations of one kind or another. The research process itself is subject to the same stipulations: that it should not employ methods oppressive either to researchers or to the researched, and should be oriented towards the production of knowledge in such a form and in such a way as can be used by women themselves (Acker *et al.* 1983; Roberts 1981). These strictures are also a formula for 'good' research practice as applied to human subjects in general. However, the practice of feminist research is often located by its advocates on one side of the divide between 'qualitative' and 'quantitative' research methods. Qualitative methods involving in depth interviewing are seen to be more suited to the exploration of individual experiences – the representation of subjectivity within academic discourse and to facilitate (in practice if not in theory) a nonhierarchical organization of the research process (Oakley 1981). Conversely, quantitative methods (large-scale surveys, the use of prespecified scoring methods, e.g., in personality tests) are cited as instituting the hegemony of the researcher over the researched, and as reducing personal experience to the anonymity of mere numbers. The feminist/masculinist and qualitative/quantitative divisions are paralleled conceptually by a third, that between the physical and the social sciences. As Hedges (1987: 443) has commented: 'Those of us in the social and behavioral sciences know intuitively that there is something 'softer' and less cumulative about our research results than those of the physical sciences.'

. . . The problem about the feminist rejection of quantitative methods as necessarily alienating, is that it bars discussion both of the ways in which these methods are used, and of those in which they could be used to generate knowledge relevant to the exercise of improving women's situation. Although feminist research practice requires a critical stance towards existing methodology . . . at the same time it has to be recognized that the universe of askable research questions is constrained by the methods allowed. To ban any quantitative (social) science therefore results in a restriction to certain kinds of questions only; this restriction may very well be counter to the same epistemological goal a code of feminist research practice is designed to promote. . . .

. . . Existing published work and the experience drawn on in this paper suggest that RCTs pose three particular problems for feminist researchers. Firstly and most obviously, there is the principle of *random allocation*, which uses chance 'the absence of design' (O.E.D) to determine the treatment received by participants in the research. The extent to which individuals are able to choose the form of their participation in the research is thereby limited. Linked with this is the much debated issue of *informed consent*. What is the meaning of consent, and how much of what kind of information is required by whom? The third problem concerns the epistemology, ownership and distribution of *certainty*. As already noted, the rationale for undertaking an RCT is uncertainty about the effectiveness/acceptability of a particular procedure. But the professionals may be certain and the lay public not; or the lay public may be convinced about the benefits of a procedure which meets with professional scepticism. It would appear that this issue in particular has provoked a good deal of unclear thinking among those concerned with the promotion of women's health.

Before examining each of these problems in turn, I shall briefly outline the study which highlighted these specific areas of conflict between the practice of *feminist* research on the one hand, and the model of *randomized controlled evaluation*, on the other.

Who cares for women? An RCT of social support

. . . The broad aim of the project was to establish whether social support provided as a research intervention has the capacity to make things better for women and their babies. Most previous work on this topic is problematic, because of the repetitive methodological problem that, although better health is generally associated with more support, it is impossible to rule out the explanation that healthier, more supported mothers are different in other ways from less supported, less healthy mothers and babies (Oakley 1985; Oakley 1988). Although the better done observational studies make multiple adjustments for confounding variables, still one can only adjust for those variables known to confound; there may be others, equally confounding, of which the researcher is ignorant. For this reason, the study was planned as an *intervention* study, in which the intervention of providing additional social support would be offered to some women and not to others, and various indices of their experiences, including their health and that of their babies, would be compared at the end of the study. Over a fifteen month period, a total of 509 women agreed to take part in the study. Random allocation was used to determine who received the intervention, and social support was given by four research mid-wives who visited women at home during pregnancy, offered a listening ear for individual problems, provided various forms of practical and emotional help when required, and were available 24 hours a day to be contacted in case of need. . . . The 'effectiveness' of this social support intervention in terms of a range of outcomes, including women's satisfaction and infant birthweight, was evaluated after delivery, using obstetric case note information from the four hospitals where the study was done, and by sending all the women a long and detailed postal questionnaire. . . .

Chance or causation? The role of random numbers

The first of the three problems referred to earlier in combining a feminist research consciousness with the technique of an RCT concerns the process of random alloca-tion itself. We had some interesting and some disturbing difficulties with this. . . .

Unpredictably, our first battle in the study was with the (then) Social Science Research Council, the main body funding social science research in Britain. When asked to fund the study, the SSRC did not understand why we were not proposing to 'match' the social support group in our study with a nonsupport group on the usual criteria of age, social class, obstetric history, etc. We were thus obliged to defend to one group of scientists the advantages of a technique borrowed from another group.[1]

Having acquired research funds[2] we then needed to discuss use of the method with those we were asking to use it, namely the four research midwives. In our discussions with them, we emphasised the dual facts that (a) it was by no means clear that social support was of global benefit to pregnant women (too much social support might be too much of a good thing: at least it was a research question as to which sub groups of women might benefit); and that (b) we wanted to be able to say something definite about the usefulness of giving social support to pregnant women at the end of the study; use of this method was more likely than any other to enable us to do this. Randomization was done by the midwives telephoning us at TCRU with the names of women who had agreed to take part. The study secretary had sheets of allocations derived from a table of random numbers, and she entered each woman in order, then informing the midwife of the result of the allocation.

---

1 As noted above, RCTs have been carried out by social scientists concerned to mount proper evaluation of other professional services. However, it remains the case that social scientists appear to be more easily persuaded by the results of studies using more familiar methodologies, and less ready to adopt a stringent approach to the assessment of accepted knowledge.

2 We are extremely grateful to the DHSS for agreeing to fund the study.

As the study progressed, we had many discussions about how everyone felt about this procedure. The midwives were sometimes unhappy about both the process and the results of the randomization. They considered it a problem that random allocation was being used to determine which women received additional social support, as this meant that the women themselves could not choose their fates; it also meant that, in agreeing to participate in the study, they were agreeing to a 50% chance of either receiving additional social support or not doing so. Secondly, the midwives worried because sometimes women they thought were in need of social support were allocated to the control group (standard care) or those they considered had enough of it already were allocated to receive it. . . .

My own concern as project 'director' on the study, on the issue of random allocation was, and remained, confused. In the first place, I was committed to the goal of evaluating the effectiveness of social support in a manner acceptable to the scientific community and to policy-makers; this raises its own problems – for instance, about the ethics and relevance to women's situation of targeting research at those in power. It is arguable that the usefulness of research in terms of effecting change is greatest when made accessible to the powerless, rather than the powerful. However, the escalating use of unevaluated technology in the maternity care field is a compelling reason for focusing at least some attention directly on those responsible for formulating policy. Because of this goal of reaching policy-makers, I felt it *was* important to carry out the study according to the rules. . . .

Consenting adults?

The issue of randomization is closely bound up with the question of to what extent participants in a research project (either an RCT or any other) consent on the basis of full information to take part in it. The issue of informed consent is the second area of conflict between the principles of feminist research practice and the use of the RCT technique. . . .

We encountered various difficulties with the method and content of the informed consent procedure we used. Much the most important of these was the extent to which our informing women who were subsequently allocated to the control group what the study was about may have resulted in their feeling deprived. One example is this experience described by one of the midwives:

> Dawn Benn (Control). She was absolutely desperate to be intervention and she was so upset when I phoned her because of her social circumstances that when she asked me if I knew the address of any mother and toddler groups, NCT groups, anything, because she's just moved into the area, I gave her a couple of phone numbers before I'd even got her allocated. She was heartbroken.

In other instances, control group women got in touch with the midwives for help even though they knew they had been assigned to the no-support group. We asked the midwives to respond minimally in such situations, conscious that responding fully would be to jeopardize the aims of the study. . . .

Because we gave information to all the women the midwives identified as eligible for the study, the women in the control group *were* part of a research project in which they had *chosen* to participate. In this sense, it is probably true to say that rigorous testing of the hypothesis that social support can improve pregnancy outcome is at odds with the principle of informed consent. A further complication is that the standard scientific model of RCTs presupposes that there is no 'contamination' of the control group by the experimental group; the purpose of the control group is, after all, to act as a 'control' for the experiment. . . . Again, the actual practice, as opposed to theory, of research reveals the chimerical nature of this model. It is assumed, for instance, that people do not talk to one another. In our study, had we not told the control group women about the study, we would have needed to rely on the intervention group women remaining silent about their receipt of social support – at home, with friends and neighbors, in antenatal clinics. But women are not silent. Although this human tendency to communicate may be overcome by randomizing groups (areas, institutions) rather than individuals, the tension between the scientific requirements of research and the humane treatment of individuals remains, and is expressed in the very strategy of designing an experiment so as to restrict people's freedom to discuss with one another the commonality of the process in which they are engaged. . . .

A second problem we encountered with our informed consent procedure was in deciding how to present the aims of the study to the women we asked to take part in it. . . . We decided to enlist the midwives' confidence in the aims of the study from the start: not to have done so would, we felt, not only have been unethical, but also intuitively counter to its aims. For the same reason, we were also open with the women in the study about what we were trying to do. In saying that we wanted to see if social support could achieve the stated aims we were conscious of the tension with the principle that women allocated to the control group should not feel deprived. Thus, we also stated what we also believed, that we did not *know* whether social support could improve the health of all women and their children in this sense.

The importance of being (un)certain

Thirdly, we come to the last of the issues raised at the beginning of this paper as especially problematic in this type of research – the question of uncertainty. . . .

RCTs have an ethical advantage over routine medical practice [because] they subject to external assessment the medical claim to therapeutic effectiveness. . . .

However, certainty is not the prerogative of medical professionals. It is also possessed by lay people and by women. The women's health movement has been guilty of a fair amount of misguided certainty over the years, as for example in the recently fashionable demand that cervical screening programs be made more readily available to all women. As Robinson (1987: 51) has noted: 'Neither the ethics, the efficacy, nor the adverse effects of screening have been adequately discussed by women's organizations.' In the childbirth field, many attempts systematically to evaluate different modes of care have been shipwrecked on the rock of women's certainty about the effectiveness of apparently natural and innocuous methods such as childbirth education, vitamin supplements, or raspberry leaf tea. (While such methods may have this effect, there is, as yet, no scientific evidence, and even some to the contrary [see Chalmers 1983].)

Perhaps best-publicized of recent examples in Britain has been the response of maternity service user groups to the Medical Research Council's RCT on vitamin supplementation in pregnancy. The trial was designed to test the hypothesis that such supplements, taken around the time of conception, can reduce the chances of a baby having a neural tube malformation. User groups such as the National Childbirth Trust and the Association for Improvements in the Maternity services contended that the need for a good diet in pregnancy was well-established, making the trial unethical (Micklethwait et al. 1982). The point is, that, whatever form it takes, and whoever professes it, certainty blocks progress towards greater understanding of the role of chance versus causation in the patterning, and human experience of events and processes, including those responsible for health or its absence.

Genuine scepticism about something is probably rare. It appears that researchers must merely possess sufficient *uncertainty* about something in order to want to find out about it. The issue of certainty was complicated in our study. . . . While it may seem almost axiomatic that social support, like love, is something we all want, what is at issue is the range and type of event/process social support is capable of affecting, and the mechanism by which it does so . . . Assumptions about the inevitably therapeutic effects of social support may prove unfounded when subject to systematic evaluation. . . .

Conclusion

The RCT is a method of *experimental* research, and the term 'experiment' has been linked with what Chalmers (1983) has called the 'Auschwitz' view of scientific inquiry, according to which all experimental research is inherently suspect. The view of experimental research as inherently unethical is central to the feminist critique (Spallone and Steinberg 1987; Birke 1986) but also comes from other quarters (see Silverman 1986). Much of it misses the absolutely crucial point that the condemnation of experimentation under the heading of 'research' allows a great deal of experimentation to pass unnoticed under the heading of standard practice. The frequency with which doctors impose on patients experiments of an uncontrolled nature has been one of the strongest objections to professionalized medicine made by the women's health movement over the last twenty years in Europe and North America (Rusek 1978). The fact that very large numbers of women have been treated with medical and surgical procedures of unknown, or suspect effectiveness, and potentially, or actually harmful, consequences has been taken to signal both women's status as a minority group, and medicine's essentially unscientific standing. For this reason, women have been, and continue to be, important beneficiaries of the advocacy of randomized controlled evaluation within medicine. One significant example concerns the treatment of breast cancer, a disease which affects one in twelve women in the United Kingdom at some point in their lives. Analysis of the results of trials of breast cancer treatments has been responsible for the production of persuasive evidence that 'conservative' treatments are superior to 'radical' treatments both in prolonging life and in assuring a better quality of life. Overviews of RCTs concerned with systemic treatment (chemotherapy or endocrine therapy) of the disease show important differences between the effectiveness of such treatments in older and younger women. They also provide evidence that short courses of treatment are as effective as longer courses – an important consideration, given their sometimes unpleasant side-effects (Consensus Development Conference 1986). It is, however, crucial to note that the benefits that accrue to women as a result of their willingness to participate in such studies cannot be held out as a carrot to those who do except by trading on altruism. While a trial protects 50% of participants from receiving ineffective or hazardous treatment, it is in general *future* health of *other* women that stands to benefit by the willingness of *some* to be experimented on *now*.

What our experience with an RCT of social support in pregnancy has shown is the need to subject every precept of the traditional scientific method to scrutiny. Is it necessary? Do its benefits outweigh its hazards? It is as important to ask these questions of a trial of something as apparently harmless as social support as it is of trials of other more obviously ambiguous therapies. The argument against 'methodolatry' is then transformed into the case for an *appropriate* methodology which, like its namesake, appropriate technology, requires that individuals involved in it be treated with sensitivity and respect, and *that there be no division between this ethical requirement and other requirements of the method*. This is not, of course, to say that the procedure of randomized controlled evaluation is the *only* means to reliable knowledge, is *sufficient* in itself, or is *always* the right approach; for the pursuit of truth in human affairs is, as we all know, ultimately an illusion, and reliable knowledge definitely not a good in itself. The point is that what Rowbotham (1985: 51) has called 'the attraction of spring cleaning' should be seen as a means to an end, not an end in itself. The frenetic housewife is unable to enjoy the product of her labours. In Evelyn Keller's words:

> The intellectual danger resides in viewing science as pure social product; science then dissolves into ideology and objectivity loses all intrinsic meaning. In the resulting cultural relativism, any emancipatory function of modern science is negated, and the arbitration of truth recedes into the political domain.
>
> (Keller 1982: 593)

References

Acker, J., Barry, K. and Esseveld, J. (1983) 'Objectivity and truth: problems in doing feminist research.' *Women's Studies International Forum* 6, 4: 423–35.

Birke, L. (1986) *Women, Feminism and Biology*. Brighton, Sussex, Wheatsheaf Books.

Chalmers, I. (1983) 'Scientific inquiry and authoritarianism in perinatal care and education.' *Birth* 10:3, 151–164.

Consensus Development Conference: treatment of primary breast cancer (1986) *British Medical Journal* 293: 946–7.

Hedges, L.V. (1987) 'How hard is hard science? How soft is soft science?' *American Psychologist* May, 443–455.

Keller, E.F. (1982) 'Feminism and science.' *Signs: Journal of Women in Culture and Society* 7, 3: 589–602.

Micklethwait, P., Jenkins, C.C., Flanagan, G.L., Mansfield, R., Beech, B., Wynn, A. and Wynn, M. (1982) Letter to the *Observer*, 25 July.

Oakley, A. (1981) 'Interviewing women: a contradiction in terms?' In: Roberts, H. (ed.) *Doing Feminist Research*. London, Routledge and Kegan Paul.

—— (1985) 'Social support in pregnancy: the "soft" way to increase birthweight?' *Social Science and Medicine* 21, 11, pp. 1259–1268.

—— (1988) 'Is social support good for the health of mothers and babies?' *Journal of Reproductive and Infant Psychology* 6, 3–21.

Roberts, H. (ed.) (1981) *Doing Feminist Research*. London, Routledge and Kegan Paul.

Robinson, J. (1987) 'Cervical cancer – doctors hide the truth?' In: (ed.) S. O'Sullivan *Woman's Health: a Spare Rib Reader*. London, Pandora Press.

Rowbotham, S. (1985) 'What do women want? Women-centred values and the world as it is.' *Feminist Review* 20: 49–69.

Rusek, S.B. (1979) *The Women's Health Movement*. New York, Praeger.

Schwarz, D., Flamant, R. and Lellouch, J. (1980) *Clinical Trials*. London, Academic Press.

Silverman, W.A. (1985) *Human Experimentation: A Guided Step into the Unknown*. Oxford, Oxford University Press.

Spallone, P. and Steinberg, D.L. (eds) (1987) *Made to Order: The Myth of Reproductive and Genetic Progress*. Oxford, Pergamon Press.

Chapter 79

Maureen Cain and Janet Finch

TOWARDS A REHABILITATION OF DATA

From Abrams, P., Deem, R., Finch, J. and Rock, P. (eds.), *Practice and Progress: British Sociology 1950–1980*, London: George Allen and Unwin (1981).

IN THIS CHAPTER WE argue, with some temerity, for the re-establishment of empirical research as central to the sociological task. We argue for a new standard of utility. In so doing we risk the suspicion and opprobrium of fellow sociologists so it is necessary to be clear. Our position is not the counterpart, from within the discipline, of the current ideological position of spokespeople of government agencies who fund the work of social scientists. These latter appear to demand increasingly that the discipline should legitimate its continued existence, and even secure its survival, through the practice of 'relevant' research which produces 'useful' knowledge. . . . We firmly reject this view of sociological knowledge. Indeed, by contrast, empirical research is necessary precisely in order to create a radical and critical sociology. . . .

A central tenet of our argument is that data are always created, never found or collected. . . . A further implication of our concept of data is that data are not value-neutral. The very selection of particular entities involves an interpretation, and the process of constituting those entities as data is inextricably part of these data. Data are never collected but always created, and they are created in terms of an on-going historical discourse (Foucault 1970 and 1972). The facts, the data themselves, are alive and full of the values with which that discourse is imbued, and in terms of which they are created: the data themselves embody and constitute this discourse. These values in turn are related to the social/political organisation which carries them.

The whole process of research is value-full. Research starts with preconceptions and moves to refined concepts; and it is only after this fundamental value-full work has been completed that one can examine empirically the relationship between concepts. Possible 'results' are contained in the prior and value-full formulation of the questions. . . .

Thus we argue that data – the basic 'facts' – are riddled with values and that there is no escape from this. Because of this, however, the onus is on the sociologist to be both *objective* and *scholarly*.

In so arguing for the constitution of data in terms of a theory we do not want to neglect the advances made within subjectivist traditions. Patterns of thought are and have always been crucial objects of sociological analysis. What we deny is that the subjects of these thoughts and behaviours can provide in themselves validation of the sociological correctness or of the absolute correctness of their thoughts. The thoughts and accounts of those investigated have no ontological primacy. Patterns of thought, in order to be objects of sociological inquiry, must be converted into data. . . . The verbal signs with which people represent their thoughts are thus inert entities to the sociologist until he or she converts them into data by constituting the speakers as relevant subjects, or the remarks as part of a relevant discourse, and providing a theoretical context which these remarks can be deemed to have a bearing on and, when theorised, a place within. . . . Subjects' accounts are objects of study. They are not self-validating, and they are not sociological explanations. They may be constituted as data; but that is all.

Subjects' accounts have no special or primary explanatory status, although they are important objects of study. But for a number of reasons subjects' accounts rarely yield sufficient data for a sociologically adequate explanation. . . . Saying different things in different settings is a normal part of social life, rather than a sign of peculiar deviousness or the will to deceive: the researcher can learn a great deal from discovering what remarks are considered appropriate in what setting.

Thus we regard what people actually do and are recorded as doing as harder data than what they say they do. . . . Observations, properly recorded, yield 'harder' data than interviews. Ideally, therefore, observation should be a component of all research projects. However, we recognise that in many research situations interviewing subjects and using pre-recorded materials are the only possibilities. Since all of these sociologically inert entities in conjunction with theory can yield data, the impossibility of observing does not preclude research.

On eclecticism and pragmatism

There are good theoretical grounds for preferring some kinds of sociologically inert entities and certain techniques in the processes of data constitution. But theory also directs the researcher to make use of whatever appropriate inert entities are available. Such eclecticism now becomes epistemologically possible because of the central place which we allocate to theory in the constitution of data. . . .

In constituting data by a variety of methods, one is not asking which is the true or best indicator of some absent essence but rather what these data, having been converted into evidence, have to say. What place can be made for them in the initial theory? How can it grow to take account of them? What refinements does this evidence necessitate and precipitate? These questions make a virtue of the qualitative differences between the items of evidence collected.

So answers to questions can be usefully accommodated, once their status as data is established. This applies to the whole range of sources from which data can be constructed. A further paradox, then, is that *theory makes pragmatism possible*. If one wants to know about the prior socialisation of playgroup leaders, then the only data which can be constituted are answers to questions about schooling, work experience, friendship networks, and so on. If one cannot gain access to discussions between Common Market officials and civil servants in the Department of Trade and Industry, to analyse the relationship between capital and the state, then one must use newspaper reports, official statistics and accounts given by anyone prepared to be talked with. The doctrine seems a comforting one. We consider it to be both realistic and theoretically correct. . . .

But in spite of our welcoming acceptance of value-laden facts, and our happy-go-lucky eclecticism in relation to sources, we insist on theoretical objectivity and a high standard of scholarship involving both technical competence and methodological rigour. Indeed the very lack of neutrality and the qualitative variation which our position forces us to accept are two main reasons for our insistence on objectivity and scholarship.

Scholarship: the sociologist's task

On purposes

To be correct, knowledge must fulfil the purposes for which it was constructed. Knowledge thus defined guides people about what to do next by describing and elucidating where they are now, and it enables policy to be formulated for a given standpoint. Such knowledge, for example, could tell one how to formulate appropriate policies for a government of which one approved and whose standpoint one shared, although many sociologists might for various reasons not wish to work from the standpoint of officialdom, and many official policy-makers might for various reasons reject our attempt to make usefulness theoretically possible.

Thus useful knowledge must be valid, in our sense. Courses of action cannot be usefully or successfully shaped on the basis of invalid (inappropriate or inadequate) knowledge, nor is it helpful to tilt one's lance at abstract as opposed to abstracted opponents.

If, then, the aim of knowledge is to assist in devising a strategy for action by theorising and comprehending developments in society, this can only be done if distortion is minimised. Publicity and debatability achieve this.

On publicity

Publicity – openness to continuous critical reappraisal – is a fundamental criterion of scholarship. Publicity makes possible assessments of the representativeness (adequacy) of data, of the objectivity of theory and of the processes of data constitution. This is why publicity is the key to scholarship.

. . . The objectivity of relationships between concepts and objects within a theory is crucial. Conceptualisation must be clear, rigorous and explicit. It is a responsibility of every researcher, therefore, to be a theorist. If he or she is not, valid data and knowledge cannot be created. If he or she is not, therefore, useful knowledge cannot be created. This leads on to a consideration of the other, more frequently neglected, part of the sociologist's task.

Theory breathes life into sociologically inert entities and data are created. The mechanisms by which this is achieved must also be public if the data and the knowledge describing and situating them are to be adequate and capable of being valid and useful which will depend on their being appropriate as well. Great care must therefore be taken to specify in detail all sources, whether of theory or of inert objects. Technical proficiency in accordance with rules which are made public must be shown in relation to how these sources are first identified and then culled. This relates particularly to the criterion of representativeness of inert entities, but also in a different way to the use and formulation of theory. It is for this reason that sampling theory, comprehensiveness of the search for written sources and the rules governing their selection, the manner of recording field diaries and, always, close specification of the data base are essential. It is important if the knowledge is to be valid and therefore useful, to know, for example, if a researcher spend twelve half-days in a court or a hundred and fifty-two, and in either case whether the days were consecutive or spread over as many weeks. It is important because it enables both the researcher and other people (not just sociologists) to assess the representativeness of the inert entities likely to have been available to the researcher, and therefore the representativeness of the data and thus the adequacy and appropriateness (validity) of the new knowledge for the purposes for which it was produced. This point is crucial. Sloppy research is dangerous because it can lead to wrong policy decisions. Sloppy research can only be identified, and politically ignored or counted as necessary, if *both* constituents of the data, of the fundamental 'facts' of the new knowledge, are open to public appraisal, evaluation, criticism and debate.

Technical proficiency is important, but it is apposite to regard the sociologist as a craftsperson (Mills 1959) rather than a technician. For although sociological research practices must be governed by rules which can be made public, or the data produced will not be valid, these rules need not necessarily be fixed in advance. . . . If timeless technical rules are fixed absolutely and in advance they will end up being inappropriate to the ever-changing inert objects which they are supposed to reconstitute as data.[1] Technical rules, rules of practice, must often be developed by the sociological craftsperson as he or she goes along, though he or she would be just as unwise to ignore altogether the rules developed by previous craftspeople as to ignore altogether all previous theory. Both will be adapted in relation with the inert objects of which they are making sense. The good sociologist will not beat an egg with a wooden spoon just because he or she believes in wooden spoons. What is important is that he or she can tell us afterwards whether he or she used a fork or a whisk. The rules of technique, however newly elaborated, must be capable of public representation, and must be so represented.

---

1 Here we take issue with Feyerabend (1975), despite our agreement that fixed technical rules can inhibit the growth of knowledge. The problem lies not in rules as such, but in the fetishism of already existing rules.

Even quantification, that masochistic pastime in the modern sociological world, can now be advised to stand up and brush itself down and take its place with dignity amongst the legitimate practices of sociological researchers. For while repetition can never demonstrate truth, and *what* has been counted must always be assessed by criteria of appropriateness, quantitative distributions of data may well be important, and whether they are or not in a theoretical sense, it is essential that they be produced in order to meet the criterion of publicity. A statement of the order: 'I went to court on twenty-eight occasions when squatting cases were being heard. On twenty-one of these occasions such-and-such happened. In six of the remaining seven cases the squatters were students . . . (etc.)' carries more weight, it is averred, than 'courts are usually harder on immigrant and working-class families than they are on students. On one occasion the judge said . . .' This is obvious, but it is not often done. And we submit that an even larger number of cases would leave readers and users of the research in an even better position for judging its adequacy and appropriateness. Statistical tests of significance may well help in this process. If numeracy is one among many ways of achieving publicity, then these skills are welcome indeed in the battery of sociological practices. What we are providing is a new context of use for quantitative data. It must be apparent by now that the imperialism of any technique can only retard the growth of useful knowledge.

Our plea for scholarship is therefore based on the fact that good theory and knowledge, as well as data, are impossible without it. In sum, research must be scholarly, and theory must be scholarly and its relations objective, if the knowledge generated is to meet the criteria of validity which we have established. These criteria themselves are largely derived from the fact that knowledge is constructed from a standpoint and for a purpose. The criteria are: appropriateness to the purpose of inert objects constituted as data: adequacy of inert entities in terms of their representatives as guaranteed by technical proficiency and publicity; structurally adequate theory, that is, theory which is of and in time, aiming for internal consistency and objective: and appropriate theory in terms of the purpose for which the new knowledge is being made. Sociologists must be both scholars and craftspeople.

On accountability

The sociologist emerges from our arguments as a highly responsible person. He or she is responsible for his or her own theory and research practices. He or she alone can ensure that the knowledge he or she produces meets the criteria of validity which will enable it to be used by him/herself and by others within his or her standpoint. Moreover, although we have established criteria, the sociologist alone can decide when his or her theory is consistent enough, when his or her data include sufficiently representative inert entities, and so on. And while we can offer no rigid tests or guarantees, we insist at the same time that because of this every aspect of the process of knowledge constitution must be public and open to debate. Our sociologist is at risk indeed.

We welcome both the risk and the responsibility, for they add dignity to our chosen task. For too long sociologists have evaded these responsibilities, first in the myth of value-neutrality, in the idea that the world properly approached will speak for itself, and later in the myth that the truths of subjects' worlds could be frozen

and apprehended, and that subjects could and would validate sociologists' representations of their knowledge. For these so called 'objective' and 'subjective' tests we
can substitute no certainties. The sociologist cannot abdicate from his or her
responsibility for the knowledge he or she produces. He or she must validate it, and
must assist the knowledge users, of whom he or she may be one, both in assessing it
and in interpreting its political messages.

To the competent sociologist anything does not go, eclectic and pragmatic
though he or she may be in his or her choice of methods and sources: only valid
knowledge counts. These assessments of adequacy and appropriateness (validity)
cannot be made entirely within science, and the truly scholarly sociologist should
make sure he or she is vulnerable to the judgements of those sharing the standpoint
from which he or she claims to be working. However, these external and changing
criteria of adequacy and appropriateness necessitate rather than subvert the maintenance of clear standards of practice in social scientific research.

The sociological researcher is therefore both responsible and accountable. His
or her accountability is not to 'the profession' but to those who need the knowledge,
and from whose standpoint it was made. We have argued that sociology and all
knowledge is political [but] not adventitiously so. This makes scholarship crucial in a
way that for the positivists was unnecessary, and for the relativists impossible. In
arguing that the task of sociology is to provide useful descriptions of the world as it
is, we reassert our confidence that, in the task of intellectual production, sociologists
can, indeed must, be scholarly craftspeople.

References

Feyerabend, P. (1975) *Against Method* (London: New Left Books).

Foucault, M. (1970) *The Order of Things* (London: Tavistock).

Foucault, M. (1972) *The Archaeology of Knowledge* (London: Tavistock).

Mills, C. Wright (1959) *The Sociological Imagination* (London: Oxford University Press).

Index

Page numbers in **bold type** refer to individual readings.